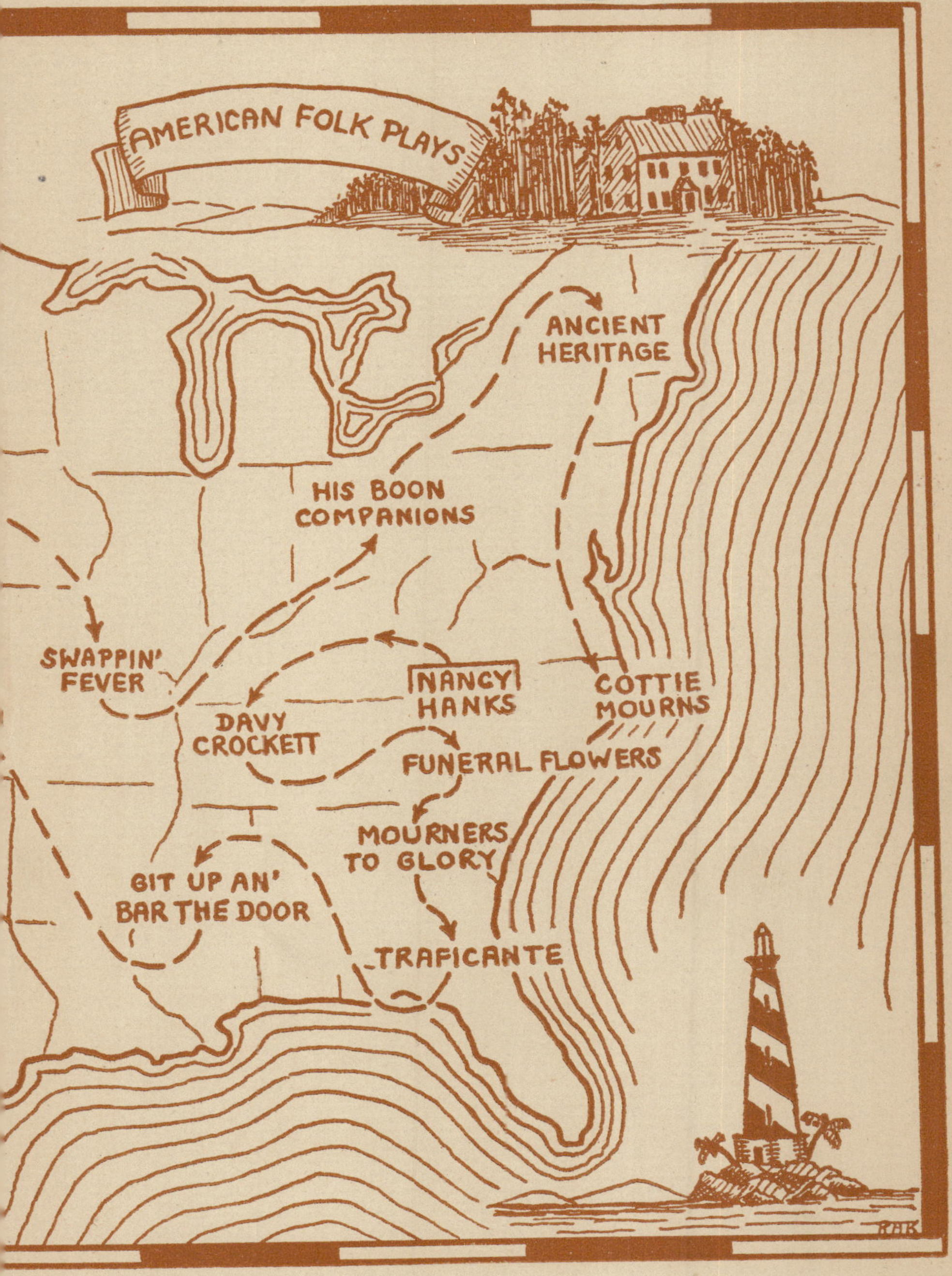
AMERICAN FOLK PLAYS
ANCIENT HERITAGE
HIS BOON COMPANIONS
SWAPPIN' FEVER
NANCY HANKS
COTTIE MOURNS
DAVY CROCKETT
FUNERAL FLOWERS
MOURNERS TO GLORY
GIT UP AN' BAR THE DOOR
TRAFICANTE
RAK

AMERICAN FOLK PLAYS

Wootten-Moulton
THE PLAYMAKERS THEATRE AT CHAPEL HILL, NORTH CAROLINA
The first theatre building in America to be dedicated to the making of its own native drama.

AMERICAN FOLK PLAYS

Edited, with an Introduction,

"AMERICAN FOLK DRAMA
IN THE MAKING"

by

FREDERICK H. KOCH

FOUNDER AND DIRECTOR OF THE
CAROLINA PLAYMAKERS

ILLUSTRATED WITH PHOTOGRAPHS OF
THE ORIGINAL PRODUCTIONS OF THE PLAYS

Foreword by

ARCHIBALD HENDERSON

D. APPLETON-CENTURY COMPANY
INCORPORATED
New York   London

1939

COPYRIGHT, 1939, BY
D. APPLETON-CENTURY COMPANY, INC.

All rights reserved. This book, or parts thereof, must not be reproduced in any form without permission of the publisher.

WARNING

These plays are for reading purposes only. The fact that you have purchased this book does not give you permission to produce any play here published, unless you have received permission to do so from the owner of copyright in the play. Directions are given concerning the name and address of the owner of copyright.

The plays are fully protected in all countries by the copyright law, all requirements of which have been complied with. No performance, professional or amateur, no public reading, no radio broadcast, may be given without permission of the owner of copyright, D. Appleton-Century Company, Inc., 35 West 32nd Street, New York City, or D. Appleton-Century Company, Inc., 34 Bedford Street, Strand, London, England.

Performances of these plays are subject to royalty. Any one presenting any one of these plays without the consent of the owner of the copyright will be liable to the penalties provided by law:

> "Section 4966:—Any person publicly performing or representing any dramatic or musical composition for which copyright has been obtained, without the consent of the proprietor of said dramatic or musical composition, or his heirs and assigns, shall be liable for damages, thereof, such damages, in all cases, to be assessed at such sum, not less than one hundred dollars for the first and fifty dollars for every subsequent performance, as to the courts shall appear to be just. If the unlawful performance and presentation be willful and for profit, such person or persons shall be imprisoned for a period not exceeding one year."—U. S. Revised Statutes: Title 60, Chap. 3.

PRINTED IN THE UNITED STATES OF AMERICA

TO
ARCHIBALD HENDERSON

CONTENTS

		PAGE
INTRODUCTION	Frederick H. Koch	xiii
FOREWORD	Archibald Henderson	xxxi

NORTH CAROLINA
NANCY HANKS, BONDWOMAN . . Janie Malloy Britt   1
A Legend of the Great Smoky Mountains

TENNESSEE
DAVY CROCKETT . . . . . John Philip Milhous   29
Half Horse, Half Alligator

SOUTH CAROLINA
FUNERAL FLOWERS FOR THE BRIDE . . . . . .
                    Beverley DuBose Hamer   59
A Comedy of the Blue Ridge Mountains

GEORGIA
MOURNERS TO GLORY . . . Rietta Winn Bailey   85
A Negro Ritual Drama

FLORIDA
TRAFICANTE . . . . . . Maxeda von Hesse   113
A Play of Spanish Florida

MISSISSIPPI
GIT UP AN' BAR THE DOOR . Arthur Palmer Hudson   143
A Ballad Comedy

OKLAHOMA

LAST REFUGE . . . . Noel Houston 179
  An Outlaw Comes Home

TEXAS

WEST FROM THE PANHANDLE . . . .
  Clemon White and Betty Smith 217
  A Tragedy of the Dust Bowl

MEXICO

THE RED VELVET GOAT . . . . Josephina Niggli 247
  A Tragedy of Laughter and a Comedy of Tears

NEW MEXICO

STICK 'EM UP . . . . Gordon Clouser 277
  A Comedy of Frontier New Mexico

ARIZONA

CONCHITA . . . . . . Rosemary Shirley DeCamp 301
  A Romance of a Copper Mining Town

CALIFORNIA

DAY'S END . . . . Alice Pieratt 317
  A Drama of a Mountain Woman

UTAH

SPRING STORM . . . . Mary Cottam Hatch 343
  A Comedy of a Country Girl

MONTANA

MONTANA NIGHT . . Robert Finch and Betty Smith 365
  A Drama of the Old West

CONTENTS

CANADA

STILL STANDS THE HOUSE . . . Gwendolyn Pharis 389
  A Drama of the Canadian Frontier

NORTH DAKOTA

SIGRID . . . . Margaret Radcliffe 419
  Farm Woman of the Prairie

MISSOURI

SWAPPIN' FEVER . . . . . . Lealon N. Jones 445
  A Comedy of the Ozarks

OHIO

HIS BOON COMPANIONS . . . . Lynn Gault 471
  A Small-Town Temperance Comedy

MASSACHUSETTS

ANCIENT HERITAGE . . Philip Goddard Parker 497
  A Drama of a New England Family

NORTH CAROLINA

COTTIE MOURNS . . . . . Patricia McMullan 529
  A Comedy of Sea Island Folk

APPENDICES

I. *The Carolina Playmakers: A Selected Bibliography* 557
II. *The Carolina Playmakers: Production and Tours* 571

ILLUSTRATIONS

THE PLAYMAKERS THEATRE AT CHAPEL HILL,
NORTH CAROLINA . . . . *frontispiece*

	FACING PAGE
THE AUDIENCE: THE PLAYMAKERS THEATRE, CHAPEL HILL, NORTH CAROLINA	16
NANCY HANKS, BONDWOMAN	17
DAVY CROCKETT	60
FUNERAL FLOWERS FOR THE BRIDE	61
MOURNERS TO GLORY	150
GIT UP AN' BAR THE DOOR	151
WEST FROM THE PANHANDLE	256
THE RED VELVET GOAT	257
STICK 'EM UP	372
MONTANA NIGHT	373
STILL STANDS THE HOUSE	452
SWAPPIN' FEVER	453
ANCIENT HERITAGE	524
COTTIE MOURNS	525

AMERICAN FOLK DRAMA IN THE MAKING

THE plays in this volume present exciting historical backgrounds, folk legends, and scenes from contemporary life—from the early days of the Spaniards in Florida to the tragic plight of refugees from the Dust Bowl of Texas. Here are such romantic figures as Nancy Hanks, mother of Abraham Lincoln; and Davy Crockett, hero of the Alamo. Dramas of the gold-rush days of the old West, of the spare ways of New England folk, of gentle Mormon people, of child-like, excitable Mexicans. Here a riotous farce of cowboys on the frontier of New Mexico, and a tragedy of a copper-mining town in Arizona. Prairie farmers of Dakota and of western Canada, fisherfolk of the Carolina sea islands, a rollicking ballad play of Mississippi, a nostalgic village comedy of Ohio, Negro ritual drama from Georgia, a back-country comedy of the Ozarks, the drama of an Oklahoma outlaw, a romance of the California hill country. New England and the South, the Middle West and the Southwest, the Rocky Mountain states and California, Canada and Mexico! The characters are indigenous to the life they portray. The playwright in every case is a native of the region about which he writes; the people in the play are his own people.

Here are eighteen plays of the American scene, one from western Canada, and one from beyond the Rio Grande in Mexico. They have been selected from hundreds of scripts written by students in playwriting at Chapel Hill and in summer courses it has been my privilege to conduct in some of our leading universities: Columbia, New York, Northwestern, Colorado, California (both Berkeley and Los Angeles), Southern California, and Alberta, Canada.

THE FOLK PLAYS OF NORTH CAROLINA

As far as we have been able to determine, the first use of the term "folk play" in the American theater was The Carolina Playmakers' announcement: "CAROLINA FOLK PLAYS," on the playbill of their initial production in Chapel Hill on March 14 and 15, 1919. The plays presented were: *When Witches Ride,* about folk superstition in Northampton county, by Elizabeth Lay of Beaufort, North Carolina (now Mrs. Paul Green); and *The Return of Buck Gavin,* concerning a Carolina mountain outlaw, by Thomas Wolfe of Asheville, North Carolina (now distinguished American novelist). His first professionally published work, by the way, was *The Return of Buck Gavin* * published in the Second Series of *Carolina Folk Plays.* That was twenty years ago. Now the term is not unfamiliar in the expanding scene of our American theater. Witness Paul Green's *In Abraham's Bosom,* Thornton Wilder's *Our Town,* Lynn Riggs' *Green Grow the Lilacs,* and Robert Sherwood's *Abe Lincoln in Illinois.*

From the first our particular interest in North Carolina has been the use of native materials and the making of fresh dramatic forms. We have found that if the young writer observes the locality with which he is most familiar and interprets it faithfully, it may show him the way to the universal. If he can see the *interestingness* of the lives of those about him with understanding and imagination, with wonder, why may he not interpret that life in significant images for others—perhaps for all? It has been so in all lasting art.

* The author played the title rôle in the original production of this, his first play.

FOLK DRAMA IN THE MAKING

The *Carolina Folk Plays,* in four volumes,* written in the playwriting courses at the University of North Carolina over a period of years, have been widely read and produced in the United States and in England. The materials were drawn by each writer from scenes familiar and near, often from remembered adventures of his youth, from folk tales and the common tradition, and from present-day life in North Carolina. They are plays of native expressiveness, of considerable range and variety, presenting scenes from the remote coves of the Great Smoky Mountains to the dangerous shoals of Cape Hatteras. *American Folk Plays* marks the extension of our North Carolina idea of folk playmaking to other American states, to Canada, and to Mexico.

WHAT IS FOLK DRAMA?

The term folk drama, as we use it, has nothing to do with the folk play of medieval times (often attributed by scholars to communal authorship) which took the form of Christmas pantomimes by village mummers, jigs, sword dances, festivals, and other community celebrations. More recently it has been applied to the peasant plays of the Irish Renaissance written by a single artist. Each of the *American Folk Plays* in this volume is the work of a single author dealing consciously with his materials, the folkways of our less sophisticated people living simple lives not seriously affected by the present-day, complex social order. The plays are concerned with folk subject matter: with the legends, superstitions, customs, environmental differences, and the vernacular of the common people. For the most part they are realistic and human; sometimes they are imaginative and poetic.

* First Series, 1922; Second Series, 1924; Third Series, 1928 (New York, Henry Holt and Company); *Carolina Folk Comedies* (New York, Samuel French, Inc., 1931).

There is an impression abroad that folk drama is necessarily tragic. But such an impression is contrary to the facts. The so-called common people, generally thought of as the "folk," have their seasons of enjoyment quite as much as do their more sophisticated neighbors—perhaps more so. In the folkways and culture of country people there is a simple joy in life. They live near to the earth and make much of the good gifts of nature. Not only in their play parties, ballad-singing, tall tales, spelling-bees, square dances, fiddlers' conventions, and "long-sweetenin' " parties; but also in their communal tasks of corn shuckin', quiltin', cane strippin', and log raisin', they find a genuine zest in living. It is not without significance that, although not selected with such a classification in mind, the plays in this volume are almost equally divided between comedy and tragedy. Side by side with the tragic story of *Nancy Hanks, Bondwoman* of the Great Smoky Mountains, is the robustious comedy of the Blue Ridge, *Funeral Flowers for the Bride*.

The chief concern of the folk dramatist is man's conflict with the forces of nature and his simple pleasure in being alive. The conflict may not be apparent on the surface in the immediate action on the stage. But the ultimate cause of all dramatic action we classify as "folk," whether it be physical or spiritual, may be found in man's desperate struggle for existence and in his enjoyment of the world of nature. The term "folk" here then, applies to that form of drama which is earth-rooted in the life of our common humanity.

Drama dealing with folk subject matter is not new, and it may take the form of either tragedy or comedy. It goes back to the beginnings of dramatic history, to the dance rituals of celebrants at the altar of Dionysus. It first flowered in the tragedies of Æschylus and his contemporaries. Later,

FOLK DRAMA IN THE MAKING   xvii

folk drama flourished in the medieval Mysteries, Miracles, and Moralities, and in the rollicking comedy of a *Gammer Gurton's Needle*. Shakespeare utilized folk materials in his great tragedies: witches in *Macbeth*, ghosts in *Hamlet* and other plays, and the legendary history of Britain in *King Lear*; and in comedy he presented a lusty crew of rustics and tradesmen. Goethe translated the popular stories of the medieval magician, Doctor Faustus, in the timeless poetry of *Faust*; and from the rich store of Scandinavian folklore, Henrik Ibsen created *Peer Gynt*.

In our own day Paul Green has portrayed the epic tragedy of a Negro leader, who, Prometheus-like, fights for his people in *In Abraham's Bosom*; and Jack Kirkland has dramatized Erskine Caldwell's novel of the degenerate poor-white sharecropper of the backlands of Georgia in *Tobacco Road*, presenting the tragicomic figure of an irrepressible Jeeter Lester. Side by side with Lulu Vollmer's stark tragedy of Carolina mountain people, *Sun-Up*, we have Lynn Riggs' refreshing comedy of the country people of frontier Oklahoma, *Green Grow the Lilacs*—and the joyous Negro pageantry of the perennial *Green Pastures*.

AMERICAN FOLK DRAMA

For many years our playwrights were imitative, content with reproducing the outlived formulas of the old world. There was nothing really *native* about them. Whenever they did write of American life, the treatment was superficial and innocuous.

When Augustus Thomas wrote *Alabama, Arizona,* and *In Mizzoura,* optimistic heralds announced the arrival of the "great American drama"; but the playwright barely skimmed the surfaces of these colorful states. His next play, *The Witching Hour,* had something of the jessamine perfume of Kentucky romance, but the ghost of the old well-made melodrama was lugged in to resolve the plot. Then there was *Uncle Tom's Cabin,* a grand old theater piece, but its treatment of the southern Negro was sentimental. It remained for William Vaughn Moody to give us the first significant American folk drama, *The Great Divide*—the conflict of the Arizona frontier with the puritan conscience of New England. And for such contemporary American playwrights as Eugene O'Neill, Elmer Rice, Paul Green, Lynn Riggs, and Maxwell Anderson to create an authentic folk drama of American life.

OUR WAY OF PLAYWRITING

First, let me say that I am aware that playwriting cannot be *taught*. But I am confident that the impulse to make a play is a natural one, that it should be cherished, and that it may be wisely directed.

I believe that when the Good Book says, "God created man in his own image," it means that God imparted to man somewhat of His own creativeness; in a sense He made man a co-creator with Him—potentially an artist! In our way of playwriting we try to cherish the creative spark in the student. We encourage him to examine, with understanding and imagination, the eventful happenings of his own experience, the characters of his own neighborhood. Then, with patient practice, we guide him in shaping his materials in an appropriate and interesting pattern for the stage. Such has been our practice from the first.

Elizabeth Lay, the author of the first play produced on our Carolina Playmakers' stage, was a young school-teacher in the back-country of Northampton County near the Roanoke River. She found the materials for *When Witches Ride* in the characters and folklore of her neighbors and

FOLK DRAMA IN THE MAKING

friends there. The Prologue she wrote for our initial play aptly states the point of view of the playwright:

> We mock with facts the Southern folk-belief,
> And so forget the eternal quest that strove
> With signs and tales to symbolize the awe
> Of powers in heaven and earth still undefined.
> Yet we may catch the child-like wondering
> Of our old Negroes and the country folk,
> And live again in simple times of faith
> And fear and wonder, if we stage their life.
> Then witches ride the stormy, thundering sky,
> And signs and omens fill believing minds;
> Then old traditions live in simple speech,
> And ours the heritage of wondering.

The playwright must know his characters intimately. As Thomas Wolfe, a member of our first playwriting group in Chapel Hill, wrote in a foreword to his first play, *The Return of Buck Gavin:* *

> It is a fallacy of the young writer to picture the dramatic as the unusual and remote. ... He is likely to choose for the setting of his first effort a New York apartment house, the Barbary Coast of San Francisco, or some remote land made dramatic by all of the perfumes of Arabia.... But the dramatic is not unusual. It is happening daily in our lives. We toil on a mountain farm to think bitterly on the unvaried monotonous grind of our existence. Here is material for drama in the true sense.

And Dorothy Canfield avers, "I can write nothing at all about places, people or phases of life which I do not intimately know, down to the last detail. If my life depended upon it, it does not seem to me I could possibly write a story about Siberian hunters or East-Side factory hands without having lived among them." When the writer por-

---

* *The Return of Buck Gavin* by Thomas Wolfe is included in the Second Series of *Carolina Folk Plays*.

trays characters and scenes with which he is familiar we share with him the life he knows and feels. And his drama becomes our own.

THE PLAYMAKING IMPULSE

Every child is a "little actor" in his play, as Wordsworth suggests in the famous *Ode*. And his instinct for playmaking may easily be directed by the teacher. This was vividly brought to my attention at five o'clock one winter morning when the first of our sons, Fred, Jr., aged nine, awakened me and his mother from sound sleep by loud conversation with his brother in the next room.

I went in to stop the racket and Fred piped up, "Dad, I've written a play, and I want you to type it for me, so I can get it published!" His eyes were shining.

"Ye gods! Must I be wakened at five in the morning by this playmaking business? What is this play? How did you come to write it?"

"We made it up in school. First we acted it out, then we wrote down the words; and now I want you to type it, so I can get it *published!*"

Then I learned that the play concerned the conflict of three birds over a favorite nesting site in an apple tree: a cardinal, a mocking-bird, and a blue jay.

"Well, which one wins?" I asked.

"Why the blue jay, of course!"

Well, I didn't stop to analyze the structure of Fred's play, but I was obliged to admit that it had a conflict and a beginning, a middle, and an end! And I made a silent prayer then for more teachers like the one who recognized and put to work the child's *making* instinct, his natural impulse to create something of his own.

Our approach to playwriting is frankly empirical. There

is no textbook to inhibit the young writer, to make him overconscious of the complicated structure of the dramatic form. Like Lope de Vega we "put the rules aside and lock them up." Technique seems to be the big bugbear of the beginner. At first the student must trust his own natural instinct for form. Otherwise he is likely to entangle himself in the intricacies of technique—like the poor centipede who "was happy quite until the toad for fun said, 'Pray which foot comes after which' [and] threw her mind in such a pitch, she lay distracted in the ditch, considering how to run." Without consciously studying technique as such, the potential playwright may in time, with wise encouragement and sufficient practice, become proficient in the difficult art of writing a play. But he must sing his own song in his own way! For, as Edmund Spenser avers,

> ... Of the soul the body form doth take,
> For soul *is* form and doth the body make.

THE PLAN

In playwriting then, we follow no formulas. But we do proceed with what seems to us a logical plan, a plan which rests on the assumption that the student is by nature creative. Our method is inductive, rather than deductive; the way of the laboratory, rather than that of the textbook. The chemical and physical sciences have shown remarkable progress since the introduction of teaching by laboratory experiment. So, too, law and sociology by case study; medicine by clinical and hospital practice; and geology, anthropology, and archeology by field work. Our way of playwriting is not an upstart then, but a tried and approved educational procedure.

We begin with the one-act form, using a volume of *Carolina Folk Plays*. (We choose our own simple plays rather than those of professional playwrights, because they are nearer to the student's point of view.) We suggest that the student read these plays with a view to visualizing them on the stage. We ask him to write down his honest impressions of an assigned play—of its subject matter and form. It is then presented on the stage in a rehearsal performance, the students in the course, books in hand, enacting the parts as well as they can. In this way the prospective playwright learns that the impact of character on character, that the stage business and the pantomime are quite as important as the dialogue—sometimes more so. And his kinetic imagination is set to work. He realizes, as he failed to do in his written criticism, that a play is not merely written, that it is *designed* to be *acted;* that what happens between the characters on the stage is the important thing; that the action of the play is a unified composition designed to interest and hold the attention of an audience, in terms of action.

Drama is not a solitary but a social art. It comes alive only through the response of an audience. It would be safe to wager that were there no audience, the drama would not long survive. In the final analysis, drama is the response of an audience to the actor's embodiment of the playwright's design.

By participating in the classroom performances, the student comes to realize that he must write his dialogue and carefully set down his pantomime with the actor, director, and audience constantly in mind—and the technical director, too!

More short plays are read and discussed, and more plays —all kinds—throughout the course. This with a view to cultivating in the student a *feeling* for good dramatic form, and with the hope that he may find a way for himself in his own playmaking.

THE PLAYWIGHT, HIMSELF

The student must realize at the outset that he, *himself*—his own view of life—should be his first consideration. Early in the course he is called upon to write down the story of his life in all its "horrible details," in the hope that he may discover the interestingness of his forebears, his immediate family, his eventful childhood, and the influences of his environment in the country, little town, or city. And, of course, the impact of other people on him, the rememberable things that have happened to him.

Lynn Riggs, in an article he wrote for *The Carolina Play-Book* * some time ago, holds the dramatist to be—a "curious cellular synthesis"—*the man himself*—which determines nearly everything about his work: the locale, the point of view, the tone, the comment it has to make, the characters it has to explore, and the luminosity by which it dazzles or offends. There on the lighted boards or on the open page is the man [the playwright], his dark and shambling and monstrous essence. For his mortal satisfaction, the man who is a dramatist too may hope to make the revealment less dark, less monstrous, more like a radiance in which a few lambent realities may cluster. It's a decent ambition, it seems to me. And that's the reason I go on writing plays, call them "folk" or whatever you will.

And Thomas Wolfe holds, in his preface, "To the Reader," in *Of Time and the River*. †

If any reader should say that this book is "autobiographical" the writer has one answer for him: it seems to him that all serious work in fiction is autobiographical. ... We are the sum of all the moments of our lives—all that is ours is in them: we cannot escape or conceal it. If the writer has used the clay of

---

* Lynn Riggs, "When People Say 'Folk Drama,'" *The Carolina Play-Book* (Chapel Hill, June, 1931).
† Quoted by permission of the publisher, Charles Scribner's Sons.

life to make his book, he has only used what all men must, what none can keep from using. Fiction is not fact, but fiction is fact selected and understood, fiction is fact arranged and charged with purpose.

This frank statement of Wolfe's credo may well be taken to heart by the beginner in playwriting.

Early in his study of playwriting, then, the student is impressed with the importance of writing honestly from his own materials. He is reminded again and again that the structure of the play he is writing must grow logically out of familiar scenes and from characters intimately known to him. That *himself* is the most important element in the play he may write, that there is something elusive beyond the structure of the play, beyond the technique—the "curious cellular synthesis that is the man."

I asked a musician the other day, "Can you work out the forms—the patterns that Beethoven used in his symphonies?"

"Oh, yes, with almost mathematical precision; we have the formulas," he replied blithely.

"Then why can't you give them to your students and let them write music as Beethoven wrote?"

"Oh, no, 'Proff'... behind the formula there is *still* Beethoven!"

Behind Beethoven's symphonies is the mystery of the artist. In his art Beethoven touches the undiscovered country where two and two may make *five!*

PLAYMAKING IS COMMUNAL

Important as the individual artist is, we must bear constantly in mind that the dramatic art is essentially a social experience. That is, in its very origins, it is communal. In playwriting the highest individualism on the part of the playwright must be the highest socialism also. He must

FOLK DRAMA IN THE MAKING

always have in mind the audience for whom he is writing. The art of the theater is not an individual experience; it is the embodiment of the desire of a human being to communicate his emotions to his fellows.

The students come to the playwriting course with vague ideas of plays-in-the-making. There is much lively discussion and the unsuspecting novice is often surprised by the reactions of different members of the group. But no matter how astounding the criticism may be, it is usually honest and does present a potential viewpoint of an audience. It challenges the young author and gives him a new perspective in his work. In this way his conception is tested and enriched by the varying viewpoints of his fellows. Perhaps the following lines, written by one of our young Playmakers in the early days in Dakota, will suggest our mode of approach:

> If you can see the world with me
> And I can see the world with you,
> I'm sure that both of us will see
> Things that neither of us do.

Perhaps the boy from the Piedmont section will begin: "I know about a country boy's courtship which ought to make a play. The old man used to stamp on the floor of his bedroom upstairs as a signal for the boy to go home. One night the boy—we'll call him 'Lem'—conceived the idea of pretending to leave. He called out to the girl a loud 'good-bye' and banged the outside door. Then, after a little, he slipped in through the window in his stocking feet to finish saying 'Good-night.' But the father came down and discovered the trick."

"That's a good one," some one shouts. "But how did the father happen to come down?"

And another pipes up, "I think you ought to make use of

the little brother who is always butting in on the courtship."

"That's good," from the prospective playwright. "The girl had two brothers, and I can work them both in for some good laughs."

A rival suitor is added to complicate the action, and a few days later, when the embryo play comes back to be read to the group, it has the elements of a real plot.

A lively discussion ensues: "The ending is weak." "Why not have the little brother steal Lem's shoes, so he can't make his get-away?"

"That's bully! I'll do it."

And—with the assistance of one of the co-eds in the course in phrasing the speeches of the girl—with much reshaping of the plot, revising of the characters, recasting of the dialogue, the comedy of *In Dixon's Kitchen* * finally emerges. Of course it is rewritten again and again before it is ready, at last, for the Playmakers' stage. And it must undergo still further changes in the process of rehearsal before it is given a public production.

So the play is not merely written, it is communally rewritten. It is really a composite product of all the members of the group, with the experience of the instructor to guide the young playwright in the complex process of building a play. We have found in our way of playwriting and theater arts that the essential thing is harmonious collaboration—a happy working together of all the members of the group.

EXPERIMENTAL PRODUCTION

The final test of the play lies in its appeal to an audience, hence experimental production of the best plays. In these informal presentations the audience has an active part.

---

* *In Dixon's Kitchen* by Wilbur Stout is included in the Third Series of *Carolina Folk Plays*.

FOLK DRAMA IN THE MAKING

Audience participation in the play harks back to the good old days of the Greeks and the Elizabethans; and to the boos, hisses, whistles, and foot-stamping of the nineteenth-century theater. But in our experimental theater it is a new kind of participation in which every member of the audience may become a critic, giving his honest impression of the play to the new playwright.

Before the performance begins, the author is introduced to the audience and he has an opportunity to preface his play with any statement he may wish to make about his sources and purpose. Thus he takes the audience into his confidence and bespeaks the collaboration of the spectators while he follows closely their reactions to what he has written.

Knowing that he [the playwright] will have a chance to have his say, or, if he himself prefers to remain silent, that he will want to weigh the criticisms of others, the author watches the play keenly. He is alert to a false note, quick to respond to a telling point....

When the curtain falls on the play, there is the usual applause as the house lights come up. Then the Playmakers' Director rises near the front and turns to the audience with: "Well, what did you think of that one?"

Cigarettes are lighted. There is a moment of thought. Then, perhaps from a Jewish lad from New York, a German girl from Berlin, or a Chinese girl from Nanking, comes the suggestion: "The ending was bad. We had been led to believe Marie was honest and sincere. We sympathized with her. Then she turns out to be just a flirt. That wasn't fair!"

"How many agree with that?" the Director asks. A show of hands. "What do *you* think, John?" John, who may be a village grocer or the dean of the school of music, slowly takes his pipe from his mouth and gives his opinion.

To all this the young playwright, seated and silent, listens intently. No need for him to speak; his voice came from the stage. The author will not accept all the suggestions made, of course. Should he do so, the final play would likely be a hodgepodge. But pertinent suggestions for changes, or those overwhelmingly insisted upon by the audience, may be adopted in his revised script.*

Such a form of audience criticism during the change of scenery offers perhaps the best advice available for the young playwright.

"AMERICAN FOLK PLAYS"

By way of introducing the author of each of the plays in this volume, and the sources from which the playwright has drawn his material, I have prefaced each of the plays with an introduction which will, I hope, enrich the reader's and the student's understanding and enjoyment of the plays.

It has been impossible in the limits of a single book to present plays of all of our United States with their diverse and multifarious aspects. To attempt to cover this whole field of our national life is quite beyond the province of one volume. If, however, these little plays of seventeen American states, Canada, and Mexico, reflect faithfully certain facets of our many-sided American life, its intention will not have been in vain.

The plays included in the volume are arranged in the form of a transcontinental journey beginning in the Great Smoky Mountains of North Carolina, going by way of Mexico to California, and returning by way of western Canada to Ocracoke Island off the eastern coast of North Carolina.

It is our hope that *American Folk Plays* may contribute somewhat to our regional literature. The plays have been written honestly by young Americans about the lives of

* Noel Houston, "Experimental Production," *The Carolina Play-Book* (Chapel Hill, March, 1938). Mr. Houston is the author of *Last Refuge*, included in this volume.

plain people well known to them; not infrequently the local has been transferred into the universal. For their authenticity of native traditions, both historical and contemporary, it is hoped that this book may be of interest and value to students of folklore. For its examples of challenging student achievement in the technique of writing the one-act play, it is our hope that it will prove of real help to students of playwriting and play production. And in its appealing characters—untouched by modern sophistication, good sturdy people who laugh or cry or remain stoically mute, but always people at grips with the realities of life—we believe it will interest all who love America.

It is our hope that these homespun plays may contribute somewhat to the making of a living theater of the people worthy of our American dream—of "the copiousness, the individuality of The States, each for itself," as Walt Whitman aptly phrases it.

FREDERICK H. KOCH

Chapel Hill, North Carolina

FOREWORD

I

ONE of the most often quoted of Oscar Wilde's penetrating epigrams is to the effect that life imitates art.
Perhaps Barrie never thought of his responsibility when he wrote *Peter Pan*. I have known two Peter Pans in real life. I once called Bernard Shaw a weird composite of Peter Pan and St. Francis of Assisi, of Puck and Euripides. I believe it was the late Montrose Moses who once called Frederick H. Koch a sort of Peter Pan in modern dress. That was my first vivid impression of him—gay, cordial, beaming, effervescent, naïve; in Norfolk jacket and lavallière knot—with a pipe prominent in the foreground. When I was introduced to him in 1918 by my colleague, Edwin Greenlaw, then head of the English department, who had brought him from North Dakota to North Carolina, Koch immediately assured me of the enormous influence exerted upon him by my *The Changing Drama*.

"Why, Dr. Henderson," he said, convincingly, "while studying that book, I underlined every passage that I considered important and wished to study further. Only the other day, I looked through my copy once more, and discovered to my astonishment that very few passages in it remained unmarked!"

Koch's chief concern on arrival in Chapel Hill was to discover a stage whereon to produce folk dramas. Dr. "Johnny" Booker of the English department escorted him over the University and showed him the only stage on which plays were ever given: the platform of Gerrard Hall, where chapel exercises were held.

"But you can't produce plays here," exclaimed Koch, incredulously. "There is no stage, no curtains, no footlights, no dressing-rooms, no anything!"

"But we do," replied Johnny, reassuringly. "We build an apron in front of the platform and rig up a string of electric bulbs for footlights; the players dress and make up in an adjoining building, and climb in through a window behind the curtain, on to the stage!"

Koch got busy and soon designed and constructed a fully equipped stage and proscenium arch in the auditorium of the Chapel Hill High School building, some distance away from the college campus, and there the first Carolina Folk Plays had their baptism. I shall never forget the gaunt, gangling, towering figure of Tom Wolfe, later to win fame as a novelist, impersonating his first artistic creation, the moonshiner, Buck Gavin, from his own western Carolina mountains. Or the inspired acting of Elizabeth Taylor, a veritable reincarnation in living reality of an imaginative character, the shrewd but kindly hag, slatternly and snuff-dipping, Mag Warren, in Harold Williamson's tragedy of the tenant farmer, *Peggy*. Those were the days, indeed, when the bizarre, unkempt Hubert Heffner, only recently made head of the Department of Drama at Stanford University (but then looking like a primitive being who had strayed from the German *Urwald*), displayed his remarkable talents as a character actor, weirdly quaint in his rurality; and when Paul Green, now a leading American playwright, made his bow as a dramatist in that still-gripping one-act play of authentically native theme, the tragedy of the Croatin outlaws, *The Last of the Lowries*. During the twenty years which have elapsed since that day of exciting beginnings, Koch has become an American classic. Not that

I mean he is, as the darky says, "powerful old": I mean that he is "powerful young" (exactly my own age, and so, indubitably young!), and the witness of his own immortality. He was once introduced to an audience at the University of Michigan by James Holly Hanford, a former colleague, as a "monomaniac." "This monomaniac's obsession when he came to Chapel Hill," explained Hanford, "was faith in the fantastic plan of trying to induce Americans to write their own drama. The real point of the joke is that Fred has actually succeeded."

The present volume is an imposing demonstration that Koch has succeeded. This is no mere collection of piffling playlets from the backwoods, representing revolting aspects of sex, feral perversities, drab degradation and tragic degeneration, from some primitive backwash of the tides of the life of the forgotten folk. I well remember coming away from Eugene O'Neill's *Beyond the Horizon* one night in New York, in company with Roland Holt who, in his boyish way, was not only vibrant with enthusiasm but eager to share it with others. Encountering in the aisle a friend, he inquired: "Well, old man, how did you like it?" The friend, who was born in the country, somewhat arbitrarily replied: "All I got out of the play, Roland, was that life on a farm is hell. And I knew that already!"

When Frederick broached to me the idea of this collection, on continental lines, I waxed enthusiastic, but made one condition precedent to writing this foreword. I told him the Roland Holt story, and said that I wouldn't foster any project which inculcated the idea that life on a farm was hell. As walker, hunter, fisherman, horseback rider, nature lover, life on a farm for me was always paradise. I discovered that there was more interest, joy, excitement, thrill in the lives of the simple folk who live close to the earth and commune intimately with Nature and Nature's

God than in the monotonous grind of many a city-pent, white-collar slave of capital. I have often shared the joys and sports, the hardy tasks and wearing labors of these patient people, as well as their sorrows and misfortunes, under conditions which to the uninitiated seem only depressingly drab and enervating. But amidst all the poverty and squalor, joy kept triumphantly breaking through and could never be permanently repressed. One bitter night of zero temperature after a glorious quail-hunt, I was offered a drink of orange juice, meaning Orange County raw corn whiskey, by the old farmer on whose plantation I was a hunting guest. I drank it off at a gulp and, in hope of relief, gave a great shout when the fiery stuff scorched the tender lining of my throat. "Why, Doctor," grinned my highly amused old farmer friend, "many's the night I've sat here before this fire with a gallon jug between my legs; and when morning came, what between a couple of cronies and myself, the jug was empty." Joy: vivid, inexhaustible, irrepressible!

Here is a volume of folk plays, continental in scope, and bearing evidence of friendly raids into both Canada and Mexico. Fred had kept his word to me. Indeed, his pledge was kept for him by the playwrights themselves. For on perusal the plays in the volume reveal themselves to be almost equally divided between joy and sorrow, comedy and tragedy. And they reveal another striking feature: the amazing number of points on the North American continent where Koch's influence has been exerted to fertilize the soil of native inspiration and stimulate the writing of authentic, autochthonous folk plays. In the field of dramatic art, Frederick Koch is a shining counterpart of that half-legendary, wholly real character, Johnny Appleseed, who roamed hither and yon over this vast country of ours, planting seeds—apple seeds (not the apple of human discord, but of human harmony)—to bring a helpful and abundant orchard. In this volume of American folk plays is found Koch's rich and happy harvest.

II

Koch is the arch-foe of the cut-and-dried, the academic, the specifically prescribed. All his life he has demanded room for the random, outlet for the unexpressed, free play for the genius. It is a sort of universally shared joke that this sprite of a man, this least academic of instructors, is affectionately called by his students "Proff" Koch (as Koch sometimes says: "With two f's, please—my only distinction!")—a name first given him by Paul Green. One of my own private jokes is that I spell it differently; for to me he is "Proph" Koch—playful abbreviation for prophet. Somehow there is an element of the prophetic, of star-pointing destiny in his career. From the first he knew what he wanted. He has never failed to get it. He will never cease to get it—until he dies. Emerson crystallizes the thought in a perfect epigram, illuminating the intimate sequence of aspiration and consummation: "The soul contains the event that shall befall it, for the event is only the actualization of its thoughts; and what we pray to ourselves for is always granted."

When I came away from the Studebaker Theatre in Chicago in 1903, after *You Never Can Tell,* my Shavian baptism, I felt as if I had passed through a stray beam of cosmic rays. My soul turned white in a single night. When Koch, a senior in an Illinois high school studying Shakespeare, learned that Alexander Salvini was coming to play *Hamlet* in the Grand Opera House (how grand we all were in the flamboyant 'nineties!), he dared greatly and besought his parents, both devoutly religious, to allow him to attend the performance. His good Methodist father, who proscribed the theater and relaxed only so far as to allow Fred to gaze starry-eyed at an occasional circus parade, relented when the eager boy fervently pled: "But, Dad, how shall I ever understand Shakespeare? How shall I ever know what a supreme dramatist he is, if I am not allowed to see his plays produced in a theater on a stage before an audience?" This bit of amazingly precocious criticism, although perhaps not expressed precisely in these words, tipped the scales in Fred's favor.

"You know how I feel about these things," mused his father. Then he boomed: "You go on your own responsibility!" What a dangerous concession was that! Fred came out of the theater that night, after the *Hamlet* of a supreme genius by a world-shaking player, a changed boy. Fred was now a Man: a Player, in Negro lingo, "des fum den on." The boy Fred, stirred to soul-depths unrealized by the myriad-minded dramatist and the fulgurant player, was the father of the man Koch, actor, lecturer, teacher, begetter and leader of the folk-play movement in the United States.

III

When Koch arrived at Grand Forks in 1905 to take up his duties as instructor in English at the University of North Dakota, at the princely annual salary of eight hundred dollars, there seemed nothing in particular to distinguish him from countless other ambitious,, indigent scholars. He was born at Covington, Kentucky (another bond between us, because my great-great-grandfather, founder of Boonesborough, is historically known as "the political father of Kentucky," and I rejoice in the rank of Admiral in the Kentucky State Navy!), September 12, 1877 (only three months later than myself). Fred had gone through the familiar academic mill, being graduated at Ohio Wesleyan University in 1900. But after graduation he had enjoyed an experience rich and strange: a study of art and architecture in Europe, North Africa, and Syria. Art had somehow got into his blood-stream: already this early he burned with the love of acting, of drama, of dramatic composition, and of that most alluring to the moth of all candles—that "palace of light and sorrow," the theater.

How callow and naïve he was! The particular brand of "snipe-hunting" to which he was at once introduced at Grand Forks was initiation into the Young Men's Club. It was a friendly frame-up, a mischievous net to catch the unwary. At two A.M., while hilariously enjoying himself in a ring-side seat at a boxing-match—staged for his especial entertainment on the third floor of the old Odd Fellows Hall—the place was "pulled" by two preternaturally stolid cops, and Fred, terrified and unprotesting, was haled off to the magistrate's court. The charges were: (1) aiding and abetting a prize-fight; (2) violating the Sabbath law; (3) aiding and abetting a public nuisance. The Young Men's Club and the shrinking and unsuspicious culprit were vigorously defended by the Club's young lawyers, before a fine old Irish J. P. (who was in the secret). The winning argument was the unanswerable declaration that the case was illegal and could not be continued, as it had all been conducted on Sunday.

"Well," said the magistrate most unctuously, in his rich Irish brogue, "in view of that circumstance, the case will be quashed."

Fred, panic-stricken by the dread of a resumption of the case and the loss of his job, faltered: "But does that mean the case will come up on Monday?"

"No," replied the magistrate genially, with a Celtic

twinkle in the eye, "you may dismiss your fears. The case is quashed—forever."

Koch, the heavy coating of verdure soon wearing thin, plunged with ardor at his task. His first important step was the immediate establishment of the Sock and Buskin Society which, after five years found reincarnation in the Dakota Playmakers in 1910. The date is historic, following by only five years the renaissance of pageantry, originating in England and spreading thence throughout the United States.

Maxwell Anderson, to-day justly famous as one of America's leading playwrights, was then serving as editor of the college newspaper, writing reams of free verse, and acting (euphemistically speaking) as a very humble, indeed a charter member of the Sock and Buskin Society. Years later, chatting and drinking beer together after the smashing success of *What Price Glory*, in which Anderson collaborated with Lawrence Stallings, Anderson interjected: "Proff, don't you remember that I had my beginnings with you at Grand Forks? I was an actor for you once."

"You *were* not," exclaimed Proph skeptically.

"Yes, I was," retorted Anderson. "Don't you remember the production of *Twelfth Night* by the Sock and Buskin? You cast me for the smallest part in the whole show. I was the Captain, who appeared in Act I, Scene 1, only. But as an actor I was so rotten that after the second rehearsal you fired me."

Proph felt himself put "on the spot" for the moment by this glamorously successful playwright, and dexterously changed the subject.

"Max, what are your royalties now on *What Price Glory?*"

"A thousand dollars a week," preened Anderson. "But we're planning to have a second company open in Chicago soon, also to send out five road companies."

FOREWORD

"As a playwright," ruminated Fred, "I'll say you're not doing so badly. At least, Max, please give me credit for firing a rotten actor to save a good playwright!"

That is all the claim Proph advances for the making of Maxwell Anderson as a playwright. But he must have moved Anderson by his class-room readings in a course in pre-Shakespearean drama, for in a reminiscent poem, "1908-1935," which Anderson inscribed "For F. H. Koch," one verse significantly describes Koch:

> Reading with emphasis aright
> The Faustian decasyllabon
> Of Tamburlaine's long last good night....

Through "barnstorming" tours of Dakota, in 1906 and later, in classic comedies, the ground was cleared for the making of true people's drama. At this time Koch was primarily concerned with coöperative authorship, acting and production. Individual plays utilizing local history and tradition were written; but also pageants of communal composition. Eighteen collaborated in the historical *Pageant of the Northwest* (1914) and twenty in the tercentenary masque, *Shakespeare, The Playmaker* (1916). An original contribution in stage technic was the Bankside Theatre, the first theater in the world, so far as known, to utilize the natural curve of a stream between the stage and the audience. This added another dimension to the stage, in that the stream permitted entrances and exits by water. There was always the picturesque beauty by day and night of the reflection of the stage scene, and the skies above, with fixed stars and floating clouds. Moreover the acoustics were virtually perfect, the water acting as sound reflector.

In a country of treeless prairies, it was but fitting that plays written in such a setting should have been termed by Koch "Prairie Plays." These simple folk plays written by

Koch's students, portraying scenes from ranch life, the adversities of pioneer settlers, and incidents along the cowboy trails, set in motion there an impulse which, after twelve years of experience in North Dakota, slowly gained momentum; and, later, from the vital focus at Chapel Hill, has now swept the country.

This fertile idea of stimulating the writing of plays, of the people, by the people, for the people, found lodgment in Koch's mind during his first years at North Dakota. Soon after his arrival an upperclassman startled him by the comment: "Last year at Commencement, we did *The Merchant of Venice,* up-to-date."

"Up-to-date!" stammered Koch. "What do you mean?"

"Oh! we had a lot of hits in it on the faculty!"

Although dejected at first by this picture of the low estate of drama in Dakota, the idea clicked in a somewhat different form.... "Why not up-to-date?" Fred argued with himself. "We should create drama about the people and the life we know and live—here and now." We are reminded of Shaw's long and stirring panegyric to journalism in *The Sanity of Art,** from which I allow myself to quote one passage:

The writer who aims at producing the platitudes which are "not for an age, but for all time" has his reward in being unreadable in all ages; whilst Plato and Aristophanes trying to knock some sense into the Athens of their day, Shakespeare peopling that same Athens with Elizabethan mechanics and Warwickshire hunts, Ibsen photographing the local doctors and vestrymen of a Norwegian parish. Carpaccio painting the life of St. Ursula exactly as if she were a lady living in the next street to him, are still alive and at home everywhere among the dust and ashes of many thousands of academic, punctilious, most archaeologically correct men of letters and art

---

* G. Bernard Shaw, *The Sanity of Art* (New York, 1908).

who spend their lives haughtily avoiding the journalist's vulgar obsession with the ephemeral.

When Koch sent Maxwell Anderson, then a newspaper man in California, a printed playbill bearing the legend "Native Prairie Plays," Anderson replied elatedly:

"What! Native folk plays of Dakota—like the Irish? If I thought that, I would walk all the way back to Dakota, to put my foot on the old sod!"

IV

The story of the last twenty years and more, since Koch arrived in Chapel Hill, is part of the history of the national American drama. But few people know that when Koch arrived in Chapel Hill, he had in his pocket the text of a play on a theme vitally related to North Carolina. Sir Walter Raleigh personally visited Guiana and despatched three colonizing expeditions to North Carolina. In 1918 extensive plans were under way for the Raleigh Tercentenary Celebration when Koch accepted the call here; and Greenlaw cannily conscripted him to write a full-length historic play, which he entitled *Raleigh, Shepherd of the Ocean*. One day in class soon after Koch's arrival in Chapel Hill, Paul Green, endlessly searching and inquisitive, sang out: "Proff, as long as you are in the business of teaching playwriting, why don't you show us how by writing plays yourself?"

It was Fred's glorious moment. He was not compelled to quote Shaw's destructive epigram: "He who can, does; he who cannot, teaches." With a deceptive air of modesty and diffidence, Proph drew the script of *Raleigh, Shepherd of the Ocean* from a drawer of the long table around which the playwriting class habitually gathered, and, handing it to Paul, murmured:

"There is a play I don't set much store by, but I wrote it—and it is about Sir Walter Raleigh. So you see, I have actually written a play and indeed, about the greatest figure ever associated with North Carolina, even before I ever set foot upon North Carolina soil."

Green was startled into silence and went off into a daydream. Suddenly he shot forth a question: "Where is this thing going to lead us to, Proff?" Proph prophetically replied: "I can't tell you, Paul; but I believe we are on our way."

Among the many answers are Paul Green and this volume of *American Folk Plays*.

The story of Koch's Carolina adventurings, struggles, and triumphs, has been admirably told in innumerable articles in the press, essays in magazines, the introductions to three volumes of *Carolina Folk Plays,* one volume of *Carolina Folk Comedies,* and one volume of *Mexican Folk Plays,* and in the notable periodical, *The Carolina Play-Book,* of which already eleven volumes have appeared.* I shall comment here on only a few salient features of his work during the last two decades. The present volume is a mark of the enormous stimulative and creative influence he has exerted, in many parts of this country, in Canada, and even in Mexico. From the three volumes of tributes sent him by friends and admirers, at the time of the great honors paid him at the University of North Dakota Commencement in 1935,† from which I made a selection published in *The Carolina Play-Book,* I venture to quote here

---

* For a rather comprehensive study of Professor Koch's activities, see Archibald Henderson, "Koch," *The Carolina Play-Book* (Vol. VIII, No. 3), September, 1935, pp. 87-92.

† On this occasion Frederick Koch was the recipient of a Litt.D. degree and honorary membership in the University of North Dakota chapter of Phi Beta Kappa. The subject of his Commencement address was "Making an American Folk Drama."

FOREWORD   xliii

only two. Arthur Hobson Quinn, historian of the American drama, who has long supported Koch's work with restrained approbation, wrote him outspokenly:

> You have done something which no one except yourself and your pupils have been able to do, and I believe your success is due largely to your unquenchable spirit that has never been discouraged by circumstances and that never truckled to anything that was base or banal in the theater. The best way to epitomize your service is to try to imagine what the American drama would have been during the last twenty years without you!

Among those letters, perhaps the most memorable, from Carl Carmer, of *Stars Fell on Alabama,* contained this passage:

> I remember that it was my knowledge of and admiration for your work in North Dakota and North Carolina which first interested me in the folkways of Alabama. In the seed which you planted then, long before I came to know you personally, lay the beginnings of whatever success I may have had in the field of American letters. And I know that, just as your influence was felt in the deep South, it was felt throughout the nation.

Worthy of permanent record here, also, is an editorial tribute in *Holland's Magazine,* July, 1936:

> His wide influence—not for a long time yet to be fully assayed—has spread indubitably into the associated fields of the novel, the short story, and even nonfiction works. From the basic idea underlying his work and philosophy stem such writings as those of Caldwell, Heyward, Miller, Bradford, Faulkner, Stribling, and other and younger novelists. Not that many more influences have not impinged sharply and deeply on Southern writers and on Southern thought generally; but Frederick

FOREWORD

Koch and his example have been a centralizing, crystallizing, and vitalizing force unequaled in Southern literature to date.

The influence of Koch, who took a Master of Arts degree at Harvard in 1909, has been personally exerted from one end of the country to the other, in lectures on countless platforms and at many universities, notably Columbia, Chicago, Pennsylvania, Michigan, Minnesota, Iowa, Texas, New Mexico, California, Southern California, Toledo, Northwestern, New York, Colorado, Manitoba, and Alberta. The Carolina Playmakers have successfully produced native folk plays of North Carolina in theaters from Massachusetts to Louisiana, and have given memorable productions of plays of Koch's students at the National Folk Festival at St. Louis and at Dallas. This year was held at Chapel Hill the Sixteenth Annual Dramatic Festival of the state-wide Carolina Dramatic Association Festival; and next year, delayed twelve months because of the disastrous fire in the Carolina Playmakers Theatre, which happily has now been completely restored, will occur the Second Southern Regional Conference and Drama Festival, at which time will be staged the celebration of twenty-one years of Koch's activities as founder and director of The Carolina Playmakers. All states east of the Mississippi River and south of Mason and Dixon's line will be invited to present plays by native playwrights in competition at the Festival. In this way, it is hoped, may be revealed a cross-section of the dramatic South, may be woven, let us say, a colorful tapestry of native dramatic design. I shall always remember sitting between Brooks Atkinson, drama critic of the New York *Times,* and Professor George Pierce Baker, head of the Department of Drama at Yale University, at the First Southern Regional Conference, during the performance of

Gertrude Wilson Coffin's amusing and highly local North Carolina folk play, *A Shot Gun Splicin'*.

"Very interesting, indeed," commented Atkinson afterwards; "but I didn't understand more than one-third of your outlandish North Carolina dialect"—one more illustration of the patent truism: "Who can the American language know who only New York lingo knows?" After the Festival was over, Baker remarked:

"If I could organize New England dramatically only half as well as Koch has organized North Carolina and elicit there such a remarkable outpouring of dramatic talent as has been exhibited here at this festival, I should feel well content."

When all is said and done, the secret of Koch's spectacular success is one word: enthusiasm. Koch has undying faith in the immortality of drama and the unquenchable flame of dramatic inspiration. He is a naïve and vibrant press agent for The Carolina Playmakers, and innumerable stories are told on him in proof thereof. One night, after a highly successful production in Greensboro, North Carolina, Koch dropped in on Gerald Johnson, then editorial writer on the Greensboro *Daily News*. It was Johnson's hour to write editorials: but Koch burbled happily on for an hour or two sounding the praises of his boys and girls. Later on in the week, Johnson described the incident amusingly in an editorial in the course of which he remarked that, had he caught Koch by the scruff of the neck and flung him through the window into the street, Koch would have landed on his feet, with arm upraised, uttering these words: "The Carolina Playmakers . . . !" On another occasion, Barrett Clark, Koch, and Paul Green were all at Green's home discussing the drama until the wee sma' hours. Koch fell sound asleep on the sofa, and in the course of the conversation The Carolina Playmakers were mentioned. Koch instantly awoke out of a sound slumber, Barrett declares, and asked suspiciously: "What's that about The Carolina Playmakers?"

Many have spoken in high terms of Koch's work, his philosophy of dramatic composition, his method of inspiring students and evoking latent dramatic talent. In his admirable work, *Footlights Across America,* Kenneth Macgowan, after describing Koch's approach to the problem, comments:

"This is the way of folk-playwriting, the way of the local drama. I do not know of a sounder. The dramatic instinct is close to being inborn. A man may train himself to craftsmanship if he can go to the theater enough. But a point of view like Koch's is a creative short cut. It is an invaluable contribution." In a penetrating article, "The American Note in the Drama," in *Current History,* October, 1933, the late Montrose Moses generously, yet justly, says:

Much of the credit for the awakening of local consciousness must go to Professor Frederick Koch, who, starting his experimental playwriting courses in North Dakota, brought them finally to fruition at the University of North Carolina.... Professor Koch has been faithful to that first ideal of his, and he has so thoroughly taught and demonstrated it all over the country that to him we owe not a little of the authentic honesty that has come into American drama.... Professor Koch has every reason to exult that his private idea of folk drama as first practiced in North Dakota has been so thoroughly assimilated throughout the land.

Archibald Henderson

Chapel Hill, North Carolina

NORTH CAROLINA

NANCY HANKS, BONDWOMAN
A LEGEND OF THE GREAT SMOKY MOUNTAINS

BY JANIE MALLOY BRITT

OF MARION, NORTH CAROLINA

Written in the playwriting course at the University of North Carolina and originally produced by The Carolina Playmakers at Chapel Hill on February 25, 26, and 27, 1937, under the title of *Leavin's*. *Nancy Hanks, Bondwoman* was included in the repertory of The Playmakers' Northern Tour, November 22 to December 4, 1937. Special performances were given in the Playmakers Theatre, Chapel Hill, for the Southeastern Arts Association on April 8th, for the American Chemical Society on April 12th, and at the University of North Carolina Commencement on June 7, 1937. It was first published in *The Carolina Play-Book*, March, 1937.

THE CHARACTERS

NANCY HANKS..................Marion Hartshorn
LEMMER, *a neighbor*...............Jessie Langdale
ABRAHAM ENLOE.....................Don Watters
SARAH ENLOE, *his wife*...........Janie Malloy Britt
TOM LINCOLN.....................Sanford Reece

SCENE: *The* ENLOE *house in the Ocona Lufta settlement in the Great Smoky Mountains of western North Carolina.*
TIME: *Late afternoon on October 5, 1808.*

Copyright, 1937, by The Carolina Playmakers, Inc.
All rights reserved.

A LEGEND OF THE GREAT SMOKY MOUNTAINS

FOR more than a hundred years now the tradition has persisted—passed down from fireside to fireside—that Abraham Lincoln was the son of Nancy Hanks and Abraham Enloe of the frontier settlement of Ocona Lufta in the mountains of western North Carolina. The great log house of Abraham and Sarah Enloe still stands, hard by the river of the same name, on land which is now a part of the Cherokee Indian Reservation.

Abraham Enloe and Sarah Edgerton were married back in their native county of Rutherford. There they adopted a child, Nancy Hanks, one of a large family of Bill Hanks, a cobbler who was so continuously drunk that he was compelled to move his business of mending shoes to the local jail. The story goes that his wife, because of their poverty, was forced to hire out some of her children. So Nancy was bound out to Abraham Enloe, and her sister to Abraham's brother, Isaac, a mountain preacher.

The Enloe family migrated west to the Ocona Lufta section of Buncombe (now Swain) County in the Great Smoky Mountains. There Abraham became a prosperous landowner and stock-raiser—so prosperous indeed that he purchased lands in the State of Kentucky to provide a stopping-place on the old cattle trail. In the Kentucky settlement Enloe set up a gristmill and hired as miller a man named Tom Lincoln, or "Linkhorn," as he was more commonly called.

The years passed and Nancy Hanks grew to womanhood, comely in form and features, of unusual charm, admired by all. Mrs. Enloe, of an intensely religious nature and constantly "ailin'," proved herself little more to her husband than a nagging wife, so Abraham turned to Nancy Hanks. And a strong attraction grew up between them, which flowered in an enduring love.

When Sarah Enloe discovered that Nancy Hanks was "in a state of increase" she insisted that the girl must leave her household. Then Abraham gave Tom Lincoln, his tenant, $100 and a mule to take Nancy with him into Kentucky as his wife. There in a rude log cabin in the wilderness the child was born, a man-child named by his mother, after the father, Abraham.

The legend that has come down holds that Nancy was cruelly beaten by her husband and died when the boy was only eight years of age. It is said that Lincoln never revealed the mystery of his origin and early youth, that he thought he was born out of wedlock and that a silence and sadness enshrouded him whenever the subject of his birth was mentioned.

"In storm and pain Abraham Lincoln was born," Miss Niggli, who directed the première production of *Nancy Hanks, Bondwoman*, was moved to write. "In storm and pain he died.... But what of Nancy Hanks, the woman who bore him? What did she think of in those nine long months while she carried him under her heart? Did she know then somehow, in vision and dream, that her son was to walk the earth as a greater man than any his century knew? Did Tom Lincoln, the stumbling, stuttering father, realize that his name was destined to be carved in granite, bronze, and gold? How could they know such grandeur in those dim days of 1809?

"The play is simply the story of a man and woman who loved each other. That their names were Nancy Hanks and Abraham Enloe is perhaps only a legend. But fate or legend or truth, the nine-months dream of Nancy Hanks, and the nine-months truth of Nancy Hanks, belong with the songs the Sirens sang, and what Achilles said when he walked among women."

Janie Britt, the author of the play, comes from a long line of Scotch highlanders. She has heard the strange story of Nancy Hanks by many a fireside since her earliest childhood. She tells us that her purpose in writing the play was "to clothe the traditional love story of Abraham Enloe and Nancy Hanks with warm living flesh." This she has done with sincerity, and with restraint rare in so young a writer.

NANCY HANKS, BONDWOMAN

The afternoon sun pours its golden dust through the narrow glazed window at the right, but it cannot pierce the shadowy layers cast by the rugged pine-log walls and the great stone fireplace at the rear. A fall chill is in the room, moderated somewhat by the glowing wood in the fireplace. Pulled up close to it is a rigid wooden rocker on the left with an upturned box facing it on the right. Near the box, between the window and the outer door in the right wall, is a weather-beaten bench, a bench on which children have carved their names, on which old women and old men have crouched, and young people have proudly sat. A good bench, a strong bench, a bench that has about it the same sturdy pioneer spirit as the grotesque, unpainted, tall, wooden loom that stands in the upper left corner. It is threaded with orange and green and blue and yellow lists, the only spot of color in the brown and gray room.

In the left wall, to the side of the loom, is a wall-cupboard, an "ark of the covenant," guarding within itself its precious burden: the family Bible. Beside it is a door leading into the bedroom.

Here is a room in which children have been born and died. A room that knows no compromise, that has rooted itself into the soil, as the trees from which it is carved had once been rooted. There is no luxury, no cultivated beauty, no sense of the loveliness of old grace and delicacy. This is no pattern of fragile half-blown flowers, but rather the bleak beauty of wind-stormed mountain tops, of pines

still green in spite of winter tearing at their hearts. *Here
is strength. The strength of a Nature and a God who
know nothing of compromise. The strength of a people
who read life in terms of good and evil, who dread no
future save Hell, no past save sin. The strength of
pioneers who tear their living from the wilderness, and
who look for Beauty in the splendid glory of God.*

[*As the scene opens,* NANCY HANKS, *a tall, awkward girl,
sharp-featured, blue-eyed, with dark, straight hair, is
seated at the loom. Her body, as she bends over her weaving, radiates intensity.* NANCY *works intensely, loves intensely, and hates intensely. She knows no compromise,
and the stoic strength of her spirit has never broken.*]
[*She quickly and deftly sets about her work of selecting a bit
of colored twist, and weaves it in and out across the
thickly-spun strings of the loom. She straightens it and
pushes the shutter into place with the rest of the material.
After a moment she bends over the basket of lists beside
the loom, sorting out the different colored skeins. Her
bending body is itself a rock foundation from which
might spring stoic fearlessness, mighty strength and ageless
wisdom.*]
[*The door leading to the outside opens and a fat, sloppy,
unkempt woman,* LEMMER, *waddles into the room. She
comes to a stop when she sees* NANCY *at work over the
box and stares at her intently for a moment, with disdainful curiosity.* NANCY *looks up in time to receive the full
benefit of the stare.* LEMMER, *caught unawares, gives a
"Humph," turns and goes out through the door she has
just entered.*]
[NANCY, *a look of puzzled resignation on her face, resumes
her work at the loom. A thin, shrill, sickly, middle-aged*

voice from the adjoining room wails out, excitedly inquisitive.]
SARAH [*from the bed-room at the left*]. Nancy—Nancy?
NANCY [*wearily*]. Yes'm, Miss Enloe...?
MRS. ENLOE [*relieved*]. I thought you... [*Suddenly.*] Who was that come in?
NANCY [*patiently*]. Hit was Lemmer.
SARAH [*sounding a bit embarrassed*]. Ah... Nancy, I do wish't ye'd come in to this fire when ye draw a breath. Hit's the wu'st coggled-up fire I ever laid eyes on.
NANCY [*continuing with her weaving*]. In one more list. [*Finished, she goes toward the door, right, which leads outside.*] I'll fotch a little kindlin'.
[*As soon as the sound of the closing door is heard,* MRS. ENLOE *enters the room from the left. She is a tall, bony woman, pale and consumptive. Her thin, straw-colored hair is drawn tightly in a knot directly on top of her head. Religious convention is her keynote and the God that she harbors is fire and brimstone, with never the shade of a compromise. To her, sin is black and purity is white and she sees no gray. She is clean and very primly neat, in her black dress with the starched white collar. She moves quickly to the window at the right and stands there, peering after* NANCY. *The bedroom door re-opens and* LEMMER *enters.*]
LEMMER [*brightly*]. Mornin', Mis' Enloe... ye're lookin' pearter'n common, jedgematically....
SARAH [*whining*]. Mornin', Lemmer, can't confidence my looks. [*Turning away from the window.*] Hit's the hurtin' in my chist, an' the shivers, I reckon, that keeps me a-beddin' it.
LEMMER [*kneeling by the list-basket at the loom and sorting the skeins*]. An' ye've shore had a spell of it, if'n I ever

seen one. This spell's kept ye a-beddin' hit fer nigh onto four months, hain't hit?

SARAH [*dragging her weak body to the rocking chair*]. Four months and off an' on a-fore then.

LEMMER [*sighing*]. 'Ell hit shore is hard, but the Good Man He's seen fit to send it, I reckon.

SARAH [*musing*]. Four months hit's been since I sot foot off'n this place. I reckon all the blossoms is fell away an' hit's high time fer the fall purties to be out. Hit shore is an uncommon sight to see. All purple, 'n' yellow, an' red, and blue somm'er's around, too.

LEMMER. Law, Mis' Enloe, you shore do love purties. [*Carrying some lists, she goes over and sits on the box.*] A-body'd know you're a good womern just to see your blossoms. Hit's a pity—

SARAH [*quickly becoming defensive*]. Now, Lemmer, the Lord giveth and the Lord taketh away, I ain't complainin'. . . .

LEMMER. Well, ye've shore had a sight of trouble—more'n common.

[NANCY *enters by the outer door, carrying an arm-load of kindling-wood. The two women stop speaking and gaze at her antagonistically. She returns their stare stoically. An instant passes in which a tense stubbornness fills the air. Then with a quick nod,* NANCY *mumbles a brief* "Howd'y'," *and strides across the room, closing the bedroom door after her.*]

LEMMER [*in a rapid whisper*]. I'd shore be ashamed! Thar' hain't nothin' funny about sech low-down goin's on!

SARAH. Lemmer, the Lord will see to it that she gets her punishment! Hit ain't right and hit ain't decent fer a woman to look at a man the way she looks at Abraham Enloe.

NANCY HANKS, BONDWOMAN

LEMMER [*righteously*]. An' right under your nose, an' you a sickly soul!
SARAH [*with the consolation of her stern religion*]. No good'll come of it.
LEMMER. An' I come in a hair o' tellin' her of hit that day.
SARAH. The Lord'll straighten hit out! I been a-prayin' an' a-prayin' with Abraham. Prayer'll show him the way.
[*The door at the left, leading into* SARAH's *room, opens. Conversation stops short.* LEMMER *begins to work at the lists. She is afraid that* NANCY *has overheard her conversation with* SARAH *and squirms uncomfortably.* SARAH *draws her mouth down into a thin, tight line, intolerance flaming through the look she gives* NANCY. NANCY *meets her gaze directly and speaks in a quiet unruffled manner.*]
NANCY [*at the loom now*]. Yer fire's goin' right good now.
SARAH [*rising*]. I'd better git to hit. [*Whining as she goes into the bedroom.*] The shivers 'll set in if'n I don't.
[NANCY *resumes her work, quietly efficient.* LEMMER, *unable to stand the silence any longer, speaks abruptly.*]
LEMMER. Well, an' how is Mis' Enloe this mornin', do you think?
NANCY [*without looking up*]. Well as common.
LEMMER [*still working as she talks*]. As good a womern as ever lived! [*She glowers narrowly at* NANCY.] The Lord only knows where we-uns would a-been 'thout'n her. [*There is a pause, then* LEMMER *adds spitefully, unable to resist this opportunity for nagging.*] Now take yourself when your ol' pappy was a-layin' in the Rutherford County jail, an' your pore old Ma had nothin' to do but hire you-uns out. Mis' Enloe didn't 'specially need a young-un, but she took you in, and they've been good to ye. Course they've been good to me, too, but ye've got a

right good eddication. Ye read the Bible in meetin' an' they've learned ye to back letters.*

NANCY [*quietly, but firmly, as if to close the matter*]. I'm satisfied.

LEMMER [*quickly following up this lead*]. An' ye shore ought to be. Mis' Enloe an' her man hev' had a sight of trouble what with their girl a-runnin' off an' a-marryin' thet Thompson feller—allus will say that done more to put Sairy Enloe flat of her back than anything else. She's shore got enough worries on her now to send her soul to torment. Not many gals is had your chanct. 'Course, I reckon they aim fer ye to pay—

NANCY [*rising*]. I have paid! The way I aim to keep a-payin'. I've done my work here every day since I've been a young-un. An' I aim to keep a-doin' hit! [LEMMER *gasps in amazement at this outburst.* NANCY, *seeing the consternation her words have caused, takes a breath of triumph, then bends over the list basket.*] Hev' ye made them green lists yit?

LEMMER [*sullenly*]. They're ag'in' the smoke-house. They ought to be dry. [NANCY *walks out the outer door, never for a second losing her stoical calm. As the door closes after her,* MRS. ENLOE *comes in from the bedroom.*]

SARAH. Who was that? Did Nancy go out ag'in? [*She crosses quickly over to the window at the right and peers out.*]

LEMMER [*rising and coming over to the window, stands behind her. They are two figures of self-righteousness and livid hate, as they bend slightly to stare through the window*]. Humph, hoists that head o' her'n prouder'n a lady!

SARAH [*sinking weakly down on the bench by the window*]. She's a-walkin' in sin an' she'll pay fer hit! She's brung misery to this house, and I reckon she'll take misery wherever she goes.

* To address envelopes.

NANCY HANKS, BONDWOMAN

LEMMER [*venomous in her disgust*]. She's jist *leavin's,* a man's *leavin's!*
SARAH. An' she's goin' t' find hit out. The Lord don't let no such go on fer long 'thout's He puts a stop to hit.... [*Pleased with the thought.*] That's what she is—*leavin's!*
LEMMER [*shuffling to the loom*]. Well, I better get them lists. She'll not git 'em done with jest her.
SARAH [*again peering out of the window*]. Abraham ought to be here soon....
LEMMER [*paying no attention to* SARAH, *who is looking admiringly at the loom*]. This shore is a-goin' to be a pretty carpet.
SARAH [*wistfully*]. I do aim to have me a listed carpet, if'n hit's the last thing I gets a-fore I die... all listed with as many colors as there's herbs in these here hills.
LEMMER [*smiling gently at her*]. Yes'm.
[*With a sad shaking of her head, she leaves through the outer door.* SARAH, *left alone, sighs, then slowly crosses to the wall-cupboard and takes from it her eternal comforter: the Bible. Rubbing her thin, stiff fingers across its cover, she seats herself in her rocking-chair. Opening it, she reads a verse; then, unable to keep her mind away from* NANCY's *flirtation with* ABRAHAM ENLOE, *she sinks back, her hands folded on the open page. As though in answer to the thought in the woman's mind,* NANCY *enters.*]
NANCY [*shivering slightly as she closes the door*]. Hit's a-turning cold.
SARAH [*speaking slowly, as though the doom of judgment were flowing through her mouth*]. Nancy, ye're a-goin' to hell, if ye don't get right with God—
NANCY [*quietly*]. Mis' Enloe—
SARAH. Ye needn't to think I don't know. I do. Nancy, the word o' God says that a deceitful woman is damned, and a

sinful woman will burn in hell-fire. God'll give ye a chanct, Nancy, if'n ye'll go to your knees an' tell Him ye've sinned.

NANCY. Mis' Enloe, God ain't—

SARAH [*beginning to preach*]. Nancy, there was another woman—a woman livin' in scarlet shame—the people of the town drug her out to rock * her to death, but the Lord saw to hit they never did. [*Her enthusiasm for her religion mounts to a high pitch.*] He scratched out these letters in the dirt: "Let he who is amongst ye without sin cast the first stone." He forgave her, Nancy, and he showed her soul salvation. He'll show you, if'n ye come to Him, girl. Tell Him of yer sins an' that ye're sorry.

NANCY [*sincere in her innocence*]. Hit ain't a sin, Mis' Enloe—

SARAH [*horrified*]. Ain't a sin? Ain't a sin to drag a man from the path o' glory down to the road to hell? A man with a family? [*Standing now.*] Hit is a sin! Hit's the blackest of sins—an' hit's blasphemy for ye to deny it. Ye'll burn in fire and brimstone fer it if'n ye don't confess.

NANCY [*aroused by this time*]. Mis' Enloe, God ain't namin' hit a sin to love like I do.

SARAH [*turning away in disgust*]. Love!

NANCY. God would know I was a-lyin', if'n I said I was sorry. I hain't sorry.

SARAH [*harshly*]. God help ye, girl. Ye're defying the Power when ye talk this way. God'll not put up with it. Ye'll come to a bad end because ye're a disciple of the devil. Ye're stubborn, ye're deceitful and ye're full of lust!

NANCY [*angrily*]. Hit's a lie!

SARAH. God'll see to hit that ye're put where you cain't drag decent folks to hell. He'll stop—

* Stone.

NANCY [*her voice hard and firm*]. Mis' Enloe, things *is* an' you can't change 'em.

SARAH [*her voice rising*]. Ye've had your chanct, an' ye won't listen! Ye're the whore o' Babylon ridin' the green dragon to the bottomless pit!

NANCY [*sharply*]. The Good Book has a name in this, too: "Jedge not thet ye be not jedged."

SARAH. God'll jedge ye. You shall be utterly burned with fire, for in—

NANCY. Ye'll not change things; ye've got your Abraham and your God—they'll save you. I've got my Abraham and my God. He'll take care o' me.

SARAH [*contemptuously spitting out the words*]. Who are you to speak the name of God?

NANCY [*slowly*]. Mis' Enloe . . . [*Almost reverently.*] I'm a-goin' to birth a child for Abraham. . . .

[SARAH *shrinks back from her in horror, the Bible clasped against her thin breast as though it were a buckler between herself and sin. Feeling the blasphemy of this, she looks down at the Book, then turns and puts it carefully away in the cupboard. Not until that moment can she trust herself to speak to* NANCY.]

SARAH [*in a horrified whisper*]. You git out'n this house!

NANCY [*quietly*]. Ye've got your God. But ye'll never have what we've got.

[*Some one is heard stamping on the front porch. Then* TOM LINCOLN'S *lazy drawl is heard off right.*]

TOM. Anybody home?

[*At the sound of his voice, the tension in the room is broken.* NANCY *goes quietly to the fire and begins to replenish it with wood.*]

SARAH. Who's there?

TOM [*outside*]. Tom Lincoln.

SARAH [*exultation begins to burn in her as she sees an answer to her problem*]. Come in. [*The door opens and* TOM LINCOLN *is framed in the doorway. He is slouched and dirty, small and wizened. The big, brimmed hat on his head seems to rest half-way down on his neck onto his stooped shoulders. His eyes are small and closely set; his forehead is low and narrow; and his chin recedes. All in all, he presents a picture of a cruel, weak man.* NANCY *goes to the door, and he is forced to step aside for her. She goes out, right. He looks after her with surprise, but turns to* SARAH.]
TOM. Howd'y'.
SARAH. Howd'y', Tom Lincoln.
[LEMMER *enters quietly and goes up to the window where she peers out after* NANCY.]
TOM. I was a-wantin' to have a few words with Mister Abraham. Is he about?
SARAH. He went to Soco, this mornin', but I'm lookin' fer him now. [*Very cordially.*] Won't ye set?
TOM. Well, I'm in right smart of a hurry. I reckon I'll walk on up the road a piece an' meet him. You say he ought to be back?
SARAH. Hit's long after time fer him. Set if ye will. . . .
TOM. No, I thank ye. I better be a-gittin' on. If'n I don't meet him, I'll come back. [*He leaves as abruptly as he came.*]
LEMMER. I reckon he's doin' right well over thar' in Kaintucky, a-grindin' for you-uns.
SARAH [*joyfully*]. Lemmer, the Lord's seen fit to send an answer to my prayers!
LEMMER [*puzzled*]. What ye a-meanin'?
SARAH [*dropping to her knees*]. Go to yer knees, woman, an' thank the Lord fer a-savin' us from this hour o' misery.
LEMMER [*kneels at the box*]. Praise the Lord!

SARAH [*exultantly*]. Thank ye, Lord, fer sending this man—
this Tom Lincoln—from Kentucky to take Nancy to his
bosom as his wife. Thank you, Lord, fer givin' her this
chance to bathe in the blood of the Lamb. Yea, to bathe
her red sins in blood, so that they shall be white....

[*At this moment* ABRAHAM ENLOE *enters from the porch. He
is a tall, slender man, with dark hair, deeply sunk eyes,
beetling brows, and a short, clipped beard. Dressed in
rough, homespun clothes, he is a homely man whose facial
ugliness has been submerged by a burning love of beauty.
Patriarchal, he is tortured by the thought that God is not
repentance, but redemption. His spirit is like* NANCY'S,
honest, clear, strong as ice in winter. SARAH *rises and turns
to him, her eyes burning with religious fervor.*]

SARAH. Rejoice! Rejoice! The Lord has seen fit to send us a
sign.

ABRAHAM [*puzzled*]. What are you sayin', woman?

SARAH. The Lord has seen fit to lift the sin from this house!

ABRAHAM. Woman, what ails ye?

SARAH [*with intense scorn*]. Don't you think I know? Don't
you think I've seen?

ABRAHAM. What do you know, and what have you seen?

SARAH. All the times I've had to be shushed on account o'
what folks hereabouts would think. All the times I've had
to set an' hold my feelin' in—all the times the man I married with her I raised!

ABRAHAM [*warningly*]. Mind your tongue, woman!

SARAH. Her I took from out'n her mammy's arms—her I
took when her pappy was a-lyin' drunk in jail!

ABRAHAM. Do you hear me, woman?

SARAH. Her, that's a bastard!

ABRAHAM [*roaring*]. Sarah!

SARAH [*more quietly*]. She is, an' ye know it.

LEMMER [*righteously*]. Her you've taught to read and write.

SARAH [*sinking down on the rocking-chair*]. Her I've done my best to make a Christian woman.
ABRAHAM. Nancy's a good, God-fearing girl.
SARAH [*scornfully*]. God-fearin'!
LEMMER [*sniffing*]. Devil-fearin', ye mean.
ABRAHAM [*angrily to* LEMMER]. Go tend to the lists.
SARAH. She ain't to go.
ABRAHAM [*decisively*]. I'm headin' this house! There's words between you and me, Sarah, that've got to be spoke. Lemmer, go tend to the lists.
LEMMER [*with a frightened glance at* SARAH]. Yes, Mr. Abraham. [*She scuttles out of the door, right. He shuts it after her and turns to* SARAH.]
ABRAHAM. You're makin' black what ain't black.
SARAH. Do you call what you and she've done God-fearin'?
ABRAHAM. What Nancy and I have done is between us and God, and nobody else!
SARAH. The Devil's got a hand in this. Ye can't lay hit all to the Lord.
ABRAHAM. Ye're talking about somethin' ye ain't got no knowledge of.
SARAH. I knows whorin' when I sees it.
ABRAHAM [*takes a step toward her, then pauses, his eyes dark with fury*]. Ye're passin' jedgment, Sarah, on somethin' ye ain't got no right to touch, no more'n you got the right of jedging the Lord God, Himself.
SARAH. Take not the name of the Lord in vain.
ABRAHAM. What do you know about God. He ain't nothing to you but fire and damnation.
SARAH [*vindictively*]. He punishes where punishment is fit.
ABRAHAM [*with firm, religious belief*]. God don't punish nobody. He can't.
SARAH [*scandalized*]. Abraham!

Wootten-Moulton

THE PLAYMAKERS THEATRE, CHAPEL HILL, NORTH CAROLINA

The audience at the Fifty-sixth Experimental Production of New Plays on July 20, 1938. The figure, standing at the right conducting the discussion, is Frederick H. Koch. The bald-headed figure seated in the row nearest Dr. Koch is Archibald Henderson.

NANCY HANKS, BONDWOMAN

NANCY [*reciting from the Bible*]. "And God said unto Abraham. Let it not be grievous in thy sight because of the lad, and because of thy bondwoman;...of the son of the bondwoman will I make a nation, because he is thy seed."

Wootten-Moulton

ABRAHAM [*doggedly*]. He can't I tell you. God's made out of love, there ain't no hate in Him.

SARAH [*in horror*]. She's been doin' this to you. [*Rises.*] Nancy's been eatin' your soul.

ABRAHAM. She's been showin' God to me, like I never seen Him to be.

SARAH [*preaching*]. Turn away from this sinnin', Abraham Enloe, before it's too late. This white witch is pouring the green oil of damnation over you. Turn to the paths of righteousness.

ABRAHAM [*goaded*]. I ain't walkin' to hell backwards like you're doin'.

SARAH [*firmly*]. You're a-walkin' to hell as straight as Ruben Lassiter.

ABRAHAM [*puzzled*]. Lassiter?

SARAH. Him as took his servant girl, Chloe, in adultery— just the same as you've took Nancy. Him as died in his sin.

ABRAHAM [*slowly*]. Chloe....

SARAH. Chloe that was sent out in her sin, same as Nancy should be sent out in her'n.

ABRAHAM [*in torment*]. I hadn't thought about Chloe.

SARAH. Chloe as bedded a bastard, same as Nancy will bed one.

ABRAHAM [*the word is torn out of him; he is forced to catch the loom for support*]. A bastard....

SARAH [*softly*]. But Nancy will have what the Lord God never seen fit to send to Chloe.

ABRAHAM [*almost pleading*]. What is that?

SARAH. A husband!

ABRAHAM [*stupidly*]. A husband?

SARAH. I tell you the Lord God has visited us with a sign. [*Raises her hand.*]

ABRAHAM [*painfully*]. Say it plain, woman.

SARAH [*with the fire of the Lord*]. Tom Lincoln!
ABRAHAM [*steps back horrified*]. Lincoln!
SARAH [*calmly*]. The same. He needs a woman to care after him in Kentucky. Nancy can do that.
ABRAHAM [*quickly*]. Not with Tom Lincoln. He's a liquored-up, lazy—
SARAH [*harshly*]. And he kin give a name to your bastard! Had ye thought on that?
ABRAHAM. Give a name... [*He turns desperately from her.*] Nancy and Tom.... It ain't right.
[*A sound of heavy footsteps is heard on the outside porch.*]
SARAH. Hit's Tom!—God's givin' ye this chance, Abraham. Leave it, an' ye dare! [*She goes up to the fireplace chair as* TOM *enters.*]
TOM. Howd'y', Mr. Abraham.
ABRAHAM [*dully*]. Howd'y'.
TOM. Come to see you 'bout my driving the stock.... Missed you down the road.
ABRAHAM. I cut across the field.
SARAH [*suspiciously*]. The field close to the barn where the lists are kept?
ABRAHAM [*sharply*]. No! The field across the door here. [*He relaxes and turns to* TOM.]
SARAH. Take a chair and set a while.
TOM [*sitting on the bench*]. Don't mind if I do. Cold a-crossin' them chimbleys, and smokier'n a coggled fire! Snow on ol' Baldy.
SARAH. Looks like it might be a hard winter. Reckon you-uns in Kentucky 're fixed?
TOM. A-h-h, I reckon. Folks in thar've been smarter'n common with their crops. Sure got a chanct o' hawg-meat laid by. Killed hawgs day a-fore I started. Fine a chanct of hawg-meat as I ever seen. Corn ain't lackin' none, neither, and the like o' dried fruit beats all! We'll not go hungry.

SARAH. Well, I'm right glad Abraham bought that piece of land in Kentucky. After all, it's come in good. [*There is a pause.*] Good for a stoppin' place 'gin he starts to drive them cows. [*Her attempt at making conversation is ignored.*]

ABRAHAM [*speaking suddenly*]. Tom, where ye aimin' to stop this winter?

TOM [*aroused from his nodding again*]. Huh?

ABRAHAM. Are ye aimin' to stay at the mill this winter, Tom?

TOM. A-h-h, I reckon so. Right quiet there. Nothin' 't all to fuss about ... kind o' lak' it thar' too.

ABRAHAM. U-m-m, reckon folks keep a-bringin' ye corn to grind. Ye seem to be a-doin' right well over there.

TOM. Nothin' to complain about. Folks know hit's your mill an' I'm a-workin' fer ye ... [*Grinning.*] ... distillin' a little on the side.

ABRAHAM. Yeah, I heard. [*There is a pause.*] Ain't courtin' none over there, are ye?

TOM [*contemptuously*]. Wommern's is scaircer'n hen's teeth in them parts, an' what's thar' is uglier'n a meat-ax! Courtin'! [*Snickers.*]

ABRAHAM [*in desperation*]. Tom, ain't ye aimin' to marry?

TOM. Humph! I reckon not, Mr. Abraham. Reckon women-folks is too much of an undertakin' fer me. They're allus a-ailin', an' I ain't aimin' to have no passel of young-uns traipsin' behind my tail.

ABRAHAM. Ye ain't ag'in' wommerns, air ye?

TOM. Well, not exactly, ain't got nothin' for 'em either.

SARAH [*rises*]. You're right smart, Tom. [*Looks deliberately at* ABRAHAM.] Better take care, or a girl like Lassiter's Chloe'll snatch ye.

ABRAHAM [*quietly, but firmly*]. Go on out, Sarah. You've talked enough.

SARAH. I'm a-goin', but remember the voice of the Lord. [*She goes into the bedroom, left.*]
TOM [*staring curiously after her*]. Bein' sick makes woman-folks queer, don't it, Mr. Abraham?
ABRAHAM [*fighting his battle within himself, crosses to the fireplace*]. More than common, Tom... [*He pauses, then turns abruptly, determined to speak.*] Tom....
TOM. Eh?
ABRAHAM. Tom, I've got something to tell you.
TOM. I'm a-listenin'.
ABRAHAM. It's about.... [*He pauses, his courage failing him*]. If I told you to drive the stock through, how long would it take?
TOM. Have you got 'em rounded up?
ABRAHAM. They're in the pen over at Soco.
TOM. I can leave to-morrow a-fore sun-up.
ABRAHAM. Would you be herdin' long?
TOM. Two days. [*Crossing to the window, he peers out.*] Ordinarily, I could do it in one, but it's blowing cold and stock ain't partial to cold.
ABRAHAM. Too cold for stock. God! Too cold for a woman....
TOM [*turns*]. Eh?
ABRAHAM. Tom, I'm... I'm in trouble.
TOM [*indifferently, as he rests his foot lazily on the fireplace box*]. Aw, we all get troubles.
ABRAHAM. God sends it, and we bring it on ourselves.
TOM. More'n likely.
ABRAHAM. Tom, hev' you ever seen Nancy Hanks?
TOM [*taking his foot down in surprise*]. What's ailin' ye, Mister Abraham? Course I've seen her. Been comin' here nigh on to twelve year now and of course I've seen her.
ABRAHAM. I mean looked at her. Do you know what she looks like?

Tom. Can't say in particular. Looks right sturdy.

Abraham [*looking into fire*]. Her eyes are gold, Tom, like sand in a brook.

Tom. I ain't never noticed if they be. Got to take a good look next time I see her.

[Nancy *appears in the doorway, with lists in hand. She hears her name called and stops short. Neither man notes her presence.*]

Abraham. Nancy's as good a hand to work as ever I seen. She's a good girl, Tom.

Tom. Mebbe so. Ain't nothin' to me though.

Abraham. Tom, listen to me. She's . . . [*He pauses, his face working with emotion.*]

Tom. I'm a-hearin'.

Abraham [*desperately*]. Ye must take her, Tom. . . . I'll see to all the expenses.

Tom [*with blank amazement*]. What ye sayin'?

Abraham [*pitifully*]. Nancy'd make ye a good woman.

[Nancy *drops the lists in horror; her slight movement causes the men to turn quickly. She is white with anger. Her tall body is trembling as she advances into the room gazing with wounded eyes at* Abraham, *who is unable to face her.*]

Abraham. Nancy, ye heard! [Nancy *does not speak but continues to stare at him.*]

Tom [*snippishly*]. Eavesdroppers never hear good o' theirselves.

Nancy [*turning on him in a sudden white heat of anger*]. Get out! [Lincoln *is amazed but, at a nod from* Abraham, *he leaves the room.* Nancy *and* Abraham *stare at each other.* Abraham's *eyes are pleading*—Nancy's *hurt. After a moment,* Abraham, *unable to meet the wounded spirit in* Nancy's, *turns away.*]

NANCY [*accusingly*]. I'd make him a good woman! Him, that nobody but a dog'll live with. I'd make *him* a good woman!

ABRAHAM [*pleadingly*]. Nancy, ye can't think...

NANCY [*bitterly*]. Do you think I could be to him what I've been to you? Do you?

ABRAHAM [*drawing himself up with a desperate grasp at self-control*]. Nancy, hit ain't right. But it's got to be.

NANCY [*fiercely*]. Because of talking it's got to be? Because of folks talking!

ABRAHAM [*facing the inevitable*]. Because of God, Nancy.

NANCY. Whose God?

ABRAHAM. Nancy!

NANCY. Their God or our'n, their God that's fire and hell and hate or our'n that's gentle and kind and lovin'.

ABRAHAM. Their'n and our'n; we've sinned, Nancy.

NANCY. We've loved, Abraham, and that ain't sinnin'. Nobody can tell me that's sinnin'. Not even... [*She pauses and sinks down with a hopeless sigh on the bench.*] Not even... not even you, Abraham.

ABRAHAM [*desperately*]. Do ye think I want to say it, Nancy? Do ye think it ain't tearin' the heart out of me....

NANCY. Then why do ye think it, Abraham? [*She looks at him as though longing for negation in his face. But his face is pitiful and contorted, and drawn with the struggle inside. She knows that he does think it a sin.*] You do think it, Abraham? You do?

ABRAHAM [*trying to explain himself to her*]. If it just were we-uns, Nancy, I wouldn't let nothin' stand between us. Not even the Good Book itself....

NANCY [*desperately*]. Then, why....

ABRAHAM. But it ain't just we-uns, it's *him,* too.

NANCY [*slowly*]. Him?

ABRAHAM. Him that's a-breathin' under your heart, Nancy.

NANCY HANKS, BONDWOMAN

Him that's my blood and your blood, my bone and your bone....

NANCY [*with awe*]. Your blood and your bone....

ABRAHAM. He can't be like Chloe's young-un—spat on and sneered at....

NANCY [*moaning, she covers her ears with her hands*]. No!

ABRAHAM [*taking a step toward her*]. I've been thinking, Nancy. In the nights I've been thinking. It's like I've been hearing the voice of God tellin' me what to do.

NANCY [*wildly*]. I can't hear God! I can't hear nothin' but you sendin' me away from you!

ABRAHAM. I can hear Him as plain as I hear you. "Hit's your son," He keeps sayin'. "Hit ain't you no more, hit's your *son*."

NANCY. What you meanin', Abraham?

ABRAHAM. Hit means that we-uns don't matter no more. Hit's what we've made a-tween us. Don't you see, Nancy? We've sinned. And he can't suffer for our sinnin'.

NANCY [*piercingly*]. We ain't sinned.

ABRAHAM. We have....

NANCY. We ain't. [*She goes up to him as she tries to convince him.*] If we had, God wouldn't have given him to us.

ABRAHAM [*doggedly*]. Chloe sinned and she had a young-un.

NANCY. But our young-un ain't like her'n.

ABRAHAM. Folks won't see the difference betwixt 'em.

NANCY. I ain't thinkin' about folks. I'm thinkin' about my young-un. He's goin' to be like you.

ABRAHAM [*turning away*]. I ain't no different from Lassiter.

NANCY. You are. He didn't care nothin' for Chloe.

ABRAHAM [*with quiet simplicity*]. I've loved you, Nancy.

NANCY. And I've loved you, Abraham. Our young-un ain't built from our blood and our bone. He's built from my love and your'n.

ABRAHAM. But we can't let him grow up a... [*Turns to her pleadingly.*]
NANCY [*calmly*]. A bastard, Abraham. I ain't a-feared of the word.
ABRAHAM. Ye've got to marry Tom, Nancy. Ye've got to!
NANCY [*slowly and quietly, resolved*]. I'll marry him, Abraham. I'll go with him to Kentucky.
ABRAHAM. Ye say it so quiet like....
NANCY. 'Cause I'm not a-feared of Tom. He won't be thar'... any more than he's here in this room with us now. [*Intensely.*] He won't have no more of me than a rock cliff of the rain.
ABRAHAM [*shutting his eyes against her intensity*]. Nancy, child, you're puttin' an iron on my heart.
NANCY. I ain't had but one husband. [*She takes the Bible from the cupboard and carries it to him.*] God knows that.
ABRAHAM [*clenching his hand*]. If he raises his hand to you.... [*He looks dully down at his own hand.*]
NANCY [*stretching out the Bible to him*]. Put your hand on it. Say, "You're my..." [*Her voice breaks, then she continues quietly.*] Say, "You're my wife, Nancy Hanks."
ABRAHAM [*with all his love for her shining in his eyes*]. You're my wife, Nancy Hanks.
NANCY [*quietly*]. You're my husband, Abraham.
ABRAHAM [*with awe*]. It's like God speakin' the words, ain't it, Nancy?
NANCY [*puts the Bible on the mantel*]. He did speak 'em, Abraham, right here in the Good Book. When Sarah said unto Abraham, "Cast out the bondwoman and her son," God said to Abraham...
ABRAHAM [*taking it up*]. "God said, 'Let it not be grievous in thy sight.'" [*He pauses and they gaze at each other.*] "And Abraham took bread and a bottle of water and gave it unto the bondwoman...."

NANCY HANKS, BONDWOMAN

NANCY [*softly*]. Ye'll never send me away, Abraham, 'cause ye can't. I'll take ye with me... under my heart.
[*He draws her gently to him and bending, kisses her mouth. The bedroom door opens and* SARAH *enters.*]
SARAH [*horrified, catches at the loom for support*]. A-whorin' in my own house! Ye might have the decency, Nancy Hanks, to git out'n the house with yer low-down...
ABRAHAM. Hold yer tongue, woman! I've listened to ye long enough.
SARAH [*pleading with them*]. Abraham, ye're rebukin' God A'mighty when ye talk this way. Go to yer knees you-uns, and tell Him ye've sinned!
ABRAHAM. God—
NANCY [*stops him with her hand*]. Mis' Enloe, God ain't wantin' penance. Hit'd be a sin to ask fer forgiveness fer the things you ain't aimin' to fergit. [*Her eyes turn towards* ABRAHAM.] My God'll take keer o' me....
[LINCOLN *opens the outside door and comes in. He is followed by* LEMMER. LEMMER *realizes that there have been "goin's on" and looks curiously from one to the other.*]
TOM [*breezily*]. Well—gittin' kind o' late... better git started 'gin I aim to reach Felix Walker's a-fore dark.
ABRAHAM [*with hopeless resignation*]. Yes, Tom, reckon ye had.—Lemmer, you go fetch that first ham o' meat hangin' jest inside the smokehouse door. [LEMMER *goes out, right.*] Tom, ye're to take that gray mare with ye. With the ham o' meat an' what corn ye got on hand ye ought to make out. That ought to do fer the two of ye....
TOM [*blankly*]. But I ain't aimin'...
ABRAHAM [*quickly*]. An' when ye come back I'll have a hundred dollars fer ye... [*Choking.*] a hundred dollars!
SARAH. Abraham!
ABRAHAM [*looks at her in a blaze of fury*]. Would ye send

the girl out 'thout'n a mouthful to eat and no way to get nothin'?

TOM [*eagerly*]. A hundred dollars. And the mule?

ABRAHAM. And the mule.

TOM [*seizes* NANCY's *arm. She breaks away*]. You were sure right, Mister Abraham. Her eyes are sort of gold.

LEMMER [*entering*]. I tied the ham on the back of your saddle, Tom.

TOM [*laughing*]. Seems as how you'd make a better wife'n Nancy, Lemmer.

SARAH [*righteously*]. No one goes journeyin' from this house without the comfort of the Good Book. [*Looks straight at* NANCY.] It don't matter if they ain't no more'n a—

ABRAHAM. Sarah!

SARAH [*finishes triumphantly*]. Than a bound girl. Let us go unto our Comforter. [*She drops to her knees. So do the others. Her prayer is a fervent bit of advice to God.*] Give this woman strength and maintenance in this new land of Canaan.

TOM AND LEMMER. Amen.

SARAH. Make her unto this man a good wife. Let her do him good, and not evil, all the days of her life. She layeth her hands to the spindle and her hands hold the distaff.

TOM AND LEMMER. Amen.

SARAH. She looketh well to the ways of her household and eateth not the bread of idleness. Favor is deceitful and beauty is vain, but a woman that feareth the Lord, she shall be praised.

TOM AND LEMMER. Amen.

SARAH. Pray, Nancy.

NANCY. Go with me, O my God, my Shepherd. . . . I shall not want. . . . Yea, though I walk through the valley of the shadow of death, I shall fear no evil. [*She turns her head, and she and* ABRAHAM *face each other.*] Thy rod and thy staff shall comfort me, and I shall dwell in the house of my Lord forever.

SARAH [*handing the Bible to* ABRAHAM]. Read from the book, Abraham. This bound woman shall go from us wrapped in the white cloak of the Lamb.

NANCY [*looking at* ABRAHAM]. And he "took bread and a bottle of water and gave it unto the bondwoman." [*As she speaks* ABRAHAM *moves up to her.*]

SARAH. Read, Abraham.

ABRAHAM [*looks sharply at* SARAH, *then quietly opens the Book with the calm certainty of one who knows exactly for what he is searching. His voice is clear and true as he reads*]. "Wherefore she said unto Abraham, Cast out this bondwoman and her son; for the son . . . [*He pauses, his voice breaking slightly, then gaining power*] . . . for the son of this bondwoman shall not be heir with my son, even with Isaac. [*He is not looking at the Book now but straight at* NANCY.] And the thing was very grievous in Abraham's sight because of his son." [*He pauses,* NANCY *takes a step toward him, and raises her hand, then lets it drop. He quietly extends the Book and she drops her hand on it. She begins to speak gently.*]

NANCY. "And God said unto Abraham, Let it not be grievous in thy sight because of the lad, and because of thy bondwoman; in all that Sarah hath said unto thee, hearken unto her voice; for in Isaac shall thy seed be called. And also of the son of the bondwoman will I make a nation, because he is thy seed."

SARAH [*suddenly starting as though having just become conscious of what is being said*]. Nancy!

[NANCY *looks at her a moment in triumph, secure in her knowledge of* ABRAHAM'S *love. Then, without a glance at* ABRAHAM *she starts toward the door, hesitates, lifts the* shawl over her head, and leaves the house. TOM *drags out after her.*

ABRAHAM [*blinded by the realization that he will never see her again, starts abruptly toward the door*]. Nancy!

SARAH. Abraham!

ABRAHAM [*looks at her, dully, his body drooping, his spirit without hope. Then he drops on the bench, opens the Bible, and begins to read softly*]. "And God said unto Abraham, Of the son of the bondwoman I will make a nation."

THE CURTAIN FALLS

TENNESSEE

DAVY CROCKETT
HALF HORSE, HALF ALLIGATOR

BY JOHN PHILIP MILHOUS
OF FAYETTEVILLE, TENNESSEE

Written in the playwriting course at the University of North Carolina and originally produced by The Carolina Playmakers at Chapel Hill on December 8, 9, and 10, 1932. *Davy Crockett* was included in the repertory of The Playmakers' tour of eastern North Carolina, February 26, 27, and 28, 1933, and it was revived at the University of North Carolina Commencement on June 5, 1933. *Davy Crockett* was first published in *The Carolina Play-Book*, March, 1933.

THE CHARACTERS

UNCLE DICK, *a tavern-keeper*..........Robert Proctor
KATE, *Dick's niece* ....Eugenia Rawls
TIM, *a young frontiersman* ....Alfred Barrett
MARTHA, *an old woman*...............Betty Barnett
SAL .... Phoebe Barr
ESTHER .... Jo Orendorff
BILL .... Frank McIntosh
LEE .... Edward Martin
UNCLE BEN, *an old Negro* ....William Bonyun
DAVY CROCKETT .... Foster Fitz-Simons
MARY, *his wife*.....................Marion Tatum
A GOVERNMENT AGENT.................William Pitt

SCENE: *A tavern in western Tennessee.*
TIME: *The fall of 1835.*

Copyright, 1933, by The Carolina Playmakers, Inc.
All rights reserved.

THE YELLOWEST FLOWER OF THE FOREST

THE author of *Davy Crockett*, John Philip Milhous of Fayetteville, Tennessee, has given us a colorful drama of the Tennessee frontier—of Davy Crockett, "Half Horse, Half Alligator," pioneer settler, Indian fighter, adventurer, statesman extraordinary, congressman, candidate for the presidency of the United States, and romantic hero and martyr of the Alamo!

The author tells us that he has endeavored to adhere as closely as possible to the known historical facts, "disdaining the use of fictitious situations and even the invention of speeches wherever the actual words of the man could be forced into the dialogue." If the play has suffered as a result of such a course the young playwright feels that at least he has "spared his cowardly conscience a great deal of misery."

His parents were born in Lincoln and Giles counties in Tennessee. As a child he hunted rabbits, quail, and other small game over the hills and in the canebreaks where David Crockett once chased the buffalo and the deer—where he killed three bears in a half-hour, sixteen in a week, forty in a month, and one hundred and five in a season!

The name of David Crockett has become little more than an obscure legend. Our young playwright of the Tennessee mountains does well to recall him to life on our stage—a man of all his tribe we cannot afford to forget.

He died at the Alamo in far-away Texas. With his little band of one hundred and eighty-two men he held the Alamo for eleven days against two thousand and five hundred trained soldiers, the flower of the Mexican army. On the sixth of March, 1836, they were brutally massacred. His body was found hacked to pieces in a corner of the fortress, his rifle shattered, and it is said a half-smile upon his face. "Thermopylae had its messenger of defeat; the Alamo had not one," is inscribed in stone on the State Capitol of Texas.

I quote in closing from the playwright's article, *Davy Crockett*, published in *The Carolina Magazine* for December 11, 1932:

"And so I close this little story of Davy Crockett, this tiny sketch that began in the sunlit forest of Tennessee and ended in the Texas sand. And no one has told me any more to say, but my heart goes out and my two eyes are bright for seeing yet another chapter. The scene shifts and I think I can feel something of the hurt, somewhat the silent grief of the little Irish wife in Tennessee, when the news comes back, the news that the man she had never really known, the man who was always marching away to Congress or to war, would not come back. And there are no stage lights to dim for her, no sad music to prepare the audience for her sorrow as the curtain of ninety and six years draws back upon its dark proscenium.

" 'Davy Crockett... Davy... Crockett!' The yellow flower of the forest, shattered, crimson in the desert air."

DAVY CROCKETT

Scene I

The scene is the big room of a backwoods tavern of West Tennessee on a fall night in 1835. At the left is a bar extending diagonally across the corner of the room; at the left, front, is a door leading to the interior of the tavern; at center, back, another door, the outside entrance. On the right is a great fireplace, the mantel decorated with pewter plates. To the left of this, conspicuously placed, is a rough bench, and a corresponding one between the bar and the outer door.

Uncle Ben, *an old Negro minstrel, sits in the corner between the fireplace and the door. He plays for the dance and sings the songs. With his whitened hair roached back, forehead low and narrow, flat nose protruding on either side of his face, he wears an expression of great dignity and unfailing courtesy. His pantaloons are tight, reaching only to the knee, but a ragged coat almost touches his heels, and his leg is set so nearly in the middle of his foot that, with toes on either end, nobody could track him!*

The Dancers: Martha, *a snaggled-toothed old woman, dressed in linsey-woolsey, with gray hair about her face in smoky wisps is having the time of her life.* Uncle Dick, *the tavern-keeper, is her masculine counterpart. He is bent with rheumatism and shows the stubble of a two-weeks' beard on his weather-beaten face.* Bill, *a huge tough, extremely good-natured but capable of rough action when aroused, is also unshaven.* Sal, *a fresh, young girl of the frontier and, like Bill, showing a taste for fancy colors, is bubbling over with an excess of animal spirits.*

KATE *is a rather refined, sweet girl, not long from Ireland; she is somewhat more independent, if possible, than most, and knows her power over men.* TIM *is a tall, slender youth with a delicate, sensitive face. He is a bee-hunter, that is, he makes his living by hunting out and selling wild honey in the settlements. He is also something of a poet, snatches of song being always on his lips. He and* KATE *are comparatively well educated.*

[*The dance is all life.* * *Terpischore of the frontier is ever vigorous, alive, real. It is a square dance, a modification of the universally popular Virginia reel. As the curtain goes up, the men are lined up on the left, the women on the right, clapping and keeping time with their feet.* BILL *calls the figures. The first tune:*

UNCLE BEN.

Ol' Dan Tucker was a good ol' man,
Washed his face in a fryin' pan,
Combed his hair with a wagon wheel
An' died with the tooth-ache in his heel!

Thar you go, Old Dan Tucker,
You're too late to get yo' supper.
                [*Repeat.*]

BILL. Salute yo' pardners!
Down front!
Grapevine!

[*When the grapevine figure is almost completed, they are suddenly brought up short by the breaking of a string.*

---

* As many couples as practicable may be introduced into the dance as well as into the crowd scenes throughout the play. The tune may be improvised from "Turkey in the Straw."

DAVY CROCKETT 35

All give exclamations of disgust and crowd about the minstrel, who soon knots the string and is ready to go again.]
UNCLE BEN. Aw shucks!
DICK. Hey, Marthy, give us a jig!
ALL. Come on, Marthy! Shake a leg! Hop along, Sister Marthy, hop along!
MARTHA [*waving them aside*]. Strike up a tune, Uncle Ben. —Land alive, I kin go to my death on a jig!
UNCLE BEN. Mis' Marthy, I lube to see yuh; yuh so limber on de flo'!
[MARTHA *dances,* UNCLE BEN *sings:*]
  I started off from Tennessee,
  My old hoss wouldn't pull fo' me.
  Now back step an' heel an' toe!
  He began to fret an' slip,
  I began to cuss an' whip,
  Walk jawbone from Tennessee,
  Walk jawbone from Tennessee!
  Now weed corn, kiver taters, an' double shuffle!
  I fed my hoss at de poplar trough,
  It made him cotch de whoopin' cough.
  My ol' hoss died in Tennessee
  An' willed his jawbone here to me.
  Walk jawbone from Tennessee,
  Walk jawbone from Tennessee!
[MARTHA *stops and staggers against the bar, all out of breath. They urge her on, but she has had enough.*]
ALL. Aw, come on, Marthy. You ain't started yet. Come on, give us Jim Crow!
MARTHA. Wa'n't that killin'—an' didn't I go my death!
DICK. You did that, Marthy. You sho' can go the hull animal. But I did too!
MARTHA [*exhausted, pulls up her striped hose and gratefully accepts the drink* UNCLE DICK *pours for her.*] You

shore did, Dick. Ain't you the yallerest flower of the forest though!
SAL [*taking a drink to* UNCLE BEN *who grins and bows*]. Here, Uncle Ben, swaller that alive.
BEN. Thank ye, Miss Sal.
[KATE *and* TIM *seated on the bench at the front, right, have been whispering about strange things.*]
KATE. That seems to me shameful.
TIM. Aye, shameful it is, but no more than the way you've been treating me. [*He slides closer. She pulls his hair.*] How much are your kisses worth, Kitty O'Kerry?
KATE. More than you could ever repay me, Timothy Shane. [MARTHA *suddenly takes notice. She motions to* UNCLE DICK, *who comes from behind the bar. They slip up toward the unconscious pair.*]
TIM. Then suppose I was just to be owin' you a couple. [*He catches her, but is arrested by* MARTHA *before any damage is done.*]
KATE. I'd call it a bad debt, Timothy!
[DICK *and* MARTHA *point accusing fingers.*]
MARTHA. What air ye doin' young Timmy, an' what air ye doin' sweet Kate!
UNCLE DICK. Ah-h, sparkin' in the corner—we knows you! An' a dance goin' on!
[TIM *and* KATE *have risen, good-naturedly embarrassed.*]
MARTHA. Ain't young-uns the funny things, though. They do be at that.
TIM [*with lyric flourish*]. On such a night as this methinks.
...[*The entire crowd joins in the fun at* TIM'S *expense.*]
UNCLE DICK. Aw, you an' yer poetry! Can't ye even fergit poetry when ye got a bonny lassie like Kate by yer side?
KATE [*nose tip-tilted*]. I'm not at his side—or anyway I wouldn't be if there were anybody else about. How about

you, Uncle Dick? Couldn't you stand a bonny lass at your side? [*Going to* UNCLE DICK *coquettishly.*]
UNCLE DICK [*as she takes his arm*]. Oh, ho! Wal, I beat ye, Timmy—fair and square. But you know I'm married up tighter'n Dick's hatband, I am. So ye needn't worry; I ain't goin' t' take her. But you ain't neither if you keep feedin' her on honey. Set up pert to her; that's my advice to you, an' you'll have her eatin' out of yer hand in no time. Heh, I allus was a hound with the women. [*He drops her hand and waddles over to the bar.*] Come on, folks—on the house! [*They need no second call.* UNCLE DICK *raises his glass in a toast.*]
[*The door opens silently and a* HUNTER *with a long rifle appears. He surveys the scene, leaning on his gun. He is tall, wiry, athletic, with a face that is determined, forceful; yet kind and strangely youthful. He seems somewhat a lad full of youthful exuberance for all his size and age, for he is apparently about forty-five. His is a dominant personality, so dynamic and radiant that only the crowd's absorption keeps it from feeling his presence.*]
UNCLE DICK. To the Ginril, God bless him, an' long may he flourish!
THE CROWD. Yeah, Ginril Jackson! Hurrah for Ginril Jackson!
THE STRANGER. Hurrah for hell—an' praise yer own country! [*He pauses with a fine sense of the theatrical to let the effect register, then swaggers into the room.*] How do ye do?
UNCLE DICK. Same as common, I reckon. How do ye do?
THE STRANGER. Most as I please, now that ye're askin'. [THE CROWD *resents this and murmurs angrily.*]
BILL [*slouches over. He is a tremendous fellow, apparently twice the size of his antagonist, with huge hands and arms. He is perennially good-natured but quick to resent an in-*

jury or a challenge]. Them's mighty uppity words, Stranger.

THE STRANGER. Thar's more whur they come from, case you want to hear 'em.

BILL [*bellows*]. Listen, ye runt, whur did ye come from!

THE STRANGER [*standing his ground and staring insolently and provocatively*]. I'm jist some'pm crawled out o' th' harricane to see what's goin' on 'mongst th' white folks— an' shoot off me forelock if they ain't gettin' ready to vote for old Jackson!

ALL. Down him! Down the man who dares defy Ginril Jackson!

BILL. So ye're agin' Ginril Jackson! Stranger, I don't value you. I don't, not a-tall.

THE STRANGER. Whur I come from if they don't value a man, they got ways o' lettin' him know it. An' neither does I value you. Yer all dressed up in buckskin, but ye brays like a jackass.

THE CROWD [*horrified*]. Get him, Bill! Grab him!

BILL. That ain't airy man livin' has dared to say that an' few of 'em dead ever dared. If your mammy don't know you're out in this neck of the woods, you better git home an' you better git fast, cause I'm rough an' I'm tough, an' I'll chaw ye up fer supper!

THE STRANGER. I don't know who ye air, but ye shore can *talk* a mean fight. Whur'd ye git that face ye're a-wearin', you splay-footed son of a pigeon-toed terrapin? It looks like a coon grinnin' in the forks of a tree. [*They thrust their faces together and begin to circle each other.*] I can grin too. I can out-grin any domn coon till he falls off his perch.

MARTHA. Go after him, Bill! Stomp 'im!

SAL. Git me his hide fer a fur collar!

UNCLE DICK. Turn him wrong side out'ards. (TIM *gets*

KATE *out of the way and stands protectingly in front of her. The antagonists circle each other.* THE STRANGER *flaps his arms and crows.* BILL *snarls and growls.*]

MARTHA. Come on, Bill. Finish him up!

SAL. Snatch me his gall-bladder!

UNCLE DICK. I'll have his lights and liver! Get 'em fer me, Bill.

[BILL *makes a dive for* THE STRANGER'S *legs and finds himself lifted adroitly in the air and plopped on the floor with the Terror on his back. They struggle violently, but it is no use;* BILL *is "licked."* THE CROWD *shows disappointment.*]

THE STRANGER [*holding him down*]. You're a right smart coon, you are; but you ain't nearly a bait fer a feller like me.

BILL. Think you're a ripstaver, don't yer?

THE STRANGER. Think it an' know it; what's more I can prove it. Don't ya' like it, don't ya' take it—hyar's my collar, come an' shake it!

BILL [*as* THE STRANGER *twists his arm*]. Ye-o-ow! Calf rope!

THE STRANGER [*rising and helping* BILL *to his feet*]. Ain't I the yallerest flower of the forest? I'm all brimstone but the head an' ears—an' them's *aqua fortis*.

BILL. Ye licked me plenty, Stranger. You shore air a beauty —Who be ye now? If I knowed who ye was, I'd vote fer ye shore.

THE STRANGER [*with heroic flourish*]. I'm that same Davy Crockett—half horse an' half alligator! [*The look of astonishment on the faces of* THE CROWD *changes to one of extreme pleasure as* DAVY *and* BILL *shake hands.*]

THE CROWD. Davy Crockett!!

DAVY. Yes, Davy Crockett, that lives on the crack of an earthquake, rides on a streak of lightning, can slide down a honey locust without gettin' a scratch! I can whup my weight in wild-cats, an', if any gentleman cares (for a ten-dollar bill), a panther throwed in! I can hug a b'ar too close fer comfort, an' eat any man that's fer old Andy Jackson!

THE CROWD. Yea, Davy Crockett! Drinks, Davy Crockett!

DAVY. Drinks fer my people! Come up, all ye folks! [*As* UNCLE DICK *pours the drinks,* DAVY *hesitates, then draws a lone coon skin from his belt. This he throws on the bar.* UNCLE DICK *picks it up admiringly, rubs his hands, and drops it in the box at the end of the bar.*]

UNCLE DICK. Thank you, Davy! Thank you.

SAL. Now tell us a story, Davy.

DAVY [*swinging himself up to sit on the bar*]. What'll it be?

SAL. About a b'ar!

DAVY [*leaning over*]. A big black b'ar?

MARTHA. Yes-siree, a big black b'ar—a whole flock of b'ars! [*She giggles excitedly.*]

DAVY [*confidentially*]. Thar ain't no more b'ars! [*They shout with laughter.*] They heard I was comin' an' took out from th' cane. They know Davy Crockett—half horse and half alligator—touched up a little with the old snappin' turkle—that can kill more licker, an' love more women, see more fun, an' set up later than any he-devil this side o' doom!

MARTHA. More drinks, Davy Crockett!

SAL. Drinks, an' a speech about Jackson. [DAVY *thinks quickly. He motions* THE CROWD *up, when* UNCLE DICK'S *back is turned, he fishes the coon skin out of the box, passes it behind him, and enjoys the hilarity created by his brilliant piece of chicanery.*]

UNCLE DICK. Thank you, Davy. Thank you. [*He drops the skin back in the box.*]

DAVY. Fill 'em up plenty, brother; fill 'em up plenty.... Folks, I'm askin' you to send me back to the halls of Congress. I been thar before an' I need to go back to stop Andy Jackson. Now I didn't take this course of opposin' the Ginril because it was popular—cause it shore to God ain't. He's got his follerin' an' they's folks as would die fer him. I ain't ag'in' that; no, I ain't ag'in' that. But when he sets hisself up to be *God,* an' king o' this country what's supposed to be *free,* it's Mr. Davy Crockett what's going to yell "Whoa!" [*To* UNCLE DICK.] What do ye know about Jackson, Brother?

UNCLE DICK. Why, he licked the Britishers down to New Orleans.

DAVY. Seems I remember thar was other folks thar had a hand in the fightin'. Who was some o' th' officers an' some o' th' men that fought an' bled blood besides Andrew Jackson? Who was they, Brother?

UNCLE DICK. I don't know! I allus heard Andy done most of it.

DAVY. Yes, that's what you heard. But there was others there, Brother, and don't ye fergit it. The Ginril's only a man, an' he ain't no more neither— Why, he planted a cannon in the middle of a bridge an' he says, "Davy Crockett, you'll stay whur I tell you!" Sez I, "Ginril Jackson, I'll drap ye a postal card when I git home!"

THE CROWD. Yeah, Davy Crockett!

BILL. What happened with the cannon?

DAVY. Has anybody heard of Davy Crockett gettin' shot?

SAL. Takes more than a cannon-ball to stop Davy Crockett.

MARTHA. He splits right through 'em like a scythe in the grain.

THE CROWD [BEN *leading them in a chant, keeping time with their feet*].
Ginril Jackson had a army of a hundred thousand men,
He marched 'em up the mountain an' he marched 'em down again!

BILL. But not Davy Crockett! Yeah, not Davy Crockett!

DAVY. And I'll tell you one more about old King Andy. He's stole the deposits an' disrupted our finances; an' he's got to put 'em back—or somebody else has. Him and Van Buren! I wonder how long are you folks in the backwoods goin' t' put up with these two Heavenly Twins! [*He strides back and forth in his excitement and evidences disgust when he thinks of Jackson, almost spitting out the words.*]

THE CROWD. Go on, Davy Crockett!

DAVY. Yeah, yell for Crockett—but you yell for Jackson too, and I can't swaller that.

SAL. You stop 'em, Davy.

MARTHA. You tell 'em what's what.

DAVY. That's what I'm asking you—give me the chance, an' ring off m' neck if I don't twist their tails till they holler calf rope. They ain't a whole lot I got done up to date, but they's one thing shore—they ain't nobody yet hung a collar round my neck sayin': "MY DOG, (*Signed*) Andrew Jackson!"

THE CROWD. Hooray! [DAVY *waves them up.*]

DAVY. Soak 'em up, folks. Have a drink on th' Senator!

TIM. Let's drink to Davy Crockett—the yellow flower of the forest!

[DAVY *again fishes out the coon skin. The crowd enjoys the joke, as before.* UNCLE DICK *rubs his hands like a bloated plutocrat.*]

DAVY. As I was a-comin' along up here, I met a old man at the forks of a trail. Says he, "Huntin' squirrels?" Says I, "Naw, I'm a-huntin' my way!" Says he, "Yes, sir, I think they's some up thar." Says I, "Hell fire, I'm askin my way. Can ye tell me if that road leads on to the tavern?" Says he, "Most like two er three."

Now that raised my dander up even though I seed he

was deef. Says I, "I think ye're a domn fool!" "What's that you say?" says he—"I think ye're a DOMN FOOL!" "Sure," says he. "The hull woods is full of 'em!" [THE CROWD *laughs and shouts.*]

MARTHA. Did anybody ever git the better of you, Davy?

DAVY. Wal, I got a little woman back in the harricane that takes after me right spry sometimes. She sho' can scamper perditiously, that woman can. [*He is taking up his gun.*] I jest got one other thing to say to ye now before I start home, ye can all vote for Davy Crockett—or ye can all go to Hell!! [*Pandemonium breaks loose. They gather around him, shouting wildly and waving their arms. He stands in the center of the moving circle, with head thrown back and the full, rich, loud, joyous laugh of the primal backwoods roaring from his throat. No haughty Roman hero receiving the plaudits of the vulgar throng this; he is* DAVY CROCKETT, *American, Patriot, and Barbarian!*]

THE CROWD. Hurrah fer Crockett! Let's have a parade! Davy Crockett! Davy Crockett! [*All are cheering wildly as*

THE CURTAIN FALLS

SCENE II

SCENE: *The tavern, as in Scene I.*
TIME: *A few nights after the election.*
[DAVY *is seated forlornly on a stool at the right;* UNCLE DICK *is wiping off the bar. The coon skin is hung conspicuously on the wall.*]

UNCLE DICK. We'll be mighty sorry to be giving ye up.

DAVY. Sorry—I reckon....

UNCLE DICK. Come on—have a drink—but, mind ye, none of yer coon skins. This here's on me, so's I kin be sure ye ain't pullin' no fur over m' eyes. [DAVY *gets up smiling and walks to the bar;* UNCLE DICK *pours out the drink, and chuckles.*] That'll make ye whistle. Nothin' like Belle O' Lincoln when a man's blue-black inside. [*Assuming an attitude of revery, and leaning across the bar.*] I shore wish't I was younger. I'd haul out to Texas and have 'em all licked afore ye could git thar. I'd give old Santy Annie sich a belly-ache he'd fergit thar ever was a Alamo. [*He pats* DAVY *on the back.*] Man, ye're goin' t' do fine out thar in the West.

DAVY. Couldn't do worse than I've done hereabouts.

UNCLE DICK. Nah, don't ye say that. Why, gittin' defeated by two measly votes...

DAVY. Two or two hundred it's beat just the same. Now I can't go to Congress and stop Andy Jackson from ruinin' the country.... I'm beat, Uncle Dick; that's what's so irksome.

UNCLE DICK. Well, ye wouldn't have been if the Gover'mint hadn't worked against ye an' ye by yerself. That agent feller, he come hur' and wanted a room, but he shore didn't get it. Says I, "Ye varmint, go sleep in the br'ars. No man what's ag'in' Davy Crockett kin have a night's sleep under my tavern roof!"

DAVY. I'm mighty much obliged to you, Uncle Dick. I'll always remember the way you befriended me. And I've got a fine army to go with me out there.

UNCLE DICK. It ain't like 'twas goin' alone what with Timmy an'—

DAVY. Aye, a fine lad an' grand fightin' we'll see! Well, folks went to the polls and they says, "Davy Crockett, they's others better suited to be carryin' on the business of this big settled country." Maybe they're right. I never was made to set in soft seats and argue things out. There's jest one thing I does an' it's all I can do: When I'm sure that I'm right, I jest go *ahead!*

UNCLE DICK. Bedad, an' I'd like to be shakin' yer paw upon that. An' case I don't get another chance, what about now? [*He wipes his hand on the cloth, and* DAVY *shakes it heartily.*] It's all there, Davy Crockett! Men doesn't need to talk; you know what I mean. [*There is a silence between them.*] We'll be actin' like a couple o' old hens in a minute.

DAVY. Let's go down the road and see how Captain Davis is gettin' along with the preparations for the leavin'. I hate to be marching to-night but we must be in Little Rock to-morrow.

UNCLE DICK. Wait till I call the young-uns to tend bar fer me. [*He chuckles.*] But it's little attention two love-sick young folk is a-goin' to give it.

DAVY [*laughs and slaps him on the back*]. You old devil you!

UNCLE DICK [*calls*]. Hey, Timmy, bring your gal out an' tend bar fer me a while, won't ye? [*They leave when* TIM *answers.*]

TIM [*within*]. Sure, Uncle Dick. [TIM *and* KATE *enter, quarreling.*]

KATE [*pointing*]. That's the man would be goin' to Texas and getting in a war just for the fun of it.

TIM. Let's not be going over all that again. I tell you, if you'd heard him, you'd be wanting to go too—he was that pitiful, and him saying the people he'd fought for had gone back on him now. And the horrors he told about being done in that new bloody country. It made my blood boil till I just had to go. [*He takes her in his arms. She turns her face away.*]

KATE [*drawing away*]. Let me go.

TIM. Not if I can help it. [*She doesn't want him to see her cry. Seeing this he drops his restraining arm. She runs through the open door.*] Kate! [*He follows her out. She does not answer him and he returns and begins cleaning the bar, and idly half singing, half humming:*]

Oh, what is the time of the merry round year
That is fittest and sweetest for love?
Ere sucks the bee, ere buds the tree,
And primroses by two, by three,
Faintly shine in the path of the lovely deer
Like the few stars of twilight above.

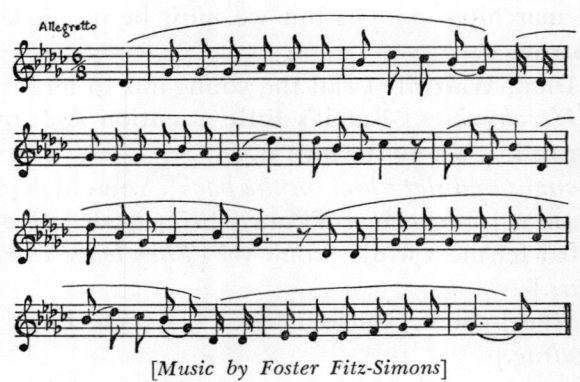

[*Music by Foster Fitz-Simons*]

[UNCLE DICK *comes excitedly into the room.*]
UNCLE DICK. Timmy! Timmy! Come here!
TIM. What is it, Uncle Dick?
UNCLE DICK. It's bad news I be bringin' ye, Timothy lad!
TIM. That's no surprise to me, what with Davy defeated and Kate not speaking.
UNCLE DICK. It's partly about Kate well enough. —You mind that slick agent feller—him as was wantin' to make love to yer Kate?
TIM. And what about him? [*A rumble of voices is heard in the distance.*]

DAVY CROCKETT

Uncle Dick. Well, he heard what ye said about him last night, and he's comin' this way to give ye a thrashin'.

Tim. Hah! And he's the man that was passing lies about Davy—is that all the bad news?

Uncle Dick. Hit's plenty to me.—Do ye think ye can handle him, Timothy lad?

Tim. Well, not till he gets here—not till he gets here! [*He continues the song.*]

> In the green spring-tide all tender and bright,
> When the sun sheds a kindlier gleam—

[A Government Agent *strides in brandishing a whip,* The Crowd *following.*]

The Agent. You young scoundrel! I'll teach you, impudent school boy! [*The expectant* Crowd *surrounds them;* Tim *continues singing:*]

Tim [*apparently unconcerned*]. O'er velvet bank that sweet flowers prank—

The Agent [*shouts*]. I say you're an infernal scoundrel, sir! —Do you hear?

Tim [*still unmoved*]. I do that. But it's news to me you are saying. [Davy Crockett *enters.*]

The Agent [*irate*]. News! You needn't think to carry it off so easily. I say you're an infernal scoundrel—and by God I'll prove it!

Tim [*with quiet reserve*]. I pray you do not. I shouldn't like to be proved a scoundrel.

The Agent. You answer me this—did you or did you not say that I was a mere—

Tim [*quietly*]. Calf? Oh, no sir. The truth is not to be spoken at all times.

The Agent. The truth! Do you presume to call me a calf, sir?

TIM [*simply*]. Oh, no sir. I call you—*nothing!*
THE AGENT [*hotly*]. It's well that you do, for if you should have presumed to call me—
TIM. A man? I should have been grossly mistaken. (THE CROWD *laughs uproariously.* DAVY, *brightened at the scent of a fight, edges in, grinning.*]
THE AGENT [*brandishing his whip*]. Do you see this? What do you think I'm carrying it for?
TIM [*winking at* DAVY]. Do you wish me to tell you just what I thought?
THE AGENT. Do if you dare!
TIM. I thought to myself—what use has a calf for a cow skin! [*He removes his knife from his belt and offers it to* DAVY.] Here, Colonel. Would you be so good as to hold this for me?
DAVY. Sure an' you could tickle his slats a long time with this and not make him chuckle! [THE AGENT *running to the bench, takes off his coat, and rolls up his sleeves.*]
THE AGENT. I'll flog you within an inch of your life.
TIM. I doubt it.
THE AGENT. I'm a liar then, am I?
TIM. Just as you please.
THE CROWD. You can't help flogging him now! Chaw him up, Timmy! We're with you.
DAVY. Man, I wisht I'd a-seen him fu'st!
TIM. You'll have to stand back, Colonel. This one's my property.
DAVY. Shore he is! You show him who's th' bull of th' woods. But if you ain't keerful, I'll lick him myself. I'll jump down his throat an' gallup through his belly like a b'ar in the canebrakes! [*He waves to the onlookers as the fighters approach each other.*] Come on up, folks, and form a ring. [*He motions to* BEN, *who shakes his head with a knowing grin and goes out.*]

THE CROWD. Gouge out his eyes, Timothy. Make liver-meat out of his fat face! Stomp 'im! Stomp th' life out o' him! Eat 'im up! Ain't he purty?

[KATE *appears in the door, frightened. As* THE AGENT *raises his whip,* TIM *catches his wrist and pins him to the floor.* BEN *runs in with a bucket of water.*]

BEN. Here, Massa Tim, give 'im a drink. [TIM *souses the water over his victim's face to the extreme merriment of the onlookers. They hoist him up and hustle him posthaste out the door, jeering after him.*]

THE CROWD. Get a rail! Tar and feathers! Sick th' army on him!

DAVY [*slapping* TIM *on the back*]. Wal, you won y'ur spurs, Timmy, my lad. I'm jist sorry I didn't git a crack at th' varmint, though. [*Scratching his head.*] I ain't had a honest-to-golly fracas in near ten days, an' I'm feelin' that wolfish about th' head and ears I'm liable to spile if'n I ain't kivvered up with salt.

KATE [*entering*]. Timothy! Fighting!

TIM. Well, you see, Kate, you went off and left me so what could I do?

KATE. Tim, don't you know I was thinking of you all the time? See—I've made you a satchel to carry your things when you go out to Texas . . . [*She offers him the satchel she has held behind her. He takes her in his arms.*]

TIM. But what's this inside it?

KATE. Your books, Timmy dear.

TIM [*taking out two of the three volumes*]. Just the Bible, Kate. I'll leave the poets with you—there may not be room for poetry in Texas. [KATE *hides her face on his shoulder.* DAVY *stands upon first one foot, then the other and slowly edges his way toward the door.*] Hey, Davy! Davy Crockett, where are you going?

DAVY. Wal, I'm jest edgin' outside. I never did hanker to

be the fifth wheel on nobody's wagon! [*He comes back and places his hands on both their shoulders.*] Suppose you two jest run your wagon into the next room—it'll run smoother in there. [*They comply. At the door* TIM *turns.*]

TIM. You'll be calling me when you're ready, Davy, for I'm going with you, and don't you forget it!

DAVY. Sure ye are, Tim; an' we'll carve 'em up plenty. Hooray for Texas! [*He chuckles to himself as they go. The door opens and* MARY *enters. A slow, sad smile comes to his face.*] Ye shouldn't have come after me now, Mary. It was hard enough to leave ye at best.

MARY. It's little ye knew of me ever, Davy Crockett—not to be tellin' me even farewell when ye're going off to that far western country and I shan't be seein' ye ever again. Did ye think I would let you? [*She kisses him gently.*]

DAVY. I know, little wife, an' I hate to be leavin' ye—but if a man waited for his wife to be willin', there wouldn't be no wars till folks was murdered on their doorsteps.

MARY [*sadly*]. And must ye go off to this strange, foreign war? Will ye be goin' an' leavin' me alone with the babies? I haven't said much afore this to ye, Davy, when ye shouldered yer rifle and marched off to the wars. I knowed ye was young then, and that ye would go. But I was thinkin' jest the same. I used to comfort myself an' th' babies, thinkin', "He'll come back some day and settle himself to smoke by my fire!" [DAVY *turns away.*] Why can't ye be doin' that now, Davy Crockett? We're old and there's not many days we've got to be livin'. Why can't you stay here an' let's get acquainted? We been sharin' the same bed for now—how many years—an' still we're like strangers. You've done your share of this world's fightin'—an' a whole lot more.

DAVY [*turning to her*]. Yes, I've done more. But there's folks in this world, God help 'em, does nothing, so a man that is willin' has got his hands full jest keepin' things goin'—an' I'm that kind of man. [*He strides across the room.*] From way out in Texas they've set up the cry. I've heard 'em a-calling an' it's not in me to set still. Nobody yet ever called on the name of Crockett an' he didn't hear 'em. Don't ask me why. Ask Him that made me. I can look out now over that bloody land of Texas and I can see great things ahead if I can help make 'em true. I've got to help make a place for women an' babies to be safe in the night time. Don't ask me to stay. I've got to keep movin'. [*He crosses over.*] It ain't like it was... you got neighbors now, an' the babies is growin'. Ye won't miss me much—if I don't come back....

MARY [*quietly*]. I've missed ye so long—seems as if I'd get used to it. [*She fumbles at her belt and gives him a hunting knife.*] Here's yer long knife that ye left on the mantel. If ye must be goin'—an' ye won't come back—remember when ye're fightin' that I brung it to ye.... God bless ye, Davy Crockett.... If I was to tell ye what's here in my heart, I couldn't get started... for the tears would be comin' to drown out the words. Jest fight like ye can—that's all I'll be askin'—an' prayin' in the night time while ye're out there....

DAVY. Thank ye, Mary....

MARY. I reckon I ought to be proud ye're a fighter. An' I am—so proud it hurts me inside—but it's only a little hurt long of what I'll be sufferin' at givin' ye up. [*He goes to embrace her.*] Oh, don't ye be huggin' me now, Davy Crockett. Then I'd know sure ye warn't comin' back.—Go on now an' leave me jest like ye were huntin'—jest like ye were huntin' and soon comin' back.... [*A bugle sounds in the distance.*]

DAVY. It's the sound of the men gettin' ready to march. No

use to say good-by to ye yet. Come with me now an' see the fine army! [*Calling.*] Tim, are ye ready? [*They go out silently, arm in arm.*]

BEN [*entering hurriedly calls*]. Massa Tim! Oh, Massa Tim!

TIM [*appearing in doorway with* KATE *on his arm*]. What is it, Uncle Ben?

BEN. 'Scuse me, but you all ain't deaf, is you? Massa Davy say if'n you don't fergit about women an' come on purty soon, he gwine to sick the whole Mexikin army on you sho'—that's what he say!

TIM [*amused*]. All right, Uncle Ben. Tell him he'd better not if he wants to get a turn at them himself.

BEN. All right, I tell him. Man, them boogers make a ha'nt out o' you. [*He goes out chuckling.*]

TIM [*softly*]. Be brave, little Kate.

KATE. I'll try it, poor Timmy. But many's the time in this settled country I'll be sitting alone in the red moonlight and eating my heart out for you away.

TIM [*half facetious*]. But you mustn't be doing that now you're loving a hero.

KATE. What's it to me if I'm loving a hero and him in the grave. For you aren't coming back, Timmy. You aren't coming back. Something keeps telling me the lie of it all the time that I'm trying to hope.

TIM. It's the new country calling and the blood of the slain ones. I couldn't be deaf with that call in my ears—to have people say, "He stayed here at home with his girl and his hunting and let Crockett die, because he was afraid!"

KATE. I know how it is, Timmy. It was so in the old country when our men fought, and then when they died. It's just the woman in me keeps wishing you'd stay. But there's something else in me that's proud you're a man! [*A sound of marching men is heard in the distance.*]

TIM. Colonel Crockett is waiting! [*He kisses her again, picks up his rifle, and hurries to the door. The sound of the marching men grows louder. He stops, flings up his hand with a gallant gesture.*]

All saddled and bridled and booted rode he
With a plume in his cap and a sword at his knee!

KATE [*trying to match him, but her voice quavers and there are tears in her smile:*]

And hame cam' th' saddle all bluidy to see
And hame cam' th' horse, but hame niver cam' he.

Tim! [*She runs to him and buries her face on his shoulder.*]
TIM. What is it you're thinkin'?
KATE. Do you remember the times I—I was hateful to you? —the mean little things I said? I—I'm sorry for them ... now....
TIM. Kate! [*He takes her in his arms. She is sobbing softly, when the company of* CROCKETT'S *men halt outside.*]
AN OFFICER. Companyee! Halt! Rest! [*The tramping ceases and* THE CROWD *pushes into the room with* DAVY *in the lead.* UNCLE DICK *goes behind the bar carrying the Bonny Blue Flag of Texas which he places in a bracket on the outer edge of the bar.*]
THE CROWD. Drinks! And a speech! A speech, Davy Crockett! [DAVY *is about to comply when old* BEN *rushes in, a terrified look on his face.*]
BEN. 'Fore Gawd, Massa Crockett! 'Fore Gawd, I is lost!
DAVY [*more or less amused*]. Most likely you're drunk again, Uncle Ben. What's the trouble? I'll save you.
BEN. De Shadder of Death! I seen it! Hit's de Shadder of Death!

DAVY. What about it, Uncle Ben—what about the Shadow of Death?
BEN. Lawd, Massa Crockett! Ain't you never heard of de Shadder of Death? You ain't never heard, an' you goin' to de wars!
DAVY. Well, now, maybe I've seen it. I fi't some mighty strange critters in my time. Maybe Death was one of 'em, but ye'll have to refresh my memory a little. I don't seem to recall it. [*He winks knowingly at the others.*]
BEN. Lawd, de Shadder of Death come out when a man is a-gwine to die! I see him in de clearin' jest back of de woods. He come into de moonlight, an' de moon look at him till hit git sick an' pale. [*He weaves about as the excitement of the thing he has seen grows upon him.*] He stan' still at fust an' den he creeps into de clearin', come slow in de clearin', jest a shadder in de moonlight, a shadder creepin' in. An' den he move—Lawd, how he move! He tear out'n de woods, out'n de tangled briars an' de bamboo canes, past de new dogwood trees. He stop an' look. Lawd! He stop an' look in de moonlight. Fust you don't see him—but you know he dere, he dere jest de same, standin' an' lookin' fo' de man he gwine ha'nt!
MARTHA. Ha'nts! I've seen 'em too. I've seen 'em!
BEN. Den he come faster, round and round, he come fast in de moonlight! You can't tell whar he comin'; jest stan' still an' wait. Stan' still in de moonlight, can't move, scared to death, all scrunched up to yo'self!

Den he give a jump, an' he jump clean *through* de moonlight! He run up de bark ob de white oak tree! Up! Up de tree! He scramble up de bark an' he git to de top! [*Slowly and in a hushed voice.*] But he ain't dere. He ain't dere, an' he ain't left dere. He jest *ain't!* He daid maybe. He gone. But dey's plenty mo' in de woods where he come from, layin' low in de bamboo briars, an' drinkin'

black water out'n de daid pools! Dey out dere now, waitin' by de clearin' to git at you! ...
    Dey comin' all right. Never you mind—dey comin' to git you. You goes on about yo' business an' den you fergits—but dey don't fergit. By'n'by yo' time comes, an' de Shadder comes wid hit, out in de moonlight, an' wrop de threads 'round you till dey scrush you to death!

DAVY. Phew! I've fi't with black b'ars an' I've fi't with panthers, but by lickety-splits I ain't never fi't with no Shadow of Death!—Uncle Dick, let's pour some drinks! An' one for old Ben that'll loosen his tongue a bit. Give him that banjo there—got to have a song from Uncle Ben before we go.

THE CROWD. Yea, a song, Uncle Ben, a song! [TIM *hands him the banjo.*]

BILL. Give us a fast one, Uncle Ben.

UNCLE DICK. Let's have Jim Crow.

BILL. Or "Walk Jawbone from Tennessee!"

BEN [*shaking his head and moaning to himself as he strums the banjo*].

[*Music by William Bonyun and Foster Fitz-Simmons*]

Goin' down in de valley of de Shadder, Lawd.
Goin' down in de valley of de Shadder.
Goin' to walk on Jacob's ladder, Lawd,
From way down dere in de Shadder!

Comin' out'n de valley of de Shadder, Lawd,
Comin' out'n de valley of de Shadder.
Goin' to walk on Jacob's ladder, Lawd,
From way down deep in de Shadder!

[*As the final chords die away, leaving a deathly quiet in the room, the tramp of the men returning to their posts is heard and the voice of an* OFFICER *calls:*]
THE OFFICER. Are you ready, Colonel Crockett?
DAVY. Ready, Captain Davis.
THE OFFICER. Fall out, all ye troopers. [*They make a concerted movement toward the door,* DAVY *in the lead. He reaches the door and the passing of the flag held by* UNCLE DICK *in front of the lantern casts a shadow over him and* TIM. *Old* BEN *cries out and the women scream.*]
BEN. 'Fore Gawd! Hit's de Shadder of Death! [DAVY *wheels, half ready to shoot, but instead he puts his hands on his hips and laughs heartily when he sees the cause.*]
DAVY. It's a fine soldier I'm making would be going off and forgetting his flag! [*He motions to* BILL *to take it.* BEN *goes out the door with his banjo moaning.*]
BEN. Oh, Lawd! Oh, Lawd!
MARTHA and SAL. Yer speech, Davy Crockett! You're forgettin' yer speech!
DAVY. And so I was. —Well, there ain't much that's in me to say to you now. Ye may be wonderin' why I'm goin' off an' leavin' my wife an' babies back home. But it's for babies like them I'll be fightin', an' mothers, an' for Kate, an' the girls that come later. We'll fight an' we'll slay till the whole western country will be safe for the weak because we've been strong.

Then let the Almighty look down on us now. I don't know what He thinks about killin' an' slayin'. I never was one to stick close to the church, but I'll take my chances.

He thinks we are right. An' if we've got to die, well, there's men died before us, an' there's men will die after. As long as there's men there will always be fightin', an' as long as there's women there'll be hearts that are broken.

But we can't think of that. Are you ready to fight, men? Are you sure that you're ready?

ALL. Yeah, Davy Crockett! Lead us on!

DAVY [*smiling and taking* TIM *by the arm*]. He's as sorry an excuse as I ever see, Kate. You're lucky to get rid of so ornery a critter!

KATE. You'll be takin' good care of him for my sake, won't you, Davy?

DAVY. Oh, I'll take good care of him—not that he's worth it. Now, don't ye be cryin'—leastways, not till he's gone. Good-by, everybody! —Good-by to ye, Mary—[*They do not touch; she only looks at him.*] An' if the Shadow has got me as Uncle Ben thinks, why, I'll die—*NO!* I'll not die! I'll grin down the walls of the Alamo, and we'll lick up the Mexies like salt! Come on, men! [THE CROWD *swings through the door, leaving* KATE *and* MARY *alone in the room. The column gets under way singing the "Bonny Blue Flag of Texas" as they march.*]

KATE [*turns slowly toward* MARY *who is standing in an almost military pose of attention. The moonlight floods into the room, blue through the windows, and red from the flares*]. Did you love him like I . . .

MARY [*quietly, resigned*]. Yes . . . I loved him . . . like . . . but that's all I can say. I got babies to tend to. That's all he left me, all I can show. And there ain't any Davy Crockett . . . no more . . . there never was any. He's just something I heard about—something was big, and something was fine—bigger than I knew, and so fine I couldn't come close to him. It's others he thought of, and others he will when he draws his last breath... "As long as there's men, there will always be fightin'...."

KATE. "And as long as there's women, there'll be hearts... broken!" [*She sinks her head on* MARY's *shoulder.*]

MARY. Aye, but that's where he's wrong. Our hearts may be broken, but how should we know our hearts—they ain't with us; they took 'em away—an' there ain't much that's left, Kate.... There... ain't much that's left.... [*She strokes* KATE's *hair; her own eyes are dry. On a gust of wind the song is lifted and borne backward to fill the rough tavern with the voices of men that know how to die.*]

"We are a band of brothers native to the soil
Fighting for our liberties we gained by honest toil.
Hoorah! Boys, Hoorah! For Texan Rights, Hoorah!
Hurrah! Hurrah! For the Bonny Blue Flag
That bears a single star!"

THE CURTAIN FALLS

SOUTH CAROLINA

FUNERAL FLOWERS FOR THE BRIDE
A COMEDY OF THE BLUE RIDGE MOUNTAINS

BY BEVERLEY DuBOSE HAMER

OF EASTOVER, SOUTH CAROLINA

Written in the playwriting course at the University of North Carolina and originally produced by The Carolina Playmakers at Chapel Hill on February 25, 26, and 27, 1937.

Funeral Flowers for the Bride was repeated at the meeting of the American Chemical Society on April 12th, at the University Commencement on June 7th, and by the Carolina Playmakers Repertory Company at the Island Theater, Nantucket, Massachusetts, on August 9th and 10th. It was also included by the Playmakers on their Thirty-Fifth Tour, November 22—December 4, 1937. It was first published in *The Carolina Play-Book*, September, 1937.

Recently *Funeral Flowers for the Bride* won first place in The International One-Act Play Competition over two hundred and sixty-six entries. It was produced for the first time in London at the Duchess Theatre on November 27, 1938.

THE CHARACTERS

ZEKE GASH, *a widower*.................Harry Davis
RUBY GASH, *his daughter* ....Janie Malloy Britt
SADIE JOHNSON, *a neighbor* ....Evelyn Snider
THE REVEREND R. C. HOLMES......Bedford Thurman

SCENE: *The Gash home at Pine Grove, a small summer resort in the Blue Ridge Mountains of South Carolina.*
TIME: *The present. Late afternoon in early spring.*

Copyright, 1937, by The Carolina Playmakers, Inc.
All rights reserved.

DAVY CROCKETT

THE STRANGER [*with heroic flourish*]. I'm that same Davy Crockett—half horse an' half alligator!

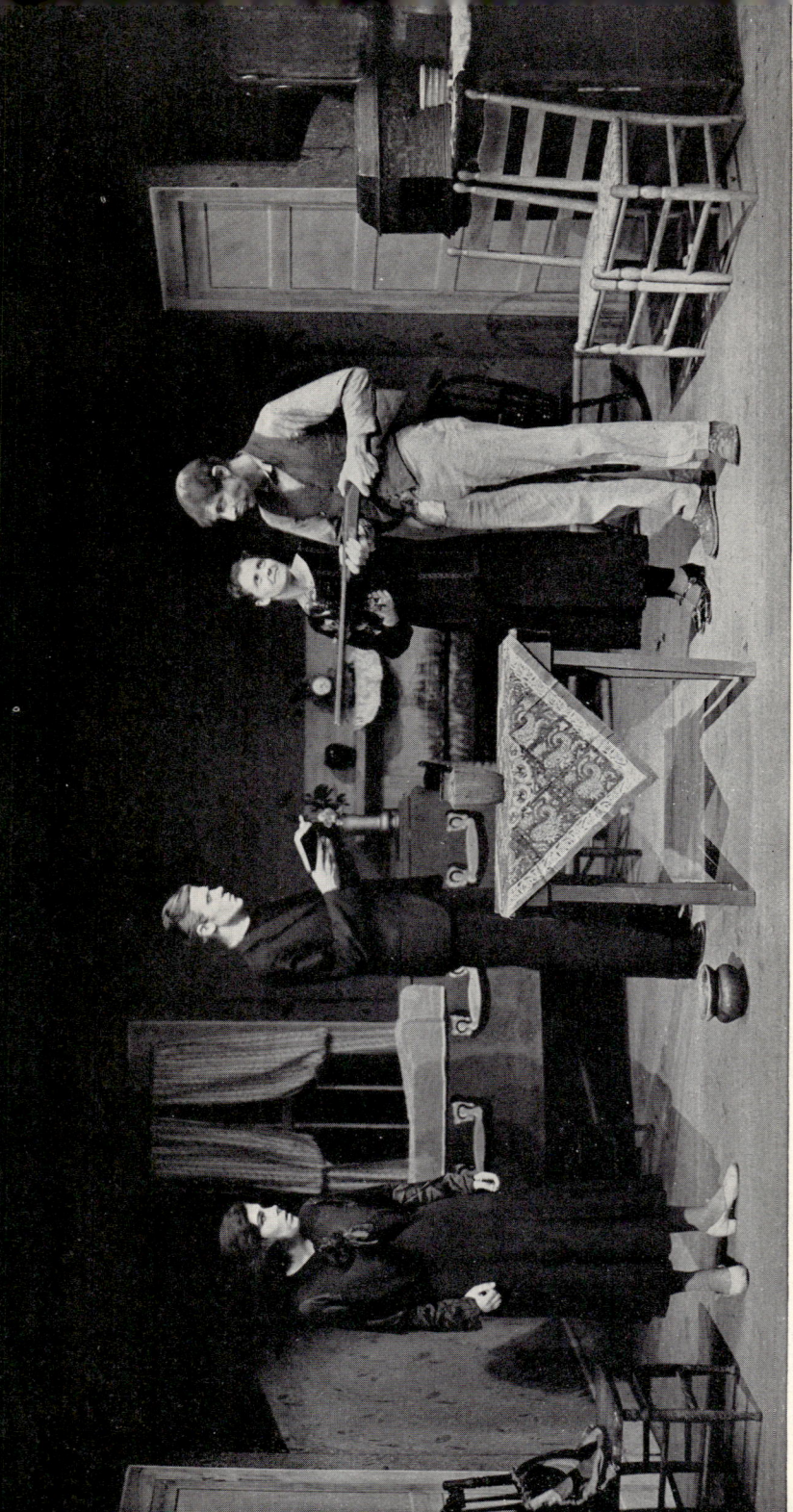

FUNERAL FLOWERS FOR THE BRIDE

ZEKE [*pointing his rifle at* RUBY]. Shet that door and come here, you—you snake-in-the-grass. Stand right there where I kin keep my eyes on you—an' my gun, too!

SOUTH CAROLINA MOUNTAIN FOLK

THE achievement of *Sun-Up* and *Hell Bent fer Heaven* is responsible, perhaps, for the prevailing notion that the drama of the Blue Ridge Mountains is necessarily tragic. *Funeral Flowers for the Bride* by Beverley DuBose Hamer of Eastover, South Carolina, is a refreshing mountain comedy quite as indigenous as are the tragedies of Lulu Volmer and Hatcher Hughes.

The author of the play has known the mountain people intimately since her earliest childhood. She soon discovered beneath their homespun ways a sturdy character, true neighborliness, and a sly humor—in their corn-huskin's, quiltin'-bees, and log-raisin's. In sickness she saw them send the best food from their scant cupboards, and come often "to set a spell."

In *Funeral Flowers* we have a survival of the ancient wake. The mountaineer, Miss Hamer tells us, very often marries a second time and has been known to take a third, fourth, or even a fifth wife. More than most men he needs a woman to help him with the field work, to take care of his cabin, his children and his stock. For this reason he is not so prone as most men to be conventional about the lapse of time between wives.

The characters in the play—Zeke, Ruby, Sadie, and the good Reverend R. C. Holmes—the author has modified somewhat for dramatic purposes. They live in a neighborhood to which her family has been going every summer for the past thirty-five years. "My summer world of the blue hills has peopled my waking dreams with characters as lovable, humorous, and fantastic as any in *Alice in Wonderland*," she says.

When Beverley Hamer was informed that a course in playwriting was required of all candidates for the Master's degree in the Department of Dramatic Art at the University of North Carolina she gasped, "But I'm not interested in *playwriting;* only in acting and directing. I never *could* write a play!" Then we tried to explain to her that a good director should have the point of view of the playwright and that we feel here that the best way of securing this is for the student-director to go through the process of writing a play himself.

We have always held the actor to be the central figure in the theater and the successful playwright, in the very nature of the case, to be *potentially* an actor. Now Miss Hamer had created a number of unusual comedy rôles and we suggested that she utilize her histrionic talent in playwriting. *Funeral Flowers for the Bride* is the surprising result.

When the play was first produced, Paul Green, sitting in the balcony, chortled all the way through it and laughed right out when the curtain fell. "By golly, I wish I could write as good a comedy as that myself," he exclaimed.

But the most surprising thing about *Funeral Flowers for the Bride,* perhaps, is that when the author read her first draft in the playwriting class and everybody laughed vociferously she insisted, "I don't see anything funny about it. I wrote these characters to be taken *seriously!*" The fact is, she had done the characters so well that she didn't realize how amusing they were in perspective.

The young playwright was so much heartened by the unusual reception of her little play that she decided to develop it further. This she did and the resultant full-length drama proved highly acceptable to the Department of Dramatic Art in lieu of the traditional thesis required of all candidates for the M.A. degree. And its première at North Carolina Agricultural and Engineering College, Raleigh, on July 14, 1938, made a very palpable hit.

This is how the young lady who said, "I can't write a play," came to write *Funeral Flowers for the Bride.*

FUNERAL FLOWERS FOR THE BRIDE

ZEKE GASH *is unaccustomed to seeing his living room in such disorder as it now stands. For one thing,* ZEKE *is not —as we conclude from the furnishings—so poverty-stricken as most mountaineers. For another, the potted jewel plant on the window-sill at right, blue satin tie-backs on the white curtains and unframed pictures of flowers, fruits, and sunsets on the walls suggest that a feminine hand has tried—though perhaps more sincerely than artistically —to beautify* ZEKE'S *home.*

Yet only a small fire whimpers dejectedly in the fireplace at rear; wood is carelessly piled at one side and trash from it litters the floor. ZEKE'S *gun is propped against the wall by the door at left, which opens on a hall. The splint-bottomed rocker,* ZEKE'S *favorite chair, has been left closer to the fireplace than a woman would allow; and the ladder-backed straight chair near the window no longer stands precisely beneath the picture on the wall above. On the unpainted pine table at center, beside the ancient phonograph which is wont to hold undisputed sway there, stand an overflowing basket of darning and a pile of clothes needing the attention of needle and thread.*

But ZEKE *is not deeply troubled by the condition of the room. For whatever order it still possesses is further menaced by the presence, on three chairs between the fireplace and the front door, at right, of a very plain but none the less ominous white board coffin.*

[*As the curtains open, we see* ZEKE *standing by the coffin, twisting his battered old hat in his hands. He is rather gaunt and stoop-shouldered, with hair the color and texture of straw. His straw-colored mustache tends to hide the expression of his face and to muffle his words. His eyes have retained the brilliant blue often found among mountaineers; and though he usually suppresses his feelings, when he is deeply moved, his eyes clearly reveal them. His apparent stoicism, due to the mountain code of accepting things without a great deal of fuss and furor, does not disprove that he has great capacity for feeling— love, anger, tenderness, and perhaps most of all, loyalty— loyalty to what he thinks is right and to those whom he loves. He is of even disposition and slow to make decisions; but once aroused, he quickly both makes and executes them. He loves children; and his great sorrow is that although he has had three wives, he has only one child, RUBY, who is not her father's pride.*]

[ZEKE *is wearing his regular work clothes: overalls, boots, and a faded blue shirt open at the neck. To him chewing tobacco and, consequently, spitting, are as necessary and as natural as breathing—so that he continues them even now in the deep sorrow in which we find him.*]

ZEKE. Pore Mary. Reckon your troubles 're over now. You won't have to be cold and sick no more, and wear yourself out a-workin' and a-worryin'—[*Suddenly, as a frightened child might, he thinks of his own loss.*] But what am I goin' to do without you, Mary? I can't go on, right by myself. [*Hearing a noise inside the house, as if ashamed of his emotions he wipes his eyes, looks toward the hall door, then turns back to the coffin.*] Hit's all right, Mary. Don't you worry none. I'll find a way. I'll fix it so we won't have to give up everything me and you's been a-workin' for. [*He walks toward the fireplace and, picking up his gun, begins to polish the barrel with his handker-*

FUNERAL FLOWERS FOR THE BRIDE

chief—absently, as though he must have something to do with his hands.]
[*The door into the hall opens, and* RUBY GASH *comes in.* RUBY, *his daughter by his first wife, is a thoroughly disreputable, slovenly looking woman of thirty. She shows the results of years of dissipation and has a mean, selfish disposition. She carries some flowers in one hand and a cheap blue vase in the other. For a moment she stands watching her father; then with a toss of her head and a scornful sniff expresses her opinion of him and stalks to the table, where she begins to arrange the flowers.* ZEKE *wheels about, his gun still in his hands, and eyes her with suspicion.*]
ZEKE. Where'd you get them flowers. If you've been a-botherin' Mary's—
RUBY. I ain't been a-botherin' nothin', Pa. And put that fool gun down when you talks to me. Go off and blow my brains out, for all you care.
ZEKE. You got no brains to blow out. How come me to have a daughter like you is a mystery to me. [*Lowering the gun and patting it lovingly.*] I kin handle this here gun, I reckon, and I ain't aimin' to blow out nobody's brains. What I want to know is where you got them flowers. If you think just cause Mary's dead—
RUBY. Who's to hinder me, I'd like to know?
ZEKE. I am, that's who.
RUBY. Yeah? You out in the field all day? [*Scornfully.*] Hain't nobody to hinder me from nothin' now. Anybody I want kin come here. I kin do what I wants when I wants to do hit, 'thout Mary's a-yappin', "It's not respectable."
ZEKE [*quickly*]. Mary didn't yap.
RUBY [*paying no attention*]. Eff'n I want a drink o' licker, I don't have to step over to Miss Metcalf's for it no more. [*While* ZEKE *is horrified at the turn things are taking,*

RUBY *prances about like a spiteful child, rather overwhelmed, but pleased at her new importance. To the coffin*]. Course I ain't aimin' to speak no ill of the dead, but I shore am glad to be boss in this house again. Yes sir, I shore am!

ZEKE [*startled*]. You boss? What about me? It's my house, ain't it?

RUBY [*laughing rather indulgently*]. Lawd, men *is* a passel of fools! Shore it's your house, but ain't nobody ever told you it's the woman what rules the house? [*Shaking her finger at him as her voice becomes hard.*] And that goes here, too—even if you air the clerk of court and a officer of the law.

ZEKE [*sharply*]. Well, you ain't the only woman in the world. Hain't nobody ever told you *that?* [*He marks his victory by spitting.*]

RUBY [*maliciously*]. I'm the onliest one you're apt to git in this house, for all your smart talk, yeah! [*She snarls.*]

ZEKE [*as if accepting a challenge*]. I don't know about that, now—I don't know. I been a-studyin' 'bout that ever since Mary was took worse. Me an' her talked it over, even. [*Sighing heavily.*] I just don't know what's the best thing to do. [*Suddenly remembering that they have strayed from their original argument.*] An' for all *your* smart talk, you ain't told me where you got them flowers.

RUBY. Well, if you'll shut up an' give me a chanct, I'll tell you. A bunch of women come to the kitchen door with 'em—said they was for Mary because she liked 'em. Humph! Much good they'll do her now. [*More vitally interested.*] They said they was comin' back when the men come for the sittin'up. Said they was goin' to bring back cakes and pies and stuff with 'em.

ZEKE [*mollified*]. Well, now, that's real kind of 'em. There's a heap o' goodness in the world even if you ain't got your

FUNERAL FLOWERS FOR THE BRIDE 67

rightful share. [*Nodding diffidently toward the flowers.*] They're purty, ain't they? She'll like 'em.

RUBY. Humph! Her likin' days is over. And how come you ain't got nobody to preach her funeral?

ZEKE. How you know I ain't got somebody?

RUBY. Mr. R.C. ain't comin' to preach no mountain funeral. He thinks we ain't wuth it. [*Stepping behind the rocker.*] Him an' his city churches—

ZEKE. That's a lie, and you know hit! R.C. and me was boys together, and we growed up together. ... You ain't never had a friend—you can't understand it.

RUBY [*cynically*]. Yeah, friends.

ZEKE. Many's the day we went chinquapin huntin' and swimmin' down yonder in the creek, and didn't I put wet tobacco on him when the hornets near 'bout ate him up that time? Why, I've done fought for him. I ain't never let anybody say nothin' 'bout R.C. or none o' the Holmeses, and I ain't goin' to. [*Almost to himself.*] There ain't nobody like R.C.

RUBY [*impatiently*]. Well, what's that got to do with it?

ZEKE [*jerked from his revery*]. I'll tell you, if you kin get it through that thick head of yours! Hit means there ain't nothin' I wouldn't do for R.C., an' the next time I catch you a-sellin' his wood to them thievin' Metcalfs—Why, they ain't worthy to walk on his dirt!—I told them, and I'm a-tellin' you. I'm here to see they don't do hit no more, neither. [*He spits.*]

RUBY [*changing the subject from her guilt*]. Shore, I know you're a plumb fool about *him,* but that ain't sayin' he's a-comin' up here to bury Mary. They's plenty'll take favors without givin' 'em, you know.

ZEKE [*with disgust*]. Yeah, I reckon you kin understand that all right without taxin' yourself none. [*Rising loyally to the bait about* MR. HOLMES.] But R.C. ain't one of 'em.

Why, he's done more for me than anybody'll ever know, 'cept me an' him. Who you think give me this here house, or this here land to farm? Who you think started the summer folks a-buying milk an' vegetables from me, eff'n it warn't R.C. an' Miss Janie? An' who you think got me this here clerk o' court job, so's I could be makin' a little cash money all year?

RUBY. That never put him out none. But to come all the way up here just 'cause you wants him—that's diff'rent.

ZEKE [*with assurance*]. They ain't nothin' R.C. wouldn't do for me if I needed him. An' I don't want no more back chat out o' you 'bout that or nothin' else. No need o' you gettin' uppity. They's ways of fixin' it so's you won't be the only hen on the roost. [*He pauses, then turns to the coffin.*] Women folks is shore quare.... Come to think of it, 'fore she died, Mary *said* you was goin' to be worse 'n ever. She downright *begged* me to git Sadie or some other woman here to help me. [*Almost unconscious of* RUBY, *he follows his puzzling train of thought.*] Reckon—reckon she could o' meant—[*As though making a surprising discovery—softly, incredulously.*] Well, I swan—I'll shore swan!

RUBY. Pa, if—[*She makes an impatient gesture, dismissing his words as incomprehensible.*]

ZEKE. R.C.'s a-comin', you can count on that, and I'm a-countin' on hit. An' when he gits here, I dunno as it won't be best to git it over with right then. [*Thoughtfully, to the coffin.*] If I just knowed for shore that was what Mary was tryin' to tell me—

RUBY. I don't know what you're aimin' to do, and I ain't a-carin'; but you'd better git yourself spruced up some. All them people'll be here come sundown. [*Tauntingly.*] Looks like after you'd done buried two women 'fore

Mary, you'd know how to act now, 'thout nobody tellin' you.

ZEKE. 'Tain't no use fer me to fix up none, Ruby—can't do Mary no good. And what's I got to fix up with? Took all the money R.C. sent me Christmas to buy Mary's medicine and pay the doctor. And you're too lazy and shiftless to wash me out a shirt or fix up the house and tend the children. Where are the children?

RUBY. I sent 'em over to Miss Metcalf's.

ZEKE. That ain't no fit place for children.

RUBY. Well, they was a-takin' on so, a-snivellin' 'round here, gettin' under foot all the time. Why, I don't believe they'd o' took on so if it was me, their own ma, in that there coffin, 'stead o' Mary.

ZEKE. Well, it's been Mary that tock care of 'em all these years, ain't it? An' tried to raise 'em decent and give 'em some learnin'? Don't know what would o' become of 'em eff'n it hadn't been for her—with you all the time projeckin' round * with fust one no 'count man an' then another.

RUBY [*trying in vain to interrupt*]. Aw, Pa, you—

ZEKE. An' what's to become of 'em now is more'n I know, pore little nameless chillun—[*Fiercely to her.*] But I ain't a-goin' to let 'em grow up to be like you. I'll fix it so's they'll have a good home. [*Musing.*] That 'Lizabeth's a real nice little gal, an' she's been a sight o' comfort to me. [*He starts to think out his problem again, and says, as though trying to get* RUBY *out of the room:*] Git some chairs for the folks to set in when they come.

RUBY. Yeah, reckon I better. [*As she goes out,* ZEKE *looks tenderly toward the coffin.* RUBY *returns with two straight chairs.*] Reckon who'll wash for Mr. R.C. an' Miss Janie, now Mary's dead? [*Defensively.*] I'm shore *I* ain't a-goin'

* Amorously experimenting.

to wash nobody else's dirty clothes and clean house for 'em.

ZEKE. Naw, when you ain't got pride enough to wash your own.

RUBY. Guess ol' Miss Metcalf kin do it now. He! He! He!

ZEKE. Not one o' them gawdless Metcalfs is a-goin' to set foot in Miss Janie's house, an' you kin lay to that! Why, they'd steal the spectacles off'n her face.

RUBY. That'd be good for 'er, with her highfalutin ways.

ZEKE. An' she ain't highfalutin, neither. She's a good woman, and honest as a penny. Ain't I been a-carryin' milk up there every summer nigh on thirty years, an' her a-figurin' up how much it costs and payin' me cash money?

RUBY. Well, she's got to get it some'rs. Maybe Miss Metcalf kin—

ZEKE. An' look at all the stuff she sent Mary at Christmas— warm clothes an' things for the chillun. Highfalutin? Humph!

RUBY [*abruptly*]. You say Mr. R.C.'s a-comin', huh?

ZEKE [*firmly*]. I did.

RUBY. Well, I'll be right glad if he does. He'll want somebody to open up the house for him, an' git things fixed up. Then now's the very time to get Miss Metcalf started. I'll just step over there an' tell her how she kin make some good easy money.

ZEKE. You'll do no such thing!

RUBY. Once she gits started up there, it'll be easy for her to stay an' do the washin' this summer. Yes sir, that'll be jest right for that highfalutin Miss Janie!

ZEKE. I said you'll do no sech thing. I'll get somebody that'll open up the house an' wash for 'em, an' do hit right! It won't be Miss Metcalf. . . . Yes sir, that's what Mary meant, all right. I'm sure of hit now. She'd never rest easy in her grave if them Metcalfs was a-washin' for Miss

FUNERAL FLOWERS FOR THE BRIDE 71

Janie. She kept a-sayin' I'd have to git somebody to look after the children, an' tend her flowers, an' do Miss Janie's washin'—
Ruby. Well, if you're aimin' for me to do hit, you kin aim again. I done told you—
Zeke. I ain't aimin' for you to have nothin' to do with it. [*From outside we hear the voice of* Sadie Johnson, *calling.*]
Sadie. Mr. Zeke.
Ruby. Then what in the name of—
Zeke. You'll know soon enough what I'm aimin' to do, an' eff'n you finds out, you'd best not git me r'iled. [Sadie *calls again, then knocks.*] Now, go see who that is. And if it's Sadie, send her on in here and you clear out. I got to see her 'bout somethin'.
Ruby [*turning to go*]. Pa, what you want with that fool? She ain't got the sense God gives a grasshopper.
Zeke. She's got sense enough. Now, you git out o' here an' do like I tell you. [*Perplexed,* Ruby *goes out.* Zeke *looks around the disorderly room. Taking a pen and an official-looking paper from the table drawer, he begins to write. Looking toward the coffin.*] Guess you knowed all the time I'd have to do this. [*He bends over the paper.*]
Ruby [*greeting* Sadie *outside*]. Howd'y', Sadie. Go on in— Pa wants to see you 'bout somethin'.
Zeke [*to the coffin*]. It'll be hard, Mary, 'cause won't nobody else ever take your place. But if it's got to be [*Sighing resignedly.*] hit's got to be, that's all. The ways o' the Almighty ain't to be questioned, I s'pose.
Ruby [*still outside*]. Don't stand there like a bump on a log. Go on in!
[Sadie Johnson *scurries into the room. She is about thirty years old and shows remnants of what once was real beauty. Though she is sweet and good, and probably*

never had an unkind thought, she is not overly endowed with intellect; therefore, and because of her gentleness, she is accustomed to being treated as a door mat. She is intensely romantic but starved for affection, even attention; and if given the slightest opportunity, she will dramatize herself endlessly. What happiness she has found in life has been from the dream world of her own creation. She carries a bouquet of spring flowers. Entering, she looks around timidly—like a wide-eyed and adoring child, and yet with something of a woman's understanding and sympathy for ZEKE in his grief.]

SADIE. Howd'y', Mr. Zeke.

ZEKE. Good evenin', Sadie.

SADIE. I come to see if I could help anyways. An' I brought these here flowers. Miss Mary, God rest her, used to love 'em so.

ZEKE [tenderly]. You like purty things too, don't you, Sadie?

SADIE [nodding her head]. Yes sir, I do.

ZEKE. Well, now, that's good. [Calling.] Ruby, come here an' git these flowers an' fix 'em. [RUBY enters, eyes SADIE haughtily, snatches the flowers from her, and crams them into the vase on the table. ZEKE watches her with narrow eyes, then bursts out angrily.] Now, git on out. Go on! [RUBY stalks out, chin in air.] Here, Sadie, set down.

SADIE. Thank you, sir. [She sits on the edge of her chair, very ill at ease.]

ZEKE. An' you just as well take off your hat. I'm glad to see you, Sadie. You're the very one I wants to see, an' I got somethin' to ast you.

SADIE [beginning to thaw a little]. Yes sir?

ZEKE. Maybe it's a little sudden—I dunno. But I ain't much on talk, an' I—[Groping for words.] Well, I'm in trouble, and I need your help an' Mr. R.C.'s. He's a-comin'.

SADIE. Mr. R.C.'s a-comin' up here?

ZEKE. I'm looking for him any time, now. I kin count on him, an' what I wants to know is kin I count on you?

SADIE [*earnestly*]. You needn't ast me that, Mr. Zeke. Eff'n it's anything I kin do for you, I'll shore do hit. Miss Mary, God rest her, was always kind to me. An' I ain't forgot that time you stood up for me when they was about to put me out'n the church. I been aimin' to tell you, Mr. Zeke, I ain't done wrong no more.

ZEKE. That's all right, Sadie.

SADIE. I ain't never took up with just anybody, the way Ruby does. I was deceived that time, and it grieved me sorely. I'm glad the little mite died. If it hadn't been for you an' Mary, I'd 'a' died, too. I knows that, and I'm grateful to you both. [*She works herself into a frenzy of self-pity and gratitude.*]

ZEKE [*trying to hide his embarrassment*]. You know that's all right about that, Sadie. We'll forget that. You's a good woman. I know it, an' Mary knowed it. What I wants to know now, is you skeered o' work?

SADIE. Land o' mercy, Mr. Zeke, if you knowed how I have to work at home, you'd 'a' spared your breath askin' me that. Why, them sisters o' mine is too high an' mighty to lift their fingers—an' they so much smarter an' more educated than me. I has to do everything that's done—

ZEKE [*breaking in*]. Kin you wash?

SADIE [*laughing delightedly like a child, rocking back and forth, thoroughly pleased at the novelty of having some one's undivided attention*]. Wash? Land yes, Mr. Zeke. And if I do say it as shouldn't, I kin sure turn out a passel of clothes as purty and white! Why, one time I remember I was—[*Troubled by a sudden thought, and looking at him sharply.*] Why you askin' me all them questions?

ZEKE [*hurriedly*]. Jest one more. You like children, don't you?

SADIE. Yes, Mr. Zeke. I loves 'em. [*Puzzled.*] But why—
ZEKE [*solemnly, and looking her squarely in the face*]. Well, Sadie, it may seem a little sudden, like I said; but I done got my mind made up, an' 'tain't no use beatin' around the bush. I aims for you an' me to git married.
SADIE [*astonished*]. *Married!*
ZEKE. Uh huh.
SADIE. Do Lawd! You fair take my breath, Mr. Zeke.
ZEKE [*his seriousness lightened by a slight twinkle*]. May as well cut out the Mister stuff, Sadie. [*He walks over to the fireplace and spits.*] If you is goin' to be married to me you might as well start callin' me Zeke.
SADIE [*getting up, still incredulous*]. You mean *marry, me?* An' let me come here in this house an' live—an' have flowers in the yard, an' play the music box Miss Janie gave to Mary, an' [*Her voice trails off as her glance embraces the room.*]
ZEKE. I *said* marry you, didn't I? An' I never says nothin' 'lessen I means hit.
SADIE [*sitting, in the same chair*]. Hain't no man never ast me to marry him. [*To* ZEKE, *earnestly.*] But you know, they's always said I ain't real bright. I wouldn't want you to take me under no false pretenses. [ZEKE *looks at her sharply.*] Why, you're a fine, upstandin' man, Mr. Zeke. You've done had three good wives, an' right now you could have your pick o' all the women in Oconee County.
ZEKE [*pleased, but embarrassed, he spits into the fire*]. Aw—
SADIE [*for the first time thinking of the coffin*]. But look— Mary on yon side of the room. Why, it don't seem right, when she's been dead scarce two days.
ZEKE. Don't you worry your head 'bout that. [*Softly.*] It'll be all right with her. She knows I got to have somebody to help me with the work, an' look after Ruby's young-uns —Ruby ain't a-goin' to do it—an' somebody's got to do

the washin' for Miss Janie an' R.C.'s family. An' besides, I ain't a-gettin' no younger, an' it's lonesomelike for a man to come into a cold house after his work's done, an' no woman 'round about.

SADIE. Yes sir, I reckon it is.

ZEKE. Mary knowed all that—I believe she knowed it 'fore I did. An' it ain't a-goin' to trouble her where she's gone. Don't *you* trouble none about it.

SADIE. But what'll folks say? They'll sure think that I—

ZEKE [*firmly*]. What they think is their own business, I reckon; but what they say is mine, and I'll tend to that. Now you an' me 'll just git R.C. to marry us soon as he gits here. I didn't aim to do hit so sudden, but Ruby's gettin' mighty uppity. I'll give you a good home, Sadie, an' be kind to you, and if you're willin'—

SADIE [*now radiantly happy*]. Oh, Zeke, that'll be just grand! [*They are about to kiss.* ZEKE, *embarrassed, breaks the strain by moving away.*]

ZEKE. Well, I'll just finish gettin' the license drawed up. This here job o' mine is comin' in handy.

SADIE. An' to think—you'll give me back my character, and I'll be a respectable married woman—married to the best man in Oconee County! Oh, I'll work hard, Zeke, an' keep the house an' do the washin' and have me a garden an' chickens, an' flowers, an—[*Looking down at her dress, she is suddenly dismayed.*] But I ain't purtied up none. An' got on this old dress.

ZEKE [*laconically*]. You'll do.

SADIE [*dreamily*]. To think—me a-gittin' married!

RUBY [*bursting in, raging, and mimicking* SADIE]. To think —you a-gettin' married. [*Pausing.*] To think no such thing! You'll do it over my dead body. I heard what you been a-sayin', an' 'fore God, you'll not do it! [SADIE *cowers in her chair.* RUBY *turns her wrath upon her father.*]

Pap, have you lost your mind? Marry this here drivelin' idiot? An' Mary here ain't been buried. [*She points at* SADIE.] Why, she ain't even respectable. Everybody knows—

ZEKE [*threateningly*]. Shut up! I warned you not to git me all r'iled up, and if you know which side your bread's buttered on, you'll heed what I say.

RUBY. Gawd A'mighty, Pap—you can't let this here connivin' old hag git hitched up with you, an' Mary not yet cold in her grave.

ZEKE. Mary's as dead now as she'll be ten years from now. [*Spitting, he leans back against the wall, crosses his ankles, and calmly taps one foot.*]

RUBY [*finding* ZEKE *impregnable, and turning to* SADIE, *who begins to whimper and twist her skirt with her workworn hands*]. Of all the snoopin', vile, base creatures I know, you is the low-down basest of 'em all. An' I suppose you're aimin' to turn me out o' my own house. [*With "dramatic" self-pity.*] Here I've spent my life a-slavin' an' toilin' for Pap—why, you ought to be drove out the county. Comin' here in a time of sorrow like this, when me an' Pap is a-grievin' ourselves sore over pore Mary!

ZEKE. Pore Mary is all right now. It's the livin' what we got to think about. [*Softly.*] And it's who *she* was a-thinkin' about. Now, Ruby, as long as you behaves yourself, you'll be all right. But my mind's made up not to take no more foolishness off of you.

RUBY. It's you that's actin' the fool.

ZEKE. I'm goin' to marry Sadie, an' marry her now. If you wants to stay here, well an' good; but you'll do like I say from now on. You done been the cause o' me buryin' three women, and I ain't aimin' for you to bother Sadie none. Your mammy died a-bornin' you, an' 'Lizabeth an' Mary you jest plumb worried to their graves—all the

FUNERAL FLOWERS FOR THE BRIDE

time pesterin' an' naggin' an' frettin' with your sinful ways.

RUBY. Sinful ways!

ZEKE [*rising*]. Things is a-goin' to be diff'rent from now on. You ought to know that when I puts my foot down, I puts it down flat.

RUBY. Pap, have you lost all your damn senses?

ZEKE. We'll git married right here in this very room. [*Looking at the coffin as though telling Mary that at last he understands, then he turns fiercely on* RUBY.] An' you'll be one o' the witnesses!

RUBY. Married in this room—[*Desperate, she tries to frighten* SADIE.] Well, I hope Mary'll rise up out o' her coffin an' call down the curses of Gawd A'mighty on you both. [*She snatches the vase from the table, throws the flowers in* SADIE's *face and the vase to the floor.*] Here, you won't have to buy no bride's bouquet. Jest use these here flowers that was meant to go on Mary's grave!

[SADIE *shrinks from her in terror.* RUBY *laughs hysterically.* ZEKE, *who has turned to the coffin, now advances on* RUBY *savagely.*]

ZEKE. Here, you—[*A knock is heard at the front door.* ZEKE *stops, and all turn,* SADIE *as though another horror were expected.* RUBY *breaks off in the middle of her wild laughter.* ZEKE *draws a deep breath.*] That must be R.C. You'd better thank the good Lord he come when he did. One more word out o' you, and I'd 'a' [*He walks quickly to the door and opens it.*] Howd'y', R.C., I'm glad to see you—I shore am.

HOLMES [*Outside*]. I'm glad to see you, too, Zeke.

ZEKE. Come on in.

[HOLMES *enters. A minister whose family has been summering in the mountains for many years, he is a man of* ZEKE's *age whose very presence inspires confidence. His education and position as minister of a large city church have not let him lose "the common touch." He is quick to understand another's troubles and to give himself in sincere sympathy.*]

HOLMES. I was very sorry to hear of your trouble. [*Looks toward the coffin.*] Little one can say at a time like—

ZEKE [*for the moment so concerned with* RUBY *that he has almost forgotten the coffin*]. What trouble? [*Remembering, he walks back to the coffin and lays his hand upon it as if asking for forgiveness.* HOLMES *comes to him and stands at the other end of the coffin.*]

HOLMES. Little one can say at a time like this, I know, makes things much easier, but you know without my telling you that I've come to help in every way I can.

ZEKE. I knowed that, and I knowed it 'fore you come. I done told Ruby and Sadie so.

HOLMES [*bowing to the women*]. How are you, Ruby?

RUBY [*jerking her head in response, but resenting the presence of this outsider whom she regards with suspicion*]. Howd'y'.

HOLMES [*to* SADIE]. And you're Sadie Johnson, aren't you?

SADIE. Yes, sir.

RUBY. She's Sadie Johnson, all right.

HOLMES. I'm glad to see you, Sadie.

SADIE [*going toward him, greatly embarrassed, and trying to smooth out the wrinkles in her dress*]. Thank you, sir. But you must excuse my poor plight. I didn't know I was goin' to see Zeke's landlord.

HOLMES [*trying to put her at ease*]. That's quite all right, Sadie. Your apologies are unnecessary. I feel a bit untidy myself after that long trip. But like you, I'm Zeke's friend, and I came for the same reason, I'm sure, you did.

SADIE [*surprised*]. Why, you're real kind an' understandin'-like, ain't you? No wonder Zeke sets such store by you.

I didn't know summer folks could be that-a-way. Ruby, here, said you was highfalutin an' biggity.

ZEKE [*angrily*]. Ruby says a lot 'sides her prayers, and if she don't—

HOLMES [*relieving the tension by interrupting*]. Thank you, Sadie; I hope I'm not biggity and highfalutin, as you call it. I've lived long enough to see the futility of that. And now, Zeke [*With a gesture toward the coffin.*] what plans have you made?

ZEKE [*gulping*]. Well, I'm—[*Unable to continue.*]

HOLMES. Or perhaps you would like to talk it over alone with me. I'm sure the women will excuse us. It helps, you know, to unburden the heart to a friend—get it off your chest.

ZEKE. 'Tain't no use for 'em to go. I done told 'em anyhow.

HOLMES. You mustn't let it whip you, Zeke. No one knows better than I how hard the death of a loved one is. But God in His mercy never sends more than we can bear. You believe that, don't you?

ZEKE [*with resigned agreement*]. I reckon you're right, R.C. Bein' a preacher, you know more about such things than I do. Hit's just too big for me to understand.

HOLMES. It's too big for all of us, Zeke, unless we turn elsewhere for help. [RUBY, *who with* SADIE *has been listening, much impressed, shows her inner rage now only by her sullen expression as she watches the men out of the corners of her eyes.*] I suppose you are not planning to have the funeral this afternoon.

ZEKE. No, I ain't.

HOLMES. It *will* be better to have it to-morrow. But I could have a simple prayer now, if you like.

ZEKE. You kin pray all right, eff'n you think it'll help any. But what I wants you should do now—[*He eyes* RUBY *sternly a moment, then continues.*] What I wants you to do is marry Sadie an' me.

HOLMES. What—do you mean—marry now?

RUBY [*running to* HOLMES]. Don't listen to him, Mr. R.C. Don't let him do it! He don't know what he's sayin'. He's gone crazy, I tell you, or he wouldn't want to do no such unlawful thing!

ZEKE. Hit ain't unlawful. The Good Book says hit's all right for a man to take another woman unto himself eff'n his wife dies. Hain't that right, R.C.?

HOLMES [*stunned by what is happening*]. Yes, it's perfectly legal, I suppose. You're a widower and at liberty to marry again if you choose.

ZEKE [*calmly*]. Well, I've chose.

RUBY. It ain't right, I tell you. And if you don't stop 'em, I will. I'll take Sadie yonder, and I'll squeeze the livin' daylights outen her with my naked hands! As Gawd's my witness, I'll—[SADIE *puts her hands to her throat as though for protection and gives a terrified gasp.* ZEKE *wheels toward* RUBY *threateningly and* SADIE *begins to cry.* HOLMES *takes charge of the situation.*]

HOLMES [*sternly*]. Hush, Ruby. Stop it this minute. It can do no earthly good to talk like that. [*Under his firm voice and manner* RUBY *cowers. He turns to* ZEKE.] But, Zeke, don't rush into this blindly. [*With a kind look at* SADIE.] I'm sure Sadie will make a good wife. If you love each other, and want to be married *later,* why, no one will be gladder than I. But, to say the least, it's hardly conventional to take a step like this now.

ZEKE. That's as may be, R.C., but we're gettin' married now.

HOLMES. You mean immediately?

ZEKE. Just as immediately as you kin git that little book out of your pocket and git it done. You said you'd do whatever you could to help me, and it ain't like you to back out. I've knowed you a long time, an' you ain't never failed me yet.

HOLMES. No, and I don't mean to start now. But after all, Zeke, you will have to wait at least until to-morrow: you need a license, and witnesses. You think it over to-night. Then, after Mary's funeral, if you and Sadie still want to get married, I'll perform the ceremony for you.

ZEKE. Whatever ceremony's performed 'll have to be done now. I've done drawed up the license, and it's legal. Ain't I the clerk of court in Oconee County? I got my reasons all right for gittin' married now.

HOLMES. Well—

ZEKE. Besides, if we wait till to-morrow, folks'll hear 'bout it, an' there'll be a lot o' jawin' around. I'll maybe have to git in some fights, even, an' remind some folks to tend their own businesses. I don't want nothin' like that to happen. I tell you, it's better this way, R.C. An' Ruby here can witness.

RUBY [*wildly*]. I'll not do it, I'll not! Ain't no power on God's green earth kin make me! [ZEKE *quietly reaches for his gun and puts it in the crook of his arm.*]

ZEKE. You'll do as I say. I've took 'bout enough off of you!

SADIE [*terrified, but coming between them*]. Don't shoot her, Zeke!

RUBY [*compelled to back down, but sullen still*]. I'll do it since you're so sot. I don't believe you'd stop at nothin'— killin' your own chil', even—'long with your other sins.

HOLMES [*trying for comic relief*]. Well. This is the first time I've ever officiated—at a shot-gun wedding—or is that a rifle?

ZEKE. Hit'll shoot, all right, whatever it is. Now let's git goin'. There's a passel o' folks comin' in, an' I wants you to be marryin' us when they comes—so they can't butt in an' say no harsh words. I ain' in no mood for hit, and I don't want nobody to git hurt.

SADIE. Air you shore it's all right, Mr. R.C.?

HOLMES. Yes, Sadie, it's all right, I suppose. [*Sighing.*] At any rate, you seem to have no choice in the matter.

SADIE. Zeke here is so headstrong, he kind o' sweeps me off my feet.

ZEKE. I'm shore glad to hear you say that, R.C. And I'm glad you're goin' to do the marryin'. Mary would ruther you did hit. And ef it's all right with her, an' you think it's all right, it don't make no diff'rence what nobody else says.

HOLMES. Well, I know you well enough to know it's no use arguing with you if your mind's made up. And [*Patting him on the shoulder.*] I think I understand.

ZEKE [*officiously*]. You come here, Sadie, an' stand by me. [*Shifting his gun in his arm.*] I aim to be a-facin' the door where I kin hush 'em as they come in. R.C., you git your book an' stand there. [HOLMES *takes "Ministerial Acts" from his pocket and stands by the table where* ZEKE *has indicated, his expression at once amused, sympathetic, stunned, and slightly incredulous.*] Ruby, you go see eff'n the folks ain't a-comin'.

RUBY [*going to the front door and looking out*]. Yeah, here they're comin', shore 'nough. [*As a sudden inspiration strikes her, she puts her hand to her mouth and shrieks.*] Come on, you all, an' come a-runnin'! Pap's gone out o' his mind, an' you got to help me!

ZEKE [*aiming at her, and speaking fiercely*]. Shet that door and come here, you—you snake-in-the-grass. Stand right there where I kin keep my eyes on you, an' my gun, too. [*Reluctantly* RUBY *obeys.* ZEKE *turns, with an air both weary and triumphant, to* HOLMES, *who is somewhat dazed by the proceedings.*] All right, R.C., let 'er go! [*He lowers the gun once more to the crook of his arm, pats* SADIE *on the shoulder, and looks squarely at* HOLMES, *who begins in solemn tones to read the marriage ceremony. Voices are heard outside].*

HOLMES. "Dearly beloved, we are gathered together— [*Knocking is heard at the door.* RUBY *turns as if about to make a dash for it.* ZEKE *raises the rifle on her. She stops.* HOLMES *looks up at* ZEKE, *who nods for him to continue.*] to join this man and woman in holy wedlock—"

THE CURTAINS CLOSE

GEORGIA

MOURNERS TO GLORY
A NEGRO RITUAL DRAMA

BY RIETTA WINN BAILEY

OF COCHRAN, GEORGIA

Written in the playwriting course at the University of North Carolina and originally produced by The Carolina Playmakers at Chapel Hill on March 3, 1938. *Mourners to Glory* was originally produced under the title of *Wings to Fly Away*.

THE CHARACTERS

VIOLET .... Lois Latham
ETHEL, *her daughter* .... Frances Roughton
BUCK KINNEBREW .... John Morgan
MR. HUDSON .... Wieder Sievers
SIS' EMMA .... Marguerite Lipscomb
SIS' JERRIE .... Jane Hunter
SIS' NETSIE .... Jean Brabham
BROTHER MAC .... Eugene Langston
BROTHER JIM .... Clifton Young
BROTHER NAP .... Henry Bluestone

SCENE: *A Negro cabin on a farm in middle Georgia.*
TIME: *The present. An evening in August.*

Copyright, 1938, by The Carolina Playmakers, Inc.
All rights reserved.

NEGRO RITUAL DRAMA

MOURNERS TO GLORY is something new in our southern folk drama. It calls to mind the Mystery Plays designed by the religious brotherhoods of the Dark Ages to vivify the Bible stories of an unlettered audience. Miss Bailey's drama, however, suggests rather the Miracle and Morality Plays, more specifically the Moralities. She uses, not a story of Bible characters or saints' miracles, but an abstract moral idea —the salvation of man by faith.

Have we, perhaps, in *Mourners to Glory* an interesting parallel with such plays as the redemption of *Everyman,* famous fifteenth-century morality play? The drama of ancient Greece began at the altar of Dionysus in the market place. The religious drama of medieval Europe was born at the high altar of the Christian church. Perhaps the student of dramatic folklore can show us that our Negroes in the South are unconsciously following the great tradition of religious drama in the history of Western culture.

The author of *Mourners to Glory* comes from the little town of Cochran in middle Georgia. She graduated from Wesleyan College in Macon in 1934, and became a case-worker for the Federal Emergency Relief Administration in Harris County. There in the Pine Mountain Valley rural community she worked among the farm laborers, both black and white. For six weeks she did relief work in the textile strike at LaGrange, and in 1936 went on the Recreation Division of the Works Progress Administration in West Georgia, traveling over several counties organizing recreation programs. In June, 1937, she came to Chapel Hill for the summer course in playwriting at the University of North Carolina. Her first Negro ritual drama, *Washed in de Blood,* was produced by The Carolina Playmakers on December 9, 1937, and published in *The Carolina Play-Book* for March, 1938.

Of the people in her play the young author says: "I think I

have known about Negro sinning and Negro religion as long as I have known about anything. My mammy told me many tales about 'de Lawd' and 'de heabenly glory.' Her faith was as much a part of her everyday life as her work."

The songs in the play the author heard at Mount Zion Church in her home town. She says: "I cannot sing them as they came to me; nor can any white person. There is a beauty, a haunting, unfinished melody, which varies every time the songs are sung. There is no music which comes as freely, as naturally, as this.

"On Sunday the bells in the Negro church begin ringing by sundown and soon the singing comes soft through the night. It was a long time before I was old enough to go and sit inside the church and watch them 'get filled wid' de sperit' and see the 'shout-holders cotch 'em when dey falls.' Once the yard-man told me I was invited to come to the meetin', because 'dey gwine have a orchestry—one man he beats de drum, one 'oman she sing, and one 'oman she shakes de tangerine!'

"From the first I have loved them and depended on them—found them faithful and kind. Now I find some powerful force still deep down which lifts itself in their beautiful, haunting music, and snarls on a Saturday night—which bows its head to the white man's paternalism and dances in abandon when they are among their own kind. I have seen beauty of physical strength and beauty of humble hands and kinky old white heads, brown eyes, deep and soft.

"Once I saw a black man hanging from a tree and white men around him with hatred in their eyes. I got a hurt inside me then that does not go away....

"No load is too heavy to 'tote,' no work is done that is not set to music. Far across the cotton fields I have watched them bending over the rows, the sound of their singing coming soft and beautiful. In the rock quarries the ring of the pick on stone is marked by a loud 'Ha!' and they sing again as they lift the pick, break the rock. Yes, some are trifling and sleep all day in the sun. They fish in the creek all afternoon and do not seem to care when they come away empty-handed.

"Saturday afternoon near the Silver Moon Café I've seen them fill the street of the town. I remember one nigger gal wearing a rose satin evening dress with fur around the tail on a hot August afternoon. Whatever they wear takes on the flowing grace of their bodies, and a yellow blouse seems to like the red skirt under it.

"Yes, we love them, we laugh at them, we use them, we take care of them—after a fashion. They remain a dark thing hovering around town in poverty of material goods but rich in emotion and forever unknown to us."

Rietta Bailey has written *Mourners to Glory* with understanding and sincere appreciation of the religious beliefs of the Negro people, with a deep respect for their faith, and with an abiding love for their music. "I am not sure," she holds, "that any white person can write from the point of view of the Negro —an uneducated one, I mean. Their world is one of imagination and their emotions are strong and short-lived. I have known them faithful and kind, humble, care-free, and happy. Some steal and lie. Some are mean and dirty and stupid. I have seen them cruelly mistreated by white men. I have seen others loved and protected. I don't know what we are going to do about them but I do know that they will always be a colorful, warm, and interesting people to me. And I hope I shall always live near them."

MOURNERS TO GLORY

*Negro cabins dot the cotton plantations in middle Georgia.
VIOLET WARD's cabin, on the edge of a wide field which
lies white and hot in the late August twilight, is shaded
by tall pine trees. Behind it the woods deepen to the
river swamp, dark and dangerous to those who do not
know their waters. The cabin door, in the center of the
rear wall, stands wide open. The window to the right
of it is also open. In the right wall is a fireplace of rough
field-stone. On the low chimneypiece are a kerosene
lamp, a vase of paper roses, a box of snuff, and a jar of
hair-straightener. In front of the fireplace is a rough pine
bench. The doorway in the left wall, leading to the bedroom, is curtained off by a faded blue counterpane.
There is another pine bench by the left wall and a pine
table, with a water bucket on it, in the corner.*

[VIOLET WARD *is kneeling behind the bench, at the left,
scrubbing it. She is a middle-aged woman, comfortably
fat but energetic. She sings with joy as she works. Religion and work in the fields make her life complete. Her
soul has been delivered to the "Lawd"; she is a Christian
and her soul would find peace here below, if it weren't
for the fractious ways of her daughter,* ETHEL.]
[ETHEL *is seated on a low stool by the doorway, her feet
cooling in a tub of water. She is young with the wildness
of youth still rampant in her blood. She has the restless
feet and the wandering eye. Leaning against the door-*

jamb, she gazes into the twilight now, too weary and too bored to stir.]
VIOLET [*singing—scrubbing with the rhythm of her song*].

Oh, Lawd, I wants two wings to veil my face,
Oh, Lawd, I wants two wings to fly away,
Oh, Lawd, I wants two wings to veil my face,
An' de world can't do me no harm.

ETHEL [*sighing*]. Two wings! Lawd, I wish I had 'em now—Two wings to fly 'way from here!
VIOLET [*abruptly*]. Well, you ain't 'bout to come nigh no wings.
ETHEL [*turning to* VIOLET]. Pour some of dat water in de tub, Ma; dis done got hot.
VIOLET [*reluctantly taking the bucket and sloshing water into the tub*]. You gits mo' triflin' an' good-fo' nothin' ebery day dat pass. What ail you, droop-moufin' all de time?
ETHEL [*staring out the door to the cotton fields*]. Dere dat cotton fiel', stretchin' ha'f way 'round de worl'. I done bent over dem rows till my back is broke, my feets is blistered, an' my head is gwine roun'.
VIOLET [*returning to the bench, she gets down on her knees and begins scrubbing again*]. Dat ain't de trouble. I ain't notice you doin' no powerful pickin'. I see you settin' under de shade tree till de sun ease up. Don' you talk to me 'bout no work. You ain't done it.

ETHEL. Lawd, Lawd, de sun drive down!

VIOLET. You hesh up callin' on de Lawd. He ain't hearin' you. Gits yo' feets out ob dat tub an' sweep dis flo'.

ETHEL [*not moving*]. My Jedus, Ma, dey ain't a speck ob dust on dis' flo'.

VIOLET [*sitting up on her knees and turning on her*]. You move when I says move. De chief mourners comin' here fo' a meetin'. De house gwine be 'spectable when dey gits here.

ETHEL [*wearily taking her feet out of the tub, she throws the water out of the front door*]. What dey comin' here for? All you keeps on yo' min' is dat buryin' society.

VIOLET. Da's jist what you gwine do from now on. Git it on yo' min' right shortly. You gwine be present at dis meetin'.

ETHEL [*crossing to the right corner, places the tub on the floor there*]. Dat I ain't. I ain't neber fool wid no buryin' society an' I ain't startin' now.

VIOLET [*her hands on her hips, she faces* ETHEL *and speaks with authority*]. You listen to me, Ethel Ward, and hesh dat sass! From dis night on you gwine be a 'nitiated member of de "Sons and Daughters ob Rest." You gwine moan wid 'em—you gwine pay dues—you gwine rise and face de Lawd.

ETHEL [*taking the broom from the corner, begins sweeping down right*]. You ain't got no coaxin' han' on me no mo', Ma. Dey ain't no use in you wastin' yo' breaf.

VIOLET [*threatening*]. Who gwine bury you when you die? Who gwine sit up wid you on de sick bed? Who gwine moan yo' soul to glory?

ETHEL [*not impressed*]. I ain't nowhere near to dyin', an' I ain't worryin' none 'bout it.

VIOLET [*scrubbing the bench with vigor*]. No, you ain't. You gots yo' min' on nothin' but traipsin' roun' de countryside. You gwine burn in eternal fire ef you don' change yo' ways.

ETHEL [*carelessly*]. My way suits me.

VIOLET [*fixing her eyes on* ETHEL]. Yeah, dey suits you. Whar was you las' Sunday ebenin'?

ETHEL [*sweeping indifferently*]. I disremembers.

VIOLET. You disremembers all right. You was down to dat convict camp, hangin' onto de gate, passin' sweet talk wid dat convict, Buck Kinnebrew.

ETHEL [*she stops sweeping*]. Who been totin' lies home now?

VIOLET. You de onliest one totin' lies. I passed dere an' seen you, myself.

ETHEL [*sweeping again, accenting her words with strokes of the broom*]. Well, you seen me den. An' mos' lak' you gwine see me dere some mo', case I'se gwine back.

VIOLET [*rises*]. My Jedus, Ethel! Ain't you had enough ob low-down, mean niggers widout gwine roun' chasin' up mo' ob 'em?

ETHEL. Buck ain't no low-down, mean nigger. [*She is sweeping toward the door.*]

VIOLET. How come he settin' in de chain gang?

ETHEL. My God A'mighty! You talk lak' you ain't never had nobody on de gang.

VIOLET. I ain't talkin' 'bout me, I talkin' 'bout you.

ETHEL. You ain't got no room to talk about me nor Buck. Yo' son Abraham ain't makin' you no livin'.

VIOLET. You listen to me. Abraham is a good boy. He is wanderin' lak' all chillun. When he come home, he be totin' money and not wearin' no convict suit.

ETHEL. He ain't so smart. I don' reckon you never wore yo' heart out pinin' fo' no man shet up 'hind de bars. Reckon you ain't neber stood outside de gates an' hearn him sing outer de cage lak' he heart gwine break.

VIOLET. I'se moaned fo' him—yes, I'se moaned an' griebed. Dey ain't no sense to it. Dey comes an' goes lak' de summer an' de fall. Dey ain't faithful—dey don't last. And dere ain't no man on earth you gwine stay wid fo' no juration ob time.

ETHEL [*looking out of the door*]. Buck de only man I eber see make me shet my eyes to all de res'. [*She seems to dream.*] An' he workin' de roads by day an' locked up in de night wid chains on he feets. Dey sleeps 'em in boxcars, dey ain't no room to walk roun'. Dey ain't no sweet air to cool he face in de heat ob de night. Buck so strong an' tall, he kiver up de doorway when he stand dere lookin' out. He hol' onto de bars lak' he gwine tear 'em loose an' walk away from dere.

VIOLET. You workin' yo' self into a moan now. You don't know nothin' 'bout dat nigger—whar he come from, what he done. Last year you was courtin' Nelson Copeland; de year befo', who? I tell you right now, Ethel, I put up wid dem, but ef dat convict set he foot inside dis yard he gwine leab here wid a stick ob stove wood 'hind he haid. You ain't gwine mess roun' wid no sich trash.

ETHEL. He ain't no trash, I tol' you. De jedge sont him to de gang fo' stealin' a automobile; he ain't nebber seen dat car.

VIOLET. Das what he tol' you. I don't care what he done or what he ain't done, you ain't messin' wid him.

ETHEL. I got a min' to court who I please to court. Long as Buck stay shet up in de gang, I visits him. When he come out, I goes wid him wheresomever he go. He comin' out ob dere, too. He bust loose once and dey caught him. De next time he be moving keerful and fast. Ain't no white man livin' will run him down.

VIOLET. You gwine weep fo' dat talk. You gwine moan mo'

dan you moanin' now. I done tol' you de Lawd visit pain on dem dat turn dey back to Him and cavort wid sinners. Yours been a long time turned.

ETHEL. Hesh dat yellin', Ma. Here come de folkses. Sis' Netsie and Sis' Jerrie. [ETHEL *stands looking out the door.* SIS' NETSIE *and* SIS' JERRIE *pause before they enter. The long wail of a dog is heard coming through the night. They stand silent.* VIOLET *listens,* ETHEL *shows fear.*] What dat? Listen to dat soun'—hit a hootin' owl.

[SIS' NETSIE *and* SIS' JERRIE *enter slowly, solemnly. They are both tall, thin, and very black. Their presence seems to bring an atmosphere of gloom into the room.*]

SIS' NETSIE [*prophetically, solemnly shaking hands with* VIOLET]. I knowed de hootin' owls was gwine cry dis night. Dey been two funerals dis week. Brother Mose and Aunt Viny done gone to dey reward. It time for de third to be called. [*She crosses to the bench, down right, and sits.*]

SIS' JERRIE [*solemnly shaking hands with* VIOLET]. Jedus have told me! De owl signify dat de angel ob death am flyin' roun'. [*Following* SIS' NETSIE, *she sits beside her.*]

VIOLET [*warning her*]. Tie a knot in yo' apron string, Ethel. Dat owl soun' lak' he restin' nigh to dis house.

ETHEL [*tying the knot quickly, she tries to throw off the gloom*]. My Jedus, you all calls death in de door.

SIS' NETSIE. De angel ob death gwine visit us all, Ethel, gwine visit us all.

SIS' JERRIE. Best make yo' peace wid de Lawd. Yo' days am numbered on dis yearth.

ETHEL [*starting out the door*]. I gwine over to Beulah's while de meetin' gwine on here.

VIOLET [*commanding*]. You ain't gwine set yo' feets outside dis do'.

SIS' JERRIE [*looking at* ETHEL *with a superior, all-knowing expression*]. I wouldn't be trompin' roun' no woods dis night, Ethel.

Sis' Netsie [*with the same expression*]. I hearn talk in de south fiel' dat Lucy Roberson done ask fo' a spell to be sot on you, Ethel.

Ethel. Lucy Roberson don' bother me none. I handle her any day ob de week.

Violet. Wa'n't she messin' wid dat Buck Kinnebrew?

Sis' Netsie. Da's right. De man what thought he could bust loose from de gang—dey cotch 'im tryin'.

Sis' Jerrie. Lucy never had him down in no han' writin', but she claim him. Her gran'ma kin cast a powerful spell.

Sis' Netsie. De Sons and Daughters of Rest is glad you gwine ride de gospel train from now on, Ethel.

Sis' Jerrie. Yo' soul be saved fo' glory. We is glad to come moan wid you.

Ethel [*turning to* Violet, *walks down center*]. So dat's it. You brings 'em here to moan ober me. Well, I ain't gwine hab no moanin'. I ain't ridin' no gospel train, and I am leabin' 'fo' de res' ob 'em gits here. [*She turns, goes to the door where she meets* Sis' Emma *and* Uncle Mac *coming in.* Sis' Emma *is a little woman; she carries white robes over her arm.* Uncle Mac *is very tall, very thin, and more than solemn. He carries a large Bible in his hands. They stand for a moment as if warning* Ethel *with their eyes.* Sis' Emma *forces her to back into the room.* Ethel *sees the white robes. She watches them fearfully.*]

Sis' Emma [*nodding to the sisters*]. Evenin', sistren. [*To* Ethel.] Evenin', sinner.

Brother Mac. Evenin', sistren. [*To* Ethel.] De Lawd have mercy on yo' soul!

Violet [*walks behind the table, followed by* Mac]. The table am sot an' waitin' fo' de Good Book, brother.

BROTHER MAC [*carefully places the Bible on the table, takes a pair of spectacles from his coat pocket and places them on his nose*]. Brother Nap and Brother Jim be comin' on; dey burden slow 'em down.

SIS' EMMA [*placing the white robes on the table*]. Dey nine here. Brother Mose' robe be waitin' for de nex' mourner. Sis' Viny's robe waitin' fo' you, sinner, to git inside and face de Lawd. [*She crosses to the bench, down right, and sits*].

ETHEL [*wildly, looking at the robes and backing toward the door*]. I ain't puttin' on no dead folkses' robe! I ain't doin' it. Dey ain't nothin' but grave clothes, an' I ain't wearin' 'em.

BROTHER MAC [*firmly*]. You put it on, sinner, you gwine see repentance.

ETHEL. I done seen enough; I gittin' out ob here whether de owl hootin' or no. [*As she starts for the door* UNCLE NAP *and* UNCLE JIM *enter solemnly bearing a coffin. When she sees it, she shrinks back in terror.*] Oh, my Jedus! Oh, my Jedus! What you bringin' de body here fo'?

BROTHER MAC. Evenin', bretheren.

BROTHER JIM AND BROTHER NAP. Evenin', brother. Evenin', sistren.

VIOLET. Rest it 'side de wall, bretheren.

ETHEL. Who ridin' dat coffin?

BROTHER JIM [*they walk down center with the casket and cross the room to the left*]. Dey ain't nobody inside, sinner. Death ain't called, yet.

ETHEL. What you bring it here fo'? Ma, git it out ob dis house; we got to sleep here to-night.

BROTHER NAP [*they place the coffin against the wall, then come to sit on the bench*]. De coffin belong here, Ethel.

It's part ob de services. You gwine see de las' restin' place you habes on dis earth. It turn yo' thought to de Lawd an' Salvation.

ETHEL. I ain't gwine stay nowhere dey is a coffin standing up 'side de wall an' grave clothes lyin' roun'. I ain't gwine stay!

BROTHER MAC [*using the full power of his voice*]. De sperits of evil is at work outside in de night; de spirit ob de Society am inside dis house; you is in dat spirit, an' you ain't gwine out ob it. De services will commence. Brothers, put on de robes. Sisters, put on de robes.

ETHEL. I cain' stan' no mo'!

SIS' EMMA. De sin inside yo' soul is what you cain't stan'. We is here to sabe you.

SIS' NETSIE. De night outside holds ghostes and sperits.

BROTHER MAC [*pointing to* ETHEL, *commanding*]. Stand where you be, sinner. We prays fo' you to see de light. Let de service start. Dis sinner gwine face death and her Maker.

ETHEL [*thoroughly frightened*]. I stands here, den. I stands here. [*She stands in the door as far away from the coffin as she can get and as close to the door as she can without being on the outside, her back half-turned to the mourners.* VIOLET *gives each a robe. They put them on slowly, then gravely take their seats on the benches—the brethren on the left, the sisters on the right.* UNCLE MAC *presides behind the table. They sing.*]

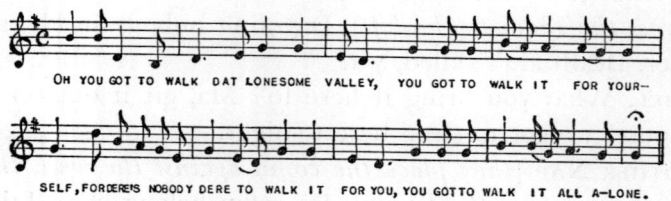

OH YOU GOT TO WALK DAT LONESOME VALLEY, YOU GOT TO WALK IT FOR YOUR-

SELF, FOR DERE'S NOBODY DERE TO WALK IT FOR YOU, YOU GOT TO WALK IT ALL A-LONE.

MOURNERS TO GLORY

> Oh, you got t' walk that lonesome valley;
> You got t' walk it fo' yo'self,
> Fo' dere's nobody dere to walk it fo' you.
> You got t' walk it all alone.

[*As they begin singing softly,* ETHEL *turns on them, walks down center, crying first to sisters, then to brethren.*]

ETHEL. What all you sing dat song? Buck cry out in it. Sing something else. [*They pay no attention to her but sing lustily and more mournfully. She backs away, slowly.*]

> Oh, my Jedus had to walk dat lonesome valley,
> He had to walk it fo' Hisself,
> Fo' dere's nobody dere to walk it fo' Him.
> He had to walk it all alone.

BROTHER MAC [*closes his eyes and begins to pray as the mourners fall to their knees and begin swaying and chanting*].

> Lawd, look down; Lawd, look down.
> We bows de head an' prays;
> Holp dis sinner struggling here;
> Holp her to mend her ways.

SIS' NETSIE. She labor in de fiel' by day, Lawd.
SIS' JERRIE. She walk in de light ob de sun.
SIS' EMMA. She res' in de cool ob de night, Lawd,
  When her day's work am done.
VIOLET. She see de daylight wid her eyes, Lawd;
BROTHER NAP. She hear de soun' ob de mawnin' creep,
BROTHER JIM. But her heart am deaf to de call, Lawd;
SIS' EMMA [*pointing to* ETHEL]. Her sinful soul am 'sleep.
THE MOURNERS [*clapping their hands in the rhythm of the song*].

Wake up de sinner, Lawd, Lawd;
Wake up de sinner from sin.
Wake up de sinner, Lawd, Lawd;
Call de wanderer in.

BROTHER MAC [*pointing to* ETHEL].
Listen, sinner to de word ob de Lawd;
De jedgment day gwine roll aroun',
THE SISTERS.
An' de blessed answer: "Ready, Lawd,"
THE BRETHREN.
But de sinner-man cain't be found.
BROTHER MAC.
De jaws ob hell be open up wide
Wid de fire a-roarin' high,
THE SISTERS.
An' de sinner cry out: "Here me, Lawd,"
THE BRETHREN.
But de Lawd he pass 'em by.
SIS' NETSIE [*rising to her feet*].
De sperits ob de sinner rise from de grave;
Fly roun' lost at night.
SIS' JERRIE [*rising*].
Dey howls an' moans
In de dark, black swamp,
THE BRETHREN AND SISTERS [*rising*].
But de blessed sees de light!
BROTHER MAC.
Oh, see de light ob heaben shine;
THE MOURNERS.
See de pearly gates—see de glory.
BROTHER MAC.
See St. Peter, waitin' at de gates.

THE MOURNERS.
    See de pearly gates—see de glory!
[ETHEL, *having been drawn into the rhythm of the clapping hands, begins to turn slowly toward* THE MOURNERS *as if in a trance and begins to walk down toward them.*]
[BUCK KINNEBREW *appears suddenly in the doorway. He wears the striped suit of a convict. His big body is drooping with fatigue. He leans against the door and calls* ETHEL. *She does not hear him. He calls again. She hears him, turns quickly, and stops when she sees him. The shouting ceases abruptly.* THE MOURNERS *stare at* BUCK, *while* SIS' NETSIE *and* SIS' JERRIE *turn away quickly, afraid.*]
ETHEL. Buck! Buck, you ain't dere?
BUCK. Let me come inside, Ethel. It me, Buck.
ETHEL. Buck, come here. [*She runs to him and pulls him into the house.* VIOLET *gets her stove wood and comes at* BUCK. ETHEL *steps between them.*] Buck, you run away—you hurt!
BUCK. Jist in de shoulder; I ain't hurt bad.
VIOLET. Stop dis; stop dis I tells you! You git out ob dis house, you convict!
ETHEL. Leave him alone, Ma.
SIS' NETSIE [*dolefully*]. De service ob de Lawd be stopped by a sinner.
SIS' JERRIE. De jedgment ob de Lawd be against him.
ETHEL. Hesh up, all ob you! Move 'way from dem benches. You come set down, Buck. [*She leads him to the bench. The women back away from him, afraid.* SIS' NETSIE *and* SIS' JERRIE *turn their backs on the sinner but their curiosity makes them face him again.*]
VIOLET [*standing over him*]. Dey ain't no convict gwine sit on de mourner's bench in my house.

BUCK. I cain' go no further. I ain't got no breaf. Dey after me!

ETHEL. Cain' you see he wore out?

BROTHER MAC [*walking down center*]. Let de sinner rest. How long you been out, boy?

BUCK. Since befo' day dis mawnin'. . . .

VIOLET. You hurry up and ketch yo' breaf an' make tracks 'way from dis place.

ETHEL. You ain't gwine turn him 'way from here, Ma. You ain't gwine do it.

SIS' EMMA. Yo' sins is rise to face you, Ethel.

ETHEL [*wildly, as she walks down center away from* BUCK]. I repents of 'em! I says 'em all out loud! I'll be 'nitiated! Put me on de prayin' robe.

VIOLET. You repents, does you?

ETHEL. I repents 'fo' God—I repents 'fo' everybody. I does what you say from now on. Yes, I gits in dat coffin, ef dat what it take. Jist don't turn Buck away from here.

BROTHER MAC. Is you a sinner, boy?

BUCK. Naw sir, I ain't.

VIOLET. You been baptize'?

BUCK. Yes ma'm, I been baptize'.

SIS' EMMA. Is you been sprinkled or dipped?

BUCK. I been under de water all de way. I ain't done no big harm. I couldn't stand bein' shet up no longer; I broke loose dis mawnin'. I ain't got no place to go now. I been in dat swamp. Please Jedus, let me res' here a minute. De mens done lost my trail; I got a breavin' space now.

BROTHER NAP. How many ob 'em after you?

BUCK. I don't know; dey got de bloodhounds loose on me. I swum through de swamp—dey lost de scent.

BROTHER JIM. Dat swamp bad, 'less you knows it.

BUCK. I couldn't find no way out de other end. I hearn de

dogs bark. I lay low 'til dey die away, den I make fo' de clearin'.

VIOLET. Ef you cain' stay whar you belong, 'hind de bars wid de convicts, you bes' stay in de swamp wid de res' ob de varmits.

ETHEL. Ma, whar yo' son, Abraham? What ef he wanderin' roun' lost somewhere and nobody dere to 'friend him? Ain't you think on that?

SIS' NETSIE. You *is* got a wanderin' boy, Sis' Violet.

SIS' JERRIE. De same as dis one.

SIS' EMMA. Maybe he cryin' for he home and he friends. Maybe he find trouble.

VIOLET. He ain't no chain-gang nigger.

ETHEL. How you know what he done or whar he be? You ain't heard no word from him.

BUCK. Don't turn me out, Miss Violet. Let me res' here 'til I gits my breaf, den I go back to de swamp.

BROTHER MAC. Be merciful, Sis' Violet. He yo' color—he in need!

SIS' NETSIE. He a wanderin' lamb.

SIS' JERRIE. Strayin' from de fold.

ETHEL. Ain't he tol' you he been baptize'? Ain't he got religion?

BUCK. Yes, Lawd, lak' *yo'* boy, Miss Violet. Mayhap he in need somewhar.

VIOLET [*softening*]. I ain't seen him. I don' know whar he be, in grief or no. I don't know nothin' 'bout him.

SIS' NETSIE. De Lawd say don' turn de stranger 'way from yo' do'.

SIS' JERRIE. Holp dem what suffers and falls by de way.

VIOLET [*determined*]. Is you willing to jine up wid dis society? Will you face death in dat coffin? Or is you scared ob de Lawd same as you is ob de white man's law?

BUCK. I ain't scared. I face Jedus—I face de coffin!

ETHEL. You hears him, Ma. Keep him here, den Brother Mac and Brother Jim show him out ob de swamp.

BROTHER NAP. I gits him through to de outside. My brother'll haul him 'way in he wagon befo' day.

VIOLET [*lifting her head and praying*]. Lawd, I takes dis sinner in my house; I sabes him ef I can. Lawd, look down on Abraham and rest he soul from pain. [*She speaks to* THE MOURNERS *abruptly.*] Now git on wid de 'nitiation. De white mens won't find you here, boy. Dey know I don' hide no convicts. [*She brings the robes, handing one to* ETHEL, *one to* BUCK.] Here de robes.

ETHEL. You puts your'n on—I puts mine on. De chains hurt you bad?

BUCK. Dey ain't soft. I broke 'em loose.

BROTHER MAC. De sinners kneel befo' de mourners. Lawd, dese lost lambs is bowed down befo' you. Watch dey sorrowful heart. Hear de promise dey makes befo' de sperit. Sabe 'em, Lawd, when dey is laid by in death. [*To* ETHEL *and* BUCK.] Does you repent for all de sin you done?

ETHEL AND BUCK [*kneeling before him*]. We repents... we repents.

BROTHER MAC. Does you see de angel ob death draw nigh?

ETHEL. Yes, Lawd!

BUCK. I hear de soun' ob he wings.

BROTHER MAC. Will you set up nights wid de sick and de dyin'? Will you moan fo' dem when dey gone?

ETHEL. I will, Lawd.

BUCK. I set up wid 'em on dey dyin' bed. I bring de coolin' balm to heal dey head.

BROTHER MAC. Will you comfort de widow an' de orphant chile? Will you 'ten' de Lawd's house? Will you pray?

ETHEL. I promise, Lawd; I does it.

BUCK. I set in de house ob de Lawd by day and by night.
I pray now an' forever mo'.
THE SISTERS. Pray den, Brother. Let him hear you call.
BUCK.
    Lawd, I steal away in de early mawnin'—
    I creep 'way from dat cage.
    Lawd, I wallow in de swamps and de cane brake.
THE SISTERS.
    He trabel, Lawd; he weary.
BUCK.
    Lawd, I prayed to you in de water ob de swamp;
    I hide my face from de sun.
    Let me res' here, Lawd, 'neath yo' arm;
    Lawd, let dis race be done.
ETHEL.
    Lawd, sabe him, keeps him safe.
    Lawd, sabe him, Lawd, Lawd!
BROTHER NAP.
    He trabel wid a load, Lawd, trabel far.
BUCK. Bress dese sistren an' bretheren, Lawd, dat hides me here. I live fo' yo' glory, Lawd, fo' yo' glory from now on.
THE SISTERS. Hallelujah, he coming roun' to de Lawd!
BUCK. I see you sit in de jedgment seat, Lawd. I been a sinner—I walk de earth an' fergit you dere, but I see you, Lawd, I sees you. I ain't had no big sin, Lawd; ain't mean no harm. Put de shelterin' arm aroun' me, Lawd. I didn't mean no harm.
THE BRETHREN. Hallelujah, he confess!
BROTHER MAC. Rise, Brother. Get ready fo' de march. Open de casket, dat final bed; let him see Death inside.
[THE MOURNERS *rise from their knees.* BROTHER NAP *and* BROTHER JIM *pass the blindfold around* BUCK'S *head. They turn him around three times.* THE MOURNERS *fall in line behind him.* ETHEL *takes his hand and leads him*

around the room to the coffin. He steps inside. BROTHER JIM *and* BROTHER NAP *put the lid on and* THE MOURNERS *fall on their knees. They sing.*]

In my dyin' room I know
Somebody gwine a moan,
All I want you to do for me
Is give that bell a tone.

[*As they sing softly, the sound of a dog barking is heard.* ETHEL *raises her head and listens. The others continue.*]

When I'm dyin', don't you moan;
When I'm dyin', I'll be dead.
When I'm dyin', don't you moan;
Jedus gwine to make up my dyin' bed.

[ETHEL *stops them.*]
ETHEL [*getting quickly to her feet*]. Listen, listen to dat! Hit a bloodhound howling! Git him out ob dat coffin —git him out!
[*They stop. The barking of the hounds draws nearer.* BROTHER JIM *and* BROTHER NAP *let* BUCK *out. He takes*

the blindfold from his eyes. He hears the sound. They listen silently.]
BUCK. Oh, my Jedus, dey done picked up de trace! Oh, my Jedus, dey got me!
ETHEL [*quickly, thinking fast*]. No, dey ain't! No, dey ain't.
BUCK. Where I gwine hide? Where I gwine hide?
ETHEL. You gits back in de coffin, Buck Kinnebrew! We be havin' a funeral when dey gits here. We be moanin' for de livin' 'stid ob de dead!
VIOLET. What ail you, Ethel?
ETHEL. Ain't nothin' ail me. Give me dem benches. Lay dis coffin twixt 'em.
[BROTHER NAP *and* BROTHER JIM *bring up the benches and place the coffin across them.*]
BROTHER NAP. I don't know what ail her, but she talk lak' she know what she mean.
SIS' EMMA. What gwine on here? Fast as we gits to de knees to moan, somethin' stop us.
SIS' NETSIE. Jedus gwine study 'bout why we ain't never finish de moanin'.
BUCK. I'se finish now.
ETHEL. You ain't. You git in dat coffin an' res' dere lak' it yo' last sleep. Don' you move nary toe. We gwine be havin' moanin' fo' de funeral when de mens come in here. Git in, Buck Kinnebrew!
BUCK [*getting into the coffin*]. I leave my soul to you an' de Lawd, Ethel.
VIOLET. Dey ain't no funeral, Ethel.
ETHEL. Dis is a funeral. Stand dere an' hold de lid, brother, an' when you hears de footsteps let it drap. You ain't gwine smother, Buck, dey breathin' holes dere. Git aroun', sistren, you ain't never moaned lak' you gwine moan now. Ma, you been tellin me all dis time you was a

chief moaner—all yo' all is chief moaners. Well, out-moan *me* now.

BROTHER MAC [*crossing down right, stands and watches the door*]. Bretheren, stand roun' de casket. I talks to de white gentlemen when dey comes in. Dey knows me.

ETHEL. Ma, in dis casket is yo' son, Abraham. Dey brung de body home; he dead wid de fevers an' we moanin' fo' him. Git on de knees, sistren; don' nobody rise from here. Uncle Mac, keep yo' eyes on dat do'. Here we goes. [*She begins a loud, high wail which builds throughout the scene. The* SISTERS *and the* BRETHREN *moan an accompaniment.*]

  Oh, my Jedus, Lawd in heaben,
  Dis heart am griebin', griebin'!

[*She looks at the casket; sees its bareness; gets up from her knees to get the cover from the table and a vase of flowers from the mantel and hurries back with them. Moaning all the time, she spreads the sheet over the casket, sets the flowers at the head.* THE SISTERS *follow her movements; the wailing is continuous.*]

ALL.
  I nursed him, Lawd, an' I seen him suffer;
  He cried out, Lawd, in pain;
  De las' word he said on dis earth, Lawd,
  He were callin' out yo' name.
  He pinin' fo' glory; he soul won't rest;
  Take him, Jedus; take him, Lawd.

[JAKE HUDSON, *the sheriff, appears at the door and stands there watching the moaning in amazement. Recognizing* MAC, *he crosses to him.*]

HUDSON. Stop this noise, Mac. Mac, stop this infernal noise!
BROTHER MAC [*raising his head calmly, looks innocently at the* SHERIFF]. Evenin', boss.
HUDSON. Get them niggers on their feet, Mac.
BROTHER MAC. I ain't sure dey can come out ob it quick, boss.
HUDSON. They better come out of it.
BROTHER MAC. I tries, boss. Dey moanin' fo' Miss Violet's boy, Abraham. Dey brung him in dead ob de fevers.
HUDSON. Well, hurry up.
BROTHER MAC. Boss, I ain't wantin' to stop de sperit off short. Dey moanin' Abraham into glory.
HUDSON [*turning to the* MOURNERS]. Git up, all of you, git up, I say.
[*They pay no attention to him.* ETHEL *begins a louder wail, rising from her knees and flinging herself across the coffin.*]
ETHEL. Lawd, I cain't find de way, I cain't find de way!
BROTHER MAC. Was you wantin' somethin', boss?
HUDSON. I want Buck Kinnebrew.
BROTHER MAC. I don't know him, boss. Maybe Jim or Nap does. Dey be out ob it soon.
HUDSON. You go in there and get them on their feet. Move them away from that coffin.
ETHEL [*sending up a louder wail*]. Listen, Lawd, listen. I prayin' fo' a guidin' spirit. Show me de way, Lawd, show me de way.
BROTHER MAC. Jes' wait, boss, she won't las' long; den dey all calm down.
[HUDSON, *seeing that* MAC *is not going to move, walks toward the coffin.* ETHEL *suddenly raises her head and faces him. Her eyes have a glassy stare; she moves as if in a trance toward him. The* SISTERS *watch her, amazed. As* ETHEL, *with arms outstretched, a sort of glory shining*

in her face, walks toward him, the SISTERS *rise and follow her.* HUDSON *stops.*]

ETHEL [*with a high wail*]. Yes, Lawd; yes, Lawd! I sees it now; I sees de way! Here de angel sont from heaben!

SIS' EMMA. She in de trance! Hallelujah, she in de trance!

ETHEL. He hab' come, sistren, de angel of de Lawd! He hab come to dis earth!

HUDSON [*feebly, unable to take his eyes off the march of* MOURNERS *bearing down upon him*]. Shut up this fool—

ETHEL [*with a beatific smile upon her face, absolutely confident*]. I sees de wings sprout from de shoulders. [*She makes a gesture with her hand the way she sees the wings grow.*] I sees de golden crown, resting on he head! [HUDSON *takes a step back as the* MOURNERS *advance to him.* ETHEL *advances slowly, surely.*] Oh, de Lawd sont de angel!

THE SISTERS AND BRETHREN [*pushing in upon him, thrust out their arms to him*]. Praise and glory be!

[HUDSON, *now almost completely surrounded, is at a loss what to do. He draws out his pistol and points it toward them.*]

ETHEL [*indicating the pistol*]. He got the blessed key to heaben in he hand! [*She holds her arm out, pleading for the key. The others do the same. Slowly,* HUDSON *lets the pistol drop, moved by their fervent supplication.*] You be the guiding angel sont from Abraham. Is he rest well; find he peace?

[HUDSON *is aghast. He begins backing toward the door.* ETHEL *begins shouting with a marked rhythm. The* MOURNERS *follow her lead and march with her pushing him to the door.*]

> Oh, de worl' roll roun'
> An' de debil roll wid it!

MOURNERS TO GLORY

THE MOURNERS. De Lawd look down from de sky!
ETHEL. De angel passin' wid a whirrin' wing!
THE MOURNERS [*shouting*]. Lawd, we standing by!
[HUDSON *stands in the doorway surrounded by the* MOURNERS. ETHEL *falls to her knees before him; the others do the same. He stares at them, then turns and rushes out.*]
ETHEL [*exultant*].

>Oh, gather roun' de saint of de Lawd,
>Tech de hem of he flowin' robe!

THE MOURNERS.

>Hallelujah, he wearin' de robe!
>Hallelujah, be praise!

ETHEL [*at the door, lifting her arms high to the night*]. Don' fly away, angel, we seen you here; we comin' wid you to the glory!
MOURNERS. Yes, Lawd.
ETHEL [*triumphant, to the* MOURNERS]. We want two wings lak' he wearin', Lawd; two wings to fly away! [*She runs to the coffin.* BROTHER NAP *and* BROTHER JIM *throw back the lid,* BUCK *sits up, and the* MOURNERS *sing "Two Wings To Fly Away."*]

Two Wings To Fly Away

>Oh, Lawd, I wants two wings to veil my face,
>Oh, Lawd, I wants two wings to fly away,
>Oh, Lawd, I wants two wings to veil my face,
>An' de worl' cain't do me no harm.

THE CURTAIN FALLS

FLORIDA

TRAFICANTE
A PLAY OF SPANISH FLORIDA

BY MAXEDA VON HESSE

OF WINTER PARK, FLORIDA

Written in the summer session at Northwestern University, 1934, and originally produced by The Carolina Playmakers at Chapel Hill, North Carolina, on November 15, 1934.

THE CHARACTERS

FELIPE, *a lighthouse keeper*............Fred Howard
ARMANDO, *a trader among the Timuquan Indians*
                                             Philip Parker
ROSA, *Felipe's wife*..................Louise McGuire
JUAN, *the small son of Rosa and Felipe*
                                             Danny Hamilton
A SERVANT-GIRL, *a half-breed slave*......Ellen Deppe

SCENE: *The kitchen of* ROSA *and* FELIPE's *home, the small shell-house of the keeper, nestling at the base of the lighthouse. Both are builded on one of the tiny islands of the Keys in the Florida Straits.*

TIME: *September, the month of the great winds, in the year 1607. Late afternoon on a stormy day.*

Copyright, 1938, by The Carolina Playmakers, Inc.
All rights reserved.

OF SPANISH FLORIDA

THE author of *Traficante*, Maxeda von Hesse, holds that no American state has a richer background than her state of Florida—in the deepest South.

There, held in dark secret by the impenetrable sloughs of the Everglades, are Seminole villages still unvisited by white men—trails once trod by the moccasin of the fierce, aboriginal Timuquan. There the history, written in the blood, of wandering Franciscan priests; of volatile Huguenots; of adventuring hidalgos from the golden courts of Spain's morose Philip the Second—history written darkly in blood spilled by the proud, slow-learning Timuquan caciques who were forced to deal with the bearded ones, the white gods who had sailed in tremendous canoes over the great water from the village of the Sun. There pirating rogues who once lay in wait in the little coves of the Florida Keys to pounce on lumbering merchantmen returning to the Old World laden with rich cargo out of Mexico—sea-going brigands with no scruples and less manners who buried their treasure-chests jealously upon the sands of the Dry Tortugas where no fresh water was to be had, then or now. There the Seven Golden Cities of Cibola for which many hopeful ones lost their lives in the seeking.

In these, our years of living, one may watch from the docks of Miami in Biscayne Bay sea-going yachts, ex-rum-runners, auctioned-off freighters, sloops—anything that floats on water from an out-rigger canoe to a three-masted whaling ship—clearing port with an escort of porpoises playing before them. Out to sea, to the warm waters of the Gulf Stream, the Florida Keys, and pirate treasure!

Now to take half a leg-stride between the long past and the mercurial present: what of the lean, brown settlers driving their oxen before them down-coast from the Virginias? We name them Florida Crackers, for once they wielded bull-whips from twenty to forty feet in length over their cattle—whips that could too easily cut a man to ribbons—and sometimes did.

So it is that the history of *La Florida,* Land of Flowers, has been written by the war-ax, the crucifix, and the whip.

Of the story of *Traficante* the author says: "This particular tale has haunted my mind's peace for a period of years. It was first told me by a ragged beach-comber in the very shadow of the ancient Spanish lighthouse about which the play is written. The beach-comber was a Harvard graduate, an irritatingly slow story-teller with a lazy twinkle far back in his sea-blue eyes. There was no way of knowing whether he was thirty or seventy years old. He had two valuable possessions: namely, a beautiful Irish setter named Lord Jim, and a weird watch-fob of seven silver skulls linked together. I coveted both the dog and the skulls and do to this day, likewise the twinkle—but nothing else, I may add.

"There is no doubt in my mind that he did embroider the legend with his own unrest and fancy. Perhaps it was because of this that my imagination caught fire from the telling. *Quién sabe?* An historian, particularly after the fact, would find the tale shockingly spotty. And yet there is a deal of truth here which I have verified to the best of my ability. You see, the Timuquan Indian, the Spaniard, a beach-comber, and I have all made our contributions to it."

TRAFICANTE

ROSA'S *clean-scrubbed kitchen, the roof of which is thatched with palmetto leaves above the dark stained rafters. Small red peppers, strings of native onions, and dried gourds of all sizes and shapes hang suspended from the beams. A hooded fireplace commands the rear wall of the room. On either side of the fireplace, trenchers and drinking cups stand neatly ranged on racks high against the shell wall. Smoke-soot streaks up the hood and darkens the Spanish tiles of the hearth. Suspended from an iron crane, a pot hangs over the coals simmering and giving off a delicious odor of stewing meats and vegetables. An oven of the early Dutch type squats on one side of the hearth opposite the split pine and oak logs of firewood. Directly in front of the fireplace stands a rough-hewn table naked of cloth and empty of dish. There is a small window on either side of the fireplace, and a rude bench against the wall. Another bench stands with its legs spraddled under the table. On the left wall, near the door to the bedroom, hangs a crucifix. Over the door* FELIPE'S *gun, a Spanish arquebus, rests on wooden pegs. A weather-stained cloak hangs limply on another peg. A door, up right, opens into the garden and the palm forest beyond. Earthen pottery bulges in a corner cupboard behind this door. A skin of the small red deer is stretched on the window-bench. A sea-chest, wondrously carved, is beneath the cloak. The entire room is colorful, a happy mingling of Old World grace and New World strength. Simple people have steeped this room with the personalities of their lives.*

[FELIPE, *a dark slender man of thirty-four years with the forehead of a dreamer and a gentle yet firm mouth, stands looking out across the garden patch, one knee resting upon the bench. He pays* ARMANDO *scant attention, having withdrawn into a protective silence.* ARMANDO, *a lean man, taut as a rope in a gale and as active if loosed, with dark eyes above a hawk nose and red lips, sits tilted back against the wall in one of the crude kitchen chairs to the left of the hearth. He is busily picking his strong, white teeth with the point of his belt-knife and enjoying himself as he talks of himself.* FELIPE, *with his silent cat-stride, crosses to the door facing the sea and leans against the door-jamb.*]

FELIPE [*speaking more to himself than to* ARMANDO]. It is too hot... too still.

ARMANDO. Your manhood is a pale thing, Felipe. You fear each change of wind. Forget it and listen to my—

FELIPE [*quietly interrupting*]. It is the month of winds. The air has changed. Not a leaf stirs in the palm-forest. It is too hot, I say... too still.

ARMANDO [*sniffing*]. You mistake it. The wind freshens.

FELIPE. No.

ARMANDO. Storm may not visit us yet. It is too early, man. [*He yawns.*]

FELIPE [*with cold courtesy*]. You ever had a small capacity for knowledge, Armando. The storm will break upon us soon, I say.

ARMANDO [*peevishly yet shrewdly*]. Very well, you say it! From your manner, Felipe, I see you have grown away from our early friendship... yes?

FELIPE. Aye. [*He turns, and his voice is dry with distaste as he regards* ARMANDO.]

ARMANDO [*wholely unperturbed*]. Well, I have something

to thaw the ice of your philosophic heart. Listen to a tale rich for the telling—

FELIPE [*turning back to watch the sea*]. I listen....

ARMANDO. At noon I set out... listen you, Felipe? I am not so old I enjoy talking to myself.

FELIPE [*shifting in the doorway*]. Forgive me, *traficante*. Storm ever makes me restless.... I can smell it in the air. But I will put my mind to trading. Go on.

ARMANDO [*chuckling*]. Trading, say you? *Cierto*, rare trading! [*He laughs, relishing his humor.*] But I would share the spice of my tale with you, my brother—[*He breaks off and regards* FELIPE *with growing disgust and irritation.*]

FELIPE [*forgetful of the braggart's presence, talking out his own thoughts*]. In the villages the drums of the *butios* will be calling the women in from the fields, the men from their games and hunting trails. [FELIPE'S *voice rises in a soft-rhythmed chant.*] Oak and *yaquila* will be burned to appease the wrath of the Storm-Gods. The drums will go throbbing through the tunnels of the swamps till the leaves of the trees tremble with the beat. There will be the chanting of the bronze people and the gourds rattling out staccato prayers. An ancient *paracoussy's* wife, many seasons in this life, will rise and, shuffling in the circle of the council fire, will tell the legend of the tribe. The throats of the drums will sing to the blood as the prayers rise on the smoke of the sacrifice. [*He breaks off abruptly.*] And yet who knows? Each man his god, his way of worship. What would you tell, Armando?

ARMANDO [*sullenly*]. Your ears are the ears of an old man who thinks only on his own thoughts.... I am of half a mind to tell you nothing. [*He looks hopefully at* FELIPE.]

FELIPE. Hah! Some woman adventure, I warrant. You and your petticoats! They'll trip you some fine day. [ARMANDO *opens his mouth eagerly, then shuts it as he remembers he is offended.*] What windy tale is this, *traficante?*

ARMANDO [*alertly interested*]. *Cristo!* She is a pretty wench. And a handful to manage, I tell you. [*He stops and fingers his jaw with a lean forefinger.* FELIPE *turns away to the sea. A thin wind whistles in the palm-grove, but for all that it rests deathly hot and still.*]

FELIPE [*wearily*]. One of the servant-women again, Armando? I thought your taste overfed in that quarter.

ARMANDO. Ah, she can fight like a swamp-cat, I tell you; but they always fight who are worth the taking. It makes surrender the sweeter. She and others had been bathing in the river. They were drying their bodies with the soft plumes of the river-grass when I came upon them at the bend. She is very good to look upon ... most as good as your Rosa, Felipe.

[FELIPE *disregards the other man's baiting. He feels the green hush. Over the sea he watches clouds form out of nothing and go scurrying to the northwest.*]

FELIPE. The sea has turned dead man's color! I like not this low murmurous groaning that fills the air. [*A line of sharp worry creases his forehead as the wind rises and the surf grows stronger.*]

ARMANDO [*tilting back perilously in his chair*]. The others ran like startled brown deer before the hunter. Ah, Felipe, she was like a young panther. Fierce she was and strong in her anger and fear of me. Beneath my hand her heart beat like a small rain-drum. And of kissing she knew nothing! [*He balances his knife in his hand.*] Ayiiiiih! [*He yawns widely and stretches, flipping his belt-knife point down into the wood of the table.*]

FELIPE. The storm has us now rightly enough. The whole world moves. Mayhap you will finish your long-winded tale another place, *traficante,* ... warmer than this? [*He looks on* ARMANDO *as a stranger.*]

ARMANDO. Ah, Felipe, her mouth! [*He moves with ecstasy.*] Red as the pomegranate, and on her arm a pricked circle. [FELIPE *starts at this.*] The women made deference to her as though she were a queen. I vow she bore herself with grace as regal as Britain's royal hussy.

FELIPE. Armando!

ARMANDO [*sighing lustily*]. Man, man! She is worth more love! Perchance...? But the ship comes soon.... Ah! her body is sweet as nutty Spanish ale!

[*The wind is another surf in the trees. Rain falls in splashing torrents against the house. There is no thunder nor flare of lightning lancing the air; only the rising wind in the turbulent trees and the sea and the rain. A strange luminescence plays about the house as though the hurricane itself carried light. And yet through that evil glow the darkness increases over the cowering land and furious waters. Rain falls with a fury unequaled as though the heavens held an ocean, then loosed it suddenly upon the earth.* FELIPE's *face is white under its swarthiness as he faces the* traficante *across the still-quivering knife-blade.*]

FELIPE. How was this, Armando? Come, fellow, make answer. [*His voice is heavy with command.*]

ARMANDO [*his eyes narrow, as* FELIPE's *hand closes suggestively about the upright knife-hilt*]. Man! It is nothing to tremble over!

FELIPE. Continue! Quickly, *traficante!*

ARMANDO [*angrily*]. *Por dios!* I did not kill the girl. I left her safe enough upon the trail. She won't be telling the tribe of our... encounter.... Not if she values her own skin...!

FELIPE. You did not go on, then, to the inner village? [*His face is intent and strained.*]

ARMANDO. No! I returned to the island shortly, having no need to trade again. Postpone your worry, Felipe, until a grief comes worth the worrying!

FELIPE. It has come, *traficante,* and with you! [*He would add more but checks himself.*]

ARMANDO. Bah! The day is lazy and life is good. [*He stretches luxuriously.*] The caravel is due and soon I shall be back in Spain with a tidy store of gold and enough of this brown weed tobacco, feathers, and skins to delight the court of any king, even our long-nosed Philip of the sensitive belly! [*He pats his own lean stomach with humor.*] And sassafras, too, for his royal tea. Man, I have fared well in your raw country. Am I not the lucky one?

FELIPE [*darkly*]. Until this ill-born day, Armando.

ARMANDO [*wroth*]. Now by the beard of Philip, I'll not look down my nose and fashion empty fears!

FELIPE. *Traficante,* this girl you took by force...!

ARMANDO [*carelessly, his quicksilver temper cooled by the other man's anger*]. Force is a good persuader. He argues well enough for me.

FELIPE. Evil enough, mean you.

ARMANDO [*sullenly*]. I live in mine own fashion.

FELIPE. A Yamassee runner from the north country has brought evil talk to Hyllispilli, the cacique, concerning the treachery of all Spaniards, and now you.

ARMANDO. Bah! Give you rumor and you eat it like a bear the honeycomb!

FELIPE [*starting up*]. Listen, the Yamassee message made our post here precarious enough without this to inflame the tribe to massacre us.

ARMANDO. Your fears are wearisome. Between the wind howling outside the walls and you...in, *Diablo!* You were ever frightened of your own shadow, Felipe!

FELIPE. I must tell Rosa, even though it worry her. [*He starts up from the bench, undecided.*]

ARMANDO [*snarling his disgust*]. Then do not tell her. The heat has made you foolish in the head. Your fear has scuttled your wits. Take stock of yourself, Felipe. This comes of your dreaming too much by day.

[FELIPE *draws himself up to his full height and addresses the outlaw trader with hidalgo hauteur as the wind rattles on the roof and buffets the house.*]

FELIPE. *Traficante!* I have bridled my tongue, reminding myself you were a guest beneath my roof, but now I must speak. You do not know nor understand the South Timuquans. Spain is opening up this new world too ruthlessly. The iron of her own fist will strike her down in the end. When you first landed on these shores, saw you an Indian bowed in slavery? Within this year a Timuquan slave has died under Spanish whips for every foot of length added to the irrigation ditch. My brown brothers will not—

ARMANDO [*sneering openly*]. Brothers? For a race of servants you bespeak them very lovingly...!

FELIPE. They are proud hunters, not servants. I have lived in friendliness with them before you rested here... with your trading.

ARMANDO. I am as eager to end my visit as you seem to be. And it will end soon, good mine host.

FELIPE. Aye. But not as you planned. You have taken more on yourself than this woman now. Remember my words.

ARMANDO [*with his old mocking smile*]. Your variety of fears is wonderful. First a great wind is to blow us away, and now our scalps are to be lifted... by brown brothers!

FELIPE. I fear me this was Ho-Ti-Chee, the cacique's daughter, you attacked. The pricked circle assures me of it for she let blood in betrothal not two moons past.

ARMANDO [*contemptuously*]. Even so?
FELIPE. Our only hope lies in standing them off until the caravel arrives. Pray God we can make the tower before the attack.
ARMANDO. You sicken me! I've heard enough old wives' worry.
[ARMANDO *grunts in disgust and swings out the sea-door into the teeth of the wind. Gnawing his mustache and heartily wishing the keeper dead with his worrisome fears, he makes for the lighthouse, his tall body bent in a question-mark against the force of the storm.*]
[ROSA, *a young, handsome, olive-skinned Spanish woman on the north side of thirty years, enters from the inner room. Her full skirts billow gracefully about her as she walks. She is plump and pleasant. Her face in repose is sweet and rather sorrowful. One is given the impression of sleeping temper and purposeful strength. She comes into the kitchen quietly and immediately goes to the simmering pot, lifts the lid with a cloth, and stirs with a long spoon, adding a pinch of pepper.* FELIPE *knows, without turning, it is she.*]
FELIPE. Rosa?
ROSA [*stirring*]. A moment, Felipe. [*She busies herself at the hearth.*]
FELIPE [*his back towards her*]. I have need of you, Rosa . . . as ever.
ROSA [*going to him quickly*]. You are anxious, my husband?
FELIPE. Aye. [*He puts a gentle arm about her waist.*]
ROSA. Then tell me that I may share your trouble. [*She nestles in the circle of his arms and watches with him the fury of the storm over the sea.*]
FELIPE. It is the old trouble. . . . Women! [*He sighs and rests his cheek against her shining hair.*] Ah, *Rosa mia*, I thought this a pleasant place once. But I did not forsee

that such a man as this Armando would make our home his, trading with the Indians only to enrich his own purse, giving no thought to gaining their respect and friendship and living the while on us like any thirsty leech.

ROSA. An entertaining leech, methinks. [*She slants her eyes at him.*]

FELIPE [*his voice harsh*]. Armando is one of those who live by other men's strength, gathering the fruits of other men's toil and leaving empty husks for those who labor.

ROSA [*softly*]. What then, my husband?

FELIPE. I have small liking for the soft looks you send him, Rosa. You vowed your love to but one man.

ROSA [*smiling wistfully*]. My love belongs to the one who holds me thus within his arms. I could never give to another the love I have for you, my Felipe... but the *traficante* has a way of pleasing me with small considerations.

FELIPE. He has lost the way of pleasing me, if ever he had it. I feel only displeasure concerning him... but then I am no woman. [FELIPE'S *voice is gruff. His face darkens as he probes his own wounds farther.*] How would you like him for a lover?

ROSA [*twisting out of his arms furiously*]. Felipe! You have a sad wit! [*Her mood changes and she turns to him, reaching up her hands to touch his face and force his eyes to meet hers.*] I have but one lover, and want no other, Felipe. [*She sighs and lays her head against his chest.*] Why is it a woman must always be reassuring a man?

FELIPE [*unwilling to bury the subject*]. Armando is a wild fellow. And not to be gentled by any woman.

ROSA. He is wild, that one, but there is good in him.

FELIPE. It would bring comfort to believe that, but I cannot.

ROSA. Evil or good—I can read his thoughts as though a

journey-book were open to my eyes and so anticipate his moods. He is disturbing, aye, but not all evil as you would make him out.

FELIPE. Disturbing is the word for such as he. I like him not.

ROSA [*she leaves his arms and considers his face*]. Your sudden strong dislike is passing strange.... [*She crosses to the hearth and stirs the contents of the pot with the long-handled spoon.* FELIPE *seats himself on the sea-chest.*]

FELIPE. Even little Juan takes to him kindly, but I am no longer of the same mind. I shall be far more content when he has taken himself and his free ways to Spain.

ROSA [*looking up from the stew and speaking sharply*]. You let your worry own you, Felipe! As for my liking of Armando... I meet in him no stranger such as I wedded in Cadiz!

FELIPE. What mean you? [*His eyes are alert, his words deliberate.*]

ROSA [*wiping her hands on her apron*]. Just that, my husband!

FELIPE. I am slow to understand, wife.

ROSA [*she faces him, her voice pleading with him to understand her sorrow*]. Many times, when I stretch out my hand and feel you near me in the night, I sense the spirit of you roving. I know not what distant far-off land you see nor what soft voices call you from me. [*She crosses to him and places her hands on his shoulders as he rises.*] I only know you go alone; I may not follow. And so I lose you, beloved. Your mind journeys in strange ways, and there are times I needs must think the heart is its companion, leaving me lonely and afraid. Nor may all my love be yours until you will it.

FELIPE. I listen, Rosa.

ROSA [*pleading, begging for his understanding*]. I... I am

all woman, Felipe! Without you life would lose its meaning, yet have I vainly asked my heart how to know the stranger who sleeps at time in my arms. [*She turns away from him, not bearing to see his grave and saddened eyes. Going to the window she presses her cheek against the pane to hide her tears.*]

FELIPE [*passing a hand across his forehead and not looking at* ROSA]. I perceive this has long troubled you.

ROSA [*in a small, sad voice*]. You go apart ... withdraw into yourself. [*She whirls and her voice trembles with passion.*] Then do I hate you, Felipe! Hate you as much as I fear this barrier of silence you raise between us!

FELIPE [*sitting upon the sea-chest and lowering his head into his hands*]. You find me a cold lover and lacking, I know it's truth. It is my way ... this going apart as you name it ....

ROSA [*brokenly*]. It is your way ... but, oh ... the lost feeling it leaves me!

FELIPE [*raising his head and looking at her*]. Yet I warrant you know full well I love you better than life itself?

ROSA [*flashing him a quick, warm smile*]. I know, and am content. More so than in the love so easy met and read in other men. But I would go with you always, forever and all ways.

FELIPE. That ... one may never do with another. Within one lives his own life, for the most part. It is God's truth, my Rosa, and grieve not for it.

ROSA. I will try, ... but begrudge not my small liking for Armando.

FELIPE [*impatiently*]. Hark to my words, wife. I say he is too well versed in pretty phrasing.

ROSA [*mockingly*]. Music to a woman's ears and wine to her lips, Felipe. More so when starved she is for the hearing of them.

FELIPE [*highly disgusted*]. You speak truth! And no compliment to your sex!

ROSA. Oh, I grant you we are foolish when we love, else where would you find yourself, my husband? [*Laughing, she makes him a low curtsey.* FELIPE *pulls her roughly into his arms.*]

FELIPE. I mistrust his eyes... his looks slide out from under a straight glance. And you... [*He shakes her gently.*]... with your light talk of liking him...! Rosa, the *traficante* has brought Indian war upon us, I fear.

ROSA. Blessed Mother of God! Let that not happen! What say you... Armando?

FELIPE. Aye. The *traficante*. He drinks war like wine, but this vintage is not to my liking... nor will it be to his, I vow, when the drinking of it comes.

ROSA [*crossing back to the hearth, she lifts the lid of the pot, tastes the stew speculatively and replaces the lid.*] The ship is due, Felipe, unless it be delayed by this ill weather. [*She lays down her spoon and goes to him.*] You are worried because of Rosa and the little Juan? I have brought you much unhappiness before... and seem to have made it my dowry! [*She turns in his arms and lays her saddened face against his heart.*]

FELIPE. You have brought happiness, my sweet one, beyond my wildest dreams! I would have found life a dull and sorry venture without you and the small son by my side. [FELIPE'S *face relaxes in tenderness.*] The storm climbs and thickens. Perchance it may cheat the Timuquans of their revenge....

ROSA [*going again to the window and looking down the beach*]. Look here, Felipe, the great oak is riven but a bow-shot from our door! Think you the house will stand against such a wind?

[*The wind has mounted to a sullen roar that hurts the ears.*

The tempestuous rain may be heard on the thatched roof like so many small hammers pounding. And over and above the wind and the rain may be heard the crashing of the waves against the breakwater.]
FELIPE. We will be safer now the rain has come.
ROSA. How it falls! As though it would make another flood and in much less than Noah's forty days. [*She faces* FELIPE.] What has the *traficante* done to arouse the Indians to war against us, Felipe? You are their friend, accepted even in their councils.
FELIPE [*sighing*]. It is the old, old story... the world knows it well. Man and woman and man's imperfections....
ROSA. And Armando?
FELIPE. Armando took by force Ho-Ti-Chee, and she is this month plighted in troth to the young *paracoussy,* Tomo Chici, of the North Timuquans.
ROSA. And for this?
FELIPE. She will die. The maiden has no choice. Only may she choose to die honorably by her own hand or under the knife of the *butio* in tribal justice. It is more fitting a cacique's daughter die by her own intent since she must give up this life because of Spanish contamination. [*A small groan escapes him.*] All old ways are broken! All our life is broken by this... *traficante!*
ROSA. No, no, Felipe! Surely...?
FELIPE [*somberly*]. It is the age-old lust for gold that visited Armando upon us. *Cristo!* We hold too dear this shining hand-held metal.
ROSA. I am afraid, my husband....
FELIPE [*summoning false cheer to his aid*]. Do not fear. I will find a way of safety. At times my brain is like to crack, I have so cudgeled it, but there must be some manner of escape from such a needless death.

ROSA. If God and the Holy Mother desire it, a way will open unto us.

FELIPE. Aye, of that I am assured. The boy sleeps?

ROSA [*gesturing to the inner room*]. I have hopes he will sleep through the afternoon until the fury of the storm passes. [*She starts towards the bedroom door at the left, but pauses to peer out into the garden through the small window.*] How dark it is for day. One would believe it night, Felipe.

FELIPE [*taking down his gun and inspecting it carefully*]. Aye. Storm brings night in his company.

ROSA. Rain falls in drops as large as plums!

FELIPE. 'Tis better so. This place is hard on a gun. I grease and oil it like the pig for the roasting and the rust eats in regardless.

ROSA [*turning to face him by the garden window*]. What will become of all this, Felipe?

FELIPE [*sighting down the gun-sights*]. The caravel will sail ... and take us off ... and we shall have to stand Armando's company as far as San Marco. [*He lowers the gun and looks at her sardonically.*] Methinks you will not find that hard.

[ROSA *walks huffily into the bedroom, reappearing immediately, her nose sharp with anger and her tongue quick.*]

ROSA. For one so wise you are exceeding stupid! [*She disappears only to dart out again.*] I often wonder why I ever listen to you—[*In again, to* FELIPE's *amusement, and then reappearing.*]—an evil habit!

FELIPE [*sighing and replacing the gun on its pegs. He ignores* ROSA's *small show of temper*]. It saddens me to think we must say good-by to old ways here. But I will talk with *el capitán*. He will put me within leg-stride of the present....

ROSA [*reëntering and taking down trenchers and cups from*

their racks, setting them on the tablecloth]. And then, my husband?

FELIPE. And then?... I know not. Spain holds uncertain welcome for me now. But be of good cheer. There is a deal of life left us to live.

[ROSA *makes* FELIPE *no answer but continues preparing an early meal. The rain has stopped and the high wind has abated.*]

[FELIPE *takes his weather-stained cloak from its peg by the door and hesitates on the threshold.*] I go to examine the safety of the well, Rosa. I fear a tree may have fallen across it. [*He cranes his head out the door, regarding the sky.*] 'Tis clear, now. The storm rides to the north of us. The sun hangs a smoking lantern in the west. Well, no matter.... [*He pulls the door to behind him and goes, singing beneath his breath,* "Santa Maria, madre de Dios."]

ROSA [*musingly, as she gazes after her husband*]. Hmm, Felipe walks like an Indian. Odd that he should praise God for the love he has found in these savages.

[*From the inner-room,* JUAN *calls softly,* "Mamá!" ROSA *leaves her cooking to go to him. She reappears with the boy in her arms all rumpled from his nap. She kisses him and sets him down. He crosses the room to the corner where his shells are scattered on the floor, but finds them uninteresting.* ROSA *is busy mixing batter in an earthenware bowl when* JUAN *tugs at her skirts.*]

JUAN. Mamá! Mamá!

ROSA [*patiently*]. Play with your pretty shells, Juanito. I am busy with supper.

[ROSA *does not look up as* JUAN *slips out through the door facing the beach.* ARMANDO *comes in by the same door, turning to smile and murmur something to the boy before shaking the water from his great-coat. He leans* against the door-jamb and casually watches ROSA moving about her pots and kettles. She, however, pays him scant attention, speaking only to give crisp orders to the SERVANT-GIRL who has slipped into the room behind ARMANDO.]

ROSA [peevish with the girl's tardiness and well guessing where she has been.] Nita! Watch what you do! Stir it well, baggage! And look sharp or it will stick to the bottom of the kettle and burn.

[ROSA kneels and slides a tray of flat dough into the Dutch oven resting to one side of the coals. The SERVANT-GIRL moves to obey. ROSA rises and busies herself with the table. ARMANDO utterly ignores the SERVANT-GIRL as she sends him sly, amorous glances the while she stirs the pot, round and round and round. When he glares at her in disgust, she hides her head in her apron and giggles, whereupon he glares more fiercely as she giggles and stirs. ARMANDO, unable to endure ROSA's indifference longer, crosses to her and caresses her arms with his dark hands.]

ARMANDO. You are angry with Armando? Yes? It is very becoming!

[Stooping over the pewter trencher heaped with yellow squash which ROSA carries before her, he kisses her full upon the mouth as she twists aside from his descending caress. ARMANDO laughs at her as she stamps her foot in exasperation, undecided whether to crown him with the dish or set it safely down for the usual use of excellent garden squash. ARMANDO, half-laughing, half-serious, walks beside her as she carries the dish to temporary security and bends to her, speaking softly.]

ARMANDO. Come to me to-night, my beautiful one, while the stupid Felipe sleeps through his nose.... I would teach you much of love! Ah, Rosita, your breasts bring memories of the hills of...

ROSA [*tossing her head contemptuously*]. And your nose makes me think of a Pyrenees vulture! [*Her breathing quickens.*]

[*The* SERVANT-GIRL *simpers... and the dull red of aroused anger and passion creeps under the* traficante's *swarthy skin. Never before has any woman found him less than irresistible! He gestures angrily in dismissal and, unnoticed by* ROSA, *the* SERVANT-GIRL *leaves the room wide-eyed, her simper cut off by* ARMANDO's *look. As* ROSA *crosses to the table carrying a copper carving knife, the* traficante *reaches out a long arm and gathers her to him.*]

ROSA [*panting in her struggle*]. Mother of God, Armando, are you mad? Let me go! Felipe will kill us both!

[*As* ROSA *makes to strike him,* ARMANDO *knocks the knife from her hand with easy strength and bends her back over the table as though he would break her in two.* ROSA's *black hair tumbles down as she struggles under his kisses, covering his arm like a warm mantle. His voice mocks her efforts to free herself.*]

ARMANDO. Rosa! I have not fully appreciated your beauty! And to think I have denied myself your sweetness these many dull and weary weeks. I must be getting old and blind!

[*Lamenting thus, he bends his head to her lips and kisses her rapturously until she pants for breath, lying spent in his arms and quivering beneath his touch. A scraping sound upon the threshold causes* ARMANDO *to raise his head from* ROSA's *trembling lips and espy* FELIPE *crouched in cold fury in the door.* ROSA *cries out as* FELIPE *strides across the room and tears his wife from the* traficante's *arms, sending her reeling against the wall with such force as to make her sink to her knees in weakness and terror.*]

FELIPE. *Renegado!* You are to leave my wife alone ... or I kill you with my bare hands, God witnessing!

ARMANDO [*in graceful resignation to his fate.*] Women ... ! They are always after me! ... Come, Felipe, you have as much pepper in your disposition as your Rosa has in her cooking. [*He wets his lips nervously, sends a venomous look at* FELIPE *and a calculating one at* ROSA.]

FELIPE [*advancing like a panther deliberately on his kill*]. Words! words! words! I am of a mind to tear the dirty, lying tongue from out of your empty head! Go easy with your words, *traficante*. The love of killing you runs strongly in my veins.

ARMANDO [*laughing hollowly*]. Rosa is yours, Felipe! For so small a virtue ... such a defense! She is yours, man—and a trifle fat! But let us eat. A lean belly breeds too good a hate, and Brother Noah himself knows love never flourished on an empty stomach. [*So saying, the* traficante *sits himself down to* ROSA's *table and helps himself generously to the squash. He takes a large mouthful and immediately spews it forth on the floor, complaining wrathfully.*]

ARMANDO. This! ... This squash never saw fire in its history! Woman, would you poison me with *raw* vegetables?

ROSA [*regaining her composure but still fearful*]. You know well why it never saw fire. And as for poisoning you ... you anticipated my desire.

[ARMANDO *chuckles and regards* ROSA. *She turns away from his mocking eyes.* FELIPE's *countenance is stern.* ARMANDO *hurriedly continues his solitary eating.* FELIPE *glowers, standing over this man so intent on carrying food to his mouth.* ROSA *brings wine and fills the drinking-cups in trembling silence.* FELIPE *never takes his eyes from* AR-

MANDO, *who bears the scrutiny with discomfort, losing his appetite rapidly.*]
FELIPE [*speaking in a low monotone as his eyes brood over the man opposite him at the table*]. Once...when I was standing by my father's table, I plucked a cluster of purple grapes from the great bowl and stood eating them slowly when one who had turned traitor came and gave me the insult to my face. I bore it, knowing that if I killed him, those I loved would suffer for his death...so I did not kill him—not then. The grapes within my palm burst their skins and oozed between my fingers. I have always had very strong fingers, *traficante,* very strong indeed, and I would close these fingers on your treacherous neck and squeeze until your eyes burst their sockets! [FELIPE'S *hands clench and unclench upon the table.* ROSA *is plainly frightened.* ARMANDO *gets to his feet.*]
ARMANDO. I...I think I will...ah, go to salt some skins in the tower;...the dampness does them no good....
[ARMANDO *leaves by the sea-door with as much grace as he can muster.* FELIPE *does not move.* ROSA *busies herself with* JUAN'S *food in a small trencher, stealing timid glances at her husband the while.* FELIPE *has fallen into a dark meditation. Finally,* ROSA *ventures to question him as she recoils her dark hair with nimble fingers and pins it up.*]
ROSA. Perchance the Indians will not come before the caravel is here, Felipe?
FELIPE [*rousing himself with obvious effort*]. Timuquans strike in the heat of revenge. Only such a storm as to-day's could have delayed them. They dared not attempt the crossing of the Bay in their war canoes with the waters so high and troubled.
ROSA [*sighing*]. The waiting is hard.
FELIPE [*bitterly*]. You will not find the waiting hard with

the glib Armando to beguile away the time. [*The great need to hurt her grows on him.*] Shall I call him back for you, Rosa? I realize, in comparison with the romantic *traficante*, I am dull company!

ROSA [*turning away to hide the quick tears*]. Felipe! You are cruel!

FELIPE [*grimly*]. Aye. Cruelly slow to comprehend treachery in mine own house . . . in mine own wife! And with such as he!

ROSA. Ah, you are mad as well as cruel. Armando presumed upon my friendship and glad I was you came . . . but that you should turn against me! Your jealousy blinds you.

FELIPE. I am *not* jealous of my wife! There is no need . . . or is there? Perchance I have been a long time blind. [*His hand clamps down upon her wrist.*] Look you, Rosa . . . you may not dishonor me in mine house, before our son. Rather would I see you slain by any warring Timuquan than that. What is this *traficante* to you? Speak out!

ROSA [*wrenching her arm free and speaking in hot, tearful anger*]. You know not what you ask, Felipe!

FELIPE. Answer me, woman, or I think the worst.

ROSA. I will not!

FELIPE. Answer!

ROSA [*brokenly*]. He is nothing to me . . . and you shame me by the asking.

[ROSA *turns to leave* FELIPE, *tears forcing their way beneath her hot eyelids, wetting her cheeks.* FELIPE'S *fierce mood passes, and he is ashamed of his anger. He pulls her down onto his lap, kisses the nape of her neck and the curve of her shoulder, murmuring endearments until she turns and weeps softly upon his breast and lies quiet. He holds her gently and once more life is sweet and good. A great peace descends upon him and he is glad.*]

[*Just then the garden door is flung open and the* SERVANT-

GIRL *stumbles terror-stricken into the room. Running to* FELIPE *and* ROSA *where they are seated on the sea-chest, she falls on her knees and babbles incoherently. The garden door is open behind her and* ROSA *rises and closes it dutifully as the* SERVANT, *fright tripping her tongue, tells her message to* FELIPE.]

SERVANT-GIRL. Master! The garden! In the garden as I worked ... I saw a shadow move ... ! A branch I thought it was at first, but then it moved and became a man's arm and I saw a hideous painted face. ... Master! Filled with a terrible fright I ran in.... What has come? [*She bows her head and beats it against the floor, rocking to and fro and moaning.*]

[ROSA *whirls and goes into the bedroom.* FELIPE *strides to the window, looks once, then drags the heavy sea-chest before the door opening out into the garden.* ROSA *returns instantly, her face wild and desperate.*]

ROSA [*crying out as though wounded*]. Felipe! He is not there!

FELIPE [*peering out the window*]. Who, Rosa? Armando, mean you?

[ROSA *runs to* FELIPE *and beats upon his breast with her fists as though to wake him to action.*]

ROSA. Juan! He is gone! [*Distractedly she crosses to the beach-window, looks out and sucks in her breath sharply. She makes for the sea-door, her full skirts gathered up in one hand.*] There! Far down the beach I see him playing —Felipe!

[FELIPE *reaches for his gun as* ROSA *runs to the door. He leaps to hold her back from certain death but, with desperate strength, she throws him off and gets free. As she runs out the door, the* SERVANT-GIRL *rouses from her state of petrified fear. She twines herself about* FELIPE'S *legs to prevent his going out. He drags her a few steps,*

straining to follow ROSA, *when her words register on his feverish brain.*]
SERVANT-GIRL. Master, the Indians fire the house from the west! They wait for us to come out! Do not leave me! Please God, do not leave me, Master Felipe!
FELIPE [*roughly*]. Out of my way.
[FELIPE *throws the* SERVANT-GIRL *off and gains the door. Throwing it open he recoils as a Timuquan arrow buries its head in his shoulder. The piercing cry of mortally wounded* ROSA *rises in a thin crescendo and is cut off... abruptly. The war-drums begin a soft rhythm, surrounding the house with their throbbing song of kill, kill, kill. ...* FELIPE *raises his gun painfully and fires, then leaps back and is closing the door when* ARMANDO *gains the entrance. The two men fight with the door partially closed between them—one to enter, one to bar the other out. Smoke has commenced to curl through the windows and cracks of the garden door. Finally* FELIPE *jerks open the door and* ARMANDO *falls into the room. He is uninjured, but grimy with powder-stains and his clothes torn and disheveled. He stumbles to his knees and* FELIPE *yanks him in by the collar, closing and bolting the door after him.*]
FELIPE. In with you, *renegado!* [*The drums beat faster and stronger. The crackling of hungry flames may be heard.*]
ARMANDO [*rising and dusting himself off. Then sarcastically*]. Ever my friend in need! But what ails the shoulder? You have let blood!
FELIPE [*pointing to the arrow lying headless between them on the floor*]. Aye. The poison bites deep. But it is of no matter to you. Saw you ... Rosa?
ARMANDO [*crying out*]. Aye. Aye. God forgive me! [*He beats his forehead with his open palms.*]
FELIPE [*leaning against the wall and sinking a little*]. How

like you the results of thy woman-hunger? [*He sinks lower against the wall, his eyes beginning to glaze with pain and loss of blood and grief.*]
ARMANDO [*belting himself tightly*]. Little, Felipe, little. [*He leans toward the dying man.*] Can you find the mercy in your heart to forgive me, Felipe . . . forgive?
FELIPE [*smiling faintly*]. I can forgive no . . . one.
ARMANDO [*turning on the* SERVANT-GIRL, *whimpering and moaning in a corner, and roaring at her*]. Leave off, wench! God's mercy, may not men die without *you* mewing in their ears!
[*She shrinks away from him. He regards her cynically.* FELIPE *sinks down on the sea-chest against the door. His left shoulder is darkening with an ever-widening circle of blood. His head is tilted back as he watches the* traficante's *last dealings with a woman.*]
[ARMANDO *picks up the copper carving knife he but lately knocked from* ROSA's *struggling hand and balances it suggestively in his palm. Then he thrusts it hilt-foremost at the cowering* SERVANT-GIRL.]
ARMANDO. There! Sheathe it in your breast, unimportance. But spare us the trouble of watching you. Get out or I'll drive it home myself in a less comfortable place. A speedy death to you!
[ARMANDO *bows mockingly. He motions her into the inner room. She has taken the knife from him like one hypnotized. The smoke in the kitchen has thickened. The men cannot talk without coughing. The drums grow more insistent.* ARMANDO *is light-headed with the intoxication of death and danger.* FELIPE, *though the finger of Death is on him, dominates the room with a quiet force.*]
FELIPE. Well played, traficante. And now I accept the invitation of mine host, Death. . . . You see I may be dramatic, too? But Death is an old friend of mine and Rosa waits

me... and the small son. [*His voice weakens as he smiles at* ARMANDO.] For me it is the beginning... this putting off of the clumsy flesh, but for you... *traficante,* for you...?

ARMANDO. The last trade, amigo! [*He laughs and picks up* FELIPE's *fallen gun, priming it.*] The last trade, say I! And a dear one for yon savages.

FELIPE [*smiling still*]. I warrant you will ferret out some way to cheat a few of them of life, yes? As for me, *traficante,* I have lived a full outward life and, I dare swear, a full inward life. I never thought to say it to you, but now... the sands of your life, as mine, have run the hour through... Go with God, *traficante....* [*He seems to faint, but rouses himself as* ARMANDO *pauses before the closed door.*]

ARMANDO [*still chuckling*]. To be blessed by you in my last trade! I mean to sell my stores most dearly! You know me well. [*The drums grow louder, fierce in their bloodlust, and the* traficante *raises his fist and gun and shouts at them.*] Hold off, you devils! I come, by God, I come! [*He turns back to* FELIPE, *his voice loud and ringing through the smoke.*] Go to your Rosa in peace, amigo. You are a strange man, but a man, and I a careless rogue. Think not too hard of me in your strange heaven. I'll be meeting old friends in hell! [*He tears down the barricade at the door.*] And now, by Santiago,* I go to my trading!

[ARMANDO *unbolts the door and bounds out through the smoke, crying out against the savages.* FELIPE *straightens up and half rises as the cry of the warring panther sobs higher and higher in sorrowing passion on the lips of a painted Timuquan brave.* FELIPE's *lips move silently. He reaches out as though to grasp an unseen hand.*]

* The usual Spanish battle cry is, "Santiago, y cierra España!"

FELIPE. Yes, Rosa! I come, I come! The light...! *In manus tuas Domine commendo spiritum meum....*
[*The drums beat loudly. Smoke swirls in clouds about* FELIPE *as he sinks back upon the old sea-chest and slips to the floor.*]

THE CURTAIN FALLS

MISSISSIPPI

GIT UP AN' BAR THE DOOR
A BALLAD COMEDY

BY ARTHUR PALMER HUDSON
OF KOSCIUSKO, MISSISSIPPI

Written in the playwriting course at the University of North Carolina and originally produced by The Carolina Playmakers at Chapel Hill on November 6, 7, 8, and 13, 1930. It was first published in *The Carolina Play-Book*, December, 1930.

THE CHARACTERS

BURRUS STUBBS, *a Mississippi hill farmer*
                                                          Charles Elledge
JENNY, *his wife*.................Bess Jones Winburn
RETT STARNES, *a neighbor*............Marjorie Good
PINK ARMSTRONG ⎱ *the Armstrong* ⎰ Kent Creuser
TOL ARMSTRONG ⎰ *Gang* ⎱ Peter Henderson
JACK ARMSTRONG ⎰ ⎱ Lubin Leggette

SCENE: *The kitchen of a simple farmhouse in the hills of central Mississippi.*
TIME: *Thirty years ago, about dusk of a November day.*

Copyright, 1930, by The Carolina Playmakers, Inc.
All rights reserved.

MISSISSIPPI BALLAD COMEDY

THE author of *Git Up an' Bar the Door,* Arthur Palmer Hudson, tells us the play is about "Southern farm folk who lived in the good old days before the need for farm relief was discovered. These people were poor, but not poverty-pinched; exploited, no doubt, but not down-trodden; oppressed, but not cowed. Living close to the land which they and their fathers had but recently won from the wilderness, they tasted the full-flavored sap of its soil and breathed the easy freedom of its air. They accepted life cheerfully, and they made it tolerable, even enjoyable, by the free play of a rude, broad, physical humor. These people, such as they were, and their humor, such as it was, this play seeks to present."

The plot is based on the old popular ballad which gives the play its name. Mr. Hudson has localized the settings and the characters in his native hill region of central Mississippi. The development of the plot is his own invention and the additions to the original story, it goes without saying, have their source in the author's first-hand knowledge of his characters.

The character of the gossipy neighbor, Rett Starnes, is drawn wholly from life. Burrus and Jenny Stubbs are composites of several portraits in the gallery of the author's boyhood memories. The Armstrongs correspond in a number of traits to a gang once notorious in central Mississippi. The dialect, thinned down somewhat for dramatic presentation, is authentic for the period indicated—that is, the beginning of the present century; but it is not to be regarded as normal Mississippi speech to-day. The two song fragments, "There Was an Old Man Who Lived in the Wood" and "Hog Drovers," sung in the play to their traditional tunes, are genuine folk songs current in Mississippi.

"Chitlins" (dialectal form of *chitterlings*), Stubbs's favorite dish, are the "smaller intestines of swine, esp. as cooked" (Webster). Throughout the South they are still esteemed as a country delicacy and as a subject for bucolic humor.

GIT UP AN' BAR THE DOOR

[*The light of a November sunset, streaming through the window in the rear wall near the right-hand corner, ruddies the interior of* JENNY STUBBS' *kitchen and shows* JENNY *stooping over her cook-stove, at the center of the right wall, singing to herself:*]

There was an old man who lived in the wood
    As you may plainly see.
He swore he could do more work in one day
    Than his wife could do in three.

"Very well," the old woman said,
    "If that you will allow,
To-morrow morn you stay in my stead,
    And I'll go drive the plow."

[JENNY'S *kitchen, of "boxed" construction (i.e., made of wide planks nailed upright to horizontal supports and serving as clapboards and ceiling in one), is rude enough by present-day standards of home comfort; but the ruddy light from the window, and the aspect of simple furnishings that hearty folk have made and lived with a long*

GIT UP AN' BAR THE DOOR

time, not only redeem it from any suggestion of squalor but give it an appearance of old-time, homely cheer. To JENNY's left, by the wall, are a wood box and a small home-made wooden bench. On the wall in front of her hang a few cooking utensils; to her right and higher up, a chromo and a nondescript wrap. The window, already mentioned, has a white curtain over the lower sash; the upper sash is unshaded and lacks one glass. Under this window is a good-sized bench upon which sits a large jug. Close to the window, against the rear wall, is a movable, tin-doored, wooden cupboard (locally known as a "safe"), with glass jars of preserved fruit, an old-fashioned coffee-mill, and a lamp sitting on top of it. Somewhat to the left of the center of the rear wall is a plank door which opens into the back yard. A bar with a large nail through one end hangs along the left door jamb because the notch catch at the other end has been broken off. Between the door and the corner of the room a lantern hangs from a nail in the wall. Midway of the left-hand wall of the room is a second plank door which presumably leads into the bedroom and the front of the house. Upstage from this door stands a split-bottomed hickory chair; downstage is a wash-bench, with a basin, a bucket, and a soap dish on it, and a slop bucket beside it on the floor. On the wall, over the bench, hang a mirror and a towel. A little to the right of the center of the room is an eating-table, with two chairs standing with their backs to JENNY.]

[JENNY, *singing at her stove, is preparing supper. She is a plump, comely matron of forty, clad in a faded blue calico dress and a cook apron that do not muffle the pleasing rondures of a good-looking country wife. Her brown, abundant hair is pulled back tight over her head and* knotted behind. *The profile of her face, kindly and humorous in its general contours but firm of chin and cheek, the brisk competency of her bodily movements, and the quiet energy of her song suggest an unsoured, wholesome, high-spirited daughter of the old pioneer stock. But something has annoyed her, for, stooping over the wood box, she stops singing, picks up a few sticks of wood, lays them on the stove, kicks the wood box vigorously, seizes it and shakes it over the stove, puts the few sticks in the fire-box of the stove, and slams the door loudly. Then, resuming her song in a somewhat altered key, she crosses to the cupboard, opens it, takes out a bowl, sets it on the table, goes for another, takes this one to the wash-bench, pours water in it, and sets it on the table beside the first. From the first bowl she extracts some white, flabby-looking objects and begins washing them. At this point she hears a step in the front of the house, at the left, off stage, looks at her wet, greasy hands, and waits.*]

RETT [*offstage*]. Hello!
JENNY. Hello!
RETT. Anybody at home?
JENNY. Nobody but the cat. That you, Rett?
RETT. Uh-huh. But 'e ain't got your tongue, I reckin. [*Apparently lingering within.*] My, what a purty quilt you're a-piecin'.
JENNY [*recognizing a neighbor, resumes her work, taking one of the bowls, crossing to the slop bucket, and emptying it of water*]. Onlatch the door an' come on in.
RETT [*enters through the bedroom door, left. She is a spare, sharp-faced housewife of fifty, dressed in a tight-fitting gray garment of nondescript material, with a shawl of undyed wool on her shoulders and a blue splint bonnet*

on her head. *She wears a snuff-brush* * *in her mouth. As she enters, the back door, center, flies open*]. Been a-renderin' up lard. I smelt hit at the front gate.

JENNY. Uh-huh. Pull off yer bonnet an' drag ye up a cheer. [*Closing the kitchen door.*]

RETT [*draws a chair near the table, and sits down, sighing*]. I shore feel like floppin'.

JENNY [*still standing at the table*]. Well, how air ye all? [*Resumes her work.*]

RETT. Callie's baby's got the whoopin' cough. Been a-nussin' him all day. Tried coal ile an' sugar; wouldn't work. Then ri'clicted ol' Aint Cindy's remedy an' drug 'im through 'is pappy's britches leg, an' 'e qui'ted off rat away like 'ed tuck chloryform. [*Going to the slop bucket and spitting into it.*] I been jes' dyin' to gab with ye about the news.

JENNY [*with interest*]. News? What news?

RETT [*shrilly*]. News! Whar's that no-'count husban' o' yourn?

JENNY [*stops work*]. Gone to Vaiden with a load of cotton. Rett Starnes, what you drivin' at?

RHETT. To Vaiden? Well, the Lord persarve 'im. Has 'e gone batty?

JENNY. Naw. He heerd Alexander Brothers was a-givin' two or three p'ints more'n the Kosciusko merchants, and—Rett Starnes, ef you don't tell me what you're a-talkin' about, I'll choke ye. [*Going over to* RETT.]

RETT. Don't you make lack you ain't heerd.

JENNY [*leaning over* RETT]. Make lack nothin'! If you don't tell me, I'll— [*She makes as if to shake* RETT.]

---

* The habit of "dipping snuff" is common among the poor whites in all sections of North Carolina. A twig, chewed into shreds at one end, is known as a snuff-brush, snuff-stick or "toothbrush." This is dipped into the powdered snuff and then rubbed over the gums and teeth. The practice is common among the women and they seem to get much pleasure from it.

RETT. W'y, the Armstrong boys, so folks say, helt up ol' man Dick Stegall in Scoopy Chitty bottom las' night an' robbed 'im of 'is cotton money.

JENNY [*straightening up*]. W'y Rett!

RETT [*rising; but instead of continuing her story, she goes to the slop bucket, spits deliberately, and returns to her chair*]. Shore did. Charley heerd hit at the sto' this mawnin'. You-all so buried in the woods down heah you don't heah nothin'. Yes-sir, robbed 'im! He was a-comin' home hossback from Vaiden. The niggers had done went ahead with the waggins. Cotched 'im in that dork place 'twixt the fust an' the secon' bridges this side o' the creek. Taken 'is money away from 'im. Tied 'im back'ards on the ol' hoss—ol' Bodger—an' sont 'im lopin' down the big road ridin' back'ards! [*At this point the door blows open again, but the two women do not notice it.*]

JENNY. Ef that ain't jes' lack them Armstrong boys—playin' devilish pranks on folks. Lan' sakes! How'd 'e git home?

RETT [*turning and spitting into the slop bucket again*]. Might' nigh daid. Ol' Bodger lack to a knocked ol' man Dick's haid off when 'e drug 'im under the lot gate, but the niggers caught 'im an' got ol' man Dick off befo' Bodger made it to the stable door or 'e'd a shore brained 'im thar.

JENNY. Was 'e bad stove up? [*Resuming her work at the table.*]

RETT. Right smart. But he was a-restin' easy this evenin', the mail rider said. He stopped thar on 'is way back.

JENNY [*crossing to the slop bucket to empty the bowl again*]. How much did they git offen ol' man Dick? [*Returning, she goes to window, and gets a dish cloth from a nail on the wall.*]

RETT. 'Bout two hundred dollars, the mail rider said. Sold

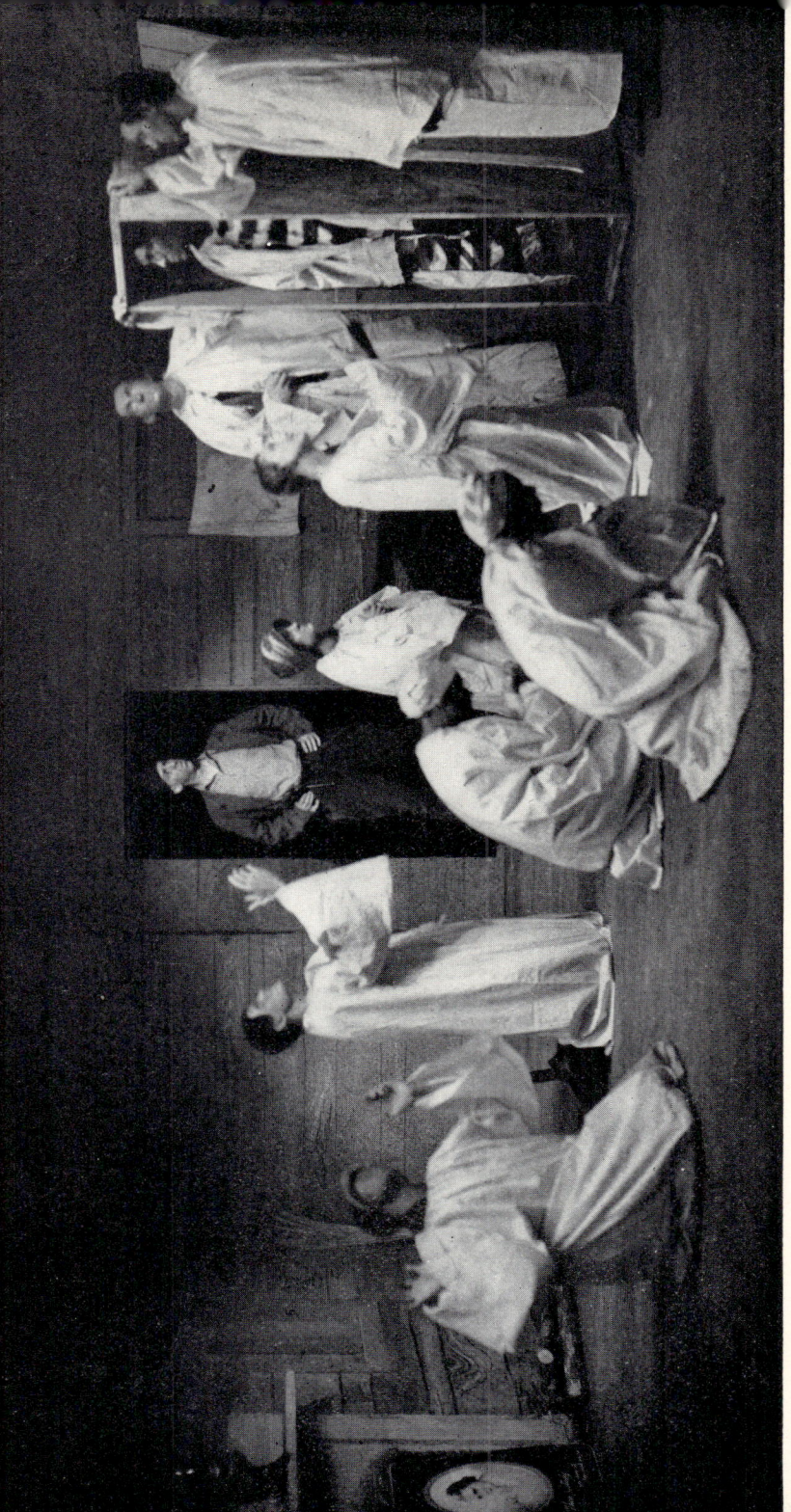

Wootten-Moulton

MOURNERS TO GLORY

ALL. He pinin' fo' glory; he soul won't rest!
Take him, Jedus; take him, Lawd!

GIT UP AN' BAR THE DOOR

JACK [*advancing on* STUBBS]. 'Tain't nothin' but a lye-soap-an'-barlow-knife shave, but I reckon the ol' boy won't complain; he's gittin' hit fer nothin'!

Wootten-Moulton

fo' bales. [JENNY *is now wiping the bowl with the cloth.*]
JENNY [*solicitous*]. Which way did the gang go?
RETT. Some 'possum hunters heerd a passel o' hosses lopin' down Big Black swamp, below whar Scoopy Chitty runs in, 'bout a hour later. But a nigger up the Eupory road 'lowed 'e seen 'em up thar. Ain't you skeered 'bout Burrus?
JENNY [*straightening up decisively*]. Not much, I reckin. [*Sets the bowl on the table and starts toward the window.*] Lightnin' don't strack twicet in the same place. Besides, ain't the menfolks up thar a'huntin' 'em? [*Hangs the dish cloth on its nail and returns to the table.*]
RETT. Yeah—all over that end o' the county an' to'ads Choctaw. Charley lit out soon's 'e heerd 'bout hit. [*Rising, she crosses in front of the table, goes to the stove, and raises a lid.*] Still an' all, they say them Armstrongs is the owdaciousest gang 't ever rid the roads. [*She spits into the fire-box.*] Wouldn't put nothin' past 'em. W'y, they're apt 's not to git Burrus on his way back from Vaiden ef 'e comes through Scoopy Chitty bottom atter dork. [*With rising voice.*] They mought rob you rat chere in your house to-night. [*She sits in the chair at the right of the table and adds in a lower tone:*] Mought a come *down* the river atter all an' hid in the swamp. [*Meanwhile,* JENNY *has been getting meal, sifter, and salt and pepper shakers from the cupboard.*]
JENNY. Shucks, no danger o' neither one. [*Sifting meal.*] Burrus left 'arly an' 'll come home 'arly. Lookin' fur 'im ever' minute; 's w'y I storted supper. Nobody but a neighbor lack you 's li'ble to poke roun' this place in the dork. [*Pauses.*] Still an' all [*Sighs.*], I will be glad when Burrus does git back. [*A strong flurry of wind blows leaves into the kitchen through the still open door.*] I'll be switched ef I will, either. Drat that door! Ugh [*Shiver-*

ing.], the kitchen's gittin' cold as floogins! [*She goes to the kitchen door, closes it, and sets a chair against it.*]

RETT. Jes' noticed 'twas. How come you ain't storted a far?

JENNY. Ain't got nary stick o' stovewood in the box. [*Sitting in the chair at the left of the table, facing* RETT.] Jes' laid a far with what was lef' from renderin' the lard this mornin'—turned the box bottom side up'ards—an' I said to myself I'd be plague-taked if I'd git any more. Tol' Burrus las' night 't 'd take more'n usual to render up that air lard an' all, an' to be shore to git enough to las' till in the mornin'.

RETT. Do 'im lack I done Charley that time. Fust year we was married. Promised faithful when he was a-courtin' me 't 'e 'd alluz keep me in stovewood. Fust time 'e missed choppin' hit 'cause one o' the mules tuck sick on the road back from town an' throwed 'im late gittin' back. Secon' time the woods cotch afar back o' the newgroun'. I chopped hit both times myself. Third time 'e clean fergot hit 'fo 'e went off fishin'. An' then I went back home to my mammy's. Sont 'im word the only way I' go back home was a-ridin' on top of a two-horse waggin load o' stovewood—chopped stove len'th. He come fer me nex' day—an' the wood was heart pine, an' dry. Cuored him. [*The wind blows the door open again, pushing the chair before it.*]

JENNY. Plague take hit! [*Rising, she slams the door shut, and replaces the chair.*]

RETT. Why 'n't ye bar hit?

JENNY. Bar nothin'! [*Banging the chair against the door.*] The ketch 'as been broke since las' summer. [*Returning to the table and resuming her work.*] Done my best to git Burrus to fix hit, an' he said they wa'n't no use so long 's the weather was warm.

RETT. Jes' lack Charley 'bout fixin' our roof—weather dry,

GIT UP AN' BAR THE DOOR

don't need hit; rainin', too wet to work. Ain't menfolks the triflin'est critters God A'mighty ever made? [*She goes to the slop bucket, spits, and returns to the chair. Then she sits in the chair at the left of the table.* JENNY *has gotten the coffee mill from the cupboard and sits in the other chair by the table, holding it between her knees.*]

JENNY [*turning the coffee mill vigorously*]. When they ain't the contrariest. He won't fix it 'cause I vowed I wouldn't, an' here we air the fu'st o' November, an' us a-proppin' that door. [*Returning the coffee mill to the cupboard, she takes a platter therefrom, and stands by the table.*] Burrus is a good pervider an' a sharp hand in the field, but the triflin'est scamp roun' the house an' the wust tease 'bout little things I ever seen.

RETT. Ri'clict that time at the school-house raisin' when Burrus cotched a rusty-back lizard from the timber an' put 'im down your collar?

JENNY [*smiling*]. Uh-huh.

RETT. Never will fergit how hacked 'e was when you grabbed up that scantlin' an' punched 'im when 'e whirled, 'n 'e had to back off to the woods fer the boys to pin up the seat of his britches with nails so's 'e could go home an' git 'em sewed up. I allus tol' Charley that was Burrus' way o' startin' to court ye. Looks like 'e'd larnt better'n to pester ye by now.

JENNY. Well, 'e ain't. An' he's shore got the best of me 'bout that door—so fur. [*She begins rolling the chitterlings in the sifted meal.*]

RETT. What ye fixin' fer supper?

JENNY. Chitlins.

RETT [*rising and peering into the bowl*]. My, how purty!

JENNY. Reckin so—fer chitlins. [*Returning the sifter and the salt and pepper shakers to the cupboard.*] From that Polan' Chiny shote Burrus kilt day befo' yistiddy. Been a-soakin', an' ready fer fryin'. They was so tender tol' Burrus they wan't no use to parebile 'em.

RETT [*picking up a piece*]. Ain't they peenk an' juicy-lookin'. [*Waggling snuff brush in her mouth.*] Make my mouth worter to look at 'em. [*She removes snuff brush, goes to the slop bucket, and spits.*]

JENNY. Ought to be, ef any chitlins is. [*She takes the platter to the little bench by the stove and sets it down.*] Burrus tapered the shote off on clabber. Been a-honin' to eat 'em. Be hongry as a wolf to-night, atter 'is sto'-bought snack o' crackers and cheeses. Got off so 'arly I didn' have no time to scrape 'im up no grub. Et up the liver an' the lights las' night fer supper. [*Getting the coffee pot, she crosses to the wash bench, and pours water into it.*]

RETT. But this mess o' chitlins ain't more'n three nigger fiel' han's could eat, or I'd stay fer supper with ye.

JENNY [*chuckling*]. Do. I'll make Burrus piece out 'is supper on spare-ribs.

RETT [*chuckling, too*]. Jes' jokin'. Burrus'd feel lack takin' a plow-line to me ef I was to stay an' make 'im whack up on 'is clabber-fed chitlins. Know how well 'e loves 'em. Ric'lict when you-all was to our house atter the fust hog-killin', an' Burrus et chitlins an' et chitlins, an' said 'e b'lieved 'e could eat a elephant's chitlins [*Cackling.*]—by his-self [*Cackling.*]—ef they was as good as hog chitlins [*Cackling more shrilly.*]?

JENNY [*eager to complete the story*]. Uh-huh. An' vowed an' 'declared 't that night he drempt 'e had 'is mouth full o' one end of a chitlin down at New Orleens, an' was a-eatin' 'is way up to Memphis [*Laughing.*]—an' woke up a-chawin' the bed-sheet! [*Sets the coffee pot on the table, takes the tray out of the coffee mill on the cupboard, returns, and measures coffee.*]

RETT [*laughing perfunctorily at an old joke*]. Lawzee! But

he can beat you a-tellin' hit. [*Looking toward the window, and noticing that night is approaching.*] Well, I got to be moseyin' along.... Jenny, long's I'm here, reckin I mought be borryin' from ye, so ye won't fergit me. I'm plumb out o' 'east cakes, an' I 'lowed to have some light-bread fer dinner a Sunday. Got any to spare?

JENNY. Shore. [*She goes to the cupboard and starts back with a small tin can.*] Got anything to wrop 'em in?

RETT. Uh-huh. My pocket handkerchief—but I reckin hit's clean. [*Producing it from her apron pocket, she receives the yeast cakes, and wraps them up.*] Well, I must be goin'. Gittin' dork.

JENNY. Oh, it's 'arly yit. Leavin' lack ye borryed a chunk o' far. [*She is pinching and patting the biscuit dough.*]

RETT [*setting the chair back to the wall*]. Bound to. Chinned with ye too long a'ready. Got to go home an' min' the baby while Callie milks. We ain't expectin' Charley back till late, but reckin we'll have to skeer up somethin' fer 'im to eat.... Shore enjoyed that mess o' backbone ye sont over yistiddy.... Tell Burrus I hope he'll enjoy his chitlins—arter he 'arns 'em. [*Laughing.*] Spunk up to 'im, Jenny. L'arn 'im a lesson, like I done Charley.

JENNY. Good min' to. But Burrus is a ol' dog to teach new tricks to.

RETT. Well, I ain't never seed a man too old to be tetchous 'bout 'is stummick. You kin alluz ketch 'im thar. [*As she opens the door to the bedroom, the kitchen door bangs open again. She turns in the doorway.*] An' git 'im whar the wool's sho't 'bout that do', too. [*She goes, chuckling.*]

JENNY. I'm 'feard I won't git no holt on 'im lack that. [*She wipes her hand on her apron, moves the chair from the door, and sets it by the table.*]

RETT [*offstage*]. Well, good-by Jenny. Come to see us—ef Burrus don't whup ye up too bad—or ef the boogers an' the robbers don't git ye 'way off down here in the woods. [*Cackling.*]
JENNY. I can take keer o' myself, I reckin. Come back ag'in. [*Looking at the door for a moment, she forms a plan.*]

"Very well," the old woman said,
"If that you will allow,
To-morrow morn you stay in my stead,
And I'll go drive the plow."

[*She has gone to the stove, lifted one of the lids, selected a wedge-shaped splinter of wood, and wedged it under the offending door, kicking it vigorously. She lights the lamp, replacing it on top of the cupboard, then stands a moment, and listens. The crunch of wagon wheels and the rattling of trace-chains are heard off stage, left; then the joyful barking of a dog.*]
STUBBS [*offstage, at the rear—presumably in the back yard*]. W'oah! [*Whistles to the dog. Makes sounds as if unhitching his mules.*]
JENNY [*going to the window, looks out, crosses to the stove and gets a biscuit pan, then busies herself putting biscuit in the pan*].

"You must milk the tidy cow
For fear that she'll go dry,
And you must feed the pigs in the sty,
For fear that they will die."

[*She takes the biscuit pan to the stove and sets it beside the bowl of chitterlings. She is clearing off the table, lay-*

GIT UP AN' BAR THE DOOR

ing a red cloth upon it, and setting it from this point until STUBBS *makes his threat to force the door.*]

STUBBS [*still offstage*]. Hello, puppy! [*He whistles.*] Ain't been runnin' no rabbits, air ye? [*After a moment.*] Git down, suh! Git down!

JENNY.

> He then went to feed the pigs in the sty,
> For fear that they would die.
> The old sow jumped between his legs
> And throwed him into the mire.

STUBBS [*making sounds as if collecting his purchases from the wagon—putting sacks, cans, packages, and bottles in a box*]. What ye got the door shet fer, Jenny? Cain't see how to git my things outen the waggin.

JENNY. Pull your waggin up under the winder, then.

STUBBS. Light won't shine through that curtain you put over the lower sash.

JENNY [*glancing at the window*]. Nothin' to keep hit from shinin' through the upper one, [*In a lower tone.*] where you ain't put that missin' pane.

STUBBS [*outside, singing an old play-party song*].

> Hog drovers, hog drovers, hog drovers we air-r,
> A-courtin' your darter so neat and so fair.
> Can we git lodgin' here, O here?
> Can we git lodgin' here?

Open up, Jenny. [*Waits a moment. Shakes door.*] Better lemme in; mought have a purty fer ye. Unbar hit, I say! Got my arms full. [*Gets no reply.*] Well, I ain't goin' roun' to the front. I'll bust in if ye don't open hit. [JENNY, *who has finished setting the table, tiptoes to the door, silently removes the wedge, and slips to the bedroom door, where she stands and peeps at what follows.*] Look out. [*Chants rapidly.*]

> Up the hill an' down the track!
> Clear the way fer Fanny an' Jack!
> Hooray, here we come!

[*The door gives to his charge and, losing his balance, he falls sprawling into the kitchen, the box flying toward the middle of the room, its contents scattering and rolling over the floor. He sits up, groaning, looks ruefully at the door, and lets out a string of imprecations.*] Holy Roller hell an' high worter! Oh-uh-uh! [*He picks himself up, rubbing his hurts and groaning.*] Ugh-ugh! Lockjaw an' hyderphoby! [*He advances toward the door, kicks it, and stares at it.*]

[*In normal circumstances* STUBBS *is a waggish-looking, heavy-set farmer of forty-five, dressed in jeans breeches and coat, hickory-striped shirt with sleeves rolled up to show a red undershirt, and brogans. He sports a forward-thrusting, broad, black beard. His hat, which has fallen off, discloses a disheveled mane of the same color.*]

JENNY [*stepping out of the doorway and speaking sharply, her voice suddenly arresting* STUBBS'S *second impending kick*]. Well! Did a harricane blow ye in? What's the matter?

STUBBS [*not being sure that* JENNY *has seen all, he decides that his best cue is to treat his discomfiture as an accident rather than the result of a trick of his wife. He swaggers cavalierly toward her*]. Jes' rejoicin' before the Lord. So glad to git back home! Howd'y'! [*Suddenly seizing her and kissing her resoundingly.*]

JENNY [*catching her breath*]. Ugh! Air ye drunk?

STUBBS. Aye grabs! I bet I busted my bot—... [*He catches himself, feels ruefully along his left thigh up to the pocket, lifting his coat so as to reveal to the audience, but not to* JENNY, *the neck of a bottle.*] Shore, I ain't drunk.

JENNY. Cain't fool me. I smelt it on your breath. Your rotten ol' whiskers is full of it. I'll bet you bought a bottle of—

STUBBS. Lyddy E. Pinkham's Vegetable Compound [*Handing a bottle to* JENNY, *who snatches it out of his hand and puts it in the cupboard.*]—coal ile [*Setting the can down near the wash bench.*]—sugar an' salt, sody, coffee an' black pepper, rice, matches [*Holding up each article in turn and replacing it in the box.*]—an' Dr. Granger's Liver Regulator, fer you. [*Handing the package to* JENNY, *who disposes of it as of the bottle.*] Ever'thing you said. Didn't fergit nothin'. An' I got somethin' else [*Patting his hip pocket.*]—ain't gonna tell ye what—ain't gonna give hit to ye neither ef you don' treat me right. —What about my chitlins? [*He smacks his lips.*] Chitlins an' biscuit! Hongry as a she fox in suckin' time. [*Starting toward the stove.*]

JENNY. Thought mebbe you'd lack 'em raw—with dough biscuit.

STUBBS. Why, you ain't even storted a far. [*With some irritation.*] Aye God, have you gone crazy, ol' woman?

JENNY [*sitting down in the chair and folding her hands*]. Thar's your supper. That's all I'm a-goin' to do to hit till you git me some stove-wood to cook with. I tol' you las' night—

STUBBS. I chopped enough wood to far a freight engine from Kosciesko to Chiny. Why, you must a-been burnin' hit lack you was runnin' a 'lasses pan.

JENNY. You know I had to render up that shote lard.

STUBBS [*eagerly*]. Did you make any cracklin' bread? [*Going to the cupboard.*]

JENNY. Ne' mind whether I did or not. Wa'n't enough wood to make a far under the big pot down to the worsh place, an' I had to burn up all the stove-wood. You can git me some more or do with'ut your supper fer all I keer. I'm plumb tord o' choppin' wood.

STUBBS [*having opened the cupboard and failing to find the bread, looks hungrily at the uncooked food on the stove and crosses room to the chair, left*]. Aye God, I reckin I'm tord, too. [*He bangs the chair on the floor and sits down, stamping his feet.* JENNY, *without getting up, turns her chair so that its back will be to* STUBBS, *brings it down with a bang, and stamps her feet too.* STUBBS *eyes her a moment, scratching his head, ponders over the situation, and then rises, slaps his thigh, and speaks with assumed bluff humor.*] Well, I reckin ye got me this time. [*Starts toward her.*] Dang my boots ef'n you ain't. [*Leans over* JENNY, *caresses her awkwardly, and begs in a wheedling tone.*] Will ye cook 'em fer me, ol' lady, ef'n I git you some stove-wood?

JENNY [*in an indulgent tone, pushing him away*]. Go on, you triflin' rascal. I've sp'iled ye till you're rotten. Go on an' chop that wood. [*She smiles as he goes out, singing with a suggestion of malicious triumph.*]

> He then went to feed the pigs in the sty,
>   For fear that they would die.
> The ol' sow jumped between his legs
>   An' throwed him in the mire.

[*She strikes a match and lights the wood in the stove. Takes the frying pan, wipes it, and sets it on the stove. Outside,* STUBBS *is heard chopping violently. Presently he comes in with a small armful of wood.* JENNY *surveys the load of wood critically.*] Wa'n't you afeerd of gittin' a stick too much in the dork?

STUBBS [*advancing to the wood box*]. Naw—I counted 'em. [*Drops the wood and blows.*] Phew! [*Crosses the room to the chair, left, sits down, leans back comfortably, and begins to fan himself with his hat.*]

JENNY. Did you git that winder-light in town lack I told ye?

STUBBS [*stops fanning in the midst of a stroke and looks foolish*]. What winder-pane?

JENNY. *What* winder-pane? Look at that string I tied on your finger this mornin'. [*Waits while* STUBBS *looks at his hand and remains stubbornly silent.*] Answer me: Did you git that pane?

STUBBS [*sheepishly*]. Naw—fergot hit. [*Resumes fanning himself.*]

JENNY [*advancing toward him*]. Fergot hit! Burrus Stubbs, you're the triflin'est white man I ever seen. You're the [*Turning in disgust.*]—oh, I don't know what to call ye. [*Looks at the kitchen door. Points.*] Shet the door. You ain't too triflin' to do that, air ye? [*Returns to the stove and picks up the bowl of chitterlings.*]

STUBBS [*pigheadedly*]. Too hot! [*He leans back and fans himself vigorously.*]

JENNY [*witheringly*]. I reckin ye air, with your skin as full o' whisky as a tick on a Jersey yearlin'. Well, I ain't. That draf' will be givin' me the mis'ry. Go an' shet that door, if you think you've got sense enough. I been a-tryin' to keep it shet all day. [*Starts putting the chitterlings in the frying pan.*]

STUBBS [*in a tone of self-pity*]. Well, you shore had it shet when I come home. Shet ag'in your husband, when, for all you keered, I mought never 'a' come home, with them Armstrongs—

JENNY. I know all about the Armstrong gang. Pity they didn't git ye, or somethin' couldn't git hold of ye now. Shet that door, I say. All summer you been a-promisin' to fix that ketch, an' now hit's the fust of November—

STUBBS [*interrupting*]. Thar you go 'bout that danged door ag'in. Ridin' your high horse.

JENNY [*forking the chitterlings into the frying pan*]. Well, I reckin I got a right to ride a high horse 'bout hit. Ef you'd been pestered with the thing all day lack I been, proppin' an' unproppin' hit ever' time I went fer a bucket o' worter or stepped out o' the kitchen fer anything, you'd be hot about hit too. Shet that door, I'm a-tellin' you.

STUBBS. *Hot* about hit? I thought you 'lowed you was cold.

JENNY [*forking up one of the frying pieces and brandishing it*]. Burrus Stubbs, I'm a good min' to slap this hot chitlin in your face. [*The wind blows a scurry of leaves into the kitchen.*] Shet that door or I'll stop cookin' this minute and leave the house. I won't be mistreated by no man like this.

STUBBS. Light a shuck, then. I'll be danged ef I'll shet hit.

JENNY [*throwing the frying fork violently on the table and unbuttoning her apron*]. You can stay here an' do your own cookin', an' the dogs an' the cats an' the chickens an' the ducks an' the cows an' the hogs can traipse through the house [*Throwing her apron on the chair.*] before I'll shet hit. [*Starts for the door, rear.*]

STUBBS [*Overtaking her in the doorway, seizes her, hugs her, bear-like, and speaks to her in a wheedling tone expressive of assumed good humor and real fear.*] Aw, come on back, ol' lady. Don't git lack that.

JENNY [*struggling*]. Turn me a-loose!
STUBBS. Now, honey!
JENNY. Turn me a-loose, I say, or I'll bite your hand off.
STUBBS [*realizing that she is becoming hysterical, releases her, and he gazes at her ruefully for a moment, then gingerly lays his hand upon her shoulder, and speaks in a conciliatory tone*]. Don't git mad lack that, honey. Le's don't have no racket.
JENNY. Do lack I tol' ye, then: Shet the door. [*She pushes STUBB's arm off her shoulder and faces him.*]
[*There is a slight pause. STUBBS studies his wife in some bewilderment, realizing that matters have gone too far. JENNY points toward the door. Then STUBBS remembers something. From the breast pocket he extracts a package, unwraps it with his back to JENNY, making the paper crackle audibly. It is the "purty" to which he referred when he was seeking admission at the door—a large pink "tucking comb" with false brilliants. He grins at this, then, over his shoulder, at JENNY. JENNY points again to the door. He faces front, shielding the comb from JENNY's view, lays his peace-offering upon the table, and grins broadly at JENNY, who now has her back turned on him. Then he starts for the door, watching JENNY over his shoulder.*]
[JENNY *has meanwhile given way to her curiosity and turned back toward the table. Seeing that* STUBBS *is watching her over his shoulder, she stamps her foot and points inexorably at the door.* STUBBS *jerks his head around and resumes his slow progress.*]
[*Then the comb, in all its splendor, catches her eye, and she picks it up. Mollified by* STUBBS's *peace-offering and, like* STUBBS, *realizing the absurdity of their conduct, she puts the comb in her hair, walks rapidly over to him, pats him on the arm, and speaks to him in a softened tone.*]

JENNY. We ought to be 'shamed o' ourselves—carryin' on like little chaps or new-married folks. Go on an' shet the door, Burrus, while I see ef your supper ain't sp'iled durin' the rookus. [*She pats the comb in her hair and returns to her apron.*]

STUBBS [*Scratching his head and looking at her like a spoiled boy trying to save his face*]. Now, lookee here, ol' lady. I wouldn't 'a' minded shettin' the door; but you was kind o' bossy, and I, I—

JENNY [*tying the apron around her*]. You what? Go . . . on . . . an' . . . shet . . . the door—you big ol' gander you! [*Seeing* STUBBS *start in the direction of the door, she resumes her work at the stove, singing:*

> He swore by the sun and the moon and the stars
>   And the green leaves on the tree
> That his wife could do more work in a day
>   Than he could in three.

STUBBS [*Advancing to the door, puts his hand on it, as if to shut it, glances at* JENNY, *registers a stubborn resolve not to obey, then tiptoes to the wash shelf, and washes his face noisily. Drying his face with the towel, he faces* JENNY]. Uh, honey, don't the Good Book say somethin' 'bout keepin' your oaths?

JENNY [*glances at him, then at the still open door*]. It says a lot more about not swearin' none. [*Stamps her foot and points to the door.*] Shet the door.

STUBBS [*going toward her, grinning*]. Now, lookee here, honey, I chopped the stove-wood fer ye, an' I give ye a purty, an' . . . well, you know how it is with a man. You don't want me to—

JENNY [*breaking in*]. I don't want ye to do nothin' but shet the door. That's all. [*Stooping over and opening the oven door.*] An' ef you don't, the oven won't never git hot enough to cook these biscuits.

STUBBS [*starts slowly toward the door; then, encouraged by* JENNY's *tone, looks shrewdly at her.*] Honey, you don't want to brow-beat your husband, do ye?

JENNY [*on her way to the cupboard for a dish*]. Brow-beat ye? No. I want ye to shet the door.

STUBBS [*chucking her under the chin*]. Listen, honey. It's this-a-way: I swore I wouldn't, an' you—

JENNY [*striking his hand, but half-playfully*]. I didn't swear nothin'. 'Twas you done the swearin'. An' ef your words don't taste good when you have to eat 'em, 'twas you done the cookin' of 'em. Besides, you don't have to eat no words. Jes' shet the—

STUBBS [*boyishly*]. Tell ye what, honey. We ain't gittin' nowhere with this here thing.

JENNY. You mean *you* ain't gittin' nowhere, you hard-headed rascal.

STUBBS. Le's try a new deal. You said somethin' while ago 'bout us actin' lack little chaps or new-married folks. Le's settle hit that-a-way.

JENNY. What way?

STUBBS. You see, you're allus a-sayin' that I love to wag my tongue much as you do yourn. I'll give ye a chancet to prove hit.

JENNY. What's that got to do with shettin' the door?

STUBBS. Le's make a trade: that the fust one that says anything atter we draw a deadline will have to shet that door.

JENNY. If you lose, or if I lose, no matter which, will you fix the door fust thing in the mornin'?

STUBBS. Shore as sun-up.

JENNY. An' promise, cross your heart an' hope to die, that

you'll git a pane o' glass fer that winder the very nex' time you go to town, an' fix hit when you git back?

STUBBS. Shore as the Lord lets me live. [*Eagerly, putting his arm around her.*] Now is hit a trade?

JENNY [*pushing him away*]. Not yit it ain't. One more thing. I want you to git the bucket an' go to the well fer a bucket o' worter.

STUBBS. What fer?

JENNY. So you kin heat some worter fer a bath.

STUBBS. A bath? [*Snorts.*]

JENNY. Yes, a bath.

STUBBS. Who fer?

JENNY. You, you stinkin' rascal. You ain't worshed since you kilt hawgs, an' you smell wuss 'n a polecat. I don't know when you *have* worshed.

STUBBS. Right atter layin'-by time. [*Seating himself by the table, left.*] You know when I worsh: when I peel off my winter drawers an' undershirt in the spring, Fo'th o' July, layin'-by time, an' Chris'mas. Worsh reg'lar as any man.

JENNY. Well, ef you don't worsh to-night an' git them mule sheers an' trim up your nasty ol' whiskers, I'll throw these here chitlins [*Motioning with the skillet.*] out the winder, an' make you sleep on the floor.

STUBBS. Hol' on a minute! One at a time, like the feller said when the doctor showed 'im his two twins. I'll worsh fer my chitlins, but I'll be danged ef I'll tetch scissors to a hair o' my whiskers fer you nor fer chitlins nor fer nothin' else. I'll sleep in a holler tree an' eat acorns fust.

JENNY. You ought to shave 'em slick 'stead o' trimmin' em. you look wuss 'n ol' Jacob in the Sunday-school book.

STUBBS [*getting up*]. Give up my beard, woman? Finest beard in Attala County [*Stroking it.*]—finest set o' whiskers in the State o' Mis'sippi—ain't a better one in the

Nunited States. Cut off my beard! W'y, woman, hit's my manhood. Where'd ol' Sampson be 'thout his whiskers?

JENNY. Oh, stop that ol' rigmarole an' git me that worter ef you want any supper. [*Going to the table with a dish in her hand.*] Do you want me to throw these chitlins out?

STUBBS. Looks like ye got me ag'in—'bout the worshin'. But I got you 'bout my beard till the cows come home... Where's the bucket?

JENNY. Been so long since you filled hit you fergot where hit is?

STUBBS. An' I'm a-goin' to git you 'bout the door, too.

JENNY. Go on, now; the biscuit'll be ready in a minute.

STUBBS [*bucket in hand, starts slowly toward the door, singing*]. "Hog drovers, hog drovers, hog drovers we air," etc. [*Stops near the door, sets the bucket down, and turns to her.*] Atter I leave the door, the game's on. No king's ex.

JENNY. Not a word 'bout nothin'?

STUBBS. Naw: 'bout nothin'—to nobody—nohow. No crossed fingers, neither. [*Fumbling in his pocket, he extracts the whisky bottle. Trying to set it behind the preserved fruit on top of the cupboard, he strikes one of the jars.*]

JENNY [*turning at the sound*]. Don't you knock down them quince persarves. [*Recognizing the bottle.*] Uh-huh. That won't help you much. Never heerd o' licker tyin' up nobody's tongue. [*She resumes her work at the stove.*]

STUBBS. Well, we'll see if this here bar-the-door game'll keep you from sayin' what you allus say 'bout me drinkin'. [*Chuckles, takes a drink, and sets the bottle on the cupboard.*] Shore will be good atter I eat my chitlins. [*Picks up his bucket.*] Atter I leave the door is the deadline. [*Turns in the doorway and recites in staccato, schoolboy fashion.*]

Las' night an' the night befo'
Twen'y-fo' robbers at my do'.
Ol' woman opened an' let 'em in,
Knocked 'em in the head with her rollin' pin.
—ALL AIN'T HID HOLLER I!

[*He makes a face at* JENNY, *who motions him out. He goes.*]
[*While* JENNY *is putting the rest of the supper on the table,* STUBBS *returns with the water, sets the bucket on the table, and makes himself comfortable in his chair.* JENNY *shakes him, points at the bucket, and then at the stove.* STUBBS *gets up reluctantly, sets the bucket on the stove, and makes himself comfortable again, this time in the other chair.* JENNY *prods him with the frying fork and points from the bucket to the kettle, directing him to pour the water from the one into the other, then supervises him while he is doing so. In performing this task,* STUBBS *manages to spill a pint or two on* JENNY'S *feet. She suppresses herself with difficulty.*]
[STUBBS, *having resumed the chair just vacated, leans back expansively, and cocks one of his feet on the corner of the table.* JENNY *indignantly seizes the foot and pushes it down. As she returns from the stove, the foot confronts her again. Thrusting it down again, she stamps it with her own foot. No sooner than she turns her back,* STUBBS *eases it up once more.* JENNY *sighs, returns meekly with the coffee pot, fills her own cup, then* STUBBS'S, *and suddenly empties the pot on* STUBB'S *foot.* STUBBS *howls inarticulately and* JENNY *suppresses herself with difficulty, stuffing the corner of her apron into her mouth. She finishes putting the food upon the table,* STUBBS *watching her covertly.*]
[JENNY'S *face is now calm. She seats herself, folds her hands in her lap, and bows, as usual, for grace.* STUBBS, *through*

force of habit, does likewise, and has opened his mouth with a half-articulate invocation like "O Lo—" when he catches himself. JENNY *insists by proper motions that* STUBBS *has lost the game, and points triumphantly to the door, but* STUBBS *shakes his head stubbornly and begins reaching for his favorite delicacy. Just as he has taken the first mouthful with relish, and washed it down with coffee from his saucer, the dogs bark in the front yard. The two listen,* STUBBS *chewing vigorously.*]
[*The tramp of horses and two or three low "w'oa's" are heard; then the following dialogue, offstage.*]
PINK. Hello!
TOL. Hello!
JACK. Hello, in thar!
TOL. Don't seem to be nobody thar.
PINK [*more loudly*]. Hello!
TOL. I could 'a' swore I seen a light through a open door when we come round a bend in the road back thar.
[*During this conversation* STUBBS *and* JENNY *are making frantic but silent gestures commanding each other to shut the door.*]
PINK. Stay here, boys, an' I'll ride roun' to the back.
TOL. Go ahead. We'll watch the front.
[*At the sound of the horse's tread, the dogs bark more furiously outside; and inside,* STUBBS *and* JENNY *look at each other in alarm.* JENNY *kicks* STUBBS *on the shins and, failing in this effort, pulls him out of his chair and is trying to propel him toward the door when a leering face appears, peering cautiously around the corner, eyes blinking in the light. At sight of this, she pulls* STUBBS *back violently into his chair. The two continue to stare as the figure of a man emerges and stands in the door—that of a large, unshaven, scowling ruffian, dressed in slouch hat,*

mud-bespattered boots and corduroys, with a big revolver in a holster at his side.]

PINK [*in a tone suggesting some slight effort to be civil, but scarcely the less gruff*]. Evenin', folks. [STUBBS *and* JENNY *stare at him and remain still. It is clear from their expressions that they are alarmed by a strong suspicion as to the stranger's identity; but either from fear or from remembrance of their pact about the door, they remain mute.* PINK *speaks again, more loudly.*] Evenin'! [*Getting no response, he strides boldly across the kitchen, eyes the couple balefully, then, very loudly.*] Air ye deef? Dumb too? [*Laughs, then opens the door, left, and calls through it.*] 'S all right, boys. Jes' a couple o' deef an' dumb ol' eejuts. Ride roun' to the back an' hitch your hosses to the fence.

[*The other two members of the gang are heard obeying the order.* PINK *completes his survey of the room, seizes food from the table, eats ravenously, and, as the figures of the other two appear in the doorway, calls out a muffled order to his confrères.*] Better feed the hosses fust; they's in wuss shape than us. [*The other two members of the gang poke their heads through the door, staring curiously at the couple.*] One of ye—you, Tol—come git the ol' man [*Making an amused appraisal of* STUBBS.]—ol' Black-byeard heah—an' make 'im show ye his cawn crib. [*Leans over and shouts into* STUBBS's *ear.*] We're cattle men. [*The other two* ARMSTRONGS, TOL *and* JACK, *attired somewhat like* PINK, *and as mud-bespattered, but more visibly weary and bearing Winchester rifles, enter.* STUBBS's *glance travels from the Winchesters to* PINK, *registering obvious disbelief.*] Rid all the way from Canton. Tord an' hongry. Want supper fer ourselves an' feed fer our hosses. Got to make hit to Vaiden to-night. [*At the mention of Vaiden* STUBBS *and* JENNY *look at each other with*

GIT UP AN' BAR THE DOOR

expressions showing that they know they are facing the worst; but neither speaks or moves.]

TOL [*who has been watching* STUBBS *suspiciously*]. Ol' Whiskers may be dumb, but I got my doubts 'e ain't deef. [*Seizing* STUBBS *by the beard, he points to the door.*] Come on, ol' mill post, an' show me your cawn crib.

[*As the two near the kitchen door,* TOL *notices the lantern hanging on a nail and points to it.* STUBBS *lights it. Then, Winchester in hand,* TOL *marches* STUBBS *out.* JENNY *still sits fast in her chair.*]

PINK [*calling after* TOL]. Make 'im git some tubs or boxes, tie 'em with the halters, an' feed 'em in the yard thar.

JACK [*placing his Winchester against the side of the cupboard, drags a chair close to the wall, left, and tips back in it.*] Ugh! Gawd, I'm tord!

PINK [*To* JENNY]. Git busy, sister. Another plate an' sich. [JENNY *sits mute and still.* PINK *shouts at her, at the same time pushing her roughly in the direction of the stove.*] Git busy! [*Points at the plates, then indicates a vacant place at the table.* JENNY *rises and busies herself as commanded.* PINK *sits down, facing front, and resumes eating.*]

JACK [*notices for the first time that* PINK *is eating*]. Grub! [*Rises, comes to the table, and snatches a biscuit.*]

PINK [*with his mouth full*]. Lay off till Tol gits back. [*He pushes* JACK *away.*]

JACK [*reaching and snatching another morsel*]. Aye Gawd, reckin I'm hongry too.

PINK [*threateningly*]. Git along.

[*Outside,* STUBBS *and* TOL *are heard shucking corn for the horses. Presently they return.* TOL *sets his gun near* JACK'S.

[STUBBS, *who entered in front of* TOL, *stops at the door and blows out the lantern. Now, making as if to return it to*

its nail, he tries to slip out the door; but he is discovered.]
TOL [*snatching up a rifle*]. Halt!
PINK [*whipping out his revolver*]. Uh-huh! Ol' boy heerd that, I reckin. [*Turns to* TOL, *who is near the back door.*] Go git that rope off'n my saddle. [*To* JACK.] Look in the next room thar an' fetch out another cheer. [*To* STUBBS.] Shuffle back heah, Sandy Claus, an' keep 'em up. [*Indicates a spot in front of the wood box. Takes a chair from the table, all the while keeping his gun pointed at* STUBBS, *and when* STUBBS *reaches the point indicated, steps behind him and suddenly pushes the chair against his calves, making him drop down suddenly into it.*]
TOL [*returning with the rope*]. Heah. [*Throws it to* JACK, *who by this time has returned with another chair and, seeing that* PINK *has taken one from the table, sets it down instead.*]
PINK. Tie 'im in the cheer, Jack—feet to the front rounds, hands behind 'im.
TOL [*looking on*]. Wisht we had another ol' hoss to tie 'im to like we done that ol' boy on the Vaiden road las' night.
PINK [*laughing*]. Never will fergit how the ol' feller looked when they went humpin' down that road, him a bobbin' up an' down an' bumpin' 'is chin on the hoss's crupper. [*Guffaws.*]
TOL [*guffawing too*]. Yeah, an' the way he was a-talkin' to his hoss: "W'oah! [*Loudly.*] ... W'oah! [*Shrilly.*] ... W'oah, Bodger! W'oah, ol' boy!" [*In a coaxing tone, diminishing as if by distance.*]
PINK [*To* JACK, *who is on his knees tying up* STUBBS]. Hurry up thar, kid, if you want any supper. We'll eat an' then see what's in the house.
JACK [*pausing and pushing* JENNY *away from* STUBBS]. Git away from heah, ol' woman! [*He rises and surveys his job.*]

PINK. Yeah, you better not let me see you meddlin' with your ol' man. [*Seating himself, facing front.*]

TOL. Now, le's eat. Make yourselves at home, boys. [*He seats himself at the end of the table, right.*]

JACK [*approaching the table and examining the food*]. Aye Gawd, chitlins! An' biscuit an' coffee! [*He seats himself and eats ravenously, looking the while at* STUBBS. STUBBS *stirs violently, attracting the attention of the others.*]

PINK. Bet the ol' son-of-a-gun's mouth is a-worterin' for these heah chitlins. [*He raises his empty cup and motions to* JENNY, *who pours coffee for all.*]

TOL. Damn ye, Jack. Go easy on them chitlins. Don't have to make a hawg of yourself jes' because you're a-eatin' a hawg. They won't be enough fer the rest of us. [*To* JENNY, *pointing at the empty biscuit plate.*] Hey! More biscuit! [JENNY *obeys; on her way back to the stove she slips a biscuit into* STUBBS's *mouth.*]

JACK [*rising*]. The las' chitlin. Le's see ef we cain't piece out this meal. [*Going to the cupboard, he fumbles around, and brings out two dishes.*] Cracklin' bread an' collards! [*Sets the dishes on the table and helps himself. At the mention of crackling bread,* STUBBS *glowers at* JENNY, *then at the men.*]

TOL [*rising*]. Le's see what I can find. [*Goes to the cupboard.*]

PINK. You won't find nothin' Jack didn't.

TOL [*examining the jars while* JENNY *glares. He holds up one of them*]. Quince persarves! [*Advancing toward* JENNY.] Ol' woman, bake me a bushel mo' biscuit an' git me a pound o' butter. [*He fondles* JENNY *with his free arm.* JENNY *glowers at him and opens her mouth as if to speak, but remains silent.* TOL *fumbles behind the jars, finds the whisky bottle, uncorks it, and smells of it.*] Hooee! Look what ol' Sandy Claus brung us.

[STUBBS *leans forward, his head trembling with rage.*]

PINK. Fetch it heah! [*As* TOL *approaches, he snatches the bottle from* TOL's *hand, pours himself a stiff drink, and passes the bottle to* TOL. TOL *empties his coffee cup over his shoulder, in* STUBBS's *face, helps himself, and passes the bottle to* JACK.]

JACK [*filling his cup*]. Fust 'is chitlins, an' now the ol' boy's licker. [*Toasts* STUBBS.] Heah's lookin' at ye, ol' Black-byeard. Them whiskers shore is a eye full.

PINK [*wiping his mouth with the back of his hand*]. Got to be movin', boys. Jack, see ef the hosses is done.

JACK. Aw, hell, what's the hurry? [*Continues eating and drinking greedily.*]

PINK [*pushing* JACK *away from the table*]. Hump it, you lazy hound.

JACK [*stuffing his mouth full and rising*]. Allus a-peckin' on me. [*Over his shoulder as he goes to the door.*] W'y in hell cain't you do somethin' yourself? [*Glances out the door.*] Ain't done yit; still a-chompin'. [*Starts back with alacrity.*]

TOL. Shet the door. Cold in heah. [JENNY *and* STUBBS *exchange significant glances.*]

JACK [*returns and fumbles at the door*]. Damn thing's busted. [JENNY *looks spitefully at* STUBBS.] Damn it! [*The door refuses to be fastened.* JACK *kicks it shut and starts back toward the table. The door flies open again behind him.*]

PINK and TOL [*roaring*]. Shet hit!

JACK [*turning to* JENNY]. You shet hit. Reckin you ought to know how. [STUBBS *solemnly nods his head.* JENNY *looks daggers at* JACK, *then at* STUBBS, *who grins at her; she refuses to move.* JACK *advances toward her, arm raised threateningly; but she stands fast.*] Shet hit, I said. [*Seizing* JENNY]. Git a move on ye. [*Propelling her toward the door.*] An' don't you try none o' your ol' man's tricks. You won't git no stort lack ol' Whiskers had. [JENNY *goes over and pretends to shut the door, but she actually leaves it visibly cracked open. As she returns,* STUBBS *grins at her triumphantly, and she glares back at him, shaking her head. The men resume eating and drinking—chiefly drinking.*]

TOL. Lemme kill this soldier an' lay 'im to rest. [*Puts the bottle to his lips, drains it, and lays it down in front of* STUBBS. *The door flies open suddenly, banging loudly against the wall. The three* ARMSTRONGS, *startled, leap to their feet, knocking over chairs,* PINK *snatching his revolver out of the holster.*]

PINK [*disgustedly*]. Aw, hell! Nothin' but the wind.

TOL. Shet it ag'in, ol' woman. 'S cold in heah. [STUBBS *nods at* JENNY, *who glares at him, not at* TOL.]

PINK [*looking suspiciously at* STUBBS]. Naw, leave hit open. [*To* STUBBS.] What you got up your sleeve, ol' Whiskers? [*To the others.*] Leavin' toreckly, anyway—soon as we see what ol' Whiskers has got in the house heah.

JACK [*feeling the effects of the liquor*]. Whiskers is right. [*Belching and pushing back his plate.*] B'lieve I'll shave 'em off'n 'im. [*At this remark,* JENNY *smiles, in spite of herself.*]

PINK and TOL. Shore. Go ahead an' shave 'im.

JACK [*rising unsteadily*]. May 'a' been a-talkin' all this time an' [*Hiccups.*] we ain't heerd 'im through them whiskers. [*Takes out a big jack-knife and starts toward* STUBBS.] Git them off'n 'im, and mebbe 'e kin tell us whar 'is money is. [*Putting one foot on the wood box, he proceeds to whet his knife on his boot.*]

TOL. Put some mo' wood in the stove, sister. Gittin' cold in heah.

JACK [*gathers* STUBBS'S *beard in one hand and with the*

knife in the other tries to cut it off. But the knife is too dull. STUBBS *grimaces and grunts.* JENNY *now looks on indignantly.*] Whar's the ol' boy's soap? Cain't shave 'im dry, I reckin.

PINK. Over thar on the worsh bench, mebbe. Bet hit's lye soap.

[JACK *sticks the blade of the knife in the side of the wood box and crosses to the wash bench.*]

[*Meanwhile,* JENNY *has gone to the wood box. As she stoops over for the wood, she sees the knife, snatches it up, picks up a few sticks of wood, and glances swiftly around. The two men at the table are idly looking at* JACK, *who has found the soap. To prepare for her next act,* JENNY *deliberately drops the wood behind* STUBBS's *chair.*]

[*The men look round, but having seen only a part of what has happened, and thinking that the dropping of the wood was an accident, turn their attention again to* JACK, *who has found the soap and is making up a lather.*]

JACK. Lye soap's right. Bet this'd soften the bristles on a bo' hawg's back.

[*While* JACK *is making this observation,* JENNY, *stooping over as if to pick up the wood, swiftly cuts the rope binding* STUBBS's *hands, but of course does not try to loosen his feet, which are left with the slackened rope around them. She replaces the knife where it was, puts the wood in the stove, and takes up her position between the table and the cupboard.* STUBBS, *keeping his hands well behind him, chafes his wrists to restore circulation.*]

TOL. Don't be stingy with your lather.

JACK [*advancing on* STUBBS]. 'Tain't nothin' but a lye-soap-an'-barlow-knife shave, but I reckin the ol' boy won't complain. He's gittin' hit fer nothin'. [*Lathers* STUBBS *copiously, filling his beard and mouth with lather,* STUBBS *grunting and spitting meanwhile.*]

PINK [*rises to watch the fun, walks over to* STUBBS's *left, and stands rather close to him, the revolver within easy reach of the latter*]. Nothin', hell. When you git through with 'is Irish shave we'll collect from 'im, all right. Wonder 'e ain't turned over in 'is sleep some night an' smothered 'is ol' woman in all them whiskers.

JACK. Bet 'is ol' woman'll run off an' leave 'im when I finish with 'im. [*Whets the knife on the palm of his hand.* JENNY *watches expectantly.*]

TOL [*rising, picking his teeth with his fingers*]. Well, let 'er come to me. I et the las' biscuit, an' they say the guy what eats the las' biscuit has got to kiss the cook. So while you-all are a-shavin' the ol' man, I'll kiss the ol' lady. [*He seizes* JENNY *suddenly and kisses her loudly.* JENNY *slaps him with a sharp smack.* JACK *and* PINK *turn, guffawing,* PINK *with his holster side very close to* STUBBS.]

STUBBS [*snatching* PINK's *revolver, leaps to his feet, pushing the chair back as much as possible, and waves the gun at them.*] Hands up! [*They comply.*] Back out thar in the middle of the room. [*The men do so.*] An' now ... you lousy cut-th'oats [*Chokes with rage and soap.*] ... et my chitlins ... drunk my licker ... cut my byeard ... an' [*Blowing lather from his mustache.*] ... now, Gawd blast ye, ye kiss my ol' woman! [*Waves the gun at them and almost loses his balance.*] Jenny, ontie my feet. We'll tie 'em up in their own rope an' ... [*He tries to shift his feet a bit so that* JENNY *can get at the knots better, loses his balance, and falls, the gun going off*] ... hell!

PINK. Git the guns! [*The ruffians jump for the rifles near* JENNY, *but she is too quick for them. She snatches the kettle from the stove and scalds them, but says not a word.* STUBBS *writhes on the floor, roaring and cursing. Meanwhile, the ruffians, howling with rage and pain, have escaped from the kitchen, mounted, and ridden off amidst an uproar among the dogs in the yard.*]

STUBBS. Damn 'em, they got away! They got away! They got away! [*He punctuates each sentence with a groan.*] Ontie me, Jenny. They got away!

JENNY [*releasing him, and speaking for the first time since the two made their silence wager,* STUBBS *pointing each of her assertions with a groan*]. Yes, they got away. An' they et your chitlins... an' drunk your licker... an' kissed your ol' woman. An' you've lost the game. But I'll cook ye some more chitlins... if you'll... jes' [*Tugging at* STUBBS's *collar.*] ... GIT UP [*Pulling him erect, and pointing at the door.*] AN' BAR THE DOOR!

[STUBBS *tries to kiss her, but she fights off his soapy face and points inexorably at the door. He is on his way as*

THE CURTAIN FALLS

OKLAHOMA

LAST REFUGE
AN OUTLAW COMES HOME

BY NOEL HOUSTON
OF OKLAHOMA CITY, OKLAHOMA

Written in the playwriting course at the University of North Carolina and originally produced by The Carolina Playmakers at Chapel Hill on May 26, 1938.

THE CHARACTERS

JOE HEATHERSTONE, *a bandit killer*....Howard Bailey
WILMA, *his sister*..................Janet Pendleton
UNCLE LEV, *his uncle*..................Fred Meyer
WADE, *his brother*.....................John Morgan
RUBY, *his wife*...............Madeline Haynsworth
GORDON, *his son*....................Tommy Hearn
LARITA LAMONTE, *his companion*.......Helen Bailey

SCENE: *A cabin in the Cookson Hills of eastern Oklahoma.*
TIME: *The present. A bright Saturday morning in October.*

Copyright, 1938, by The Carolina Playmakers, Inc.
All rights reserved.

OKLAHOMA OUTLAW

THE Cookson Hills of eastern Oklahoma, scene of *Last Refuge*, are thickly forested and interlaced with tortuous roads and winding trails. Noel Houston, the author of the play and a native of Lawton, Oklahoma, tells us that these hills have served as a hideout for outlaws for many years. A not-unusual ending to a story in an Oklahoma newspaper, he avers, is: "The officers were in close pursuit until the bandit-killer reached the safe refuge of the Cookson Hills." Beyond the hills is the Arkansas River and the city of Muskogee on the distant plain.

This region is a part of the old Indian territory. As early as a hundred years ago settlers made the long trek from North Carolina, South Carolina, Georgia, Alabama, Tennessee, and Kentucky, to this new country. Here they cleared the forests, built their cabins, and planted their crops.

But the soil lay thin on the rocks and, before many years, the heavy rains sent the plowed earth sluicing down the hillsides. The land produced less and less, the families became poorer and poorer. Shiftlessness and ignorance, whisky making, and petty crime followed. And before long this region began to breed some of the most notorious Midwestern outlaws— among them Charles "Pretty Boy" Floyd.

The hills became a haven for desperate outlaws. Four years ago the State Peace Officers Association of Oklahoma massed five hundred police and five hundred militiamen to throw a cordon around the hill country in an attempt to ensnare the bandits and murderers known to be hiding there. Great secrecy surrounded the project, but when the "army" closed in, nothing was found but deserted cabins, old men and women too feeble to be moved, and a few straggling cows and chickens. The "grapevine telegraph" had sent out the warning, and a sudden migration eastward into Arkansas followed. The "army" left, and the hill folk moved back to their cabins.

Some say the land should never have been used for farming. The plight of the Cookson Hills folk is like that of hundreds of others living on submarginal land. The Resettlement Administration has bought up thousands of the denuded, rocky acres and is turning them back to forest and grazing land; millions of trees are being planted over scrawny corn and cotton patches; and the families are being moved away to the rich bottom lands along the Arkansas River. The character of the Hills is to be changed. The old whisky maker, the puny children, the sickly crops, the lurking outlaw—all must go. In their place, the game will run again and the forest will reclaim its own.

Noel Houston is a young newspaperman on the staff of *The Daily Oklahoman* of Oklahoma City. His interest in playwriting brought him to Chapel Hill. Besides *Last Refuge* The Carolina Playmakers have produced three other plays from his pen: a domestic comedy, *Penny for Their Thoughts,* on December 9, 1937; a play of condemned men on Death Row in the Oklahoma State Penitentiary, *The Last Christmas,* on February 2, 1938; and *The Long Ago,* a comedy of a wealthy Oklahoma couple, on January 11, 1939.

The sad fate of "Pretty Boy" Floyd is recorded in a contemporary balad:

> Pretty Boy was born in the Oklahoma hills,
> Where the beautiful flowers grow wild.
> He was christened Charles Arthur by his parents so proud,
> Who thanked God for their beautiful child.
>
> . . . .
>
> Pretty Boy will learn on that last great Judgment Day
> That a life filled with crime doesn't pay.

LAST REFUGE

The mountain cabin of the Heatherstones has been lived in for a long time. It is sturdily built of chinked, split logs, designed to weather the changes of the years. The scene is the living room. An ample fireplace made of round native stone occupies the center of the rear wall, at the right of it a door leading outside, at the left a window which looks out on a forest clearing and on distant mountains.

Incongruously enough, at the left of the fireplace is a handsome chintz-covered easy chair, a footstool, an expensive floor lamp with a gaudy shade, and a large, ornate radio cabinet. On the other side of the fireplace is a small old-fashioned rocker. The hearth is cold but there is a pile of pine kindling just by.

At the right is a table and two splint-bottomed chairs; at the left, an old iron cot covered with a soiled patchwork quilt, and a door to the kitchen. A woman's nightgown hangs from a nail above the cot and two long cotton-picking bags hang on the kitchen door.

The walls are decorated with several skins of small animals.

[UNCLE LEV, *an old reprobate, sits at the end of the table facing us, a bare foot crossed over his overalled knee, a dilapidated brogan shoe on his lap. He is intently searching through a Chicago newspaper, a stack of other newspapers on the floor beside him. Occasionally, he digs dirt from between his toes, then gives his thumb a lick as he turns a page.* WADE HEATHERSTONE, *a husky fellow of about seventeen, sits on the edge of the cot. Naked to the waist,* WADE *is sewing an athletic letter "B" on a pullover sweater.* WILMA, *about forty, is removing breakfast dishes from the table and taking them into the kitchen. Weariness has become a part of her nature, malnutrition and overwork show in her whole body, and she speaks from a deep sorrow. Long suffering and patient,* WILMA *is mother, sister, and servant to the two men. She wears a simple dress, over it an apron made of faded flour sacks. Like* WADE, *she is bare-footed.*]

UNCLE LEV [*impatiently turning a page*]. This here paper's sorrier'n a old mule; hain't a damn word 'bout Joe in it. They lost money on *this* paper; people wants to read about *Joe.*

WILMA [*wearily going out with the dishes*]. Better git your mind off'n them papers and git out in the field.

UNCLE LEV. Hain't goin' to the field to-day ... got to work a *money* crop. [*He chuckles.*] Got a hundred gallons of mash to run.

WADE [*brightly*]. You goin' to work your still after Jimmy Goforth warned you this mornin'?

UNCLE LEV [*chuckling*]. Jimmy's the friendliest feller! There I was, just a-gittin' off o' my mule—there in front of the five-and-ten-cent store—when Jimmy come up. It was still dark but the street light wa'n't off yit and I seen it was Jimmy. He come up and he says, "Well, I still say if I can just git the vote of the good folks back in the hills I'll be elected sheriff next time." [WILMA *returns and continues clearing the table as he goes on telling the story he has told three times already this morning.*] I says, "Jimmy, we folks back in the hills goin' to vote for you, 'cause your record as deputy sheriff shows you're fair and square and knows what a man's rights are." Then he sidles up to me and he says, "It may not be nothin', but they's a crew of strangers come into town yesterday, and they *might* be revenue men—alcoholic tax agents," Jimmy called 'em—he's always one for the fancy stuff. "So maybe," says Jimmy, "you'd better not run any mash for a couple of days."—Yes, sir, looks like we're goin' to have to make Jimmy sheriff; he's a mighty good officer.

WILMA [*going out with the plates*]. Wade, you finished your molasses?

WADE. Yes'm. [*To* UNCLE LEV]. Mightn't they be revenooers?

UNCLE LEV. What if they are? I ain't scared of 'em. I got her hid where they couldn't never find her.

WADE [*grinning*]. I reckon so.

UNCLE LEV. Can't tell nothin' 'bout strangers in Beulah no more no way. The way the guvament's all the time sendin' in men, tellin' the folks down around Beulah how to raise their crops, how to cut their timber, how to dam their streams, how to build their privies.

WILMA. They might do well to come up in the hills and show *you* how to build one, seein' we been without one for two months now.

UNCLE LEV. I'll git around to it. [*He slaps down the paper and picks up another.*] Here I go all the way down to Beulah to git these papers and they ain't nothin' in 'em about Joe!

WADE. Less said about Joe in the papers the better for him. He don't like publicity.

UNCLE LEV [*sarcastically*]. He don't like publicity! Ain't a man alive doin' big things don't like the world to know it. [*He chuckles.*] Last week now, Joe give 'em some news. The President ain't never had no bigger headlines. Joe was the biggest man in Chicago last week.

WADE. He's gettin' himself too big.

UNCLE LEV. You can't argue with success. Wilma, bring me

that scrapbook. I want to read them last week's stories about Joe.

WILMA. You done read the print clean off'n 'em. Now you clear out o' here and git about your business.

UNCLE LEV [*taking up another newspaper*]. Just got one more.

WILMA [*going*]. Git to hustlin', Wade. We ought to finish pickin' that top-side patch to-day.

WADE [*calling after her*]. I'll get on it, Sis, soon's I finish this sweater. I ain't goin' t' overdo pickin' that skimpy cotton to-day, though. Got basketball practice to-night.

UNCLE LEV. You 'n your basketball! Looks like Wilma's the only body thinks o' work 'round here.

WILMA [*entering with a dust cloth*]. Basketball's mighty important work to Wade.

WADE. 'Tis if I'm going to A. and M. next fall.

UNCLE LEV. College! Acorns and tarnation. Learn all that fancy farmin' stuff. Now if you'd step out lively and make sumpin o' yourself—like Joe!

WILMA [*at the fireplace*]. That's fine advice to give a growin' boy. Here's Wade, one member of this family looks like he's got gumption enough to amount to somethin' without livin' in dread of the law, and you advisin' him—

WADE [*going to her, smiling*]. Don't worry, Sis. I'm payin' no mind to the old coot. I got my plans. Farmin' suits me—if I can get off these worn-out hills and get me some good land.

UNCLE LEV. Ain't no good land left. Ain't nothin' in it but hard work and starvation. Fust they say a man can't make liquor out'n his own corn. Now they say he can't make bread out'n his own wheat. Man can't move no more from bein' hedged in by the guvament. Hey, here's sumpin 'bout Joe! Now, le' me see, le' me see. [*He reads laboriously,* WADE *leaning over his shoulder,* WILMA

standing beside him, fearing that JOE *has been killed.*]
"Joe Heatherstone, No. 2 man in the Lustree gang, was believed to-day to have fled from Chicago. G-Men have kept a fu-*tile* vigil around Heatherstone's lux—"

WADE [*rapidly*]. "—luxurious apartment and searched his night-spot haunts in vain since the $65,000 robbery of—

UNCLE LEV. Damn it, I can read! "—since the $65,000 robbery of the Merchants Bank & Trust Co. in which three bank employes and two customers were slain."—Eh! "The authorities were reported working on a tip that the dapper Heatherstone had fled into hiding at a Minnesota lake resort. Orders were to shoot him on sight."

WILMA [*sorrowfully*]. He's errored this time.

UNCLE LEV [*chuckling*]. They can't catch ol' Joe.

WILMA. He'll go runnin' and hidin' and runnin', but they'll git him at the last.

UNCLE LEV. Not ol' Joe. He'll out-smart 'em.

WILMA. It ain't like it was back here in the hills. He's out there in a world where a man lives as others say for him to, and if he don't they're all against him—and they git him and they kill him.

UNCLE LEV. If they do, he'll make 'em pay fust. [*Imitating a machine gun.*] Putt-putt-putt-putt! Putt-putt-putt-putt! Putt-putt-putt-putt!

WADE. Sis, I wonder if I shouldn't ought to ... go help Joe. I could hitch-hike up yonder and, well ... maybe it's what a brother should ought to do.

UNCLE LEV [*contemptuously*]. How'd *you* find him?

WADE. I could try.

WILMA. No, ain't two Heatherstone brothers goin' to' be killed outside the law.

WADE. [*doubtfully, going to the cot*]. Well....

WILMA. You're the one Heatherstone people's goin' t' look up to.

UNCLE LEV. Wade'll have to go one hell of a way to be as big a big shot as Joe. *Ever*'body knows about Joe—more'n if he's a movie star.

WILMA [*resentfully*]. Yes, everybody knows about Joe. His name, his picture, and what he's done. He went out to get whatever he wanted and now he's runnin' before the pack, not knowin' what minute they'll close in.

UNCLE LEV. Ain't no use criticizin' your brother. Folks here in the hills got admiration for Joe. They *respect* the name of Heatherstone in these parts.

WILMA [*sadly*]. Folks are like you—sittin' up here away from danger—wantin' him to go on and on out yonder, makin' bigger and bigger headlines, gettin' himself deeper and deeper in trouble, while you sit up here a-chucklin', makin' out like it's yourself bein' a hero.

UNCLE LEV. Can't tell me nothin' about my feelin's for Joe!

WILMA. I was thirteen years old when he was a baby. I fed him and washed him and I put on his diapers.

UNCLE LEV. That's a sickenin' way to talk about a man. Why I was more a daddy than a uncle to that boy. I braced the rifle for 'im the day he killed his fust game—a nice doe down at the *pre*serve.

WILMA. Yes, and you was the one got him to hangin' around that pool hall down in Beulah. And you was the one that give him a pistol for helpin' you run your still.

UNCLE LEV. Ever' man's got a right to have his own pistol.

WILMA. But you wasn't with that boy—just the age of Wade he was—when he went on that spree robbin' fillin' stations. And you wasn't with me when I walked sixty miles barefoot in the cold to visit him at the penitentiary.

UNCLE LEV. Your Ma went with you.

WILMA. And you wasn't with Joe when he was shot—in that bank holdup—at Okmulgee. And you wasn't with me when I went to see him—in that apartment at Tulsa—

and found Ruby a-nursin' him—and Joe out of his head with the pain.

UNCLE LEV. Well, now, I'm an old man, Wilma. Way you talk against how Joe's seen fit to live his life, a person'd think you was leanin' toward the law.

WILMA [*bitterly, turning away*]. I hate the law!

WADE. What do you all want to argue here for—right after breakfast?

UNCLE LEV. I just say we folks ought t' be proud of Joe— Name me another feller in these hills could go to a city like Chicago and git himself sixty-five thousand dollars in one day! And besides, Joe—

[RUBY *appears in the front doorway with her son,* GORDON. RUBY *is twenty-seven with a quiet appealing simplicity about her, despite an old dress, a faded coat sweater and bare feet.* GORDON *is a ragged little lad of ten with tousled hair and a thin face.*]

RUBY. What's this about Joe?

WILMA. Hello, Ruby.

WADE. Mornin', Ruby.

UNCLE LEV. We's just a-talkin' about what's in the paper here, Ruby.

RUBY. Has anything happened to him?

UNCLE LEV [*handing her the paper*]. Hell-fire no! It's just—

WILMA. Gordon, you go out and play.

GORDON [*by the fireplace*]. I don't want to.

RUBY. No, go on and play, Gordon.

GORDON. I want to hear about Daddy, Mamma. Why can't I hear about Daddy?

RUBY. Just because. Now go.

GORDON [*going reluctantly*]. Aw, hell!

RUBY. Where is it?

UNCLE LEV. Right there! It says he's gone to Minnesota.

Reckon he's gone up there to do a little fishin', eh Ruby? [*He chuckles.*]

RUBY. I wish *I* could laugh. I wish it was funny. [*She hands back the paper.*] Are you tellin' me the truth, Wilma? [*Eagerly.*] Ain't you heard from him, askin' about me?

WILMA. We ain't had a word since Ma died eight months ago.

RUBY. I don't believe you! He's wrote for me and you ain't told me. Joe said he'd send for me.

WADE. Take it easy, Ruby.

UNCLE LEV. Why'd we lie to you, gal?

RUBY [*sadly*]. He's forgotten me.

UNCLE LEV. I ain't sayin' he ain't, 'cause I don't know. But maybe he ain't had a chance to send for you— Joe's been a mighty busy man, managin' them night clubs and headin' up that restur*ant* association for Lustree. He told you he'd send fer you soon's he got settled good, didn't he?

RUBY. It's been five years. Three years he was in St. Looey and K.C. and now two years he's been in Chicago. A woman shouldn't ought to be away from her husband like that. I could be a help to him. I stood by him through thick and thin before he quit Oklahoma.

WILMA. You was a good wife to Joe. That's why I told you to come here when you run out o' money.

UNCLE LEV. We're all fond of you, gal. I can't think of another human bein' besides yourself I'd help Wade build that cabin over yonder for. 'Y God, it tires me out now just a-thinkin' about it. [*He sinks into a chair.*]

RUBY [*to* WILMA]. *You* think he's forgotten me, don't you?

WILMA. Men do sometimes quit carin' for a woman. It's somethin' they can't help.

RUBY. I know it. [*She puts a hand to her face.*] And I wouldn't put no blame on him if he has.

UNCLE LEV. That shows a fair spirit.

RUBY. If I could just see him and talk to him five minutes, I'd know. I wouldn't humble myself to him. I wouldn't let him see my heart. [*To* UNCLE LEV.] Is there anything in the other papers?

UNCLE LEV. Nope, that's the latest one.

GORDON [*returning with a knife and a whistle*]. I ain't goin' t' stay outdoors no longer. [*He stands by the fireplace, quietly whistling.*]

RUBY. All right, dear. [*To* WILMA.] I just run over to borrow a pot to boil a mess of greens in.

WILMA. Why, sure. I got one in the kitchen you can keep. I'll walk back to your cabin with you. I'm on my way to the cotton patch—[*Takes one of the cotton-picking bags from the kitchen door.*]—the only one there is now.

WADE [*calling after them as they go*]. Sis, I'll be out in two shakes of a dead lamb's tail. [*He turns to* UNCLE LEV.] I feel awful sorry for Ruby.

UNCLE LEV. Mmm-hm. [*To* GORDON.] What's on your mind, Sonny?

GORDON. This danged old whistle I'm a-whittlin'—can't make her blow.

UNCLE LEV. Let me see it. [*He takes the whistle and knife.*] You ain't cuttin' the notch right. I've showed you and showed you, and you don't get it right. [*He goes to the door and takes down his hat from the wall.*] Come on down to the still with me and I'll show you agin.

GORDON. I want to hear some more about Daddy, too.

UNCLE LEV [*putting on his hat, he takes* GORDON *by the hand*]. Come on, Gordon.

WADE. Wilma'll break your skinflint neck if you tell Gordon any more o' them stories.

UNCLE LEV. [*spitting*]. Aw, shut up.

[GORDON *sticks out his tongue and he and* UNCLE LEV *leave by the kitchen door.*]

[WADE *sits by the table, sewing on his sweater. He sticks himself, jumps, sucks his finger, then resumes his sewing. The door at the rear opens slowly.* LARITA LAMONTE, *a blond, hard-featured young woman, wearing an expensive mink coat, tiptoes into the room.* WADE *hears her and turns quickly. She halts abruptly.*]

LARITA. Don't move—what's your name?

WADE. Wade Heatherstone. Who ... are you?

LARITA. You Joe Heatherstone's brother?

WADE. I don't know anything about Joe. I haven't seen him.

LARITA. Who else is here?

WADE. Nobody just now, I think.

LARITA. Is there any law around?

WADE. No.

LARITA. Has there been any?

WADE. No.

[LARITA *goes swiftly to the door, right, and looks off, then crosses to the door, left, and looks off.* WADE *is amazed and bewildered.* LARITA *then goes up to the window and waves her handkerchief to some one outside.*]

WADE [*rising and going to the fireplace*]. Say, who are you?

LARITA [*trying to throw off her nervousness*]. So you're Joe's little brother. I didn't know you was a Tarzan.

WADE. I'll—I'll just put on my sweater. [*Starts to pull it on.*]

LARITA. Ah, don't do that. I like to see the muscles of a man.

[*An automobile is heard approaching.* LARITA *looks out the window.* WADE *slips on his sweater. The automobile stops.* LARITA *wearily takes off her hat and looks around the room.*]

LARITA. So this is the place we drive halfway across the country to get to. What a dump!

[JOE HEATHERSTONE *appears in the doorway. He is carrying two traveling bags in one hand and holds a Luger pistol in the other. He is flashily but immaculately dressed. Wears a snappy hat and two-tone black and tan shoes. Wears a diamond in his tie and his hands are gloved. Though not tall, his solid figure speaks of an out-of-doors vigorous boyhood. At present he is in need of a shave and his eyes betray insufficient sleep. Cruelty, depravity, nervousness, fear are in his face, but something bewildered, pathetic, utterly lonely, is there too. He walks with a slow, stalking grace, and in his first speech he reveals several sides of his character: a domineering manner, hunger for his boyhood home, sensitiveness to disappointment, and delusions of grandeur.*]

LARITA. It's okay.

WADE. Joe!

JOE. Nah, stay where you are! [*He looks eagerly about the room.*] I want to see it. I want to look at it. [*He comes down a step farther into the room.*] It's smaller than I remembered it. Dirtier, too. Why don't you get it painted? Ah, but it's home. Home! [*He puts up his gun and places one of the traveling bags on the table.*] Larita, did Abraham Lincoln ever go back to his log cabin, do you know? [LARITA *is exasperated.*] Nah, you wouldn't know.

WADE. Joe! Where did you drop from?

JOE. From around. [*He puts the other bag on the table.*]

WADE. But Joe... ain't it bad... comin' here like this?

JOE [*lashing out*]. Where ain't it bad? Ain't nobody here goin' t' squeal on me, is they?

WADE. You know better'n that.

JOE. Jesus Christ, can't a guy come home?

WADE. Why, sure, Joe. We're glad to see you. We been wantin' to see you a long time now.

JOE [subsiding]. You have, unh? Well, good. [He hangs his hat on a nail by the door and begins pulling off his gloves.] I been wantin' to see you all, too—to see the place. I got down in this country—and decided to come over.

WADE. That's swell, Joe. How long can you stay?

JOE [hard suddenly]. Why? You want me not to stay long?

LARITA. Ah, lay off the kid. He's tryin' to be nice.

JOE [a quick thrust]. Did I ask you to put your mouth in? [LARITA sits on the cot. JOE shakes off his temper.] I'm sorry, kid. [He pats WADE's arm.] You've got husky. What's that letter? You an athlete now?

WADE. I got this for baseball. But basketball's my main game. I'm on the Beulah team.

JOE. Basketball? What kind of a game's that for a man? With a build like yours, you should be swinging leather. You could come up to Chicago and I could get you some bouts. [Remembering.] That is, I could 'a' ... before last week.

LARITA [sarcastically]. Yeh, you could 'a' before last week.

WADE. I don't want to be a fighter. I'm goin' to A. and M. next year. That's why I'm playin' basketball—to help me get a job workin' my way through.

JOE. Hey, look! If you want to go to college, you don't have to work your way through. A brother of mine can go through like the rest of them guys—easy, with the fraternities and all that stuff. I'll put up the dough.

WADE. Well, gee—that's swell, Joe. But you see ... I ... maybe you better not.

JOE. Hunh?

WADE. Well, you see... there's been some talk... that is, I might have a little trouble... uh... gettin' in. And uh....

JOE. What's that?

LARITA. He means on account of you're his brother, you dope!

JOE. What?

WADE. No, it ain't that, just...

JOE. I get it. And you're goin' t' go to a cow college that's snooty about your brother. Well, that's up to you. But if it was me, I'd tell 'em to take their college and—y-a-a-anh!

WADE. Look, Joe, let's not get in no argument. Hell fire, I don't want to argue.

JOE. Okay, kid. Where's Uncle Lev? Don't tell me. I know. Runnin' his still.

WADE. [grinning]. Reckon he is.

JOE. But where's Wilma?

WADE. She's over in the top-side cotton patch. I'll go get her. That'll be your room. [Indicating bedroom.] I'll straighten it up a bit. [He goes to the bedroom door.]

LARITA. Hey, wait a minute! [To JOE.] Are we goin' t' hang around here?

JOE [to WADE]. Go on. [WADE goes into the bedroom. To LARITA.] Sit down. Relax!

LARITA [going to the chair by the table and sitting]. I tell you, this is no time to see how the other half lives.

JOE. Ya-a-anh! [His eyes fall on the cotton-picking bag hanging on the kitchen door.] Look-a there! [He takes it down and examines it in delight.]

LARITA [casually]. What's that thing?

JOE [laughs and throws the bag over his shoulder]. I hate to think of the miles I walked with one of these things, pickin' that cotton. Here I'd go. [Bent over, he limps *slowly across the room, as a cotton-picker.*] Reachin' for this'n, grabbin' for that'n, stoopin' for this'n. Sometimes I'd sing a little song—a made-up song. [*He sings an impromptu moaning Negro spiritual while picking the cotton.*] "Lord, I'm weary, in the fi-eeld." [*Turning.*] Sun beatin' down. Hotter'n hell. Mornin' to night. [*He straightens with a mock effort, holding his back.*] Oh, boy, did my back ache! But Jesus, could I sleep! [*Suddenly aware of* LARITA's *look of disgust, he covers his ecstasy with sarcasm.*] You don't know nothin' about that, do you?

LARITA. I wish I could lay down and sleep a *week*—right now.

[JOE *hangs up the bag with a caress.*]

WADE [*reëntering*]. Wilma'll sure be glad to know you're here. [*He leaves by the kitchen door.*]

[JOE *looks about the room; his eyes rest on the fireplace.*]

JOE. We found a snake up that fireplace once. [*He kneels and looks up the chimney.*] A big rattlesnake. Had fourteen rattles. And we killed him. [*He rises, takes up a piece of pine kindling, rubs the rough bark affectionately, holds the wood to his nose, and inhales blissfully.*] Mmm-mh. [*He takes it over to* LARITA.] Smell this. You never smelled no perfume as sweet as pine. Just smell it!

LARITA [*sniffs it to humor him, bored*]. All right....

JOE [*taking the pine stick back to the fireplace, tosses it on the soft ashes*]. The cold mornin's I've got up to start a fire in that baby. You never got up on a cold mornin' to build the fire, did you, Larita—when there was ice solid in the tea kettle?

LARITA [*nastily*]. No.

JOE [*seeing a folded quilt on the foot of the iron cot, goes to it and takes it up*]. Wilma and me'd sleep on pallets in here on the floor. [*He spreads the quilt on the floor and kneels on it.*] That was Pa's and Ma's room in there.

[*Lying on his back on the quilt.*] Pa'd wake up in the mornin' and he'd say, "Joey. Joey!" [*Stretching luxuriantly.*] I wouldn't say nothin', but he'd keep on 'til I grunted. Then he'd say: "Gittin' day. Better git up and start the fire." [*He chuckles.*] He'd never change it. It was always, "Gittin' day." [*He is getting to his feet.*] "Better git up and start the fire."

LARITA. Yeah? Well, we better get goin' before somebody builds a fire under you.

JOE [*coldly, carefully brushing his trousers*]. You wish you wasn't here, don't you, Larita?

LARITA. I don't see anything to sing about. Cheesy dump!

JOE [*throwing the quilt on the cot*]. All right, maybe it ain't so much. But that Chicago slums tenement of yours when you was a kid, you cried about on my shoulder one night—that wasn't so much neither!

LARITA [*springing up*]. Let's get out of here. I can't stand this!

JOE. He-e-ey?

LARITA. I can't understand you! Here we go duckin' and turnin' through the country—drivin' all night!—with you as jumpy as a cat at every headlight you see—holdin' your gun in your lap. And then you walk in here—and all of a sudden you ain't got no cares. You go moonin' around like you was a—gentleman thinkin' about buyin' a country estate!

JOE [*with hard rapture*]. I wish I could buy it—the whole of these hills—and stay here forever!

LARITA. Yeh—and what about the law?

JOE. I feel safe here.

LARITA. Well, I don't. I've lived in holy terror ever since we was twenty miles out of Chicago.

JOE. And you've done nothing but whine ever since.

LARITA. Did I ask to be brought along? I was sleepin' peaceful when you come around at three A.M. and yanked me out of bed.

JOE. [*sarcastically*]. Just a fair-weather floozy!

LARITA. I don't care about bein' filled full of lead.

JOE. It was all very sweet when I was settin' you up, but when a guy gets in a spot—

LARITA. You got value received for everything you give me. Now if we're goin' some place, let's get goin' and not sit around here in the old home place!

JOE [*conciliatory*]. Ah look, baby. I know your nerves are on edge, so are mine.

LARITA. I could pull mine out with tweezers.

JOE. This travelin' at night and snatchin' sleep down a side road by day's been a grind for both of us.

LARITA. It's bad enough out in the open, but at least you're moving. I don't like all these trees and hills around. I feel trapped.

JOE. It's just the other way. Out there I don't have no friends, no safe place I could turn into.

LARITA. Well, what are we here?

JOE. Protected. This ain't a part of the same world. Guys have used these hills for hideouts for years. I began feelin' safe when we started up Wild Dog Mountain back yonder. That's why I tell you to take it easy.

LARITA. O God, I'm tired.... How long we been drivin'? It seems like forever.

JOE. We'll get a good rest here. [*With a humoring laugh.*] The simple life'll do you good.

LARITA. I haven't had a bath for a week. Is there a bathtub in this joint?

JOE [*half-apologetic*]. We always heated water on the stove and poured it in the washtub.

LARITA. The simple life, hunh? Look at my eyes.

Joe. They're beautiful eyes. [*He takes her in his arms and kisses her with rough passion, and with crude tenderness.*] Look, baby, maybe I shouldn't have yanked you out on this trip with me, but I had to have you along. I couldn't a-stood bein' down here with you a thousand miles away.

Larita [*responding to the physical bond between them*]. I appreciate that, honey. Don't think I'm plain yellow.

Joe. Lustree can square this thing if we give him time. We'll lay out here—until things are sweet again for me and you. [Joe *kisses her savagely, then his lips gently brush her cheek, eyelid, and forehead.*] It's when guys get itching pants and can't stay in one place that they get knocked off; they ain't nothin' to be scared about here.

[*Running footsteps are heard outside. They spring apart,* Joe *reaching for his holster.* Uncle Lev *and* Gordon, *hand in hand, appear in the front doorway.*]

Uncle Lev [*amazed, radiant*]. Joe! Joey boy!

Joe [*laughing, happy*]. Uncle Lev!

Uncle Lev [*to him*]. Dang it, Joey, I can't believe my eyes! [Gordon *is standing by the fireplace regarding his father wonderingly.*]

Joe. Well, it's me. Home at last.

Uncle Lev [*pawing* Joe]. I seen that whoppin' big Cadillac rollin' up to the place and I come a-tearin'. 'Y God!

Joe. How'd you like that big hay-burner?

Uncle Lev. Mm-mh! Say, let me look at you. Turn around. [*He turns like a mannequin.*] 'Y God! Guess you got a private tailor, ain't you? [Joe *laughs.*]

Larita. Who's this? The Old Man of the Mountains?

Uncle Lev [*looking* Larita *over*]. Mmmm-mh! Who's she, Joey?

Joe. This is Larita La Monte, Uncle Lev.

[Gordon *comes quietly over to where* Joe *stands, halts,*

hands on hips and legs apart, and regards JOE *with wondering looks.*]

LARITA [*coldly*]. Hello.

UNCLE LEV [*surprised*]. She your woman, Joe?

JOE [*casually*]. She's a friend of mine.

UNCLE LEV. We-e-e-ell! Well... I'll say this, she's sure purty. Purttier'n a picture! Looks like a movie actress.

LARITA [*haughtily*]. It so happens I *am* in the theater.

JOE. Yeh, a burly strip-tease!

LARITA [*hotly*]. Now listen here!

UNCLE LEV. Eeeh-uh! Got spirit, too. That's the way I like 'em.

GORDON. Say, [JOE *turns in surprise.*] are you my Daddy?

JOE. Who'r—? Are you little Gordon?

UNCLE LEV. That's your boy, Joe!

JOE. They sure grow fast. [*He tries to tousle* GORDON'S *hair, but the boy backs away from him. To* UNCLE LEV, *his eyes on the lad.*] I knew when I went North that Ruby was goin' to send him to you, but I forgot about it. Come here, sonny.

GORDON [*simply*]. I don't think I will.

JOE. Hunh?

GORDON. I don't like you.

UNCLE LEV. Here now. Here, here, here!

GORDON. You're not our folks. You ain't like my Daddy.

JOE. Hey, what the hell?

LARITA [*laughing*]. Did *you* ever get told!

JOE. Listen, I'll talk to you later, kid. You git now.

GORDON. I'm goin'. [*He stalks out the front door.*]

JOE [*going to the door and looking after* GORDON]. Say, who's been poisonin' my own kid's mind against me?

UNCLE LEV. Nobody, Joey, nobody. Swear, I can't understand it. I ain't told him nothin' 'cept what a big-shot you are.

JOE. Fresh brat.

LARITA. Well, if you *gentlemen* will excuse me, I think I'll go flop the bones. [*Taking her bag, she goes into the bedroom.*]

JOE [*changing the subject*]. Still rottin' out your guts on that stinkin' corn you make?

UNCLE LEV. That's good corn, Joey. That's lip-lickin' corn. I'll fetch a jug.

JOE. Nanh. I brought along somethin' better for you. [*Opening his bag.*]

UNCLE LEV [*in admiring imitation*]. "Nanh. I brought somethin' better for you." 'Y God, you sure got that up-North talk down pat. Sounds tougher'n a boot.

JOE [*bringing out a bottle*]. I brought you some genu*ine* Scotch.

UNCLE LEV. Scotch whisky? [*He fondles the bottle.*] I've heerd of it, but I ain't never seen none.

JOE. Go on, open it.

UNCLE LEV. Reckon I should ought? Sure is purty.

JOE. You can't drink it with the cork in! [UNCLE LEV *pulls the cork, sniffs speculatively, then takes a long swig, lowers the bottle, and takes on an expression of hopeful expectancy.*] Well, how's it go?

UNCLE LEV. Hell, Joey, it hain't got no taste to it. Tastes like clear runnin' brook water.

JOE [*closing the bag*]. Your cast-iron guts is hopeless. [UNCLE LEV *puts the bottle on the chimneypiece, still smacking his lips in vain.*]

UNCLE LEV. Scotch, huh? Purty fancy. Say, Joey, how'd you manage to git here, anyway. *I* read you's in Minnesota.

JOE. Yeh? That was a plant to shake 'em off my tail.

UNCLE LEV. We'll take care of you. Yes, sir. You tell me about that bank stick-up?

JOE [*coldly*]. I wasn't in on that job. [*Nonchalantly.*] Here, have a cigarette.

UNCLE LEV. Lord God, look at that cigarette box! Pure gold, ain't it? [*He sniffs the cigarette to* JOE's *amusement.*] Ain't goin' t' smoke it. I'll save it. I'll put it in my scrapbook. Say, Joe, you ain't seen my scrapbook, have you? [*He gets it from the foot of the cot and takes it to the table.*] Got every big thing in it that you've been doin' up there in Chicago. Your whole life as a man is right there between these covers. Look-a here! That picture's taken right after you got there and they hauled you up on suspicion of being mixed up in that Loop massacree. Turned you loose, though!

JOE [*quietly*]. I didn't have nothin' to do with it.

UNCLE LEV [*chuckling*]. Yeh! You were too smart for 'em, Joe—and here you are at that hearin' where Oklahoma tried to extradite you and couldn't do it. I figured that was Lustree sittin' back there, ain't it?

JOE. They tried to hang a string of bank robberies a yard long on me.

UNCLE LEV [*excited*]. I know it. Barber Slim—you remember him—down at Beulah? He gets the Chicago papers and saves 'em all for me. All the folks are mighty proud of you, Joe.

JOE. Sure 'nough?

UNCLE LEV. God, yes! I can't get my work done from people wantin' to know what Joe's doin' now. There you are!—'od damn, that's a whizz—look-a there—all dressed up in a monkey suit and a high hat!

JOE. Yeh.

UNCLE LEV. You got them fancy duds with you?

JOE. I got some clothes in the car.

UNCLE LEV. I got an idea. Let's throw a barbecue. A whinger! Folks from all over the hills'll come. We'll have a singin' and dancin'. [*He executes a couple of shuffling steps.*] You and your gal friend—you dress up in your steppin'-out duds and your high hat. Eee-uh! That'll knock 'em stem-windin'.

JOE. What are you talkin' about? You want to tell the whole world where I am? You want the law pourin' in on my tail?

UNCLE LEV. Can't no law get up here without you knowin' it, Joe. Jimmy Goforth is the deputy sheriff down at Beulah now. He lets all the folks know whenever they's a law comin' into the hills. Why, Jimmy was a-talkin' to me just this mornin', tellin' me I'd better not run any mash for a couple of days—'cause they was strangers in town.

JOE. Strangers!

UNCLE LEV. Ain't no use bein' startled. 'Tain't like the old days. Time was when a stranger in Beulah was bound to be a revenooer.

JOE [*sharply*]. What'd these guys look like?

UNCLE LEV. Hell, I didn't see 'em. Nowadays they's more strangers than local folks down yonder.

JOE [*dubiously*]. Yeah?

UNCLE LEV. Yeah. They's buildin' new roads, them C.C.C. boys,* and they's others layin' out resettlement projec's, and reservoirs, and a-terracin' the land, and stringin' highlines—dangdest things you ever seen! They's a-comin' and a-goin'. Nowadays when you see a stranger on the main street of Beulah most likely he's a cannin' expert or a mosquito engineer. [JOE *laughs drily*.] Times is changed. But they ain't goin' t' get back in the hills, Joey. No sir—not without us knowin' it!

JOE. Yah, these hills 'll never change. That's what pulled me back here. I knew that no matter how much of a

---

* Young men in the Civilian Conservation Corps.

jam I was in—I could come back here and it would be just like it was when I was a kid. There was one thing I wanted to see especial.

UNCLE LEV. What was that?

JOE. That big hickory at the edge of the clearing. I thought of that all night last night—while I was drivin'. It was like a beacon light, a-pullin' me home. I thought if I could just see that old hickory tree again I'd get rid of my jitters. [*He paces a few steps to the window and looks out.*]

UNCLE LEV. That so?

JOE. I figured it'd give me a feelin'... a kind of feelin'— [*He stops suddenly; incredulous, shocked, his back to the audience. Evenly.*] Uncle Lev.

UNCLE LEV. Yes?

JOE [*with deadly calm*]. Where is that big hickory?

UNCLE LEV. It's gone, Joey.

JOE. Where'd it go?

UNCLE LEV. Why—there was a blight hit it. There was a big wind one night and it blew down. We cut it up for firewood.

JOE [*rigid*]. That *tree* was the thing I wanted to see!

UNCLE LEV. What's got you wrought up, Joey? It was just a big ol' tree.

JOE [*half turning to him*]. It wasn't just an old tree. I spent the first half of my life under that tree, and up in it, and all around it.

UNCLE LEV. You sure God did. I remember one day you fell out o' that tree and broke your arm. And before you'd even let your ma take you to Beulah to have it set, you threw a rope 'round one of its limbs, hitched on a mule, and broke the limb off. Henh! You did do the queerest things sometimes....

JOE. I was mad at it. It broke my arm, didn't it?

Uncle Lev. Why do you care now then?
Joe. I'd lay under that tree and try to figure things out. How to be somebody—how to make people sit up and take notice of me. And that tree had the answer. Stand on your own feet and go shootin' right on up, big and strong, and to hell with the weaklin's around you! There wasn't nothin' growin' near that tree. It took what it wanted for itself.
Uncle Lev. I never knew you felt all that about it. [*He pulls the whistle and knife from his pocket and goes to* Joe.] Remember when I showed you how to whittle a whistle off'n that hickory? I'm showin' your little Gordon how to make hickory whistles now. [Uncle Lev *passes the whistle and knife to* Joe, *who looks stolidly down at them.*] Here, take it.... [Joe *still gazing out the window, takes them.* Uncle Lev *stands indecisively for a moment, then shuffles to the table.*]
Joe [*quietly*]. I used to lay up in that tree whittlin' on one of these thinkin' I'd go nuts if somethin' didn't happen besides the same old thing day after day.
Uncle Lev. You was always one for action, all right. I remember we'd go fishin' on Bear Creek and after a time when the fish wouldn't bite you'd jump up and down yellin': "Let's get some dynamite and *blow* the bastards out!" [Joe *laughs drily.*]
Joe. It's funny when a guy is in a jam, he gets to thinkin' about an old tree....
Uncle Lev [*remembering*]. I got an ol' pencil here, Joey. Wonder if you'd mind autographin' my scrapbook. You know—like them movie stars do! Here—on the last page —only page ain't got a story on it yet. Got t' get me a new book. Write sumpin in it for me, Joe!
[Joe *puts down the whistle and knife and stares at the pages of the scrapbook. Then he seizes the pencil, writes.*]

Uncle Lev [*reading*]. "This is all a lie—Joe Heatherstone." [*Then chuckling.*] Won't the hill folks get a kick out o' seein' that!

[Wilma *appears in the kitchen doorway. Joy, sorrow, fear, and unbelief cry out in her. She takes two hesitating steps toward* Joe.]

Joe [*embracing her*]. Wilma!

Wilma. Oh, Joe! Joe!

Joe. Take it easy, Sis.

Uncle Lev [*grimly*]. Yes, don't git so messy.

Wilma. You're in danger, Joe?

Joe [*dismissing the idea*]. No.

Wilma. Do they know you're in this country?

Joe. They think I'm a thousand miles north of here. Now just relax, Sis; everything's okay. [*He leads her to the easy chair and seats her in it. He sits on the footstool by her holding her hands.*] Now let's just you and me talk.

Wilma. Oh, Joe. You poor boy!

Joe. Ah now, let's not worry about me; let's talk about you.

Wilma. What happened, Joe? I thought you was through with the bank hold-ups and killin's.

Joe. Lustree needed some dough—he laid out this job for three of us guys—something went wrong—that's all.

Wilma. I can't believe that every law in this country has orders to—s-shoot you on sight.

Joe [*irritated, weaving his hands*]. A-h-h-h....

Uncle Lev [*listening and turning through his scrapbook*]. Don't prod a man that-a-way, Wilma.

Joe [*avoiding her look*]. You ain't lookin' so well, Sis.

Wilma [*quietly*]. I ain't been well.

Joe. All this work's too much for you, takin' care of Wade and Uncle Lev since Ma died.

Wilma. I don't mind. There ain't much to do no more; the land's all gone.

UNCLE LEV. Soil's all washed right off'n the rocks.

JOE. Uh . . . what you got in cultivation now?

WILMA. Well, Uncle Lev had five acres of corn.

UNCLE LEV. And I'm tellin' you, it wasn't worth shuckin'—mostly thumb nubbins.

WILMA. Wade and me's got ten acres of cotton we're pickin' now.

JOE. Ten acres? That top-side patch is forty acres.

WILMA. We seeded the forty three times, and we got ten acres.

JOE. What you gettin' for cotton?

WILMA. Six cents a pound.

JOE. God a-mighty! I remember we once got thirty-five bales off that forty at thirty cents a pound.

WILMA. We won't make two bales. The farm's all gone, Joe.

JOE. I hate to think that. But maybe you need a new place. I got plenty of dough now. I'll leave it with you, and you can buy you a new place.

UNCLE LEV [*excited*]. Sure 'nuff, Joe? 'Y God, that's generous of you. We'll git us a hundred and sixty acres of bottom land in McIntosh County, and—

WILMA. No.

UNCLE LEV. Eh?

WILMA. I said no.

JOE. What you mean, Wilma?

WILMA. There's a way of doin' it that's slower, but I like it better. When Wade goes to A. and M. he'll learn things about farmin' we never knowed, and we'll take a new start then.

UNCLE LEV. There you go. Always, Wade's goin' t' do this, and Wade's goin' t' do that! Let him get filled up with that perfesser stuff and a fine farmer he'll make.

JOE. That's all right. I don't put much stock in it, but if that's the way you want it, that's all right.

UNCLE LEV [*grumbling, goes to get his hat*]. Have them long-legged guv'ament men all over the place, tellin' you how to do everything, even to buttonin' up your pants. I'm goin' out and see your autymobile, Joe.

JOE. Okay.

UNCLE LEV [*looking off*]. 'Od damn, I'd sure like to ride with you in 'er. You'd drive 'er and I'd lean out the back and shoot 'em off our tail. [*Chuckling, he goes out the front door.*]

JOE. At least you're goin' t' let me give you money to get yourself some things.

WILMA. I don't want any of your money, Joe.

JOE. You ain't ashamed of it....

WILMA. I'm afraid of it. It's caused you enough misery without bringin' it on us.

JOE. I don't know. I ain't done so bad. That chair and lamp—and that radio there—they ain't caused you no misery, have they?

WILMA. No....

JOE [*striking a more cheerful note*]. How'd you like that stuff anyway?

WILMA. Fine, Joe. It was nice of you to send it.

JOE. I should-a been doin' more for you. I didn't know you was this bad off. Get some good music on that radio?

WILMA. We don't have ... electricity.

JOE [*rising, walking down right*]. What? Now—wasn't that dumb of me? Wasn't that dumb of me. 'Course that lamp wouldn't work neither.

WILMA. No.

JOE. Aw, nuts! I got that lamp for Ma to sew by.

WILMA. They're all purty, anyway.

JOE [*sitting in the rocker*]. Did Ma get to sit in the chair before she died? [*Indicating the easy chair.*]

WILMA. A little. She didn't set in it much, though.

JOE. No?

WILMA. She'd set in it a while and then she'd get to thinkin' and worryin' about you...then she'd cry. So she'd get up and set in her own little rocker there—said it fit her better.

JOE. I bought a box of flowers for her grave at a place on the way last night.

WILMA. That was nice—

JOE. But when I opened 'em this mornin' they'd wilted—so I throwed 'em away.

WILMA. Don't you want to see her grave?

JOE. Maybe I will after a while.

WILMA. It's in a pretty spot above the spring draw over yonder a piece—willows growin' around it. [*After a pause.*] You're awful unhappy, ain't you, Joe?

JOE [*resolutely*]. I don't know.

WILMA. Then why'd you decide to come back here?

JOE. Ah, there was a kind of loneliness hit me. A fellow gets in a jam, and he knows every place he goes they're lookin' for him and a-waitin' for him. A guy gets tired....

WILMA. You *are* tired, Joe.

JOE. I ain't slept. I thought I'd just come home for a spell to get a feelin' of peace again.

WILMA. Have you got it—a feelin' of peace?

JOE [*rising and pacing away a few steps*]. No, things ain't the same; the place is beginning to give me the jitters.

WILMA. Have you *ever* had a feelin' of peace, Joe?

JOE. Hunh?

WILMA. Even as a boy you were never at rest. You was born under a strange star. Wherever you are, there's always a storm comes up. You bring sorrow, wherever you go.

JOE. That's a hell of a way to talk....

WILMA. How long's it been since you've really laughed, Joe?

JOE. You ain't doin' so much to cheer a guy up.

WILMA. It's been many a year since thinking of you brought a happy look to the face of any one here at home—except to your Uncle Lev.

JOE. You mean... you don't want... me here? [JOE *is obviously nervous in his movements now.*]

WILMA. We want you as long as you'll stay.

JOE. I thought this was the one place in the world I could come to. I can't understand you, Wilma; you've changed somehow....

WILMA. Did you expect to come back here and find everything just as it was when you left?

JOE. I did, but things ain't like I remembered 'em....

WILMA. You picked one way to go, and left us to go another. We been walkin' down our road; you went runnin' down yours. Now you're tired of runnin' and you don't see nothin' at the end. And you thought you could turn back to the startin' place and we'd be there just the same.

JOE. A man should ought to be able to come back to his own home—to his own folks when he needs them.

WILMA. A man like you can't. The home you left ain't here any more. And it's not that we've changed so much; it's you that's different. You don't see it the same, that's all.

JOE. You don't see me the same, I guess.

WILMA. I can see you, Joe—plain. It's been growin' in my heart, and it grieves me to say it, but I know it's true. You chose to live by violence, Joe, and when a man goes out and destroys, he goes on until he's destroyed the same way.

JOE [*grimly*]. I can take care of myself.

WILMA. There's a thousand pistols out yonder—waitin' to be aimed at your heart.

JOE [*abruptly*]. God damn it, you drive a man nuts!

WILMA. Have you seen your little Gordon?
JOE [*vaguely*]. I saw him....
WILMA. What way will he go? Your way, or the way Wade's goin'?
JOE. Wade! Wade! Why throw him up to me? What's so wonderful about a guy that wants to be a farmer?
WILMA. He's goin' the way you could have gone.
JOE [*in sheer self-defense*]. I *like* the way I'm goin'.
WILMA. Have you seen Ruby?
JOE [*surprised*]. Ruby?
WILMA. Didn't you know she was here?
JOE. No, I didn't.
WILMA. She called to me as I passed her cabin. She ought to be over in a minute.
JOE. What's she doin' up here?
WILMA. Strange that Wade or Uncle Lev didn't tell you.
JOE [*looking toward the bedroom door*]. I know why they didn't.
WILMA. Why?
JOE. Look, I been goin' with a dame. I brought her with me; she's in the bedroom there now.
WILMA. Joe! This'll bring more tears.
JOE. Ah, well, I want to see Ruby anyway. I want to talk to her ... about divorcing me.
WILMA [*shocked*]. You don't care for Ruby any more, Joe?
JOE. Ah, Ruby's all right. [*Reflective.*] We had some swell times together.
WILMA. She was a good wife to you.
JOE. Yeah, but we were just kids then.
WILMA. You think you've outgrown her.
JOE [*defending himself*]. If you knew the big town, you'd see she wouldn't fit in there; she wouldn't like it.
WILMA. She'd embarrass you...?
JOE [*a false denial*]. Nah, but the women up there—they're

different. They got t' know how to wear snappy clothes, how to act. Lustree's even got a box at the Op'ra, and asks me to go there with him sometimes. Can you see Ruby in an op'ra box?

WILMA. No....

JOE. There you are— Ruby'll take it all right, she's a good kid. But she's not the woman for me any more. You said yourself that things are bound to change—some things a man has to put behind him.

[RUBY *appears in the front doorway. Incongruously she wears high-heeled slippers, but no stockings, has on a tight-fitting dress which seems altogether unsuited to her, and has tidied up her hair neatly.*]

RUBY [*simply*]. Honey...!

JOE [*not unkindly, but not easily*]. Hello, Ruby.

RUBY [*the timid woman before her master*]. Gordon told me you was here. I'd a-been over sooner, but I stopped to pretty-up a bit.

JOE. I didn't know you was livin' out here.

RUBY [*naïvely*]. I run out of money. I worked as a waitress in Muskogee and Henrietta and some other places, but [*With a little laugh.*] every time I'd get a job, the law'd tell the boss who I was—and he'd fire me.

JOE. If I'd a-knowed where you was, I'd a-sent you some dough.

RUBY [*kindly*]. I wrote you a lot of letters.

JOE [*lying*]. I must not a-got 'em.

RUBY. Joe....

JOE. Yeah...?

RUBY [*from her heart*]. If you're in trouble... if you need me... you know I'd—

WILMA. Wait, Ruby. Joe has something to say—

JOE [*interrupting her*]. I'll handle my own affairs, Wilma.

RUBY. Joe... you... ain't kissed me yet.

JOE. A-h-h-h... Well, I don't know how to put it except straight out. Look, Ruby, since we saw each other last, I been a lot of places and seen a lot of things.
RUBY. I know.
JOE. Bein' away that long, and meetin' different people—
[LARITA *enters from the bedroom. She is wearing a trailing pink negligée and bedroom slippers.*]
LARITA. Your yammering woke me up. [*With all the stateliness of a burlesque queen she comes up beside* JOE *and carelessly puts an arm around his shoulder.*] Are these the ladies of the Heatherstone clan?
JOE [*in surrender*]. Okay. This is Larita. My sister, and Ruby.
LARITA. Oh, the little wife! [*Angrily.*] Did we come here so you could see her?
JOE [*annoyed*]. No, I didn't know she was here.
RUBY [*naïvely*]. Is she... travelin' with you?
JOE. Yes, she is.
RUBY [*turning away*]. Oh...!
WILMA [*going to* RUBY]. Joe, wherever you are, you bring trouble and tears.
JOE. This ain't nothin' to bawl about.
RUBY [*simply*]. I ain't goin' to cry.
JOE. You see, it's okay with Ruby.
WILMA. Yes, it's okay with Ruby, because she's always thought of you as her man—and her man couldn't do wrong to her—even though somebody else might think so.
JOE [*quizzically*]. What does that make me?
WILMA. Just blind, Joe, blind. It's a good thing for Ruby you are. She'll be safe and at peace with us here—with us and her boy.
LARITA [*sneering*]. Keepin' the home fires burnin'.
WILMA. I'd like you better if you didn't gloat.
LARITA. Gloat? I should be stuck up because the guy I'm

with turns his nose up at somethin' like that? [*Indicating* Ruby.]

Joe. Hey-y-y!

Wilma [*looking* Larita *over*]. You were right, Joe. Ruby ain't like the kind of women you've come to know.

Larita. Listen, lay off those hill-billy wisecracks about me.

Joe. What's the idea jumpin' on Larita?

Ruby [*simply*]. Don't quarrel over me, Wilma.

Wilma. I ain't pickin' your women for you, Joe. That's your business. But before you get to actin' too superior to Ruby, I think you ought to realize that Ruby here is a woman who'd go acrosst the world for you—and, on the other hand I don't know about Miss Lamonte! Maybe she is the right woman for you—I ain't so used to women in silks and satin—but—

Larita. You don't need to know about me, sister—I'll tell you! I didn't ask to be brought on this little junket. I'm a hothouse plant myself—and it don't make me so happy to think about bein' in that front seat when the tommies start sprayin'. So if you'll just hitch up the horse and buggy, or whatever you ride in around here, and get me to the nearest railroad station, I'll—

Joe [*in a rage*]. Shut up!

Wilma [*quietly, after a pause*]. Well, Joe...?

[Joe *stands tense, trembling, his last defense gone. He turns to* Wilma *and* Ruby, *then lashes out at* Larita.]

Joe. Get your things. We're gettin' out of here.

Larita. But where?

Joe [*desperately smothering hysterical fury*]. I don't know. Some place. Any place. Get goin'.

Larita [*retreating in fear*]. No. No!

Joe. Get your bag—you can dress in the car. Go on! [*She goes into the bedroom.*]

Wilma. Joe, don't! Calm down. You mustn't go like this.

JOE. Calm down! Good God! I knew this was my last chance! I knew there wasn't no place else. I figured this was the one place—but it's all wrong. It's all wrong. It didn't work—you're all against me!
WILMA. We're not against you, Joe.
JOE. You want to drive me out. My own son don't like me and you run my wife in on me. [UNCLE LEV *enters the front door, startled.*] And you, cacklin' about strange guys bein' down in Beulah. [*He seizes* UNCLE LEV *by the front of his overalls.*] Who was those guys?
UNCLE LEV [*hesitant*]. I don't know, Joey....
JOE. How do I know you're not in with 'em—tryin' to put the finger on me!
UNCLE LEV [*deeply hurt*]. Joey!
JOE. Anh-h-h-h! [*He pushes* UNCLE LEV *away.* WADE *enters from the kitchen.*] And Wade! [*Crossing to him.*] Wade, the little darlin', the farmer boy—the guy I could-a been, hunh? [*The two brothers stand facing each other,* WADE *puzzled,* JOE *trembling with hate as he studies his brother from bare feet to athletic sweater. As if to destroy a ghost of his own lost soul, he suddenly slaps* WADE *hard.* WADE *spins away.*]
WILMA [*as* JOE *looks at* WADE *in bewilderment*]. I think that's enough, Joe.
JOE. Anh-h-h-h. [LARITA *reënters from the bedroom, her mink coat over the negligée, her hat and bag in her hand.* JOE *goes to the table for his bag.*] Come on!
LARITA. I don't want to go. I'll be killed. I'll be killed!
JOE. What of it? [*He goes to the front door.*] Get out to the car.
LARITA. I'm afraid to go out there. You said yourself we must stay here.
JOE [*bluntly*]. I've changed my mind.
LARITA. I won't go! You can't make me go!

JOE [*drawing his Luger*]. I can't? [*Coldly.*] Now come on! [*In abject terror,* LARITA *goes, knowing death awaits them outside.*]

UNCLE LEV. Joey boy, don't leave us like this. You're makin' a mistake.

JOE [*staring at* WADE, WILMA, *and* RUBY]. I've made a lot of mistakes.

[GORDON *edges into the doorway opposite* JOE, *slides on past him and goes to* WILMA *who takes him in her arms. The lad looks fearfully at* JOE. JOE, *with a gesture of despair, goes out the door.*]

WILMA [*quietly*]. We'll never see him again. He'll go tearin' through the country till they get him.

[UNCLE LEV *goes to the door and looks off as the automobile starts and roars off.*]

UNCLE LEV. Joe always did all right till he lost his temper. Maybe he'll cool off.

WILMA. Joe knows his string's run out.

UNCLE LEV [*sadly*]. It's hard to think of ... but if it is, we'll give him a funeral, Wilma. It'll be the biggest funeral these hills has ever seen. Thousands of folks will come! It'll be a big story—a hell of a big story! The last one ... in my scrapbook.... [*With tender finality.*]

[UNCLE LEV *starts shuffling up to the front door, hat in hand.* WILMA *sits in the big easy chair, holding* GORDON *to her.* WADE *sits disconsolately on the iron cot, and* RUBY *sits on the footstool weeping silently.*]

UNCLE LEV. Was you ... goin' t' say somethin' ... ?

WILMA. No. I ... ain't got nothin' to say....

[WILMA *looks straight ahead, dry-eyed.* UNCLE LEV *puts on his hat and shuffles out the front door as*

THE CURTAIN FALLS

TEXAS

WEST FROM THE PANHANDLE
A TRAGEDY OF THE DUST BOWL

BY CLEMON WHITE AND BETTY SMITH
OF LUFKIN, TEXAS, AND CHAPEL HILL, NORTH CAROLINA

Written in the playwriting course at the University of North Carolina and originally produced by The Carolina Playmakers at Chapel Hill on May 26, 1938.

THE CHARACTERS

CLINT DEATON.........................Sam Hirsch
FRONIE, *his wife*......................Gwen Pharis
MAY BELLE, *his elder daughter*........Rietta Bailey
HOOVER, *his younger son*..........Merwin Van Hecke
CALVIN, *his older son*.................Julian Hayes
ROSE, *his younger daughter*..........Hilda Lawrence
DAVE JOHNSON, *a stranger*............Henry Nigrelli

SCENE: *Somewhere east of Santa Fe on the highway from Amarillo, Texas, to Los Angeles.*
TIME: *The present. An early evening in autumn.*

Copyright, 1938, by The Carolina Playmakers, Inc.
All rights reserved.

THE TREK FROM TEXAS

THE first pioneers to Texas packed their belongings—the high chest that came over from England, a bundle of rosebush cuttings, the heirloom quilts, the musket, the ax, the little one's rag doll, and the half-grown dog that the boy smuggled into the canvas-top wagon—and turned their horses westward.

There the land was rich and fertile and could be had for the taking. They cleared the land, chopped down the trees, and burned off the timber. The grass was plowed up and the roots left to wither. The rich land was plowed, sowed, and the crops harvested. This cycle was repeated again and again. Succeeding generations used the land greedily with no thought of replenishing it.

The floods came, then the droughts. The wind blew and brought the dust storms. The driving rains loosened the life-giving topsoil. The sun dried it to a fine powder. The furious winds blew up a cloud of never-ending dust and rode the soil down to the river. The muddied waters joined the mighty river, the Mississippi, and the land was carried south and deposited in the Gulf of Mexico.

And the people who owned this land—our people who lived in the Texas Panhandle—packed their belongings and turned their faces westward. They had heard tell that there was new land to the west. They trekked west, trying to out-trudge the oncoming winter.

You may see them on the highway from Amarillo to Los Angeles. They have left behind them the Panhandle dust bowl and are traveling west. They travel in families. Sometimes, they ride in a broken-down, twenty-dollar Ford. More often they are afoot, with a two-wheeled, high-sided push-wagon holding their tattered quilts, their cooking pans, a rifle, and perhaps a child too sick or too young to walk. There is the father, a tall, angular, beaten-looking farmer; a ragged, wasted-looking woman walking by his side; a young girl, her sweet, fresh face with already a tracing of bitter lines; a youth, impatient with the old order, who believes he will fix things right when he grows up. Sometimes there is a smaller boy leading a half-starved dog.

They are walking westward into the sunset, where there is new land to be had. They are not factory people, not office people, not city people; they are land people. They are going west looking for a new land.

Sometimes a child is born along the road. More often one dies, coughing its life away, a victim of dust pneumonia. Sometimes there is a meeting along the way: a restless, young man going west falls in with the family. The young man looks at the daughter of the family. Little is said, but much is understood. And at night when the tired old ones are sleeping along the side of the road, the young people watch the moon riding across the prairie sky, and they make plans for the future. "We'll be different, we two," they assure each other. And the soft prairie wind mocks them.

West from the Panhandle is an American tragedy of people driven from their homes by the dust. They are the children of those who left their homes over a century ago to tame the wild land. They trudge the dusty road seeking a new frontier. They live their lives walking to the west. They dream of happiness again: a whitewashed house in a broad field, a little road coming up to it, and a mailbox a few hundred yards down the public road. And on the road of their wasteland is a whitened cow's skull with a prairie rose growing from it.

WEST FROM THE PANHANDLE

It is the fall of the year and the DEATON *family with a push-wagon full of household supplies is trekking westward. They are walking along a concrete highway in that part of western Texas known as the Panhandle. The road being the Amarillo to Los Angeles highway. On either side is the expanse of prairie earth, its rounded bareness broken only by a few bleached boulders. The road descends from the left, in the rear of the scene.*
It is just before evening and the tendrils of a red and yellow sunset shatter the chill blue of the sky.

[*The* DEATON *family is coming up over the rise. They are walking westward to California.* CLINT, *the father, is in the lead, pushing the cart. He is a tall, angular, beaten-looking farmer.*]
[CLINT *has just pushed the cart over the rise and is shouting to the people who are coming after him. It is the call of a man driving against time.*]
CLINT [*shouting*]. Come on. They's sure to be a town on the other side.
[ROSE, *a frail girl of ten, lies quietly in the cart along with some of the family's possessions.* CLINT *stops, leans heavily against the cart, pulls his hat off and strokes his unkempt face. High above is heard the faint "Honk! Honk!" of wild geese. He throws his head back and follows their flight with his eyes.*]
CLINT. Going south. Flying down to God and plenty.

[HOOVER, *a ragged lean lad of eight, runs over the rise, lugging a battered shotgun.*]

HOOVER. Papa, it's geese. Shoot them!

CLINT [*shading his eyes to see them*]. They're flying too high, boy, and it's getting too dark. We can't be wasting no shells.

HOOVER. But we could eat them. It would be better than eating prairie dog.

CLINT [*looking back over the rise.*] God Almighty, why don't they come on? We got to make a couple more miles 'fore night falls.

HOOVER [*disconsolately*]. You said there might be a town just over this hill, Papa.

CLINT [*heedless of the boy*]. Might as well stand still and wait for the winds to tote us to California.

[FRONIE *comes trudging over the rise with tattered quilts folded and strapped to her back. She is a ragged, wasted woman with a face of eternal stone, all the warmth, color, and vibrancy wiped out of it.*]

FRONIE. We're all worn out trying to keep up with you, Clint.

CLINT [*doggedly*]. We got to keep moving. [*Pointing.*] You see them geese, Fronie? Angling across the red in the southwest?

FRONIE [*rubbing her eyes*]. They's so much New Mexico dirt in my eyes, I can't see nothing. [*She takes the quilts off her back and sits down on them wearily.*]

CLINT. That means that winter is on its way down. It'll fall on us 'fore we know it. We got t' push on.

FRONIE. If it would only wait till we get to California.

[MAY BELLE *comes over the rise, a haunting wisp of a girl about seventeen. She has a beautifully chiseled face, quiet and composed. She wears torn overalls and carries a large* cardboard carton. *She sets this down and drops exhausted upon it.*]

FRONIE. Where's Calvin, May Belle?

MAY BELLE. Coming.

CLINT [*making a megaphone of his hands*]. Hurry up, Calvin. That boy's so slow, he couldn't catch the seven-years-itch.

[ROSE, *in the cart, coughs deeply. She tries to twist her cramped body.*]

FRONIE [*bending over her*]. How you feeling, Rose?

ROSE. Water, Mama.

CLINT [*looking over the countryside*]. I wouldn't give God one grand hallelujah for any of the land I've seen since we left the Panhandle.

FRONIE. Clint, we ain't got a drop of water. We ain't passed a filling station since noontime.

HOOVER [*sitting on the ground, out of the way, the gun beside him*]. Papa, I'm tired.

CLINT. We'll have to send Calvin after some water. [*He goes to the rise and looks back.*] You see that clump of cottonwoods along that draw?

FRONIE [*looking patiently*]. That's just this side of where we left from early this morning.

HOOVER. We ain't never going to get to California, are we?

CLINT. Not if we don't keep moving. We got to make it on to the next filling station or town 'fore we stop.

MAY BELLE. It's getting dark. Papa, let's stop right here.

[*From this point on, the sunset fades gradually and night comes on.*]

HOOVER. I like this hill. You can see half of the world from here. But I'm tired and I got a gnawing feeling like my stomach had teeth.

MAY BELLE [*stretching out by the road*]. I could sleep right here on this road forever.

FRONIE. Get up from there, May Belle. A car might come along.

MAY BELLE [*sitting up*]. I ain't seen a car in over an hour.

HOOVER. I saw one back yonder awhile ago.

CLINT [*to* CALVIN, *who is coming on over the rise*]. Shake a leg, boy. We got to keep moving.

[CALVIN *is a spindly, gangling boy of fifteen, dressed in ragged overalls which flap loosely on his weather-beaten frame and wearing a cap on his shaggy head. His face is drawn.*]

CALVIN. I'm petered out, I tell you. I'm tired.

FRONIE. Since it's getting dark and all of us is tired, and Rose is worse, don't you think we better stop?

CLINT. We can't stop.

FRONIE. If you'd only listen to us—

CLINT. If I listen to you all and we quit walking every time one of you complained, we'd be in one hell of a fix.

CALVIN. What do you think we're in now?

CLINT. We're getting along. We ain't dead, and we're going somewhere.

CALVIN. Rose ain't far from dead.

FRONIE. We got to take care of Rose.

CLINT. I'm the one that has to worry about you all.

CALVIN. And you got to kill us all 'cause you're set on going west. How do you know they's any promised land there?

CLINT. Is there anything for us back in that dust bowl? About the time a man plants his feet down and thinks he's standing on bottom at last, along comes a whirlwind out of the north and blows the land from under his feet.

FRONIE. You complain too much, Clint.

CLINT. A man's got a right to complain now that the land's all drifted away from us. [*He grasps the handles of the cart.*] Come on. We're going to travel this highway west.

CALVIN. This ain't no open highway. Didn't you see that detour sign back yonder? It said the highway is under construction. Why don't you read what the signs say?

CLINT. Boy, why in God's name didn't you tell me? We may have to turn back.

CALVIN. I been trying to catch you for an hour to tell you. I yelled, but you was high-tailing it right on down this road.

CLINT. Troubles! Troubles! [*Wiping his forehead.*] I guess we better stop here, then. Hoover, see if you can find a few mesquite limbs to build a fire with. [HOOVER *goes off.* FRONIE *and* MAY BELLE *form a circle of small boulders in which to build a fire.*] Calvin, push the cart out there so's it'll shut off a little dust if the wind gets started to raisin' hell.

CALVIN [*trying to move the cart*]. Give me a hand, May Belle. [MAY BELLE *helps him move the cart out of the way.* ROSE *stirs.* FRONIE *goes to her.*]

FRONIE. Are you asleep, Rose? [*She feels her forehead.*] Maybe we'll soon be getting some place where we can stop for a few days to let you get better. Some place where the dust ain't blowing.

[MAY BELLE *spreads out a newspaper and weights it down with stones.*]

CLINT [*taking a lantern from the cart, he lights it and hangs it on the back of the cart*]. We'll leave early in the morning.

FRONIE [*looking at* ROSE]. She's as patient as all eternity. I kind o' wish she'd complain a little.

MAY BELLE [*looking into the cart*]. She must be suffering awful. Look at that sweat on her forehead.

CLINT. It's a cool time of year for a person to be sweating.

CALVIN [*looking at* ROSE. *Now all excepting* HOOVER *are by the cart*]. It ain't a natural sweat. It's in big beads.

CLINT. It's wrong for a human being to have moisture on his body when there's nothing but dry dust floating across the country. We got the dry floor of every puddle hole from Oklahoma to California damming up our lungs. [FRONIE *is staring at him, frightened about the child.*] Quit looking at me like that.

FRONIE. I wasn't looking no way, Clint. [*Befuddled.*] I had a dream last night. Seems like the Panhandle was just like it used to be when we started out there together before we had the children. Only in my dream, there was trees.

CLINT. Don't get started telling dreams again. [*The spell is broken. All move away from the cart.* CALVIN, *exhausted, sits on the ground.*] Boy, get off your hind end and go find some water.

CALVIN. I got to rest some first.

CLINT. The world wasn't made to rest in, boy.

[CALVIN *takes the jug and goes off over the rise to look for water.* CLINT *unloads the cart. He takes out a cooking pot, another lantern, and other cooking utensils.*]

MAY BELLE. Mama, are we going to eat prairie dog again to-night?

FRONIE. Maybe not.

MAY BELLE. Thank God!

FRONIE. Maybe we ain't even got any of that left.

MAY BELLE. I can't eat it again. My stomach turns inside out just thinking of it.

FRONIE. Be thankful your papa is good enough with a gun to kill one of them.

CLINT. Might be able to kill us a rabbit to-morrow, if the shells hold out.

FRONIE. Aye, Lord! If anybody had a-told me five-six years ago when we was planting seventy-five acres to cotton and that much to wheat, that to-day—

CLINT [*interrupting*]. May Belle, go help Hoover find some brush. [*He places a folded quilt on the ground upstage.*]
MAY BELLE [*going after* HOOVER]. Mama, why don't you set down and rest yourself?
FRONIE. Rose is cramped in that cart.
CLINT. We'll take her out and put her down over here so's she'll be close to the fire when we build it. [*He lifts* ROSE *from the cart and places her gently on the folded quilt.*]
FRONIE. I dreamed about her dying out in this desert. I dreamed she never saw California.
CLINT [*gently*]. Soon she won't need worrying about no more. [*Passionately.*] I worry more about the rest of us with winter getting restless in the north and us with no clothes, no money, nothing to eat and away out here at nowhere. We just *got* to get to California.
FRONIE. We can take care of ourselves. She can't! She, that was never any too strong, she can't!
CLINT [*awkwardly putting his hand on her shoulder*]. You're a pitiful thing to look at, Fronie. But one time you were as purty as one of them prairie roses.
FRONIE [*with shame-faced affection*]. Why you can't help it if I ain't now.
CLINT [*quietly*]. I know that. But a man can't help but feel like—a man never knows what's ahead of him. He gets to wondering about it all.
FRONIE. Maybe God will get it all figured out some day.
CLINT. God ain't heard Hisself thunder in the last twenty years.
HOOVER [*entering with a few small faggots*]. Papa, let's build a big fire and set around and talk. [*He gives them to* CLINT *who starts the fire*].
CLINT. Can't build much of a fire with just that handful of wood.

HOOVER [*ready to cry*]. I couldn't find no more. Seems like I walked a hundred miles to get this.

CLINT. Never mind, son. May Belle will find some more.

HOOVER. Make it shoot out sparks, Papa.

FRONIE. I'll be glad for the fire. It's lonely and cold out here with so much space.

MAY BELLE [*entering with a few sticks of wood which she gives to her father*]. Away from this spot, you'd think all the world was dead. There ain't nothing moving and the prairie is empty of everything. [*She smiles.*] Except I saw a whitened cow's skull with a prairie rose growing out of it. Somehow ... it looked awful pretty.

HOOVER [*flattening out on his stomach*]. I saw a star fall last night.

MAY BELLE. Maybe it was the same one I saw. It fell like something that went dead.

FRONIE [*bringing the stewing pot down to the fire*]. We'll warm this over again. Wish we had bread. But there's no corn meal and no water if we had meal.

HOOVER. See, Papa, you traded off my dog for meal. And now *it's* gone and we ain't got the dog either.

[FRONIE *and* CLINT *look at each other for a long moment. Then they turn away.*]

FRONIE. To-morrow, if we come to a town we can stop. Maybe you can get a few hours of work and we can buy some meal.

CLINT. No chance of getting work. [*He moves about restlessly.*] We've got to keep moving down this streaked road even if we have to suck dry sticks to keep our bellies from growling.

FRONIE. *We* can keep going a while longer, but Rose, she'll have to have something.

[HOOVER *has fallen asleep.* CLINT *crosses to look down at* ROSE.]

CLINT. We'll try to get something for Rose. [*Passionately.*] But I don't expect to run into no lake of wheat or any wonder city with banana towers or mountains of pure gold.
MAY BELLE. Why did we leave home if we can't expect better?
CLINT. 'Cause we couldn't stay. That's the onliest reason.
[DAVE JOHNSON *enters from over the rise. He is about twenty-five, rather shabbily dressed, and carries a bundle, neatly wrapped in newspaper and tied with white string, under his arm.*]
DAVE. Hello! [*They all stare at him.*]
CLINT. Howd'y'.
DAVE. There's a chill in the air and your fire looks mighty good.
CLINT. Come around and get closer to it.
DAVE [*crossing to the fire*]. Thanks. I'm hitch-hiking to California. My ride stopped back at the detour. Thought I'd walk to the next town, but it don't seem very close to hand. Would you mind if I stopped off here for awhile? It's been a long day.
CLINT [*uncomfortably*]. It's a free parking place. Nowhere to sleep but on the ground, though.
DAVE [*staring at* MAY BELLE]. There's a whole family of you here. Where you heading for?
CLINT. California. We come from the Texas Panhandle where we was drove out by dust storms.
DAVE. The Mississippi Delta Flood put me on the road empty-handed and homeless.
CLINT. Seems like the soil, the sun, the wind, and the waters do what they want with us.
DAVE [*not taking his eyes off* MAY BELLE]. I lost my folks.
CLINT. I hear tell they don't have dust storms and floods in California.

DAVE. They will when folks use up the land there like they did everywhere else.

CLINT. They's a lot of new land to the west. We're a-going west. My folks moved away from Georgia when the land gave out.

DAVE. Soon there will be no west to move to. What will happen when you wear out California?

CLINT. We'll all be dead and gone by that time.

FRONIE. That's what your Pa said about the Texas Panhandle.

CLINT. They's always more land to the west.

DAVE. No. The day when we got out and burned timber off land because we wanted to plant a cotton patch is gone forever.

CLINT. Boy, you talk way over my head. [*To* FRONIE.] Time to eat?

FRONIE. I'm worried about Calvin. He was so tired, he might have fallen asleep somewhere.

MAY BELLE. I suppose he had to go a long way after water.

FRONIE. What we've got to eat is setting out here.

CLINT [*sitting down to the food*]. Will you eat with us?

DAVE. Like to. Smells good. I got part of a loaf of bread here.

MAY BELLE. Tell him what it is first, Mama.

FRONIE [*patiently*]. It might change his taste, May Belle.

DAVE. That's a sweet name.

FRONIE [*slowly*]. We're eating dog meat. Prairie dog.

DAVE [*hesitantly*]. I never ate any dog meat. [*As if to dismiss any repugnance.*] But I don't guess it's as bad as some of the stuff I got handed to me in the back streets of Philadelphia—or Charleston—or Mobile.

CLINT [*starting to eat*]. We have to live on what we can get along the road.

[DAVE *takes part of a loaf of bread from his packet and hands it to* FRONIE. *He sits next to* CLINT.]

DAVE. Maybe there'll be enough bread to go around.
FRONIE [*tearing the bread into portions and setting it in the middle of the newspapers. She takes a small piece of the bread*]. It's the first flour bread we've had in a long time.
MAY BELLE [*as the men eat*]. Hoover's asleep. Are you going to wake him?
DAVE. To a man that's been traveling since the crack of red dawn, even a dry marrowless bone, hard as paint rock, seems sweet and soft.
MAY BELLE. Wake up, Hoover.
HOOVER [*sleepily*]. Leave me alone.
CLINT. Come and eat, boy.
DAVE. Traveling must be hard on you with the young ones.
CLINT. Yeah. We been walking weeks now. But we're still on a dusty highway between two ditches.
[HOOVER *arouses himself and sits next to* CLINT *and eats.* MAY BELLE *stands leaning against the cart.* FRONIE *sits near* ROSE, *fanning her with her hand, chewing on the bread and watching the men.*]
DAVE. Won't you eat too? [*He hesitates before saying her name.*] May Belle? [MAY BELLE *shakes her head.*] A young girl has got to eat a lot to keep going.
MAY BELLE. I can't eat it.
CLINT [*gnawing on a bone*]. I wish myself it was something besides a half-starved prairie dog.
DAVE. A wonder you hit him, they're fast as greased lightning.
[CLINT *stops eating.* FRONIE *stops what she is doing. They exchange a long glance.*]
FRONIE. If there was just a little soup to it, we could feed Rose.
CLINT. Give her a bone and let her suck the juice from it.
DAVE. You got one sick?
CLINT. Dust pneumonia.

DAVE. I thought she was just sleeping over there.

[FRONIE *takes a bone and goes over to* ROSE.]

CLINT. She sort of don't take notice. Ain't talked in two days except to ask for water. Last thing she said she asked was it raining. She was the worst one I ever seen about liking it to rain. She'd stand out in the rain and hold her little hands up like this. [*He holds up his palms.*] To catch 'em full.

DAVE. How old is she?

CLINT. Be 'leven some time this month. I remember the day she was born. Me and the landlord took my fiftieth bale of cotton to be ginned. That very evening we had our first dust storm. Not a bad one. The dust blowed around some and you could see it skipping like hard blown smoke across the field towards our house. [FRONIE *is trying to get* ROSE *to take the bone.*] At first, we thought they was just common whirlwinds like we always had in dry spells. [*He looks towards* ROSE *and is silent a moment.*] Yes, when she was born, we had a whitewashed house setting out in a broad, green field, a little road coming up to it and a mailbox a few hundred yards off down the public road.

FRONIE. I'm wishing now that we'd stayed and fought it out on the Panhandle.

CLINT. You can't fight dust, Fronie.

[MAY BELLE *is clearing away the supper and putting things back in the box. She listens to the conversation.* HOOVER *has eaten and gone back to sleep.*]

FRONIE [*miserable, turning aside*]. I don't know. We could have kept on trying.

CLINT. It comes down on you like a Norther and you run in the house and lock the door. But it sifts in through the shingles or under the doorjamb.

MAY BELLE. It used to get in the food. You covered the

churn and put it in the cellar, but it always got in the butter.

CLINT. You can't fight wind and drought and dust. 'Specially dust. You can see it there in front of you. You feel it in your eyes and throat. *But you can't get your hands on it.* You can't fight dust, 'cause it ain't nobody.

DAVE. If enough people got together on it, they could fight it.

CLINT. No. You can't fight dust, 'cause it ain't nobody.

DAVE. If we plant trees again—if we sow grass again where they plowed it up and left the roots to wither, we might get our land back again.

CLINT. We'll all die while we're dreaming about it.

MAY BELLE. Talk some more about it, Papa. It's all gone now, but I like to remember everything.

CLINT. A man can think he's got the world by the tail on a downhill pull, and lose his hold and find out he's got nothing but a stray tail-feather. [*To* FRONIE.] Can't you wake her up?

FRONIE. She's awful quiet. She ain't even coughed in a good while.

CLINT [*going to* ROSE, *and kneeling beside her*]. Baby? [*The child stirs slightly but makes no sound.*] She must be suffering so much that she's unconscious.

FRONIE. We got to get something into her.

DAVE [*crossing to look at the child*]. She's awfully pale and thin. Looks like she's suffering a lot.

CLINT. Sights like this set a man's mind to wondering . . . wondering what they is to living anyway.

DAVE. There comes a time when death is more merciful than suffering.

CLINT. She'd be better off dead all right. It ain't enough that the dry winds take the land out from under us and leave us nothing for scenery but a bobwire fence and hills piled high with brown cotton stalks. It's got to go further than that. It's got to fill young-uns lungs with dirt and powdered leaves. [*Poignantly.*] It's an inhuman world that lets things like that happen.

FRONIE [*quietly*]. Like she's dying here, while we're pushing on to a new place to *live*.

DAVE [*as if to himself*]. Some day they'll have good crops in the Panhandle again. Even if they have to pipe water from Lake Erie to do it.

FRONIE. But what about now—to-day—this night? [*She is almost in tears.*]

MAY BELLE. Mama, you try to rest some and go to sleep.

FRONIE [*patiently*]. I guess all of us had better lay down and rest.

CLINT. We'll need it. We got to hit the concrete with the first yellow streaks in the morning. Got to get a good start before the east is red.

MAY BELLE. I'll set up with Rose.

DAVE. You all had a harder day than me. I won't mind doing it.

CLINT. We can take turns about.

DAVE. Sure. You go ahead and sleep awhile.

[CLINT *stoops to spread a quilt over* HOOVER. *He stops suddenly, tense. He looks at the other three with a stricken face.*]

CLINT. There's dust on that wind!

[FRONIE, MAY BELLE, DAVE, *and* CLINT *stand rigid with their faces tense, lifted, and facing north. They stand waiting. A faint breeze ruffles their hair.*]

FRONIE. I could taste it awhile back.

DAVE. I been feeling it. Inside my nose has been dry and burning.

CLINT. It's such a fine silt you can't see it.

FRONIE. I hope Calvin finds his way back 'fore it gets too heavy.

MAY BELLE. We don't have no water to wash our throats with.

DAVE. Put your rags and quilts in the open so's they catch some moisture if we have a dew to-night.

CLINT. What moisture they is will be wasted riding that dust to the ground.

DAVE. It might quit before morning and there'd be a little dew.

CLINT. We got to rest before it gets too thick.

[FRONIE *stretches on the ground.* DAVE *sits beside* ROSE. MAY BELLE *sits near her mother.*]

FRONIE [*starting to get up*]. Here, I was just about to forget the quilts.

CLINT. May Belle, you put them out for your mother.

[MAY BELLE *goes to the cart and takes out a ragged quilt and two flour sacks.* DAVE *helps her spread them out.* CLINT *takes his hat from his head and kneels beside* FRONIE.] Use this hat for a pillow, Fronie.

FRONIE. I like to have something to prop with and I reckon that'll do. [CLINT *places the hat under her head.*] A bed is a sacred thing. I'd never get used to this way of living.

CLINT [*stretching himself on the ground*]. It won't always be like this.

FRONIE. That's what you used to say when I had to churn the butter by hand.

[*They grow quiet.* HOOVER *is sound asleep.* ROSE *lies still.*]

MAY BELLE [*going to the fire,* DAVE *following her*]. I don't want to sleep.

DAVE. A girl like you needs sleep, to keep her beauty.

MAY BELLE. A chance to wash up with some soap and water and a clean dress to put on would be all the beauty treatment I'd want.

DAVE. You look fine.

MAY BELLE. My face feels dirty. [*She crosses to the cart.*]

DAVE [*following her*]. That's part of your prettiness.

MAY BELLE. You have a nice way of talking. [*She leans against the cart.*]

DAVE. No. You're the one that has the way of saying pretty things. Just before I came over that rise this evening, I heard you tell about the bleached skull and the prairie rose growing out of it. [*They are leaning against the cart with the rays of the lantern illuminating their faces.*]

MAY BELLE. I was listening to all the things you said to Papa. Where did you learn so much about things?

DAVE. Knocking around. I've read a bit, heard a lot, and seen a good many things.

MAY BELLE. Maybe you're somebody famous that I don't know about.

DAVE. I'm just a nobody working my way down to California because a man promised me a job there. If I get it, I'll work hard, save my money, and buy me a little ground.

MAY BELLE. No, you won't. Young fellows spend all they get as fast as they make it.

DAVE [*looking at her steadily*]. If they ain't got nobody to work for. May Belle, I'm hoping to work hard, settle down some place. [MAY BELLE *understands. She is embarrassed, and delighted.*]

MAY BELLE. Hope is free. [*She moves away from him.*]

DAVE. Why don't you stay still awhile? You've been walking all day. [*He goes to her. Suddenly he puts his arm under her knees and lifts her in his arms. He holds her still a second, then carries her to the cart.*]

MAY BELLE. Oh. . . .

DAVE [*placing her on the cart.*] It's more comfortable sitting there than on the ground. I can talk to you better this way too. [*He leans against the cart looking up into her face. Then he becomes silent.*]

MAY BELLE. You said you could talk better this way, but you aren't saying much.
DAVE. I was listening to the wind. It's coming stronger. [*Both of them turn their faces to the north and listen intently.*]
MAY BELLE. It makes a pretty sound coming across the prairie.
DAVE [*as if to himself*].

> The wind is the prairie father,
> Riding wild and free.
> We are his children,
> Why should we stand rooted like a tree?
>
> When the wind is riding south to-night,
> We are his children.
> We should be going with him,
> Singing his song.

MAY BELLE [*quietly*]. That was nice.
DAVE [*embarrassed*]. Those were just some words I put together one spring when times were a little easier. I keep remembering them even though I know now what the wind brings with it when it comes.
MAY BELLE. Even the wind that brings the dust and death makes pretty sounds.
DAVE. You got a way of looking at things.... Like seeing that prairie rose growing out of the whitened skull and saying how pretty it was. That was wonderful!
MAY BELLE. I don't see nearly so many wonderful things like you do though.
DAVE. There's something sweet about the way you look at people. I noticed that first when I was standing off out there and I said hello and your papa said howd'y' to me. I saw it then. I knew I could like you.

MAY BELLE. I saw you and I said something to myself. I said, "He's a man that's got something besides a dust storm to make him move somewheres." It was just a feeling I had.

DAVE. Could I walk along the highway with you to California?

MAY BELLE [*shyly*]. I reckon.

DAVE. Then there'll be lots of time to talk to you. [*He smiles.*] It's a funny first meeting. It should have been another way. I should have called at your house; had a home of my own to offer you. A safe place.... [*As if thinking aloud.*] But maybe we could find some place of safety—could make it for ourselves; a place of our own in this desert waste of America. And we could go there.

MAY BELLE. We could go away from all this land that's so wasted.

DAVE. No. We grew up out of the wastelands. Our new life must come from them. It will be like that prairie rose growing out of the whitened skull—so much the prettier because it is in that place.

MAY BELLE [*holding out her arms*]. Lift me down. [*He does so. He sets her on the ground and takes her hand. They walk to the rise. She points off.*] It's there. Growing there. If there was a moon you could see it from here.

[*They stand hand in hand looking off to where the prairie rose is growing. Breaking this quiet,* ROSE *coughs deeply. The cough ends in a strangling sound.*]

DAVE [*as they turn to look at her*]. The dust is getting heavier.

MAY BELLE. For a little time I forgot there was so much heartbreak in the world. [*They come to* ROSE.]

DAVE. If we put a quilt over her, it'd keep out some of it. [*They draw one of the quilts up over her and hold up the end that is at her head.*]

MAY BELLE. She can't live much longer. [ROSE *makes a harsh, strangling sound.*]
DAVE. Poor little one.
MAY BELLE [*passionately*]. If only that dust wouldn't keep coming on.
FRONIE [*getting up*]. Is she getting worse?
DAVE. She has a hard time getting her breath.
FRONIE [*touching the child*]. She's worse all right.
MAY BELLE [*running to* CLINT *and shaking him*]. Papa, Papa! [*He wakens instantly and sits up.*] Rose is a lot worse.
[CLINT *goes to her. The child coughs occasionally, a harsh cough that ends in a queer, strangling sound.*]
CLINT. Lord God, I wish this poor child was out of her misery.
DAVE. There's not a chance she'll live another day. There's no hope when dust pneumonia sets in that deep.
FRONIE [*kneeling*]. She's trying to open her eyes, Clint. She's trying to say something.
ROSE [*weakly, as* CLINT *lifts her head*]. Was it a big rain, Papa?
FRONIE. She's had a dream, too.
CLINT [*bitterly*]. Her mind's been wanderin'.
ROSE [*her voice high and distant*]. Everything is clean and blue now.... [*The words go off into a queer strangling sound.*]
DAVE [*softly*]. She's dying. She won't last more than another day at the most.
FRONIE. We can't move her now, Clint.
CLINT [*pacing restlessly towards the rise*]. If we stay here, we'll all get it. We've got to keep moving.
FRONIE. A little water would do a lot of good. A body never knows how much water is worth until they ain't none.

MAY BELLE. Calvin will find some. He won't come back till he does.

FRONIE. Her lungs must be all full of dust by now.

CLINT [*violently, turning to her*]. Do you think I like to see her suffering? Or hear you tell of it?

FRONIE [*quietly*]. I know it, Clint.

CLINT. I killed old Drummer, my horse, when he was sick and had that same look in his eyes.

FRONIE [*fearful*]. Clint!

CLINT. People are merciful to dumb beasts.

MAY BELLE. You can't kill a human being.

CLINT. If a dog was laying there suffering, I wouldn't think twice about it. You'd all say go ahead and do it and hate me if I didn't.

MAY BELLE. There won't be much longer to wait.

FRONIE [*putting her arm across the child*]. She's our child, Clint!

CLINT. If we stop here a week and wait for her to die, we might as well dig a grave deep enough for all of us.

MAY BELLE. Somebody might come along and give us a lift.

CLINT. The road's closed to traffic. Besides, in the weeks we've been walkin', no one ever gave us a lift.

DAVE. He's right, May Belle.

MAY BELLE [*turning on him*]. You can't mean that? You seem to understand so much. [DAVE *turns away. She turns to* CLINT.] Don't listen to him, Papa. He's a stranger.

FRONIE. It ain't right! It ain't right!

CLINT. What's right and what's wrong don't count no more with me. It's whether we live or die.

MAY BELLE. She liked you so much. Remember how she'd follow you down a mile-long furrow when you was plantin' cotton.

CLINT. This ain't no time to tie me down with a bunch of memories when I know what I got to do. [*To* FRONIE.]

Start packing up so's we can leave in a hurry. [*Automatically,* FRONIE *picks up a quilt, folds it, and puts it in the cart.*]

MAY BELLE [*frantically*]. Don't let him do it, Mama.

CLINT. She's unconscious now. She won't know.

MAY BELLE [*screaming*]. No! No! Please, Papa!

CLINT. Where's my gun? [MAY BELLE'S *eyes go to the gun on the ground. She makes an instinctive move to get it. He picks it up. He starts to load it.*] Everything's against us. We got to take things in our own hands and do the best we can for the sake of the rest of us. [MAY BELLE *coughs suddenly. Terrified, she puts both hands over her mouth to strangle the sound. All turn to look at her, terrified. She coughs again.* CLINT *is desperate.*] She's coughing now. We can't wait. We got to get moving. She'll be the next one.

[FRONIE *kneels in front of the child. She is desperate and firm.*]

FRONIE. Put that gun down and wait till Calvin comes back with the water.

CLINT [*looking at* ROSE *over* FRONIE'S *shoulder*]. I'd like her to taste water once more before ... she goes. [*Slowly he sets the butt of the gun down.*] But I ain't waitin' all night. We got to bury her before daybreak.

DAVE. The boy that went for water will be back soon.

CLINT [*setting his gun against the cart*]. It's just like it is. She'll never sing another song nor paddle her feet in no more water holes. We can't help it. Maybe there are people that could, but they ain't caring about us.... [*His voice breaks. He passes his hand across his face.*]

FRONIE [*patiently*]. Set down and rest awhile, Clint. Give your feelings time to wear off. [*She picks up a few more things and stores them in the cart.*]

[MAY BELLE *leans against the cart.* CLINT *comes over to*

stand next to her. She gives him a frightened look and moves away from him.]

CLINT. What you shying at, girl?

MAY BELLE. Nothing. . . . [*She presses her hands over her mouth to hold back a cough.*]

CLINT. What you get scared for?

MAY BELLE. I was thinking what might happen if I get sick.

CLINT. We got to get you out of here. Away from the dust. We can't wait till morning.

DAVE [*gently*]. All the brush is gone. I'll get some more for the fire. You come with me, May Belle.

[CALVIN *now appears on the rise. He moves like a dazed person. The jug hangs from his right hand.*]

MAY BELLE [*going to him*]. Calvin! Didn't you get some water?

CALVIN. Seems like I walked a thousand miles.

MAY BELLE. Did you find water?

CALVIN. I found where water used to be. A spring beneath the yuccas at the foot of the mesa. But the bottom was cracked and dry.

FRONIE. Wasn't there a filling station?

[MAY BELLE *takes the jug from him and holds it upside down. It is empty.*]

CALVIN. All I saw was prairie, and more prairie, and this hill when I looked back

MAY BELLE [*angrily*]. Why didn't you keep on going till you found some?

[HOOVER *is still sleeping through all the discussion.*]

CALVIN [*whimpering*]. I couldn't. I was tired and the dust was coming and I was afraid I wouldn't be able to find you all again. I can't stand up a second longer. [*He sinks to the ground.*]

CLINT [*quietly*]. There'll be no more talking about it. [*To* CALVIN.] There's one more thing you have to do, boy.

I know you're tired. But you must do it. [CALVIN *sits up and stares at* CLINT.] We ain't got no tools to dig with. [FRONIE *and* MAY BELLE *glance fearfully at each other.* CLINT *reaches in the cart and takes out a short-handled goose-neck hoe.*] But take this and go out there and scoop out enough dirt to make a hole.
[CALVIN *is about to protest. He stares at* CLINT *as though hypnotized. The women watch* CLINT *fearfully.* DAVE *turns away. As if in a dream,* CALVIN *gets to his feet, takes the hoe and goes off over the rise.*]
MAY BELLE [*throwing her arms about* CLINT *to hold him back.*] No, Papa, don't!
FRONIE [*kneeling by* ROSE, *clutches the corner of the quilt and moans softly*]. O Lord!
CLINT [*to* FRONIE]. Get away now. [*He shakes her loose.*] My mind is fixed. We'll have it over with in a little while.
MAY BELLE [*clutching* DAVE]. You got the kind of words that make people listen to you. Talk to him. Tell him he can't do it.
DAVE [*gently*]. Your father is a good man—and a wise man. His way is best. [*She turns away from him.* DAVE *touches* CLINT *on the arm.*] Hadn't we better take her out there —first? [*He indicates the rise.*] Where you sent the boy?
CLINT [*thinking; he looks at* FRONIE]. Reckon so.
DAVE [*stooping over*]. I'll carry her.
CLINT. No! She's my own young-un. I'll have the last holding of this little one. [*He hands his gun over to* DAVE, *stoops and takes up* ROSE. *She hangs limp. He stares down into her face. He holds her closer to him. His expression changes. He looks at her more closely. He bends his head and puts his ear to her breast. He lays her down again, gently, on the quilt.*] I . . . I . . . don't have to do it . . . now. . . . [MAY BELLE *sobs.* DAVE *puts the gun away in the cart and goes to the rise.*]

FRONIE [*quietly*]. The Lord is good.

DAVE. I'll help the boy out there. [*He goes out over the rise.* MAY BELLE *and* FRONIE *kneel by* ROSE. CLINT *stands over them, brooding.* HOOVER *continues sleeping.*]

FRONIE [*patting* MAY BELLE's *shoulder*]. Let's don't grieve so hard. It's all for the best, maybe. There's still you, and Hoover, and Calvin left.

CLINT [*dully*]. May Belle.... [*He pauses, searching for the words that will make her understand.*] If she hadn't died this way, I would have done it... I would have killed my own young-un that I cared about... If you don't know why, I ain't got the words to make you understand it....

[DAVE *comes over the rise with the hoe on his shoulder.*]

DAVE. We'll have to hurry; the dust sifts back into the hole as fast as we scoop it out.

CALVIN [*appearing on the rise*]. She's filling up again, fast! Hole won't stay in the ground more'n a minute.

CLINT [*looking down on the dead child*]. First the earth kills them off and then it won't take its dead back.... The earth has something against us, maybe.... We tore the trees out of her and ripped out the grass. Now she won't take us back to her....

CALVIN. Hurry, Papa, I'll scoop it out again. [*He takes the hoe from* DAVE *and disappears over the rise.* CLINT *stoops over, wraps the quilt around the child and takes her in his arms.*]

DAVE [*to* CLINT]. I'll help you.

CLINT [*shaking his head*]. No, it's my place to do it. You stay here with the women... and maybe speak a few words while I put her away.

FRONIE [*tucking in a loose edge of the quilt*]. Wrap the quilt tight around her, Father. [CLINT *goes over the rise with the child and disappears on the other side.* FRONIE *follows and stands on top of the rise looking down over it at the grave. She stands alone on the rise and speaks as if to herself.* MAY BELLE *and* DAVE *stand near the cart. The girl has her hands over her face and is weeping silently.*] I remember when she was born. I turned my head and the first thing I noticed was her little hand all curled up like a new rose. [*Her voice rises.*] I died four times. I died each time I gave birth to one of my children. I made a bargain with God. I told Him I would take all the suffering, that I wouldn't cry out in my pain. I told Him I would stand all the suffering there was in the world if He would see to it that no harm came to my young-uns. [*Then quietly.*] He didn't keep His bargain. [*Passionately.*] But He's making me keep mine! He's making me keep mine! [*A huge sob is torn out of her body. But she gets herself in hand and stands alone, an image of suffering cast in stone.* MAY BELLE *and* DAVE, *hand in hand cross to her.* DAVE, *after awhile, looks to the east and speaks the few words for the dead.*]

DAVE.
    Down in the earth, the deep, deep earth,
    shall the hungry one, the weary one, rest.
    The soft rains will come again,
    replenish the earth again.
    Now, O, clean earth, close about her,
    let her bones know their final kinship.
    The sweet and eternal
    embrace of maternal
    earth
    Shall wrap her arms securely about her.

[*There is a pause.* FRONIE *sighs, shudders. All is quiet.* DAVE *takes* MAY BELLE *by the hand and leads her back to the cart. He picks up whatever possessions are still on the ground and stows them away in the cart.* FRONIE *stands alone on the rise for a moment. Then* CLINT *appears with the hoe in his hand. He puts his hand on her shoulder and they come down the rise together.* CALVIN *is behind them.*]

HOOVER [*waking up and rubbing his eyes*]. Is it time to go, Papa?

CLINT [*gently*]. Just about, son.

HOOVER [*starting to get up*]. I'll carry the shotgun. Where is it?

CLINT. No, son, you can ride in the cart to-night. [*He gives the hoe to* FRONIE, *picks up* HOOVER *and puts him in the cart, covering him with a quilt.* CALVIN *picks up the water jug and a folded quilt.* MAY BELLE *takes up her cardboard box.*]

DAVE [*taking it from her*]. I'll carry it the rest of the way.

[FRONIE *seeing there is nothing left for her to carry, takes her place behind the cart next to* CLINT. *He looks to see if all are ready.*]

CLINT. You young-uns go first for awhile. [DAVE *and* MAY BELLE *line up in front of the cart, side by side, with* CALVIN *behind them.*]

FRONIE. Did you wrap the quilt warm around her?

CLINT. I wrapped it good and tight. [*Softly.*] And we found a prairie rose to go on top. [*He grasps the handles.*] Are we ready, Fronie?

FRONIE. Yes. [*She grasps the handle, her hand next to his.*]

DAVE. The wind's turning to the east now.

CLINT. Then we'll have the wind behind us while we're walking west.

[FRONIE *looks back towards the rise as she starts to walk. They take the first step towards the west as...*

THE CURTAIN FALLS

MEXICO

THE RED VELVET GOAT
A TRAGEDY OF LAUGHTER AND A COMEDY OF TEARS

BY JOSEPHINA NIGGLI

OF MONTERREY, NUEVO LEON, MEXICO

Written in the playwriting course at the University of North Carolina and originally produced by The Carolina Playmakers at Chapel Hill on April 25, 1936. *The Red Velvet Goat* had its first professional production by The One Act Repertory Company at the Hudson Theatre, New York, beginning January 20, 1939. It was first published in the *One-Act Play Magazine,* July, 1937.

THE CHARACTERS

ESTEBAN, *who longs to own a goat*..William Chichester
MARIANA, *his wife*....................Hester Barlow
LORENZO, *their son*..................Robert duFour
LOLA ⎱ *village girls, friends* ⎰ Audrey Rowell
CARMEN ⎰ *of Ester* ⎱ Frances Johnston
ESTER, *a village girl with whom Lorenzo is in love*
  Ruth Mengel
RAMON, *a peddler of women's clothing*
  Holman Milhous
DON PEPE, *the mayor of the village*..Gerald Hochman
DOÑA BERTA, *a neighbor and grand lady of the village*
  Janie Britt
OTHER VILLAGERS: Herbert Kane, Mary Delany, Kenneth Bartlett, Jean Walker, George Starks, Conrad Poppenhusen, and Thomas O'Flaherty.

SCENE: *The patio of* ESTEBAN's *house on The Street of the Arches in the town of The Three Marys, Mexico.*
TIME: *The present. Six o'clock of an afternoon in June.*

Copyright, 1937, by The Carolina Playmakers, Inc.
All rights reserved.

MEXICAN VILLAGE COMEDY

THE author of *The Red Velvet Goat*, Josephina Niggli, is a new poet in the theater, a maker of Mexican folk drama.

Although only twenty-five years of age, she has written for the stage at Chapel Hill six plays which reveal the colorful lives of her people with vivid realism and lyric intensity. The titles of her plays suggest the range of her imagination: *Tooth or Shave* and *Sunday Costs Five Pesos*, gay comedies of Mexican village life; *The Red Velvet Goat*, a *saenete*, a popular form of village entertainment, a tragedy of laughter and a comedy of tears; *The Cry of Dolores*, a play of the impassioned leadership of Father Hidalgo for Mexican independence in 1810; *Azteca*,* a tragedy of the pre-conquest period (1412) in the great convent of the Earth-Mother Goddess; and *Soldadera* † *(Soldier-Woman)*, the tragedy of Mexican Valkyries in a mountain pass at Coahuila in 1914; "the women whose stories have never been written down and whose bravery is shrouded by legends told about the fireside at night by men who knew them." In addition to the above one-act plays, Miss Niggli is the author of two full-length plays produced by The Carolina Playmakers: *Singing Valley*, a comedy of Mexican village life and *The Fair-God (Malinche)*, a play of Maximilian of Mexico, both produced in 1936.

Josephina Niggli was born in Monterrey, Neuvo Leon, Mexico. From childhood she looked so much like her father that she is still known to all his friends as "Little Niggli." Her mother, a former concert violinist, is well known throughout

---

* *Tooth or Shave, Sunday Costs Five Pesos, The Red Velvet Goat, The Cry of Dolores,* and *Azteca* were produced by The Carolina Playmakers originally on April 25, 1935. *Tooth or Shave* was taken on tour by them in 1936, *Sunday Costs Five Pesos* in 1937.

† *Soldadera (Soldier-Woman)* was produced originally by The Playmakers on February 27, 28 and 29, 1936, and taken by them on their Thirty-sixth Tour in 1938.

the Southwest as a teacher of music for children. Her home is an old Mexican estate with a *casa grande* (great house), *La Quinta del Carmen* (The House of Flowers), of many acres and many servants. The favorite in the family is her grandmother, affectionately known to every one as *La Mama*. On Sunday evenings an orchestra conducted by the gardener's son-in-law comes to the great house saying, "We have come to serenade *La Mama*." Miss Niggli says, "If any one has plans of doing anything other than listen to the music, he may just as well forget about it for the time being."

In the summer of 1935 she came to Chapel Hill and wrote her first play in the playwriting course. Her decision to join The Carolina Playmakers was endorsed by Señor Pinza, attaché at the Bolivian embassy in Mexico City, himself a well-known playwright in his own country. Miss Niggli has acting talent, too. She has played a number of parts in her productions and has directed some of her own plays. She plans on her return to Monterrey to establish a Mexican Folk Theater, utilizing her own repertory. The increasing tide of American visitors will have a better understanding of the Mexican people by seeing her plays.

The Red Velvet Goat is a *saenete,* a Spanish type of drama unknown to the English-speaking stage, but widely popular in Mexico. Miss Niggli tells us that the term *saenete* cannot be translated exactly into English, although it is vaguely defined by the dictionary as a kind of farce, that it is simply a picture of what we call the "lower classes" lifted from reality to the stage. It is a comedy, written in poetic dialogue with a romantic flavor. Perhaps its best classification is that of Lorenzo in his prologue to Esteban's play, "a tragedy of laughter and a comedy of tears."

"It is a home-made play such as one can see in any village from Quintana Roo to the Rio Grande. When a Mexican goes to a play he goes, not as a spectator, but with the firm intention of being as much a part of the drama as the actors on the stage. It is the prompter, however, who bears the full burden of the performance, and so, to him, health and wealth.

"All of the characters, with the exception of Mariana, are drawn from life. Esteban, whose real name I have forgotten, I often used to see at dances playing a saxaphone which he had bought from a Sears, Roebuck catalogue, because, as he said, 'it looked so much like a worm.' He called it a 'sasafone,' and when he blew into the mouthpiece it rested with God as to what note would come out at the other end.

"Lorenzo, Ester, Don Pepe, Doña Berta, are all people whom I have known and loved since infancy. I can still see in memory the various Esters sitting primly at dances while their fans flashed back and forth in signals at the various Lorenzos grouped about the doors, while the Doña Bertas sat in magnificent grandeur ready to pounce on the first couple which did not behave in a manner befitting young ladies and gentlemen.

"If there is a moral to be found in this play, I think it is this: that we may thank God that there are still grown people who retain the hearts of children."

THE RED VELVET GOAT

The late afternoon sun has thrown a golden haze over the patio of ESTEBAN'S *home. It is not a magnificent patio. There is no fountain with flowers banked around it, as in the home of* DON PEPE, *although there are pots of flowers on the stoop of the door which opens into a bedroom on the right. If it were noon, there would be chickens scratching about, and perhaps a baby pig or two, but it is evening, and the livestock have been closed up in the corral which is beyond the gate on the left.*

There are benches in front of us, and two rocking-chairs swaying back and forth in front of a platform that is made of planks resting on saw-horses placed against the outside wall of the house at the back. This platform, these chairs, these benches are not usually found in ESTEBAN'S *patio, but they are here this afternoon because he is going to present a play of his own composition. The platform is in a very convenient place, since there is a door leading into the living room which serves very well for the actors to make their entrances and exits. That funny little box in front of the platform is for the prompter, and those gray blankets dangling from the rope attached to the posts at the two front corners of the platform serve as curtains.*

To the left, now partly closed, is the great wooden door that opens directly on the street from the patio, and if you care to peer through the iron barred window in the right wall you will see MARIANA'S *dress, which she intends to wear in her husband's play, laid out on the bed.*

THE RED VELVET GOAT

The boy standing on the platform, clutching the stool in his two hands is LORENZO, *very brown of eyes and skin and very black of hair. He wears the white pajama suit of the tropics, with a red bandana knotted at the throat. Because he is twenty-two, old enough to have a sweetheart, he has on a pair of bright yellow shoes that hurt.*

That woman standing to the right with her hands buckled on her hips, that flaming, flashing woman is MARIANA, *his mother. Although she is forty there is no gray in the black satin cap of her hair; there are no wrinkles in the smooth golden cream of her skin; and as for her body... well, even the loose white blouse and the billowing red muslin skirt cannot hide the youthful fire in that pretty body.*

It seems almost impossible to think of ESTEBAN, *the man leaning against the edge of the platform to the left...it seems almost impossible to think of this funny, fat little man as being* MARIANA'S *husband. Sometimes he wakes up in the night, especially after feast days, and wonders himself how he ever came to marry such a gorgeous creature. Poor* ESTEBAN *with his funny little blob of a nose perched in the middle of a round moon face, is no match for* MARIANA *and he knows it. His hands are always aimlessly clutching at each other. They are doing it now as he watches* LORENZO *with the stool.*

MARIANA [*impatiently to* LORENZO]. No, fool! Where are your brains? Remove the chair and place it in the corner to the right. Esteban, speak! You are the master of the play.

ESTEBAN. To hear you rattle on, a man would think it was your scene. [*Points left.*] The stool goes there.

MARIANA [*points right*]. No, there! Would you have it hide the door?

Esteban [*angrily*]. I say it goes there! Lorenzo, place it where I say or I will break your head!

Lorenzo [*who, through the argument has been standing still patiently holding the stool, now bangs it down in front of him on the platform*]. Holy saints! Whom am I to obey? I'll put it here, and you can change it where you like. I am an actor, not a doll on strings. I must go read my part again. [*He then goes out through the platform door, slamming it behind him.* Mariana *hides a laugh.*]

Mariana. He says he is an actor. Haha! Then I am queen of tragedy. What hour does it grow to be?

Esteban [*taking a large gold watch from his pocket*]. My watch says eight, so then it must be six. [*Bends toward her, clasping his hands tightly together.*] Does all the world know of the benefit?

Mariana. Musicians played before each door in town. I sent Lorenzo out with notices this morning. Do you think our guests will pay enough to buy a goat? [*Sinks down on the end of one of the benches.*]

Esteban. We only need ten pesos for a goat. Don Pepe said he'd sell us one of his. With the money from its milk and cheese we'll have enough to buy another one, and soon we'll have a flock. Then we'll be the richest two in town.

Mariana [*scornfully*]. Just with one goat? What silken dreams you can build from air. To hear you speak no man in all the northern part of Mexico will be so rich as you when this play is done.

Esteban [*with modest pride*]. My talents are so varied, Mariana. Perhaps we should not buy a goat at all. Any one can own a goat, but I, and I alone, can compose such drama.

THE RED VELVET GOAT

MARIANA. A truth, a little truth indeed, my 'Steban. No other man could write such plays... [*Flares at him.*] ... because he would not write them. I think it best to buy the goat.

ESTEBAN [*shocked*]. Have you no soul, no breath of genius blowing through your feeble brain? In time the world shall hear of this Esteban and mourn the fact that he possessed such a blockhead for a wife.

MARIANA [*peeved*]. Who gave you hints of how to write it best but me, me, me! Who furnished you with chairs, and clothes, and men? Yes, men? [*Goes to him, her eyes burning with anger.*] Lorenzo is my son as much as yours. Oh, when I wept and cried the night that he made his first entry in the world I did not think that he would grow to be an actor.

ESTEBAN. Do not fear. My son has failed to grasp my talent. He—

MARIANA. Is better, far, than you will ever be.

ESTEBAN [*grandly ignoring her*]. Did you bring the vase from Doña Berta's?

MARIANA. It is on the table in the house next to my red and blue one. You see, I do not forget, even if you do. [*Goes into the bedroom right.*]

ESTEBAN [*following her to the door and calling after her*]. Now what have I forgotten?

MARIANA [*from inside*]. Just a prompter, that is all. [*She enters, goes to the platform and places the vases on the prompter's box, standing back to see the effect.*] A little prompter to aid us with his book when we forget.

ESTEBAN [*with a gasp*]. I meant to ask Don Pepe...

MARIANA [*sarcastically*]. Did you indeed? Don Pepe, the mayor of The Three Marys! Perhaps you would prefer to have the President of the Republic, or the great civil judge to read our lines for us! Where are your wits, fool?

Hanging from your nose like Spanish moss upon an ancient wind-blown tree?

ESTEBAN [*wringing his hands*]. It grows near the hour of our performance! Why did you not remind me of this small detail?

MARIANA [*flings her arms above her head*]. Remind you! Saints in Heaven! Holy Mary, aid me! Oh, what ass is this dressed in man's clothing? Must I remember everything? Or was the play of your invention?

ESTEBAN [*maliciously*]. Who gave me hints of how to write it? Who gave me chairs, and clothes, and men, but you, my little, darling wife?

MARIANA [*furious*]. But even I could not give you wit, my love. Each day I watch your ears grow longer and more pointed. Some day they will fall down and slap your cheeks, like that... [*Gives him a resounding slap.*]... and then you will remember Mariana.

ESTEBAN [*ruefully*]. You are the whip I wear here at my belt, my sweet... [*Rubs his face.*]... a whip that does not need my hand to wield its power.

MARIANA. Enough of arguments. The crowd will soon be here. Go out and hunt a prompter.

ESTEBAN [*scandalized*]. At this hour? Have you no thought at all for my great art? Am I not the hero of this play? In a short time I must walk across that stage, and even now my poor heart is beating in my chest, and see my hands... [*Wiggles them loosely*]... shaking at the wrist.

MARIANA [*firmly*]. Am I not the tragic lady of this play? I will not speak a line of your great drama until a man is safe within that box.

ESTEBAN [*imploring aid from Heaven*]. Why did I marry such a woman, who loves an argument more than her soul's salvation?

Wootten-Moulton

WEST FROM THE PANHANDLE

CLINT. The earth has something against us, maybe.... We tore the trees out of her and ripped out the grass. Now she won't take us back to her.

THE RED VELVET GOAT

MARIANA. My husband! I may no longer call you husband!
LORENZO. What news is this? What sad words beat against my brain?

Wootten-Moulton

THE RED VELVET GOAT

MARIANA [*also imploring Heaven*]. Why did I marry such a lazy fool who would rather sit in the sun and watch the goats feed on the mountain side than make an honest living for his family?

[LORENZO *opens the platform door and sticks his head through.*]

LORENZO. There are some people coming up the hill.

MARIANA [*giving a startled shriek. Runs toward bedroom door*]. The audience! And I not dressed!

ESTEBAN [*stopping her*]. Mariana, Lorenzo can find the man we need. [*As* MARIANA *pauses, he turns to* LORENZO.] My son, we need a prompter. Go into the town and search for one.

MARIANA. Bring back a man who can read, and not some ignorant fool.

LORENZO [*comes out on the platform, a large square piece of red velvet in his hands*]. I have already spoken to Don Pancho's son, Ramon. The one who peddles silks and threads to all the women in the towns nearby. He can read, yes, and write, too.

MARIANA [*her eyes fixed on the velvet, and speaking in a strangled voice*]. Lorenzo! Lorenzo, for what is that red velvet?

LORENZO [*innocently*]. To cover the prompter's box, my mother, so that all the world shall know we give a play.

MARIANA [*stalking up to the platform*]. Where did you get it? Where did you find that strip of goods?

[ESTEBAN *frantically signals to* LORENZO *to keep quiet.*]

LORENZO [*looking curiously at his father*]. What is it, sir? Why do you not speak out? I can not read such wavings of the hands.

[ESTEBAN *sinks down on one of the benches with a helpless gasp.*]

MARIANA [*swings on him*]. So! It was you who gave it to him, eh? Well, search your brain for clever, useless answers. Where did you find the velvet?

ESTEBAN [*pleadingly*]. Mariana, you have not worn that dress in many years. Not once have you worn it since our wedding day.

MARIANA [*slowly*]. My dress. My beautiful red dress. The dress I wore when I first met the man I loved. [*Glares at him.*] From which part did you cut it?

LORENZO [*helpfully*]. From the back. [*Turns around and makes an effort to show her how high up the cut came.*] You could replace the goods with a piece of red silk. Besides, when you are talking to your friends, they would not peer behind to see the difference.

MARIANA [*bursting into tears*]. Oh, love of God and all the little angels! When was a woman so afflicted with such fools for a family?

ESTEBAN [*awkwardly patting her shoulder*]. I know my sweet, my heart's queen, my little cooing dove, that you have kept it out of sentiment. But you have other gowns that you first wore at our early meetings.

MARIANA [*jerking away from him*]. I said I wore it when I met the man I loved, not the ass I married! [*Blazing out at them.*] Get out of my sight, the two of you! Oh, saints in Heaven, you and your plays and goats, and my red velvet gown. [*Her voice drops to a quiet deadly tone.*] I will make you pay for this, my friend.

[*Girls' voices are heard in the street.*]

LORENZO [*excitedly*]. We must draw the curtains. The audience arrives.

MARIANA. Will you leave before I break a piece of wood across your heads? [*Screams.*] Get out!

ESTEBAN [*jumps up on platform*]. We had best leave, my son. Your mother feels a little nervous.

[*As they start out* ESTEBAN *looks at* MARIANA *who has walked to the gate and has her back turned to them. He runs to the prompter's box, drapes it with the velvet, then hastily pulls the curtains as the girls appear at the gate. He and* LORENZO *disappear through the platform door.*]

MARIANA [*opening the gate*]. Enter, enter. Our house is yours.

[ESTER, LOLA, *and* CARMEN *enter. Their skirts are of striped material, their blouses very white and clean. Their hair falls in two plaits over their shoulders, and they possess the wild, shy beauty of young deer. All three have on shawls. When they speak their voices are high and shrill and sweet, and they have the habit of giggling behind their hands.*]

ESTER. Here is our money, Doña Mariana.

LOLA. Will Lorenzo play a part?

[*All giggle at* LOLA's *boldness.*]

MARIANA [*beaming on them*]. He will indeed.

CARMEN. May we sit anywhere we like?

MARIANA [*nodding*]. Wherever you may choose to sit save in the rocking-chairs. They are for Doña Berta and Don Pepe.

[*The girls giggle as they find their places.* RAMON *comes to the gate.*]

[RAMON *is very handsome and knows it. He wears a stiff straw hat, a bright pink shirt, a black tie, brown trousers, and shoes that are more orange than yellow with button tops. His voice drips with personality.*]

RAMON. Is this the house of one Esteban Elizondo? Is this the house where there will be a play?

MARIANA [*gazing thoughtfully at him. To her, any new man is subject to conquest. It is perfectly harmless. She has never been unfaithful to* ESTEBAN. *She just likes to know that she could be if she wanted to*]. So you are old Don Pancho's youngest son, Ramon.

RAMON [*makes her a low bow*]. Your servant, señorita.

MARIANA [*smiling faintly*]. I am Lorenzo's mother.

RAMON [*steps back*]. Impossible! Why, you do not look so old as he. [*Lifts her hand.*] Allow me to press a kiss upon your hand from my dirty mouth.

[ESTEBAN, *sticking his head through the curtain, sees this gallant gesture and glares at them.*]

LOLA [*tittering*]. Good evening, Don Esteban.

ESTEBAN [*grumpily*]. You may not speak to me. I am not here. I am behind the curtain. [*Trying to show his authority.*] Mariana! Take his money and let him in.

MARIANA [*shrugs her shoulders*]. He is the prompter.

ESTEBAN [*snapping at her*]. Then he should be safely in his box, and you changing your gown. I will not have you roll the eye at every man who comes along.

RAMON. Would you be jealous of me, Don Esteban, and I only a poor peddler of woman's goods?

ESTEBAN. I trust no man when Mariana rolls the eye. Lorenzo will stand at the gate.

[LORENZO *sticks his head through the curtains below* ESTEBAN'S.]

CARMEN. Good evening, Lorenzo. [*The three girls giggle.*]

LORENZO. Good evening, Carmen, Lola... [*He gives a deep sigh for he is in love with* ESTER] ... Good evening, Ester.

ESTEBAN [*sharply*]. You may not speak to them. Are they not the audience? Are you not on the stage? You must stand at the gate and take the money in your mother's place.

LORENZO. But I cannot stand at the gate and learn my part.

ESTEBAN [*yelling, since the poor man is irritated beyond endurance*]. You should know your part! You will stand where I direct you. [*Gives him a push, and* LORENZO, *who is holding the curtains, swings out, falling off the platform, taking curtain and* ESTEBAN *with him. The girls scream and stand up on their bench.* MARIANA *and* RAMON *laugh.*]

ESTEBAN [*from below the mass of curtains*]. Help us up!

LORENZO [*wailing*]. Aye, Father, you are sitting on my stomach.

MARIANA [*strolling over to the jerking heap of curtains*]. Do I stay and take the money, my dear love?

ESTEBAN. You will change your gown.

RAMON. Here comes Don Pepe climbing up the hill. He will enjoy this drama. Not every hero can be wrapped in blankets.

[*A low murmur of voices from the road at the left can be heard growing louder and louder.*]

MARIANA. Speak quickly, my sweet turnip.

ESTEBAN [*frantically fighting with the curtains*]. Help me up and you can own the goat.

MARIANA [*trying to hide her laughter*]. Will you lend your hand, Ramon?

RAMON [*makes her a deep bow*]. For you, dear lady, I would cage the sun in a crystal lamp, and borrow a star's five points to bind your hair.

LORENZO [*moaning*]. Father, will you get off my stomach?

ESTEBAN [*as* RAMON *helps him up*]. I will, when peddling fools remember how to act instead of speaking airy verses to the moon's left ear. [*Moving threateningly toward* RAMON.] As for you, my fine friend—

MARIANA [*hastily*]. No time for speeches now. Aid Lorenzo with the curtain.

LOLA. May we help?

MARIANA. You may indeed with Don Pepe at our gates. I will hold him off until the task is finished.

Ramon [*gallantly*]. My arm, lady?

Mariana [*takes it with a smile meant to infuriate Esteban*]. Thank you, Ramon. [*They exit through the gate. Esteban hangs over it gazing jealously after them. Lorenzo is putting up the curtain.*]

Ester [*watching Lorenzo*]. You are very strong.

Lorenzo. In all the valley there is no man so strong as I.

Lola [*helping Lorenzo with the curtain*]. So Ester said yesterday. [*She giggles.*]

Ester [*snaps at her*]. You have no right to repeat my words.

Lorenzo [*forgetting the curtain steps down from the platform in front of Ester*]. You spoke of me ... yesterday?

Carmen [*helping Lola with the curtain*]. You are the constant subject of her speech.

Ester. Who gave you leave to tell such tales of me? [*Flounces over and sits on bench. Lorenzo follows her.*]

Lorenzo [*softly*]. Will you be at the plaza to-night?

Ester [*turns her back on him*]. I do not know.

Lorenzo [*moving around to see her face, but she promptly turns her back again*]. If you are there, will you walk around with me?

Ester [*pleasantly shocked*]. Alone?

Lorenzo [*boldly*]. Alone. Three times around.

Ester [*gasping for breath*]. But that would say to all the world that we were engaged!

Lorenzo [*sitting beside her*]. My father soon will have enough to buy a goat, and then two goats, and then a herd. He will give me money to buy a wedding gown for you, and slippers ... small white slippers. [*As the final tantalizing bit, since any beggar could have real flowers.*] And orange blossoms fashioned out of wax.

Ester [*turning away her head*]. Who can marry any one without a house?

Lorenzo. We will have a house with floors of blue tile.

THE RED VELVET GOAT

There will be a patio with white flowers growing in it. And, at night, when the moon is shining, there will be a light of pure green silver on your face. The locusts will hum their scratchy tunes, and the gray mocking-birds will wake and sing to us.

ESTER. What will they sing?

LORENZO. Of other lands they've seen beneath the moon. Of dusky jewels shining on white arms. Of fields of flowers sweet in bloom. Night-blooming jasmine, and the pale filagree of oleander. Of lilies, fragile as your hands, and blossoming thorn too sweet for any man to know its fragrance.

ESTER [*moves to another bench and stands looking down at it*]. Is that all?

LORENZO [*following her*]. Perhaps they will sing of mountains like purple ships against the soft pink evening sky ... of cities that are pearls on the golden breasts of distant valleys....

ESTER [*whispering*]. Is that all?

LORENZO [*softly*]. Perhaps they will sing of blue tiled floors, and you and me. [*Catches up her hand.*] Will you walk around the plaza, three times, alone?

ESTER [*facing him and once again the flirt*]. With you?

LORENZO. With me.

ESTER. To-night?

LORENZO [*steps closer to her*]. To-night.

ESTER [*draws back; she hears voices in the street*]. There is Don Pepe.

LORENZO [*catching her wrist*]. But will you come?

ESTER [*jerks away from him, then laughs up into his face*]. Perhaps! [*Runs up to* LOLA *and* CARMEN *at the platform.*]

LORENZO [*catches his breath, then flings back his head and begins to sing triumphantly*].

> Shadow of our lord, St. Peter,
> The river lures me,
> The river lures me.
> And thus your love
> Would my poor love allure...
> My love allure.

ESTEBAN [*turning*]. Stop your crackling. Behind the curtains with you, and you, señoritas, to your chairs. [*The girls giggle as they return to their bench.*]

LORENZO [*as he passes* ESTER *he whispers*]. To-night?

[ESTER *tosses her head at him.* LORENZO *and* ESTEBAN *disappear behind the curtains as* DON PEPE, *the mayor of The Three Marys enters with* DOÑA BERTA *on his arm. She is a large impressive woman, while he is a tiny spry little man. A crowd of men and women follow them. The men wear various colored bandanas knotted about their throats, and the white pajama suits of the tropics, while the women are in colors as brilliant as the birds of the jungle country. They are all in a very gay humor, ready to enjoy the play.*]

DON PEPE [*impressively*]. I have not seen a play upon the stage since I was last in the United States. [*He leads* DOÑA BERTA *to the rockers.*] Good evening, Carmen, Lola, Ester.

LOLA. Do they have plays upon a stage in the United States?

DON PEPE. They have the photographs of people who walk across a screen and talk like you or me.

CARMEN [*giggles*]. Oh, Don Pepe, what a tease you are.

DON PEPE. And what is more they can make their water hot or cold with merely the turning of a handle.

MAN IN CROWD. Now, Don Pepe, would you play with us?

THE RED VELVET GOAT 265

Don Pepe [*with a luxurious sigh*]. Aye, it is an education to travel.

Doña Berta. I prefer my own bed every night.

Ester. Is it true that girls can walk with men, even though they are not engaged?

Don Pepe. It is indeed.

Doña Berta [*scandalized*]. A most immoral custom. Put not such foreign thoughts in our girls' heads, Don Pepe.

Don Pepe [*rises and makes her a low bow, then sits down again*]. Always your obedient servant, Doña Berta.

Mariana [*to* Ramon]. You had best into the prompter's box, while I change my gown.

Ramon. If you need aid....

Mariana [*tosses her head*]. Then I will not call for you, my saucy lad. [*She goes into the bedroom, right.*]

Ramon [*as he steps into the box the audience claps loudly. He holds up a modest hand*]. I am but the prompter, my friends.

Man in Crowd. Long life to the prompter. [*The audience claps loudly again.* Ramon *makes another bow, and lowers himself into the prompter's box.*]

Lola [*whispers*]. Ester, did Lorenzo ask you anything?

Ester. Why should I tell you what was said?

Carmen. We would keep your words as secret as a priest at confessional.

Doña Berta. What would you keep secret, Miss?

Carmen. Ester spoke with Lorenzo all alone.

Doña Berta [*scandalized*]. What?

Don Pepe [*startled*]. Eh?

Ester [*defensively*]. Lola, Carmen, and Don Esteban were here.

Lola. But just we three. That is almost the same as being alone.

Doña Berta. That is your wild advice taking root, Don Pepe.

Don Pepe. Girls and boys must speak together. How else would marriages arrange themselves?

Doña Berta. When I was young, girls listened to their parents.

Man in Crowd. Is that why you have remained a spinster, Doña Berta? [*Loud laughter from the crowd.*]

Drunk in Crowd [*sings tune of* La Cucaracha].

> All the maidens are of gold
> And the married ones of silver.
> All the widows are of copper
> And the others merely tin.
> *La cucaracha, la cucaracha....*

Doña Berta [*stands; she is furious*]. Is this the gathering place of drunks?

Don Pepe [*standing*]. Take out the fool.

Drunk. I paid my money....

Don Pepe [*in his most thundering voice*]. What did you say?

Drunk. I said... I need another drink. [*He staggers to the gate, then staggers back and shakes his finger at* Doña Berta, *as he sings tauntingly*]

> And the others are of lead....

[Don Pepe *signals to a man in the crowd who drags the* Drunk *outside the gate and then returns to his own bench.*]

Doña Berta [*reseating herself*]. Such common men deserve to stay in jail, Don Pepe.

Don Pepe [*flinging out his hands*]. He stays in jail so much, Doña Berta, that he keeps his clothes there and calls it his hotel. I gave him the key to his cell, yesterday. I became quite bored with locking it to keep him in, and then unlocking it to let him out.

[LORENZO *sticks his head through the curtains. There is loud applause from the audience.*]

LORENZO [*grinning and nodding his head, then to the prompter*]. Ramon. [RAMON *sticks his head above the prompter's box.*] Can you perform on the harmonica?

RAMON. Alas, my only talent is for the drums.

LORENZO [*woefully*]. But who will play the applause music?

MAN IN CROWD. We will sing it for you.

LORENZO. Thank you, my friend. [*Steps in front of the curtain.*]

AUDIENCE [*sings lustily*].

>Now the duck is in the pot
>Bubbling for the fire is hot,
>Lifts his head and calls for savor,
>Adds an onion for the flavor.

[*They applaud loudly.*]

LORENZO [*bows and shakes his own hands over his head to the audience*]. This is a tragedy of laughter, and a comedy of tears.

MAN IN CROWD. Long live the drama! [*Shouting and applause from the crowd.*]

LORENZO. Its story I need not tell you, for you will see it for yourselves upon the stage. We ask you to laugh where laughter is needed, and for your tears where you should weep. If you go home contented, our labor has been repaid. [*Retires behind the curtain. More shouts and applause from the audience.*]

MARIANA [*strolls in from the bedroom, dressed in a brilliant costume and with flowers in her hair*]. I am the heroine. Will some kind gentleman aid me to the platform?

Don Pepe [*hastening to her*]. May I be of service? [*Whispering as he lifts her to the platform.*] Was there enough to buy the goat?
Mariana [*laughs*]. Quite enough, my friend. Thank you. [*Disappears behind the curtain.*]
Lola [*nervously tittering*]. Oh, I am so excited.
Carmen. Some one is pulling back the curtain.
Esteban [*a large straw hat on his head, a gaily striped blanket over one shoulder, and carrying a gun now pulls back the curtains. There is loud applause from the audience.*]
Crowd [*sings*].

> Beans and corn and sweet potatoes,
> Add a touch of red tomatoes.
> Forget your sobs and your great sorrow,
> We will all be drunk to-morrow.

[Esteban *strikes an heroic attitude. There is a silence. Again he strikes an attitude. Again there is silence. He leans over and knocks on the prompter's box.*]
Ramon [*pops out his head*]. Eh?
Esteban [*impatiently*]. Well... begin.
Ramon [*blankly*]. Were you ready?
Esteban [*takes a deep breath*]. St. Peter give me patience! [*Thunders.*] We are ready!
Ramon [*lightly*]. I have no book.
Esteban. And you call yourself a prompter!
Ramon. No, a peddler. [*Seizing the opportunity, he stands and faces the audience*]. Ladies of the audience, I have silks and satins, wedding gowns, and gowns for mourning, threads and pins to make you beautiful—
Esteban [*screams*]. Enough! [*More quietly.*] This is a noble drama, not a sale of women's clothes. [*Calling through the door.*] Lorenzo, the book.

THE RED VELVET GOAT

LORENZO [*tosses the book through the curtains*]. Here you are, Father.
ESTEBAN [*hands it to* RAMON *who sinks down into the box. Again* ESTEBAN *strikes an attitude*]. Begin!
[*The prompter speaks rapidly in a clear, monotonous voice with the actors, but he is usually just a word ahead of them.*]
ESTEBAN AND RAMON. I am a soldier home from war...
AUDIENCE. Bravo!
ESTEBAN AND RAMON. I am the bravest man in Mexico!
AUDIENCE. Long live the Republic! Long live Mexico!
ESTEBAN AND RAMON. I am returned after twenty years to see my wife and child.
MAN IN CROWD. The Revolution only lasted eight years.
ESTEBAN [*glaring at him*]. Is this my war or yours?
[*Here* ESTEBAN *reads one speech and* RAMON *another.*]
RAMON. How I love my beautiful wife...
ESTEBAN. I am returned after thirty years.... [*Bangs on prompter's box.*] You are ahead of me, Ramon.
RAMON. Did I know you were going to repeat? [*Reading.*] To see my wife and son.
ESTEBAN [*exasperated*]. I have already said that.
RAMON. Well, say it again.
LORENZO [*sticking head through the door*]. Father! [*Crooks a finger at him.*]
ESTEBAN [*walks to the door*]. Well, what do you want?
LORENZO [*in a loud whisper*]. You entered too soon. We are supposed to be ahead of you.
ESTEBAN [*who is rapidly losing his patience*]. I wrote this play, and if I wish to be ahead of you, I will be first.
LORENZO. Mother says that if she does not enter now she will not act at all.
ESTEBAN [*who recognizes defeat when he sees it, sighs*]. Very well. [*Comes down to the edge of the platform and*

speaks to the audience.] Pretend I have not been here. I will return in a little while. [*Goes through door to much applause from the audience.*]
[MARIANA *and* LORENZO *enter.*]
MARIANA AND RAMON. I fear your father soon returns from the distant wars.
LORENZO AND RAMON. Father? You told me that he died long years before I was born.
MARIANA AND RAMON. There is a weight within my breast. I have always felt it there before I saw your father. [*Loud stamping noise behind platform door.*] I hear him now, the ghostly beat of horse's hoofs. [*Falls to her knees.*] Oh, Holy Virgin, save me from his wrath.
LORENZO AND RAMON. I will see who comes. [*He runs out through door.*]
MARIANA AND RAMON. [*She beats her chest.*] Aye, aye, aye.
[LORENZO *enters immediately wearing a false mustache.*]
LORENZO AND RAMON. My wife!
MARIANA AND RAMON. My husband! [*They fall into each other's arms. She draws back.*] I may no longer call you husband.
LORENZO AND RAMON. What news is this? What sad words beat against my brain?
MARIANA AND RAMON. I fear Lorenzo's father does return to-day.
LORENZO AND RAMON. You told me he was dead.
MARIANA AND RAMON. And so I thought, but in the cards I read of a dark man, a dangerous man, and he is very dark, and very dangerous.
LORENZO AND RAMON. Your speech has stabbed me....
LORENZO [*in a loud whisper to* RAMON]. Speak louder, Ramon.
LORENZO AND RAMON [RAMON *is laughing so hard his words are muffled*]. My heart is rent in twain.

LORENZO [*to* RAMON]. How can I hear you if you laugh, you fool?
LORENZO AND RAMON [*both begin to shout, but* RAMON *wins*]. I die, I die ... I am dead! [LORENZO *stretches himself carefully out on the platform.*]
MARIANA AND RAMON. Help, help, he is dead. [*She kneels beside him. Lifts up her arms, then looks at the audience.*]
MARIANA. Silence, please. This is the sad speech.
MARIANA AND RAMON. Oh, saints in Heaven, protect me from the wrath of man. Guard in your arms this poor sweet soul whose only sin... [*She gives a long sob*] ... was loving me too much.
ESTER [*wailing*]. Oh, Carmen, Lorenzo is dead!
LORENZO [*sitting up*]. I will return to life if you will walk around the plaza with me.
MARIANA [*pushes him down*]. Lie down, you fool. You are dead. [*To* RAMON.] What happens next?
RAMON. You carry him out.
MARIANA [*in a loud whisper*]. Lorenzo, this is where you go out. [LORENZO *stands.*] Walk like a ghost. Remember, you are dead.
[LORENZO, *in as ghost-like a manner as possible, vanishes through the platform door.*]
MARIANA AND RAMON. I am a widow once again. Oh, Heaven. Oh, Saints. Oh, Love. [*She follows* LORENZO *out.* ESTEBAN *enters with his face turned to the side, proving that he can not see* MARIANA.]
ESTEBAN [*to the audience*]. You remember that I am home, so we will continue from where I was... [*He glares at the platform door.*] ... interrupted. I am ready to begin, Ramon.
ESTEBAN AND RAMON. I bear upon my chest the scars of war. [*Loud applause from the audience.*] Once I was

wounded.... [*Loud applause.* ESTEBAN *holds up his hand.*]

ESTEBAN. You are not supposed to clap there.

ESTEBAN AND RAMON. Once I was wounded, but my enemy was cut to bits, and now I am home again to feast my eyes upon the beauty of my wife. [*Knocks on the door.*] Are all within here deaf?

LORENZO [*without the mustache, enters*]. Father! [*Falls to his knees.*]

ESTEBAN AND RAMON [*draws back with dramatic surprise*]. And who are you?

LORENZO AND RAMON. Your son.

ESTEBAN AND RAMON. My son? Your age?

LORENZO AND RAMON. Nineteen.

ESTER. Lorenzo! You told me you were twenty-two.

DON PEPE. This is a play, child, not a truth.

ESTEBAN AND RAMON [*with a glare for the interruption*]. A son of mine nineteen, and I from home for thirty years?

MAN IN CROWD. You said twenty the first time.

ESTEBAN. Did I not write this play? If I choose to change the date then I change the date, with no advice from you!

ESTEBAN AND RAMON. Where hides the woman you call mother, and whom I once called wife!

ESTEBAN [*to the audience*]. You can applaud for that. [*Loud applause.* ESTEBAN *modestly waving his hand*]. Thank you, my friends.

ESTEBAN AND RAMON. Where is she?

[MARIANA *enters.*]

MARIANA AND RAMON. Aye, Federico!

ESTEBAN AND RAMON. Ysabela, my love....

MARIANA AND RAMON. My husband! [*They embrace.*]

ESTEBAN AND RAMON [ESTEBAN *drawing back from her*]. One moment! Explain how it is that I have a son nineteen, and I from home... [*He comes down and glares at the* MAN IN CROWD] ... forty years!

MARIANA AND RAMON. I thought that you were dead, completely dead.

ESTEBAN AND RAMON. Kneel down.

MARIANA AND RAMON [*she kneels*]. I was young and beautiful, and weak to a man's whisper.

ESTEBAN AND RAMON. I must commune within my mind, secret and alone.

ESTEBAN [*goes down and faces audience*]. What shall I do? What would you do, my friends?

MAN IN CROWD. Shoot her!

ANOTHER MAN. Chop off her head!

ANOTHER [*in a trembling voice*]. Forgive her.

ESTEBAN [*raps on prompter's box*]. What do I do now?

RAMON. You choke her.

ESTEBAN AND RAMON [*he returns and begins to choke* MARIANA]. So shall all men deal with unfaithful wives. [*Loud applause from the audience.* ESTEBAN *bows and goes down to edge of platform, shaking his own hands above his head.*]

AUDIENCE [*singing*].

> Hungry now the neighbor's look,
> Stand and wait and watch it cook.
> But, alas, they must not eat it.
> Bravo! Bravo! ! !

ESTEBAN. Thank you, my friends. [*Goes back and finishes choking* MARIANA. *She falls dead.*]

ESTEBAN AND RAMON. So am I revenged. [*He kicks her.*]

MARIANA [*sits up angrily*]. That kick was not in the play!

ESTEBAN. Shh ... lie down. You are dead.

MARIANA. Not too dead to deal with you, you ancient eater of cow's meat. [*Reaches out and grasps one of the vases on the prompter's box and throws it at him. He ducks, and it smashes on the floor. She screams.*] Aye, it was my own vase! I thought it was Doña Berta's.

DOÑA BERTA [*stands*]. So I am not only insulted, but my property is destroyed as well. I stay no longer here! [*Sweeps out of the patio with hurt dignity. The audience rises.*]

ESTEBAN [*wringing his hands*]. But the play is not finished. I have still a beautiful speech.

MARIANA [*jumps down from the platform*]. Say it alone! I am finished with your drama. [*Runs into bedroom, right.*]

RAMON [*climbs out of the prompter's box*]. As for me, I prefer a good bottle of beer in the saloon. I have money, my friends. Who joins me? [*With much cheering the audience, with the exception of* DON PEPE, LOLA, CARMEN, *and* ESTER *press forward to shake* ESTEBAN'S *hand, and then follow* RAMON *through the gate.*]

ESTEBAN [*sits down on the edge of the platform*]. My beautiful play.

DON PEPE [*comfortingly*]. It was an excellent drama, my friend. I think that we can arrange about the goat. [*To the girls.*] Shall I walk home with these three pretty flowers?

LOLA [*giggles*]. Aye, Don Pepe.

CARMEN. Will you tell us all about the United States?

DON PEPE [*beaming*]. With the greatest of pleasure.

LORENZO [*who has worked his way around to* ESTER]. Ester.

ESTER [*earnestly*]. When you died I knew the truth.

LORENZO. Will you be on the plaza to-night?

ESTER [*stamps her foot*]. No.

LORENZO [*crestfallen*]. You ... won't?

ESTER. Not unless you should be there, too. [*Runs out through the gate.*]

LORENZO. Ester! [*Runs out after her.*]

DON PEPE. My three flowers have shrunk to two...one for each arm. [*He extends his crooked arms and the girls take them.*]

LOLA [*as they exit through the gate*]. Do they have such beautiful dramas in the United States?

[ESTEBAN *sinks his chin in his hands and takes a long sniffling breath.* MARIANA *enters, dressed in a bridal gown. She parades up and down in front of him.*]

ESTEBAN [*sighs*]. The play is finished, but at least we have enough to buy the goat. [*Notices her for the first time.*] What are you wearing?

MARIANA. A bridal gown, which you could see if you were not so blind, my fool.

ESTEBAN. Have I seen that gown before?

MARIANA. I think not. It has only just been purchased. [*Preens herself.*]

ESTEBAN [*springing up*]. From Ramon? [*He catches her wrist.*]

MARIANA [*pulling her hand away*]. From the peddler of silks and satins, threads and pins, to make all ladies beautiful.

ESTEBAN [*narrowing his eyes*]. With what did you pay for that gown?

MARIANA [*touching her dress lightly*]. With the money that I took in at the door.

ESTEBAN [*squeaking*]. The money for my goat?

MARIANA. No, my love. [*Jerks the velvet from the prompter's box and holds it out toward him.*] The money to replace an ancient gown of bright red velvet.

[ESTEBAN *grasps his head and moans as*

THE CURTAINS CLOSE

NEW MEXICO

STICK 'EM UP
A COMEDY OF FRONTIER NEW MEXICO

BY GORDON CLOUSER

OF ROSWELL, NEW MEXICO

Written in the summer playwriting course at the University of North Carolina and originally produced by The Carolina Playmakers at Chapel Hill on July 20, 1938.

THE CHARACTERS

SHERIFF BOB, *the "law" of El Centro*......Don Muller
HENRY, *an old-timer*..................Arthur Persky
MARK, *owner and operator of The Oriental Bar*
　　　　　　　　　　　　　　　　　Robert Wherry
JACK, *a Horse-Lake Ranch cowboy*......Neil Hartley
CLARENCE, *a not-quite-bright tenderfoot from Kansas*
　　　　　　　　　　　　　　　　　Frank Groseclose
PINTO-EYED PETE, *desperado*..........Joe Blickman
JIM ⎫　　　　　　　　　　　⎧Milton Eller
BILL ⎬ *town characters* ......⎨W. P. Covington, III
CHET ⎭　　　　　　　　　　　⎩Claude Suddreth

SCENE: *El Centro, New Mexico: The Oriental Bar.*
TIME: *July, 1883. Late afternoon.*

Copyright, 1938, by The Carolina Playmakers, Inc.
All rights reserved.

FRONTIER NEW MEXICO

NEW Mexico has always been a land of romance and adventure. Coronado entered the land of the Zuñis and the Seven Cities of Cibola in 1540 seeking the fabled streets of yellow gold, rich stores of sparkling jewels, and glittering treasure. He found only a few ornaments of turquoise, the color of the sky, and the yellow sands of the Indian pueblos. But the love of adventuring has persisted in New Mexico, none the less, even to our own times.

After Coronado came the Franciscan padres to build their mission churches and to give Catholic names to an Indian pueblo, *La Villa Real de la Santa Fé de San Francisco de Assisi;* a range of mountains, *Sangre de Cristo* (Blood of Christ); an enchanted mesa, *La Mesa Encantada.*

The frontier period of the cowboy comedy in this volume may seem unromantic indeed against the exciting background of the Pueblo Indians and the Spanish invaders. But the history of the early settlement of New Mexico exhibits a scene of violent conflicts, of a restless pioneering folk, still unexplored by the American dramatist: nomadic Navajos; United States Army skirmishes; Hopi dance rituals; round-ups; gold prospectors; mining camps and mushroom towns, now ghosts of an outlived past; feuds between cattle owners and nesters; lonely sheep herders. . . .

Territorial New Mexico in the 1880's was the scene of restless living, daring achievement, robustious and sometimes even grim, humor. Gordon Clouser of Roswell, New Mexico, the author of *Stick 'Em Up,* likes to tell the story of a cowboy from Las Vegas who rode up to a squatter's cabin one day and called out, "Mrs. Martin, do you know where your husband is?"

The woman came to the door, "Why yes, he went after some new harness; he's in town."

"Oh, no, he ain't," the rider guffawed. "We just caught him

rustlin' some stock and he's hanging on a big cottonwood tree down on the river.— He's got a new harness all right!"

No less extravagant, but far more agreeable, is the humorous incident of frontier life recorded by the young playwright in *Stick 'Em Up.*

STICK 'EM UP

The scene is the cool, whitewashed interior of an adobe building, gratifyingly dim in contrast to the brilliant glare of the afternoon sun outside. On the rear wall, somewhat left of the center, is a large mirror with "ORIENTAL BAR" and "TWO FINGERS—TWO BITS" lettered in white upon it. Flanking it are shelves stocked with bottles of wine, whisky, and cognac, a row of beer mugs, wineglasses, and the "bet box." Above, to the right of the bar, is a poster with the likeness of an outlaw pictured on it, and the legend, "DEAD OR ALIVE—PINTO-EYED PETE, $5,000 REWARD." In front of the mirror is a small, rather crude bar incongruously sporting an elegant brass footrail. A large brass spittoon is tucked behind the rail, and the splotched area around it testifies to the fact that even here in the frontier country of New Mexico not every one is a dead shot.

Set at an angle across the right corner of the room are two blue-shuttered swinging doors. On the right wall is a chromo-painting of a voluptuous lady in the nude. She is reclining on her side, her very yellow hair discreetly draped to conceal enough of her nudity to make her appear tantalizing. By the right wall are a table and two chairs.

In the left wall, opposite the bar, is a door leading outside to the alley. Downstage from it are several sad, bullet-riddled beer kegs. On the wall is a four-inch strip of paper crudely lettered with the words: OLD THUNDERBOLT WHISKY.

[*As the curtain opens,* MART *is behind the bar, the* SHERIFF *sulking in a chair by the table, and* HENRY *is standing at the end of the bar, midway between them.*]

[MART *is the none-too-savory bartender. He wears a large, soiled apron, is unshaven, pudgy, and possessed of a generally greasy appearance. One is certain that his hands are always moist and disagreeable; it is better to simply say "Hello" to him.*]

[*The* SHERIFF *is a tall, blustery individual who relies upon his manner and his fierce mustache to extricate him from awkward situations. He does not possess a surplus of physical courage, but he is really a very likable fellow for all that. There is something ingratiating about him. He wears corduroy trousers outside his cowboy boots, a holstered gun, tan shirt open at the neck, and a broad-brimmed brown hat.*]

[HENRY *is an elderly man, rather stooped and walking with a slight limp but endowed with an amazing store of energy. There is nothing decrepit about him. He is the wiry type of oldster who, dried-up though he may seem, can still out-ride and out-rope many a younger man if necessary. He is wearing a flat-crowned black hat shoved well back on his head, a once-white shirt, dark vest (open), baggy trousers, and high-heeled riding boots. It is five or six days since he has shaved, and his face is covered with a thick stubble considerably grayer than his hair.*]

HENRY [*to the* SHERIFF]. Yes sir, she sure is slippin'! This here Territory's just like an old mossback steer what has to have a cowpoke * come along and tail him up to keep him on his feet. Take the Governor, for instance. Why did President Hayes send Lew Wallace out here five years ago? [*He looks to* MART, *who spreads his hands,*

* Cowboy.

palms up.] You know as well as I do. [*He turns to the* SHERIFF.] The Lincoln County war'd got so's the county couldn't stop it, Governor Axtell couldn't stop it, and the whole blamed Territory couldn't stop it! Axtell lit out, and Wallace loped in.... Take Billy the Kid, who finally got him?

SHERIFF. Yeah, we know, but—

HENRY [*interrupting*]. Pat Garrett, that's who! And who's Pat? A New Mexican? Not by a stack of blues,* he ain't. A longhorn Texas hide-hunter, that's what he is; and if the buffalo hadn't give out, he'd still be peggin' out hides.

SHERIFF. Well, who cares?

MART [*shifting his tobacco cud*]. Don't make much difference, does it?

HENRY [*turning on him*]. Just goes to show what I been a-sayin'. New Mexico's slippin', always got to call in some hombre from the outside. Look at John William Poe, another Tejano.†... Half a notion he'd be a good one to get over from Lincoln County to catch Pinto-Eye there. [*He motions to the poster on the wall. The* SHERIFF *rises, stung.*]

SHERIFF. Now listen here, Henry; you keep a tighter rein on your lip. Mebbe New Mexico's slippin', but El Centro ain't—[*With a malevolent glare at* MART.]—or wasn't 'til yesterday. [MART *looks away uncomfortably.*] And what's more, I don't need Poe or Garrett or any one else to help me get Pinto-Eyed Pete. Understand? [*He strides across to the bar.*]

HENRY. Well, all right then, Sheriff Bob; you needn't get on the prod.‡ But you ain't done nothing since Pete was here last—and you didn't do much then!—Now I'm talkin'

---

* Blue poker chips.   † A Texan.
‡ A colloquial phrase meaning to get angry.

for the voters of El Centro, and what we want is some action, pronto, [*He spits loudly;* MART *leans over the bar to see if he has hit the spittoon.*] not just a lot of talk! [*He turns on his heel and limps out. The* SHERIFF, *disgusted, turns to* MART.]

SHERIFF. There you are! No wonder we're slippin', with people like you and Henry 'round here, not givin' any support to the law. [MART *tries to say something, but the* SHERIFF *is ahead of him.*] Yes, and of the two I think you're the worst. It's a disgrace, that's what it is—a disgrace to the town of El Centro! Here we are in the state's best cattle range and right next to good gold minin' country. Right in line to become the queen city of New Mexico, we were, and you let this thing happen! Ain't you got no civic pride?

MART. Aw, but Bob, I couldn't 'a' done nothin' about it. Four o'clock ever'thing was all right. Then them crazy Texans blowed in, and ten minutes later I could see just what was goin' to happen.

SHERIFF. And what did you do then? Nothin'! That's what makes me so danged mad.

MART [*almost in revolt*]. Well, good hunk! What in thunder *could* I do?

[JACK, *a tall, blond cowboy, strolls in from the street in time to hear the* SHERIFF's *rejoinder. He wears a broad-brimmed gray Stetson, red-checkered shirt, and blue jeans tucked into the tops of decorative cowboy boots. The shirt and trousers are workaday, faded and worn, but the rest of his outfit has the appearance of having been carefully saved for trips into town; his bright spurs jangling as he walks. He is clean-shaven and clear-eyed, a jovial youth who loves to relax against the bar and tell a joke or rag some one.*]

SHERIFF. You could 'a' called on me, your sheriff—on the

reg'larly constituted law of the country—that's what you could 'a' done! And that's what you should 'a' done—what you would 'a' done if you'd 'a' had any sense! [*During this speech the* SHERIFF *has crossed to the table. He sits down.*]

JACK. Them's powerful hard words, Sheriff. What's he done to deserve 'em?

SHERIFF [*snorting*]. Hunh? Him?

JACK. Yeah. [*To* MART.] Schooner of beer, Mart?

SHERIFF [*stung*]. Beer! Gah! Beer! Do you know what that double-dyed son of an orey-eyed * maverick's † went an' done? He's run out of *beer!*

JACK [*incredulous*]. Run out of beer? [*He looks hard at* MART, *who shrugs, spreads his hands deprecatingly, and continues wiping the bar.*]

SHERIFF [*turning away*]. To my everlastin' shame I admit it, Jack. It's a blow El Centro ain't goin' to recover from in a hurry; matter of fact, I don't s'pose we'll ever live it down. Folks don't forget things like that in a hurry.

JACK. Don't know as you can blame 'em either, Sheriff. A fellow sort of counts on somethin' cool when he rides into town these hot days— How'd it happen?

SHERIFF. Ask him; he's the one responsible.

JACK [*to the* BARTENDER]. How about it, Mart?

MART. Aw, they was plenty of beer to 'a' lasted, but a bunch of Tejanos blowed in yesterday. They drunk all they could, and then old Shanghai Pierce—you know 'im, don't you?

JACK. Yeah, I've saw 'im around a couple o' times—the bird that paid a two-thousand-dollar fine over in Dodge City once, ain't he?

MART. Yeah. Well, he tossed me a hunnerd dollars to pay for everything and then started salivatin' ‡ the kegs.

* Wild-eyed.   † A motherless calf.   ‡ Shooting.

Wasn't one of them he didn't shoot plumb full of holes.

JACK [*laughs and goes to look at the bullet-riddled kegs*]. Boy howd'y'! He sure does things up brown when he gets started, don't he?

MART. Yeah, you must 'a' not been in town long, not to 'a' heard about it.

JACK [*leaning against the end of the bar*]. Naw, just rode in to get some blank cartridges—[*He slaps the box down upon the bar.*]—and fireworks for the Fourth out at the ranch. Old Man Singer was pretty busy, so I hunted up the stuff myself; didn't talk to nobody much.

MART [*wearily*]. Everybody here knows all about it—and danged if they don't most of them blame me for it—just like Sheriff Bob here!

JACK [*amused*]. He always did like his beer. [*He moves over to the* SHERIFF]. Well, how about it, Sheriff? Caught up with Pinto-eyed Pete yet?

SHERIFF [*rousing*]. Pete, did you say? Not yet, I ain't, but I'm sure goin' to! Yes, sir, and I'm a-goin' to do it soon.

JACK. Better not take too long; election's comin' up this fall.

SHERIFF [*putting on the pompous pose of the politician*]. Gentlemen, you mark my words, Pete'll be in jail months before election time. You know me, boys; when I go after a man, I get 'im! You know my record.

JACK. Let's see ... your record was a half-mile in nineteen seconds, wasn't it—the last time you saw Pete? Fellow told me he never thought that ol' nag of your'n could run so fast. Said you sure *got away* in a hurry! [*With a loud laugh.*]

SHERIFF [*snarls*]. Who said that?

JACK [*at the bar*]. I don't rightly remember. Fellow did say, though, we sure elected a good rider! [*Another laugh.*]

SHERIFF. There, Mart, you hear that? That's the kind of

slander some of them low-down, side-windin' politicians spread around. Everybody knows why I come back—I'd forgot my rifle. Time I could get back there with it, Pete'd pulled his freight. He got away that time, but the next time I see 'im I'll...

[HENRY and JIM *rush in through the swinging doors.*]

HENRY. Hey, Sheriff!

[BILL and CHET *run in. The* SHERIFF *is annoyed by the interruption.*]

SHERIFF. Now what?

HENRY. He's come!

JIM. Just rode into town! Ben Thompson seen 'im!

SHERIFF [*with complete self-assurance*]. All right, now. Who rode into town, and who'd Ben see?

JIM. Pete!

CHET. Pinto-Eyed Pete!

SHERIFF [*rising abruptly*]. What?

BILL. Sure has.

HENRY. Yeah! Rode in from the south, Ben says, and we hurried after you, 'cause we knowed you'd want to get right after 'im.

JIM. 'Tain't long 'til election, Bob. Be a cinch if you got Pete.

SHERIFF [*hesitantly*]. Yeah...ah...why, yeah! Sure!... Sure thing! I been waitin' for a chance at Pete, but... ah...we got to be careful.... [*In quick explanation.*] Ah...daren't let 'im get away....

HENRY. Sure dassen't.

SHERIFF [*stalling*]. Let me see, now.... You say he rode in from the south, Jim?

HENRY. That's what Ben said.

SHERIFF. He did, huh? From the south...hmmm...Goin' to take some real figurin' now to catch that bird.

JACK. Goin' to take a little action too, ain't it, Bob?

SHERIFF. You're just like the rest of these wild punchers 'round here—long on rampagin', but mighty short on thinkin'. . . . Goin' to take strategy to get Pete. . . . C'm' on, you fellows, out this way.

JACK. Hey, Bob; they said he come from t'other way, from the south!

SHERIFF [*furiously*]. This here's strategy, you idiot! We got to circle 'round and cut off his retreat. [*He turns away disgusted, and leaves.* JACK *calls after him.*]

JACK. Well, don't forget your rifle this time.

[HENRY *watches the exit of the others, then turns toward the front door.*]

MART. Ain't you goin' to go see the fun?

HENRY. Hunh! Bob ain't goin' nowheres near Pinto-Eye—not if he knows it. He'll hole up some place till he hears Pete's left town. . . . We'll have a new sheriff, though, come election. [*He leaves by the front door.* MART *turns to* JACK.]

MART. I don't know about that. Ol' Bob's right smart of a politician.

JACK [*crossing to the chair and straddling it*]. Politician or not, he's done for in El Centro; he ain't got a chance in the 'lection. Why, I wouldn't bet on him if you gave me ten to one.

MART. Would you bet ten to one the other way?

JACK. Sure thing; I'd give ten to one against him right off—only nobody'd be fool enough to bet with me that way.

MART. I'd take a little on ol' Bob at ten to one. How much you got?

JACK. Couple o' months pay. You goin' to be fool enough—

MART. Aw, we'll find that out election time. I got a ten-spot here. [*He pulls it out.*] Got a hunnerd to cover it with?

JACK [*hesitant*]. Yeah, but—

MART. Let's have it, then. We'll put it in the bet box. [*He takes from the shelf the cigar-box which serves that purpose.*]

JACK. But that leaves me awful close, Mart.

MART. You backin' down?

JACK. Aw, hell, then! [*He rises and goes to the bar, pulling out his money as he does so. He counts the hundred out.*] Here you are. [*He tosses the money to* MART, *who adds his ten to it and places the whole amount in a cigar box on a shelf by the mirror.*] Reckon it's safe enough. You won't catch Bob takin' a chance if he don't . . . if he don't have to.

[CLARENCE, *the not-quite-bright tenderfoot from Kansas, enters disconsolately, carrying an old, double-barreled shotgun. He is slightly built and there is a wistful quality about his peaked face; he looks as though he has missed something, knows that he has, but is unable to do anything about it. His mind works slowly and he must concentrate carefully on anything he wishes to understand. His movements are correspondingly slow, except when he has an end clearly in view and a purpose which to him seems sufficiently worthy. He is poorly dressed in old shoes, ragged trousers and shirt, and a floppy, broken-brimmed soft straw hat.* JACK *looks him over.*]

JACK. Howd'y'.

CLARENCE [*meekly*]. 'Lo.

JACK. Stranger here in town?

CLARENCE. Yeah . . . sort o'. . . .

JACK. Mind sayin' where from?

CLARENCE [*petulantly*]. From Kansas—an' I wish I was back there, too! [MART *moves out from behind the bar, to get a better look at the lad.*]

JACK. Don't sound like you thought much of El Centro.

CLARENCE [*aggrieved*]. Well, gee whiz, this ain't like the

West ought to be! There ain't any shootin', or stage-robbin', or anything!

JACK. Oh, ... I see. [*He gets an idea, and turns to* MART *with a wink.*] Say, listen, Mart; give me my gun—I ain't drunk now.

MART [*not understanding*]. Huh?

JACK [*winking again*]. My gun—you know, the one you put down there on the shelf for me.

MART [*still not comprehending*]. But that's—

JACK [*interrupting*]. Yeah, sure, I know it's against the law, but then nobody obeys the law nohow. [*He winks again.*] Come on, Mart; give me the gun—you wouldn't want to let some gunman kill me, would you?

MART [*still puzzled*]. You don't look drunk, but—

JACK. I'm not drunk, Mart; it'll be safe to give me my own gun. It's right down there. [*He indicates the shelf under the bar.*]

MART. Well, ... all right. [*He goes back, takes up a gun with belt and holster from under the bar, and gives it to* JACK.] But you be careful with that there gun!

JACK. Thanks, Mart; I'll go easy with it. [*He buckles it on as* MART *returns to his place behind the bar.*] There, now I'm dressed again!

CLARENCE [*naïvely*]. But you were dressed all the time!

JACK [*with gusto*]. Young fellow, in this here town ain't no man dressed 'thout his gun. Mart always coaxes mine away from me when I get drunk 'cause he don't want me ruinin' his mirror, but I'm sure glad to get it back— Better look it over, though, I guess. [*He draws the revolver, punches out the shells, and places them on the bar, then proceeds to load it with blanks from the box he had previously set out.* CLARENCE *rises and watches him with great interest.*]

CLARENCE. What're you doin' that for?

JACK. Safety first. Can't take no chances on old shells; might miss fire.
CLARENCE [*impressed*]. Oh....
JACK [*holstering his gun and looking* CLARENCE *over*]. You don't carry a hog-leg, hunh? Couple of derringers up your sleeves, mebbe?
CLARENCE. Me? Hunh-unh! They cost too much.
JACK. Shoulder holster, then? Or a bulldog?
CLARENCE. Why... uh... no—
JACK [*pretending astonishment*]. Nothin' but that ol' shotgun? An' you come right through town and got here alive?
CLARENCE. Well... well... well, why not? [*He advances a step or two towards* JACK.] This place ain't wild, is it?
JACK. Ain't wild? Great snakes and rattlers, man! Why, this here's the toughest town in $72\frac{1}{4}$ states—mebbe in $72\frac{1}{2}$! El Centro has a couple of men for breakfast ever' day, a few more for dinner, and never less'n half-a-dozen for supper—one for each course, you might say—'cept'n mebbe in Lent. [*To* MART.] Who got it to-day?
MART [*finally catching on*]. Oh... uh... only Spear Heller and Dumpy Vanpelt this mornin'. Guess the real gunmen ain't woke up yet.
JACK. That's about the way of it. It ain't very late yet.
MART. Yeste'day was a real lively day, though. Bunch of killers blowed in from Texas, and they sure made things hum. Thirteen, I think it was altogether—or mebbe fourteen, was it? Let's see—[*He uses his fingers to count.*]—them six longhorns, Jim Bryant, Al Mossman—
JACK [*turning to* CLARENCE]. There, you see what kind of a place this is? And Pinto-Eyed Pete, the outlaw, is in town, too!—You got to be tough to get along in El Centro—real tough.—Like me! [MART *hides a grin, but* CLARENCE *is all attention.* JACK *pulls his gun and "throws down"*

on the boy, who is alarmed and tries to raise his shotgun.] No, you don't! No, you don't! Put 'at gun down! [CLARENCE *lowers the muzzle.*] Now you come up here. [*He moves up cautiously.*]

CLARENCE. B-b-b-b-but-but, mister, I-I wasn't aimin' to do anything.

JACK [*his hand reassuringly on* CLARENCE's *shoulder*]. Don't be scared, boy. I'm tough, I am, but I sort of cotton to you. I'm goin' to help you out. [*Impressively.*] Son, you wouldn't last ten minutes with that ol' scatter-gun; you can't swing it around fast enough. Now I'm goin' to give you some good advice: To keep a-kickin' here in El Centro they's only one thing to do—get the drop on the other fellow 'fore he drops you! Understan'?

CLARENCE. Yeah, but—

JACK. Now that's all right, son; I'll take care of that. I'm goin' to give you a couple of lessons, 'cause I sort o' like you, and I don't want you to get killed right off.

CLARENCE [*gratefully*]. Gee, mister, would you? [MART *takes a chew from a plug of tobacco.*]

JACK. Sure thing. Here, like I told you, the first thing's to get the drop—this way, see? [*He flips the gun to a level several times to demonstrate, then passes it to* CLARENCE, *who stands his shotgun against the bar.*] You try it. [CLARENCE *is very awkward at it.*] Naw, that'll never do! [JACK *takes the gun back.*] First fellow you met'd blow you to Kingdom Come! We got to think up somethin' else for you.... Here, how'd this be? [*He illustrates, taking the revolver in his right hand and folding his arms.*] You fold your arms, see—like this—and there can't nobody see your gun. Then all you do is this—[*He then swings the gun out from under his left armpit.*] Stick 'em up!

CLARENCE [*grinning*]. Sure, I can do that! Here, let me show you. [JACK *surrenders the gun, and* CLARENCE *rehearses.*] Stick 'em up! [*Another swing.*] Stick 'em up! [*And again.*] Stick 'em up! Gee, this's easy!

JACK. Well-l-l-l-l, that's fair.... But here's another important thing; it ain't enough just to get the drop, 'cause lots o' times fellows'll take the chance of beating you to the trigger. You got to let 'em have it!

CLARENCE [*beaming, gratefully*]. Gee, thanks a lot, Mr.... Mr....

MART [*behind the bar and leaning over it*]. Jack's his name.

CLARENCE. Mr. Jack, you're sure an awful big help to me!— Like this, huh? [*He fires point-blank at* JACK, *who sags, clutching his breast, and slips to the floor as dead.* MART *stares, open-mouthed, and then hurriedly disappears behind the bar.* CLARENCE *is delighted.*] Ye-e-e-e!!! It works! [*He looks around, then starts for the door.*] Boy, oh, boy, wait'll I find some of those tough Texas fellows! [*He scurries out.* JACK *sits up and stares after him.*]

JACK [*feelingly*]. Why, the damned idiot!... Sure lucky I put blanks in that gun! [MART *rises and comes around the right end of the bar, choking.*] What's the matter, Mart?

MART [*in a very small voice*]. I... swallered my cud!

JACK. What?

[MART *nods. As* JACK *stares in amazement, he ducks his head, clasps a hand over his mouth, and rushes straight ahead out the side door.* JACK *slaps his thigh and bursts into loud guffaws, rises, dusts himself off with his hat, and finally, still laughing, sits down at the table.* MART *returns rather slowly, and unsteadily.*]

MART. So you think it's funny, eh?

JACK. Oh, Lord, yes! [*He continues guffawing.*]

[*A shiver passes over* MART's *body; his eyes widen and his hand goes to his mouth as he fights off another threatened revolt of his stomach. He conquers it, but* JACK *has gone off into a violent fit of laughter.* MART *regards him malevolently.*]

MART [*glaring*]. You and your bright ideas!—That there cud wasn't half chewed out neither!

CLARENCE [*from some distance outside comes the faint command*]. Stick 'em up!

JACK. Listen! [*There is a shot, followed by a terrified yell.* JACK *slaps his leg again, rises, goes to the swinging doors, and looks out.*] Blamed if he ain't got some one else! Ain't he the damnedest? [*He comes back to the bar.*]

MART [*blackly*]. He's goin' to cause trouble, an' don't you forget it. Some one'll kill the poor fool!

JACK [*casually*]. Aw, well, the world'll just be rid of another idiot.

MART [*meaningly*]. Yeah, but not the right one! [*Another distant shot is heard.*]

JACK. Aw, you're gettin' crabby in your old age, Mart. You can't—

[*He breaks off as a tall heavily-built* STRANGER *appears, framed in the side doorway. He wears a big Mexican sombrero pulled low over blazing eyes and swarthy features. He has a heavy black mustache; and a gun is slung low on his thigh.*]

STRANGER. Howd'y'.

JACK. How you?

MART. Howd'y'. [MART *only stares at the* STRANGER *and backs away as he advances. The* STRANGER *halts.*]

STRANGER. What's wrong with you, friend?

MART. Why...uh...heh...uh, sort o' funny, but you kind o' remind me of Pete...Pinto-Eyed Pete...there. [*He indicates the poster, wild-eyed.*]

STRANGER [*calmly*]. Looks sort o' like me, does he?
MART [*suspicious*]. Yeah, matter o' fact, if you didn't have that mustache—
JACK [*edging away*]. Mustaches can be bought, or growed!
STRANGER [*advancing to the bar*]. Well, you boys needn't be scar't o' me; I'm not your outlaw. [*His foot on the rail.*] Ben Thompson did tell me, though, he seen this Pete you're talking about ride into town not so long ago.
MART [*relieved*]. Oh, then you been in town quite some time? [*He and* JACK *relax and advance a little nearer to the* STRANGER.]
STRANGER. Sure, come in yeste'day, 'bout mid-afternoon. Been down by the corrals most of the time, jawin' with the boys.
MART. Well, that's about the best way to catch up on the news, I reckon. What'll you have, stranger?
STRANGER. Glass of beer, if it's good and cold.
JACK [*starting*]. Huh?
MART [*tense*]. What'd you say?
STRANGER [*emphatically*]. Didn't you hear me? I said good, cold beer.
MART [*straining against the rear wall*]. You been here since yeste'day, an' you don't—
JACK [*excited*]. It must be Pete! [MART *ducks behind the bar. As* PETE *draws his gun,* JACK *makes a dash through the swinging door. He yells outside.*] Hey! Hey, you over there! Pete's down here—in The Oriental.
PETE [*puzzled and disgusted, scratches his head*]. Now how in the devil did they find out?
SHERIFF [*outside at a distance, purposely misunderstanding* "*Oriental*"]. Go north on Central, men! We'll head 'im off!
[PETE *listens intently.*]
JACK [*yelling*]. No, down here! Here in the saloon!

[*All the lines from this point on, until the entrance of* CLARENCE, *are outside.*]

HENRY. Down there, he says, Sheriff.

[PETE *settles his hat more firmly on his head and runs to the side door.*]

SHERIFF. Eh? Down there?

JIM. There!

[*The sound of a shot is heard.* PETE *slams the side door shut, and prepares for a siege. He scoops up the shotgun and sees that it is loaded, turns the table on its side downstage left, and piles the chairs around it. From behind this improvised barricade he commands both doors. He squints along the barrel of the shotgun. His mustache bothers him and he snatches it off, wincing a bit at the pull of the glue. Then, completely ignoring the hidden* MART *he begins laying out cartridges on the floor where they will be handy.*]

HENRY. Hog-tie me if I didn't miss the varmint!

JACK. Needn't be scared, Bob; Pete ain't got his rifle.

SHERIFF. That's him in The Oriental, you say?

JACK. Well, who'd you think it was? Billy the Kid? 'Course it's Pete!

SHERIFF [*in command*]. All right, then, boys; spread out a little. Some of you go 'round the back, so's he can't get out of that window.

CHET. Okay, Bob. He won't get out while we're a-watching.

SHERIFF [*raising his voice, alternately demanding and pleading*]. Pete, we got you surrounded. You might as well give up.... [*No answer.*] We know you're in there, and you haven't a chance to get away. You might as well be reasonable. [*No answer. The* SHERIFF *is becoming desperate; if he cannot persuade* PETE *to surrender, he'll be in as tight a place as* PETE *is.*] Listen, Pete, be sensible. Come on out with your paws in the air, and we'll treat you right. We'll sure salivate you, though, if you put up a fight. [*Still no answer.*]

HENRY [*derisively*]. Smoke 'im up, Sheriff!

JACK. Sure thing, Bob! Go right in there and pull 'im out by the heels!

SHERIFF [*hedging*]. Well, now, wait a minute—

JACK [*mocking him*]. What're you tremblin' for, Sheriff? Did you forget your rifle again?

SHERIFF [*stalling again*]. Who...who'll volunteer to run 'im out of there?

JACK. We elected *you* for that sort of thing; that's what we're payin' you for!

JIM. He's 'bout right, Bob; it's your job, sure as shootin'.

JACK. Remember election's in a couple of months, Sheriff!

SHERIFF [*desperately*]. All right then, you all get back out of the way.

JACK. Creep up on 'im, Sheriff!...Well, damned if he ain't!

[*The heavy breathing of the* SHERIFF *is now heard and his hat appears above the right swinging door, poked in on the muzzle of his revolver.* PETE *points at it, but doesn't fire. The* SHERIFF *withdraws the hat and replaces it absent-mindedly on his head—then peeps over the door.* PETE *fires twice and the* SHERIFF *pops back from view, thrusts his revolver over the door and shoots it blindly.* PETE *grins and decides to take advantage of the incident. He rises, kicks over a chair, gives a loud groan, and falls heavily to the floor, pretending to be dead. Then he bounds quietly to his feet and takes his station at the left of the bar, pointing his gun at the main entrance, his back to the side door.* MART *pops up from behind the bar, sees a decidedly live outlaw, and ducks back again.*]

SHERIFF [*outside, with a triumphant shout*]. Boys, I got 'im! Didn't you hear 'im fall? I got 'im!

JACK [*none too well pleased*]. Well, drag 'im out, then.

[*The side door opens quietly behind* PETE.]

SHERIFF. Hold your hosses, hold your hosses! Give me time to load my gun!

[CLARENCE *peers in at the side door and his face lights up at the prospect of another victim. Arms folded, he tiptoes in and jabs the muzzle of his gun into the small of* PETE'S *back.*]

CLARENCE [*sharply*]. Stick 'em up!

[PETE *stiffens, quickly weighs the chances, and decides against resistance. Dropping his gun on the bar, he raises his hands.* CLARENCE *turns away, closes his eyes and plugs an ear with his free index finger, then stops—in the very act of pulling the trigger—to count on the fingers of his left hand the number of shots he has already fired. He finds to his dismay that he has used up all six cartridges so he pushes the gun still harder into* PETE'S *back.*]

CLARENCE. An'—an' *keep* 'em up!!

[*The* SHERIFF *peeps in, blinks at the sight of the supposedly dead outlaw with his hands in the air; then, covering him with his gun, he takes charge.*]

SHERIFF. Well, Pete, you tried to pull a fast one on me, didn't you? You might 'a' knowed it wouldn't work—not on me!

[MART *rises again and appropriates* PETE'S *gun. The* SHERIFF *motions* PETE *away from the bar without seeing* CLARENCE, *who, deciding that he can't fight the rest of the town without cartridges, slips down at the end of the bar.* MART *watches in silent amazement. The others enter, fearfully at first, then confidently.* CLARENCE *squats on the floor and pulls the empty shells from his revolver. The* SHERIFF *is bulging with pride over his achievement.*]

JACK [*incredulously*]. Well, hail and hallelujah!!!

CHET. Sheriff, you've done yourself proud! Danged if I thought you had it in you!
SHERIFF [*preening himself proudly*]. Hah! Reckon I can count on your vote now too, Henry, come election?
HENRY [*coming to the fore with his rifle*]. Bob, any one that can do what you just done's the man we need for sheriff!
BILL. I'll say!
JIM. Bet your boots!
HENRY. 'Ray for Sheriff Bob!
ALL. Yipee!!! 'Ray for Sheriff Bob!
[*The* SHERIFF *joins in the cheer.* CLARENCE *feels in his pockets and looks around for more shells.*]
JIM [*after looking* PETE *over carefully*]. I thought you pinked 'im, Bob, but he ain't bleedin' none.
SHERIFF. Just a little trick of his, gents, but it didn't work —not on Sheriff Bob! No sir... Hah! Believe it or not, they was some folks in this town thought I was scared of Pete—that I was runnin' from him when I went back for my rifle. Hah!... [*With mock courtesy.*] Well, Pete, ready to look at your room in our little stone hotel?
[MART *takes another chew of tobacco.*]
ALL. Ha! Ha! Ha!
JIM. Soft bed, good home cookin', an' lots of peace and quiet!
[*They guffaw loudly.*]
HENRY. Rates mighty reasonable, too!
SHERIFF. All right. Let us out of the door, boys. [*They open a path and the humbled* PETE *goes out, the* SHERIFF *following.*] Guess the folks 'round here know what's what now, don't they?
[CLARENCE *peeks over the bar and sees the shells upon it. Jubilant, he slips around the end of the bar, out of sight.*]

OTHERS [*outside*]. They sure do, Bob! Absolutely! Bet your boots, Sheriff!

[JACK *remains disconsolately behind, propped against the bar.*]

JACK. I can't understand it, damned if I can.

[CLARENCE'S *hand comes up, gropes around, and finds the shells. He comes back into sight and squats at the end of the bar, loading his gun. Grinning,* MART *opens the bet box, takes the bills out, and, when he is sure* JACK *is watching, kisses them fondly.*]

MART. Mm-m-m, Baby! [*He stows the wad of bills away in his trousers pocket, then thinks of something, and pulls the dinero* out again. He peels off a bill and leans down to* CLARENCE.] Here, son. [JACK *stares in amazement, then leans over the bar to see what this is all about.* MART *turns toward him and is riffling the bills in his face as* CLARENCE *pops up from behind the bar, swings up his revolver and jams it into* MART'S *back.*]

CLARENCE. Stick 'em up!

[MART'S *mouth drops open, and his roll of bills falls from his hand. He gulps involuntarily, and the second cud of tobacco goes the way of the first as*

* Money.

THE CURTAIN FALLS

ARIZONA

CONCHITA
A ROMANCE OF A COPPER MINING TOWN

BY ROSEMARY SHIRLEY DeCAMP
OF JEROME, ARIZONA

Written in the summer session of the University of Southern California in Los Angeles, 1931, and originally produced at the Touchstone Theater on the campus there on July 22. It was first published in *The Carolina Play-Book* of September, 1931.

THE CHARACTERS

MANUEL, *a Mexican chauffeur, pro tem*..John J. Frisch
JOSE, *a Mexican miner*..............Charles Patmore
MARIA, *a Mexican matron*.............Hazel Baird
MEXICAN WOMEN.......Phyllis Pierson, Ruth Weyand
MRS. CONNOLLY, *the policeman's wife*
                                     Florence Chubbuck
THE SUPERINTENDENT'S WIFE..........Ruth Boerger
JESUS, *the best man at the wedding*....Harold Herson
CONCHITA, *a Mexican fandango dancer*
                                   Rosemary Shirley DeCamp
PEDRO, *the groom*....................Russel Brooks
ROSITA, *the bride*..................Dorothy Taylor
CONNOLLY, *a policeman*...............W. F. Stuckey
THE OLD MEXICAN SEXTON............Lloyd Waltz
AN OLD WOMAN....................Edith Brandeis
SPANISH PRIESTS.........Alpheus Lincoln, Jerry Blunt
THE WEDDING GUESTS.....Laurence Bachmann, Alice Bowers, Vera Booth, Mildred Culbertson, Edith Brandeis, Edna Day, Mary Hollingsworth, Alida Larson, Myrtle McLeod, Maybeth Fyle, Mamie LaRoque, Marian Morgan, Nancy Naumburg, Florence Sprenger, Marie Stubbs, Evelyn Towne, Emily Wyatt, Merrill Windsor, Nellie Smith, Mildred Silver, Martha McMillin.

SCENE: *The doorway of the old Catholic church in Jerome, Arizona.*
TIME: *Just before noon on a July morning.*

Copyright, 1931, by The Carolina Playmakers, Inc.
All rights reserved.

ARIZONA MINING TOWN

CONCHITA, an Arizona folk play, was written and produced in the course in playwriting and experimental production at the University of Southern California in the summer of 1931. Five other plays, written by the students that summer, were produced experimentally: *The Fatted Calf,* a Dakota farm play, by Charles Upham Patmore; *Object—Matrimony,* a folk comedy of Wyoming, by Coza Clausen; *Weather-Beaten,* a tragedy of the Montana plains, by Phyllis Pierson; *Stoves,** a Utah farm comedy, by Mary Cottam Hatch; and *Casting Office,* a play of Hollywood, by Harold Hersom. All the plays were presented in the Touchstone Theater on the University campus. Six new plays representing six different states in the West! It was really a thrilling adventure.

The author of *Conchita,* Rosemary Shirley DeCamp, was born in a little town in northern Arizona, the daughter of a mining engineer. Packed into the most convenient bundle by her mother, she was carried about from camp to camp. She recalls vividly now the strikes, Mexican uprisings, and mine disasters that were all too common in her childhood days.

The scene of her little play of Conchita is the doorway of the Catholic Church opposite her home in Jerome, Arizona, and the incident she recalls here she herself witnessed from the window of her home. "A great deal of my youth," she tells us, "was spent in the house across the street from that doorway. Through it I saw every kind of creature walk, limp, or being carried. Some dramatic incident took place on those steps almost every day.

"The town is made up almost wholly of Mexicans and Spaniards with every other race and breed thrown in, hot-headed, passionate people very near their primitive ancestors. So near that the thin varnish of their civilization will bear no strain, and is often melted in the warmth of a friendly argument. Man-

---
* Renamed *Spring Storm.* See page. 343.

uel, Mrs. Connolly, The Old Woman who faints in the play, and The Superintendent's Wife are still living in Jerome, Arizona. Conchita is the essence of her kind. I have seen, met, and ordered her about in mining camps all over Arizona and Mexico.

"This atmosphere, combined with the natural drama of one of the largest copper mines in the world, created for me a tremendously dramatic childhood—murders, explosions, fires, and escapes were a part of my daily life. For that reason I beg your understanding of this seemingly melodramatic incident."

CONCHITA

The little sprawling town of Jerome, Arizona, a mining camp near the Mexican border, clings to a bare mountainside, and the Catholic Church is high above the town. Over the doorway is a large gilt cross. Just now the high tower of the Church casts a cool blue shadow across the scene. The rest of the town lies stifled and quiet under the broiling noonday sun.

Devout Catholics climb the steep stairs and the long walk that leads to the Church door, two and sometimes three times a day—some from love of God and some from fear of their sins.

The roadway continues up the hill slope beyond the Church, right, out of sight. A railing on the far side of the ascending walk is silhouetted sharply against the soft turquoise of the distant mountain ranges. This rail serves as a support for the foot-weary worshipers. At the left side a narrow stairway leads down to the living quarters of the priests.

Rose petals, scattered over the steps, pink and red, mark the path of the bride within. The outer doors are thrown back and the sound of an old organ and a chorus of voices singing a minor chant comes from the cold, musty depths of the Church.

[*The aged, white-haired* MEXICAN SEXTON *in faded blue jeans climbs wearily up the stairway from the left. He carries a broom and begins sweeping the rose petals from the steps and walk.*]

[MANUEL, *in dusty, green serge "store suit" saunters down the hill from the right. When he comes within the shadow of the Church he pauses, looks up at the gilt cross, and removes his hat. He mops his brow, twists his drooping mustachios and sits on a boulder at the right of the steps. He pulls a toothpick from an inner pocket and goes to picking his shining gold teeth with complacent care.*]

THE OLD SEXTON. Agh! Twice already I have cleaned these steps—trash—all day long nothing but trash!

MANUEL. Well, the steps of the Church must always be clean.

[THE OLD SEXTON *grunts and wobbles down the stairs, left, with his broom.*]

[*The sound of hobnailed boots tramping down the walk from the mine pits above becomes louder and louder. A Mexican miner,* JOSE, *comes into view, right. He is covered with gray dust. His face is unrecognizable. He carries a lunch bucket and wears a cap with a carbide lamp on his forehead.*]

JOSE [*removing his hat as he observes the cross*]. Cómo está, Manuel? How are you?

MANUEL [*his real interest in the toothpick still*]. Cómo está, José? You come from the graveyard shift?

JOSE. Sí. Sí. We mucked fifty yards last night and I am tired. But you, *mi amigo*, why do you wait at the door of the Church? You feel it perhaps more fit? No? [*His rich Mexican voice breaks into a low laugh as he leans against the railing near* MANUEL'S *boulder.*]

MANUEL. No. *Seas tonto.* Don't be foolish. I wait to drive the bridal party of Pedro Rodríguez who marries Rosita Fernández y Mayogotia within at this same hour. You have not heard? It is a big wedding so they have it at regular mass. Half the camp is inside. A very grand affair!

[*One feels in his satisfaction that he is responsible for it all.*]

MANUEL. No. Pedro has at last plucked the young virgin from the arms of old Fernández. He has done well. Ah! And Rosita, too. She has not got for herself a young devil? Handsome and gay?—The women, they have worn a path to his door on their knees.

JOSE. *Sí.* And he's take what he wanted and throw the rest out to rot on the street. Oh! If I could have had such luck, José would not have been so selfish—so unkind. *Dios, no!*

MANUEL. Hmm-m-m. It is a great pity the women of the town know so little of the greatness, the goodness of your heart. [*He is lost in admiration of his own sarcasm.*]

JOSE [*seating himself on the railing, toes caught on the second bar so that he may hang by his knees—a position one may retain for hours with care*]. But, Manuel, have I not heard there was one who loved him more than the rest? One whom he seemed always to return to when he was weary of the pay-day nights and fandango women?

MANUEL [*taking up* JOSE'S *lunch bucket from the ground and starting to open it.* JOSE *looks up in surprise*]. If you don't mind, señor? I have such a hunger, and I have worked so hard to-day. [*He finds bits of old sandwiches and munches them between sentences.*] Yes, there is such a one—and she is good, though the men from the mines call her many other things. Conchita gave to Pedro everything—but all she gets from him is beans and a shed, and Pedro perhaps one night a week.

JOSE [*he is young and these things are sad to him*]. I have heard—but what of her now? What becomes of her? The streets again?

MANUEL. Ah, señor, why do you ask me? I know not the future. Besides, such people always take fine care of themselves. [*He finishes the end of a very old banana with quiet enthusiasm and disposes of the skin and papers by rolling them in a ball and throwing them over the railing.*] Here comes the fat Mrs. Connolly to mass, and the Superintendent's wife behind her. They are always late.

MRS. CONNOLLY [*enters from the left. She is large and florid, as is her dress. She breathes rather like a thoroughbred bull-dog at the steep ascent*]. Well, shure, I was telling you we'd be late.

THE SUPERINTENDENT'S WIFE [*enters. She is anemic and short, and wears an old tan dress*]. Oh, I don't think it matters much. Some said they was a-havin' a wedding, so it's apt to be long and tedious.

MRS. CONNOLLY. You know, before you be after climbin' the hill again I'd be that pleased if you'd drop around and write the recipe fer that new spinach hash you're givin' the kids. The Doc' has been saying how my Paddy needs a bit of somethin' rough in his di-et. [*She sweeps her skirts away from the Mexicans with elaborate care.*] Ugh! Filthy, greasy things! OO-oo! [*As she stands in the doorway.*] The weddin' is shure a purty sight! [*She passes on into the Church, followed by* THE SUPERINTENDENT'S WIFE.]

MANUEL. Ah! *Madre de Dios!* It is those who will never understand our race. Calls us greasy, the pasty one! And, too—that fat one—she talks *all* the time. My wife now, she is quiet. *I* talk or there is nothing. [*As he speaks* MARIA *and two other* MEXICAN WOMEN *come up the hill from the left. When they approach the Church they unfold black mantillas.*]

JOSE. *Buenos días, señoras.*

THE MEXICAN WOMEN [*very much alike—thin, sallow, in long black dresses*]. *Cómo está,* señor?

MARIA [*smaller and more energetic than the others. She*

wears a long white dress with her black mantilla]. We have been helping at the home of Rosita for the reception. The bridal party, it is still within?

MANUEL. *Sí*, señora. The mass began sometime ago.

MARIA [*seating herself on the steps in heated weariness while the others stand near the men in the shade*]. This wedding, it will bring no good to any one. It is bad—*malo!* This morning, it is said, the groom lost the ring and had to find another. That is very bad—*malo!*

THE MEXICAN WOMEN. *Sí. Sí.*

MARIA. And what of the beautiful Conchita? Does she not know down there in the town that her Pedro stands at the altar with Rosita?

ONE OF THE WOMEN. She is good—but there is that in her eyes that sends my prayers to the Holy Mother when she looks at the unfaithful Pedro.

THE OTHER WOMAN. He is her man and she would give her life for him if she thought he was true. And she stays with him, too—as long as she knows he will come back to her. But now—*Quién sabe?* Who knows?

MARIA. Our people, they love too much. And they hate too often. What is to become of us?

MANUEL. *O Dios mío!* Stop this croaking. *Miren ustedes!* Look! It is a day of the Virgin herself, and in one hour we have the reception. And all night the fandango while the bride and groom lie in half the bed! *Es verdad, amigo mío?* [*Giving* JOSE *a lewd look and a nudge.*]

JOSE. *Sí.* And *to-day?* He is *pay-day!* One grand night we have! Eh, Manuel?

MARIA [*rising*]. Ah! These pay-days! May the Mother of God throw them back into the arms of the Devil! He made them for drinking and shooting and red women. Come, let us go in. [THE WOMEN *drape the black mantillas over their heads and enter the Church.*]

JOSE. The words of María fall heavy and cold on the heart, no?

MANUEL. Ugh! Women! They talk from sun to moon and ward off the time when their men have grown tired of them. But pay no attention. Well, *mira!* Look! Some one has fainted again.

[*The limp figure of a little* OLD WOMAN *is carried out of the Church. The veil has fallen from her head, showing her hair pure white, her thin yellow face, and the slender gold rings she wears in her little shrunken ears. The man places her gently on the steps and motions casually to* JOSE *and* MANUEL *as he returns to the service within. The little, wasted figure lies limply on the steps, apparently lifeless.* JOSE *and* MANUEL *simply move over from the stones by the sidewalk on to the steps.* JOSE *leans against the pillar and* MANUEL *seats himself with care for his green suit. He produces another toothpick and an old bandana handkerchief, which he calmly waves over the face of the little* OLD WOMAN *without looking at her.*]

MANUEL [*shrugging his shoulders*]. They don't eat enough. They can't breathe enough in there and then they have a surprise when they faint. Humph!

[*Feet are heard tramping down the walk above once more.* TWO MINERS, *dressed like* JOSE, *and carrying wood faggots on their shoulders for their fires at home, approach.*]

THE MINERS. *Cómo está?* [*They see* THE OLD WOMAN.] She faints?

MANUEL. Umm... Ummm. [*Waving the bandana calmly.*] How goes the work?

THE FIRST MINER. The ore—she has faded away in my drift. Do not know where we work to-morrow.

JOSE. Ah! She is hard times.

THE OTHER MINER. *Sí.* The rock was hard in my stope and I made no bonus last night. *Adiós.* [*He moves away.*]

MANUEL AND JOSE. *Adiós.* [THE MINERS *tramp off down the hill.*]
THE OLD WOMAN [*flutters to life, stands unsteadily, looks up at the Church, makes the sign of the cross and mutters weakly*]. *Madre de Dios!*
JOSE. You better go home now. No?
THE OLD WOMAN. And miss all the wedding and *la procesión?* *Dios! No!* [*She totters back into the Church with no more protest from* JOSE *or* MANUEL.]
MANUEL [*thoughtfully wiping the buttons on his shoes with the bandana*]. I think it would perhaps be very wise for Señor Pedro to go out of town for a little honeymoon, no?
JOSE. Oh, when he is married he is safe. The beautiful Firecracker can do nothing now.
MANUEL. A Mexican woman jealous is bad. I want nothing to do with such a one. They stop at nothing. Have you, then, had so little experience in the dance halls that you don't fear their glances? Or, perhaps, *mi amigo,* yours is not the face that brings the green fire into their black eyes, eh?
JOSE. You are insulting, my friend, but I am too lazy to be angry. You will perhaps have a cigarette? [*Offering him a bag and some papers.*]
MANUEL. *No, gracias,* I buy them from the store. [*With heavy superiority he lights one and pastes it on his lower lip for future reference, then cleans his nails with the match.* JOSE *rolls his own carefully and tucks away the implements.*] You are staying, then, with me?
JOSE. *Sí, sí.* Parties like this are rare. I will stay and see it all. Who is the best man of Señor Pedro?
MANUEL. Oh, a gay young fellow, the brother of María, who just entered the mass. He has come but lately to the camp. Pedro knows him only a little but Rosita asked that he be the "good man" for the wedding.

Jose. Ah! I hear "Ave María!" They kneel now for the wedding service. So soon she will be all done. I hope she goes well and there is no mistake. You must drive them quickly away in the machine, Manuel, for Conchita, she must know by now. Oh, it's a sad to be a woman! [*He turns to sit on a boulder.*]

Manuel. *Dios!* Who comes up the hill? Look, it is—Can you see?

Jose. One minute. The sun is very white. [*They stand peering down the walk.*]

Manuel. It is *Conchita! Caramba!*—Something must be done, and quickly. She comes not to congratulate.

Jose. Everything is quiet within. It will not now be long.

Manuel. I will go down through the rooms of Father Ramón. I can perhaps get a word to Pedro upstairs that she is here. *O Madre de Dios!*

Jose. *Sí! Sí!* I will talk to her here. [*He seats himself with apparent ease as* Manuel *strolls casually around the Church, left, and goes down the stairs to the priests' quarters.*]

[*A woman of about thirty years comes up the long walk. She walks with a swift quietness that suggests something sinister in the folds of her clinging coarse gray dress. The customary black mantilla is thrown back from her proud, smooth head. Her face is white and set, the eyes half closed, the lips drawn and pale. She walks more slowly as she approaches the doorway. Her arms are folded across the graceful curves of a slender, lithe body.*]

[Jose *smokes thoughtfully, but sits so that* Conchita *cannot enter the Church without crawling over him.*]

Jose. *Buenos días*, señorita. You are a little late.

Conchita [*tensely*]. Is it crowded within?

Jose [*almost eagerly*]. O, yes—much too crowded, as you see. I couldn't get nearer than the door.

CONCHITA. But why do you wait? There are no more services until night. And it is warm.

JOSE. You find it so? Hmm... mm... mm?

CONCHITA [*quietly, ironically*]. I will *stay* and see some one.

JOSE. But señorita? There will be so many people—you—why, you will have trouble finding the one you wish.

CONCHITA. I will stay. And I will have *no* trouble in finding him.

JOSE [*looking nervously within; decides he must divert her soon if at all*]. Ah! Conchita, you are very beautiful and very proud.

CONCHITA. That is none of your affair.

JOSE [*plunging, with many fears*]. There was a time when it was the affair of any one who noticed, no?

CONCHITA [*snarling*]. Agh! What do you mean?

JOSE [*realizing how unfit he is for the rôle*]. Tell me—you who are so proud—what were you doing five years ago, eh? [*She is silent, disdaining to answer.*] Ah, my *bonita*, may *I* not perhaps come to see you some night—to-night—when it is dark—and you are all alone?

CONCHITA [*opening her amazing black eyes*]. O *tú desgraciado! Tú piensas que yo soy una puta!* You vile wretch! You think I am only a courtesan!—Like the rest of them, the women down there? That I am for any one, every one,—to be passed about like a public towel for every one to wipe their hands on! It is not *so!* I belong to one man. I *love* him. You dogs! You know not the meaning of the word. I don't sell it. —It can't be sold. He belongs to me—and he *always* will. [*Her voice has risen to the breaking pitch, and she speaks with such rapidity that* JOSE *is frightened and rather hurt at being so turned upon.*]

JOSE. Sh! Conchita—the Church—all the people—one must be quiet about these things. Everything, she will be all right—in a little time. [*He is surprised at his own hypocrisy.*]

CONCHITA. Stop babbling, you fool! You know nothing. This is my life! All I have! Everything! This man, I have slaved and worked for him—eaten only scraps—bent my back to wash for him—worn rags. And I *loved* him! And I have been so glad to do these things, because he always came back to me. Always the others have been *nothing!* —When I was a dancer, in the streets, he took me to his house. And we were to be married—he swore it—and I stayed. And now? *Now!* He marries a *child!* He told me no word of it. Yet it is on the tongue of all—every one knew—all the world knew but me. Until an hour ago—a little boy told me—told me, and *laughed!*

JOSE [*trying to stem the tide of her fury*]. But for you—the world, she holds everything. You are beautiful—not too old—any man—I, Conchita, I am sorry.

CONCHITA. You! Sorry for me! Bah! I want none of your pity. I have had him—I loved him. And now I will have him once again. [*She smiles and speaks with a deadly quiet.*]

JOSE [*shivers and makes the sign of the Cross. He speaks with determination*]. Come, señorita, you and I must go below to wait the confessor.

CONCHITA. Don't touch me! This is to you nothing! Stand aside! [*She gives him a shove.*] They are coming. I hear the music. I hear the *procesión* moving down the aisle. Listen. They laugh and talk. [*She has pushed* JOSE *back to the wall at the right of the doorway and she stands facing him at the left side, her arms folded, staring at him fixedly. He seems transfixed.*] They come! They come! Laughing! My Pedro—comes laughing to me—to me—down the aisle of the Church he comes to *me!* [*Her voice is about to break but is drowned in the confusion of the wedding throng.* CONCHITA *stands behind the doorway, where she cannot see or be seen.*]

THE WEDDING GUESTS [*entering*]. Hola! Felicitaciones! Rosita—Pedro—Felicitaciones! Felicidades!

[*The wedding throng appears at the door. Some one throws rice and, whether by accident or perhaps because* MANUEL *has accomplished his mission, laughing* JESUS, *the best man, is pushed before the bride and groom through the narrow doorway.*]

JESUS. Stop! Fools! [*He laughs and dodges the shower of confetti and rice.*] You push so! [*He half backs down the stairs ahead of* PEDRO.]

PEDRO [*standing on the top stair, turning to the little bride*]. Ah! Now you are mine, my dear, *mi querida!*

[*In the midst of the confusion the best man's shoulder has come level with* CONCHITA'S *gaze and, as he turns to come out, her right arm darts swiftly from her scarf, with the cold gleam of a knife. It rises and falls in an instant!* JOSE *steps across and catches the young body before the boy falls.*]

[*Suddenly everything is quiet. The crowd stands frozen.* CONCHITA *stares at the boy at her feet, and moans. Then she slowly drags her eyes upward and sees* PEDRO *standing aloof, with his bride, on the upper step.*]

[PEDRO *wears a pseudo-Tuxedo of rusty black serge, funeral white cotton gloves, and a large cabbage rose in his buttonhole. He is the average greasy type of good-looking peon, tall, with blue-black hair and sideburns, lazy, heavy-lidded eyes, and a coarse mouth.*]

[ROSITA *is dressed, or rather draped, in white satin, yards of white lace, and carries a formidable bouquet of lilies. She is little, pretty, and dark—at least, it appears so, for she is heavily rouged and powdered.*]

CONCHITA. Pedro! [*And in her startled cry is all the irony of her mistake, and all the tragedy of her love.*]

PEDRO [*almost whispering*]. Conchita! You cat from Hell! [*He starts down the stairs toward her, forgetting everything. The crowd murmurs. He looks up at* ROSITA *and, remembering his place, shrugs, glances at the dead boy with a growing discomfort. He loosens his collar.*] God in Heaven! This is no sight for the eyes of *mi amada*. —Come, my beloved! They will take care of Jesus. —The car waits. [*He leads her up the hill to the waiting automobile, after one insolent backward look at* CONCHITA. MANUEL *and the bride and groom drive up the hill out of sight.*]

[CONCHITA *stands staring after them.* MARIA *tears through the crowd to* JESUS, *sobbing.* CONNOLLY, *the policeman, steps out from the crowd.* CONCHITA *wakens from her daze and looks wildly around.*]

CONCHITA. *Cristo! Señora!* They will take me—and *he* lives! And this boy! Oh, tell me he will not die! [*She pleads with the faces around her, but the* TWO PRIESTS *are already directing the removal of the body downstairs. And every one turns from her as* CONNOLLY, *the policeman, puts his hand on her arm. She sobs brokenly as he leads her down the hill.*]

[*The crowd finally pours out of the Church door and disperses rapidly, murmuring and chattering excitedly as* CONCHITA *is led away.*]

[*The stage is soon cleared and* THE OLD SEXTON *comes up the stairs, left, with a mop, a bucket of water, and a broom. He is weary and disgusted. He goes to the puddle of blood and sloshes water on it, mops it up, reaches for his broom, and sweeps the rice and confetti off the steps and walk, picks up the mop, pail, and broom and departs. The scene is exactly as it was when the play began. And*

THE CURTAIN FALLS

CALIFORNIA

DAY'S END
A DRAMA OF A MOUNTAIN WOMAN

BY ALICE PIERATT

OF CAPELL VALLEY, CALIFORNIA

Written in the summer session of the University of California at Berkeley in 1927 and originally produced by The Carolina Playmakers at Chapel Hill on March 30 and 31, 1928.

THE CHARACTERS

SARAH KROAN, *the wife*..........Josephine Sharkey
MOLLY, *her sister-in-law*..........Katharine Darling
SALLY, *Molly's daughter*..............Helen Dortch
SKIFFENSON, *an old mountain peddler*.Hubert Heffner

SCENE: *The kitchen of the* KROAN *ranch house in a remote mountain region in California.*
TIME: *Late afternoon of a day in winter.*

Copyright, 1929, by Frederick H. Koch.
All rights reserved.

CALIFORNIA VALLEY

IN *Day's End* Alice Pieratt gives us an authentic drama of California valley folk, well known to her family. She cherishes her early remembrances of old Skiffenson, the mountain peddler, and his funny old wagon with an oiled canvas top in which he carried everything from heavy woolens to fine white lawn for wedding dresses. Her grandmother, she recalls, bought from him doilies and curious old bedspreads. She also remembers that he never gave up hope of selling, and he never came down in his prices.

The young schoolteachers who came to the valley fresh from normal school often married substantial farmers. Sometimes they were happy and prosperous, sometimes they were not. Sarah Kroan was not. From small snatches of conversation heard at the dinner table and from the fact that Sarah's husband whistled for things and spoke only when it was absolutely necessary, the author surmised the story of Sarah Kroan's married life. Surely Sarah must have had some reason for remaining on the lonely ranch so long to care for old "Gran."

"Life in our mountains," Alice Pieratt tells us, "has changed greatly in recent years. Old Mount George still looks down upon Napa Valley. The distance to town runs about twenty miles. It used to take three hours to reach Napa in the spring wagon. Grandfather always made quite a ceremony of the trip. Three hours to town, three hours to attend to his various affairs, three hours to get home again, and the day was gone. Now the trip is made by automobile in an hour.

"Sometimes the boys would start for town on a summer evening with a great load of hay. I used to love to find a comfortable place on top of the load and jounce along under the stars, dozing in snatches, sometimes fearful of the deep gulches cutting sharply from the road which always seemed too narrow to hold our great wagon and a passing, home-going team—perhaps eight mules with a jerk-line. We'd reach town in the early morning, hungry and warm with the fresh odor of hay clinging to us.

"I spent my girlhood in the city. Perhaps for this reason, I loved the mountains and saw things which people born there and accustomed to them did not. I know Grandmother did not approve of those night hay rides. She thought I'd rest much better at home in bed.

"Now we have an electric stove in the kitchen, a radio in the living-room, and the older children go to town to school. Grandmother says that women don't know what work is any more, and it's too bad for them that they don't."

The dominant figure of *Day's End,* "Gran" Kroan, is drawn with admirable skill. Though dead, she rules her little household with a "powerful mind."

DAY'S END

The interior of the ranch house kitchen. An old oak tree covers the one window with its heavy foliage allowing what little light the day affords to fall in fantastic shadows on the floor and on a large, much-worn armchair. To the left, well downstage, a door opens onto the back porch. There is a door to the living-room at the right. A cupboard, a table, a stove, and a few chairs complete the furnishings.

The kitchen is quite dim, then as though the sun had broken through the clouds, a few rays of light play into the room and upon the old chair.

[SARAH KROAN *enters, followed by* MOLLY *and a minute later, the reluctant* SALLY.]

[SARAH, *in her late forties, is dressed simply in black. She seems the typical, hard-working farm woman thirty years back, but this impression is belied by the deep tones of her voice and a peculiar lightness in the movements of her hands.*]

[MOLLY *is about the same age as* SARAH, *though her round eyes and slightly petulant mouth might indicate that she was considerably younger. She is also dressed in black but not so simply as* SARAH. *Jet ornaments dangle from her hat and there is a bit of fur on her coat.*]

[*Her daughter,* SALLY, *is eighteen, and her black outfit is a makeshift affair, as though the various garments had been gathered from as many people to serve for this emergency.*]

SARAH [*going to the range*]. I put plenty of wood in the stove this morning so's there'd be some coals left. [*She adds fresh fuel.*] It'll catch in a minute.

MOLLY [*dabbing at her eyes with a black-bordered handkerchief*]. That range always did hold the fire. I remember when Gran bought it. She bought it from Skiffenson, when I was still a girl home here on the old place. Poor Gran! She always was a good customer to Skiffenson. And you know, Sarah, I think she missed him not coming up here the last few years. Just last week she was trying to mumble something about him to me—when I brought her over that cheese cake...remember? It was the last thing she ate from me.... She always liked cheese cake.... [*She weeps and sniffs.*]

SALLY [*holding the door open slightly*]. Aw, now Moms!

SARAH [*standing very still by the range, her eyes away, a light on her face; at* SALLY'S *voice she turns*]. Better come in, Sally, and shut the door.

MOLLY. You're letting all the heat out, Sally. It's cold enough in here.

SALLY [*does so unwillingly*]. Moms, you said you wouldn't stay.

MOLLY. Now don't go tellin' me what I said or didn't say at a time like this. I can't remember nothing from one minute to the next. My mind's all in the past. [*She wipes her eyes and moves toward the table.*] You know, Sarah, I was thinking of Peter Farrel.

SARAH [*straightens swiftly and turns. She looks at* MOLLY, *then down at her hands*]. This wood—is splintery.

MOLLY [*not heeding*]. And I haven't thought of Peter Farrel for years. I guess it was passing the old hermit's shack on the way to the cemetery that brought Peter to mind. You remember, Sarah, he—

SARAH [*with a quick breath*]. Shall I...make some tea?

DAY'S END

MOLLY [*with an apprehensive glance toward the large chair*]. I... yes, make some, Sarah. [*She sits on chair near the range.*] A body feels the need of something hot after a funeral.

SALLY. Oh, now we'll be here for an hour. I want to go home.

MOLLY. Listen to her, Sarah. The way that young one talks!

SARAH. She's tired.... The water's getting ready to boil.

MOLLY [*weeping and settling herself comfortably*]. I've seen Gran sitting in that old chair for so many years, seems I see her sitting there still. It don't seem real... she's gone.

SARAH [*moving toward the sitting-room door*]. Yes... she's gone. [*Her voice rises on a note of pain.*] She's dead... at last. [*Her eyes fall for an instant on the old chair and a haunting doubt creeps into her voice.*] You... are gone? [*She turns from the chair and faces* MOLLY.] Like you, Molly, I thought for an instant I saw her sitting there.

MOLLY. Sarah, you take it so queer. I know you're just her daughter-in-law and blood's thicker'n water, but you've lived with her for nearly thirty years. And God knows you been good to her. Better'n Otto, her own son, ever was. He's terrible anyhow. He wouldn't speak at the funeral this morning. Anybody'd think he was dumb, the little he talks. Making motions for this and making motions for that....

[*A sudden sharp whistle is heard from without.* SARAH *takes a quick step forward, then stands with a quick intake of breath.*]

MOLLY [*drops her wet handkerchief*]. What's that?

SARAH. It's Otto. It's the whistle he uses when he wants Chad to help him in the field. One long whistle... like that.

SALLY. No wonder he can't keep a hired man on the ranch.

Chad said he wouldn't stay here any longer than it took to get a job somewhere else; he likes some sociability. [*She turns to* SARAH.] Then I guess Uncle Otto will have *you* working out in the fields.

SARAH [*with an eager look*]. No, no, Sally, no. I'll not be working in the fields any more. I'll not plow the near-end orchard this spring to come, nor ever again, not ever any more.

MOLLY [*picking up her handkerchief*]. You're too old to work in the fields, Sarah. [*She looks belligerently toward the door.*] If that ain't just like Otto! Blowing a whistle when he wants the hired man. And what right's he got working the fields to-day? With Gran not cold in her grave . . . her own son not showing more respect. . . . He's my own brother but I . . . I'd like to tell him what I think of him. [*She weeps again.*]

SARAH. The water's boiling. You make the tea, Molly. [*She is at the living-room door.*] I'll be right back. . . . There's something I want to. . . . And, Molly, put out the old blue cups, I'm going to use them to-day . . . Gran's precious old blue cups. [*She goes quickly.*]

MOLLY [*getting to her feet*]. Blue cups! Sarah, did you say the old blue cups? [*There is no reply.*] Did she say the blue cups, Sally?

SALLY [*listlessly turning over the pages of a catalogue*]. I don't know. I wasn't listening.

MOLLY. I don't know what's got into Sarah. She don't act natural. I don't like the look on her face. What does she want to use Gran's old cups for . . . at a time like this. Gran never used them blue cups except for weddings and christenings and . . . farewells . . . like when your Uncle Joey went away to sea. . . .

SALLY [*rather flippantly*]. Maybe Aunt Sarah's going away. She hasn't been off this ranch in thirty years.

MOLLY. Tisht! Sarah going away. Where'd she go, who's she got to go with? How many times did we invite her to take the trip down the valley with us, but you couldn't budge her from this place.

SALLY. Well, why don't you use the blue cups if she wants 'em. What good are they up on the shelf?

MOLLY [*straightening the table*]. Them cups are valuable, Sally. More'n a hundred years old they are. I know Gran wouldn't like 'em used at a time like this and I ain't going to set 'em.

SALLY. I wish we were home. How Aunt Sarah ever lives in this place is more'n I can see.

MOLLY [*waving her wet handkerchief*]. Where else would she live? This is her home, the only home she's known in thirty years. She ain't never left these mountains since she came up here to teach in the old school that was burned down before you was born. She was teacher here a few months ... and then she married Otto ... and I tell you we never thought she'd have him.... But Gran said Otto was like herself and always got what he wanted.... [*She weeps again.*]

SALLY. Oh, well, I wish you'd stop crying. Poor old Gran is better off dead and you know it. Last few years she couldn't do anything but sit and mumble. And I didn't see the family coming over and doing anything for her either. They left all that to Aunt Sarah. Gran's better dead.

MOLLY [*puts her wet handkerchief on the oven door to dry and takes a fresh one from her pocket*]. I never thought to hear you speak so heartless. Now I know it'll be the same when I'm gone. Never a tear nor a word of praise for all the years I've raised you young ones ... just nothing but "she's better dead."

SALLY [*comes over and fusses with her mother's hat*]. Now,

Moms, don't feel bad. I didn't mean it—the way you took it up.

MOLLY [*brightening, continues to clear the table*]. Well ... I know Gran lived a full life and it was her time to go. But she did hold on, Sally. I never knew any one so strong for wanting her own way. And she was hard to the end. [*She sniffs.*] She wouldn't send a word of forgiveness to your Uncle Joey—and him off in a heathen land across the sea.

SALLY [*with conviction*]. I think Uncle Joey is one member of this family I'd have liked—besides you, Mom, of course.

MOLLY. Your Uncle Joey did a terrible thing. Gran never forgave him and she prayed extra for him every day of her life. He married a divorced woman.

SALLY [*simply*]. What's so terrible in that?

MOLLY. Sally! That's a mortal sin. When people are married they have to stay married no matter what.

SALLY [*significantly, turning her head toward the field*]. There's some people I wouldn't stay married to—no matter what!

MOLLY [*weeping*]. Sally! Wherever do you get such ideas? Anybody'd think I didn't raise you right. Seems you're always crossing me here lately.

SALLY. Oh, don't cry, Moms. I didn't mean it. [*She pats her shoulder as though she were the older.*] Make the tea for Aunt Sarah.

MOLLY [*fussing with the table*]. Yes, poor Sarah. She's been a good wife to your uncle, Sally. She's never crossed him by a word.

SALLY. Hmm! Might have been better all around if she had.

MOLLY. Sally! I can't stand the way you are talking. Where do you get such thoughts? You can't say things without thinking 'em first. [*She weeps again.*] I declare!

SALLY [*with a sigh*]. I'm sorry again, Moms. Anyhow I'm going outside and wait for you. I don't want any tea.

MOLLY. But it's cold out there, Sally.

SALLY. Maybe it is, Moms. But this coat that you borrowed from Mrs. Anders would keep me warm on top of Shasta. [*She spreads her arms and turns about displaying the size of the garment.*]

MOLLY [*with appreciation*]. I don't know what we'd do without Mrs. Anders. She's that good-hearted about lending her coat for funerals. For all of twenty years it's been goin' the rounds in these mountains. She's getting on herself, Sally. I don't think she'll last many more winters. Then I guess her sister down in Wooden Valley 'll get the coat. [*Reflectively.*] Though I've done a lot for Mrs. Anders myself.

SALLY. Well, I hope I never have to wear it again.... Make the tea, now, Moms, and I'll be outside. [*She moves to the door.*]

MOLLY. I guess it's all right, Sally, but I think you ought to stay in, if only to show respect.

SALLY [*has opened the door*]. Moms, here comes old Skiffenson with a pack on his back.

MOLLY [*with interest*]. Skiffenson? Why he never peddles these mountains in the winter. And as I was sayin' to your Aunt Sarah he hasn't been up this way for a couple of years. [*As though expecting credit for her perception.*] I know what, Sally, somebody in the valley must have told him that Gran... was gone. Lots of the old-timers heard about it. Some one must have told old Skiffenson. Bad news travels fast. [*She shakes her head dolefully.*]

SALLY. Maybe that's it, Moms. But he didn't forget to bring his pack. Leave it to that old peddler to mix business with pleasure.

MOLLY [*sinking into a chair*]. Sally, you keep saying such things!

SALLY. I won't say another word, Moms. But listen now, don't buy anything for *me* from *him*. He's carried the same stock around since the year one. He might have been all right in the old days, when you couldn't get to town and they didn't have stores in the valley, but no one wants his stuff now.

MOLLY. You just be still, Sally. Gran traded with old Skiffenson all her life and so did I up until...a few years ago. Let me tell you his stuff *wore*. [*She weeps again.*] Anyhow who's thinking of buying anything at a time like this?

SALLY [*with a sigh*]. I just wanted to tell you. It might be a good idea if you let me keep your purse. You got the butter money in it.

MOLLY [*indignantly*]. I can take care of my own purse. You ...you're too sassy, miss. [*She rises.*] Come in or go out, but shut the door!

SALLY. Don't be mad at me, Moms. I'll wait out in the rig. [*She smiles as she is about to go out.*] You like me, don't you, Moms?

MOLLY [*pleased but determined not to show it*]. Go on with you, Sally, you're letting all the cold in. [SALLY *is half through the door.*] If you sit in the rig, wrap the buggy robe around you.

SALLY. All right, Moms. [*She goes.*]

[MOLLY *pours water into the teapot and puts fresh wood in the stove. There is a knock on the door and at* MOLLY's "Come in" SKIFFENSON *enters. He is bald-headed and old and long and thin. His glasses rest almost on the tip of his pointed nose. He has a habit when talking of blowing upward and so placing the glasses higher. But they never stay there long, and most of the time he peers over them, his head swaying on his long neck when he wishes to emphasize his words.*]

SKIFFENSON [*surprised at seeing* MOLLY]. Hah! Well, for all! You here, Mully? [*He takes the pack from his shoulders and slips it onto the floor.*] Wh-r-r. [*He shivers.*] The cold right through this stuff what they sell for wool now, goes. [*He slips off his scarf with contempt and holds it up.*] Wool what never saw a lamb's back, Mully.... My! My! How is't with you, Mully?

MOLLY [*wipes her eyes*]. Well....

SKIFFENSON. My! My! The years like the birds they go, hah? In this kitchen I ain't seen you since you was married with Salvin. I brung your weddin' linen. Thirty years, I bet, Mully.

MOLLY. Thirty-two, but it seems longer.

SKIFFENSON [*reminiscently*]. Yah! Yah! In them times I did the good business, Mully, and had no rheumatiz and all. Skiffenson was the man to buy off in them days. Now all's got rigs, or wasting money in damned autymobiles, and down they go buying, to the valley. [*Excitedly.*] And them storekeepers what are reapin' benefits from trade what I built...they ain't givin' no tick...they ain't trustin' nobody...and they don't sell honest but set traps in winders to catch fool people what don't know wool from shoddy. [*He kicks the scarf, which has fallen to his feet, away from him.*]

MOLLY [*sniffing*]. Times change. The young ones want things different....

SKIFFENSON [*has not listened to her. His eyes are on the old chair now. A fantastic pattern plays upon the worn back cover. He speaks slowly*]. My!...My!

MOLLY. Course you knew about...Gran?

SKIFFENSON. Yah. Yah! Poor womans! [*He blows his glasses.*]

MOLLY. Yes. But it was her time. We all got to go. Too bad

you missed the funeral. Lots came, even if it did look like another storm. And we had one wreath made special at the valley florist's, too. Mrs. Anders led the singin'—but she always sings too high. Still it was nice. It's too bad you didn't get here earlier.

SKIFFENSON. My! My! For funerals I wouldn't take this long trip the mountains over. Not anyways till it comes summer and good roads. [*He touches his heart.*] In here I keep what I feel for old customers like what Gran was.

MOLLY. You didn't come for the funeral? Then what brought you?

SKIFFENSON [*peering over his glasses*]. Long in the past I promised Mis' Kroan to come right here... when the old lady... went.... [*He raises his finger upward with a simple gesture.*]

MOLLY [*seeming to connect* SARAH'S *attitude with the old man's words*]. You got your wagon—you come up in it?

SKIFFENSON. Yah, down in the road bend I left it. [*Looks at her doubtfully.*] Bein's you're here, Mully, you know all right that Mis' Kroan goes with me down the valley?

MOLLY [*pours a cup of tea and gulps it down*]. She said something... but I think now... she changed her mind. When was it she asked you to come now? I forgot.

SKIFFENSON [*thinking that* MOLLY *knows about the arrangement*]. She asked me... come thirty years back next Easter. [*He blows his glasses.*]

MOLLY. Thirty.... Yes, that's how long she's been married to Otto.... I can see... but since then she ain't thought of going to the valley. We ask her 'n' ask her, but she won't budge a step. You made your long trip for nothing, Skiffenson.

SKIFFENSON. Yah! Right you might be, Mully. But I made promise to Mis' Kroan and old Skiffenson don't forget. My! My! Mully, I brung her up here to teach in the school and she rode in the same old wagon what's waitin' now down in the bend. My! What a smiley she was. Mind, I mean before she was married with Otto—when she was sweetheartin' with that artist man what was boarding with Mis' Anders.

MOLLY. You mean Peter Farrel?

SKIFFENSON. His name is no matter. But Mis' Kroan made no laugh on me when old like I was, even then, I asked her the way to make numbers and writing.

MOLLY. I know, we had t' laugh t' see you writing on a slate. You never held the pencil right.

SKIFFENSON [*blowing his glasses*]. To laugh was all right, Mully. But from then on I got no cheatin' done to me. But more'n that, for myself I could read words what one who once loved me, wrote me, back in the old country—far years past . . . [*There is a short pause before he adds.*] . . . and a long time she's been up. [*Again the simple upward gesture.*] And now come every Christmas I write the words over . . . it wears the paper out here . . . [*Touching his heart.*] . . . against me. And . . . it seems new again—the letter—like it was fresh from [*The upward gesture.*] her what once loved me.

MOLLY [*interested in a romance, no matter how old*]. Oh . . . poor thing. But it was long ago . . . and them things we forget . . . except sometimes . . . and then . . . we remember. . . . I know . . . how 'tis.

SKIFFENSON. So for Mis' Kroan I have thanks for the learnin'.

MOLLY. Sarah *was* a good teacher.

SKIFFENSON. Yah! I had no thought then, that long spring past, that come the next summer I'd find her married with Otto Kroan. My! My!

MOLLY. And you wasn't the only one that had no thought of such to happen. I think she had a fallin' out with

Peter Farrel and married Otto for spite. Though she never said so.

SKIFFENSON [*reminiscently*]. By the road bend she was standin' when I came that summer. "I scarce to know you, Miss Sally," I says. "You lookin' so lost in your face ... like somethin' what's been sucked dry." ... "I don't be Miss Sally any more," she tells me, "but Mis' Kroan. ... I want a promise from you—when you hear—when once you hear old Gran's dead—come in your rig what brought me here—and take me back home to the valley!"

MOLLY. I bet Sarah forgot all about it years ago. Course if she wanted to go below *then,* she might've asked you to call for her. The road was a fright and the men didn't go down month in, month out. But the last ten years, she could've gone any time. [*Meaningly.*] If you start off now, Skiffenson, you'd make the Anders place by night.

SKIFFENSON. Yah? [*Emphatically.*] Mully, here I stay till I see Mis' Kroan. [*Sighing reflectively.*] My! My! What a booty she was.

MOLLY. Yes, she was, but no more, Skiffenson. [*Firmly.*] You get the idea out of your head that she's going down with you.

SKIFFENSON [*with a stubborn look*]. Here I wait till I see Mis' Kroan. I take her, if she wants.

MOLLY [*with some excitement*]. She can't take that trip to the valley with you in that old rig. Everybody'd be talking. A woman can't get up and leave her husband like that. Gran would never stand for anything like that—she'd turn in her grave.

SKIFFENSON [*watching the weaving of the light on the old chair*]. Sit down, Mully, start no goings on. [*Briskly.*] Something fine, so fine I'll show to you. [*He lifts his pack and removes a few yards of crimson cloth.*] Now, just look and see.

MOLLY [*she sits down and watches him from the corner of her eye.*] How should I care to look ... at a time like this?

SKIFFENSON. Never will come a better time, Mully. Forty years I been through these mountains peddlin'—and at weddin's and funerals is best to look—for the eyes something better to do than weepin' it gives. [*With a quick movement he spreads the cloth before her.*] See now, hah, how is that for a bootiful?

MOLLY [*rises and feels the material expertly*]. Oh, lands! [*Her face falls.*] Such a color! Gran ... wouldn't like it. Anyway at a time like this I couldn't think to buy anythin'.

SKIFFENSON. It bootiful makes you, Mully.

MOLLY. Red always was the color I liked best ... but Gran ... [*decidedly.*] No, I wouldn't buy it.

SKIFFENSON [*folds the material*]. No? Mis' Dodgers then maybe will like it.

MOLLY [*quickly*]. Let me feel of it again. [*She does so and sighs.*] I couldn't wear it. The color ... the neighbors'd talk. I got to wear mournin' now for always.

SKIFFENSON [*blows his glasses and speaks mysteriously*]. Mully, you could wear it *under*.

MOLLY. Such a talk! Waste it under?

SKIFFENSON. Wait now, something I'll show you. [*He draws a booklet from his pocket.*] Here it tells from the people what makes the stuff that ladies can use it for under. [*She peers over his shoulder eagerly.*] Wait, I find it. Here ... here is where it says it. [*He adjusts his glasses and reads.*] "This goods is unex*celled* for the fashioning of—"

[*At this moment the same whistle, that was heard earlier, sounds piercingly, but this time there are two short blasts. They both start.*]

MOLLY [*moving away*]. That's Otto again. He must want

something. Sarah's such a long time in there. [*She calls.*] Sarah, what are you doing in there?

SARAH [*comes into the room carrying an old valise, a black hat and coat*]. It... took longer than I thought... to get ... things together. [*She sees* SKIFFENSON *and her face lights up, as she goes to him.*] I knew you wouldn't forget to come—I knew all the time that you remembered. [*She sighs.*] Although... it's been a little bit long... to wait... but you got the rig... the same old rig.

SKIFFENSON. Yah! Down at the bend I got it.

SARAH. How is it down home in the valley, Skiffenson?

SKIFFENSON [*shaking his head*]. My! My! Mis' Kroan, for me there is no business there no more.

[*The two whistles are heard again.* SARAH *stiffens.*]

MOLLY. What does Otto want, Sarah? You seem to understand his whistlin'. You must've heard him a minute ago.

SARAH. Yes... I heard... but I thought this once I wouldn't. I thought this once I won't.... [*Her eyes seem drawn to the old chair.*] But maybe.... [*Turning to* SKIFFENSON.] Two whistles short like that means Otto wants a change of horses. I... I don't want to see... him. Will you take them down for me, Skiffenson?

SKIFFENSON. To see Otto I'm not longin'. But for you I'll do it, Mis' Kroan.

SARAH [*a little breathless*]. Don't tell him that I'm going.

SKIFFENSON. Have no fear for me makin' loose of my tongue. [*He is at the door.*]

SARAH. Bring him the two grays, Skiffenson. [*As he seems reluctant to go.*] He doesn't like to wait... for things.

SKIFFENSON. I hurry. [*He goes.*]

MOLLY. My heavens, Sarah! What's all this about you going down to the valley with Skiffenson? If you hadn't been actin' so queer yourself, and having such a funny look on your face, I'd have thought the old man was crazy. He said you asked him thirty years ago to come and get you... when he heard that Gran was... gone.

SARAH [*standing very still*]. Yes, I did. I asked him then. I've been waiting all the while... to go.

MOLLY. Oh, Sarah, you could've gone down the valley for a trip any time with us. It's out of the question you going in that old rickety wagon.

SARAH [*almost whispering*]. You don't understand, Molly. It was Skiffenson who brought me here. I remember... how the... wheels crunched and crunched in the brown road... and how everything was still except for that sound. It sang "Peter... Peter... Peter... Peter."

[*The two whistles are repeated, and the animation dies from* SARAH's *face.*]

MOLLY. Can't he wait a minute? I don't see how you put up with that whistling for things. I don't see how Gran ever put up with it.

SARAH [*heavily*]. She liked it... and she liked it more and more toward the last. She used to say she guessed I wouldn't forget I was a Kroan... when Otto whistled.

MOLLY [*wiping her eyes*]. Gran was... she had a powerful mind. She was a good woman... she always made people do just what she wanted. I remember... when I didn't want to marry Salvin... when I liked... some one else. ... It might sound funny, Sarah... but I wonder how it'll seem to Gran being... where what she wants... don't count. ...

SARAH [*with a start and looking at the table*]. You didn't put on the blue cups.

MOLLY. Gran wouldn't like it, Sarah. Anyhow I wouldn't set them, now I know what you want to use 'em for. You think you're going to stay in the valley.

SARAH. I'll get one for myself. [*She takes a blue cup from the shelf and smiles strangely.*] I'll drink from it... and as it has meant godspeed to others, let it mean the same to me. [*She holds it out.*] God speed me! [*Her eyes dart to the old chair and an involuntary shiver runs through her body—and the cup crashes to the floor.*] Oh!

MOLLY. Sarah! You broke it! [*She stoops and picks up the pieces.*] I wanted them cups to pass on to Sally. [SARAH *stands white and motionless; a sudden pity stirs* MOLLY *and she goes to her.*] Here, sit down, Sarah. Now drink from this. [*She hands* SARAH *an ordinary cup and* SARAH *drinks.*]

SARAH [*slowly*]. Thanks. Where is Sally?

MOLLY. She's waiting out in the rig. She didn't want any tea.

SARAH. I'm sorry about the cup—because of Sally.

MOLLY [*fitting the pieces*]. We might be able to glue it together. Sally'll like this set. She feels worse about Gran than she lets on.

SARAH. She's a good girl.

MOLLY [*veering about*]. Well, I don't know, Sarah. It's hard work understanding your own young ones. I used to feel sorry for you not having any when mine were small but now ... I don't know ... it may be just as well.

SARAH [*dully*]. Just as well.

MOLLY [*after a pause during which* SARAH *stares straight ahead and* MOLLY *sugars her tea noisily against the cup*]. You always been a good Christian woman, Sarah.

SARAH. If you call me good because I stayed with him you'll have to begin calling me bad, I guess. I'm leaving these mountains—right away, with Skiffenson.

MOLLY [*spilling her tea*]. Sarah! If you want to go down let some one in the family take you; don't go with that old peddler.

SARAH. You don't understand, Molly. I have to go with him. If I went down into the valley with any one else ... I'd never find myself again...myself...you know...my real self that got lost when I married Otto. [*She draws her hand over her brow.*] You see, Molly, I...*I* have not been here at all—ever. *I* have been lost somewhere on the road to the valley and I need Skiffenson's rig to carry me over the road....I need to hear the wheels crunch and crunch....

MOLLY [*half frightened*]. Sarah, what do you mean? You better take a rest when I go. You're upset about Gran. I know you haven't had any sleep for a week.

SARAH. There'll be lots of time to sleep. I don't have to stay here any more now that Gran's gone. [*Quickly.*] And she is gone, isn't she, Molly?

MOLLY. You know she is. But if you wanted to leave Otto for so long I don't see how a helpless old woman like Gran could've held you here.

SARAH. She was strong, Molly, strong enough to do with me anything she wanted—while she lived. [*She puts an arm on the table and leans toward* MOLLY.] She knew something...and she promised never to tell...so long as I stayed here...and now she's dead...and what she knew ...is buried with her.

MOLLY. What'd she know?

SARAH. I'll never tell. I gave myself to the long slow years ...years eating into me, in and out and in and out like worms in a dead tree, so you nor anybody else would hear what...she knew.

MOLLY [*weeping*]. It's awful to hear you talk this way, Sarah. But if what she knew kept you here, when you've felt this way—it must have had something to do with Peter Farrel!

SARAH [*rising to her feet*]. She never said so! She never spoke of him to you?

MOLLY. No, but you know everybody expected you to marry

Peter Farrel. We was all dumfounded when he went off so sudden and nobody never heard from him again.

SARAH. Never again.

MOLLY. I remember it so well because Peter went the night somebody killed Aspin, the old hermit. And robbed him of the money he had sewed in his mattress. I remember Gran was the first on the scene. She always was everywhere first.

SARAH [*her hands gripping the table hard*]. Pour me a little more tea, Molly.

MOLLY [*pouring*]. But that's all past and done with. God knows where Peter Farrel is. And you're too old to begin a new life. I don't think Gran would 've died until she was sure nothing could make you break your marriage vow. "Till death do us part," was what she always preached for married people. [*She sighs.*] Gran was religious. [*She shakes her head.*] You're set now, Sarah.

SARAH [*passionately*]. That's not true! I tell you that's not true. I've been keeping watch on myself all the while. I've been waiting and waiting for her to die. In my soul, in that part of me that really lives, I've never been here at all. I've lived ever and always in a world you know nothing of—and I'm not old ... not so very old.

MOLLY. Anybody but me'd think you were out of your head, Sarah. I know you're just worn-out. Sit down.

SARAH [*glancing at the clock, her spirit droops*]. Why ... it's time to mix the bread. [*She begins mechanically to make preparations.*] It's so cold the yeast doesn't raise; my bread's been kind of heavy. [*There is a pause.*]

MOLLY. Sarah, you haven't any folks in the valley no more; it's been five years since your last cousin died. And you haven't any more blood folks.

SARAH. That doesn't matter. I have myself down there. It's myself I want to be with again.

MOLLY [*carefully*]. Suppose—even if you do go with Skiffenson—you can't find... what you're looking for down there?

SARAH. Molly, I never thought of that: I always felt so sure. [*She puts her hand to her heart.*] And while I was longing and praying to be free to go, it seemed so simple. The first few years I used to go down to the bend and I'd pretend to myself, "This is the day I am going away, this is the day, this is the hour...."

MOLLY. But you don't do that no more, Sarah?

SARAH. I've always done it in my mind.

MOLLY. Well, keep on doing it in your mind. That won't hurt nobody. But you know Sally and Ned are going to school in the valley next term and they'd feel terrible if you went off and left Otto. Everybody'd be talking— these mountains'd just buzz with the talk. The Kroans 've always held up their good name.

SARAH. I know... but I'm going.

MOLLY [*with some irritation*]. Who's going to bake the bread, Sarah, if you won't be here to-morrow?

SARAH. What? Why, that's true. I forgot for a minute. It's just... just habit.... Gran always liked the bread set at this time. [*She pushes the mixture away and goes back to her seat.*]

SALLY [*opening the door*]. Moms, are you never coming? I'm nearly froze. It'll take two hours to get home. You know Dolly's got a sore foot.

MOLLY. I'll be right out. Go on, I've got something to say to Aunt Sarah.

SALLY. 'By, Aunt Sarah. I'll come over next week and help you some.

SARAH. I wish you would, Sally.

SALLY. I sure will. Now hurry up, Moms. [*She goes.*]

MOLLY. How can you tell Sally to come next week when you're leaving? [*She rises.*]

SARAH [*with a bewildered fluttering of her hands*]. Why... that's right. I forgot again. I've dreamed of going for so long... you know... that now... I can't realize I... I'm going.... [*She starts to mix the dough.*]

MOLLY. Sarah, you keep spilling flour on the floor.

SALLY [*opening the door*]. There's a big, black cloud in the sky, Moms. Looks like a real storm's coming. You better hurry; you know how Dolly shies at thunder.

MOLLY. That horse is an old fool. I've got to go, Sarah. [*She feels the handkerchief, now dry, on the oven door and begins to weep into it afresh.*] I can't say nothing more to you, Sarah. I'm just wore out. You try to think about the rest of us a little bit. [*She moves to the door.*] Your best years are gone. You don't know enough to teach the young ones nowadays. I'm going, Sarah. [*She stands undecidedly for an instant.*] Good-by. [*She goes.*]

SARAH. Good-by, Molly. [*She crosses slowly and stares out of the window. She adds more wood to the stove, then returns to the window.*]

SKIFFENSON [SARAH *does not hear him enter the door which* MOLLY *had not closed*]. I brung Otto the Grays. And now it's better to start, Mis' Kroan. Already the storm I smell.

SARAH [*not heeding*]. Skiffenson, Skiffenson, if you knew how I've hated that tree. The branches always seemed like big, live hands choking the life out of the sun.

SKIFFENSON [*tightening his pack, folding the crimson material into it regretfully*]. These mountains is thick with 'em like that. Better to chop it down from there.

SARAH [*involuntarily*]. Oh, no! I'm used to it now. I'd feel ... queer with it gone.

SKIFFENSON. Better to put your hat on now, Mis' Kroan.

DAY'S END

SARAH [*moving to the table, her face eager*]. Skiffenson, call me, "Mis' Sally."

SKIFFENSON [*averting his face*]. Miss Sally!

SARAH [*a hurt expression on her face*]. Why... it doesn't sound the same.... It doesn't reach deep down in me... and make me sing... I....

SKIFFENSON [*gently*]. Better to put your hat on now, Mis' Kroan.

SARAH [*doing so*]. It seems so strange to put my hat on this time of day. [*She looks at the clock.*] It's almost time to feed the turkeys. [*She looks at him helplessly, appealingly.*]

SKIFFENSON [*at the door, looks at her sadly*]. I'll pass by here again... come summertime.

SARAH [*her face brightening*]. In the summer? Everything is different in the summer, isn't it, Skiffenson?

SKIFFENSON. My! My! Yes. The roads are more better.

SARAH. That's true. I didn't think of that. The wheels couldn't crunch happily in the mud. No... they'd slither along, like the years sneaking by on you.

SKIFFENSON. We better to start, Mis' Kroan... if you're going....

SARAH. Yes. [*She stoops and picks up the valise. At the same instant three long whistles ring out. She drops the valise.*] Three? Was it three whistles? Did you count three whistles?

SKIFFENSON. Three. [*He opens the door.*]

SARAH [*her eyes are drawn irresistibly to the old chair, a single line of light plays among its shadows*]. Three! [*She removes her hat slowly.*] That means Otto wants... me....

SKIFFENSON [*sadly*]. I got to go now, Mis' Kroan. No longer can I wait. The storm I feel it heavy in the air.

SARAH [*takes a few swift steps toward him*]. I'm going with you. I'm going with you. Wait for me! [*As she is about to put on her hat, again the whistles are repeated. She stands still and the light dies from her face, her entire body wilts, she looks, as* SKIFFENSON *would say, "sucked dry."*] Next time... you come... maybe,... in the summer? Everything is different in the summer....

SKIFFENSON. Yah! All's different then... in the summer. [*He opens the door.*] Good-by to you... good-by to you,... Miss Sally. [*He goes.*]

SARAH [*with a quick breath*]. Miss Sally... oh... Skiffenson, say my old name like that again. [*She takes an eager step.*] Skiffenson! Wait! [*The whistles sound again more urgently. She moves back to the table. Her eyes are no longer eager, but deeply shadowed.*] I hear you... I hear you.... [*She takes an apron from the door and puts it on, her eyes on the old chair all the while. She seems drawn to it irresistibly and for an instant she stands with a look of fear upon her face. Suddenly she straightens, her hand on the back of the chair.*] I hear you.... [*She sinks into the chair.*] But I'm not coming.... [*The light plays upon her face.*] I'm not... coming.

THE CURTAIN FALLS

UTAH

SPRING STORM
A COMEDY OF A COUNTRY GIRL

BY MARY COTTAM HATCH
OF SCIPIO, UTAH

Written in the summer session playwriting course at the University of Southern California in Los Angeles and originally produced at the Touchstone Theater on the campus there, on July 22, 1931. *Spring Storm* was first called *Stoves*.

THE CHARACTERS

MARGARET, *a young schoolteacher*...Mabel Keefauver
BARBARA, *her fourteen-year-old sister*.....Ruth Music
MRS. MARTIN, *her mother*...............Patty Baird
OBADIAH MARTIN, *her father*...........W. F. Stuckey
KEITH WARNER, *her fiancé*...........Sterling Kincaid

SCENE: *A country village in Utah. The living-room of the Martin farmhouse.*
TIME: *The present. Near noon of a raw day in early spring.*

Copyright, 1938, by The Carolina Playmakers, Inc.
All rights reserved.

MORMON FOLKWAYS

SPRING STORM by Mary Cottam Hatch of Scipio, Utah, was written and produced in the summer course in playwriting and experimental production at the University of Southern California in Los Angeles in 1931. It is a simple play of life on a Utah farm.

Of life in her home town the author writes: "To the thousands of tourists who hurry through Scipio, Utah, it is just another one of those ghastly country towns. But I know differently. Life flows there as elsewhere and I have felt its pulse. I know the struggles of its peoples, their hopes, their desires, their ambitions, their successes, their failures. I have seen life come in with the red dawn; I have seen it ebb out with the gray dusk. And I have seen it just go on ... morning ... noon ... and night.

"Scipio is small, too small to be called a town, too small almost to be called a village. Yet it lives.... It is an emerald valley; but it lies close, too close, to the vast sinister desert. Its people must fight always those long brown arms of the desert that would so gladly reach out and bring them death. In the face of this, they must needs be a strong, simple, stoical people. They come to think in the immensities of storm and sand and soil. They have no time for the shams and frivolities that bother a larger world. Eventually they develop a philosophy that the world might do well to copy.

"The struggle with the desert is as old to Scipio's people as their oldest pioneers long since laid to rest in the depths of a narrow, rocky canyon. Now they face another problem. But for the pass which leads to the desert, Scipio is hemmed in by steep, rugged mountains. Once the place was almost inaccessible ... mountain heights to be scaled or desert heat to be conquered. So people lived and died and were happy knowing nothing of the outside world. Now things are different. A smooth white-ribboned road scales the mountains and runs straight and fleet across the desert. It does not bother the old folk, this long, smooth road; their roots strike too deep into their own soil. But it calls to youth, and youth feels stirred to follow it... west to the sea, east to the tall cities.

"Sometimes youth never returns. More often it does. And it returns with complexes that those who stay behind cannot understand. It is ashamed of its people, its town, its entire background. It takes simplicity for simpleness, strength for crudeness. Situations result which are sometimes tragic, sometimes amusing. I have seen both.

"*Spring Storm* is the simple story, partly amusing, partly serious, all true, of one girl who returned from following the shining highway, to find the simple ways of her own people to be the best."

Mary Cottam Hatch might have written the obvious Mormon tale of the man who went to prison because of his three wives, and liked it so well that he begged to stay; the story of the woman who hung herself when another bride crossed the threshold; the legend of the three Nephites; the saga of her grandfather's life and his five wives, one who was Swedish and died young with longing for the salt spray and the flowered loveliness of Swedish spring, one who was Scotch and sensible, and one whom he had never seen alive, but who he thought had come to him in a vision... or the stories of the long searches for water holes, or the strange madness that the desert silences wrought in human minds.

I was eager to have her write plays peculiar to her own Mormon people. Instead she chose to write *Spring Storm* to show us that the folkways of the people in Utah are not unlike those of other American states.

When I went to Utah and observed the gentle dignity of this remarkable people, I could not but agree with the young playwright.

SPRING STORM

The MARTIN *living-room is an old room in which attempts have been made, somewhat tastefully, to give it a less old-fashioned appearance. At the rear of the room toward the left is a door leading to the front porch. Two windows, draped with gay little curtains, look out on the front lawn. In the left wall, downstage, is a door which leads to the kitchen. In the right wall is a door leading upstairs. Under the windows is an old-fashioned couch covered with an imitation tapestry. A heavy, golden-oak library table, relieved by a dyed scarf and a slender glass vase, occupies the center of the room. About the table are several Victorian chairs. Easily the most conspicuous object in the room is a large, friendly, wood-burning Franklin stove. Near it is a comfortable, plush-covered easy chair. Several hand-woven rugs give the room a final touch of coziness.*

[*As the curtain rises,* MARGARET *is seen on the stage struggling to take down the pipes of the stove.* MARGARET *is a pretty girl, but her prettiness is lost behind the grim, desperate look which now clouds her face. She is dressed in a faded house dress, and her hair is tied up with a towel.*]
[*After considerable tugging and straining, she succeeds in getting the stovepipes down. Then she begins wrestling with the stove, but her efforts are fruitless, and she calls out in desperation.*]
MARGARET. Barbara! Barbara! Oh, where is she anyway?

She's never around when you need her. Barbara! Barbara! [BARBARA *finally appears in the kitchen doorway.*]
BARABARA [*indifferently*]. What do you want?
MARGARET. Come in and see. [BARBARA *saunters in.*] And hurry!
BARBARA [*taking her time*]. Now, what d'y'want?
MARGARET. Come in and get hold of this stove.
BARBARA [*in surprise*]. Come and get hold of it?
MARGARET. Yes. —Right around on this other side.
BARBARA. But what d'y'want me to get hold of it for?
MARGARET [*annoyed*]. Heavens, Barbara, why do you have to ask so many foolish questions. What do you suppose I want you to get hold of it for?
BARBARA. I don't know. If I did I wouldn't ask you.
MARGARET. It's to help me out with it, that's what for.
BARBARA. You mean clear out of the house so's we won't use it any more this year?
MARGARET. Yes, that's it.
BARBARA. But we can't take it out. It's too cold to take it out yet.
MARGARET. It isn't too cold either. It's the last of April. Come on, get hold of it.
BARBARA. No, I'm not going to. I don't want to be freezing to death.
MARGARET. You won't be freezing. Good Heavens!
BARBARA. I don't see why you want it out anyway.
MARGARET. You do see why I want it out. You know Keith is coming, the boy I met when I was teaching last winter.
BARBARA. Sure I know he's coming. That's all you've been talking about for a week. But what's that got to do with taking out the stove?
MARGARET. Just this: I want things looking a little bit nice for him when he comes, and they can't look nice with this squatty, old-fashioned stove sticking around.

BARBARA. It looks all right to me.
MARGARET. Of course it would. You've never seen anything any different.
BARBARA. Well, has he?
MARGARET [*sarcastically*]. Now, what do you think? With loads of money and a fifteen-thousand-dollar home in Salt Lake City.
BARBARA. Sure, but he still has to keep warm, doesn't he?
MARGARET. Yes, but not with a funny, old-fashioned stove.
[MRS. MARTIN *enters right. She is a cheerful little woman in her early fifties. She shows the wear and tear of hard work, but none of it has corroded the pleasantness of her spirit; it has merely worn away the bloom of her maturity. She wears a faded dress and a dark working apron. Her gray hair is drawn straight back from her face and fastened in a knot at the back of her head. This coiffure might be severe, but her hair has a natural, fluffy curliness; it loosens itself and falls gently about her face. Her manner is brisk and decisive. But it is also gracious and calm.*]
MRS. MARTIN [*surprised*]. Why, Margaret, what are you doing, taking the stove down?
BARBARA [*speaking up*]. She thinks she's going to take it out.
MRS. MARTIN. She thinks she's going to take it out?
MARGARET AND BARBARA [*together, but in different tones*]. Yes.
MRS. MARTIN. But why?
MARGARET. Mother, do you have to have everything explained to you, too?
MRS. MARTIN [*laughing*]. I hope not. But—
BARBARA. I'll tell you why, Mama. She doesn't think the stove's nice enough for Keith.
MARGARET. Barbara, you keep still.

Mrs. Martin. Oh, that's it, is it?

Barbara. Yes, m'am, it is.

Mrs. Martin [*placatingly*]. I don't suppose it is as comfortable and modern as what he's been used to.

Margaret [*vehemently*]. I should say it isn't! If you'd see the house his folks live in—air-conditioned and an automatic gas furnace!

Mrs. Martin. I know it must be grand. And I know we haven't anything like it. But then, we still have to keep warm.

Margaret. But it'll be warm enough now. My goodness, it's almost summer.

Mrs. Martin. I know. But if it should rain—

Barbara. Yes, and I bet it does rain. It's awfully cloudy outside right now.

Margaret. But it won't rain. It never does in this desert country. [*Defiantly.*] Anyway, rain or no rain, I won't have this stove in here when Keith comes—that I won't!

Mrs. Martin [*giving in*]. All right then, dear. If you want it out, we'll see that it gets out. But dear, you can't pull it out by yourself. Wait and let your father do it when he comes.

Margaret [*shaking her head impatiently*]. But then it might be too late, Mother. Keith'll be here in another two hours. Besides, you know what a fuss Dad makes about having to help take out the stove.

Mrs. Martin [*reluctantly admitting it*]. Well, yes....

Margaret [*dramatically*]. And I simply can't bear hearing Dad go on a rampage. I'm so nervous now I could scream.

Mrs. Martin [*soothing her*]. Well, then, I'll help you pull it out.

Margaret. I asked Barbara to.

Barbara [*saucily*]. Golly, it's too heavy for me!

MRS. MARTIN [*calmly*]. Never mind, I'll help Margaret now. Which side do you want me to take, Margaret?

MARGARET. You take the back and I'll take the front. [*They do so.*] But don't you lift too hard. I don't want you to hurt your back. [*They begin dragging the stove toward the door.*]

MRS. MARTIN [*to* BARBARA]. Barbara, you can open the door for us.

MARGARET [*as* BARBARA *pokes toward the front door*]. And don't keep us waiting.

[*As* BARBARA *goes to open the door, it is thrust open from the outside, and* OBADIAH MARTIN *enters.* MR. MARTIN *is a sharp-tongued man, but one whose bark is worse than his bite. He is obstinate and brusque at times, but under ordinary circumstances he is good-natured and easy-going. He is a thin, stoop-shouldered, and leathery man and wears a worn felt hat and bib overalls. His chin is covered with a thin stubble beard. But he is upstanding for all his bent figure. If he is one of the country's "forgotten" farmers, he is unaware of it. He bears himself with a masculine, master-of-the-house air.*]

MR. MARTIN [*without any suspicion of what is taking place*]. It looks like— [*Stopping dead still in astonishment.*] Say, what's going on in here?

[MARGARET *shudders, looks about in despair, then pulls herself together and clutches at the stove with grim defiance.*]

MRS. MARTIN [*as though nothing is happening*]. Are you home already, Father?

MR. MARTIN [*brusquely*]. Sure, I'm home. I always come home at noon, don't I? But you haven't answered my question— What's going on around here? What're you doing with that stove down?

BARBARA [*enjoying the situation*]. Margaret—

MARGARET [*at the same time*]. What does it look like?

MRS. MARTIN. Now, girls. [*To* MR. MARTIN.] We've just been doing a bit of spring house-cleaning, Father, and we thought while we were at it we might as well get the stove out of the way. [*Still tugging away at the stove.*]

MR. MARTIN. You thought wrong. It's too early to take the stove out yet.

MARGARET. It isn't either too early. My goodness, do you think Utah is the North Pole?

MR. MARTIN. Mighty dang near it, I can tell you—especially after a spring rain, and that's what we're going to have before the day's over.

MRS. MARTIN. I don't think it'll rain, Father. Anyway, I think we can manage without the stove.

MR. MARTIN. Maybe we can, and maybe we can't. But we ain't going to take any chances. That stove's going to stay right here in this room.

MRS. MARTIN. But Father, now that it's down—

MR. MARTIN. That don't matter. It can be put up again.

MARGARET [*defiant*]. But I won't let you put it up again, I won't!

MR. MARTIN [*his paternal ire aroused*]. You won't, huh? Well, now, young lady—

MRS. MARTIN. Oh, Father, come on now, don't be obstinate.

MR. MARTIN. I'm not being obstinate. I'm just being sensible.

MARGARET [*in high dudgeon*]. Yes, you're being sensible. You—[*Beginning to cry.*]—but go on, have it your own way, I don't care. [*She runs to the couch and sinks down on it in tears.*] Do whatever you want. I don't care. I don't care.

MR. MARTIN [*sputtering*]. Now, now, what you starting crying for? Just because I want to be sensible and keep you all from dying of pneumonia. [*He edges over toward* MARGARET *to soothe her.*] It's beginning to rain already.

MARGARET [*motioning him away*]. You don't need to make excuses. Go on, do what you want. I don't care. Put a dozen old stoves up in here; it's all right with me.

MR. MARTIN. If you're so set on having the stove out of the way for your young man that's coming, I guess we'll have to give in to you. But there ain't no sense to it.

MRS. MARTIN. I knew you wouldn't stand in the way, Father.

MARGARET. It doesn't matter; I don't care any more now.

MRS. MARTIN [*placating* MARGARET]. Yes, you do care. Now come on Margaret, I'll help you out with it.

MR. MARTIN. You don't need to help her. I will. Come on, Margaret, let's get it out and over with.

[MARGARET *gets up slowly. She takes her end of the stove, and with much puffing and some protestation on* MR. MARTIN's *part the stove is carried outside.* MRS. MARTIN *hovers near, and when the stove is finally out of the house she drops down on the couch with a sigh of relief.*]

MRS. MARTIN. Thank goodness, that's over with!

BARBARA [*at the window*]. What'd you let Margaret take the stove out for, anyway? I'm cold already. And I bet it's going to rain, too. Yes, sir, it's starting to rain already.

MRS. MARTIN. Don't say anything about it.

BARBARA. Margaret's always got such funny ideas. I wonder where she gets 'em, anyhow?

MRS. MARTIN [*vaguely*]. You see, Barbara ... you see, it's....

BARBARA. You see it's what?

MRS. MARTIN. It's ... oh, I don't know just how to explain it.

BARBARA. Does she get that way from having a beau?

MRS. MARTIN [*with a bit of a laugh*]. I guess that might have something to do with it.

BARBARA [*emphatically*]. I bet that's it, all right. Gee whiz, does everybody get funny ideas when they're in love?

MRS. MARTIN. Most everybody does, I guess.

BARBARA. Then, I'll never have a beau.

MRS. MARTIN. We'll wait and see about that. But listen, Barbara, will you do something for me right now?

BARBARA. Maybe. What is it?

MRS. MARTIN. I want you to dust this room.

BARBARA. Oh, shoot!

MRS. MARTIN. Now, Barbara. . . .

BARBARA. Seems like that ought to be Margaret's job. She's the one that wants everything fixed up. It isn't my beau that's coming.

MRS. MARTIN. I know, but she's got so much else to do. Come on, say you will.

BARBARA [*reluctantly*]. All right. But I won't do it next time.

MRS. MARTIN. The duster's in the kitchen; you can run in there and get it. And hurry, we haven't any time to lose.

[BARBARA *goes slowly.* MARGARET *returns from the porch wiping soot from her hands.*]

MARGARET [*triumphantly*]. At last that old stove's out of the way!

MRS. MARTIN. That's fine. But you look all tired out. Don't you want to take a bit of a rest so you'll be fresh when Keith comes?

MARGARET. Certainly I'd like to, Mother, but I haven't time. I've got to dust in here.

MRS. MARTIN. Barbara's going to do that.

MARGARET. Oh, she couldn't do it good enough.

MRS. MARTIN. Yes, she can. You go on.

MARGARET [*starting out*]. All right then. But maybe I'd better get all ready before I rest—all but putting on my dress and shoes. What do you think?

Mrs. Martin. Yes, that might not be a bad idea. Get your bath over with and then the washtub won't be in the way in the kitchen right when I'm finishing dinner.

Margaret. I'll bathe, then. But let me see. [*Looking over the room.*] Is everything going to look all right in here?

Mrs. Martin. It's going to look lovely as soon as Barbara finishes dusting.

Margaret [*anxiously*]. I hope it will look all right. If it doesn't, and Keith doesn't care about me any more, I... I don't know what I'll do.

Mrs. Martin. It's going to look fine, dear. You don't need to worry.

Margaret. If he were just an ordinary fellow—if he'd never had anything any better....

Mrs. Martin. I know, dear. But everything's going to be all right. The room really looks lovely now. Don't you think it so?

Margaret [*nodding agreement*]. Yes, I... I think it does look right nice now. But with that old stove—

Mrs. Martin. I know. But we don't need to worry about the stove any more. That's past history now.

Margaret [*grimly for a moment*]. It'd better be.

[Barbara *enters left.*]

Barbara [*holding up the dust cloth*]. Is this the duster?

Mrs. Martin. Yes, that's it. [Barbara *begins dusting.*]

Margaret. And be sure you do it decently.

Barbara [*truculently*]. If you don't like the way I do it—

Mrs. Martin [*interposing quickly*]. She'll do it all right, Margaret. You go on and get ready.

[Margaret *goes into the kitchen.*]

Barbara. Do I have to dust everything?

Mrs. Martin. It won't take long. You'll be sure and get in all the corners, won't you?

Barbara. Oh, I guess so.

Mrs. Martin. And do the windowsills and doors.
Barbara. All right. [*A pause.*] But listen, Mama!
Mrs. Martin. Now what is it?
Barbara. It's raining harder than ever outside. You can hear it on the roof. You can see it just pouring down out there. [*She points to the window.*] It's getting cold in here, too.
Mrs. Martin [*throwing up her hands*]. Oh, dear, I didn't think it would pour down like that. I wonder where your father is? If he's out in it—
Barbara. I bet he is. He's not in the kitchen.
Mrs. Martin. It'd be just like him to be out in it. If he comes in here like a drowned rat—
Barbara. Oh—
Mrs. Martin. Heavens! What is it now?
Barbara. Here Father comes. He's on old Dan, riding as fast as he can. [*She laughs.*] He sure looks wet!
Mrs. Martin. Gracious! He'll be wet to the skin. He'll have to change his clothes and everything. And he always makes such a fuss!
[*The outside door opens and* Mr. Martin *blusters in, shaking himself.*]
Mr. Martin. Jumping grasshoppers, but that's some rain out there!
Mrs. Martin. Oh, dear! You're soaking wet.
Mr. Martin. Yeh, and freezing to death, too. You'd better get me a fire. [Mr. and Mrs. Martin and Barbara *all remember simultaneously. All stare at the spot where the stove was.*] Oh, hang it all, no stove! Now what'll I do?
Mrs. Martin. It's not too cold in the bedroom upstairs to change your clothes, is it?
Mr. Martin. Of course it is. It'd freeze a brass nigger. You know that as well as me.

Mrs. Martin. Then you'll have to change in the kitchen.

Mr. Martin. Who wants to be cooped up in the kitchen? If Margaret'd left the stove in here like I wanted her to—

Mrs. Martin. I know, Father. But the stove didn't look so very nice. And when she wanted things fixed up for her beau—

Mr. Martin. Things was fixed up fine! Margaret and her fool notions! Well, come on, let's get in there and get these wet things off. I can't stand here all day talking about it and catch my death of cold. [*He starts toward the kitchen, grumbling as he goes.*]

Barbara [*excited*]. You can't go in the kitchen now. Margaret's taking a bath.

Mr. Martin. What's that—what's that you say?

Mrs. Martin. She's almost through by now, I'm sure.

Mr. Martin. I'll bet she isn't. It takes her all day long to do anything.

Mrs. Martin. She's hurrying to-day. I know she's nearly finished. I'll go and see.

Mr. Martin. You don't need to bother.

Mrs. Martin. Then you'll go upstairs and change?

Mr. Martin. No, I won't do that. I'll bring the stove back in.

Mrs. Martin [*alarmed*]. You'll bring the stove back in?

Mr. Martin. Yeh, that's what I said.

Barbara [*jubilantly*]. Oh, goody, goody.

Mrs. Martin. But, Father, you don't mean *that*!

Mr. Martin. I sure do mean it. Come on, Barbara, you can help me. [*He starts for the porch.* Mrs. Martin *holds him back.*]

Mrs. Martin. Obadiah, it's foolish to bring it back in when it's already out.

Mr. Martin. Yeh, I guess it'll still be foolish when I die of galloping pneumonia!

Mrs. Martin. Oh, nothing like that'll happen. You can get in the kitchen right now. I'll tell Margaret she'll have to let you have it whether she's through or not.

Mr. Martin. No, m'am! I ain't going to be cooped up in that kitchen. Come on, Barbara.

Mrs. Martin [*pleading*]. But Obadiah, when Margaret's expecting company—can't you leave things the way they are —just this once?

Mr. Martin. No, I can't. I ain't going to die of the chills for anybody. Come on, Barbara. [*He pulls away from* Mrs. Martin *and goes out.* Barbara *follows him.*]

Mrs. Martin [*distracted*]. Oh, dear, if that man weren't so obstinate. Now I don't know what'll happen.

[Margaret *enters wearing a dressing-gown, and looking gay and excitedly thrilled.*]

Margaret. Mother! Mother!

Mrs. Martin [*with a start*]. Oh, it's you, Margaret!

Margaret. What dress do you think I ought to put on? I —what's the matter, Mother, don't you feel well?

Mrs. Martin [*quickly, to hide her distraught feelings*]. Oh, yes, yes, of course. I'm all right.

Margaret. But you look so queer—

Mrs. Martin [*pulling herself together*]. I'm all right— Now listen, Margaret, there's something I've got to tell you.

Margaret [*alarmed*]. What is it, Mother? Has something happened to Keith?

Mrs. Martin. No, it isn't that.

Margaret. Mother! Tell me, what is it?

Mrs. Martin [*gathering her courage to deliver the blow to* Margaret]. Oh, I hate to tell you, Margaret. Poor dear, you'll have to know sooner or later, and we might as well get it over with.

MARGARET. Oh, Mother! Hurry up and tell me!

MRS. MARTIN [*taking a deep breath before she speaks*]. Your father's bringing the stove back in.

MARGARET. Bringing the stove back in! Mother, you don't mean that!

MRS. MARTIN. I'm sorry, Margaret, but—

MARGARET. Mother! You *can't* mean it. Why Dad helped me take it out, and everything was all settled!

MRS. MARTIN. I know. But he came home dripping wet, and—

MARGARET. It is true, then. It is! Oh dear! Oh dear! What are you letting him do it for?

MRS. MARTIN. I tried to stop him; but you know how your father is when his mind's made up. You might as well argue with a stone wall.

MARGARET. But I can't have that stove in here. I can't! I'll go out and stop him! I don't care what he says.

MRS. MARTIN [*detaining her*]. You can't do anything, Margaret. You'll only make things worse.

MARGARET. I stopped him once to-day.

MRS. MARTIN. You can't do it again. His mind's set on it.

MARGARET [*in despair*]. Then I give up. [*She drops into a chair.*]

MRS. MARTIN. You mustn't feel that way about it, dear.

MARGARET. I don't know how else I can feel.

MRS. MARTIN. I'm sure it won't make any difference to Keith.

MARGARET. It will too. It'll make him feel sorry for me because we haven't got anything decent around here. And I won't have people feeling sorry for me. I won't! I won't marry some one just because he thinks I need help!

Mrs. Martin. He won't feel sorry for you, I'm sure.

Margaret. He can't help it, Mother, he can't! I— [*Hysterically.*] Oh, I wish I hadn't invited him to come. I wish I'd never seen him. I wish I was dead! [*She rushes off upstairs.*]

[*A loud thumping and banging is heard.* Mr. Martin *shouts loudly outside.*]

Mr. Martin. Open the door, somebody!

[Mrs. Martin *stiffens in defiance and starts off right. Another shout from* Mr. Martin *stops her, and she loses her courage. She shakes her head, turns around, and goes to the door and opens it.*]

Mr. Martin [*in the doorway*]. Well, it's about time! Hold it open wide now, so we can get this thing through. [Mr. Martin *pulls the stove through the door.* Barbara *follows with the pipes.*]

Mr. Martin [*struggling to get the stove in place*]. Come on, Ma. Give me a hand here.

Mrs. Martin [*about to refuse*]. I think— [*Then relenting she goes to give him a lift.*] All right. There you are. [*The stove is in its place again, and* Barbara *picks up the pipes.*]

Barbara [*after relinquishing the pipes*]. Shall I get some kindling and wood for it now, Papa?

Mr. Martin. Yeh, sure.

[Barbara *goes into the kitchen for dry wood.* Mr. Martin *stands on a chair and fits back the pipes.* Mrs. Martin *helps him, but grimly and with reluctance. The pipes are difficult to adjust, and* Mr. Martin *blusters. He would swear if it were permissible.*]

Mr. Martin [*when the job is finished*]. Well, now, that's over with. Could have saved all this bother though, if I hadn't been so soft-hearted. It won't happen again, anyway. I can assure you of that.

MRS. MARTIN. I don't suppose there'll be any need for it to happen again. Margaret feels so terrible.

[BARBARA *enters with wood, paper, and kindling.*]

MR. MARTIN. That's a good girl, Barbara. Now we'll have a fire in no time. [*The fire is soon burning brightly.*]

BARBARA. Oh, goody! That'll feel swell, won't it?

MR. MARTIN. You're blame right, it will.

MRS. MARTIN. Now that it's done, go on and get your clothes changed.

MR. MARTIN. Yeh, that's what I'm going to do.

MRS. MARTIN. You'd better do it in the kitchen though. It's still too cold in here.

MR. MARTIN. Sure, that's what I'm going to do. But you come along with me and get my clean clothes. [*He goes.*]

MRS. MARTIN. I shouldn't have given him an ounce of help. But to keep peace— [*She follows him into the kitchen.*]

BARBARA. Boy! this fire sure feels good.

[MARGARET *enters. She is wearing a pretty afternoon frock, but there are lines of bitterness about her mouth and her eyes look weary. She glares at the stove, then shrugs resignedly and drops into a chair.*]

BARBARA [*persistently*]. Now, aren't you glad we've got a good fire?

MARGARET. It doesn't matter to me. Nothing matters to me any more.

BARBARA [*in surprise*]. Gee, but you've sure changed all of a sudden. A little while ago you cared about everything, and now— [*There is a knock at the door.*]

MARGARET. Go to the door.

BARBARA. But it's for you.

MARGARET. It won't be for me now. Go on. [BARBARA *goes to the door and opens it.*]

KEITH [*on the porch*]. Is this where Margaret Martin lives?

[*At the sound of his voice,* MARGARET *starts and goes quickly upstairs.*]

BARBARA. Um-hm.... Sure....

KEITH. I'm Keith Warner.

BARBARA. Then you're her beau, aren't you?

KEITH [*laughing good-naturedly*]. I hope she feels that way about it.

BARBARA. She does—at least she did. Come on in. She's right here.

[KEITH *enters. He is a well-dressed young fellow and carries a suitcase. In the doorway, he shakes the rain from his hat.*]

BARBARA [*looks around the room in surprise*]. Now, that's funny; she was here a minute ago. Golly, maybe she doesn't want to see— [*Catches herself.*] I mean, maybe Mama called her or something. I'll go see.

KEITH. Thank you, I wish you would.

[BARBARA *starts to the kitchen,* MARGARET *comes in, pretending to be unaware of* KEITH'S *presence.*]

BARBARA. Well, it's time you showed up.

KEITH. Well, Margaret, it's good to see you. [*Dropping the suitcase and going eagerly toward her.*]

MARGARET [*As though seeing him for the first time, speaking very formally and without animation.*] Oh, hello, Keith.

KEITH [*He takes her hands in his, but she fails to respond*]. I... I could just about eat you up. [*He starts to take her in his arms, then backs away.*] I forgot, I'm sort of wettish. I was soaked just coming from the car to the house—

[MR. MARTIN *comes in from the kitchen, followed by* MRS. MARTIN. *He is now in dry clothes.* MR. MARTIN, *unaware of* KEITH'S *arrival, is in an expansive mood.* MRS. MARTIN *still appears worried and concerned.*]

MR. MARTIN. Now, with a good fire—

[KEITH *looks up expectantly;* BARBARA *dashes over to her mother and father;* MARGARET *is exasperated.*]

BARBARA [*blithely*]. Look who's here!

MR. MARTIN. Well, well, well!

[MRS. MARTIN *says nothing, but attempts to conceal her concern for* MARGARET *with a cheerful manner.*]

MARGARET [*stiffly*]. My mother and father, Keith—Mother, Mr. Warner.

MRS. MARTIN [*extending her hand warmly*]. I'm surely glad to meet you. Margaret has told us all about you.

KEITH. I hope she hasn't told you all. I'm very glad to meet you, too.

MARGARET. And my Dad.

KEITH. How do you do, Mr. Martin.

MR. MARTIN. How d'y-you do, Mr. Warner, I'm glad to see you. Say, you're all wet, ain't you?

KEITH. I did get a bit of a sprinkling.

MR. MARTIN. Yeh, you sure did. But it don't matter, because we got a good warm fire here. [*Pointing to the stove.*]

KEITH [*with delighted surprise*]. Say! let me take a good look at that stove. [*Goes over to the stove and looks at it admiringly.*]

[MR. MARTIN *nods approvingly;* BARBARA *giggles;* MARGARET *looks on, fearful, suspicious, surprised;* MRS. MARTIN *is uncertain.*]

KEITH [*delighted*]. Yes, sir, that's what it is, exactly—a Franklin! Who would have thought it?

MR. MARTIN. What's the matter? Not seeing something you recognize, are you?

KEITH. Yes. My grandmother had a stove like this at her place in the country.

MARGARET [*with a little cry*]. You don't mean to say you really *like* it?

KEITH [*excitedly*]. Exactly like this one! [MARGARET *is happy;* MRS. MARTIN *relieved.*]

MR. MARTIN. Sure, it'd be like this one. And the Franklin's the best stove ever made.

KEITH. It sure is. At least I thought so when I was a kid and went to stay with grandmother for Christmas vacation. She'd let me put wood in it and poke around in the coals and do all the things kids like to do. When I think about it now, it all comes back.

MARGARET [*taking his hand*]. I know just how you felt because I like to poke the fire, too. Don't I, Mother?

MRS. MARTIN [*with a sly smile*]. Yes, indeed, you certainly used to!

BARBARA. But you don't any more.

KEITH. Don't you, Margaret?

MARGARET. Oh, of course I do. There's nothing I like better. [KEITH *gives her hand a little squeeze and looks at her adoringly.*]

MR. MARTIN. Well, here now, here now, wait a minute!

MRS. MARTIN [*beaming at the happy turn of events*]. I think I'd better go back to the kitchen now and finish dinner. Barbara, you and Father come along. I'll need your help. [*She starts left, but* MR. MARTIN *and* BARBARA *do not follow her. She comes back and rounds them up.*] Come on, come on. [*They follow reluctantly.*]

MARGARET [*perfunctorily*]. I'll come and help you if you want me to, Mother.

MRS. MARTIN [*in doorway*]. You stay right here by the fire and enjoy yourselves. We'll manage without you.

[MRS. MARTIN, MR. MARTIN, *and* BARBARA *all leave.* KEITH *draws* MARGARET *toward the fire and put his arms about her. They should have a few moments completely to themselves.*]

THE CURTAIN FALLS

MONTANA

MONTANA NIGHT

A DRAMA OF THE OLD WEST

BY ROBERT FINCH AND BETTY SMITH

OF DILLON, MONTANA, AND CHAPEL HILL, NORTH CAROLINA

Written in the summer playwriting course at the University of North Carolina and originally produced by The Carolina Playmakers at Chapel Hill on July 20, 1938.

THE CHARACTERS

STEVE GALLAGHER, *a young road agent, or robber*
    Cy Edson
BOONE BENSON, *his partner, another road agent*
    Don Muller
BOB COOPER, *a young miner*........John Roughton
WASH BIEDLER, *an old prospector*.......Glenn James

SCENE: *The supply station of Gallagher and Benson in Virginia City, Montana Territory.*
TIME: 1863. *New Year's Eve.*

Copyright, 1938, by The Carolina Playmakers, Inc.
All rights reserved.

MONTANA GOLD RUSH

JACK GALLAGHER, notorious road agent, lies buried on a sunny wind-swept hill overlooking the city he depredated. They call it Boot Hill because those buried there died with their boots on. Men who were companions to Jack Gallagher in life, lie close by: Club-Foot George Lane, Haze Lyons, Frank Parish, and Boone Helm. All of these desperadoes were hanged by the Vigilantes in Virginia City, Montana Territory in 1864. They rest quietly after a violent life. Their plain headstones face Virginia City, now a ghost town in a desolated valley. Nights, when a chinook wind hushes its way through the valley, carrying the scent of sage-brush, folks turn their faces to Boot Hill and say that the sage-brush growing on Jack Gallagher's grave smells sweeter, somehow, than any other for miles around. It all happened so long ago, that time has mellowed the remembrance of his desperate exploits.

Often these men reined in their horses on this very same hill and looked over Virginia City, then a crowded, booming, brawling, gold-mine town. The place had been an unsettled gulch until the discovery of the richest placer gold deposits that the world has ever known, caused ten thousand people to settle there in ninety days. Tents, cabins, and brush wikiups (shelter huts) were thrown together in the roughest form to provide shelter. Gamblers, traders, and road agents drifted into the gulch following the great stampede. They preyed on the prospectors and grew rich in one of two ways: by outright robbery or by exploiting the daily needs of the miners. Fortunes were made in a day and lost in five minutes. Hotels charged twenty dollars for a night's lodging. A small bottle of ink cost two dollars. Flour brought one hundred dollars a sack and many a buckskin cavalier paid ten dollars to dance five minutes with one of the saloon girls. Those were fabulous times. Fortunes had a way of coming quickly to men; death even more quickly.

The road agents organized murder and robbery into an efficient business. Murder was the quickest way of concealing robbery and the two crimes went hand in hand. Men were murdered because they carried gold. Others were murdered because their failure to carry gold infuriated the robbers. Murder became an hourly occurrence in the streets, stores, and saloons. A man was shot because he did not grant a request quickly enough. A miner accused a storekeeper of having a bad temper; the storekeeper was so insulted that he beat the miner to death trying to convince him that he was mistaken.

Violence was so rampant that no person was safe even in his own home. It was then that a party of fearless upright citizens organized themselves into a Vigilante Committee to stamp out crime in the Territory. They worked efficiently and courageously and soon came to be feared by the road agents. Quietly and steadily, they rounded up known criminals and after an informal but just trial, hanged them without mercy. Many of the most infamous road agents died giving their password, "I am innocent." The last speech they heard in this life was the terse command of the Vigilante leader: "Men, do your duty!" This was the signal which swung them off into eternity.

The Vigilantes executed the worst offenders and drove the others from the Territory. Peace and order reigned. Then the gold gave out. There were rumors of new discoveries elsewhere; the gulch was deserted, and Virginia City turned into a ghost town overnight.

There are perhaps two hundred people living there now. Among them are a few old-timers who, as lads of fourteen, sometimes rode out with the Vigilantes. Others, eight or nine years old at the time, recall the tales their fathers told of the road agents and the hangings. If you can get one of these old men to talk, he will tell you of the old days. He will point out Jack Gallagher's grave and tell you what a handsome man he was. He will speak of Club-Foot George who plied his trade of shoemaker in order to allay suspicion and how he betrayed the confidence of miners who mistook him for a harmless craftsman. You will hear the story of Boone Helm, alleged to have eaten his partner when the rations gave out. He might take you to the place where the road agents were hanged. You'll hear of the unfortunate boy from the East whose partner was murdered and who, unwittingly, walked into the hands of the murderers. The murderers tried to get his claim away from him but he was befriended by a kindly prospector and saved from death. The old man will grow reminiscent and tell you that men aren't as brave nowadays as they were then. He will swear that the winters aren't as cold or the summers as hot as they used to be. To him, the Ruby Mountains do not seem as high as they seemed sixty years ago and the Ruby River does not run as swiftly.

"It all happened once," he'll sigh. "But it could never happen again. No, it could never happen again."

In this play it happens again.

MONTANA NIGHT

Virginia City, Montana Territory, site of the greatest placer gold strike in history, is preparing to celebrate the New Year's Eve of 1864. GALLAGHER AND BENSON'S *supply station is still open but no one is trading there. The proprietors do not encourage small trading because the station is really a blind for a band of road agents. Under the guise of selling supplies and cashing in the gold of those prospectors who have "panned out wages," the proprietors are able to obtain information which they pass on to their leaders or else use themselves. They hear of miners who have struck it rich and carry large fortunes about with them. They find out the routes taken by freighting outfits carrying large shipments of gold. They get information of newly discovered rich claims, as yet unfiled, which may be jumped after the owner has been done in. Protected by their alleged status as traders, they plunder and murder, unsuspected and unpunished by the Vigilantes.*

The station is a crude one-room cabin. The walls are weather-worn logs chinked with mud. A wide, heavy door is in the center of the rear wall. To the right of this door, is a window with snow clinging to it. A large animal skin is stretched on the right wall. A lighted kerosene lamp stands on a small table. A crudely made bench stands downstage of the table. Next to the bench is a round-bellied heating stove with a stool before it and a box of wood beside it. There is a jog in the opposite wall into which a counter has been built with several shelves behind it. These hold a lighted kerosene lamp, a pair of gold-weighing scales, several new knives in sheaths, short-handled axes and a stack of chewing tobacco plugs and some coiled leather straps or belts. Downstage of the counter is a narrow door which leads outside behind the station. Pegs have been driven into the wall-space upstage of the counter. On these hang a new saddle, a bright plaid blanket, a new holster belt, a deerskin jacket, a heavy coat, and a hat or two.

[GALLAGHER is a young road agent or robber. He is a handsome man, thirty years of age. His hair is rather long and jet black, and he has a small mustache. He is nervous and quick-moving. He wears frontier clothes of a better quality than average; well-made doeskin breeches tucked into expensive high boots and a fringed doeskin coat. His partner, BOONE BENSON, another road agent, is forty years old. He is a cruel-looking, slow-moving man with a short, unkempt beard. He wears the usual frontier clothes consisting of rough trousers stuffed into high boots, a coarse shirt, and colored neckerchief.]

[It is just before midnight of New Year's Eve. A blizzard has been howling down from the mountains all evening. But the bitter cold night has not prevented the miners from coming into town to celebrate. Tin-panny dance music is coming from the saloon called The Last Chance. A lively frontier air called "Oh, Suzannah" is being played. The supply station is empty. The smoky lamps are turned low. Some reflected light from the snow comes in through the window. A man with his head bent to the storm is just passing the window. Two men are close behind him. One carries a knife in his upraised hand. The knife comes down in the man's back. He falls without a sound. A man has been murdered but nothing more has been seen of the murder than a blurred silhouette outside the window. The door is opened and voices are heard.]

GALLAGHER [*off*]. Wait a minute, Boone. I'll turn up the light. [*He enters and turns up the lamp on the table.* BOONE *stands in the doorway, looking back.*] Now I feel better.

BOONE. There's nothin' to be afraid of.

GALLAGHER. There's plenty to be afraid of as long as he's above ground.

VOICE [*comes from way off. It is weird and faint and mingles with the music*]. John-ne-e-e-eeeee....

GALLAGHER [*alarmed*]. What was that?

BOONE [*listens*]. I didn't hear nothin' exceptin' that music from the dance hall.

GALLAGHER. No. Listen! [*They listen.*]

VOICE. John-ne—-e-eeeeeee!

GALLAGHER. Get him in here quick before some one comes along.

BOONE [*talking as they go out*]. It's just some fool down to The Last Chance objectin' to the way the Professor's playin' the piano. [*As if to bear out his words, the music stops abruptly.*] See? The playin' stopped.

[*The room is empty for a second. They reënter, carrying the body of a man between them. His red woolen scarf hangs trailing to the floor.*]

VOICE. John-ne—e-eeeeeee!

[GALLAGHER *closes the door and peers out the window.* BOONE *kneels and ransacks the pockets of the murdered man. He takes out two filled buckskin bags.*]

BOONE. Look at this! He was packin' about fourteen ounces of gold dust!

GALLAGHER [*as he takes the bags and stuffs them into his own pockets*]. That was worth doin' him in for.

STICK 'EM UP

Sheriff. Well, Pete, you tried to pull a fast one on me, didn't you? You might 'a' knowed it wouldn't work—not on me.

Wootten-Moulton

Wootten-Moulton

MONTANA NIGHT

BOONE. Look at this! He was packin' about fourteen ounces of gold dust!

BOONE [*searching further*]. Must have staked himself out a rich claim somewhere. But there ain't no map or papers on him tellin' where.

GALLAGHER. Sure wish I knew.

BOONE. Maybe he works with a partner?

GALLAGHER. What if he does? We got the one packin' the gold.

BOONE. The partner might come around lookin'.

GALLAGHER. Well, let's get him underground, then. [*He pushes the body with his foot.*] Come on.

[*Just as they are about to pick up the body, there is the rumbling roar of a snowslide outside. It lasts a few seconds. The two men listen, startled.*]

BOONE [*relaxing*]. There goes some more snow off the mountains.

GALLAGHER. I hope none of them snowslides hit this shack.

[*They carry the body out by way of the door downstage of the counter which leads to the back of the station. The red scarf slips from the body unnoticed and lies on the floor.*]

VOICE [*quite close*]. Johnny! [*Then it is just outside the door.*] Johnny!

[*The road agents reënter stealthily and crouch behind the counter.* BOB COOPER *enters from the rear door. He is not quite twenty. He is handsome and given to quick changes of mood. He is cheerful and trusting one moment and in the depths of despondency the next. He has a thin, sensitive face and dark eyes which are nearly always wide open and he wears the usual frontier clothes, breeches, boots, coat, and white shirt.*]

BOB. Johnny, are you here?

BOONE. Reach for the ceilin'! [BOB *stands petrified.*] Quick! [*The boy's hands go up.*] That's better. Gallagher, turn up the light.

GALLAGHER [*as he turns up the lamp on the shelf*]. Watch him!

BOB [*naïvely*]. You needn't be afraid of me. [*He smiles.*] I just nearly got caught in that snowslide out there a-ways.

BOONE [*snarling*]. What do you want?

BOB. I'm lookin' for my partner.... Is Johnny here? I followed his tracks for miles until the snow covered them. [*The men stare at him.*] I'm awful tired. Can I sit down awhile? Maybe he'll find me here. [BOONE *hesitates about putting his gun up. Finally he returns it to his holster and* BOB's *hands come down.*] Don't be afraid. I wouldn't hurt you. Johnny don't let me pack no gun. Not since the accident when I hurt my head. [*He presses his hand to his forehead as he sits on the stool.*] But it don't hurt no more. I still have bad headaches sometimes. But Johnny says I'm pretty near myself again—most of the time. [*He smiles ingratiatingly at the men.*]

GALLAGHER. I guess it's all right. But you can't stay long. Him and me run this station and we got things to do.

BOB. I expect you're mighty busy, this bein' New Year's Eve and lots of prospectors in town so's they can file their claims first day of 1864. [*The road agents exchange looks.* BOB *holds out his hands to the stove.*] Well, I won't bother you. I just want to warm my hands a little. They're nearly frozen. [*As if to himself.*] My, that was a big snowslide! Yes sir. Glad we got out of the pass in time.

GALLAGHER. What's your name?

BOB. Bob Cooper.

GALLAGHER. What you doin' runnin' around out there dodging snowslides and yellin' like that? [*He shivers.*] You gave me the creeps.

BOB. Have you seen Johnny?

BOONE. Don't know nobody by that name.

BOB. I thought he might be here.

GALLAGHER. Why here?
BOB. Just a feelin' I had when I come in. That he was here.
BOONE [*as the two road agents exchange glances*]. What's he like?
BOB [*beaming at what he considers their friendly interest*]. He's an awful good-hearted fellow. You'd like him.
BOONE. How come you lost track of such a fine partner?
BOB. We were headin' for town. We come out from Black Deer Canyon way. I ain't got a horse so we were both ridin' Johnny's horse, Skipper. It was snowin' mighty hard and the trail got covered with snow. So Johnny started off on foot to find the trail. I waited for him to come back. Then I started lookin' for him. I been lookin' ever since.
GALLAGHER. What made you come to this place?
BOB. The horse sort of wanted to head this way.
GALLAGHER. What sort of a lookin' fellow was he—is he?
BOB. You wouldn't forget him if you saw him. He's wearin' a red scarf. [GALLAGHER'S *eyes fall on the scarf on the floor. Hurriedly, he kicks it out of sight.*] He's six feet tall in his boots. Boots got Spanish spurs with wheels and rowels on 'em. He's got buckskin pants on, fringed at the seams and pulled in at the waist with a U.S. belt. He's got a loaded revolver and a sheath knife in the belt. He's carryin' two— [*He stops suddenly.*]
BOONE [*craftily*]. Two what, youngster?
BOB. Nothin'....
GALLAGHER. If it's gold, you do right not to tell. Too many road agents in Montana Territory these days.
BOONE. Yes, this is rough minin' country. If you happen to be packin' money or papers or anythin' like that, it's best to be careful and not ride out alone unless you let somebody take care of your things for you.

Bob. I was sort of scared ridin' in alone from— [*He stops suddenly.*]

Gallagher. From—where did you say your claim was?

Bob [*frightened*]. I never said we had no claim. Johnny told me I must never— [*He looks from one to the other.*] Where's Johnny?

Boone. You tell us first where his claim is.

Bob. Then you know where he is?

Gallagher [*with an angry look at* Boone]. No, he don't. But you know where the claim is, don't you? [*The frightened boy steps back. The other two step up to him.*] Don't you?

[Wash Biedler *enters by rear door. He is a kindly prospector about fifty years old. He is a hard-working miner and although he has struck it fairly rich, he dresses shabbily. He is large, friendly, and good-natured although he is inclined to act a little boisterous after a drink or two. He is likeable.*]

Wash. Wash Biedler, that's me. [*The road agents relax and smile in order to deceive the newcomer.*] Whoops! I'm from way back in Pike County, Missouri. My parlor is the Rocky Mountains. I smell like a wolf and drink water out of a brook like a horse. Look out, you coyotes, I'm goin' to turn loose! [*He pushes the road agents aside with a flaying movement of his arms. He staggers to the counter and pounds on it with his fist.*] Give me a shot of tarantula juice.

Boone. This ain't no saloon.

Gallagher. The Last Chance down the road will sell you all you want to drink. And maybe you'll get to dance with one of the girls.

Wash. Ain't no gal would dance with me less'n I paid her ten dollars. [*Arguing with himself.*] But ain't I got ten dollars? Sure! [*Tosses a small bag on the counter.*] Weigh it in.

BOONE. We don't weigh gold this time of night.

GALLAGHER. Oh, give him the money, Boone, to get him out.

BOONE [*angrily; he weighs the dust grudgingly*]. Man of your kidney is apt to get plugged in the back some night.

WASH. Not for my *money*.

BOONE. No. For talkin' too much.

WASH. I'm well liked in these parts. Ain't a road agent on the frontier would harm me. [*He takes a long wicked-looking knife from his belt and plunges the tip of it into the counter. He watches it quivering as he drawls.*] Yes, sir, I'm well liked. [*He stares at the knife.*] Besides, I scalped nigh onto forty Indians in my time. [*Staring at* GALLAGHER.] And half of them white men, too!

BOONE [*eyeing the knife*]. It don't weigh quite an eagle but I'm givin' it to you, anyway. [*He tosses a gold piece on the table and points to the door.*] Now get out! [WASH *waves his hand at him and then draws the stool away from the stove and sits on it.* BOB *takes a step toward him.*]

BOB. Mr. Biedler, do you know Johnny?

WASH. Ain't seen nobody answerin' to that name—not so far to-night. But I'm sorry for him if he's a stranger and wanderin' around these parts. I heard tell there's a bunch of road agents doin' business as—

GALLAGHER [*interrupts him*]. Why don't you get yourself a room at the hotel and sleep it off?

WASH. No, I'm goin' to be drinkin' champagne while 1863's a-dyin' out. Will you gents drink with me?

BOONE. We don't want you around here.

WASH [*coming back to the subject*]. Where did you say your partner was, son?

Bob [*almost in tears*]. I don't know.

Wash [*frankly*]. There's somethin' about this place I don't like. [*He beckons to* Bob.] Come here. [*He seizes* Bob's *arm and is about to tell him something when* Gallagher *pushes himself between the two men.*]

Gallagher. Now look here, Bob, as long as you're worried about your partner, why don't you take a lantern and go out and look for him? [*He wants to get him away from the talkative prospector.*]

Boone [*taking a lantern from behind the counter and lighting it*]. Sure. And if you don't find him, you come back and let us know. Then we'll go out and help you.

Bob [*going to the counter for the lantern*]. I guess I better hurry all right. Thanks for lettin' me get warm. [*He turns and smiles gratefully at them.*] You know I was plenty scared when you pointed that gun at me. I could look right down in the barrel and see the lead gettin' ready to jump. I had an idea you were goin' to kill me. [*He takes the lantern and goes to the door.*] I guess my horse is rested by now. Good-by and thanks. [*He goes out.*]

Wash [*befuddled and scratching his head*]. There's somethin' I ought to tell that boy and I don't know what it is.

Boone [*through his teeth*]. Now you *walk* out of here unless you aim to be carried out on a board.

Wash [*putting his knife in his belt*]. I warn't calculatin' to stay. Don't like your company. Guess I know where I ain't welcome. [*He goes out.*]

[*Music from the dance hall starts playing again, this time, a lively polka.*]

Gallagher [*runs to door, opens it, and looks out to see that no one is about. He peers out the window*]. Well, they're both gone, now.

BOONE. Let's get rid of that body out there, then. Just in case the Vigilantes come ridin' around.

GALLAGHER [*shudders*]. Why do you have to talk about the Vigilantes? No one suspects nothin'.

BOONE. Maybe that boy does.

GALLAGHER. He seemed plenty loco * to me.

BOONE. But those kind have a way at guessing at things. We should have killed him.

GALLAGHER. Not until we find out where his claim is. When he gets back, we'll make him tell. Then we'll get there in a hurry, tear down the markers that stake out his claim, put up our own, and get back here by daylight and file our papers on it first thing in the mornin'.

BOONE [*drily*]. In the meantime, let's bury the body. [*He goes behind the counter and gets a shovel.*]

GALLAGHER [*nervously*]. Look! Can't we drag him out to Daylight Gulch? There's a couple hundred thousand ton of snow ready to slide down the mountain into that pass. It'll happen before mornin'. They won't find him till spring—when the snows melt. Then it'll look like an accident.

BOONE [*derisively*]. A fine idea! But would you want to drag him out to that gulch with the whole place full of prospectors in town for New Year's Eve?

GALLAGHER. Noo-o-o-o....

BOONE. We'll work fast and get him under ground, quick. Snow will be three feet deep over him by mornin'.

GALLAGHER. We can put him in that old prospectin' hole we dug out there before we built the shack. There's dry dirt and gravel in the shed next to it.

BOONE [*going to the downstage door*]. That will save a lot of time. [GALLAGHER *stands as though reluctant to move.*] Get the pickax. [*He goes out.* GALLAGHER *goes to win-*

* Crazy.

dow and stares out. *The sound of* Boone *shoveling coarse gravel is heard outside. The music plays on. The shoveling stops as* Boone *calls.*] Hurry up with that pickax.

Gallagher. I'm comin'. [*The shoveling starts again. Hurriedly he removes the two gold-filled bags from his pockets and looks around for a place to conceal them from his partner.*]

Boone [*stops shoveling*]. Well, come on, then.

Gallagher. Right away. I'm lockin' the door. [*In his haste, he picks up* Johnny's *red scarf, places the gold in it, and ties it up. He goes to the wood-box and stuffs the bundle under some sticks of wood. Then he goes to the door to lock it, but* Boone *calls.*]

Boone. Hurry up and give me a hand with him.

[Gallagher *turns without bolting the door, grabs a pickax from behind the counter, and goes out to* Boone. *The music plays on cheerfully. Now the sound of shoveling comes louder. From far away, but above the noise and the music, comes the cry again.*]

Bob. John-ne-e-e-e . . . !

[*Complete silence. The shoveling stops and the music dies away. Then there is a sound like a deep sigh made by the road agents lowering the body into the grave.*]

Boone [*from outside, as if in great relief*]. There!

[*The shoveling is resumed harder and faster for a moment, then begins to grow slower and more quiet. The large door, rear, opens and* Wash Biedler *enters.*]

Wash. Want to 'pologize for my ungentlemanly conduct. [*He is carrying a bottle of champagne in the crook of his arm. He sets the bottle on the counter.*] Would be proud to have you gentlemen drink with me. [*He sees the room is empty. He listens and hears the shoveling sound which is now growing faint. He goes to the stove to warm his hands, notices that the fire is low and replen-*

ishes it. *After a few sticks have been put in the stove, he sees the bundle. He picks it up and stares at it.*]

GALLAGHER [*from outside*]. Now we'll level off the top.

[WASH *listens. Looks thoughtful. Stares at bundle, stares in direction of the voices. Replaces bundle in the wood-box. He starts to leave quickly. Almost at the door, he remembers the bottle of champagne on the counter. He goes back to get it and then leaves in a hurry. Just as the door closes after him, the side door opens and* GALLAGHER *enters cautiously. He looks around and starts to go to the wood-box.*]

BOB [*getting closer to the station*]. John-n-e-e-eee ...!

GALLAGHER [*rushes to window, looks out and then calls back over his shoulder to* BOONE, *who is still outside*]. For God's sake, hurry! It's that boy! He's comin' back. [BOONE *comes in carrying the shovel over his shoulder. It is wet from the snow.*] I can see his lantern. He's headin' this way again.

BOONE [*as he stands the shovel behind the counter*]. I'm glad that's over with.

GALLAGHER [*hoarsely*]. I forgot the pick! Get it! Somebody might see it and wonder what we were diggin'.

[BOONE *hurries out to get the pickax. Before he returns,* BOB *comes in. He is covered with snow and looks more frightened than ever.*]

BOB [*as he puts the lantern on the counter*]. I'm glad the horse found his way back here. It's a terrible night out.

GALLAGHER. Why did you come back so soon? Don't you want to find your partner?

BOB [*nearly in tears*]. Of course, I do. But the horse, Skipper, keeps comin' back to this place all the time. Skipper had a way of always followin' Johnny around. Sometimes for miles. [BOONE *comes in with the pickax which he places behind the counter, unobserved by the boy.*] Are you sure he didn't come here?

GALLAGHER. We would have told you.

BOB. I don't know what to do! Maybe he's layin' dead under the snow right now. [*The road agents exchange glances.*]

BOONE [*craftily*]. Tell you what you do: you just stay here and rest and when the snow lets up a little, I'll bet he'll walk in here and find *you*.

BOB [*beaming*]. Do you think so? Yes, I guess he will, all right. I'm foolish to worry.

GALLAGHER. Sure, he'll come. He's mighty anxious to file that new claim in your name and his—like you said.

BOB [*sits on bench and passes his hand in confusion across his brow*]. Did I say that?

BOONE [*sitting next to* BOB]. Yes, you did, boy. I'm mighty anxious for your partner to turn up. Didn't like to talk about it when that old prospector was here. But we made a couple thousand dollars runnin' this supply station and maybe we'd sort of like to buy a small interest in your claim. That is, if you care to sell.

GALLAGHER [*leaning over* BOB]. *And* if it's a good claim.

BOB [*eagerly*]. Oh, it's good, all right. It's a wonderful pocket— [*He stop suddenly.*]

GALLAGHER [*sighs with pretended indifference*]. Some folks have all the luck.

BOB. We're sure lucky all right. Only been in the Territory a few months. We came overland together. Worked awhile in the gold-fields. Then I had the accident. We sort of drifted around after that and then came up the Missouri in a Mackinaw boat. Man gave us a job freightin' supplies. Then we got to huntin' gold again. We crossed the Black Tail Mountains and followed the Gravelly Range till we come to Alder Creek. We panned thousands of tons of gravel without raisin' the color until we got to— [*He checks himself suddenly.*]

GALLAGHER [*too eagerly*]. Yes? Got to where?

BOB. To where our claim is now. [GALLAGHER *makes a gesture of impatience.*] We had given up. Decided to go back to Bannock the next day. We made camp and built a fire. Johnny pulled up some sage-brush to burn. There was black sand on the roots. So he tried one last pan— [*He rises in his excitement.*] And sure enough, he raised the color!

BOONE. Fine!

BOB. Sixteen dollars in dust and nuggets in the bottom of that first pan. Course, we panned out even higher wages after that.

GALLAGHER. Good for you! [*Softly.*] Now just where is this claim?

BOB. I ain't tellin'. Johnny told me never to tell nobody.

[*The road agents exchange looks over his head.* GALLAGHER *nods as though he had an idea, then saunters over to the counter casually, his hands in his pockets.*]

GALLAGHER. I wouldn't be a bit surprised Johnny went back to the claim thinkin' you'd gone back there.

BOB [*hopefully*]. Do you think so?

GALLAGHER. That's what I'd do if I was lookin' for *my* partner.

BOB [*starts for the door*]. Then I'll ride back to the claim.

GALLAGHER. Look here! Seems like he wanted you in town so's you boys could file your claim first thing in the mornin'. If you go out in this blizzard, you might lose the trail or get caught in a snowslide. Johnny might show up here and then *he'd* have to go lookin' for *you*.

BOB. But you said he might have gone back to the claim.

BOONE. Maybe, but suppose you wait here and me and Gallagher will ride out to the claim and find him. You'll be here in case he comes in. If he don't, we can bring him in to you. Either you or us will find him that way.

BOB. That's mighty nice of you.

BOONE. Oh, no. We're kind of anxious to find Johnny, too.

GALLAGHER. Now what road do you take to get to the claim? [*He asks this very casually.*]

BOB. You take the pass through Daylight Gulch.

BOONE [*all attention*]. Daylight Gulch.

BOB. For six miles to just beyond the Yellow Bluffs.

GALLAGHER. Then?

BOB. Then you take the left fork till you come to a creek.— You'll have to ford it but it ain't deep there and it runs too swift to freeze over.

BOONE. On the other side—

BOB. You'll find two cottonwoods that grow together. Our claim starts there. [GALLAGHER *gets into his coat.*] We got our stakes in and if the snow ain't too deep, you can see where we were prospectin'. [BOONE *gets into his coat.*] But it won't do you no good to file a claim next to ours. Because it's just a rich pocket and it's all on our claim.

BOONE. We're not prospectors. We're storekeepers, ain't we, Gallagher?

GALLAGHER. Quit talkin' and hurry up so's we can get back.

BOB. I'll keep it nice and warm for you. [*Stoops to take wood from the box.*]

GALLAGHER [*alarmed*]. Wait! That wood's kind of green. It don't burn so good. I'll get you some drier pieces. [*He goes out to the yard.*]

BOONE [*pulling on his gloves*]. You stay right here and wait for us. And don't tell no one what you told us . . . about the claim.

GALLAGHER [*comes in with an armful of wood which he places on the floor by the stove*]. There.

BOB. I won't say anythin'. I'll wait here for Johnny. Good-by, and thanks. [*They go.* BOB *reaches in the woodbox to get a piece of wood. He remembers and takes a piece from the floor instead. He puts it into the stove. He looks around the room. He shudders. He looks out of the window. He then stands with his back to the rear door. He calls out in tense whisper.*] Johnny? [*He listens intently. He calls again.*] Johnny? [*He turns his head slowly until his eyes rest on the door through which the road agents carried* JOHNNY's *body. He seems to hear a sound coming from that direction. His face is tense as though he were being called by some one. He asks, softly.*] Yes? [*As if obeying a summons, he walks slowly to the door.*] Johnny! [*This time it is a statement. He is about to open the door, but he shudders and turns away from it in horror.*]

WASH [*coming in from the rear door.*] Where are those two high-tailin' it for in such a hurry?

BOB. They're headin' for Daylight Gulch.

WASH. Takes a reckless man to head in that direction tonight.

BOB [*as if to himself*]. He's out there.

WASH. Here you see me all sobered up. Throwin' me out of The Last Chance into the snow did it. I'll tell you how it happened. I walked into the bar and got me a drink of tangle-leg. Then, I started in actin' miscellaneously. The first thing I knew— [*He stops, noticing that* BOB *is staring at the door.*] What's wrong, son?

BOB. I think Johnny's out there and ... I'm ... afraid to go out. I called him and I thought he answered from there. ... I'm scared. ...

WASH. Take it easy. I'll go out and look. [*He goes.* BOB *stares at the door.* WASH *returns almost immediately. He closes the door slowly behind him and stares thought-*

fully at the pickax and shovel behind the counter.] Your partner was mighty good to you, wasn't he?

BOB. Oh, yes, ever since I had the accident and hurt my head, he's been awful good to me.

WASH. Youngster, I think we better get out of here. You come along with me.

[*The music starts playing "Auld Lang Syne" in monotonous waltz tempo.*]

BOB. Do you think Johnny's all right?

WASH [*slowly*]. Ain't nothin' can harm Johnny...now. [*They listen to the music for a second. Then several shots ring out from The Last Chance.*] Twelve o'clock! Well, it's a New Year!

BOB. They say whoever you're with when the old year goes will be your friend all the next year.

WASH [*kindly*]. I ain't complainin' none.

BOB [*almost weeping*]. But Johnny ain't with me.

WASH. Sit down, youngster. There's somethin' I got to tell you. [*The boy sits on the bench.*] Johnny had to go away.

BOB. No. He wouldn't go nowheres without me.

WASH. I'm goin' to try to take his place. [*He walks to the wood-box.*] He left somethin' for you. [*He hesitates before he takes up the bundle.*] Would you know his scarf if you saw it?

BOB. Oh, yes, a red one! [WASH *takes the bundle from the wood-box and unwraps the bags.*] Why, that's from our claim!

WASH. Johnny wants you to have it.

BOB. What does he want me to do with it?

WASH. I think he'd want you to go with me; to take that money and go east to Chicago. We can go to a place and pay good doctors to make you well again.

BOB. Yes, Johnny said we'd do that some day. [*He passes his hand across his forehead.*]

WASH. First, we'll file the claim in your name in the mornin'. When spring comes and the snow is gone, I'll work it for you and send you most of the money until you're well enough to come back west and look after it yourself.

BOB. Is that what Johnny would want me to do?

WASH. If he was here, he'd tell you that was the best thing to do. [*He gives the bags of gold to the boy.*]

BOB [*taking them*]. All right, then. I'll do as you say. [*He smiles.*] Lucky I didn't tell those men where our claim was. Johnny told me not to tell. I told them to go through Daylight Gulch. [*He points to the right.*] It's really the the other way—through Alder Gulch! [*He looks worried.*] I wonder did I do wrong in tellin' them to go that way? They must be just goin' through it by now. [*There is a terrific rumbling and crunching sound. It comes from a distance. Then the muffled boom of the snowslide is heard.* WASH *rushes to the door, followed by* BOB. WASH *opens it and they look off towards the right.* BOB *waits anxiously, and then asks.*] Did I do wrong?

WASH [*gently*]. No, son. I think you did exactly the right thing.

[*The music swells a little. The two go out. With a last long look in the direction of Daylight Gulch, they turn and go away in the opposite direction from it as*

THE CURTAIN FALLS

CANADA

STILL STANDS THE HOUSE
A DRAMA OF THE CANADIAN FRONTIER

BY GWENDOLYN PHARIS
OF MAGRATH, ALBERTA, CANADA

Written in the playwriting course at the University of North Carolina, it was originally produced by The Carolina Playmakers at Chapel Hill on March 3, 1938 and revived for the University of North Carolina Commencement on June 6, 1938. *Still Stands the House* was produced by the Medicine Hat Little Theatre at the Alberta Dramatic Festival at Edmonton, Alberta, Canada, on February 25, 1939, and was awarded first prize as the best native Canadian play entered in the annual Dominion Drama Festival in 1939.

THE CHARACTERS

BRUCE WARREN..................Howard Bailey
RUTH WARREN, *his wife*...............Ruth Mengel
HESTER WARREN, *his sister*............Floyd Childs
ARTHUR MANNING, *a real estate agent*..Dan Nachtman

SCENE: *Western Canada. The living-room of the Warren farmhouse in Alberta.*

TIME: *The present. Seven o'clock on a January night.*

Copyright, 1938, by The Carolina Playmakers, Inc.
All rights reserved.

CANADIAN FRONTIER

NORTHWESTERN Canada offers a challenge to the young playwright. In *Still Stands the House*, a farm tragedy of the Canadian prairie, Gwendolyn Pharis has made a brave beginning in this unbroken field. Other plays she has written of the still unexplored frontiers of this north country, among them a folk comedy of the country people of her neighborhood, *Chris Axelson, Blacksmith*,* which The Carolina Playmakers produced on May 26, 1938.

Gwendolyn Pharis comes from the little town of Magrath in the province of southern Alberta where a goodly number of Mormon people settled in the early days. She came to admire this pioneer people, their communal society, and their temple rituals. She cherishes the long summer days spent on her father's ranch. She tells me that her earliest memories are of the vast harvest of the war years on the great prairie.

After graduating from high school, she worked for a year on the Blackfoot Indian reservation and learned how simple and how terrible life can be in a primitive half-breed society. Hers was a frontier childhood.

She graduated from the University of Alberta four years ago. Her life there was none the less dramatic. She could not escape the tragedy of the bitter years of drought and the consequent economic and political conflict of a radical provincial premier who, some say, almost succeeded in establishing a dictatorship with his social credit plan.

Before coming to Chapel Hill, Miss Pharis was associated with Elizabeth Sterling Haynes, founder of the rural community drama movement in the province of Alberta.

Still Stands the House is a tragedy of the sun-parched prairies of western America—the Dakotas, Montana, Saskatchewan, and Alberta—a region once known as the "bread basket of the

---

* Awarded the Gwillym Edwards prize at the Alberta Dramatic Festival at Edmonton, Alberta, Canada, on February 24 and 25, 1939.

world"—in recent years a desert plain. The play is the struggle which has broken the spirit of many men and women in their vain efforts to make wheat grow for the markets of the world. Each spring brings a new faith in the soil, a new hope that this year when the sun comes to the snow-sheeted fields, the rains will surely follow.

I remember the prairie-spring of waving wheat fields. Wild roses everywhere on the unbroken sod, and the pale blue pasque flower at Easter time. And the roadsides gay with the song of the meadow lark! I remember, too, the long cold of the great flat in the winter time and the lonely farmhouses sheltered with wind-blown cottonwood trees standing staunch against the unharnessed blizzard. Such is the scene of *Still Stands the House*. It recalls vividly my own pioneering years on the white winter desert of Dakota.

The author tells us that the play is also the tragedy of a "woman whose life is concerned, not with present realities, but with memories of the past; not with the living, but with the dead." Hester Warren's love for the house in which she was born is the dominating factor in her life. This house, left to her by her dead father, who had loved and conquered his dry-land farm, holds still in decay its proud austerity.

STILL STANDS THE HOUSE

The icy wind of a northern blizzard sweeps across the prairie, lashes about the old Warren farmhouse, and howls insistently at the door and windows. But the WARREN *house was built to withstand the menace of the Canadian winter and scornfully suffers the storm to shriek about the chimney corner, to knock at the door and rattle the windows in a wild attempt to force an entrance.*

The living room of this house has about it a faded austerity, a decayed elegance that is as remote and cheerless as a hearth in which no fire is ever laid. The room has made a stern and solemn pact with the past. Once it held the warm surge of life; but as the years have gone by, it has settled in a rigid pattern of neat, uncompromising severity.

As if in defiance of the room, the frost has covered the window in the rear wall with a wild and exotic design. Beside the window is an imposing leather armchair, turned toward the handsome coal stove in the right corner. A footstool is near the chair. A door at the center of the rear wall leads to the snow-sheeted world outside. Along the left wall, between a closed door to a bedroom (now unused) and an open door to the kitchen, is a mahogany sideboard. Above it is a portrait of old Martin Warren who built this house and lived in it until his death. The portrait is of a stern and handsome man in his early fifties, and in the expression of the eyes the artist has caught something of his unconquerable will.

An open staircase, winding to the bedrooms upstairs, extends into the room at right. There is a rocking chair by the stove with a small stand-table beside it. A mahogany dining-table and two matching chairs are placed at a convenient distance from the sideboard and the kitchen door. The figured wall paper is cracked and faded. The dark rug, the heavy curtains, and the tablecloth show signs of much wear; but there is nothing of cheapness about them.

Two coal oil lanterns have been left beside the kitchen door. Blooming bravely on the table, in contrast to its surroundings, is a pot of lavender hyacinths.

[RUTH WARREN *is standing near the outside door, talking to* ARTHUR MANNING, *who is about to leave.* RUTH *is small, fair-haired, and pretty, twenty-five or twenty-six years of age. There is more strength in her than her rather delicate appearance would indicate. She wears a soft blue house-dress, with a light wool cardigan over it.*]

[MANNING *is a middle-aged man of prosperous appearance. He wears a heavy overcoat over a dark business suit. His hat, gloves, and scarf are on the armchair.*]

RUTH. Do you think you'd better try to go back to town to-night, Mr. Manning? The roads may be drifted.

MANNING. It's a bad blizzard, all right, but I don't think I'll have any trouble. There's a heater in the car, and I've just had the engine checked over.

RUTH. You'll be welcome if you care to spend the night.

MANNING. Thank you, but I'm afraid I've got to get back to town. I'd hate to try it in an old car, but this one of mine can pull through anything.

RUTH. I've never seen a storm come up so quickly.

MANNING. These prairie blizzards are no joke. One of my

sheepherders got lost in one last year, just half a mile from the house. He froze to death out there trying to find his way.

RUTH. How frightful!

MANNING. One of the ranch hands found him the next morning. Poor old fellow—he'd herded for me for twenty years. I never knew how he came to be out in a storm like that.

RUTH. They say when a person gets lost he begins to go round in a circle, although it seems to him he's going straight ahead.

MANNING. Yes, I've always heard that. The winters are the one thing I've got against this country.

RUTH [*wistfully*]. I used to like them in town. We went skating on the river and tobogganing. But out here it's different.

MANNING. If Bruce sells the farm and takes this irrigated place near town, you won't notice the winter so much, Mrs. Warren.

RUTH. No. I hope he does take your offer, Mr. Manning. I want him to.

MANNING. He'll never get a better. Five thousand dollars and an irrigated quarter is a good price for a dry-land farm these days.

RUTH. If only we didn't have to decide so soon.

MANNING. I talked it all over with Bruce in town a couple of weeks ago, and I think he's pretty well made up his mind. All he needs to do is sign the papers.

RUTH. I thought he'd have until spring to decide.

MANNING. I've got orders to close the deal before I go South next week. You tell Bruce I'll come by to-morrow or the next day, and we can get it all settled.

RUTH. I'll tell him. I hope he does take it, Mr. Manning.

MANNING. I know you do and you're right. I think all he needs is a little persuading. He's had a hard time here these dry years.

RUTH. I don't know what Hester will say.

MANNING. I understand she's very much attached to the place. Is it true that she never leaves the farm?

RUTH. Not often.

MANNING. She'd be better off where she could get out more.

RUTH. I don't know.

MANNING. I suppose all those years out here, keeping house for Bruce and her father, were pretty hard on her.

RUTH. The house has come to mean so much to her. But maybe she won't mind. [*Smiling hopefully.*] We'll see.

[*The door to the bedroom, left, is opened quietly, and* HESTER WARREN *enters the room. She closes and locks the door behind her and stands looking at the two in the room with cold surmise.* HESTER *is forty years old. She is tall, dark, and unsmiling. The stern rigidity of her body, the bitter austerity of her mouth, and the almost arrogant dignity of her carriage seem to make her a part of the room she enters. There is bitter resentment in her dark eyes as she confronts* RUTH *and* MANNING. *She holds a leather-bound Bible close to her breast.*]

RUTH [*startled*]. Why, Hester! I thought you never unlocked that door.

HESTER [*quietly*]. No. I keep Father's room as it was.

RUTH. Then why were you—

HESTER. I was reading in Father's room. I heard a stranger.

RUTH. You know Mr. Manning, Hester.

MANNING [*with forced friendliness*]. I don't suppose you remember me, Miss Warren.

HESTER [*without moving*]. How do you do?

MANNING [*embarrassed at her coldness and anxious to get away*]. Well, I'll be getting on home. I'll leave these

STILL STANDS THE HOUSE

papers for Bruce to sign, Mrs. Warren. Tell him I'll come by to-morrow. He'll find it's all there, just as we talked about it. [*He lays the document on the table.*]

RUTH. Thank you, Mr. Manning.

MANNING [*turning to go*]. Take care of yourselves. Good night. [*To* HESTER.] Good night, Miss Warren. [HESTER *barely nods.*]

RUTH. You're sure you ought to try it in the storm?

MANNING. Sure. There's no danger if I go right away. [*He goes out.*]

RUTH [*calling after him as she shuts the door*]. Good night.

[HESTER *watches* MANNING *out and as* RUTH *returns, she looks at her suspiciously. There is a silence which* HESTER *finally breaks.*]

HESTER. What did he want here?

RUTH [*uncomfortable under* HESTER's *scrutiny*]. He just left some papers for Bruce to look over, Hester. He was in a hurry so he didn't wait to see Bruce.

HESTER. I see. What has Arthur Manning got to do with Bruce?

RUTH. It's something to do with the farm, Hester. I'll put these away. [*She starts to take up the document on the table, but* HESTER *is before her.*]

HESTER [*after a long look at the document*]. A deed of sale. [*Turning angrily upon* RUTH.] So this is what you've been hiding from me.

RUTH [*quickly*]. Oh, no! Nothing's settled, Hester. Mr. Manning made an offer, and Bruce wants to think it over. That's all.

HESTER [*her eyes betraying her intense agitation*]. Bruce isn't going to sell this place!

RUTH. It's just an offer. Nothing has been decided.

HESTER. Your hand's in this! You've been after him to leave here.

RUTH [*trying to conciliate her*]. Let's not quarrel. You can talk to Bruce about it, Hester.

HESTER. You hate this house, I know that.

RUTH. No. [*Facing* HESTER *firmly*.] But I think Bruce ought to sell.

HESTER. You married him. You made your choice.

RUTH [*quietly*]. I've not regretted that. It's just that we're so cut off and lonely here, and this is the best offer we could get. But let me put these away. [*Indicating the deed of sale.*] We'll talk about it later, the three of us.

HESTER [*allowing* RUTH *to take the papers*]. You may as well burn them. He isn't going to sell.

RUTH. Please, Hester ... we'll discuss it when Bruce comes. [*She places the document on the sideboard, then crosses to the stove.*] I'll build up the fire.

[HESTER *takes the Bible to the sideboard and places it under her father's portrait. She stands looking up at the portrait.*]

HESTER. This house will not be sold. I won't allow it.

[RUTH *puts some coal on the fire.*]

RUTH [*shivering*]. It's so cold it almost frightens me. The thermometer has dropped ten degrees within the hour.

HESTER. I hope Bruce knows enough to get the stock in. They'll freeze where they stand if they're left out tonight. [*She moves to the window and takes her knitting from the ledge.*]

RUTH. He'll have them in. [*Crossing to the table.*] Look Hester, how the hyacinths have bloomed. I could smell them when I came in the room just now.

HESTER. Hyacinths always seem like death to me.

RUTH [*her voice is young and vibrant*]. Oh, no. They're birth, they're spring! They say in Greece you find them growing wild in April. [*She takes an old Wedgewood* bowl *from the sideboard, preparing to set the pot of hyacinths in it.*]

HESTER [*in a dry, unfriendly tone*]. I've asked you not to use that Wedgewood bowl. It was my grandmother's. I don't want it broken.

RUTH. I'm sorry. [*Replacing the bowl, she gets a plain one from inside the sideboard.*] I thought the hyacinths would look so pretty in it, but I'll use the plain one.

HESTER. You've gone to as much trouble for that plant as if it were a child. [HESTER *sits in the rocking chair by the stove.*]

RUTH [*placing the hyacinths in the bowl*]. They're so sweet. I like to touch them.

HESTER. They'll freeze to-night, I'm thinking.

RUTH. Not in here. We'll have to keep the fire up anyway. [*Leaving the bowl of hyacinths on the table,* RUTH *returns to the sideboard, taking some bright chintz from the drawer. She holds it up for* HESTER *to see.*] I've almost finished the curtains, Hester.

HESTER [*tonelessly*]. You have?

RUTH. Don't you think they'll make this room more cheerful?

HESTER. The ones we have seem good enough to me.

RUTH. But they're so old.

HESTER [*coldly*]. Old things have beauty when you've eyes to see it. That velvet has a richness that you can't buy now.

RUTH [*moving to the window*]. I want to make the room gay and happy for the spring. You'll see how much difference these will make.

HESTER. I've no doubt. [HESTER *rises and goes to the table to avoid looking at the curtains.*]

RUTH [*measuring the chintz with the curtains at the window*]. I wonder if I have them wide enough. [*The wind rises. As if the sound had quelled her pleasure in the bright curtains,* RUTH *turns slowly away from the window. A touch of hysteria creeps into her voice.*] The wind swirls and shrieks and raises such queer echoes in this old house! It seems to laugh at us in here, thinking we're safe, hugging the stove! As if it knew it could blow out the light and the fire and ... [*Getting hold of herself.*] I've never seen a blizzard when it was as cold as this. Have you, Hester?

HESTER [*knitting*]. Bruce was born on a night like this.

[*Throughout this scene* HESTER *seldom looks at* RUTH *but gives all her attention to her knitting. She seems reluctant to talk and yet impelled to do so.*]

RUTH. I didn't know.

HESTER. Father had to ride for the doctor while I stayed here with Mother.

RUTH. Alone?

HESTER. Yes. I was rubbing Father's hand with snow* when we heard the baby crying. Then we helped the doctor bathe him.

RUTH. You were such a little girl to do so much.

HESTER. After Mother died I did it all.

RUTH. I know, but it was too hard for a child. I don't see how you managed.

HESTER. Father always helped me with the washing.

RUTH. Not many men would stay in from the field to do that.

HESTER. No. [*Her knitting drops to her lap, and for a moment she is lost in the past.*] "We'll have to lean on one another now, Daughter." ... Those were his words. ... And that's the way it was. I was beside him until—I never left him.

---

* A common remedy used in the North country to alleviate frostbite.

RUTH [*at* HESTER's *side*]. You've never talked of him like this before.
HESTER [*unconscious of* RUTH]. He always liked the snow. [*Her eyes are on the portrait of her father.*] He called it a moving shroud, a winding-sheet that the wind lifts and raises and lets fall again.
RUTH. It is like that.
HESTER. He'd come in and say, "The snow lies deep on the summer fallow, Hester. That means a good crop next year."
RUTH. I know. It's glorious in the fall with the wheat like gold on the hills. No wonder he loved it.
HESTER [*called out of her dream, she abruptly resumes her knitting*]. There hasn't been much wheat out there these last years.
RUTH. That isn't Bruce's fault, Hester.
HESTER. You have to love a place to make things grow. The land knows when you don't care about it, and Bruce doesn't care about it any more. Not like Father did.
RUTH [*her hands raised to touch the portrait above the sideboard*]. I wish I'd known your father.
HESTER [*rising and facing* RUTH *with a sudden and terrible anger*]. Don't touch that picture. It's mine.
RUTH [*startled, she faces* HESTER]. Why, Hester—
HESTER. Can't I have anything of my own? Must you put your fingers on everything I have?
RUTH [*moving to* HESTER]. Hester, you know I didn't mean— What is the matter with you?
HESTER. I won't have you touch it.
RUTH [*gently*]. Do you hate my being here so much?
HESTER [*turning away*]. You've more right here than I have now, I suppose.
RUTH [*crossing over to the stove*]. You make me feel that I've no right at all.

HESTER [*a martyr now*]. I'm sorry if you don't approve my ways. I can go, if that's what you want.

RUTH [*pleading*]. Please... I've never had a sister, and when Bruce told me he had one, I thought we'd be such friends...

HESTER [*sitting in the chair by the stove*]. We're not a family to put words to everything we feel. [*She resumes her knitting.*]

RUTH [*trying to bridge the gulf between them*]. I get too excited over things; I know it. Bruce tells me I sound affected when I say too much about the way I feel, the way I like people... or the sky in the evening. I—

HESTER [*without looking up*]. Did you get the separator put up? Or shall I do it? [*Discouraged*, RUTH *turns away, and going to the table, sits down with her sewing.*]

RUTH. It's ready for the milk when Bruce brings it. I put it together this morning.

HESTER. The lanterns are empty.

RUTH. I'll fill them in a minute.

HESTER. When I managed this house, I always filled the lanterns right after supper. Then they were ready.

RUTH [*impatiently*]. I said I'd fill them, Hester, and I will. They're both there in the corner. [*She indicates the lanterns at the end of the sideboard.*]

HESTER. Bruce didn't take one then?

RUTH. No.

HESTER. You'd better put a lamp in the window. [RUTH *lights a small lamp on the sideboard and takes it to the window.*]

RUTH. I wish he'd come. It's strange how women feel safer when their men are near, close enough to touch, isn't it? No matter how strong you think you are. [*As she speaks,* RUTH *drapes some of the chintz over the armchair.*]

HESTER. I can't say that I need any strength from Bruce, or could get it if I needed it.
RUTH. That's because he's still a little boy to you. [*A pause. Then* RUTH *speaks hesitantly*]. Hester...
HESTER. Yes?
RUTH. Will you mind the baby in the house?
HESTER [*after a silence, constrainedly*]. No. I won't mind. I'll keep out of the way.
RUTH [*warmly, commanding a response*]. I don't want you to. You'll love him, Hester.
HESTER [*harshly*]. I loved Bruce, but I got no thanks for it. He feels I stand in his way now.
RUTH [*suddenly aware that* HESTER *has needed and wanted love*]. You mustn't say that. It isn't true.
HESTER. When he was little, after Mother died, he'd come tugging at my hand.... He'd get hold of my little finger and say "Come, Hettie...come and look." Everything was "Hettie" then.
RUTH [*eagerly, moving to* HESTER]. It will be like that again. This baby will be almost like your own.
HESTER [*as if* RUTH'S *words were an implied reproach*]. I could have married, and married well if I'd had a mind to.
RUTH. I know that. I've wondered why you didn't, Hester.
HESTER. The young men used to ride over here on Sunday, but I stopped that. [*A pause.*] I never saw a man I'd sleep beside, or let him touch me. And that's all they want.
RUTH [*involuntarily; it is a cry*]. No!
HESTER. Maybe you don't mind that kind of thing. I do.
RUTH [*attempting to put her arms around* HESTER]. What hurts you?
HESTER [*rising*]. Don't try your soft ways on me. [*She moves*

behind the armchair, her hand falls caressingly on the back of the chair.] I couldn't leave Bruce and Father here alone. My duty was here in this house. So I stayed. [HESTER *notices the chintz material draped over the chair, and taking it up, turns to* RUTH *angrily.*] What do you intend to do with this?

RUTH. I thought... there's enough left to make covers for the chair to match the curtains—

HESTER [*throwing the chintz down*]. This is Father's chair. I won't have it changed.

RUTH. I'm sorry, Hester. [*With spirit.*] Must we keep everything the same forever?

HESTER. There's nothing in this house that isn't good, that wasn't bought with care and pride by one of us who loved it. This stuff is cheap and gaudy.

RUTH. It isn't dull and falling apart with age.

HESTER. Before my father died, when he was ill, he sat here in this chair where he could see them threshing from the window. It was the first time since he came here that he'd not been in the fields at harvest. Now you come—you who never knew him, who never saw him—and you won't rest until—

RUTH. Hester!

HESTER. You've got no right to touch it! [*Her hands grip the back of the old chair as she stands rigid, her eyes blazing.*]

[BRUCE WARREN *enters from outside, carrying a pail of milk. He is tall and dark, about thirty years old, sensitive and bitter. His vain struggle to make the farm pay since his father's death has left him with an oppressive sense of failure. He is proud and quick to resent an imagined reproach. He has dark hair, his shoulders are a little stooped, and he moves restlessly and abruptly. Despite his moodiness, he is extremely likeable. He is dressed warmly in dark trousers, a sweater under his heavy leather coat; he wears gloves, cap, and high boots. He brushes the snow from his coat as he enters.*]

BRUCE [*carrying the milk into the kitchen*]. Is the separator up, Ruth?

RUTH. Yes, it's all ready, Bruce. Wait, I'll help you. [*She follows him into the kitchen.*]

[HESTER *stands at the chair a moment after they have gone; her eyes fall on the plant on the table. Slowly she goes toward it, as if drawn by something she hated. She looks down at the lavender blooms for a moment. Then with a quick, angry gesture, she crushes one of the stalks. She turns away and is winding up her wool when* BRUCE *and* RUTH *return.*]

RUTH. You must be frozen.

BRUCE [*taking off his coat and gloves*]. I'm cold, all right. God, it's a blizzard: 38 below, and a high wind. [*He throws his coat over a chair at the table.*]

RUTH [*with pride*]. Did you see the hyacinths. They've bloomed since yesterday.

BRUCE [*smiling*]. Yes, they're pretty. [*Touching them, he notices the broken stalk.*] Looks like one of them's broken.

RUTH. Where? [*She sees it.*] Oh, it is! And that one hadn't bloomed yet! I wonder.... It wasn't broken when I—
RUTH *turns accusingly to* HESTER.] Hester! [HESTER *returns* RUTH's *look calmly.*]

HESTER [*coldly*]. Yes?

RUTH. Hester, did you...

BRUCE [*going over to the fire*]. Oh, Ruth, don't make such a fuss about it. It can't be helped.

HESTER. I'll take care of the milk. [*She takes the small lamp from the window.*]

RUTH. I'll do it.

HESTER [*moving toward the kitchen*]. You turn the separator so slow the cream's as thin as water.

RUTH [*stung to reply*]. That's not true. You never give me a chance to—

BRUCE [*irritably*]. For God's sake don't quarrel about it. [*He sits in the chair by the stove.*]

HESTER. I don't intend to quarrel. [*She goes into the kitchen.*]

[RUTH *follows* HESTER *to the door. The sound of the separator comes from the kitchen.* RUTH *turns wearily, takes up the pot of hyacinths, and places them on the stand near the stove. Then sits on the footstool.*]

RUTH. It's always that way.

BRUCE [*gazing moodily at the stove*]. Why don't you two try to get along? [*A silence.*]

RUTH. Did you put the stock in? [*The question is merely something to fill the empty space of silence between them.*]

BRUCE. Yes. That black mare may foal to-night. I'll have to look at her later on.

RUTH. It's bitter weather for a little colt to be born.

BRUCE. Yes.

[*Another silence. Finally* RUTH, *to throw off the tension between them, gets up and moves her footstool over to his chair.*]

RUTH. I'm glad you're here. I've been lonesome for you.

BRUCE [*putting his hand on hers*]. I'm glad to be here.

RUTH. I thought of you out at the barn, trying to work in this cold.

BRUCE. I was all right. I'd hate to walk far to-night though. You can't see your hand before your face.

RUTH [*after a look at the kitchen*]. Hester's been so strange again these last few days, Bruce.

BRUCE. I know it's hard, Ruth.

Ruth. It's like it was when I first came here. At everything I touch, she cries out like I'd hurt her somehow.
Bruce. Hester has to do things her own way. She's always been like that.
Ruth. If only she could like me a little. I think she almost does sometimes, but then—
Bruce. You think too much about her.
Ruth. Maybe it's because we've been shut in so close. I'm almost afraid of her lately.
Bruce. She's not had an easy life, Ruth.
Ruth. I know that. She's talked about your father almost constantly to-day.
Bruce. His death hit us both hard. Dad ran the farm, decided everything.
Ruth. It's been six years, Bruce.
Bruce. There are things you don't count out by years.
Ruth. He wouldn't want you to go on remembering forever.
Bruce [looking at the floor]. No.
Ruth. You should get free of this house. It's not good for you to stay here. It's not good for Hester. [Getting up, she crosses to the sideboard and returns with the deed of sale, which she hands to Bruce.] Mr. Manning left this for you. He's coming back to-morrow for it, when you've signed it. [He takes the papers.]
Bruce [annoyed by her assurance]. He doesn't need to get so excited. I haven't decided to sign it yet. He said he wouldn't need to know till spring. [He goes over to the lamp at the table and studies the document.]
Ruth. His company gave him orders to close the deal this week or let it go.
Bruce. This week?
Ruth. That's what he said.
Bruce. Well, I'll think about it.

RUTH. You'll have to decide to-night, Bruce. No one else will offer you as much. Five thousand dollars and an irrigated farm a mile from town seems a good price.

BRUCE. I'm not complaining about the deal. It's fair.

RUTH [*urgently*]. You're going to take it, aren't you, Bruce?

BRUCE. I don't know. God, I don't know. [*He throws the document on the table.*] I don't want to sell, Ruth. I think I'll try it another year.

RUTH. Bruce, you've struggled here too long now. You haven't had a crop, a good crop in five years.

BRUCE. I need to be told that.

RUTH. It's not your fault. But you've told me you ought to give it up, that it's too dry here.

BRUCE. We may get a crop this year. We're due for one.

RUTH. If you take this offer, we'll be nearer town. We'll have water on the place. We can have a garden, and trees growing.

BRUCE. That's about what those irrigated farms are—gardens.

RUTH. And Bruce, it wouldn't be so lonely there, so cruelly lonely.

BRUCE. I told you how it was before you came.

RUTH [*resenting his tone*]. You didn't tell me you worshiped a house. That you made a god of a house and a section of land. You didn't tell me that!

BRUCE [*angrily*]. You didn't tell me that you'd moon at a window for your old friends, either. [*He stands up and throws the deed of sale on the table.*]

RUTH. How could I help it here?

BRUCE. And you didn't tell me you'd be afraid of having a child. What kind of a woman are you that you don't want your child?

RUTH. That's not true.

BRUCE. No? You cried when you knew, didn't you?

RUTH. Bruce!

BRUCE [*going blindly on*]. What makes you feel the way you do then? Other women have children without so much fuss. Other women are glad.

RUTH [*intensely angry*]. Don't speak to me like that. Keep your land. Eat and sleep and dream land, I don't care!

BRUCE [*turning to the portrait of his father*]. My father came out here and took a homestead. He broke the prairie with one plow and a team of horses. He built a house to live in out of the sod. You didn't know that, did you? He and Mother lived here in a sod shanty and struggled to make things grow. Then they built a one-roomed shack; and when the good years came, they built this house. The finest in the country! I thought my son would have it.

RUTH [*moving to him*]. What is there left to give a son? A house that stirs with ghosts! A piece of worn-out land where the rain never comes.

BRUCE. That's not all. I don't suppose you can understand.

RUTH [*turning away from him, deeply hurt*]. No. I don't suppose I can. You give me little chance to know how you feel about things.

BRUCE [*his anger gone*]. Ruth, I didn't mean that. But you've always lived in town. [*He goes to the window and stands looking out for a moment, then turns.*] Those rocks along the fence out there, I picked up every one of them with my own hands and carried them across the field and piled them there. I've plowed that southern slope along the coulee * every year since I was twelve. [*His voice is torn with a kind of shame for his emotion.*] I feel about the land like Hester does about the house, I guess. I don't want to leave it. I don't want to give it up.

RUTH [*gently*]. But it's poor land, Bruce.

* A steep-walled valley through which a stream runs.

[BRUCE *sits down, gazing gloomily at the fire.* HESTER *comes in from the kitchen with the small lamp and places it on the sideboard. Then she sits at the table, taking up her knitting. As* BRUCE *speaks, she watches him intently.*]

BRUCE. Yes, it's strange that in a soil that won't grow trees a man can put roots down, but he can.

RUTH [*at his side*]. You'd feel the same about another place, after a little while.

BRUCE. I don't know. When I saw the wind last spring blowing the dirt away, the dirt I'd plowed and harrowed and sowed to grain, I felt as though a part of myself was blowing away in the dust. Even now with the land three feet under snow I can look out and feel it waiting for the seed I've saved for it.

RUTH. But if we go, we'll be nearer other people, not cut off from everything that lives.

BRUCE. You need people, don't you?

HESTER. Yes. She needs them. I've seen her at the window, looking toward the town. Day after day she stands there. [BRUCE *and* RUTH, *absorbed in the conflict between them, had forgotten* HESTER'S *presence. At* HESTER'S *words,* RUTH *turns on them both, flaming with anger.*]

RUTH. You two. You're so *perfect!*

HESTER [*knitting*]. We could always stand alone, the three of us. We didn't need to turn to every stranger who held his hand out.

RUTH. No! You'd sit here in this husk of a house, living like shadows, until these four walls closed in on you, buried you.

HESTER. I never stood at a window, looking down the road that leads to town.

RUTH [*the pent-up hysteria of the day and the longing of months breaks through, tumbling out in her words*]. It's not for myself I look down that road, Hester. It's for the child I'm going to have. You're right, Bruce, I am afraid. It's not what you think though, not for myself. You two and your father lived so long in this dark house that you forgot there's a world beating outside, forgot that people laugh and play sometimes. And you've shut me out! [*There is a catch in her voice.*] I never would have trampled on your thoughts if you'd given them to me. But as it is, I might as well not be a person. You'd like a shadow better that wouldn't touch your house. A child would die here. A child can't live with shadows. [*Much disturbed,* BRUCE *rises and goes to her.*]

BRUCE. Ruth! I didn't know you hated it so much.

RUTH. I thought it would change. I thought I could change it. You know now.

BRUCE [*quietly*]. Yes.

RUTH [*pleading*]. If we go, I'll *want* this child, Bruce. Don't you see? But I'm not happy here. What kind of a life will our child have? He'll be old before he's out of school. [*She looks at the hyacinth on the stand.*] He'll be like this hyacinth bud that's broken before it bloomed. [BRUCE *goes to the table and stands looking down at the deed of sale. His voice is tired and flat, but resolved.*]

BRUCE. All right. I'll tell Manning I'll let him have the place.

HESTER [*turning quickly to* BRUCE]. What do you mean?

BRUCE. I'm going to sell the farm to Manning. He was here to-day.

HESTER [*standing up, her eyes blazing*]. You can't sell this house.

BRUCE [*looking at the deed of sale*]. Oh, Ruth's right. We can't make a living on the place. [*He sits down, leafing through the document.*] It's too dry. And too far from the school.

HESTER. It wasn't too far for you to go, or me.

BRUCE [*irritably*]. Do you think I want to sell?

HESTER. She does. But she can't do it. [*Her voice is low.*] This house belongs to me.

BRUCE. Hester, don't start that again! I wish to God the land had been divided differently, but it wasn't.

HESTER. Father meant for us to stay here and keep things as they were when he was with us.

BRUCE. The soil wasn't blowing away when he was farming it.

HESTER. He meant for me to have the house.

RUTH. You'll go with us where we go, Hester.

HESTER [*to* RUTH]. You came here. You plotted with him to take this house from me. But it's mine!

BRUCE [*his voice cracks through the room*]. Stop that, Hester! I love this place as much as you do, but I'm selling it. I'm selling it, I tell you. [*As he speaks, he gets up abruptly and, taking up his coat, puts it on.*]

[HESTER *sinks slowly into the chair, staring.* RUTH *tries to put her hand on* BRUCE'S *arm.*]

RUTH. Bruce! Not that way! Not for me. If it's that way, I don't care enough.

BRUCE [*shaking himself free*]. Oh, leave me alone!

RUTH. Bruce!

BRUCE [*going to the door*]. I'll be glad when it's over, I suppose.

RUTH. Where are you going?

BRUCE [*taking his cap and gloves*]. To look at that mare.

RUTH. Bruce! [*But he has gone.*]

HESTER [*getting up, she goes to her father's chair and stands behind it, facing* RUTH; *she moves and speaks as if she were in a dream*]. This is my house. I won't have strangers in it.

RUTH [*at the table, without looking at* HESTER]. Oh, Hester! I didn't want it to be this way. I tried—

HESTER [*as if she were speaking to a stranger*]. Why did you come here?

RUTH. I've hurt you. But I'm right about this. I know I'm right.

HESTER. There isn't any room for you.

RUTH. Can't you see? It's for all of us.

[HESTER *comes toward* RUTH *with a strange, blazing anger in her face.*]

HESTER. I know your kind. In the night you tempted him with your bright hair.

RUTH. Hester!

HESTER. Your body anointed with jasmine for his pleasure.

RUTH. Hester, don't say such things.

HESTER. Oh, I know what you are! You and women like you. You put a dream around him with your arms, a sinful dream.

RUTH [*drawing back*]. Hester!

HESTER. You lift your white face to every stranger like you offered him a cup to drink from. That's sin! That's lust after the forbidden fruit. [*Turning from* RUTH, *as if she had forgotten her presence,* HESTER *looks fondly at the room.*] I'll never leave this house.

[BRUCE *opens the door and comes in quickly and stormily. He goes into the kitchen as he speaks.*]

BRUCE. That mare's got out. She jumped the corral. I'll have to go after her.

RUTH [*concerned*]. Bruce, where will she be?

BRUCE [*returning with an old blanket*]. She'll be in the snowshed by the coulee. She always goes there when she's about to foal.

[HESTER *sits in the chair by the stove, her knitting in her hand. She pays no attention to the others.*]

RUTH. But you can't go after her in this storm.

BRUCE. I'll take this old blanket to cover the colt, if it's born yet. Where's the lantern? [*He sees the two lanterns by the kitchen door, and taking one of them to the table, lights it.*]

RUTH. It's three miles, Bruce. You mustn't go on foot. It's dangerous.

BRUCE. I'll have to. She'd never live through the night, or the colt either. [*He turns to go.*] You'd better go to bed. Good night, Hester.

RUTH. Let me come with you.

BRUCE. No. [*Then as he looks at her, all resentment leaves him. He puts down the lantern, goes to her, and takes her in his arms.*] Ruth, forget what I said. You know I didn't mean—

RUTH [*softly*]. I said things I didn't mean, too—

BRUCE. I love you, Ruth. You know it, don't you?

RUTH. Bruce! [*He kisses her, and for a moment their love is a flame in the room.*]

BRUCE. Don't worry. I won't be long.

RUTH. I'll wait.

[BRUCE *goes out.* RUTH *follows him to the door and, as it closes, she stands against it for a moment. There is a silence.* HESTER *is slowly unraveling her knitting but is unaware of it. The black wool falls in spirals about her chair.*]

HESTER [*suddenly*]. It's an old house. I was born here. [*Then in a strange, calm voice that seems to come from a long distance.*] You shouldn't let Bruce be so much alone. You lose him that way. He comes back to *us* then. He'll see you don't belong here unless you keep your hand on him all the time. [RUTH *looks curiously at* HESTER *but does not give her all her attention.* HESTER *suddenly becomes harsh.*] This is my house. You can't change it. [RUTH *starts to say something but remains silent.*]

Father gave it to me. There isn't any room for you. [*In a high, childlike tone, like the sound of a violin string breaking.*] No room. [*She shakes her head gravely.*]

RUTH [*aware that something is wrong*]. Hester—

HESTER [*as if she were telling an often-recited story to a stranger*]. I stayed home when Mother died and kept house for my little brother and Father. [*Her voice grows stronger.*] I was very beautiful, they said. My hair fell to my knees, and it was black as a furrow turned in spring. [*Proudly.*] I can have a husband any time I want, but my duty is here with Father. You see how it is. I can't leave him. [RUTH *goes quickly to* HESTER.]

RUTH [*with anxiety and gentleness*]. Hester, what are you talking about?

HESTER. That's Father's chair. I'll put his Bible out. [*She starts from her chair.*]

RUTH [*preventing her*]. Hester, your father's not here—not for six years. You speak of him as if you thought.... Hester—

HESTER [*ignoring* RUTH *but remaining seated*]. When I was a girl I always filled the lanterns after supper. Then I was ready for his coming.

RUTH [*in terror*]. Hester, I didn't fill them! I didn't fill the lanterns! [*She runs to the kitchen door and takes up the remaining lantern.*]

HESTER [*calmly*]. Father called me the wise virgin then.

RUTH. Hester, Bruce took one! He thought I'd filled them. It will burn out and he'll be lost in the blizzard.

HESTER. I always filled them.

RUTH [*setting the lantern on the table*]. I've got to go out after Bruce. If he gets down to the coulee and the lantern goes out, he'll never find the way back. I'll have to hurry! Where's the coal oil? [RUTH *goes to the kitchen and returns with a can of coal oil and a pair of galoshes.* HESTER *watches her closely. As* RUTH *comes in with the oil,* HESTER *slowly rises and goes to her.*]

HESTER. I'll fill the lantern for you, Ruth.

RUTH [*trying to remove the top of the can*]. I can't get the top off. My hands are shaking so.

HESTER [*taking the oil can from* RUTH]. I'll fill it for you.

RUTH. Please, Hester. While I get my things on! [*Giving* HESTER *the oil can,* RUTH *runs to the footstool and hurriedly puts on her galoshes.*] I'm afraid that lantern will last just long enough to get him out there. He'll be across the field before I even get outside. [*She runs up the stairs.*]

HESTER [*standing motionless, the oil can in her hand*]. You're going now. That's right. I told you you should go. [RUTH *disappears up the stairs.* HESTER *moves a step toward the lantern, taking off the top of the coal oil can. She hesitates and looks for a long moment after* RUTH. *With the strange lucidity of madness, slowly, deliberately, she places the top back again on the can and moving behind the table, sets it on the floor without filling the lantern.* RUTH *hurries down the stairs excited and alarmed. She has on heavy clothes and is putting on her gloves.*]

RUTH. Is it ready? [HESTER *nods.*] Will you light it for me, Hester? Please. [HESTER *lights the lantern.*]

RUTH. I'll put the light at the window. [*She crosses with the small lamp and places it at the window.*] Hurry, Hester! [*With a sob.*] Oh, if only I can find him! [HESTER *crosses to* RUTH *and gives her the lantern.*]

[RUTH *takes the lantern and goes out. A gust of wind carries the snow into the room and blows shut the door after her.* HESTER *goes to the window.*]

HESTER [*her voice is like an echo*]. The snow lies deep on the summer fallow.... The snow is a moving shroud ... a winding sheet that the wind lifts and raises and lets fall again. [*Turning from the window.*] They've gone! They won't be back now. [*With an intense excitement,* HESTER *blows out the lamp at the window and pulls down the shades. Her eyes fall on the bowl of hyacinths in the corner. Slowly she goes to it, takes it up, and holding it away from her, carries it to the door. Opening the door, she sets the flowers outside. She closes the door and locks it. Her eyes blazing with excitement, she stands with her arms across the door as if shutting the world out. Then softly she moves to the door of her father's bedroom, unlocks it, and goes in, returning at once with a pair of men's bedroom slippers. Leaving the bedroom door open, she crosses to the sideboard, takes up the Bible, and going to her father's chair, places the slippers beside it. She speaks very softly.*] I put your slippers out. [*She draws the footstool up to the chair.*] Everything will be the same now, Father. [*She opens the Bible.*] I'll read to you, Father. I'll read the one you like. [*She reads with quiet contentment.*] "And the winds blew, and beat upon that house; and it fell not: for it was founded upon a rock."

[*The wind moans through the old house as*

THE CURTAIN FALLS

NORTH DAKOTA

SIGRID
FARM WOMAN OF THE PRAIRIE

BY MARGARET RADCLIFFE

OF LARIMORE, NORTH DAKOTA

Written in the summer session of the University of Colorado at Boulder and originally produced in the University Theater there on August 16, 1933. *Sigrid* was first published in *The Carolina Play-Book,* September, 1934.

THE CHARACTERS

SIGRID SWANSON, *a Norwegian farm woman*
                                        Martha Ryan Beck
OLE SWANSON, *her husband*..............Hugh Scott
ALEX, *their son*....................Herbert Graves
WILLIAM NICHOLS, *a prosperous farmer*
                                        Vincent Reynolds
MRS. NICHOLS, *his wife*..............Jessie Campbell

SCENE: *The kitchen of the Swanson farmhouse situated on the rising prairie to the west of the Red River Valley in North Dakota.*

TIME: *Ten o'clock on a July morning in 1885, four years after settlement.*

Copyright, 1934, by The Carolina Playmakers, Inc.
All rights reserved.

DAKOTA PRAIRIE

HERE is a folk drama of the frontier life of Dakota—a play of the long, bitter winters, of the treeless prairie, of the bleak life of a pioneer farm woman. It tells the story of the sometimes cruel isolation of these frontier lives on the great flat.

Here is not the glory of the prairie wilderness gay with wild roses and unflecked sunshine, of fenceless fields welling over with lark song. Here is not the billowing sea of Dakota flax fields in bloom, the never-ending reaches of sun-ripened wheat. Rather it is a tragedy of the travail of the lonely, fear-driven woman of the new land.

Sigrid is an authentic folk drama which, the author tells us, is deep-rooted in the memory of her childhood days. As a country lawyer her father's business often took him to the isolated farmhouses of the prairie. Very early in his business dealings with the country people he learned the advantage of taking with him herself and her mother to draw out these taciturn and inarticulate people.

The character of Sigrid she drew from the lives of several women of her acquaintance, chiefly from a Norwegian woman who lived for many years near her home. The husband had brought his wife to live in town in the hope that she would regain her interest in life through association with others, for she had been insane in a gentle blank way for many years. She polished and scrubbed her tomb-like house and kept the little grass patch trim. Whenever people came to the house she would turn and run; her blank, white face and faded blue eyes would take on a haunted expression as she slipped quietly into the darkness of an inner room.

The author, Margaret Radcliffe, was born in Grand Forks, North Dakota, the only child of a frontier lawyer. She attended the University of North Dakota and was active in the productions of The Dakota Playmakers there. On her graduation from the university she went to Valley City, North Dakota, as a teacher of English and dramatic director in the high school. Then she was invited by Charles Rann Kennedy and Edith Wynne Mathison to assist them at the Bennett School, Milbrook, New York. After a year with them, rich in experience, she accepted a position in the North Shore Day School, one of the leading progressive schools, at Winnetka, Illinois. She is still serving as dramatic director there.

Sigrid is an epic figure in the dramatic story of the making of a new land.

SIGRID

The parting curtain reveals the kitchen of a pioneer farmhouse on the Dakota prairie. It is built of rough lumber and "sealed" with paper, without the formalities of plaster. It is not the sod shanty, or first stage of the Swansons' existence here. That home has already been abandoned to SIGRID's *half-dozen chickens, just as this one will be in a few years.* OLE SWANSON *thrives on this continual transplanting, from Norway to Wisconsin, from Wisconsin to Minnesota, from Minnesota to Dakota. Yes, from sod shanty to shack, to frame house, to brick—who can tell? But* SIGRID, *his wife, withers away because her roots are always being torn from under her. She has almost ceased to grow roots now. It is pleasanter to drift in her memories. Sometimes when she is alone for days she can almost believe she is back in her native Norway, in the mountains beyond Bergen.*

[SIGRID *comes in now from the door at the left behind the heavy square table which is covered with discolored oilcloth. She is pale and slight and more stooped than a woman of thirty-seven should be. Her fine clear skin is a network of lines from which her dim blue eyes, flitting vaguely from one object to another, stare dumbly. Sometimes her face is stolid; sometimes it is fearful. It has almost lost the power of expressing varied emotions. She crosses the room heavily, wearily, to the range which stands opposite the door at which she entered and begins to prepare the breakfast.*]

[*Behind her, through the open door and the two windows which flank it, the endless expanse of the prairie is visible. It rolls away monotonously toward the horizon, shriveling and burning already in the glare of the early morning sun. The light beats down upon the walls and low roof and streams in through the windows and open door. It envelops the soap-box wash-stand which is placed below the window to the left and climbs the legs of the table and the kitchen chairs which stand behind it and to the right of it. Perhaps its hungry fingers are reaching out after the semicircle of blossoming geraniums and petunias which, altar-like, surround the heavy Norwegian Bible. The open volume rests upon a beautiful piece of Norwegian cut-work embroidery, and a starched cap and apron from a Norwegian costume lie crumpled in the chair to the right.*]

[*When the coffee is on the stove,* SIGRID *turns to the table. A fearful look comes into her face as she hurries over to remove the traces of her play-acting. Her men have no sympathy with this pretending. She closes the Bible and is gathering up the embroidery and trinkets when her son,* AXEL, *comes through the left door, rubbing his sleepy eyes and scratching his tousled dark head. He is almost as large and strong-boned as a man and shows in all his movements the confidence which such strength bestows upon boys in this pioneer world. He blinks consideringly at the weather and then glances at his mother, who stands motionless.*]

AXEL. Hullo!

SIGRID [*clutching the Bible yet trying to divert his attention from the tell-tale collection*]. Hurry, Axel. I will have coffee now.

AXEL [*squinting at the unusual tenants of the table*]. What's all this junk!

SIGRID. Oh, I just put them by the table....

AXEL. Ya, you've been fooling again. I bet you spent all day yesterday dressing up and singing and playing "Norway."

SIGRID. But, Axel, I—

AXEL. Why don't you forget Norway? [*Gesticulating impatiently.*] We're Americans now. Can't you understand that! Why don't you forget it and be like other people?

SIGRID. Ya-a, ya-a! Be like those who go to church and—

AXEL. And what?

SIGRID [*faces her son defiantly a moment and then wavers*]. I ... I want you should let me by, now.

AXEL. You better get this junk put away before Pa sees it.

SIGRID. Ya-a ... ya-a ... [*She goes out with the Bible and the rest of her treasures.*]

[AXEL *turns to the wash-stand and begins to lather his face, neck, and ears with coarse brown soap.*]

[SIGRID *returns to the table and takes the lamp from it to the cupboard which stands along the right wall toward the front. Then she goes to the stove, watching* AXEL *stealthily.*]

SIGRID. Axel, vass there many people in the town Saturday?

AXEL [*through the soap suds*]. Ya, everybody.

SIGRID. Tal me, did you see Kirstin?

AXEL. Who?

SIGRID. Kirstin. Kirstin Olson.

AXEL. Who do you mean? The old lady was here a year or so ago? Sven Olson's ol' woman?

SIGRID [*eagerly*]. Ya ... ya! Did you see her?

AXEL [*disgustedly*]. Naw, how should I see her?

SIGRID. Oh! I just thought—

AXEL. You always are asking about her. What's on your mind anyway?

SIGRID [*fingering her plants wistfully*]. She tal me she send me some slips sometime by you. I think may ...

Axel. Well, I didn't. How do you expect me to see her, anyway?

Sigrid. But, Axel, think you go to town. You vass there, vasn't you?

Axel. Sure I was there, but I wasn't hanging around no old women.

Sigrid. Vere did you go, then?

Axel [*importantly*]. I went with Pa most all the time.

Sigrid [*unhappily*]. O-oh. . . .

Axel [*emphatically*]. Honest.

Sigrid [*wearily*]. I know. [*She is setting the table behind the disarranged flowers. She hesitates a moment and then inquires gently*]. Did you go by the church yesterday, Axel?

Axel [*looking uncertain*]. N-naw! We went to Nissen's.

Sigrid. I don't know where that is, Axel. Iss it by the town?

Axel. N-naw. . . . It's . . . it's out at the grove.

Sigrid. Way north here? [Axel *nods in the midst of toweling himself.*] But, Axel, what vass you there for?

Axel [*irritably*]. I was with Pa, I told you.

Sigrid. But I don't—

Axel [*abruptly*]. I got to water the horses. [*He slams hastily out of the door.*]

[Sigrid *looks vaguely, anxiously after him. The room sinks into stillness as she wanders back toward the table. Sighing audibly, she bends over her blossoms. She has practiced slipping away from reality so faithfully that even serious things cannot hold her any more. Fear is her only serious reality now. She smiles faintly and picking up two of the rusty tin cans starts toward the windows at the rear. The glare of the sun upon the sills is terrific.* Sigrid *shakes her head.*]

Sigrid. Ah, it iss too hot. [*She turns and looks toward the front of the stage where the two low ledges of the windows suggest the north and shady side of the house. She comes down and puts the plants on them, then returns to the table for the rest of them. She becomes absorbed in patting and pruning and bringing water from the water pail back by the stove. Her face softens a little and once, when she finds a long-awaited bud, she almost laughs aloud. Her eyes begin to look more alive as she raises them to look out across the prairie.*]

[*There is a noise of heavy boots off at the left and then the sound of a man yawning as he stretches. A moment later* OLE *strides into the room. He is a brawny, confident giant of forty, very dark and carelessly unshaven. His whole appearance and attitude suggest boundless energy and a hearty liking for people and the rough society of the frontier. The drinking, athletic contests, and especially the gambling, appeal to his adventurous disposition. He makes no distinction of race or religion and feels none. His instincts are thus at constant variance with the shrinking, sensitive timidity of his "woman," and he has little patience with her though he is not particularly brutal. He does not see* SIGRID, *and after standing at the door an instant he pulls a roll of bills from his pocket.*]

[SIGRID *struggles to her feet.* OLE *turns, surprised and a little discomfited.*]

SIGRID [*her eyes are fastened on the money and her voice is low and harsh*]. Ole!

OLE. Vhat! You here? I thought you vent to milk.

SIGRID. I vass just watering my plants. [OLE *is putting the money back in his pocket*]. Ole! Where did *that* come from?

OLE [*too easily*]. I sold some wheat Saturday. Come, now. Pour the coffee. I can't vait all day for you. [*He has gone to the wash-stand, and is splashing himself hastily.*]

SIGRID [*coming toward him*]. I know! You get that money

by the ... grove! [*She says that last word in a horrified whisper.*]

OLE. Don't be a fool. I vent to town. How can I then "get money by the grove"! [*He imitates her inflection on the last words as he hangs up the towel and then comes forward and sits in the chair back of the table.*]

SIGRID. Ole! You are a vicked, vicked man. God vill curse you, Ole!

OLE. Come now, pour the coffee.

SIGRID. Ole, listen to me! Last month you have mens here. You take their money. I saw you.

OLE. Sigrid! That's planty!

SIGRID [*coming still closer and twisting her hands*]. I tal you they vill come again, Ole. I know. They vill come in the night like the other time. [AXEL, *who has been standing in the door during his mother's last speech, opens it and comes in looking rather guilty. He seats himself at the table and tries to act as if he knew nothing of the goings on.*] Take it avay—please, Ole. [OLE *pays no attention. She turns to* AXEL.] Axel, make your father take it avay. Please, Axel.

OLE. Sigrid, I tal you I sell wheat by the town. Now you keep still.

SIGRID [*doggedly, half under her breath*]. I know! I know! [*She goes to the cupboard and begins to take something from a drawer and hide it in her full gathered skirts.* AXEL, *seeing her, nudges his father and nods toward her.* OLE *rises desperately.*]

OLE. Sigrid, you crazy fool! [*He strides across the room to her and wrenches the butcher knife from her hands. She cowers guiltily before him*]. Stop that, I tal you! How can a man live in this country with a crazy woman! [*He slams the knife on the table and pulls the milk pail down from the range and thrusts it into her hands.*] Here now.

You go by the barn and milk. [*He pushes her out the door and then turns on his son.*] You fool, did you tal her ve vent to Nissen's?

AXEL. Well... ya... kinda....

OLE. I thought I could trust you. Never can I take you if you tal all you know.

AXEL. Oh, Pa, I won't again. Honest! How will I learn right if you don't let me watch you? I never gave you away once yesterday, did I?

OLE. Ya? Well, remember, in poker game the first thing is to keep your business to yourself. [*There is a moment of heavy silence which* AXEL *breaks uneasily.*]

AXEL. What's the matter with her now, Pa?

OLE [*bleakly*]. How should I know? She is dumb and unreasonable as a wicious horse. She ban too much alone on the land—too much—too much shut up by herself... It iss bad....

AXEL. I caught her playing Norway again. I bet she did it all day yesterday. She's always worse after that.

OLE. Ya, she ban so long from Bergen now.... Too much by herself she iss on the new land... the vinter so hard, so long and cold. And now in Yuly the sun so hot... Ya, all the time she gets vorse. Always has she a knife by her now. Every night, just about, I find her taking one to bed.

AXEL. I suppose Chris and Mortimer coming to steal the pot back that night got her started. She was awful scared when you plugged that buckshot at them.

OLE. Ya, sure! That makes her vorse, and reading the Bible make her vorse, and so does everything. Always people make her vorse.

AXEL. If I hadn't seen her just in time, I believe she would have killed that peddler. She had a knife out and was standing just behind him.

OLE. Ya, ve must be careful now. She is getting sly lately. I caught her sneaking around by Hans Jenson when he came for the colt last veek.

AXEL. We best keep people away from the house more.

OLE [*rising*]. Ya.... Well, I think I put this money somewhere now. I can't keep it always by me.

AXEL. Shall I better hide the knives, too, until she settles down again? She always acts so funny after we go away. [AXEL *gets up from the table and collects the large knife and another small one and begins rummaging about the cupboard for a place to hide them.* OLE *takes the roll of bills from his pocket and begins counting them.*]

AXEL. How will it be to put these in the new sugar sack? There's plenty yet a while in the old one so she won't be looking there, will she?

OLE. Sure! Two hunderd—

AXEL [*coming over and looking admiringly at his father*]. How much did you make, Pa?

OLE [*rolling it up and laughing*]. How much you think? Three hunderd five dollar.

AXEL. Gosh! Three hunderd!

OLE. Ya, Axel, I vill fool every one of them. You see. Is it anybody can beat me at poker?

AXEL. Nobody I know, Pa.

OLE. Naw—and nobody can beat me at raising wheat, neither. You vait. The people in the valley say, "Ole Swanson iss crazy," when I come up here by the hills. They say, "He can't raise wheat up there." [AXEL *laughs.*] Sure, they say that. You see? I tal you some day ve vill have horses and cows and planty of binders. [*He looks around the room*]. And some day ve vill have the biggest house in Dakota.

AXEL. But, Pa, she's so funny we can't even have a peddler come here. What's the use of having a big house?

OLE. I know, son. [*He goes over to the cupboard and stuffs the money into a can which he then places on the highest shelf*]. We must vait. Maybe it vill be different in a few years.

AXEL. What are you going to do with the money, Pa?

OLE. I am going to buy a good team right away.

AXEL. Naw, really?

OLE. Ya, I talk to Nichols when he comes vith the feed.

AXEL [*going to the door and taking his straw hat from the peg*]. Shall I work down east to-day?

OLE. Ya. I stay by the barn and vork on the binder till Nichols comes. Go on now. I vill soon come. [AXEL *goes through the door and then looks off left, shading his eyes with his hand.*]

AXEL. Say, Pa, Nichols is coming up to the yard now. Looks as if somebody's with him.

OLE [*coming to the door and looking too*]. Ya, it iss him. Always his voman comes vith him. Go on to the field now. I talk to him.

[AXEL *goes off toward the barn at the right.* OLE *goes through the door and disappears off to the left where he can be heard booming hospitably.*]

OLE [*outside*]. Hello! Hello! Glad to see you, Nichols.

NICHOLS [*faintly*]. Good morning, Ole.

OLE [*still booming*]. Vell, it iss quite a load you have, missis. Glad to see you. Here now, I help you, Nichols. Ve just leave it by the corner of the fence and Axel and I will bring him down later.

NICHOLS. All right.—Well, Ole, how's the wheat on the hills this year?

OLE [*laughing good-naturedly as they approach the door and can be seen*]. Vell, you come and see now. I show you. First thing you know I get a threshing machine for my own crop. [NICHOLS *laughs good-humoredly but condescendingly.*]

NICHOLS. Come on, now, Ole. Look down there. It's as green as a meadow in early June. Now, look at this—burnt to a cinder, and it isn't the middle of July. Nope, no hills for me.

OLE [*laughing still louder*]. All right! All right! Now you come round the house here, and see my wheat field by the middle of Yuly. Then ve see who laughs.

NICHOLS [*stopping near the door so that he can be plainly seen. He is a tall, slender Yankee type, strong, cheerful, and keen. He looks a little thin-blooded beside* OLE's *animal physique and his animal spirits. He is quite self-satisfied, however, and looks about himself complacently. He has married a rich widow and feathered a comfortable nest for himself here on the frontier. He and his wife mix well with their numerous neighbors in the valley and find life good*]. My wife would like to step in and visit with Mrs. Swanson, I am sure. Shall I call her?

OLE. Vell, I tal you. . . .

NICHOLS [*over-riding what he takes to be the foreigner's shyness*]. I know she wasn't expecting anybody, but then our women folks don't get together very often. I'll just—

OLE. Just one minute. [*Humiliated to the depths of his hospitable nature.*] Sigrid iss not friendly by strangers, Nichols. They upset her, and ve can't let her see people.

NICHOLS. But—

OLE. You see she iss not quite right up here. [*He taps his head.*] Vith strangers she iss dangerous.

NICHOLS [*embarrassed by his own persistence and a little uneasy*]. Sorry, Swanson. Mrs. Nichols can just stay in the wagon then. We won't be long. [*He turns and waves a signal to his wife that he is going on.*] Has she been that way long?

OLE. Oh, ya—three years now. You see it iss not like Norway. And then ve lost two children vith diphtheria the first vinter. [*He sighs.*] Vell, come now. I show you the wheat. [*They disappear around the right corner of the house. Their voices fade away.*]

[SIGRID *appears now with her milk pail three-quarters full. She approaches the house from the rear right. Her manner is alert and stealthy. She has seen* OLE *with the man, and now her attention is attracted by the wagon and its occupant. She comes cautiously up to the door and turns to watch the men. Then she comes through the screen and without putting down the milk pail, hides behind the door-jamb, and watches the movements of the other stranger. Her agitation increases as she looks and she turns to peer furtively around the room. Then as* MRS. NICHOLS *comes into view looking off over the valley, she backs slowly and watchfully toward the cupboard. Once there she opens the drawer quickly and stealthily.*]

SIGRID. Aaa...ah...! [*She begins searching frantically, hastily, first among the dishes on the table, then on the stove. She hesitates between the other room and the cupboard. The cupboard is closer. She paws frantically through the shelves above, working higher with the aid of a chair. In her haste she upsets the money can on the top shelf and it rolls to the floor. She scrambles down hastily, and peers out.* MRS. NICHOLS *is still standing by the fence, and admiring the view of the valley.* SIGRID *looks at the money bulging from its can and frustratedly at the cupboard. She makes a queer noise with her breath and attacks the lower shelves. As she drags out cake pans and boxes and sacks she sees* MRS. NICHOLS *turning and coming toward the house. As she pulls at the newly opened sugar sack, it spills open onto the floor and the black handle of the knife is exposed. She snatches it and conceals it in her skirts. Rising slowly and stealthily, she watches silently as the other woman approaches the screen.*]

Mrs. Nichols [*a stoutish woman of forty, active and rather commanding, seems to belong in this setting with her colored print dress and her queer black sunbonnet-like hat. She comes quickly up to the screen door and knocks. Receiving no answer, she shades her eyes from the glare of the sun and peers into the room*]. Hello! Hello, Mrs. Swanson. Mind if I step in a minute and cool off? [*There is no response from* Sigrid *who stands backed against the cupboard. Her eyes are narrowed to sinister slits, and her breath comes rapidly.*] Funny!... Mrs. Swanson! [Mrs. Nichols *starts to shake the door, and it swings open in her hand. She looks a little startled, then steps inside.*] Mrs.——!... Oh, there you are! [*She peers toward the darker side of the room, perceiving* Sigrid *only as a dim outline after the glare of the sun. She speaks again affably.*] I just didn't hear you, I guess. Mercy, I didn't know the sun could be so hot at ten o'clock in the morning. I'm baked and that's a fact. [*She removes her black hat and wipes the perspiration from her flushed face with her handkerchief, then sinks into the chair behind the table.*] My husband and I started almost before sunrise this morning. It seems as if I must have been gone a whole day already. [*She looks over at the range and the disordered table and then a little more sharply at the woman, who becomes clearer to her as she accustoms herself to the light.*] Mercy, I don't suppose you even know who I am. You don't look very familiar to me neither. Don't believe I've ever seen you in town, have I? [*She looks still more sharply at* Sigrid, *whose watchful eyes travel fearfully from her face to the door and back again. She makes no effort to speak.*] No, I don't think so.

Well, I'm Mrs. William Nichols from down in Mary Township. We've seen a good deal of your husband off and on. Seems like I ought to have known you before this. [*She stops again, expecting a reply, but gets nothing except a still more searching and frightened look from* SIGRID, *who at once connects her with all the wickedness and danger of* OLE'S *strange life away from home.* MRS. NICHOLS *sighs and looks toward the water pail which stands between the stove and the window at the rear of the room.*] A person does get plenty thirsty riding in this heat. Wonder if I could have a drink of water?

[SIGRID'S *eyes travel slowly again from the face of the woman to the door, then stealthily down to the money on the floor at her own feet and back to the face again. They begin to gleam craftily as she moves slowly, with a sidewise crab-like movement toward the water pail.*]

[MRS. NICHOLS *smiles gratefully. She notices something peculiar in* SIGRID'S *behavior, but she has seen many shy people on these prairies. She passes her hand over her forehead and looks toward the front, where she sees the view of the rolling land to the north. She rises impulsively and steps toward it. As she moves forward her eye is caught by the disordered state of the cupboard and the sugar spilled on the floor. She hesitates for the fraction of a second, drawn by her housewifely instincts to put things in order. Then, recalling almost instantaneously that it is not her sugar, she turns to the windows and comes into full view of the blossoming plants. Her face lights with pleasure and she kneels before them.*]

MRS. NICHOLS [*with a quick indrawn breath*]. U-umph!

[*Meanwhile,* SIGRID *has been stalking every movement from behind. At the first motion, she becomes absolutely still, watching. Her gleaming suspicious eyes still glide from the woman to the door and back to the money. Her hand, which has been clutching the knife in her skirts, closes on it convulsively as* MRS. NICHOLS *hesitates. Lifting it sharply, she takes a swift cat-like step forward. As* MRS. NICHOLS *changes her course,* SIGRID *stops, swaying slightly. A baffled look replaces the craft in her eyes. Slowly, uncomprehendingly she looks at the disregarded money and then at the woman.*]

MRS. NICHOLS [*without turning.*] Why, Mrs. Swanson, they're lovely! How do you do it? I haven't seen such geraniums since I left Ohio. And petunias in blossom! How do you do it indoors?

[SIGRID *crumples a little. The hand with the knife in it sinks slowly to her side. She still stares, completely confused.*]

MRS. NICHOLS [*sitting back on her heels and smiling reminiscently*]. It certainly seems funny to sit here and look out to that barren country over geranium blossoms. You know, my grandmother used to have them in her kitchen window back home. I can remember yet how we used to pinch the leaves of the spiced ones when we were children. [*She laughs softly.*]

[SIGRID *makes one more circle of the room with her eyes and slowly slips the knife into her skirt.*]

MRS. NICHOLS. And instead of prairie, we looked out the kitchen window at a gentle slope of green grass down to a little stream. And she had five elm trees right there on that slope. [*She turns toward* SIGRID.] Think of it! Five big shade trees in your back yard.

[SIGRID *is beginning to come to herself. Her face is contorted with the struggle of long-suppressed feeling bursting into life again. Her fingers begin to twist nervously, helplessly in the folds of her skirt.*]

MRS. NICHOLS. You know when I look at this windowful of flowers it seems like I could almost hear that running water at Grandma's.

[SIGRID *starts at the word "water" and makes a quick movement with her head. Then as if slowly remembering her duties as hostess, she propels herself across the floor to the water pail and brings the tin dipper brimming with water to* MRS. NICHOLS. *It trembles and splashes but she pays no attention. Her eyes are fastened on the woman.*]

SIGRID [*humbly*]. Here iss the vater.

MRS. NICHOLS [*standing up and turning to take it*]. Why thank you! You know I'd clean forgotten it. [*She drinks and then hands it back.*] You know I don't know which cooled me off more, the water or the flowers.

SIGRID. I know. [*She nods and smiles wistfully through the tears that glisten in her eyes.*]

MRS. NICHOLS. It's lonely—this country. A person needs something . . . well—something like flowers.

SIGRID. Ya-a! [*She is suddenly seized with a desire to talk. Trembling with haste, she draws a chair close up to the flowers and offers it silently to her guest. Then kneeling beside them, she begins to show them off.*] See! See this vun. She vill have flowers on her to-morrow, I think. [*She nods happily at it and talks to it as much as to* MRS. NICHOLS.] Sax veeks now I have been vaiting for him. She iss vite too. See! Last vinter my plants nearly all froze in Yanuary, when it vass so cold, you know. And then my little vite vun vass nearly gone. And I just safe this vun little slip. But he gets big and strong before the vinter now. [*Her voice has a pitiful break in it on "vinter" and she pats the rusty can as if it were a baby in need of comforting.*]

MRS. NICHOLS. Well, it certainly is a treat to see them. I do like the pink geraniums, though. Say, there's a Norwegian woman up north has some flowers.—Hm! . . . I can't remember her name just now, but you probably know her.

SIGRID. Oh, iss it Olson, now? Do you know Kirstin Olson?

MRS. NICHOLS. That's what it was! Sven Olson was the man's name.

SIGRID. Have you seen then her flowers?

MRS. NICHOLS. Why yes, I rode over there with my husband one day this spring.

SIGRID [*putting her hands in* MRS. NICHOL's *lap like a child*]. Oh, did you see her—how do you say—her red and— p-purple— Oh, vat do you call her?

MRS. NICHOLS. Oh, I know. Her fuchsia!

SIGRID. Ya-ya! Did you see her?

MRS. NICHOLS. Yes, she has a nice one, hasn't she?

SIGRID. Oh, I am so glad it growed. Two years ago when she vass here she tal me how her sister in Minnesota send her vun.

MRS. NICHOLS. Haven't you seen it?

SIGRID. No, I have not seen her since that time. She promise to send me some slips by Axel sometime—ven he iss by the town, you know. But Axel, he never sees her somehow.

MRS. NICHOLS. But don't you go to town?

SIGRID [*tensely*]. Oh, naw. I stay by the farm, you know.

MRS. NICHOLS [*shocked*]. But you must go sometimes. Don't you go to church either?

SIGRID [*looking out the window and speaking harshly and gutturally*]. Naw-naw. I vill not go there. Ole goes there by his vicked friends.

MRS. NICHOLS. But how do you see any one? You live so far from all the neighbors. Do you—why even the Jensens are at least seven miles away. Do you see them?

SIGRID. Naw-naw. Hans Jensen iss a bad man.

MRS. NICHOLS. But don't you see any one?

SIGRID. Naw.... [*She fingers her plants again, and then, thinking of her present blessings, turns shyly to* MRS.

NICHOLS]. But I see you now. I like you. You are so kind —just like Kirstin Ol-l-lson.

MRS. NICHOLS. My dear, I am so glad I happened to ride up here. You should see more people.

SIGRID. Naw-naw! I don't like!

MRS. NICHOLS. Won't you come to see me sometime? I'd like to show you my chickens and my vegetable garden. We have had green peas already. Please come with Mr. Swanson.

SIGRID. Oh—naw! I—stay by the—farm. Naw—Ole and Axel, they come sometime.

MRS. NICHOLS. Well, I am coming to see you again, anyway. Can I?

SIGRID [*with dog-like devotion*]. Ya-a-a, I hope so-o.

MRS. NICHOLS [*striving to become less personal*]. And next time I come, I'll teach you my new crochet edge. My sister sent it to me from Ohio. Do you crochet?

SIGRID [*fingering the plants again*]. Naw—I don't.

MRS. NICHOLS. Do you embroider?

SIGRID. Eh?—Oh, ya—I do hardanger,* you know.

MRS. NICHOLS. Do you? Let me see?

[SIGRID *gets to her feet and runs into the other room. She returns almost immediately with an elaborate piece of Norwegian cut-work on which she is still working.*]

MRS. NICHOLS. Oh, it is beautiful! Is it a table cover?

SIGRID. Ya, a table cover. [*Impulsively.*] Come, I show you. I make the bedspread last year. Come, I show you. [*She takes* MRS. NICHOLS' *hand confidingly and pulls her into the other room, talking volubly as she does so.*] I show you other things too—t'ings I bring from Bergen. That's vhere I live in the old country. Oh, it iss so pretty there.

---

* *Hardanger* embroidery is Norwegian peasant work done usually on coarse, white linen. Its geometric patterns are designed by the worker as she goes along. They are often bewilderingly elaborate—so much so, that there is practically no trace of the linen foundation visible.

I like to take you and show you. Big tall hills, ve have, and trees—you know—green trees all vinter long.... [*Her voice dies away into the other room with a happy childish laugh.*]

OLE [*his voice is heard offstage right*]. Sure I remember them. That iss a good team, by God.

NICHOLS. Well, I'll sell you those bays for three hundred, Swanson, and you'll never duplicate them at the price.

OLE. I'll take them. Come, I give you the money now.

NICHOLS [*as they step through the screen door*]. That isn't necessary, Swanson. You certainly don't need to pay me until you get the team.

OLE [*striding over to the cupboard*]. Naw, I pay now. I get this money out of the house, see. Monday or Sunday I come to get the team. Iss it all right then?

NICHOLS. Surely, if you are willing to take the risk on me.

OLE [*laughing*]. Oh, that's all right. Just a minute, I— [*He stops, startled to see his precious "pot" strewn carelessly on the floor.*] Christ! Who has been at this, now? Twenty, thirty, fifty, vun hunderd—

NICHOLS [*stands waiting patiently and looking critically at his surroundings. Suddenly he spies his wife's hat and hand-bag on the chair to the right of the table. He goes over to make sure*]. I say, Swanson, my wife must have come in here. Here's her hat.

OLE. Three hunderd five dollar, saxty cent. [*He sighs*]. All safe.

NICHOLS. Swanson, did you hear me? I say my wife must have come in here.

OLE [*who has been completely absorbed in his money until this moment*]. What?

NICHOLS. Here's her hat. [OLE *drops the money and looks anxiously around the room. The sugar crunches beneath his feet, and he looks down at it.* AXEL'S *words come back*

to him and he stoops to run his hands into the sack. The
knife is gone. Just at this moment AXEL comes in at the
rear door.]

AXEL. Hello, Mr. Nichols. Is Pa getting the— [*He stops at
the sight of his father with the open sack before him and
his ear cocked anxiously toward the other part of the
house.*] What's the matter?

OLE [*dully*]. They're gone.

AXEL. Where is she?

OLE. Mrs. Nichols has been here.

[AXEL *looks horror-stricken.*]

NICHOLS. Well, for God's sake, man, what has happened?
Where is she?

AXEL. She's in there. I heard something move. [*Just then*
SIGRID's *high-pitched, hysterical, little laugh is heard coming nearer.*]

OLE [*under his breath*]. Christ!

AXEL. Pa, has she—?

NICHOLS. By God, why do you stand here! [*He starts frantically toward the door, but is stopped by* AXEL, *who can see into the room, just as* SIGRID's *voice is heard.*]

SIGRID. No—no! You take them, I tal you. I vant you should now, pleasse, I vant you should!

MRS. NICHOLS [*comes through the door laden with hardanger embroidery, a Norwegian apron, and a filagree brooch. Everything she admired has been showered upon her*]. But, Mrs. Swanson, I can't—

SIGRID. Now just you vait a minute. I give you— [*She has turned toward her plants and in so doing, comes face to face with her men and the stranger. She draws in her breath audibly and freezes in her place.*]

MRS. NICHOLS [*quick to sense the cause of the change*]. This is my husband, Mr. Nichols, Mrs. Swanson.

NICHOLS [*embarrassed at the harmless child-like glance of*

the woman he has pictured as a murderess]. Why... how do you do?

SIGRID [*looking back questioningly at* MRS. NICHOLS]. How ... you... do! [*There is a moment of awkward silence.*]

MRS. NICHOLS. Have you seen her flowers, William? They are perfectly beautiful.

SIGRID [*her face lighting again*]. Ya, I get the slips now. Just you vait a minute. [*She goes to the plants and, taking the butcher knife from her skirts, begins to cut the slips, expertly, ruthlessly.*]

OLE. Sigrid!

NICHOLS [*hastily to his wife*]. What have you been doing? Do you know she's—

MRS. NICHOLS. Hush! [*Louder.*] It is getting late, William. Hadn't we better be on our way?

NICHOLS. Yes, I think so. Don't mind about that now, Swanson.

OLE [*a trifle dazed*]. Vell, all right then. I vait till Monday or Sunday, maybe, ven I come down.

SIGRID [*turning with a handful of geranium slips*]. Now, just vun minute. I put them in a jar of vater, and then ve have some coffee, maybe.

OLE [*a great smile lighting his hospitable face*]. Sigrid!

MRS. NICHOLS [*gently*]. I'm afraid we can't stay to-day. We promised to have dinner down at Martin's, south of here, and it's getting on toward noon now.

SIGRID [*her face falling*]. Oh just vun minute. I make coffee so quick, you know.

MRS. NICHOLS [*taking the tin cup filled with geranium slips from* SIGRID'S *lifeless hand and holding her arm*]. Not this time. Next time surely, and when you come to see me. [*Turning to* OLE.] Won't you bring her with you when you come next Sunday or Monday?

OLE [*startled and then doubtful*]. Vell, I ...

[MRS. NICHOLS *summons all of her direct, forceful personality into a single look.*]
OLE. Vy, ya, I guess I can, maybe.
SIGRID [*quick to feel his doubt*]. Naw-naw! I stay by the—
MRS. NICHOLS. No! You are coming to see me next week. Promise you will come and see whether the slips are rooted.
SIGRID. Oh, I . . .
MRS. NICHOLS [*sternly*]. Promise!
SIGRID [*smiling trustfully into her face*]. Ya-a . . . t'ink . . . I co-ome.
MRS. NICHOLS [*overcome by the woman's haggard little face, takes her into her arms and kisses her forehead*]. Good-by.
[*The men nod gruffly to each other.* NICHOLS, *with unaccustomed attention, opens the door for his wife and allows her to pass through first. They pass out of sight toward their wagon to the left.*]
[AXEL, *still standing near the door, looks with a gleam of sympathy and respect at his mother, who, as if in a trance, walks slowly to the screen and watches the preparations for departure.*]
[OLE, *confused and disturbed, comes down toward the massacred geraniums. He stops. Stooping, he pulls from the can where it has been stuck, the lost butcher-knife. It glints harmlessly in his hands as he too turns to stare at the little figure pressed against the screen as*

THE CURTAINS CLOSE

A NOTE ON THE DAKOTA DIALECT

In general the voices of the Scandinavians are inclined to be guttural when they attempt to speak English. There is a pronounced lilt, or up-and-down inflection in many of their emphasized vowels. The author has indicated in the text only the most common varia-

tions in sound from spoken American. A more complete list follows.
S and *z* are always hissed sharply, never voiced.

EXAMPLES: *Was* is said *vass*.
Is is said *iss*.

This is the most characteristic and persistent variation of the Norwegian dialect and is the last to disappear from the speech of the second and even the third generation.

W is pronounced as *v*.

EXAMPLES: *Will* is said *vill*.
One is said *vun*.

J is pronounced like *y*.

EXAMPLES: *January* is said *Yanuary*.
Judge is said *yudge*.

Th (voiced) is pronounced as a combination of *d* and *th*.

EXAMPLE: *That* is said *dhat*.

Th (breathed) is pronounced like a straight *t*.

EXAMPLES: *Think* is said *tink*.
With is said *vit*.

The vowels are extremely subtle in their variations. A few hints can be noted:

The short *e* and short *a* are often confused.

EXAMPLES: *Tell* is said *tal*.
Axel is said *Exel*.
And is said *end*.

The sound of long *i* is apt to change, especially when it stands alone, to a tense long *a* sound. *I* is said nearly like *ay*. However, *like* is said almost *lak*.

Ow tends toward *ah,* a dropping of the last part of the diphthong.

EXAMPLE: *Now* is said almost like *nah*.

O long tends to become *aw*.

EXAMPLE: *Show* is said like a tense *shaw*.

MISSOURI

SWAPPIN' FEVER
A COMEDY OF THE OZARKS

BY LEALON N. JONES
OF CAPE GIRARDEAU, MISSOURI

Written in the playwriting course at the University of North Carolina and originally produced by The Carolina Playmakers on their Fifty-eighth Experimental Production of New Plays in The Playmakers Theater, Chapel Hill, North Carolina, on January 27, 1939.

THE CHARACTERS

BILL TEETERS.......................Fred Koch, Jr.
PHRONIE, *his wife*..................Frances Goforth
MOONEY BEASON, *a neighbor boy*....Kalman Sherman
CHARLEY LACEY, *a small-town business man*
                                    Wieder Sievers
BRADY, *representative of a mining company*
                                    John Morgan

SCENE: *The front porch of* BILL TEETERS' *log cabin in the Missouri Ozarks.*

TIME: *A morning in June, 1938.*

Copyright, 1939, by The Carolina Playmakers, Inc.
All rights reserved.

OZARK MOUNTAIN FOLK

LEALON JONES, the author of *Swappin' Fever*, has lived in the eastern Missouri Ozarks most of his life. In summer, as a carefree boy, he roamed the hills, swam in the Castor River, and went on many a wild romp in the woods with his country cousins. Later, as a newspaper writer and photographer, he traveled over many a mile of the Ozark country up and down the Mississippi River in search of stories, songs, and native folklore. Here, he is convinced, is a virgin field for the folk dramatist: romantic history, ballads, tales, droll humor, and racy vernacular.

There is the legend of Big Springs, which gushes forth enough water to make a small river, formed centuries ago by the tears of an Indian princess confined in a cave by her father when she refused to marry the young chief of his choice; there Spanish coins, found by the early settlers, gave rise to tales of vast buried treasure hidden away in the hills adjoining the great river; there in the Pocahontas community the tall stories of T. J. Compton are still told by many a fireside, although that master story-teller has been dead for half a century. Compton, they say, was a Mississippi Munchausen who bent his gun barrel to shoot a deer that fled around the mountain and split a tree limb with a bullet to catch the toes of ten big turkeys roosting on it; who trained a hunting dog to travel on only two legs so as to have always two legs in reserve for running down foxes. A fierce tornado once threshed all his wheat for him, they say, blew the straw into a fence corner, and left the grain lying eight inches deep all over the field.

"The Ozarks remain relatively untouched," the playwright tells us, "by a modern world of efficiency experts, split-minute schedules, super-this-and-that, two-minute eggs, and music right in the groove. Quietly the Ozarker goes his own independent way, paying little attention to an outside world which is forever striving to reach the moon. Uncle Billy Rhodes sits as quietly as ever on the dog-trot porch of his big log house, chewing copious cuds of tobacco and watching the streamlined creations burn up the highway that winds past his door. 'I heerd they was over thirty thousand people killed by them things last year,' he ruminates. ' 'Pears like that's a lot o' people to die jist on account o' somebody wantin' to git some place in a hurry.'

"Ozark religion still remains a free expression of a natural, uninhibited people. The most beautiful baptismal service I have ever seen was held in a small crystalline mountain stream one Sunday afternoon several years ago. The mountain folk crowded close to the banks of the stream and sung the well-loved hymns of their forefathers. Then eight young people reverently walked into the waters for the sacred ceremony. The shimmering light cast a benediction on their youthful faces as the mountain preacher immersed them in the stream. As one youth came toward the bank, his mother joyfully waded in and embraced his wet body.

"Rolling hills clothed in the quiet green of summer and in a color-mad riot in autumn—endless hills, the birthright always of a quiet, sturdy people in a land of peaceful friendliness—such is the country of the Missouri Ozarks."

The chief character in *Swappin' Fever*, Bill Teeters, inventor, is a "natural" man whom the author has known since his boyhood. The churning-and-fanning machine is drawn from the author's remembrances of the days when he had the irksome task of using a new invention in churning milk for his grandmother. This "contraption" was purchased by his grandfather from the man who created it. It consisted of a revolving wheel attached to a horizontal bar to the end of which the churn-dasher was affixed. Young Lealon's job was to turn the wheel (for an endless period it seemed to the lad) until the butter came. The new device worked well enough but in no way did it lessen the labor of the churning process, Lealon says. After being used a few times it was put away in the smokehouse forever.

Besides being an inventor Bill Teeters is also a master teller of tall stories, as he so well demonstrates in the play.

SWAPPIN' FEVER

The scene is the front porch of BILL TEETERS' *log cabin, in the Ozark Mountains of eastern Missouri. The porch, of the lean-to variety, extends from the lower right corner of the stage diagonally to the left rear. The house has a careless air about it. The shingles, square supporting posts, and the floor are weather-beaten and gray. The posts, sturdy ones, have felt numerous jack-knives whittling idly and carving initials on their inviting surfaces. A front door opens into the house from the center of the porch.**
Three old, splint-bottom chairs, and some claptrap oddments, a sack of corn, an old cow bell, a wooden box containing rags and newspapers, and BILL'S *"contraption" (which includes an old churn) complete the scene. The invention on which* BILL *is working consists of a foundation-board three feet long and a foot wide, two parallel uprights three feet high nailed to it. These support the rod on which a three-foot strip is pivoted by a hinge. A pedal is hinged to one end of the foundation-board and a stout string extends from the unhinged end of the pedal to the end of the three-foot strip. To this end of the strip a palm-leaf fan is attached.* BILL *is now trying to connect the other end of the strip with the churn-dasher in such a way that when the pedal is pushed down with the foot the dasher will ascend and the fan descend. The idea of* BILL'S *great invention is to keep the churner comfortably cool on a hot summer day.*

* If the director finds it impracticable to build a porch set, the play may be presented in a simple interior with a door at the left, and a window upstage, center.

[BILL *is sitting on the porch working on his invention. He is fifty or thereabouts, a thin, alert man with a big mustache and a two-weeks' growth of beard. He wears a pair of old iron-rimmed "specs," an old hat with the brim turned up, overalls and shirt that have been patched repeatedly, and an ancient pair of brogans. He is smoking a corncob pipe and happily engaged at his task, singing "Redwing" the while in a not-very-melodious voice.*]

BILL [*singing*].
  Oh, the moon shines to-night on pretty Redwing.
  The breeze is sighing,
  The nightbird's crying.
  Oh, far, far away her lover's sleeping,
  While Redwing's weeping
  Her heart away.

[PHRONIE, *his wife, emerges slowly from the house, and begins sweeping the porch. She is a small, thin woman and is slouchily dressed. She has hay-colored hair drawn stiffly back from a woebegone face. There is a dolorous air about her and she looks mournfully at* BILL.]

PHRONIE [*drawling out the words*]. Bill, ye ort to be ashamed o' yerself wastin' yer time like that when the garden needs hoein'. I seen some 'tater bugs on the 'taters 'while ago. They ort to be got off, 'fore they git a start.

BILL. Let 'em git their bellies full first. I hate to kill anything when it's hongry. I'll knock 'em off before dinner.

PHRONIE. Ye won't do no sich of a thing. All ye'll do all day'll be to fool with that old contraption that ain't worth a settin' o' rotten aigs.

BILL. Now that's where you're wrong, Phronie. Soon as I git the churnin' part put on, ye can churn and fan yerself all at the same time by jist workin' this pedal with yer foot. Think how fine that'll be durin' this hot weather. [*Enthusiastically.*] By Johnnies, I think I'll take me out a patent on this!

PHRONIE. Yes, you was a sharp one to think that up. Must have been drinkin' razor-blade soup when ye thought of it. Instead o' thinkin' about that, ye'd better be studyin' about takin' that five thousand dollars that minin' man offered ye fer minin' rights on this farm.

BILL [*evasively*]. Yeah, I've been kind o' studyin' about that.

PHRONIE. Law' me, us as pore as Job's old turkey gobbler and you turnin' down enough money to choke a cow. It shore beats me. If somebody'd give me a nickel and tell me to give it to the first crazy person I saw, I could give it away right here in this house.

BILL [*still evasively*]. Now maybe I've got some idys, if ye'll gi' me a little time.

PHRONIE. Then ye'd better be hurryin' up with 'em, 'cause that man said he'd be back ag'in to-day. Do ye reckon I can git me a nice new hat if ye sell them minin' rights?

BILL. Shore, shore....

PHRONIE. It's about time I had a new one. The bird on the one I've got is old enough now to have great-grandchildren.

[PHRONIE *goes into the house.* BILL *continues tinkering on his contraption, singing "Redwing."* MOONEY BEASON *now saunters in from the left.* MOONEY *is a boy of seventeen who has grown tall so fast that he does not yet have control of his body. He has an awkward shambling gait, a bashful manner, and talks with a dragging drawl. He grins perpetually. His eyes are large, his face lean and pimply. He has on rough shoes, patched overalls, a faded hickory shirt, and a frayed straw hat. Under his left arm he carries an old violin and a bow without strings.*]

BILL [*cordially*]. Howd'y', Mooney.

MOONEY. Howd'y'.

BILL. Come and have a chair.

MOONEY [*examining* BILL'S *invention*]. How are ye gittin' along with your churnin' machine?

BILL [*continuing his work on it*]. First-rate, Mooney, first-rate! What ye doin' with that old fiddle?

MOONEY. I brung it over to git ye to fix it fer me.

BILL. Anh hanh. What's wrong with it? [*He takes the violin from* MOONEY.]

MOONEY. Hit won't stay tuned hardly at all.

BILL. Anh hanh. Sounds like the pegs is wore down. That'll be easy to fix. I'll just whittle some new pegs.—How's the bow?

MOONEY. 'Tain't no good. All the strings is come off of it. [*He hands the bow to* BILL.]

BILL. Yes, sir! She's in a bad shape, ain't she? Cain't make no music with it that way.

MOONEY. No, sir. I want you to fix it up fer me though, so I can play on it good. Pa he wants me to learn to play "Marchin' through Georgy." He says that sure is a fine tune....

BILL. It sure is. I always liked "Turkey in the Straw," too. Now let's try to fix this bow first. Ain't you got no stringin' stuff to put on it?

MOONEY. No, sir, and I ain't got no money to buy none, neither.

BILL. Well now, it's goin' to take some thinkin' to fix this bow up. Yes, sir, some right smart thinkin'! Tell you what you do, Mooney. You go in the front room and git the scissors off o' the stand-table and fetch me that piece o' rosin off the mantle. By Johnnies, we'll jist git this bow fixed up in no time!

MOONEY. Can you fix it, shore enough?

Wootten-Moulton

STILL STANDS THE HOUSE

HESTER. They've gone! They won't be back. Everything will be the same now, Father.

Wootten-Moulton

SWAPPIN' FEVER

BILL TEETERS [*launching into one of his tall tales*]. One winter evenin' when the snow was heavy on the ground ... I set out chasin' that bee.... And what do you reckon I found? ... Some bees had a hive in a hollow tree there.... And they was makin' honey off o' them flowers right in the dead o' winter!

BILL. Yes siree, quicker'n a wink.

[MOONEY *saunters into the house.* BILL *goes over to the scrap-box and begins rummaging in it. He brings out several pieces of old cloth and examines them closely, humming and singing the while.* MOONEY *returns with rosin and scissors.*]

BILL. Now you're goin' to see some fancy fixin' done, Mooney. [*He cuts a narrow strip from a piece of calico and begins to rosin it.*] Before night you'll be learnin' to play "Marchin' through Georgy." Did I ever tell you about the time that I played it at the Bolton County Fair?

MOONEY. No, sir, you shore never did.

BILL. I played a tune on six instruments at one time. A guitar with my hands [*He pantomimes playing a guitar.*], a French harp with my mouth, a cornet out o' the right side o' my nose [*Forefinger up to his nose.*], a flute out o' the left side o' my nose [*Pipe up to his nose.*], and I beat a drum with my right foot [*Tapping his right foot.*], and picked a bass fiddle with the toes o' my left foot. [*Pawing with his left foot.*] All at one time, mind ye! Thousands o' people come to watch me play!

MOONEY [*believingly*]. I bet you shore had a fine time.

BILL. Never had a better time in my life. Now let's see how this piece o' calico works. [*He draws the rosined strip across the violin strings.*]

MOONEY. Don't make much noise, does it?

BILL. Nope, cain't use that on a fiddle bow. Cut me a strip off o' that piece o' cloth over there. [BILL *continues experimenting with the calico strip while* MOONEY *cuts a strip from another piece of cloth from the box.* MOONEY, *unsuccessful with the scissors takes out his pocket-knife to cut the cloth.* BILL *notices the knife.*] Le' me see that knife, Mooney. [MOONEY *hands him the knife.* BILL *gazes at it admiringly.*] By Johnnies, a real picture knife!

MOONEY. Hit's got a picture of a purty woman in the end of it.—Hold that little glass up to your eye. [BILL *gazes through the tiny glass near the end of the knife handle.*]

BILL. By Johnnies! Whoo-e-e, ain't she purty!

MOONEY [*giggling*]. She ain't got much clothes on, neither. If Ma knowed I had that knife, I bet she'd gi' me a whuppin'!

BILL [*eagerly*]. I'll swap ye fer it.

MOONEY [*doubtfully*]. Well, I dunno, I'd kind o' like to keep it.

BILL [*his swapping blood is up*]. How about swappin' my fortune-tellin' book fer it? You could have a lot o' fun with the girls tellin' their fortunes.

MOONEY [*bashfully*]. Aw, I don't like girls.

BILL. Well, how about one of old Sal's pups? She's a mighty good 'possum dog.

MOONEY. How old are they?

BILL. About a month old. I'll go out to the stable and git one and let ye see it.

MOONEY [*unconvinced*]. All right. But I don't believe I want no 'possum dog.

BILL. You'll want one o' these pups though. [*Enthusiastically.*] They're as purty as a picture, and they're might' nigh as smart as that 'coon dog I used to have when I lived up in Bolton County.—Now there was a smart dog if they ever was one. He's the one I learnt to run all day and all night without gettin' tired. I trained him to run on the legs on one side [*He pantomimes running with his left arm and left leg.*] while he was lettin' the other side rest. [*Raising his right arm and right leg.*] That way he could run down any 'coon he got after. Wait here a minute and I'll go get one o' them pups.

MOONEY. All right.

SWAPPIN' FEVER

[BILL *hurries into the house.* MOONEY *inspects the new "contraption" closely. Presently two men appear from the right.*]

[CHARLEY LACEY *is a good example of a small-town business man who has stayed at home and prospered reasonably by shrewd management. His dark trousers, light open shirt, and his summer hat all have the appearance of having been worn a little too long to be neat. He is middle-aged, small, thin, red-faced, and as colloquial as the hills of his home country. He moves, speaks, and chews tobacco with quick, nervous movements. He even spits "ambeer" with amazing quickness.*]

[BRADY, *his companion, an older man, forms a contrast to* CHARLEY *in grooming. From his white shoes to his panama hat, he is a perfect example of the immaculately dressed, tastefully clothed city man. His suit is an expensive tan Palm Beach. His strong, glowing face radiates the poise of the business executive. He carries a brief case.*]

CHARLEY. Howd'y', Mooney.

MOONEY. Howd'y', Charley.

CHARLEY. Is Bill around the place?

MOONEY. Yeh, he's out at the stable.

CHARLEY. How about goin' and tellin' 'im we want 'im?

MOONEY. All right. [MOONEY *ambles into the house.*]

CHARLEY [*confidentially*]. Now don't forget what I told you, Brady. Take things easy, and jist josh him along.

BRADY. All right, I'll remember.

CHARLEY. And if he starts tellin' any crazy stories about somethin' he's done, act as if you believe every word he says. That's why we couldn't make a deal when we was here last week. You got sore when Bill began to spin his yarns.

BRADY [*laughing*]. Yes, that was a mistake. But I won't

make it again. [*Musing.*] Bill's a funny fellow, isn't he? Why do you suppose he won't trade with us?

CHARLEY. We jist ain't struck him right, that's why.

BRADY. Do you think he's holding out for more money?

CHARLEY. Maybe, maybe not. I've knowed Bill a long time, but I can't say I understand him yet.

BRADY. Anyhow, let's close the deal this time. If you help me put it over in a hurry, I'll give you an extra twenty dollars for your trouble.

CHARLEY. I'll sure do my best to earn it.

[BILL *and* MOONEY *enter from the house.*]

BILL. Howd'y', Charley.

CHARLEY. Howd'y', Bill. [*They shake hands.*] You remember Mr. Brady, of course.

BILL. Yeah, howd'y'.

BRADY [*with affable executive smile*]. How do you do, Mr. Teeters. [*They shake hands.*]

BILL. You gentlemen take seats and rest yourselves awhile.

BRADY. Thank you. [*They all take chairs.* BILL *takes up the violin and resumes experimenting with the cloth strip, rosining it and trying it on the violin. It does not work.*]

BRADY [*smiling*]. Of course, you know why we're here, Mr. Teeters. We are still interested in buying the mining rights to lead ore on your farm. Have you decided to take our offer of five thousand dollars?

BILL. Nope, cain't say I have. [*To* MOONEY.] Mooney, we need hair to go on this bow.—Now, let me think.... Human hair won't do, 'tain't strong enough. [*Musing.*] Animal hair, cows, horses.... [*Excitedly.*] By Johnnies, I've got it, Mooney! A horse's tail! You go out to the stable lot and ketch old Barney and cut some long hairs out o' his tail.

MOONEY. If I can ketch 'im, I'll do it. [MOONEY *ambles back into the house.*]

BRADY. Five thousand is a big price for those mining rights, Mr. Teeters. That's quite a lot of money.

BILL. Yep, reckon it is. [*Resuming work on his fanning-churning machine.*] Now speakin' o' money, I might be able to git a right smart price for this invention when I git it patented.

CHARLEY. What is it, Bill?

BILL. This here's a machine that churns and fans a person all at the same time. When you press this pedal down with your foot, it makes the fan go down and the churn-dasher go up. When the pedal comes up, the churn-dasher goes down and the fan comes up. With this here invention a woman can churn and keep cool on the hottest day in August.

CHARLEY. Purty smart invention, Bill. [*He winks at* BRADY.]

BRADY. Yes, yes, indeed. Very clever.—Now suppose we get down to business. Would you be interested if we raise the price to fifty-five hundred, Mr. Teeters?

CHARLEY. You sure ought to take it, Bill. Why, that's four times as much as your whole farm's worth. Your land won't raise more'n ten bushel o' wheat to the acre.

BILL. That's right, 'tain't near as fertile as that two-thousand-acre farm I had when I was farmin' up in Bolton County. The clover growed so high on that place that I had to stand on a fence post to find the cows in it! [*He stands on a chair and pretends to look for the cows.*] And them cows didn't give a drop o' milk while they was pasturin' in it. No sir, nairy a drop! They didn't give nothin' but pure cream! Twelve gallons apiece ever' day! [*He holds his hat high in a gesture of exaltation.*] And wheat—I got rich off o' the wheat that that farm raised! One year I had a whoppin' big wheat crop. The day before the thrashin' a big wind storm come up and blowed hard over that wheat field. [*With wide arm gestures.*] It blowed the wheat all onto the ground, thrashed as purty as you please, and blowed the straw all over in one corner of the field! [*With a scooping motion on "one corner of the field."*] The wheat covered the ground halfway up to my knees, all over the field. [*Touching his shins with both hands.*] Gentlemen, that's the gospel truth!

CHARLEY [*laughing*]. That sure was a whoppin' big crop, Bill.

BRADY [*laughing weakly*]. Yes, indeed, very unusual. Truly remarkable.

BILL [*going over to* BRADY]. But that ain't the most interestin' crop I ever raised on that farm. No, sir, not by a long shot.—One winter evenin' when the snow was heavy on the ground, I noticed a bee flyin' out in my front yard. [*He makes a buzzing sound and darts a finger here and there as though following the bee.*] I set out chasin' that bee across my farm. He went into some woods. I follered 'im. [*He chases after the bee, in pantomime.*] And what do you reckon I found? By Johnnies, there was the purtiest patch o' sweet smellin' flowers growin' ye ever saw! [*He gets down on his knees to smell the flowers.*] Some bees had a hive in a hollow tree there. [*Pointing to the trees.*] And they was makin' honey off o' them flowers right in the dead o' winter.—Well, sir, I found what was makin' them flowers grow. They was a big hot-water spring right in the middle o' that patch. [*Points to the spring.*] Next day I fetched some garden seed down there, planted it, [*Pantomimes sowing.*] and had fresh garden stuff all winter long! Gentlemen, that's the gospel truth!

CHARLEY [*laughing*]. Never heard the beat of it, Bill.—But suppose we talk about this ore lease now. How about settlin' for fifty-five hundred?

BILL. Well, cain't say I'm hankerin' after it. No, sir, don't reckon I am.

BRADY [*resigned*]. I guess we could go six thousand, if we had to.

CHARLEY [*eagerly*]. That's a fortune, Bill—six thousand dollars! How about it?

BILL. Well, I'll think it over and let ye know some o' these days.

BRADY [*exasperated, rises*]. Good heavens, man, don't you realize we're offering you five times the value of your farm for the mining rights, and the farm will still be yours?

CHARLEY. You're the only man around here that's gettin' an offer like that, Bill. Suppose we just fill in the contract now for six thousand. Got it handy, Brady?

BRADY [*hurriedly*]. Yes, right here in my brief case. [BRADY *draws a paper from his brief case, scribbles on it and hands it to* BILL.]

BRADY. Here's the contract, Mr. Teeters. [BILL *takes the contract and they watch him breathlessly.*] Here's a pen. If you'll just sign on the bottom line, Mr. Teeters. . . . It's filled in for six thousand dollars.

BILL [*examines the fountain pen, admiring it*]. By Johnnies, ain't that purty! I ain't never writ with one o' these fountain pens before.

BRADY. Here you are, Mr. Teeters. Just try it on this. [*Pointing to the contract.*]

BILL. No, I'll jist git a piece o' paper back here to try it on. [*Taking a piece of newspaper from the box, he writes.*] It shore does write fine.

BRADY. Now, Mr. Teeters, if you'll just sign right here.

BILL. I'll think it over and let you know some o' these days.

BRADY [*exasperated, emphatically*]. Mr. Teeters, I'll make you one more offer. Will you take sixty-five hundred?

[PHRONIE *appears in the doorway.*]

PHRONIE [*casually*]. Bill, the old sow's in the garden. Ye better git 'er out 'fore she ruins things.
BILL. All right. [*To the men.*] I'll be back in a few minutes. You gentlemen just set and rest yourselves. [BILL, *apparently unconcerned, goes into the house.*]
PHRONIE [*To* CHARLEY *and* BRADY]. Howd'y'.
CHARLEY. Howd'y', Phronie.
BRADY [*smiling, though feebly*]. How do you do, Mrs. Teeters.
PHRONIE. Well, Charley, are you makin' any headway with Bill?
CHARLEY. Not a bit. Cain't you persuade him a little?
PHRONIE [*dolorously*]. I been a-tryin' to, but 'tain't no use. The other day I says to him, I says, "Bill, as pore as we are, it looks like you'd take all that money for them minin' rights." And I says to him, I says, " 'Tain't no sin to be pore, but it's terrible onhandy. You ort to take that money," I says, "and then you can be a business man," I says, "and not waste your time tryin' to invent contraptions and tellin' big windies and swappin' fer no 'count things, and I declare," I says to him, "if you ain't got the swappin' fever." Well, I guess I better go help run the old sow out. [PHRONIE *goes back into the house.*]
BRADY. Well, I'll be damned, I never saw that man's equal.
CHARLEY. Yeah, he is kind o' funny. Jist as I said though, we ain't hit him right. If we did, he'd trade in a hurry.
BRADY. Anyway, he doesn't seem interested in the money.
CHARLEY [*laughing*]. We've sure found that out. You'd think ever'body'd be tryin' to make money, but I know lots o' folks in these hills that don't seem to keer a lot fer it. It's jist as if they'd found somethin' that's a lot better. —Now there's Sherm' Applegate. He's got six kids that ought to keep any man workin' ever'day to make a livin' fer 'em, but he'll stop right in the middle of a crop and go

twenty miles to fiddle fer a dance. And if they cain't pay him nothin' it don't make any difference to him.—And there's old Aunt Ad' Newsome that doctors folks with herbs. She'll always go doctor a sick person, no matter what the weather is or how fur it is. And she never charges anything. I reckon she's got more friends than anybody else in this country.—And there's Bill Teeters here. Last summer he let his corn grow up in weeds while he was tryin' to invent a dish-washin' machine. He made one, but it broke so many dishes Phronie couldn't use it! [*They both laugh.*]

BRADY. Interesting indeed. His wife seems to be very sensible. Do you think she could handle him for us?

CHARLEY. I doubt it, judgin' from what she's jist said. [*Suddenly his face brightens.*] Say! Why didn't I think o' this before?

BRADY. What?

CHARLEY. Maybe we can git him into a swappin' deal.

BRADY [*skeptical*]. You mean we'll swap him out of those ore rights without using money?

CHARLEY [*emphatically*]. That's jist what I mean!

BRADY. What on earth would we have to trade him?

CHARLEY. Don't worry, leave that to Bill.—Will you stand behind me?

BRADY. Why, it sounds perfectly foolish.

CHARLEY. You'll admit, won't ye, that we cain't git 'im to sell?

BRADY [*doubtfully*]. Yes. . . .

CHARLEY. Then swappin's the only way out. Bill's plumb crazy about swappin'. [*Enthusiastic.*] See how it works? We'll git Bill interested in something we've got and before he knows it or what's happened, we'll make a deal with 'im.

BRADY. The company doesn't have anything he'd be interested in. Maybe you could swap him something of yours and let us settle with you for it afterwards.

CHARLEY. All right, by gollies, here's where I git rid o' that old hill-farm o' mine! The land on it's so pore that six Iowa farmers couldn't even raise hell on it, but it's good enough for swappin'. The county agent said maybe it'd raise strawberries. [*He emphasizes "maybe." and laughs. His eyes fall on the churning-fanning machine.*] Well, I'll swan! Why didn't I think o' this before? Let's try to git him to swap this old contraption in on the deal!

BRADY. That crazy thing? It isn't worth a dime.

CHARLEY. I know it. Don't ye catch on to my idea?

BRADY. Can't say I do.

CHARLEY. We'll make Bill feel like a big inventor if we try to swap for this thing along with the minin' rights. That'll make the whole deal easier.

BRADY [*laughing*]. Oh, I see! Flattery.

CHARLEY. Yeah, we'll have 'im eatin' right out of our hands.

BRADY. That's a smart idea, Charley. You go right ahead. Maybe we can make the deal for a whole lot less than the eight thousand limit the company said I could give. If we do, I'll give you an extra fifty dollars.

CHARLEY. Good! Right here's where I do some fancy swappin' and earn fifty extra!

[BILL *returns.*]

CHARLEY. Bill, we got to hurry along, I guess.

BILL. They ain't no need to rush off in sich a hurry.

CHARLEY. 'Twon't do us no good to stay, because it seems like we cain't reach any agreement with ye. But I was jist wonderin' if ye'd like to figger with us on a swappin' deal fer them minin' rights and this *invention* o' yours.

BILL. Swappin', did ye say? Shore, I'll swap the minin' rights and the invention together. Do ye think ye can sell the invention?

CHARLEY [*evasively*]. Well, we figgered we might. Cain't tell though 'til we try.

BILL. What've ye got to swap fer both of 'em together?

CHARLEY. My farm over on Zion Hill.

BILL. That old farm ain't no good. How about that thirty acres o' bottom land o' yours on Castor River?

CHARLEY. No, sir, I don't want to swap that at all. Now this Zion Hill farm ort to raise fine strawberries, Bill. Why don't ye take it and raise strawberries?

BILL. Maybe 'twould. But corn's lots easier to raise and that Castor River land o' yours is the best corn land around here.

CHARLEY. I couldn't let ye have it, Bill, because I've already rented it to Elmo Beasley for next year.

BILL. That's all right, he can farm it for me.

CHARLEY. And that ain't the worst of it, I've got sixteen head of shorthorn beef steers pasturin' on the place. If I'd let ye have it, I wouldn't have any pasture for 'em.

BILL. Don't worry about them steers. I'll take 'em off o' your hands.

CHARLEY. What do you mean?

BILL. I'll jist take them in on the deal, too.

CHARLEY. What? My beef steers too?—God, Bill, have a heart. Them's the best investment I ever made.

BILL. Now ye see, Charley, if ye let me have that bottom land, they ain't no pasture fer your steers, is they? So the thing to do is let me have the steers too.—How about it? Is it a deal? I'll bet you've got it fixed up so you'll git paid plenty fer all this anyhow. [*He glances casually at* BRADY.] Ain't that right?

CHARLEY. I reckon so. But I don't want to let that farm and them cattle go, I tell you.—Brady, ain't you got something you can swap?

BRADY [*laughing*]. I thought *you* were going to put this swapping deal over, Charley.
CHARLEY. Then, by golly, git ready to fork over a good price if I have to let them steers go.
BRADY [*much amused*]. All right. It's a deal.
CHARLEY [*reluctant*]. Well, you can have 'em, Bill.
BILL. All right, now one more thing.—How about that house o' yours in Lanceville. That one on Main Street? That'd suit me fine.
CHARLEY [*exploding*]. For Christ's sake, what are ye tryin' to do? Skin me? That's one o' the best pieces o' property in Lanceville.
BILL. Ever'body knows that. Now, Charley, supposin' ye swap me that house. It's jist like sellin' it fer cash. Then ye can buy another one.
CHARLEY. Good houses is hard to buy in Lanceville.
BILL. Lots o' people'll sell if they're offered cash.
CHARLEY. How about that Zion Hill farm instead? Why, you could make a lot raisin' strawberries on it.
BILL. 'Tain't no use to offer me that old wore-out farm. What I want is your house in Lanceville.
CHARLEY. Well, you cain't have it.
BILL. All right. Then I'll jist let somebody else have my lead ore rights.
BRADY [*urgent*]. No, no, no! Now wait just a minute, Mr. Teeters. [*Diplomatically.*] If you feel that you must have the house, I'm sure we can arrange it.—Charley, will you let him have it?
CHARLEY. What are you tryin' to do, Brady? Help him hog ever'thing I've got?
BRADY [*laughing*]. No, just helping you do some swapping.
CHARLEY. If I let that house go, Brady, you've got to give me enough to build a good, new one.
BRADY. The company will do it. Will you let it go?

CHARLEY [*reluctant*]. Reckon I'll have to, but my wife'll shore give me hell when she finds out I've sold it.

BRADY [*highly amused*]. Mr. Teeters, you've made a smart trade with our friend Charley here. Now that it's all settled, I'd like to get your signature on this mining lease. [*Offering him the paper and pen.*] Just sign on the line at the bottom.

BILL. Wait a minute, I ain't through yit.—Now, if I tend to them cattle ever' day I'll have to have me a car to go over to that farm, and some money to buy feed for 'em this fall. Your car's a right purty one, Mr. Brady, now, ain't it?

CHARLEY [*bantering* BRADY]. Yeah, it's nearly brand-new, Bill. Only twelve hundred miles on it. [BRADY *"floors"* CHARLEY *with a look.*]

BILL. Tell ye what I'll do. I'll call it a deal if ye'll swap that car in, and give me five hundred dollars and your fountain pen to boot.

CHARLEY [*jubilant*]. Now, Brady, let's see *you* do some fancy swappin'.

BRADY [*taken by surprise*]. Surely you don't need a good car like that just for feeding cattle, Mr. Teeters.

BILL. No, 'course not. But Phronie likes purty cars, so I'm kind o' wantin' to take her to town on Saturdays in it.

BRADY. Why you can't even drive a car, can you?

BILL. No, Mooney can learn me though.

BRADY [*protesting*]. Now wait a minute, Mr. Teeters. This deal hasn't gone through yet. The fact is, you want so much we can't trade anyhow. Let's see now. How much does this all amount to?—Charley, how much do you have to have?

CHARLEY. Seventy-five hundred is my lowest price.

BRADY. All right, seventy-five hundred. And nine hundred for my car—that makes eighty-four hundred. Five hundred more makes eighty-nine hundred. Good Lord! Nearly nine thousand dollars! Mr. Teeters, that's just too much!

BILL [*puffing his pipe*]. Well, bein' as you're so interested, I thought I'd give ye the first chance. They was a feller here yesterday that seemed awful anxious to buy that ore. Offered a good price fer it, too.

BRADY [*with renewed interest*]. What was his name?

BILL [*thoughtful*]. Le' me see.... Allgood, I think.

BRADY. Was he from the Superior Mining Company?

BILL. Yeah, that's right.

BRADY. Has he bought any more rights around here?

BILL. Yeah, over on Henry Bird's place.

BRADY. Then that settles it. If the Superior thinks it can beat us, it's got another guess coming.—Mr. Teeters, the car and the five hundred dollars are yours.

BILL. How about the fountain pen?

BRADY. Pardon me, I forgot. The fountain pen, of course. [CHARLEY *bursts out laughing.* BRADY *squelches him with a look.*] Now will you please sign the agreement, Mr. Teeters? [*Offering him the contract and the pen.*]

BILL. These here big words git me mixed up.—Tell ye what we'll do. I'll come into Lanceville Saturday mornin' about nine. You meet me at Lawyer Nolan's office with the deeds and sale papers and the money and we'll have him fix it up.—I'll jist keep this here fountain pen now.

BRADY. All right, Mr. Teeters. We'll be there. [BRADY *shakes hands with* BILL.] It's been a great pleasure to deal with you. [CHARLEY, *behind* BRADY, *lets out a laugh.* BRADY *frowns at him, and turns to* BILL.] I'll see you Saturday. [*He starts off right as* MOONEY *appears in the doorway with some horse hairs.*]

CHARLEY. Say, Bill, how about swappin' ye out o' them beef steers?

BILL. Ain't interested, Charley.
BRADY [*bantering*]. Come on, come on, Charley, while you've got your pants on.
CHARLEY [*as he and* BRADY *start off*]. All right, but anyhow, I didn't have to swap a fountain pen to git a lead mine. [*Laughing loudly as he and* BRADY *leave right.*]
BILL [*his eyes shining*]. Ain't that purty, Mooney? Look at that there gold band, and that there gold holder, and that there gold point! By Johnnies, I wouldn't take a purty fer this. Jist watch how it writes. [*He goes to the scrap-box, gets a piece of newspaper and scribbles on it as* MOONEY *watches fascinated.*]
MOONEY. Le' me write some. [BILL *hands him the pen; he writes with it.*]
BILL. Don't it write dead easy?
MOONEY. Shore does. Wisht I had me a fountain pen. [*And now* BILL *is ready for a swappin' deal.*]
BILL. Ye can have this'n if ye want it.
MOONEY [*incredulous*]. Shore 'nough? Do ye mean it?
BILL. Yes, sir! Why, I'll even swap it fer that old picture-knife o' yours.
MOONEY. All right, I'll swap. [MOONEY *takes the knife from his pocket and passes it to* BILL. BILL *holds it up and gazes at the lady-picture, fascinated!*]
BILL. Whoo-e-ee! [*Catching himself.*] Yes, sir, Mooney, you've made a good swap. [BILL *has what his heart desires. Putting the knife in his pocket, he now takes the horse hairs from* MOONEY *and separates out a few of them.*]
BILL. Here, you hold one end o' this while I put on some rosin. [MOONEY *obeys.* BILL *rosins the horse hair.*]
MOONEY. Old Barney was awful hard to ketch. He wouldn't go in the stable hardly at all.
BILL. Barney's a purty good horse, but he ain't as good as

airy one o' that team I used to have in Bolton County. Now there was a *real* pullin' team.

MOONEY. How much could they pull?

BILL [*astonished at such a question*]. How much could they pull? Once I hitched 'em onto a railroad engine that had got off o' the track and they got skeered and run away with it, and tore it all to pieces! Yes, sir! That's the gospel truth. [BILL *draws the rosined hairs across the strings. They make a slight sound.*]

BILL [*highly pleased*]. Listen to that, Mooney! Ain't that fine? Now all I've got to do is fasten the hairs onto this bow.—That'll take take an hour.—Then I'll have to work about three hours whittlin' out some new pegs. Yes, sir, about a four-hour job. [*He looks slyly at* MOONEY.] Guess I'll have to charge ye about two dollars, Mooney.

MOONEY. I ain't got no money, and Pa won't gi' me none to git it fixed.

BILL. Ye want to learn to play "Marchin' through Georgy," don't ye?

MOONEY. I shore do.

BILL [*enthusiastically*]. Jist think, Mooney, how proud yer pa'd be if ye could play that tune fer 'im. Then ye could play fer company, and take this fiddle to dances and play fer 'em.—Think of it! People jiggin' away, happy as mockin'-birds in June, dancin' to your music! Won't that be fine?

MOONEY. Yes, sir, it shore would! Couldn't I give ye somethin' to fix my fiddle then, so's I could play?—I could bring ye some dried beans.

BILL. Nope, we got plenty o' beans.—Tell ye what I'll do, Mooney. The work's worth more'n that fountain pen, but I'll take it back and we'll call it square.

MOONEY. All right. [*He hands back the pen.* PHRONIE *returns.*]

PHRONIE. Bill, did ye make that trade?
BILL. Shore did.
PHRONIE. What did ye git?
BILL. The purtiest knife in the country. [*He takes it out, his eyes shining.*] A genuine picture knife, Phronie!
PHRONIE. What else did ye git?
BILL. A farm, a house, some beef steers, a car, and five hundred dollars! And Phronie, do ye know what I'm goin' to do? I'm goin' to git ye a new hat with a bird on it.—No, I'm goin' to git ye *two* new hats with birds on 'em!
PHRONIE [*looking at him skeptically*]. Bill, are you sick?
BILL. Nope, never felt better in my life. Why?
PHRONIE. No man in his right mind ever promised his wife *two* hats.
BILL. Aw pshaw, I jist feel good 'cause I got this purty knife here. [*He looks through the glass again.*] Gentlemen, ain't she purty!
PHRONIE. Here, le' me see that knife. [*She takes the knife from* BILL *and examines it, then peers through the glass in the handle. A look of wonder comes over her face. She throws the knife into* BILL's *lap.* MOONEY *giggles.*] They hain't no fool like an *old* fool! [PHRONIE, *in a huff, goes into the house.* BILL *picks up the knife and gazes through the glass.*]
BILL [*musing*]. They hain't no fool like an old fool. [*To* MOONEY.] Mooney, le' me give you some good advice. Don't never grow up to be a smart man. [*He gazes through the glass, his eyes shining, and* MOONEY *grins happily as*

THE CURTAIN FALLS

OHIO

HIS BOON COMPANIONS
A SMALL-TOWN TEMPERANCE COMEDY

BY LYNN GAULT

OF NORTH JACKSON, OHIO

Written in the playwriting course at the University of North Carolina and originally produced by The Carolina Playmakers at Chapel Hill on February 2, 1938.

THE CHARACTERS

GERTRUDE .... Darice Parker
ELLA .... Gwendolyn Pharis
ISA WITHERSPOON .... Mrs. A. R. Wilson
MAECENA .... Betty Smith
HARVEY WITHERSPOON .... Fred Koch, Jr.

SCENE: *The dining-room of* HARVEY WITHERSPOON'S *home in a small Ohio village.*

TIME: *Some years ago. Early evening.*

Copyright, 1938, by The Carolina Playmakers, Inc.
All rights reserved.

A SMALL-TOWN TEMPERANCE COMEDY

SOME people think of the rolling farmlands and the little towns of our Middle Western states as drab and uneventful. But this is not true. Beneath the casual surface of the farm and the small town, strange and dramatic happenings exist for him who can find them in the lives of the common people. Tragedy and comedy, heroism and absurdity. Edgar Lee Masters found it so and recorded it in the haunting poetry of his *Spoon River Anthology*.

Lynn Gault, the young playwright of *His Boon Companions*, recalls for us an amusing incident of his childhood in his home town of North Jackson, Ohio. When only eight years of age, he was taken by his mother to a social gathering at a neighbor's home. The purpose of the party was the making of a dress form for the president of the local Temperance Society. There Mr. Gault was indelibly impressed with the process of building up a dress form on the Lady President. She stood in the middle of the room, with arms upraised in a kind of Roman salute, wearing a short-sleeved undershirt. This undershirt served as a foundation for successive layers of sticky brown tape stuck on to form a kind of papier-mâché, until the dress form was thick enough to stand alone when the lady was removed!

It occurred to the playwright that the militant Lady President of the Temperance Society might cut a funny figure parading down the street in such an armor. More absurd still would this ardent advocate of prohibition be, should she become a trifle intoxicated. The playwright insists that he would not poke fun at the good work of temperance societies, but that he is merely suggesting the extreme to which some people go in the pursuit of a worthy cause. Only innocuous amusement is intended.

The village barber of a neighboring town, a quiet, unoffending person who was thought to partake of his hair tonic as a beverage, seemed to the author a fitting husband for the militant, dress-form lady. Of the other characters in the play he says: "They are composites of neighbors, who, I hope, will not mind too much should they ever recognize a little bit of themselves in *His Boon Companions*.

HIS BOON COMPANIONS

The furniture in the dining-room of HARVEY WITHER-SPOON'S *home is early Grand Rapids, serviceable if not beautiful. The wallpaper is striped vertically with large bouquets of unidentified flowers between the stripes. The pictures on the wall are strictly dining-room subjects. One is the plentiful-year-of-fruit variety—peaches, pears, apples, grapes, oranges, a pineapple or two, and several kinds of melons conveniently split open. Another is of the fish-bowl type.*

To the left, at the rear of the scene, a door opens onto the front porch. The other doors—one, down right, leading to the kitchen and another, up left, to the rest of the house —have bright bead portières hanging in them.

The dining-room table has been pushed from its usual place in the center of the room under the acetylene hanging lamp of red-and-green mottled glass. At the right is a reed organ with a horsehair-covered stool. In the left corner, beside the buffet is a pile of placards which have been prepared for the Ladies Anti-Liquor League parade.

[*As the curtain rises* ISA (*pronounced with a long "i"*) WITHERSPOON *is discovered standing in the middle of the room with her arms raised in a kind of Roman salute. She is having a dress form made, and the process is this: The subject wears a short-sleeved cotton undershirt which serves as a foundation for successive layers of brown paper tape, which is stuck on until the dress form is thick enough to stand alone when the lady is taken out.* ISA *is only partly covered with the tape.* ELLA *and* GERTRUDE *are working on her.* MAECENA *is not helping with the dress form but is an interested spectator.* ISA *is a large woman and takes great pride in her presidency of the Ladies Anti-Liquor League.* ELLA *is small and round and housewifely.* GERTRUDE *has been "waiting" for forty-two years, and when one waits that long one does not continue to bloom. She has taken a minute out from the work to look up something in the pamphlet of directions and is leaning over the table with her back to the audience.*]

GERTRUDE [*reading*].... "and then continuing diagonally across the bust...." That's right. [*To* ELLA.] Whatever made you think we was going wrong? That's the way we made your dress form.

ELLA. I don't know. It just seemed like going the other way would make the bust stronger.

ISA. My land, the bust don't need to be no stronger'n any other place, does it?

GERTRUDE [*still looking at the pamphlet*]. I wouldn't know why.

ISA. You're sure it says to make it over a corset?

GERTRUDE. Of course, it does. What's a dress form for? You aren't going to make any dresses on it you intend wearing without no corsets, are you?

ISA. No, but it seems awfully tight through here. Don't make it so's I can't breathe.

MAECENA. If a body was to faint making one of them dress forms, it'd be as bad getting them out as the time my nephew got caught in that sewer pipe. They had to cut him out with a blow torch.

ELLA. Good night, she ain't going to faint...are you, Isy?

ISA. No, I don't think so. [GERTRUDE *laughs.*] What are you laughing at?

GERTRUDE. You know, Isy, you look like Jeanne d'Arc rigged out in all her armor.

ISA. Who?

GERTRUDE. Joan of Arc. She's that French woman who wore armor and fought with the men. Don't you remember? I used to recite a piece about her leading the men into battle.

ISA. Oh, yes. I suppose it does sort of look like armor, doesn't it? [*There is a sound from the kitchen.*] Is that you, Harvey?

HARVEY [*from without*]. Yes, Isy.

ISA. Well, what are you doing?

HARVEY. Why...I was jest going down to the shop for a minute.

[HARVEY *enters. He is a meek little man with a thin crop of nondescript-colored hair, a gentle person if there ever was one.*]

ISA. You ain't going to work to-night, Harvey?

HARVEY. No, Isy. [*He sees* MAECENA *and smiles at her in marked contrast to his meek disinterest in the other ladies.*] Good evening, Maecena.

ISA [*horrified*]. Miss Robinson, you mean!

HARVEY. Yes, Isy. I hope you're not having any more dizzy spells to-day, Maece—I mean, Miss Robinson.

MAECENA. My heart's a little better, thank you, Harvey.

HARVEY. If it ever bothers you again, come right in the shop if you're nearby and rest up.

GERTRUDE [*pointedly*]. Seems like Maecena and Harvey get along right well. [*Sniffs.*] Kindred spirits, I guess.

ISA. Humph!

HARVEY. I guess I better go. [*He starts to leave.*]

ISA. What you going down to that shop this time of night for?

HARVEY. Something I forgot....

Isa. Well, don't go nowhere else. And get yourself right back here. [Harvey *leaves the room, giving* Maecena *a significant look.* Isa, Gertrude *and* Ella *look questioningly at* Maecena, *who smiles naïvely.*] I've been married to Harvey for twenty-five years and he never smiled at *me* the way he did at Maecena when he came in.

Gertrude. Like he and Maecena had something between them.

Ella. Yes! Like they was boon companions!

Gertrude [*suspiciously*]. What about that dizzy spell of yours, Maecena?

Isa. What were you doing in the barbershop?

Maecena. I felt faint, and Harvey invited me in to rest—and we talked....

Isa. For pity's sakes, what could anybody talk to Harvey about—except liquor?

Maecena. Well, that's what we were talking about—in a way. [*The ladies look aghast.*]

Isa. What!!

Maecena. Yes! Harvey said you women in the Ladies Anti-Liquor League was making a mountain out of a molehill.

Isa. Well, of all the—I hope you gave him what for.

Maecena [*blandly*]. No, I sort of agreed with him.

Gertrude. Why, Miss Maecena Robinson, you're—you're a traitor to your sex!

Maecena. Why? I'm not a member of the L.A.L.L. Harvey said he wished you ladies would get what's coming to you. He was feeling right bad over it. I told him you're no better'n anybody else. I said if you once tasted liquor you'd lap it up like buttermilk. In ten minutes you'd all be lit like church steeples!

Isa. Why, the idea!

Ella [*shocked*]. Tch, tch, tch!

GERTRUDE. For shame!

ELLA. Some of us working our fingers to the bone in the cause and...

ISA. I guess you can see what I have to put up with. I'm going to have Harvey on hand for our Anti-Liquor League parade to-night if I have to hog-tie him. The Lord knows I've got a thorn in my flesh...and being president of the League besides. I do declare, sometimes I think it's just more than I can bear. Harvey's come home two or three nights this week when I could smell it on his breath. He usually chews Sen-Sen, but I can tell. Oh, not bad.... He ain't drunk so's he can't walk straight, but I know he's been drinking.

ELLA. Where does he get it?

GERTRUDE. That shouldn't be hard. He's in that barbershop all day.

ISA. I don't know as I should air my troubles like this, but, girls, sometimes I feel like I just have to talk it over with somebody. [*She wiggles a shoulder.*] Here, that last piece of tape is stuck on me.

ELLA. You'll have to hold that arm out a little more.

ISA. I don't know for sure, but I suspect he drinks that hair tonic. I've looked around when I've been in the shop and the bottles are always empty. [*The girls shake their heads sadly.*] As I said, I don't know for sure, but whenever he forgets the Sen-Sen, it smells just like the stuff he puts on his hair.

GERTRUDE. I can't understand menfolks...I really don't.

MAECENA. That might be the reason you never got one.

GERTRUDE. Well! If it weren't for some of us [*She looks pointedly at* MAECENA.] I'd like to ask you where the morals of this town would be. Where would the Anti-Liquor League be? I'd like to ask you?

MAECENA. You needn't look at me like that. I got no menfolks to keep out of the gutter, and I ain't likely to need no pledge myself. Although I do think a drop of spirits now and then wouldn't hurt nobody.

ELLA. Why, Miss Robinson!

GERTRUDE. I'm not surprised.

MAECENA. I didn't say as how I was sticking up for drink, but I mean if some of you Anti-Liquor Leaguers that get so he't' up on the subject would get down to earth and do something about it, instead of reading papers in your meetings on the evils of drink and singing songs— why, it's just like Harvey said yesterday, you need more of a lesson than them you're trying to reform.

GERTRUDE. You don't seem to understand. We have the curse of liquor to lift and fallen men to save.

ISA. That's what hurts me so... being president and all... and a fallen man in my own home!

MAECENA. Now, Isy, you know Harvey ain't no drunkard. He's a good husband to you. Just because he takes a little snifter once in a while—

ISA. Any man that touches a drop of the hateful poison *is* a drunkard!

ELLA. You'd think with us spending so much time for the League... like putting on this parade to-night... and working so hard in the cause... why, the last time I came home from that meeting at Miss Carson's, Henry was... well, I don't know.... Seems like the men is all linked up to do just what we're trying to keep them from doing.

MAECENA. Maybe that's why. Maybe if you was to let up on them a little—

GERTRUDE. Like Columbus, we won't give in an inch. The ship of the Ladies Anti-Liquor League must sail on!

ISA. I don't know what they see in it.

GERTRUDE. It's unbelievable what men will do.

MAECENA. Was any of you girls ever ... well, I mean, did you ever taste any of it?
ELLA. Why, I should say not!
GERTRUDE. "Lips that touch liquor...."
MAECENA. Maybe if you was to try it once.... You can't lick the enemy 'til you know where he's hiding.
GERTRUDE. Why, do you know what one little teensy drop of alcohol would do if you was to put it in your eye?
MAECENA. Yes, corn flakes are all right in their place, but put some of them in your eye and it wouldn't feel so good either.
ISA. I wouldn't touch a drop.
GERTRUDE. You couldn't *force* me.
ELLA. I don't know what Reverend Stumpfeug would say if he was to hear you going on like this.
MAECENA. Just the same if you was to have a little drop of something around the house, say a jug of dandelion wine or something, maybe a man could be sort of weaned away from liquor.
ELLA. Why, Miss Maecena, you don't seem to realize what we stand for— That would be just the same thing as—
GERTRUDE. Yes, the very same thing.
ISA. It wouldn't work ... I've ... I might as well tell you, girls. I tried that, but it's no use. Harvey wouldn't even let on it was there.
ELLA. What do you mean?
MAECENA. Dandelion wine?
ISA. Open the buffet door there, Miss Maecena, and look behind the table pad. [MAECENA *does so and pulls out an unopened bottle of gin.*]
ELLA. Well, I never!
GERTRUDE. President of the Anti-Liquor League!
ISA. Now, girls, I was desperate—don't blame me. I thought

I'd be willing to try anything [*She is almost crying.*] but it didn't work.

ELLA. Here, stop your sniffling. You can't cry in this outfit. You'll bust all the tape off.

MAECENA. This bottle ain't never been opened! And why gin? Most menfolks like whisky better.

ISA. I wanted to get something that would taste as much like the hair tonic as I could, so he could sort of taper off, and gin was what the man recommended. But Harvey never touched it. I'll empty it down the drain first thing in the morning, to take temptation out of his way.

MAECENA. If it's been hiding in there all the time I wouldn't rightly say temptation had been in his way. Seems like that would be an awful waste. [*Thoughtfully.*] My Scotch ancestry, I guess. Now, the doctor advises me to take a spoonful of sugar with a couple of drops of gin on it every once in a while, for my heart.

ELLA. Why, Miss Maecena Robinson!

GERTRUDE. I'm not surprised!

MAECENA. That makes it medicine, don't it?

GERTRUDE. I wouldn't touch the stuff if my life depended on it. [*She begins to recite from her wide repertoire.*] "No, no," the drunkard, sobered by the thought, cried out, "no child of mine, though death be near, shall touch the fatal cup."

ISA. If Doc Hyde recommends it for you—for your heart, why don't you take it along home with you . . . out of this house . . . I don't want to ever see it again.

MAECENA. Oh, I couldn't do that!

ISA. Yes, you must.

MAECENA. Well, if you're sure Harvey wouldn't mind.

ISA. Harvey! I never want him to see the stuff again! Take it.

MAECENA. Well, all right then. [*She puts it on the buffet near her large black pocket-book.*] Just as medicine, you know. It'll probably stand there in my cupboard for the next twenty years.

GERTRUDE. I doubt that!

ISA. Ain't you nearly done back there?

ELLA. Land no, we only started up the back. Can't you feel it sticking out?

ISA. I can't feel nothing through this corset. We've got to get it finished and off before time to start for the parade.

MAECENA. Are you girls going to march?

GERTRUDE. I should say so. There wouldn't be much of a parade if *we* weren't there to lead it.

ELLA. And we're all going to carry banners. Isy, I'll bet you forgot to—

ISY. No, I didn't. They're standing in the corner. [*She indicates the placards by the buffet.*]

GERTRUDE. It's nice we're starting from here. We can each pick out the one with the motto we like best.

MAECENA. What happens after the parade?

ISA. Then we all end up at the Town Hall and have some speeches and readings and songs.

ELLA. Miss Gertrude here is going to favor us with a recitation. It just wouldn't be a program without her.

ISA. Don't you think you need to practise it over once more?

GERTRUDE. Oh, no ... you'll all hear it later to-night.

MAECENA. Well, I won't and I'd like real well to hear it.

ELLA. Go ahead, Gertrude. There's lots of time yet.

GERTRUDE [*coyly*]. If you insist ...

ELLA. Here, let's move out of the way so she can have plenty of room.

[GERTRUDE *carefully places her feet in the elocutionary position—the heel of one foot to the instep of the other. Then she hooks her little fingers together with her elbows extended to the side, and announces the title.*]

GERTRUDE. "The Dying Drunkard!" [*A pause to let this soak in.*]

"Stretched on a heap of straw—his bed! [*A gesture indicating something quite distasteful at her feet on the floor.*]
The dying drunkard lies;
His joyless wife supports his head [*She supports his head.*]
And to console him tries. [*Caresses his head absently.*]
His weeping children's love would ease [*She pulls a handkerchief from her bosom.*]
His spirit, but in vain—
Their ill-paid love destroys his peace;
He'll never smile again." [*With an extremely woeful expression cast heavenward.*]

Oh, dear, me! . . . [*Her lines have left her.*]

ISA. What's the matter?

GERTRUDE. Oh, yes. . . .

"His boon companions—where are they— [*Looking hopelessly about her.*]
Who shared his heart and bowl? [*With a rising inflection.*]
They come not nigh, to charm away
The horrors of his soul. [*She indicates them.*]
What have gay friends to do with those [*Arms extended to the side and fluttering like a sea-gull.*]
Who press the couch of pain? [*She presses the couch of pain.*]
And he is racked with mortal throes; [*She registers the mortal throes.*]
He'll never speak again." [*With a dramatic silence at the end.*]

ELLA [*wiping her eyes*]. Beautiful! Just beautiful!

MAECENA. You've got an easy tongue, Gertrude. I guess that runs in your family.

Isa. You know, I used to be quite an elocutionist when I was a girl. But I haven't kept it up like Gertrude has. My favorite number was "Mrs. Jarley's Wax Works." I don't suppose I could do a line of it now, though. [*She is about to try.*]

Ella. Here, we'll have to get on or we'll never get you out of this "suit of armor," as Gertrude called it, in time for the parade. [*They begin to work again.*] I could sit and listen to you speak that piece all night, Gertrude. You do it so expressive. Girls, don't you think she ought to do it professionally? Go around and give readings like that Miss Page that come out here from Youngstown last year. [Gertrude *beams.*]

Isa. I certainly wouldn't want her taking after that woman though. Do you know what? I heard—that is, Mrs. Stroup told Effie and Effie told me, that Henry Stroup being janitor of the Town Hall, had to go back of the platform after her performance to see the windows was shut; and do you know what she was doing?

Gertrude. What? [*Ready, herself, to hear the worst.*]

Isa. She was smoking a Sweet Caporal cigarette—just as brazen a hussy as ever you see!

Ella. Ain't that disgusting? Well, she certainly could recite, but I wouldn't sit there and listen to her again, knowing that. Gertrude's a lot better than she was, anyway.

Isa. I wish Harvey could hear you speak some of them pieces. Maybe I could get him to sign the pledge after hearing something like that. He's been so obstinate, in spite of all my pleadings.

Ella. He must have a heart of stone.

Isa. I made him listen to me read a whole long chapter out of *Liquor, the Curse of Mankind* only last Sunday night, but he wouldn't sign. I've 'most give up. I guess the only way to get folks like him is just after they've been—well, when they're still feeling real bad.

MAECENA. If a man's built thirsty, he'll stay thirsty.

ISA. Land-a-mercy, I 'most forgot; I got some cookies ready to serve to you girls. I was going to make a little fruit punch to go along with them—I thought it would be sort of nice before we went to the parade. I got the stuff all ready but I didn't get the punch mixed up.

ELLA. You shouldn't ought to go to all that trouble.

ISA. Why, it ain't no trouble at all. I'll have to wait 'til I get out of this rig now, though, I guess.

MAECENA. No, let me fix it. I ain't helping none in here. You just tell me where things is, Isy.

ISA. Well, if you're sure you don't mind. The cookies is on the shelf beside the cupboard. They've got a napkin on them. [MAECENA *goes into the kitchen.*] The punch—you'll find a glass pitcher on the first shelf. The fruit juice is on the table. Sugar in the crock. If you can't find anything, just holler.

ELLA. Hold still! When you stand on one foot that way you throw your hips out of shape.

ISA. I wonder if Arabella got the torches.

GERTRUDE. I saw Charley lugging them around this afternoon. He had a great big armful.

ISA. I'm glad there'll be plenty of light. It don't do no good to parade if people can't see anything.

GERTRUDE. They'll see plenty to-night, all right.

ISA. Do you think this is heavy enough over the shoulders yet? I can move it when I wiggle them. Seems like it would need to be still there.

ELLA. Hold still and let me see.

ISA [*calling out to* MAECENA]. You'll want some cold water. Just pump it 'til it gets good and cold.

ELLA. No, I don't believe it is thick enough, quite.

GERTRUDE. You'll need another layer or two.
ISA [*There is the sound of pumping in the kitchen*]. Can you find everything all right, Maecena?
MAECENA [*from the kitchen*]. Oh, yes, indeedy.
ISA. My, this is awful making your guests do the work. I plumb forgot all about that punch.—Is it going to take much longer with this dress form? My arm is getting kind of tired out.
ELLA. Not much longer.
GERTRUDE. I better cut out some more tape, don't you think?
ELLA [*she holds a little piece up speculatively*]. Yes, it'll take quite a bit more over these hips.
MAECENA [*comes in with a black enameled tray on which are some tall glasses and a plate of cookies, and a pitcher of purple punch.*] I couldn't help nibbling at these cookies. They certainly are good. You'll have to give me the recipe.
ISA. I'll be glad to. Harvey likes them. Could you find the glasses?
MAECENA. Yes, no trouble at all. [*She places the tray on the buffet.*] Shall I pour it out?
ISA. Go right ahead. It's pretty hot in here and I'm dry as a desert.
[MAECENA *notices the gin bottle. She looks around to make certain they are not looking and quickly pours in a very liberal quantity of the gin, stirring and singing to muffle the sound of the pouring.*]
MAECENA. "Row, row, row your boat gently down the stream,
Merrily, merrily, merrily—" [*She tastes the punch and expresses her pleasurable surprise.*] If I do say so myself, I think you girls will certainly like this punch! [*She begins to pour it out.*]

Isa. I *am* thirsty, being shut up in this thing.

Ella [*pushing in on the abdomen*]. It's got too much give in here.

Gertrude [*at the back*]. You certainly haven't got any back here.

[Maecena *is ready to pass the punch.*]

Ella [*as she gets her glass*]. Henry always makes fun of our temperance punch, but I do say there's nothing like a cold glass of it to refresh you. [*The rest of the girls have their glasses.* Ella *is the first to taste it.*] Mmn.... [*Pause and swallow.*]

Gertrude [*as she tastes it*]. Mmn.... [*Pause and swallow.*]

Isa. Mmn.... [*Pause and swallow.*] I wonder did you taste the fruit juices before you mixed them together?

Maecena. Yes, they was awfully nice. I don't see how you can put them up and keep them so fresh-like.

Isa. Well, I just thought.... [*Taste and swallow.*] It has a kind of strange taste—like one of them was just a mite spoilt.

Ella. It's good though.... [*They sip and pause, sip and pause. One can see the swallow traveling downward and warming as it goes.*]

Gertrude. I should say it is.... [*Sip and pause.*] I've never tasted anything quite like it.

Ella. It is *very* good. I've never tasted anything quite like it either. [*Sip and pause.*] It certainly is a lot better than the punch Miss Carson served at the last meeting. I thought I'd never tasted such a flat concoction. [*They have finished at least half a glass of the punch.*]

Isa. It *is* good, isn't it? Maecena, I believe you can make better punch than I can out of the same things. Mine never tastes like this. Harvey always makes fun of our punch, too, but I bet he'd like this. [*The glasses are ready for refilling.*]

ELLA [*humming a little tune*]. It's wonderful how it rests you. [*A silent burp.*] Sort of takes your tiredness away just to take a few minutes out for refreshments, don't it?
GERTRUDE. I'm just as rested now. I know I'm going to feel good for the temperance parade.
ISA. Oh, yes, indeedy . . . yes, indeedy!
ELLA. It's funny how much better just a little bit of punch will make you feel.
ISA. Maecena, if anybody was to ask me, I'd say you was the best punch-maker in this town. It's too bad you don't belong to the Anti-Liquor League.
ELLA. Absolutely the best!
GERTRUDE. Never tasted anything like it!
MAECENA. Well, thank you, girls. I suppose it's just a sort of knack, what you put in it and how you mix it.
ISA. Yes, indeedy! . . . You know, girls, I think we ought to give three cheers for Maecena's punch. What do you say, girls? One, two, three! [*She pulls them into a huddle and they cheer, "Rah, rah, rah!" They laugh loudly.*]
ELLA. Anybody going along the road would think we was having a basketball game or something in here. [*More laughter.*]
ISA. Well, I guess I got on my uniform to play. [*She tosses a pillow to* GERTRUDE.] It's a mite binding in the hips, though.
MAECENA. I'd say just a bit tight.
ELLA. I'm most tempted to sit down here and play the organ. I haven't touched one in—oh, I don't know how many years. . . .
ISA. Go right ahead. There's plenty of time. We can sing a while.
GERTRUDE. Oh, yes, I want to sing. [*She sings a phrase or two of "Somewhere a Voice Is Calling."*]
ISA. I'm still thirsty. Won't you girls have some more punch?

There is lots here yet. Help yourself to the cookies, too. [*They fill their glasses.*]

ELLA. A body'd think I never e't no supper at all!

ISA. It certainly is wonderful how it's revived me. I was feeling so down in the dumps a minute ago—about Harv—and him not signing the pledge, but now I think I'll have another talk with him when he comes in before the parade.

ELLA. Yes, we'll all talk with him. Maybe in a body this way he'll listen to reason. Wouldn't it be *wonderful* for him to be saved so he could parade with us to-night?

GERTRUDE [*she gets down on the floor*]. We'll all get down on our knees and pray with him.... I can feel it coming on now.

ELLA. Yes, prayer'll do a power of good, won't it, Maecena?—Here, you're sitting there with your glass empty. You'll have to keep up with us.

ISA. It's just fruit juices. Won't hurt you a bit. Come on, girls, let's sing a while before we go back to work.

GERTRUDE. Come on, Ella, the organ's yours! [*They laugh as* ELLA *seats herself none too steadily on the horsehair seat.*]

ELLA. Woops!... I remember when I was a kid I never could sit on these horsehair stools. I fell off one day and most like to broke my— [*They laugh.*]

GERTRUDE. Ain't she a caution?

ELLA. Mom let me quit practising then for a whole week 'cause I was so sore I couldn't sit on the milk-stool to milk.—Well, let's see what we've got here. [*She examines a song book.*]

ISA. Just play anything you like....

[ELLA *attempts a bit of the "Marseillaise" but it is not very successful; neither is their singing.*]

ELLA. Oh, I never could play them hunky songs. Let's see

HIS BOON COMPANIONS

what else there is. How about this? [*She plays "Onward, Christian Soldiers."*]

ISA. Why, that's our piece! [*They all join in singing the substituted words which they use at the Anti-Liquor League meetings.*]

> Onward, Temperance Soldiers, marching as to war;
> We shall best the evil—men shall drink no more.
> On our standard royal, we all bear the name,
> Ladies Anti-Liquor League, down with liquor's shame!
> Onward, Temperance Soldiers, marching as to war:
> We shall...

[ISA *has picked up a yardstick and is beating time.* GERTRUDE *is waving her glass.* MAECENA *is swaying in time to the music and looking very much amused. Suddenly* ISA *turns and sees—of all people—* HARVEY *standing in the doorway. She stops the music abruptly by slapping a hand down on* ELLA'S *back.* HARVEY *is confused by what he sees.*]

ISA. Hi, Harv, ... we was hoping you'd get home before we left for the parade, wasn't we, girls? [*They laugh as though it were immensely funny.*]

HARVEY. Why, Isy...

ISA. Harv, we've got some good news for you. Your whole life's going to be changed from now on, ain't it, girls? You won't be the black sheep any longer.

ELLA [*swings herself around on the organ stool*]. You're going to cast your sinful robe of flesh by the riverside and be—

GERTRUDE [*hic*].... born [*Hic.*] again.

[HARVEY *looks more bewildered than ever.*]

ISA. What's the matter, Harv?

GERTRUDE. He don't want to be born again.

Harvey. Why, you don't seem ... like yourself, Isy.
Isa [*to the girls*]. I don't seem like myself. [*They laugh.*]
Maecena. She's feeling a little the worse for that armor she's wearing.
Isa. Why, Maeceny, I feel fine!
Harvey. No, Isy, you don't ... you don't look quite natural. ...
Isa [*has a sudden terrible suspicion*]. Harvey Witherspoon, come here to me. [*She drags him in front of her and makes a great show of smelling his breath.*] Just as I thought! [*A sharp cry.*] He's drunk again! [*To the girls.*] What did I tell you? [*They shake their heads sadly.*]
Harvey [*very obviously sober and more confused than ever now*]. Why, Isy, I ain't touched a drop since ... er, you know I never drink.
Isa. It's bad enough to have you come home ... like this ... but to have you lie to me besides. [*She begins to cry.*] Oh, I don't know what I'll do next. [Gertrude *and* Ella *put their arms around her.*]
Maecena. That'll be a matter of considerable speculation.
Ella. There, there, Isy, men are like that.
Gertrude. I never seen one that was worth the powder to blow him to Hades.
Harvey. Why, I almost believe— [*He looks closely at them.*] If you wasn't all such ... such ...
Maecena. Tee-totalers?
Harvey. I'd be most tempted to say you've all been sucking the bottle a bit ... all three of you.
Isa. Oh! [*A loud wail.*] What did I tell you? He *is* drunk. I knew it the minute I laid eyes on him standing in that door. [*She points dramatically to the door and weaves a bit.*] So drunk he's begun to see things. [*Suddenly frightened.*] Harv, you ain't seeing no snakes yet, are you?
Maecena. Just monkeys.

ELLA. They're just as bad. Now I had an uncle once—
ISA. Are you, Harv?
HARVEY. Good lord, no.
GERTRUDE. Oh, he's getting profane in his language. [*She makes a great point of covering her ears.*]
HARVEY. I'd be most tempted to say the whole pack of you was—
GERTRUDE. Mr. Witherspoon!
ISA. Now, Harv, just contain yourself. [*Hiccup.*] If you like, we'll all pray for you. Maybe we can still save your soul from eternal torment and shame. [*A silent burp.*]
HARVEY. You've all suddenly gone crazy or you're drunk!
ISA [*trying to humor him as one would an inebriate, with a wink and a nod to the girls*]. All right, then, Harv, have it your own way. *We're* drunk and *you're* sober, aren't we, girls? [*They nod their heads, finding it very difficult to keep from laughing.*] Now, Harv, you git down here on your knees with us. Oh, lordy, I can't git down in this armor. [*She gives* HARVEY *a push.*] You all get down and I'll stand here in the middle. [*The girls get down on the floor.*] Now before we start to pray, I'm going to ask you for the last time, Harv, will you sign the pledge? Make up your mind quick. It's hard for Ella and Gertrude to stay down there on their knees.
MAECENA. Seems like it would be easier for them to stay down than to stand up.
ISA. No, they're getting old and their knees don't work like they used to. [ELLA *and* GERTRUDE *glare at* ISA.] Now, how about it, Harv, will you sign the pledge? [*They all take a good stiff drink of punch.*]
HARVEY. I won't have you praying over me.... I'll sign your old pledge.
ISA. Whee-ee-ee! He's seen the light! Girls, girls, you can get up now. The black sheep has come into the fold. [*She*

yanks him to his feet, almost upsetting herself in the process.]

ELLA. It's a joyful day... a resurrection!

GERTRUDE. You don't know how I've prayed for you! [*She kisses him loudly.*]

ISA. Here, Maeceny, give Harv a glass of the temperance punch. Now that he's a member he'll have to learn to like it.

MAECENA. Well, Isy, there isn't much left... maybe I better make some more. [*She is starting for the door with the pitcher.*]

ISA. Nonsense, there's plenty here. [*She takes the pitcher and pours* HARVEY *a generous glass.* MAECENA *tries to signal to* HARVEY *but he does not comprehend.*]

MAECENA. Harvey, you remember... the shop... yesterday... [*Just as he is about to taste the punch.*] ... you remember the mountains and the molehills? [*She is signaling him frantically. Then he begins to understand.*]

HARVEY [*as he tastes the punch*]. Is *this* what you call temperance punch?

ISA. Yes, indeedy, isn't it good? Maeceny made it. [MAECENA *winks broadly at* HARVEY.] Oh, this is a triumphant day! The thorn is taken out of my flesh! [*She sings to the tune of "All My Sins Are Taken Away."*] "All my thorns are taken away, All my thorns are taken away."

MAECENA. You're all for temperance now, ain't you, Harvey?

[HARVEY *grins.* ELLA *has seated herself at the organ.* GERTRUDE *has picked up a shawl from a chair and draped it about her, putting on a cushion for a headdress.* ISA *grabs the fringed cover from the table for a cape to her armor.*]

ISA. And me in my armor... the armor of the Ladies Anti-Liquor League! [*She waves her yardstick sword.*] Forward into battle! [*They sing "Onward, Temperance Soldiers."*

Suddenly she stops them.] Wait, wait, the hour has come. Harvey, you're going to carry a banner.

HARVEY. Carry a banner?

ISA. In the parade ... the Anti-Liquor parade. You're the black sheep washed whiter than snow. Girls, get your signs. [*They each get a placard from the corner and line up in marching formation. The placards bear such mottoes as "Liquor, the Curse of Mankind," "Alcohol No More Shall Reign," and so forth.*] Harvey!

HARVEY. Yes, Isy ... you lead and I'll bring up the rear.

ISA. Come, my armor bearers! "Onward, Temperance Soldiers, marching as to war" ... [*They go out singing, still in their regalia, including the dress form.* HARVEY *and* MAECENA *look at each other and laugh.*]

MAECENA. There's your mountain and your molehill.

[*From the porch in the midst of the singing is heard a drunken shout,* "Harvey! Harvey!"]

HARVEY. Yes, Isy.... [HARVEY *and* MAECENA *generously help themselves to the punch. From the porch are heard shouts of* "Down with Liquor" *and* "Temperance, temperance, temperance." *This sends* HARVEY *and* MAECENA *almost into spasms. They shake hands. Suddenly they remember the placards. Selecting two which bear the mottoes* "BREAD NOT BEER" *and* "LADIES ANTI-LIQUOR LEAGUE" *with great glee they tear the tops from them so* MAECENA'S *reads* "BEER" *and* HARVEY'S *reads* "LIQUOR LEAGUE."]

ISA [*calling from the porch*]. Ain't you coming, Maeceny?

MAECENA. I wouldn't miss it for anything.

[*More shouts of* "Come on, Harvey," *and* "Come on, Maeceny." HARVEY *takes the pitch from the organ and they begin to sing* "Onward, Temperance Soldiers" *as they start out, brandishing their banners with great gusto.*]

THE CURTAINS CLOSE

MASSACHUSETTS

ANCIENT HERITAGE
A DRAMA OF A NEW ENGLAND FAMILY

BY PHILIP GODDARD PARKER

OF READING, MASSACHUSETTS

Written in the playwriting course at the University of North Carolina and originally produced by The Carolina Playmakers at Chapel Hill on February 28, March 1, and 2, 1935.

THE CHARACTERS

SARAH BANCROFT.......................Jane Cover
CARRIE BANCROFT..................Mildred Howard
EDWARD KENDALL.............Philip Goddard Parker
RICHARD KENDALL...................William Wang

SCENE: *The living-room of the Kendall homestead in an old New England town.*
TIME: *The present. A morning in June.*

Copyright, 1938, by The Carolina Playmakers, Inc.
All rights reserved.

NEW ENGLAND HOMESTEAD

NEW ENGLAND! A land of reluctant spring and relentless winter. Nowhere else in America does the weather of a place so match the character of its people—reluctant tenderness and relentless integrity! Outsiders often wrongly estimate New Englanders as unemotional and cold, unsmiling and taciturn. They are not so. They are a busy people, a conscientious people. With them work and duty come before pleasure. Long winters and a grudging soil combine to make work the life of these people.

Yet there is a great beauty in the spare firmness of their ways. They are not without humor; not the loud guffawing type to be sure, but a dry, eye-crinkly kind. They are spare of words and economical of sentiment. They are kind to a fault and honest to a great degree. They have a pride—an unspoken thing—which charts their life course.

In 1640 a man came from Old England on the *Susan and Ellen*. He built a house which is standing to-day. He founded a family. To-day, two women, descendants of this man, live in that old red brick New England mansion he built three hundred years ago. They work the land in much the same fashion as it was worked three centuries ago. They are as much a part of their land and home as if they were made of the same enduring soft-colored brick. They are proud women and their pride seems like coldness to outsiders. They keep to themselves. They struggle on through the years maintaining an heritage of independence and freedom.

Often they face the temptation to admit defeat and give up the hard life which is theirs. Each difficulty is like their winter with its drifting snow and frozen isolation; each solution is summer with the kindly shade of the ancestral elm before the house and the gentle stirring of the great trees in the pine woods. Intact, they keep the blessings of the summer; unrecorded are the desperate rigors of the winter.

"My play is about these women," the author tells us; "there is a lesson in their pride. I know them well. I admire them. I admire my understated country; the spare trees against the cold sky. I accept and understand the careful ways of my people. I am a New Englander. It is hard for me to write too freely of my people, because I am of them and as reluctant to investigate them as they are to reveal themselves."

ANCIENT HERITAGE

A musty haze of three hundred years hangs over the living-room of the four-square New England house under the elms. The furniture is old and beautiful, but it looks as if it were tired after all the years of proper decorum while the tides of life have flowed passionately by it. To the right is a door leading to the kitchen. This door is always open—as if the kitchen and this room were one. In the rear wall, at the far left, is the door leading to a tiny hall, and to the rest of the house. In the center of the rear wall is a wide fireplace with built-in cupboards and two maple ladder-backed chairs on either side. Above the fireplace are two flintlocks. There are two windows in the left wall, with the small panes of the New England house of the period. The glass is old, and gives only a wavering view of the summer fields and an ancient elm tree outside.

In the center of the room is a small, square table with Queen Anne legs. It is covered with a fine old Paisley shawl, and holds a whale-oil, glass lamp now wired for electricity and a large, metal-clasped family Bible.

Down, right, is a horsehair chair of the Victorian era. In it is seated a woman—but we shall come to her later, for she can wait—as she has done so much of her life. Between the windows at the left is a flower stand with several winter plants on it, all of them a gray-green color. Below this is another chair, a splendid example of the best Chippendale period. By the right wall is a long horsehair sofa; in the corner beyond, a great grandfather's clock,

which has read ten minutes past nine for more years
than any one can remember.
And now to the woman who is seated in the chair. She has
waited all her life for something. What, even she doesn't
know. Her face shows none of this.

[*And so, we come to* SARAH BANCROFT. *She is sixty years
old, and time has not been kind to her. Although her
face is that of a woman many years younger; her body
has been fastened to a chair for ten years—a fragile shell
kept alive only by the indomitable spirit of a proud old
lady. As the curtain rises we find* SARAH *idly playing with
her soft lace handkerchief. She seems occupied with a
problem far distant from the room in which she is seated.
It is not an unpleasant picture she makes—her calm, pale
face, her soft gray dress, with its neat white collar and
cuffs, and the startling flash of a huge garnet on her
finger.*]
[*From the kitchen comes the sound of low voices. A door
is shut, and there is the sound of some one moving china.
The quiet of the scene is broken by* SARAH'S *voice.*]
SARAH. Who was it, Carrie?
[*There is no reply, but suddenly a woman enters the room
from the kitchen. It is difficult to describe such a tragedy
in a human being as this one. She is hideous, a hag utterly
unconscious of her plight. Her face is that of a worn and
dirty witch. Her hair is stringy and fastened, with no
thought of order, in a pug on her head. She wears spectacles which are bent and mended with a string at the
corner. She wears a man's coat over a dirty apron, which
in turn hides a soiled and mended skirt. On her feet are
soft slippers which swish as she scuffs about. She speaks
with a nasal, harsh voice, monotonous and unnatural. Her
movements are stiff and ungainly, and one suspects from*

the way she sweeps her forehead, as if she were wiping away sweat and dirt, that she has been long accustomed to manual labor.]
[*This is* CAROLINE BANCROFT, SARAH'S *sister. She comes to stand above the table to talk to* SARAH.]
CARRIE [*regarding her hands and then looking away to the window*]. Mr. Hubbard, the grocer. Wanted his order, and his money. We didn't have neither.
SARAH [*speaking firmly and the hands that were playing with the handkerchief now cease moving*]. I'll see him the next time he comes. You remember now, Carrie.
CARRIE [*moving away carelessly to the window*]. Yes, I remember.
SARAH. Did you see Cousin Eddie? [*A pause. Then irritably*]. You *did* go up town, didn't you?
CARRIE [*replying with petulant slowness*]. Yes, I went up town. Eddie wasn't in the bank, so I as't them to tell him you wanted to see him—if he could come down. [*She looks out the window at the left.*]
SARAH [*thinking aloud*]. I hope he *can* get down. I do want to talk with him.
CARRIE [*turning from the window as if making an important discovery; her voice is dull, sullen, perhaps*]. It needs cuttin'—the grass.
SARAH [*with alarm*]. You musn't think of it, dear. [*It appears that* CARRIE *doesn't hear.*] You mustn't, really. It's too hot.
CARRIE [*with a vague gesture and a little smile*]. Somebody's got to.
SARAH. Well, wait 'til to-morrow.
CARRIE [*pursing her mouth and shaking her head*]. Can't; there's weedin' to be done.
SARAH [*trying to change the subject*]. What time were you up town?

CARRIE [*moving to the hall door without looking back*]. 'Bout ten.

SARAH [*watching her sister*]. Then Eddie ought to be here pretty soon—if he does come this morning. [CARRIE *starts to leave the room.*] Carrie, Carrie! Where are you going?

CARRIE [*from the door*]. Out. The grass. [*Waving her hand.*]

SARAH. I know, but— [*Then with determination.*] Carrie, come in here. I want to talk with you. [CARRIE *returns with reluctance and stands left of the table. She turns half away from* SARAH.]

SARAH. Carrie, you know why I want to see Eddie?

CARRIE [*answering as if the question were perfectly natural*]. The note's comin' due, and we've got no way of meetin' it. And the dividends don't come in like they did.

SARAH. That's part of it, but Eddie is about the only one we have left. The rest can't do anything for us.

CARRIE [*regards her coat, then looks up*]. Or won't.

SARAH. Eddie is in the bank, he may know how to help us. Anyway, he'll be able to tell us what to do about the note.

CARRIE [*dropping her hands from her coat*]. If he can't tell us, then we lose the house. [*Turning and facing the window.*]

SARAH. Hush, dear! Let's not think about things like that.

CARRIE [*standing with her hands behind her back and looking out the window*]. Can't help it if that's what you've got to think about.

SARAH [*eyeing the handkerchief in her hand*]. There isn't much left, Carrie. Just the house and the land.

CARRIE [*she straightens, but still does not turn*]. And the woods.

SARAH [*faintly*]. And the woods. [*Sighs.*] Pray God, we don't need to think about them.

CARRIE [*sniffs*]. We've got to.

SARAH. Well, not now. [*She looks around the room.*] The house, oh dear.

CARRIE [*turning her head to* SARAH]. The historical society has been after it.

SARAH [*lifting the ringed hand sharply*]. Absurd.

CARRIE [*a pause, then looking out the window again*]. That field out there would make nice house lots.

SARAH. Carrie Bancroft, stop talking that way! [*At first a little deprecating, then sharply.*] Our land cut up to make land for horrid little two-by-fours!

CARRIE. Then we'll have to sell the Kendall woods.

SARAH. Never! [*Holding out her right arm.*] I'd feel as if I were selling my right arm.

CARRIE [*turns around quickly*]. Well, I wouldn't.

SARAH. Obviously. But you forget what those trees mean to us.

CARRIE [*speaking very quickly*]. No, I don't, but I'm thinkin' . . . they might mean a whole lot more.

SARAH. It would be sacrilegious. Those pines have been in this family for three hundred years. And the new part was set down by Sam Kendall in 1785.

CARRIE [*reasonably*]. They're old enough then to make good timber—bring in money.

SARAH [*with finality*]. We're not going to be the ones to cut them down.

[CARRIE *fingers a button on her coat, and her hand drops.*]

CARRIE [*saying one thing, but thinking another, perhaps that* SARAH *tires her*]. We need money.

SARAH. Yes, but not that bad. I'd feel as if I'd be robbing the grave.

CARRIE [*turning away again, without a smile*]. Huh!

SARAH [*continuing*]. It would be just like tearing down an old ancestral monument.

CARRIE [*dryly, nodding her head*]. I can think of some I'd just as soon tear down.

SARAH. Haven't you a spark of pride in you?

CARRIE. 'Course, I got some, [*Then puzzled.*] but it's not over things you can *see*.

SARAK [*abruptly*]. Oh, go along.

[CARRIE *turns and moves to the door, right. She appears to be thinking of something else, and she turns twice to look at* SARAH *as if she were not too sure of her sister.*]

SARAH. Where are you going?

CARRIE. The grass.

[SARAH *nods and turns away as* CARRIE, *without a further glance, leaves the room. There is a sound of an automobile outside.* SARAH *takes up a letter from the table and begins reading it.* CARRIE *reappears at the door.*]

CARRIE. Here comes Eddie. Shall I tell him to come right in?

SARAH. What? [*Putting down the letter, and collecting herself.*] Yes—yes, of course; tell him to come in.

[CARRIE *goes out. Voices are heard offstage. Then a tall, well-dressed man appears. He is the spare, restrained New Englander, not uncommon in an old and honored community. He is* EDWARD KENDALL, *the cousin of* SARAH *and* CARRIE. KENDALL *is in no wise a handsome man, but his large mouth and deep, kind eyes indicate understanding and sympathy. He is the sort of man who will do for you himself, but on no condition will he, if he is in a position of trust or influence, assist you more than the regulations of that trust permit. He is a man who will grant no favor even to those nearest to him, if they do not deserve such consideration. But he will, without any fuss or feathers, go a long way to help and lend a hand.* KENDALL *comes down to shake* SARAH'S *hand, then sits on the sofa.*]

KENDALL. I brought Dick with me, Sarah.
[SARAH *turns to look at the young man who enters the room. He is a less mature* EDWARD KENDALL, *and he is obviously* KENDALL'S *son. This* KENDALL *is called* DICK, *and he is not different from most young fellows home for the summer vacation.* DICK *comes down to shake hands with* SARAH *as his father did.*]
DICK. It's nice to see you, Cousin Sarah. I'm afraid I don't get down this way very often.
[CARRIE *has followed* DICK *in at the door.*]
CARRIE [*her voice curiously flat, and speaking as if her mind were a thousand miles elsewhere*]. It's three years ago this fall, you were here last, Richard Kendall, and then you only stayed a minute.
DICK. Is it as long as that? I'd no idea.
SARAH. I know. [*Kindly.*] College does keep a boy pretty busy. Do you like where you are?
DICK. Very much, thanks.
CARRIE [*telling* DICK *something in a voice that would suggest that he doesn't know it*]. You'll be a senior when you go back.
DICK. Why, yes, I will. How did you remember? [*He is really surprised at old* CARRIE'S *remembering.*]
CARRIE [*with lack of any further interest in this subject*]. Saw it in the paper.
[EDWARD KENDALL, *thinking to find out what it is* SARAH *wants to see him about, shifts the conversation to the business of the morning.*]
EDWARD. They said at the bank that you left a message for me. Is it anything important, Sarah?
[SARAH *is evidently dreading this moment and hesitates. She shakes her head, and with a smile inquires.*]
SARAH. How's Edith?
DICK. Mother's fine, thanks.

SARAH. And how about you, Ed?

EDWARD. I haven't felt so well for years. [*Smiling.*] You're looking well, Sarah.

SARAH. I *am* well, Ed. Just once in a while now my back lets me know it wants favoring.

CARRIE [*quickly*]. Your back kept you in bed all last week. [*A pause.*] I had to call the doctor. [*She regards the doorway.*]

EDWARD [*quickly*]. We all do at times. Even Dick, here, isn't above playing sick now and then. Are you, young fellow?

DICK [*with a smile*]. 'Fraid not, Dad. But you seem to let me get away with it. [*With a little fun at the expense of his father.*] Why, Cousin Sarah, he worries worse than Mom does, and that's saying a lot.

EDWARD. The place is looking lovely, Sarah.

SARAH. We do try to keep it up, but there are so many things to do that sometimes I'm afraid we let the place go.

EDWARD. I was showing Dick the tree when we came in. [*To* DICK.] That elm hasn't changed a bit since my father was a boy. It's been right here ever since the house was built.

CARRIE. *Before* the house was built. And the house was built in 1640. [*She speaks here as if she were really interested—a little proudly.*]

DICK [*impressed*]. Gracious! I didn't know that this house was as old as that.

CARRIE [*nodding her head*]. 1640! That's when Deacon Tom Kendall put up this house. And there's been Kendall blood in it ever since. [*All this time* CARRIE *has been standing by the door at the right, throwing in her information with neither expression nor a look toward any one in the room.*]

SARAH. That's right, Dick. Everything is about the same as

it was when they were fighting over at Concord—same trees and all.

DICK. You have some beautiful, old pieces here.

EDWARD. Most of it was in this house when Lafayette slept here.

SARAH [*with considerable pride*]. His bed's in the room over this.

CARRIE [*snorting*]. Doubt if he ever slept here at all. [*She looks out over her shoulder through the door.*]

SARAH [*smiling*]. I dare say Carrie's right. It seems as if all Lafayette did in America was to sleep in somebody's prize bed.

CARRIE [*wiping her mouth with the back of her hand*]. Got to get back to my work. [*She starts to leave but hesitates.*] You'd best get to it, Sarah. [*She scuffs out.*]

SARAH [*looking after* CARRIE, *she sighs*]. Poor Carrie....

EDWARD. She seems lucid this morning.

SARAH. She is at times, and then again she lives in the past and hasn't an idea of what's going on about her.

DICK. She is very proud of this place, isn't she?

SARAH. She is, very; and she thinks of it still just as she did when she was a girl. All she does is worry about boys setting fire to the woods, or some one getting into the barn. She thinks that people are looking for her, and she is forever going out to walk up and down the road so that whoever it is won't miss her.

EDWARD. Well, I *would* hate to have those pines catch fire. [*He nods to his son.*] Dick, you've got to see those woods before we go back. I used to play in them when I was just a youngster—especially in the summer; it was so still and shady there. Some of those trees are older than anything else around here; our family is devoted to them and I, for one, don't blame them.

DICK. What good fortune spared them? I should have

thought that somebody would have cut them down before now.

EDWARD. No member of this family was ever so hard up that he would consider taking down the woods.

DICK. Rats! [*Lighting a cigarette, at which* SARAH *frowns, but says nothing.*]

EDWARD [*sternly*]. Richard!

DICK [*pursuing his point, and trying hard to understand just what he does mean*]. What good fortune spared those trees? And I think the answer is in the question.

SARAH [*vaguely*]. Dick? Ed, what *is* the child talking about?

DICK [*He reverts to his idea*]. I guess it's this way; the Kendalls have never been so hungry or known the want that would drive them to cutting off the trees.

EDWARD. That is very true.

DICK [*with a chuckle*]. I'll bet that if these trees should be cut, you'd all think it would mean the end for the family.

EDWARD [*severely*]. Your humor is out of place, Richard.

DICK. It really isn't humor. But being afraid to use the things that have been left to you by ancestors is rather dumb.

EDWARD. Strangely enough, I don't follow you.

DICK. It's this thing you call pride. I don't like it.

SARAH. Is love of family possession, pride? Of name?

EDWARD [*firmly*]. You don't know what the word means and, until you do, it might be well for you to hold your tongue.

DICK [*sincerely apologetic*]. My mistake.

SARAH [*with mock severity and affection*]. There, young man, tell your father that you're sorry.

DICK. I really am, Cousin Sarah; and I do apologize, Dad, for being so hard on you.

EDWARD [*relenting*]. Well, anyway, it shows that you have good blood in your veins.

DICK [*bowing*]. Thanks.
EDWARD [*with a gesture that says, "Oh, not at all"*]. Your mother comes of the best New England stock.
DICK [*making a face*]. Please! It sounds as if I were some breed of prize-winning cattle.
[*At this point* CARRIE *returns, carrying a decanter and glasses. She walks with one shoe off, and, coming in front of the table, she halts abruptly as though she had forgotten what she intended to do. She looks down at her shoeless foot, wiggles a toe, then looks at the decanter in surprise.* DICK *tries to conceal his amusement.* CARRIE *waves her hand in the direction of the table, after peering absurdly at it, and finally realizes her errand.*]
CARRIE. Drink up!
SARAH [*leaning forward*]. Carrie, where is your slipper? You haven't been outdoors that way, I hope!
CARRIE [*pouring, hardly heeding* SARAH]. Why not?
SARAH. Carrie! What will people think? [*She relaxes, exasperated.*]
CARRIE. Can't help what they think. [*She pours out the wine. Then she turns on* SARAH.] Don't matter, anyhow.
SARAH [*reasonably*]. But you might cut your foot.
CARRIE [*to* EDWARD *and then to* DICK]. Won't. Bottom of my feet's so hard they can't feel.
SARAH. Please! [*Her handkerchief over her lips.*]
CARRIE. Well, you started it. [*She reaches down and draws up her stocking.*]
SARAH [*shocked*]. Stop that! You ought to know better!
CARRIE. Lost the garter. [SARAH *looks volumes at* CARRIE, *then becomes the serene hostess again.* CARRIE *passes the filled glasses around.*]
SARAH. This is old dandelion wine. We only bring it out on special occasions. [*She starts to drink hers, but pauses.*]

CARRIE. And when it's hot. [*Downing hers at a gulp, and wiping the back of her hand across her mouth.*]
SARAH [*putting her glass down*]. Oh dear. Carrie, you bring the barn right in with you.
CARRIE. Better the barn than some other things. [*Looking at* DICK.] What was the fight going on in here?
EDWARD. Dick and I were disagreeing over something.
CARRIE [*nodding*]. Sounded that way. Kendall voices always carried.
DICK. Were we as bad as that?
CARRIE. Un-hunh. Who won?
SARAH [*sharply*]. As if any one won. The idea!
CARRIE [*turning and looking at* RICHARD, *giving him a level glance*]. I'll bet the youngster did.
DICK. No, Carrie, I lost.
CARRIE [*going to the window*]. Umph!
EDWARD. This is certainly delicious wine, Sarah.
SARAH [*smiling*]. Carrie made it; I think it's the best wine we've had in years.
CARRIE [*starting toward hall door; turns, frowns*]. I've got to go.
SARAH. You're not going to work on that lawn, are you?
CARRIE [*she turns back to* SARAH]. There's weedin' tomorrow.
SARAH. I know, but the lawn can go—besides, it's too hot now.
DICK [*surprised*]. You don't mow the lawn yourself, do you?
CARRIE [*flatly and matter-of-factly*]. I always have.
SARAH [*definitely*]. But not without your shoes on, not without your shoes.
CARRIE [*looking down at her feet, her eyes widen, and a smile comes. Her voice is softer, and she is utterly oblivious to* SARAH, EDWARD, *and* DICK]. I forgot . . . I for-

got.... *They* might want me to go with them, and I wouldn't have any shoes on.

SARAH. I don't know what people think. [*To* EDWARD *and* DICK.] But she *will* mow the lawn and it is so hot.

CARRIE [*still off in her thoughts; she treats* SARAH *as a mother might her little ones, telling them not to fear*]. I may not be back. Those people may want me to go with them.

SARAH [*loudly*]. Carrie, fix your hair. I declare; it's a sight.

CARRIE [*shakes her head as if in denial, but also to concentrate on those "out there"*]. It'll only come down again. [*And she swishes out.*]

SARAH. Oh, Ed, what am I to do with her? She is so...so hard to understand....

EDWARD [*smiling faintly*]. I can't remember when she was any different. It must be hard.

DICK [*breaking in*]. Who was she talking about, when she went out?

SARAH [*looking down at her hands, vaguely*]. I don't know. She thinks about them all the time, and she always says that they may be along any time and that they will want her to go away with them. I don't know who "they" are.

EDWARD. When Carrie starts to work, she can wear out any man.

SARAH. For the last few years she's kept this place going. But she...she.... Oh, it's hard to talk about her.

EDWARD. I can remember the day I saw her in town pushing a wheelbarrow. I was so upset I didn't know what to do. She never spoke to me, and really I was thankful. Sarah, I was ashamed.

DICK. Why hasn't Carrie been put in a home where she'd be taken care of?

SARAH. But Dick! I don't know what I'd have done without

her these last few years. She's fed and clothed me, and seen that I had everything I wanted. She's been an angel. Carrie put away! [*Shakes her head.*]

EDWARD [*indignant*]. A Kendall in an insane hospital!

DICK [*quietly*]. A Kendall in a home where she wouldn't know that she is any different from other people.

EDWARD [*severely*]. You seem to plan the lives of others pretty readily.

DICK [*rising, takes the family Bible and fingers it absently*]. But, I mean, you don't mind letting Carrie stay here, working as hard as she does.—Yet you would feel degraded if Carrie were put away. It's a part of your—your musty conventions—musty like this house. [*He closes the Bible.*]

SARAH [*insulted, and angry*]. I'll have you know that this house is given a good cleaning twice a week.

DICK. You can clean this house, but you can't clean musty lives. Musty things are near rot. Old families hold onto material things until they fall to pieces. And it isn't pride that makes them do it: it's vanity!

EDWARD. I don't agree. But more than that, what is it you want?

DICK [*slowly*]. That's the hard part of it. I don't know. I think that what seems to be of the greatest importance that my ancestors have handed on to me is of spiritual rather than temporal value.

EDWARD [*keenly*]. Have you proved the things you learned from me—that I learned from my father?

DICK. I think I have, but it is too early to know that yet. What I'm wondering is, are you going to teach me to respect things that aren't important, simply because *you* think they are important and because you hold them so?

EDWARD. Do you mean that you are afraid you will become attached to this old house and to the trees as we do?

DICK. Right.

EDWARD. I'll give you about half an hour out under the trees and about a day in this house, and if you don't become so attached to them that you can't give them up,—well, then I miss my guess.

SARAH [*nods and smiles as if she and* EDWARD *had a secret in common*]. I'll show him some of the old prints upstairs, and tell him a few stories about this house, and then, Eddie, he'll be a good Kendall.

DICK [*lifting an eyebrow shrewdly*]. Oh! So you're going to start a campaign to sell me the house! Well, go to it. It —never mind, you two; you've started in very well already. [*He grins.*]

[CARRIE *enters at this moment and scrutinizes each one carefully. Then, over her glasses to* DICK.]

CARRIE. At it again?

DICK. Rather.

CARRIE. And who's won this time?

SARAH [*with a faint smile*]. Youth.

CARRIE [*coming down into the room*]. Humph! It always did, whether it did or not.—Let me take these glasses out in the sink. To wash 'em.

EDWARD [*rising*]. I wonder, Sarah, do you mind if I show Dick around? I'd like him to see a bit of the place before we go back. [DICK *rises, and follows his father to the door.* EDWARD, *from the door.*] I'm going to show this boy of mine one of the real loves of my life. Come on, Son, and see the Kendall trees.

CARRIE. If you listen hard you can almost hear the pines talkin'. They're wise, those pines are. [EDWARD *and* DICK *leave.* CARRIE *starts to pick up the glasses again.*]

SARAH [*musing*]. Dick is no ordinary Kendall.

CARRIE [*rattling the glasses briskly and disturbing* SARAH]. Huh! Was any Kendall ever ordinary?

SARAH. Oh, hush!

CARRIE. Or were they all ordinary? [*She pushes a chair out of her way.*]
SARAH [*turning to* CARRIE, *to share a confidence*]. He's so surprising.
CARRIE [*with a shrug*]. His father was, when he was young.
SARAH. He thinks so...so...I don't know any words to express it.
CARRIE. Thinks with words, don't he? That's not thinkin'; that's listenin'. [*She picks up the decanter and smells of it.*]
SARAH. What are you talking about?
CARRIE. Thinkin'. [*She puts the decanter down. She takes up two of the glasses and drains them, then turns up the decanter, and drains it.*]
SARAH [*horrified*]. Caroline!
CARRIE [*paying no real attention. To her* SARAH *is far from important*]. Well, it's good and I'm hot.
SARAH. Caroline Bancroft! I don't know what to say. You have absolutely no manners, Caroline. I was dreadfully embarrassed when you came in without your shoes.
CARRIE [*almost with a sneer*]. Then what'd you say anything for? [*Suddenly her face becomes a mask.*] Did you tell 'em?
SARAH. The woods? [*She looks away.*] No, not yet.
CARRIE. Why not?
SARAH. I...I couldn't...I couldn't. [*She looks everywhere but at* CARRIE.] Ed wouldn't know what to do.
CARRIE. I should worry about that. I'm thinkin' of the grocer's bill.
SARAH [*then defiantly*]. But the woods. Eddie loves those woods as if they were human.
CARRIE. Well, they ain't! [*She stands with her hands on her hips.*]
SARAH. Oh, you don't understand.

CARRIE [*her eyes narrowing and her mouth in a straight line*]. Maybe not; but I see clear enough that some one's got to find a way for us to eat.
SARAH [*vaguely*]. Oh, we'll find a way. We've got to.—I wonder what Mother would say, if she were here—she was more Kendall than Ed.
CARRIE [*in a tone flattering to neither* SARAH *nor their mother*]. Mother would have starved.
SARAH [*proudly*]. Mother would have, before she'd admit that she'd got to live on charity.
CARRIE [*quickly*]. Who's talking about living on charity? [*Her voice rising.*] The woods are ours, aren't they?
SARAH [*vaguely*]. They're ours to *keep*.
CARRIE. And a lot of good that will do us. [*Savagely.*] We'd be just as hungry lookin' at 'em.
SARAH [*shaking herself into sharpness*]. Carrie, have you lost every speck of pride?
CARRIE [*dully*]. Hunger an' pride don't go together.
SARAH [*dogmatically*]. You can be poor and still have a little self-respect left.
CARRIE [*reviving*]. I'm thinkin' about eatin'.
SARAH [*avoiding the problem*]. We can get along somehow. I know we can, but I don't know just how.
CARRIE [*with a one-sided smile*]. That's sense.
SARAH [*as if to herself*]. If only crops sold for more, or the dividends would start coming in. . . .
CARRIE. If!
SARAH [*sternly*]. Well, we simply can't sell them; that's all.
CARRIE [*staring at the floor*]. An' why not?
SARAH. They'd think we were weak.—That's what Ed *said*. Weak!
CARRIE [*lifting her head, and moving nearer* SARAH]. You tell 'em; it won't be weak.

SARAH. I won't be the first one in this family to give in, and sell off the woods. [*She twists in her chair.*]

CARRIE [*in a different voice, higher, with no expression*]. I said long ago back that we'd lost the house—and the woods.

SARAH. You weren't thinking what you were saying. You didn't realize what it would mean to Ed.

CARRIE [*far away*]. Who's worryin' about Ed? He's not hungry.

SARAH [*almost pouting*]. Well, we're not yet. Our credit's still good. The stores will always charge things for us.

CARRIE [*smiling grimly*]. They took back the groceries.

SARAH [*aghast*]. What!

CARRIE [*still smiling, gloating over* SARAH]. Our credit has run out with them, and I don't wonder!

SARAH [*hardly believing her*]. What downright impertinence!

CARRIE [*with a nasty smile*]. No, just downright business.

SARAH. But that new store—Lufkin's? [*Arrogantly.*] They will.

CARRIE [*slowly and easily*]. How are you going to pay for all we owe?

SARAH [*coldly*]. Something's bound to turn up. Anaconda may start paying dividends.

CARRIE. And it may not.

SARAH. We could take in a school-teacher to board with us.

CARRIE. School starts in September. That's a long time off.

SARAH [*stalling*]. We could start a tea room.

CARRIE [*nodding agreement*]. And you'd wait on table, I suppose.

SARAH. We could....

CARRIE [*shaking her head*]. We won't!

SARAH [*flaring up*]. Don't you know it's not easy making

things come out? [*A little feebly.*] You don't see the things that stand in the way; how hard it is to know what to do.

CARRIE. I see clear enough. You're the one that don't see.

SARAH [*sharply*]. What are you talking about?

CARRIE. You're afraid to face the facts.

SARAH [*meeting the challenge*]. I see things so much clearer than you do, and I am thinking of Ed, and Richard.

CARRIE. Huh!

SARAH [*soberly*]. Don't you *huh* me, Caroline. You're thinking only of yourself. We can't admit we're beaten, because then we will be; then we might just as well say good-by to all this. To this house, the fields, the woods ... everything. No, Carrie, I can't tell them. And I won't; I'd be too ashamed.

CARRIE. I'm not ashamed that I'm hungry, and I'm not afraid to tell 'em—like you are.

SARAH [*her lips thinning, tugging at her handkerchief*]. You wouldn't tell them; you wouldn't dare!

CARRIE [*avoiding* SARAH's *attack*]. Then *you'd* better.

SARAH [*her hands clenching the chair-arms*]. If you even dream of telling them! If you even— Carrie, I tell you we can't!

CARRIE [*flatly*]. Then we'll starve.

SARAH [*faintly*]. Then—yes, then we'll starve.

CARRIE [*her eyes pucker, and she is almost brutal; but her mind suddenly takes her off again*]. I think you're crazy. I don't know that *I* care whether Ed's feelin's are hurt or not.

SARAH [*lifting her head*]. Never mind what I said. Not a word!

CARRIE [*turning away*]. I can't hear you.

SARAH [*leaning forward*]. I swear that if you tell them I'll— [*Her voice rising.*] I'll— [*Slowly; clenching her fists, and raising her hands.*] If you say one word—just one word—

I'll tell them you're raving. Do you understand? That you're crazy?

CARRIE [*disturbed, but not frightened*]. That wouldn't be anything new.

SARAH [*her voice is hardly controlled*]. I will, I swear I will. I'll tell them that you're mad, [*Pounding the arm of the chair.*] that you've threatened to kill me. They'll put you away.

CARRIE [*slowly, stating a fact she has just discovered*]. Yes, I believe you would.

SARAH [*controlling herself*]. Listen to me, Carrie. I tell you we mustn't; we've no right. We can't be the ones to fall down. Besides, these woods must go to Richard; we must preserve his inheritance.

CARRIE [*in a dead voice*]. That boy wouldn't care whether he had that forest or not. He's no reason why we should go hungry. I'm tellin' them the minute they get back from the woods. You and your silly pride!

SARAH [*wearily*]. Very well. Go ahead. Tell them. Tell them that we're two helpless old women, and that we don't know enough to keep food in the pantry, clothes on our back. To look at you they won't need to be told that, they'll be able to see it.

CARRIE [*challenging her*]. Now who's crazy?

SARAH. I'm sorry, but you must see that I'm right. I *am* right; I *know* I am.

CARRIE [*stubbornly*]. Your knowin' isn't enough.

SARAH [*sternly*]. I want you to tell me on your word of honor that you will do as I say, or I'll tell them you're mad. Put your hand on the Bible, and say after me—

CARRIE. I won't do it, Sarah. I won't. [*Her voice is that of a child politely, but definitely, refusing.*]

SARAH [*sternly*]. You will; you know you can't help yourself.

CARRIE [*she shakes her head nervously*]. I won't! [*Wildly.*] I'll tell them everything.
SARAH. Carrie, Carrie, don't you see I'm doing it for *you*. [*Suavely.*] I don't want them to think that you—that you're crazy.
CARRIE [*almost in tears*]. Well, I ain't.
SARAH. That's it, dear, you don't know whether you are or not.
CARRIE [*whimpering*]. I do. I do. I'm all right, I tell you.
SARAH. But what will you tell them, dear?
CARRIE [*dully*]. What you said.
SARAH. What was that?
CARRIE [*confused*]. That I'm—no, no—I mean that we're—that we have no money.
SARAH [*as if reasoning with a child*]. How strange, dear. What makes you think that? You're mistaken, Carrie.
CARRIE [*defiantly*]. I'm not. You're just trying to fool me.
SARAH [*still kindly*]. But that's silly. Why should I want to fool you?
CARRIE. Because we have no money.
SARAH. I told you, dear, we're perfectly safe. You mustn't worry about such things.
CARRIE [*with a rising voice, like the irritating sing-song chant of teasing children*]. You're afraid that I'll tell.
SARAH. What, dear?
CARRIE [*her voice higher, and leaning forward*]. That we've got to sell the woods! There, you see I did know.
SARAH. But who will believe such a thing?
CARRIE [*carried away at the fortune which enabled her to say the right thing*]. Ed and Richard!
SARAH. Will they? I wonder. [*She shakes her head.*] Carrie, do you remember the time you went up town and told people that you had found a lot of money.
CARRIE [*hotly*]. I never did.

SARAH. And then the time you got lost out in the fields, and didn't know where you were. Who are "those people," dear?

CARRIE. I don't know, but I can see them.

SARAH [*coldly*]. You'd best not say anything, Caroline. People will think you ought to be put away. Who'd ever believe you?

CARRIE. I don't know and I don't care.

SARAH. But why do you want to tell them?

CARRIE. Because I must.

SARAH [*suddenly shifting the attack*]. I wouldn't say anything about that if I were you.

CARRIE. Why not?

SARAH [*smiling tolerantly*]. Don't you see how Edward laughs at you? And Richard doesn't want to be near you.

CARRIE [*beginning to break*]. No, no, Sarah. Dick likes me.

SARAH. He said a little while ago that he thought that you ought to be put out of the way.

CARRIE. Sarah, oh, no; he couldn't! [*Her hand to her mouth.*]

SARAH. But he did, dear; and Ed said the same thing.

CARRIE [*backing away*]. I won't listen to another word.

SARAH. Why do you suppose that they come down here so seldom? Because you're always here, and they are a little afraid of you. Not that I can blame them any. You are rather wild, your hair in strings, your clothes old and dirty. Everything about you is loathsome. You're an animal! [CARRIE *touches her hair and tries to smooth out her dress.*]

CARRIE [*her eyes wild*]. And you're a cat!

SARAH [*viciously*]. Shut your mouth. You listen to me, Carrie Bancroft. All these years I've put up with you— your crazy ways—you running around here like a loon. I've felt at times like strangling you. The way you eat—

like a hog! You ought to go out in the barn with the rest of the cattle.

CARRIE. Strangle? [*Her hand goes to her throat.*]

SARAH. My sister! I'd rather have none than one like you.

CARRIE. Sarah, I won't stay. You've said enough.

SARAH. Just think how they'll laugh at you. Every time you say anything they'll laugh at you.

CARRIE [*rocking back and forth*]. I'll tell, all the same.

SARAH [*resolved, rises. At each invective she hurls at* CARRIE, *her head jerks, strikes like that of a snake. Her handkerchief flutters rapidly*]. You fool, you muddling, old hag! You think you can tell them something. You don't even know what! Do you think any one would pay any attention to a thing like you? Do you? You don't know what you want to say, or how to say it. You don't even know when you're right or when you're wrong. Stable-woman!

CARRIE. Sarah!

SARAH [*recoiling as if against something unclean*]. Witch!

CARRIE. Sarah, stop!

SARAH [*in cold black fury*]. You mad beast. You slut—you pig!

CARRIE. Stop it; God make her stop! [*Sobbing.*] I'm not. I'm not.

SARAH [*her voice deliberately unreal. She speaks slowly*]. Voices! Listen to them! People out there on the road. Those people you've been waiting for!

CARRIE [*lifting her lowered head*]. People? Them? Do you hear them?

SARAH. There they are now. Go, go, before you forget.

CARRIE [*taking up an old hat, and searching for a coat*]. Tell them to wait, Sarah. Tell them to wait.

SARAH. Hurry, hurry, dear!

[CARRIE *flies out of the room. Exhausted,* SARAH *wets her dry lips.* EDWARD *and* DICK *enter.*]

EDWARD. Where was Carrie going in such a hurry?
SARAH [*still looking toward the door*]. She thought she heard "those people" again.
DICK. Poor Carrie. She ought to be put away, where she won't have to work so hard. She seems awfully muddled.
EDWARD. It's as if she were in a dream.
SARAH. Well, young man, what did you think of the pines?
DICK. They're lovely. They're solemn, as if they had been there since the beginning, and would stay there through all time.
EDWARD. It's so cool, too—just as it was when I was a boy. The same old silence, the same old peace and contentment.
DICK. I forgive you your pride in those old trees, and in the old house. They go together, as if they were all a part of a pattern. [*He sits left of the table;* EDWARD *on the couch.*]
EDWARD. They'll be yours one day, Dick. The old house, and the great elm, the pines, and those warm fields.
DICK. Poetry, Dad?
SARAH. Poetry... and age... and things... all have their place.
DICK. And memories, too, I expect.—What a lot of life has gone on in here.
EDWARD. See to it, young man, that you live up to your heritage. They call us a new country, but much happened to America in three hundred years.
DICK [*with a smile*]. Cousin Sarah, I'm afraid Dad has become mellow.
EDWARD. And why not? I enjoy myself.
DICK. Now you must either quote the Bible, or Shakespeare.
EDWARD. I don't like to be familiar with the former, and I am not well acquainted with the latter.

Wootten-Moulton

ANCIENT HERITAGE

CARRIE. The voices! Sarah, do you hear them now? They are telling you to speak out. The woods—they're whispering to you!

COTTIE MOURNS

JERD. That there licker wa'n't quite rotten enough, Cottie. Hit hain't so hard to play dead when folks think they's helped kill you.
COTTIE [terrified, for once in her life]. Jerd, y'ain't dead?

Wootten-Moulton

DICK. In other words, Cousin Sarah, he doesn't know either.
EDWARD. Well, you don't need to be so frank about it.
DICK. I'm not; I'm just enjoying myself.
SARAH. Tell me; do you still feel the same way about family pride being foolish—I mean after seeing the woods and all?
EDWARD. Why, he couldn't—not after that.
DICK. Let's wait a bit for that. You see, I don't quite know how I do feel. It's all so grand, and I'm a little unprepared for it.
SARAH. When you get older, you'll understand why old hearts cling to things like these; they're so secure; and you always know where to find them.
DICK. It'll take a lot of living up to, to make me feel that I'm not in the wrong house.
SARAH. Then you'll have to come down more often, and try to get better acquainted with it.
DICK. I'd like to very much, if you're sure you don't mind.
SARAH. It would please me very much.
[*At this moment* CARRIE *reappears at the door, and stands listening—a vengeful* CARRIE.]
DICK [*rising*]. I hate to say it, Dad; but we ought to be thinking of getting back.
EDWARD. That's right, Son. [*He rises and goes to* SARAH.] Your mother will wonder where we are.
SARAH. Oh, don't hurry.
EDWARD. Hold on; I almost forgot, Sarah. What was it you wanted to ask me about?
DICK. That's just like you. Come all the way down here to help Cousin Sarah, and then you get to talking, and you forget what you came for.
SARAH [*with difficulty*]. Ed ... well ... I don't know how to put it really. You see, the selectmen were here the other

day, and they were talking about draining the swamp. I didn't know whether I'd better think about it this year. Money's a little scarce.

EDWARD. Why, I don't know, Sarah, I think—

[CARRIE *advances.*]

CARRIE. It isn't important what you think, Ed Kendall, because it don't matter. [EDWARD *starts.*]

SARAH. Carrie!

CARRIE [*her eyes wide, brushing her hand across her forehead intermittently*]. Are you going to tell him?

SARAH [*recoiling*]. Carrie!

CARRIE [*insistently*]. Are you going to tell him?

SARAH [*trying to escape*]. I won't, Carrie. I won't! Do you hear?

CARRIE [*nodding*]. She was afraid to, but I told her that *I* wasn't. I'll tell you.

EDWARD. Well?

CARRIE [*she looks steadily at* SARAH, *then smiles faintly*]. Poor thing, she thought she heard voices, but she didn't; I went out to look on the road, and there was no one there. [*To* SARAH.] Do you hear that? There was no one there, and— [*Slowly.*] there never will be again.

SARAH [*frightened*]. Don't listen to her; she's raving.

CARRIE [*shaking her head*]. No, I'm not. [*Slowly.*] Sarah, are you going to tell them?

SARAH [*her hands lifted, as if to ward off a blow*]. Stop it, Carrie. Stop it! Ed, make her stop!

CARRIE. The voices! Sarah, do you hear them now? They are telling you to speak out. The woods—they're whispering to you.

SARAH. My God in heaven, she's mad!

CARRIE [*sadly*]. No dear, I wish I were. [*Pausing significantly*]. I wish I were the one.

SARAH. Ed! Take me away. Take me away from her!

DICK [*his hand on* CARRIE's *shoulder*]. You're trying to tell us something, Carrie. What is it you want to say?

CARRIE. Nothing... nothing... I can't....

SARAH [*quietly*]. You may tell them, Carrie.

CARRIE. I never heard those voices. [*In a whisper.*] She's the one that heard them. For twenty years she's been hearin' them. It's she that thinks they're waitin' for her outside— that she must hurry or they'll go away. [*They look at* SARAH. *She sits quietly, eyes downcast, smoothing the handkerchief in her lap.*] I pretended I heard them... so that she would never know. All these years, I let her think it was me. So many years pretendin', takin' care of her, never lettin' her find out. [*She passes her hand across her face.*] Sometimes I forget I'm just humorin' her and believe— [*She stops and shudders.*]

SARAH [*in a faraway voice*]. There's no more food, Richard.

DICK [*shocked*]. No food?

SARAH. And the woods must go. Carrie said I must tell you.

DICK [*turning to* CARRIE *who is quietly weeping*]. Is that true, Carrie?

CARRIE. Yes.

EDWARD. And, Sarah—all these years—you never told me?

CARRIE. We didn't want to hurt you.

SARAH. I couldn't bear to admit that we were the first ones in the Kendall family to give in.

THE CURTAIN FALLS

NORTH CAROLINA

COTTIE MOURNS
A COMEDY OF SEA ISLAND FOLK

BY PATRICIA McMULLAN
OF WASHINGTON, NORTH CAROLINA

Written in the playwriting course at the University of North Carolina and originally produced by The Carolina Playmakers at Chapel Hill on February 28, March 1 and 2, 1935. *Cottie Mourns* was included in the repertory of The Playmakers' tour of eastern North Carolina and Virginia, November, 1935. It was first published in *The Carolina Play-Book*, March, 1935.

THE CHARACTERS

COTTIE CULPEPPER..............Patricia McMullan
NELLIE MERKEL BEASLEY.........Mildred McMullan
FELIX WISE........................Robert Barrett
JERD CULPEPPER....................Wilton Mason

SCENE: *The living-room of the Culpepper home, on one of the sea islands off the North Carolina coast.*
TIME: *The present. An afternoon in early fall.*

Copyright, 1935, by The Carolina Playmakers, Inc.
All rights reserved.

OCRACOKE ISLAND FOLK

OCRACOKE ISLAND, the scene of *Cottie Mourns*, a recent Carolina folk comedy, lies twenty-five miles off the Carolina coast, separated from the mainland by Pimlico Sound. It is one of a chain of narrow sandbanks which skirt the coast-line. Beyond Ocracoke are the dangerous shoals of Hatteras, and beyond that Kinnakeet. All the islands are sparsely settled by simple, God-fearing fisherfolk (self-styled "bankers") who live in remote "neighborhoods" and still speak the native dialect of their early Anglo-Saxon ancestors.*

Ocracoke stretches fourteen miles along the coast and at the most is not more than a mile across. The tiny village is safely sheltered by a heavy growth of cedars and sea-swept live-oaks. There are no streets, only clean, sandy lanes which meander aimlessly through dense thickets of overhanging sweet-scented myrtle and yaupon bushes.† The paths are fringed with a luxuriant growth of Bermuda grass and bright green dwarf palmettos. In the spring there is everywhere a riot of flowering yellow jessamine vines, and in summer in the swampy places a soft pink carpet of rose mallow in bloom.

The villagers' small, white cottages and neatly kept yards surprise the visitor at every turn. Close by each house is a small family graveyard, safe from the great storms and shifting sand dunes which sometimes change the whole topography of the "banks." In such a little house lives the four-times-widowed Cottie Culpepper of the play, now mourning the loss of her fourth husband and anticipating a fifth.

The author, "Patsy" McMullan of Washington, North Carolina, has lived each summer since her earliest childhood among the fisherfolk of these isolated sea islands. Here she has heard

---

* "Island," for instance, they pronounce "oiland"; "high tide," "hoigh toide"; and "forefather" with a short "a" as in lather.

† The smooth elliptical yaupon leaves have been used since colonial times as a substitute for tea.

many a strange tale of weird folk beliefs, superstitions, and legends of an outlived past told in the colorful vernacular of the native tongue—tales of Blackbeard, the notorious sea-robber of the early part of the eighteenth century, whose dark forbidding house with a turret looking far out to sea is called to this day "Blackbeard's House."

Simie O'Neill, chief story-teller of the Island, likes to tell the tale of Blackbeard's last stand on his daring little ship, *Adventure*, which was finally taken by Captain Maynard off Ocracoke Inlet. The place is still called by the fishermen "Teach's Hole" after the pirate's real name, Edward Teach. (Captain Maynard was sent down by Governor Spottswood of Virginia to rid the colonists of the scourge of piracy and to take the terrible marauder dead or alive.) Simie likes to climax the story with, "And when his head was cut off it had so much life left in it that it swum three times round the ship before it would sink!" The action of one of Paul Green's early plays, *Blackbeard, Pirate of the Carolina Coast*,* takes place in the hold of the *Adventure* near dawn of that fateful morning in November, 1718.

In *Cottie Mourns* the young playwright has succeeded in capturing some of the interesting folkways and Devonshire speech transmitted from our English forebears.

* *Blackbeard, Pirate of the Carolina Coast*, is included in Paul Green's first volume of plays written in the University's playwriting course at Chapel Hill, *The Lord's Will and Five Other One-Act Plays*, published by Henry Holt and Company, New York, 1925.

COTTIE MOURNS

On one of the winding paths, sheltered from the sea by the storm-blown live-oaks, is the simple dwelling of COTTIE CULPEPPER. *The scene is the combined living-and-dining-room of her home. The walls are whitewashed and the room is as clean as sand and water can make it. The door in the right wall, downstage, leads outside. Beyond it is a small shuttered window, neatly curtained. Another just like it is in the rear wall, and there is a low doorway in the left corner leading into* COTTIE'S *room. Downstage, at the left, is a door opening into the next room where her fourth husband,* JERD, *lies in state with a wax lily in his hand.* COTTIE *is preparing to give* JERD *a fine funeral. Through the window we may catch a glimpse of the fragrant myrtle bushes and the little grave-plot where* COTTIE'S *three deceased husbands: Walter, Bill Otis, and Horatio, are buried.*

The room is simply furnished. In the rear is a decrepit cupboard of antique design and a rough, hand-made table on which stands a curiously shaped bottle—probably washed ashore from a derelict sailing vessel—filled with brightly colored, artificial flowers. Occupying most of the room is a jumble of chairs recruited for the occasion. Two hand-hewn benches stand against the left wall, and in the right corner of a nondescript stand is a "talking machine" with a large cornucopia horn. A well-worn oilskin coat and seaman's hat hang on pegs at the left. Most prominent in the room, however, are the three life-size crayon portraits of COTTIE'S *three dead husbands, mounted on easels and festooned with mourning black.*

[Cottie Culpepper *is a large, loosely-built, aggressive but not uncomely woman about thirty years of age. Her face is ruddy from exposure in all weathers, and her hair is sun-bleached to a straw color. Although she is barefooted, as all the islanders are, and wears a loose-fitting black dress, she is really quite attractive in a strong, healthy way.*]

[*Her friend,* Nellie Merkle Beasely, *also sun-tanned and barefooted, has reached the age of thirty-two without acquiring a man, and shows it in her weak, plaintive way. By comparison with* Cottie *she seems thin and wistful.*]

[*The opening curtain shows* Cottie *seated in the single rocking-chair in the center of the room with an empty tomato can, which she uses as a cuspidor for spitting snuff*, beside her.*]

Cottie [*rocking vigorously, but speaking mournfully*]. And when we gits to the graveyard, Nellie Merkle, I'll git somebody to pipe up a tune fer us.

Nellie Merkle [*entering the center door with two chairs which she places in line with the others*]. What tune you goin' t' have, Cottie?

Cottie [*obviously insincere*]. Hit don't make no difference —just something real holy. [*Sighing deeply.*] Jerd may have been a heavy-drinkin' and a blasphemin' man, but come revival time, he did outshout and git religion quicker'n any husband I ever had.

Nellie Merkle [*glancing toward the door, left*]. Hit may have been religion, but I'll allus think Jerd's holy shoutin' come so easy to him on account of his a-callin' his heifersteer,† Joe, so much.

Cottie [*with a tearful voice, swaying back and forth*]. Poor

---

* See note on page 149.

† This is obviously a paradox, but the playwright insists that "heifersteer" is the term Jerd always used. Evidently it was the only one he found adequate to represent his beloved beast.

COTTIE MOURNS

Jerd, he did have so much bother with that heifer-steer, Joe, of his'n. 'Member the time he had to keep a-buildin' a fire under 'er to git 'er to move?

NELLIE MERKLE. And hit took him three hours to git across the island when I kin walk hit in thirty minutes goin' 'gin the wind. I cain't see how any man could love a dumb brute like Jerd loved that heifer-steer.

COTTIE [indignantly]. He loved that steer more'n he did me. I thought when I married him hit would be different from when I married [Looking at each picture in turn.] Walter and Billotis * and Horatio— [Then, as an afterthought.] God rest 'em.

NELLIE MERKLE. Well, wan't hit?

COTTIE. Hit shore was. He was plumb crazy in the head. He'd hafter be to act like he did—a-wanderin' round the island with that heifer-steer, Joe. He worked harder tryin' to find hit a fresh patch of grass than he did to make a decent livin' fer me.

NELLIE MERKLE. He shore did love hit. [Turning toward the left door.] But he cain't no more, fer I'm sure St. Peter ain't a-goin' t' let no heifer-steer thru' the pearly gates.

COTTIE [wailing masterfully]. But I'm sorry I said anything spiteful 'bout him, 'cause he's a-lyin' stiff and cold in yonder now. [Nodding her head toward the door, left.]

NELLIE MERKLE [going to her and patting her arm consolingly]. Now, Cottie, don't take on so. You know he's a credit to you—what with him lookin' so handsome with Elvira's wax lily in his hands and all. I swear he don't look like he's dead at all.

COTTIE. Oh, I know that, Nellie Merkle. [Suddenly practical.] Hit's a dyin' shame I didn't think of borrowin' that

---

* "Billotis" is Cottie's pronunciation of "Bill Otis."

lily 'til Hurray * died. [*Weeping.*] Poor old Walter and Billotis was buried 'thout nothin'.

NELLIE MERKLE. But *you* shore looked fine at their funerals, Cottie. Everybody's allus sayin' what a handsome widder woman you allus make.

COTTIE [*getting up*]. A-Lord, I'm glad you said something 'bout that. They'll be a-comin' round fer the funeral afore long and I've got to git my mournin' onto me. [*She starts toward the center door.*]

NELLIE MERKLE. What you goin' t' wear this time, Cottie?

COTTIE [*turning back*]. Ain't you seen my new mournin', Nellie Merkle? Hit ain't been worn afore, but I thought sure hit would dry rot afore Jerd would die.

NELLIE MERKLE [*shocked*]. How come you already had it, Cottie?

COTTIE. You needn't be so surprised— You see, I knowed he was a-drinkin' hisself to death, so I ordered my mournin' from Sears and Roebuck Co.† three month ago. Th' ain't nothin' wrong in bein' ready afore time, is there now, Nellie Merkle?

NELLIE MERKLE [*not altogether satisfied*]. I guess not, Cottie. [*Dismissing the subject.*] Well, kin I help you git into 'em?

COTTIE. No, but you *kin* hand me my snuff and my toothbrush.

NELLIE MERKLE [*looking about for them*]. Where 'bouts did you leave 'em?

COTTIE. In there on the coffin, I 'spec'. Seems like I had 'em in there when I was a-fixin' that lily under Jerd's chin.

[NELLIE MERKLE *goes to the door, left, but stops when* COTTIE *continues.*] You know I ain't never seen a man

---

* "Hurray" is Cottie's contraction of "Horatio."

† "Co." she pronounces it as it is spelled in abbreviated form with a long "o," *not* the complete word "Company."

take as long to git cold as Jerd has. [NELLIE MERKLE *looks nervously into the room, left.*] Well, what you a-waitin' fer? [NELLIE MERKLE *goes cautiously into the room, left.*] Hit was long 'bout midnight when he died, and he was still warm when I put his shroud on 'im. We put 'im into his coffin 'bout one. Hit was the licker, I 'spec'. [*She counts the chairs.*] And bring me that there chair out o' there, Nellie Merkle. This here's goin' to be the biggest funeral I've give yet.

NELLIE MERKLE [*returning with the snuff and chair*]. Here's your snuff, Cottie. [*Hesitant.*] Where'd you git a coffin so quick?

COTTIE [*taking her rocking-chair*]. Well, you see, he was a-drinkin' heavy, just like Walter and Billotis and Hurray did afore they died, and I knowed that sooner or later he'd run across some pison licker just like they did. And I thought hit was best to have my mournin' an' his coffin ready fer that day.*

NELLIE MERKLE [*placing the chair in line*]. I just cain't help thinkin', Cottie, that you shore is had bad luck with your men.

COTTIE. Hit's the truth. Seems like they just will up and die [*Meaningly.*] all by theyselves, spite of all I kin do.

NELLIE MERKLE. But there's one thing I cain't understand, and that's how come they all died from rotten licker. Hit ain't so strange fer 'em to drink, but [*Looking suspiciously at* COTTIE.] hit 'tis fer 'em to git nothin' 'cept that rotten mess.

COTTIE. There ain't nothin' strange 'bout hit, Nellie Merkle. You know that shed out back belongs to Buddy and ever since he set up his still, he's been a-usin' it to keep all the last-run licker he don't sell. I keeps the key to the

---

* The custom of such funeral preparations still survives in some remote neighborhoods of North Carolina.

shed fer 'im and hit seems like if I'd fergit to hide that key they'd all drink hit, spite of all I could do.

NELLIE MERKLE [*moving around to the table*]. But didn't you never tell 'em what rotten stuff hit was?

COTTIE [*evasively*]. Well, now I cain't remember—[*She spits.*] but they didn't have no business goin' into hit nowhow.

NELLIE MERKLE [*arranging the artificial flowers on the table*]. Well, hit's a good thing the coroner from 'cross the sound hain't been 'round when none of 'em died. He might have made you a mess of trouble.

COTTIE. I'm kind o' glad that coroner ain't been round myself. You remember when Graham Tillette up and kicked the bucket last summer when the coroner was a-stayin' at the hotel down the beach?

NELLIE MERKLE [*coming down to* COTTIE]. 'Course I remembers hit. He shore did pester Ethel—a-nosin' 'round. He was worse'n porpoises after minnows. And he's a-stayin' here now. Been here fer ten days—I seen 'im over to the hotel.

COTTIE. Well, there ain't no coroner can git nothin' on me 'bout none of my men. [*With a touch of mock sorrow.*] Walter got drunk as a coot and went down to the store on his own two feet, but they brung 'im back feet first.

NELLIE MERKLE. Wa'n't Billotis drunk when he fell out'n that boat and got drowned?

COTTIE. He was. And Hurray, he was just like Walter and Billotis. [*Suddenly changing the subject.*] A-Lord, Nellie Merkle, we ain't got no time to be a-gabbin'. [*She starts toward the center door.*]

NELLIE MERKLE. Hit 'tis gittin' kind o' late.—I swear I hope Bet and Carrie don't git next to each other at the funeral. They ain't a-speakin'. At Jethro's funeral Carrie hauled off and kicked Bet on the ankle so she hollered right out loud. An' she had to pretend like she was just a-mournin'.

COTTIE [*to her, indignantly*]. And there ain't a soul onto the island that don't know the only reason she went to the funeral was she was skeered Carrie'd git to walk with Felix.

NELLIE MERKLE [*not without evident envy*]. Hit was kind o' funny when right after that you tuk 'im right out from under their noses.

COTTIE [*peeved at the suggestion*]. I didn't take *him*, Nellie Merkle. Hit's him that's allus a-chasin' after me.

NELLIE MERKLE [*sighing*]. I shore wish he'd chase me fer a spell.

COTTIE. Humph! You'd be actin' like you was out o' wind afore you'd gone three steps.

NELLIE MERKLE [*not without some asperity*]. Well, I ain't a-noticed as how you was specially long-winded yourself.

COTTIE [*challenging her*]. Look here, Nellie Merkle, do you mean—

NELLIE MERKLE [*trying to avoid an argument*]. Now, Cottie, don't pay me no mind. You know I've got a sharp tongue and that I'm allus sayin' things I don't mean. [*Then soothing her.*] Now, come on, Cottie, we'd better git back to gettin' ready fer the funeral.

COTTIE [*vindictive*]. I swear I'll tear Bet's eyeballs out if she tries to outmourn me.

NELLIE MERKLE. Hit seems to me that them that mourns the loudest is them that don't mean nothin' by hit.

COTTIE. Nellie Merkle, you ain't insinuatin' that I wa'n't a poor bereaved widder woman after Walter, and Billotis and Hurray died, is you? Hit's true I was powerful disappointed in 'em, but I'm a *good* Christian woman and I've mourned 'em all, even if they did git just what they orter had.

NELLIE MERKLE [*placating her*]. Now, Cottie, you know I didn't mean nothin'.

COTTIE [*turning away*]. Hit sounded powerful like hit to me.

NELLIE MERKLE. Why, Cottie, even Elvira says that she'd be hanged if she'd let you have that lily another time if hit wa'n't fer the fact that she couldn't git no sleep less'n she did. She said she remembered how you wouldn't hush bawlin' after Hurray pooped 'til she flung it out the winder to you.

COTTIE [*proudly assertive*]. When I wants a thing bad enough I'm a-goin' t' git hit somehow. And hit's true I don't feel right 'bout buryin' the boys 'til they's held the lily fer a spell. [*Sitting down and beginning to mourn again.*] That seems to ease my grief somehow. Hit's just like a good dip o' snuff.

NELLIE MERKLE [*going over to the window, right*]. I'll just go over and pull to the shutters, Cottie. Hit'll help you to git to feelin' right fer the funeral.

COTTIE [*mourning*]. You shore is a jew-*el*. [*Then noticing that* NELLIE MERKLE *is not listening, but gazing intently out the window.*] What you a-spyin', Nellie Merkle?

NELLIE MERKLE. Hit's Felix Wise a-comin' up the path. [*Cunningly.*] He shore has been a-comin' round to see you right smart lately, ain't he?

COTTIE [*preening herself*]. He has been a-comin' round right regular.

NELLIE MERKLE [*slyly*]. And you sort o' like him, don't you, Cottie?

COTTIE. Well, now, he's a purty likely fellow. And that's the finest mustache he's got, hain't hit?

NELLIE MERKLE [*grudgingly*]. Hit do look right good.

COTTIE. But what I like 'bout him is he ain't like everybody else. He's the only person onto this island that's got one

COTTIE MOURNS 541

of them there disvorces. And he had one of them law fellers from Norfork fix hit up fer him, too.

NELLIE MERKLE [*trying to cool* COTTIE'*s ardor*]. Ah, that ain't so much. And anyway the only reason he's got hit is 'cause Lulu Mann's pappy that works at the Navy Yard up in Norfork got hit fer her.

COTTIE. I don't care. I think hit's grand.

[FELIX WISE *enters the door, right. He is a tall, barefooted, ungainly good-natured islander with no apparent attraction except a large bristly walrus mustache. Besides the mustache there is a look of something that verges on stupidity on his face.*]

FELIX [*speaking with a slow drawl*]. Hi there, y'all.

NELLIE MERKLE [*simpering*]. Howdy, Felix.

COTTIE [*grandly*]. Come in, Felix. Take a chair and set into 'er.

FELIX. I just got wind o' Jerd's funeral, Cottie.... I... I didn't know he was ailin'....

COTTIE [*with a quick glance at* NELLIE MERKLE]. Well, he wa'n't ailin' exactly. [*Wailing.*] Poor old Jerd.

FELIX [*bewildered*]. I... I didn't know you thought so much of...

COTTIE [*rising quickly*]. Nellie Merkle, I clean plumb forgot to order a veil to go with my mournin'. Go over and borrow that there one Ethel used when Graham died.

NELLIE MERKLE [*not at all anxious to leave* COTTIE *alone with* FELIX]. Well, I will, Cottie. But that there one was s' thick Ethel couldn't see nothin' and near 'bout broke her neck a-stumbling over things.—But I'll fetch 'er if she'll let you have 'er. You know she ain't thunk so much of you since you bawled louder at Graham's funeral than she did.

COTTIE [*grandly*]. You just tell 'er that I'm a-plannin' on killin' Jerd's heifer-steer, Joe, soon's things git settled, and I'll give 'er the hind-quarter.

NELLIE MERKLE. Well, all right. [*She leaves slowly by the door, right.*]

FELIX [*uneasily*]. Cottie, what caused Jerd to die so quick. I ... I ... well, I wa'n't exactly countin' on 'im dyin'....

COTTIE [*mournfully*]. I wa'n't exactly countin' on it myself, Felix, but he drunk so much of that rotten swill that he's left me a lone widder woman. Now I ain't got a soul to keep me company. [*With soft glances at* FELIX.]

FELIX [*evasively*]. You still got Nellie Merkle. Folks do say she's right fond of you.

COTTIE [*tearfully*]. Hit's mighty sad to have your man die drunk, 'thout saying a kind partin' word to you.

FELIX [*relieved to change the subject*]. Hit must be, Cottie. You know, I didn't think you cared fer 'im so much.

COTTIE. You cain't allus tell 'bout how I feel from the way I act, Felix. My heart's broke plumb in two. [*She "mourns" copiously.*]

FELIX [*cautiously sitting down near her*]. There now, Cottie, don't take on so.

COTTIE. I cain't help hit, Felix. He was the only man I had.

FELIX. I know hit, Cottie. But you cain't expect to have more'n one man at a time.

COTTIE. That ain't what I mean, Felix. [*Moving her chair nearer him*]. Hit's that now I ain't got no man to help me and give me advice 'bout a lot of things a woman ain't able to handle all by herse'f.

FELIX [*sliding away from her*]. There ain't s' many of them sort o' things a-comin' up. Winter's a-comin' on and you can rest up fer a spell.

COTTIE. Don't give me none of that talk. There's a lot of things a-comin' up fer a man to do.

FELIX. Well, he ain't got to be a husband, is he?

COTTIE. Well, hit's right likely he would be, hain't it?
FELIX. Hit all depends. What kind o' things is you got in mind, Cottie?
COTTIE [*slyly*]. Well, the first things is them nets of Jerd's that I ain't got no use fer now.
FELIX [*interested*]. They're fine, strong nets, too.
COTTIE [*affecting a sudden thought*]. By the way, Felix. Didn't you lose your nets in that there last blow?
FELIX [*nervously*]. I shore did. All 'cept one, and hit was so weak that that last big haul of mullets we got yesterday tore hit plumb full o' holes. [*Almost to himself.*] Hit'll be mighty hard to mend, too.
COTTIE [*slyly*]. Then maybe you could use them nets o' mine, Felix.
FELIX. Oh, I'd like to buy 'em off'n you, Cottie, but I ain't got no money right now. But if you'd let me have the use of 'em, I could make enough to pay you fer 'em in no time at all.
COTTIE [*indignantly*]. I ain't a-goin' t' do no sech— [*Then suddenly sweet.*] What I mean, Felix, is that I think you and me ought to git together and make some other kind of 'rangement.
FELIX [*backing off to safety*]. Well, to tell you the truth, Cottie, I been kind o'... uh... kind o'... kind o' plannin' on quittin' fishin' and tryin' to git into the Coast Guard. It's a heap steadier business and they do wear such purty clothes. The only thing that worries me is the shoes.... I know I cain't wear shoes all day long.
COTTIE [*shifting her sails quickly and resorting again to tears*]. Hit do look like all my friends is deserting me. I was a-countin' on your help, Felix, but if'n you go into the Coast Guard you might as well be buried under a hummock fer all your friends'll see of you. [*She sinks sobbing into a chair.*]

FELIX. Hit ain't as bad as you make hit out to be, Cottie. Maybe I'll be stationed down here.

COTTIE [*refusing such consolation*]. You and Nellie Merkle was all I was a-countin' on to help me in my grief. But, you know, hit seems like Nellie Merkle don't care fer me any more, and now ... now you're a-goin' to join up with the Coast Guard.

FELIX [*moving his chair a little to her*]. Cottie, you know a fine-looking wench like you ain't never goin' to lack fer company. Besides, folks'll allus be a-droppin' in and ...

COTTIE. But, Felix, don't you know th' ain't nothin' to most of the folks round here. [*Looking up at him admiringly.*] You're so much superior than all the rest of 'em. And you know they all say you're the handsomest man onto the island. But pore me, I ain't handsome, and I ain't brainy. I guess they might as well put me under, too. [*Wailing and dissolving in tears.*]

FELIX [*going to her, sympathetically*]. Cottie, don't take on so. You know there ain't no truth into 'er. [*He slips his chair a little nearer to her.*]

COTTIE [*reaching a grand climax in her wailing*]. I guess the rest of my days I'll set from dawn to dark 'thout hearin' a soul speak a cheery word to me.

FELIX. I'll come to see you, Cottie. I won't join up with the Coast Guard ... I wa'n't really goin' to nohow. And I'll come 'round and set with you of an evenin'.

COTTIE [*still mourning*]. You're so kind to me. [*Without hesitation or change in tone of her voice*]. And then in a week or two you and me can git hitched. [*Now she is leaning on his shoulder.*]

FELIX [*his back stiffening, slumps*]. Oh, my Lord!

COTTIE [*ignoring his tone*]. When you and me is wedded....

FELIX [*jumping to his feet*]. Wedded? [*Thinking as fast as he can.*] But, Cottie, I . . . I ain't got no wedlock into me. [*He retreats behind a chair.*]

COTTIE [*advancing on him*]. What you mean?

FELIX [*scratching his head*]. I . . . well, I ain't . . . ain't exactly able to take to myself another woman. [*He concludes triumphantly.*]

COTTIE [*blasting his hopes of any easy escape*]. How come?

FELIX [*completely flustered and bewildered*]. Well, you see, well . . . to tell you the truth, Cottie [*Suddenly inspired.*] I'm in a wedge right now. Mrs. Luark's been after me powerful heavy to marry Liz on account of that there young-'un she up and had t'other day 'thout no warnin' at all.

COTTIE [*advancing on him furiously*]. Felix Wise, do you mean to tell me that you're the pap of that there bastard of Liz's?

FELIX [*backing away, dismayed when he realizes what might come of his rash assertion*]. Why, no Cottie, I . . . I don't believe hit's true, but she do say hit's me.

COTTIE [*angry and determined*]. Then if it ain't true, I'll just go over and have a talk with Mrs. Luark right this minute. And I'll tell her a thing or two. [*She starts toward the door, right.*]

FELIX [*rushing after her and seizing her arm*]. Now don't go a-doin' that, Cottie, because . . . well . . . you see, Cottie, I just 'bout got her convinced hit ain't me. . . . And I wouldn't want you to go a-sayin' anything to 'er, 'cause hit might git her to thinkin' somethin'.

COTTIE [*seeing her chance and snatching it*]. You mean, she might know you wanted to marry me instead?

FELIX [*turning away, now completely lost*]. Well, I guess so. . . .

COTTIE [*sweetly, as if nothing had happened*]. Hit's balm to my heart to hear you say that, Felix.

FELIX [*turning to her*]. But, Cottie—
COTTIE [*advancing steadily*]. How much do you love me, Felix?
FELIX [*hopelessly*]. Well, I guess ... I guess I loves you like ... like Jerd loved his heifer-steer, Joe!
COTTIE [*somewhat surprised*]. 'Course, I'm glad to know you love me, Felix, but [*Turning away.*] I do wish you could have said it different.
FELIX. How you mean, different?
COTTIE. I just mean I wish you could use some real purty words.
FELIX [*disgruntled*]. I don't see how you come by your cravin' fer fancy words, Cottie. You hain't been to school no more'n me.
COTTIE. Oh, but I've seen 'em used, Felix. [*Sighing.*] If you just knowed the way folks talk in books.
FELIX. Humph! You cain't even write your name—much less read a book.
COTTIE [*triumphantly*]. Who was it read off the directions for a-stringin' Lum's mail-order guitar? Who was it?
FELIX [*meekly*]. Hit was you, Cottie.
COTTIE. And I've read books. Two of 'em, *Love and Destiny* and *Tempest and Tears.*—They were the finest you ever heard.
FELIX [*still suspecting* COTTIE'S *veracity*]. Where'd you ever git books?
COTTIE. I got 'em off'n Mrs. White for washin' some clothes for 'er.
FELIX. Well, you sure got cheated.
COTTIE [*heatedly*]. If you wa'n't so ignorant you wouldn't think so.
FELIX. I ain't ignorant.
COTTIE [*slyly*]. No, I guess you ain't really, Felix, but I do

wish you could use nice words. They're so much purtier than "I love you like Jerd loved his heifer-steer, Joe."

FELIX [*only for the sake of argument*]. But Jerd loved his heifer-steer an awful lot, didn't he?

COTTIE. He sure did, but hit ain't the same thing to love a woman and a steer. [*Going to him, suddenly suspicious.*] You ain't got no heifer-steer nor nothin', is you, Felix?

FELIX [*sadly*]. I ain't, Cottie.

COTTIE. I just wanted to make sure. If Jerd ever knowed nothin' nice to say, he said it to that steer. *I* never heard it. And hit seems to me, Felix, that if there's one thing sets a man off, hit's a show of larnin', like you read in books.

FELIX [*in a last attempt to save his dignity*]. I could talk like they do if I wanted to.

COTTIE [*slyly*]. Let me hear you then.

FELIX [*completely at a loss, but unwilling to admit defeat*]. Well... uh... well... I could, Cottie, but somehow I can't think how to start....

COTTIE [*eagerly*]. I'll go get a book and read her off to you, Felix. Then you'll know. [*She hurries out the door into her room.* FELIX *begins to realize the danger of his situation and grows more and more nervous. He glances cautiously toward* COTTIE'S *door and then begins to tiptoe toward the outside door. Just as he puts out his hand to open it,* COTTIE *calls to him.*] Oh, Felix.

FELIX [*jumping back guiltily, he loses all his courage and speaks sadly*]. Yes, Cottie.

COTTIE [*archly*]. Just make yourself right at home. I'm a-comin'.

FELIX [*sinking weakly into the nearest chair*]. All right, Cottie. [*He sighs deeply.*]

COTTIE [*enters the room, tenderly turning the pages of a*

book]. This here's the best one. And I'm near 'bout to the place.

FELIX. Don't trouble yourself none, Cottie. You can show hit to me to-morrow.

COTTIE. Here hit 'tis. Now this here's [*Indicating the room.*] a rose garden, Felix, and over yonder [*Pointing toward the room, left.*] is a lake and the moon is a-settin' right about over Jerd's coffin. [FELIX *starts involuntarily, but* COTTIE *doesn't notice him and begins to read falteringly*]. "My dear one, we will brave life's dangers together."

FELIX [*not realizing that* COTTIE *is reading, in an agony of nervousness*]. What dangers?

COTTIE. Not really, Felix. I just read that out of this here *Tempest and Tears*.

FELIX [*relieved, but the spell which* COTTIE *has cast over him is gone*]. Oh!

COTTIE. Then in a little while it says, "He pressed her fra-*gile* fingers in his own strong ones and said, 'You alone reign *su*-preme in my heart, my *jew*-el!'" [*Sighing.*] Ain't that beautiful?

FELIX [*miserably*]. Yes, Cottie.

COTTIE [*turning the pages*]. Then over here he says, "Rosa Lee, you are like a *fra*-grant rose kissed by the light of yon pale moon." [*Coyly.*] Am I like that, Felix?

FELIX [*defiant*]. No, you ain't!

COTTIE [*exasperated by his crude destruction of her romantic mood*]. Felix Wise, you ain't got no more fancy about you than one of Hollowell's hogs.

FELIX [*mustering his courage*]. Now look here, Cottie, y'ain't . . . you ain't . . . [COTTIE *realizes that she has said the wrong thing, but she stares him in the eye, and he finishes weakly.*] You ain't a-goin' t'start treatin' me like my Lulu did, is you?

COTTIE [*very, very sweetly*]. Felix, my love, you know I

didn't mean nothin' by hit. I just got such a cravin' to
hear purty words or a poem or somethin', I can't help
myself.
FELIX [*stalling for time*]. Oh, I know a poem. I learned it
when I went to the Graded School—to Miss Mag.
COTTIE [*all admiration*]. Oh, Felix! Please say hit fer me.
FELIX. Hit went something like this. [*At first hesitant, then
he gathers momentum and strikes an oratorical pose.*]

> Oh, the night was dark and hazy
> When the *Piccadilly Daisy*
> When down with the captain and the crew.
> Now the water must have drowned them
> Fer they never, never found them
> And I'm sure they didn't come ashore....

[*Haltingly.*] There was some more to hit, but I cain't
remember hit.
COTTIE [*sighing*]. Piccadilly Daisy! Ain't that the purtiest
name?
FELIX [*pleased*]. I think hit's kind o'nice.
COTTIE. And I can be your Piccadilly Daisy! [*Hastily turning the leaves of the book, she intones.*] "Oh, my lover,
we will stroll hand in hand o'er hill and dale."
FELIX. Huh?—[*Nervously.*] Say, Cottie, I think I'd better get
a move on.
COTTIE [*with a final effort to hold him*]. Don't you want to
take a look at the corpse afore you go?
FELIX [*reluctantly*]. Well, I guess so. [*He goes nervously
toward the room, left.*]
COTTIE [*following him*]. He's the finest looking one I've
had yet. [FELIX *stops suddenly and swallows hard, glancing from the room to* COTTIE. *Already he can see himself
as the next victim.*] Well, g'wan in, he ain't a-goin' t'

bite of you. [FELIX *enters the room cautiously. In a moment he lets out a terrified cry and comes flying back into the room.*]

FELIX [*wringing his hands, and crouching behind a chair*]. Oh, my Gawd, Cottie, Jerd's spirit's come back and hit's a-restin' in the body!

COTTIE. What air you talkin' about, Felix?

FELIX. Hit's the gospel truth, Cottie. Spirits allus go in and out through the eyes and I seen his'n a-blinkin'!

COTTIE. What are you talkin' 'bout?

FELIX [*swallowing hard*]. His eyelids—they flickered oncet and opened just enough to let his spirit in.

COTTIE [*watching* FELIX *narrowly*]. Hit's your own guilty conscience, Felix, that's troublin' you. You know you tried to court me while Jerd was alive. [*Cunningly.*] And if'n you don't do right by me now he's dead, I wouldn't be at all surprised if he didn't come back and ha'nt you.

FELIX [*retreating*]. O my Lord! I didn't stay around you much, Cottie.

COTTIE [*holding the whip hand*]. Well, I don't know. Me bein' bound in wedlock and all that....

[NELLIE MERKLE *enters rather breathlessly through the door, right, carrying a piece of heavy black silk veil which she hands to* COTTIE.]

NELLIE MERKLE. Here 'tis, Cottie, but she said don't you fergit her hind-quarter when you kill Jerd's heifer-steer, Joe.

COTTIE. Humph! That's just like Ethel Tillette. Well, I guess I'd better be a-gittin' my mournin' onto me. [*She starts out center, but turns back.*] Au revoor, Felix. [*Waving coyly at him.*]

FELIX [*dumbly*]. Huh?

COTTIE [*disgusted*]. I thought you had *some* larnin', Felix. That means, "Wait a minute 'til I comes back."

COTTIE MOURNS

FELIX [*completely cowed*]. Oh, all right.
[COTTIE *sweeps out the center door.*]
NELLIE MERKLE [*advancing on* FELIX *as soon as the door is closed behind* COTTIE]. Felix Wise, what do you mean, a-hangin' 'round here when the top to Jerd's coffin ain't even nailed down yet?
FELIX [*jumping nervously as if the "ha'nt" had already begun its spell*]. I ... I ... just ... come round to tell Cottie that I was a-mournin' with her.
NELLIE MERKLE. Humph! I ain't never noticed no great love betwixt you and Jerd.
FELIX [*looking toward the door, left, and speaking loudly*]. Oh, Jerd was a fine man. Yes, sir, a mighty fine man.
NELLIE MERKLE. Look here, Felix, you ain't a-throwin' no sand in my eyes. I know you're a-fallin' victim to Cottie's fine ways. But I ain't never seen no good come of one man a-gettin' anothern's woman.
FELIX [*subsiding into a chair*]. Nellie Merkle, what happens to men that take other men's women?
NELLIE MERKLE [*sensing the situation*]. Ain't you never heard the circuit rider a-preachin' 'gainst hit?
FELIX. I ... I guess I has....
NELLIE MERKLE. And he says when you starts to take unto yourself a woman, you'd better take one that's a decent widder, or one that hain't been married yet.
FELIX [*rising*]. But I ain't aimin' to git no wedlock into me.
NELLIE MERKLE. Now, Felix, you know hit ain't natural fer a man to live by hisself 'thout nobody to take care of 'im.
FELIX. I been gittin' along fine 'thout Lulu.
NELLIE MERKLE [*sidling up to him*]. But wouldn't you kind o' like to have a woman around to cook fer you, and wash your clothes, and air out your bed-ticking?
FELIX [*edging away from her*]. I don't want nobody.

NELLIE MERKLE. Well, Felix, I know how all the women is a-chasin' you, and I know one way of gittin' rid of 'em fer good and all.

FELIX [*eagerly*]. What is it, Nellie Merkle? My Lord, tell me what hit 'tis?

NELLIE MERKLE [*triumphantly*]. Marry yourself a fine single woman. [*Coyly.*] Somebody like me, and then. . . .

FELIX [*backing away*]. I hain't aimin' to git hitched to no wench.

NELLIE MERKLE [*following him and using all her powers of persuasion*]. I'm a mighty fine cook, Felix.

FELIX [*his appetite quite gone now*]. I know that's true, but . . .

NELLIE MERKLE. And Ethel Tillette says she ain't never seen a woman have as little swill left over as I do.

FELIX [*edging toward the outside door*]. Well, now, that's real nice.

NELLIE MERKLE. I'd make you a real good wife, Felix.

FELIX [*desperate now*]. I guess . . . I guess I'd better be a-pourin' it into 'er. You tell Cottie I'll be down to the store if she needs me. [*He leaves abruptly by the door, right, as* COTTIE *reappears at the center door carrying her hat and mourning veil in her hand.*]

COTTIE [*surprised*]. What's the matter? Where'd he go to?

NELLIE MERKLE [*meaningly*]. I don't think he was a-feelin' so good. Somethin' must 'ave upset 'im.

COTTIE. What ailed 'im? He don't most commonly do so. [*Suddenly.*] My Lord, Nellie Merkle, hit cain't be much longer till time fer the funeral and we hain't practised hit a time yet.

NELLIE MERKLE. I'll fix these here benches fer the men to put the coffin on when they come. [*She starts to arrange two wooden benches which stand against the left wall.*]

COTTIE [*putting a few of the chairs into place*]. But we got t' git hit all straight. Ethel practised fer Graham's funeral fer two days and then fergot to git somebody to pray.

NELLIE MERKLE. If I couldn't give a funeral no better'n that, I wouldn't give one.

COTTIE. Well, Jerd's a-goin' to have a decent funeral and if'n he is, we'd better git started.

NELLIE MERKLE. What you want me to do now?

COTTIE. Well, I'll stand in yonder by the coffin and mourn fer a spell while you git everybody in the right seats—and don't let none of them men set down—the chairs is fer the women.—Now you stand over here by the door.

[COTTIE *places* NELLIE MERKLE *by the door, left. Then she enters the room where* JERD *lies in state and wails like a lost soul for a few moments. Then she staggers into the room, wearing the hat and veil. She speaks now to* NELLIE MERKLE *with a great show of grief.*]

COTTIE. Nellie Merkle, my friend. [*In her natural voice.*] You're supposed to support me. [NELLIE MERKLE *seizes* COTTIE's *arm and supports her.* COTTIE *begins her mourning softly and continues with increasing vehemence, concluding with a semi-swoon into the arms of* NELLIE MERKLE.] Oh! Oh!! Oh!!! [*In a normal voice.*] Then I'll say, [*Sorrowfully.*] "Nellie Merkle, pipe up 'Nearer M'God to Thee.' "

NELLIE MERKLE. My Lord, Cottie, I done laid off singing two year ago!

COTTIE. Well, Mag Reeber kin do hit then. [*She then makes the round of the chairs shaking hands with each imaginary guest, and speaking in a sorrowful tone.*] Hit's mighty kind of you to take so much trouble with a poor widder woman in her sorrow, Carrie. [*She then turns to* NELLIE MERKLE *in her natural voice again.*] And after I've been all 'round, I'll ask Acey Partridge to go in and nail down the coffin lid [*Emphatically shaking her fingers.*] and you go in there with him to see he don't steal nothin'. And don't fergit to take that there lily out'n Jerd's hands. Elvira'd have a fit if *hit* got buried.

NELLIE MERKLE. Who you goin' t' have pray?

COTTIE. Cap'n Burrus prayed mighty well at Hurray's funeral, but folks might git to talkin' if I as't 'im again.

NELLIE MERKLE. Why don't you git Simie to? He—

[*The door bursts open and* FELIX *enters in great excitement.*]

FELIX [*stuttering breathlessly*]. Cottie, I just been over to the store and they told me that the coroner what's a-stayin' down yonder to the hotel is a-comin' over here. Acey heard 'im tell some of the summer folks he was.

COTTIE [*belligerently*]. What's he a-comin' here fer?

FELIX. Said he'd better come over and inves... inves... find out what ailed Jerd when he up and kicked the bucket. Seems like he thought hit was mighty funny you havin' four husbands die in ten year.

NELLIE MERKLE. You don't suppose he'd keep us from havin' the funeral when so many folks is a-lookin' forward to hit, do you?

COTTIE [*crossing her arms indignantly*]. They'll not stop any funeral of mine!

FELIX [*fearing for his own life*]. But... but... y' ain't been a-doin' nothin' to 'em is you, Cottie?

COTTIE [*reproachfully*]. Felix, you know I'm a good Christian woman and hit ain't in me to be glad over nobody dyin'. But hit serves Jerd right—him a-cussin' and a-swearin' all the time. I'm a *holy* woman, and if there's one thing I cain't stand, hit is profanity.

FELIX. I... I guess I'd better tell you straight out, Cottie. They's a-sayin'... they thinks... you killed him.

COTTIE [*furiously*]. Felix Wise, hit's a God damn lie, and you know hit!

FELIX [*backing away*]. Now, Cottie, you know I don't believe hit.
NELLIE MERKLE [*seeing a good chance to rid herself of* COTTIE's *competition*]. Well, I've heard some say as how hit's true.
COTTIE [*advancing on her*]. Nellie Merkle Beasley, you git outer my house and don't you never set foot in 'er agin.
NELLIE MERKLE [*retreating,* COTTIE *after her*]. But, Cottie—
COTTIE. I'll find somebody else to support me when I mourns. [*Shrieking after her.*] Now git out!
[NELLIE MERKLE *makes a quick retreat through the door, right.*]
FELIX [*placating her*]. There hain't no harm into 'er, Cottie.
COTTIE [*furious*]. I'll not have anybody a-talkin' 'bout me in my house.
FELIX [*trying to change the subject*]. Now, Cottie, quit bilin' over. Hit's near 'bout time for the funeral. I don't guess that there coroner can stop you from givin' a man a decent buryin'.
COTTIE [*resolved*]. They'll not stop me. [*Suddenly discarding her wrath.*] Felix, does you really love me? I don't see as there's any call to wait s' long to git wedded. You can kill Jerd's heifer-steer, Joe, to-morrow mornin' and we'll sell hit and . . . What's that?
[FELIX *looks forlorn thinking perhaps of four husbands lying side by side in the grave-plot. At the mention of "Jerd's heifer-steer, Joe" being killed there is a noise in the room, left, and as* COTTIE *and* FELIX *turn toward the door, left,* JERD *himself in his grave clothes suddenly appears in the doorway, a wax lily gripped in one hand.* COTTIE *stares with mouth agape.* FELIX *stares as though seeing a ghost.*]
COTTIE [*hoarsely*]. O my Jesus!
JERD [*slowly and ominously*]. That there licker wa'n't quite

rotten enough, Cottie. Hit hain't s'hard to play dead when folks think they's helped kill you.

COTTIE [*terrified, for once in her life*]. Jerd, y'ain't dead?

JERD. I sure hain't. You can pizen me all you want to [*Fiercely.*] but you dassn't lay a finger on my heifer-steer, Joe!

[COTTIE *screams wildly and faints into the arms of* FELIX *whose face breaks into a relieved grin as*

THE CURTAIN FALLS

APPENDIX I

THE CAROLINA PLAYMAKERS: A SELECTED BIBLIOGRAPHY

September, 1931, to September, 1938 *

I. PUBLICATIONS OF THE CAROLINA PLAYMAKERS

1. *Published Plays*

Carolina Folk Comedies, containing eight plays (New York, Samuel French, 1931), edited by Frederick H. Koch.

Century of Culture, A, a pageant of public education in North Carolina (Durham, N. C., The Seeman Printery, 1937), edited by Frederick H. Koch.

Lost Colony, The, a symphonic drama, by Paul Green (Chapel Hill, N. C., University of North Carolina Press, 1937).

Mexican Folk Plays, containing five plays, by Josephina Niggli (Chapel Hill, N. C., University of North Carolina Press, 1938), edited by Frederick H. Koch.

Shroud My Body Down, a folk dream, by Paul Green (Iowa City, Iowa, The Clio Press, 1935).

Ca'line, a Carolina folk comedy, by Bernice Kelly Harris, *The Carolina Play-Book,* September, 1932.

Cloey, a play of Winston-Salem folk, by Loretto Carroll Bailey; in *A Player's Handbook,* by Samuel Selden (New York, F. S. Crofts, 1934).

Common Ground, a drama of a small town boy in Iowa, by Betty Smith and Jay G. Sigmund (Evanston, Illinois, Row, Peterson and Company, 1938).

Conchita, a romance of a copper mining town, by Rosemary Shirley DeCamp, *The Carolina Play-Book,* September, 1931.

* For a Selected Bibliography of The Carolina Playmakers from 1918 to 1931 see Appendix I of the Second Series and Appendix I of the Third Series of *Carolina Folk Plays* (Henry Holt & Company), and Appendix I of *Carolina Folk Comedies* (Samuel French).

Copper Bracelet, The, a romance of old Carolina, by Betty Smith and Robert Finch (Syracuse, Willis Bugbee, 1938).

Cottie Mourns, a comedy of sea island folk, by Patricia McMullan, *The Carolina Play-Book,* March, 1935.

Country Sunday, a play of white justice, by Walter Spearman (Atlanta, The Association of Southern Women for the Prevention of Lynching, 1936).

Darkness at the Window, an Iowa folk play, by Betty Smith and Jay G. Sigmund (Chicago, Dramatic Publishing Co., 1938).

Davy Crockett, half horse, half alligator, by John Philip Milhous, *The Carolina Play-Book,* March, 1933.

Enchanted Maze, The, a play of a modern university, by Paul Green, *The Carolina Play-Book,* December, 1935 (Scene 7).

Fair-God, The (Malinche), a new play of Maximilian of Mexico, by Josephina Niggli, *The Carolina Play-Book,* December, 1936 (an excerpt from the final scene).

Fire of the Lord, a play of religious fanatics, by Frank Durham; in *Twenty Short Plays on a Royalty Holiday* and reprinted in pamphlet form (New York, Samuel French, 1937).

Fixin's, a tragedy of a tenant farm woman, by Erma and Paul Green. Reprinted in pamphlet form from *Carolina Folk Plays,* Second Series (New York, Samuel French, 1934).

Folk Stuff, a folk comedy of Iowa, by Betty Smith and Jay G. Sigmund (New York, Samuel French, 1937).

Four on a Heath, a grotesque, by Foster Fitz-Simons; in *The Gateway Series of Tested Plays* (Evanston, Illinois, Row, Peterson and Company, 1935).

Frontier Night, a drama of old New Mexico, by Chase Webb (Evanston, Illinois, Row, Peterson and Company, 1938).

Funeral Flowers for the Bride, a comedy of the Blue Ridge Mountains, by Beverley DuBose Hamer, *The Carolina Play-Book,* September, 1937.

Glendale Plantation, a play of a Maryland family, by Tom Loy, *The Carolina Play-Book,* December, 1931.

His Last Skirmish, an historical folk comedy of North Carolina, by Betty Smith and Robert Finch (New York, Samuel French, 1937).

Hunger, a tragedy of North Carolina farm folk, by Ella Mae Daniel (Published in pamphlet form by Encyclopædia Britannica, Inc., 1935).

APPENDIX I

John Brown of Pottawattomie, a play of "Bleeding Kansas," by John F. Alexander, *The Carolina Play-Book,* March, 1934.

Judgment Comes to Daniel, a folk comedy of eastern North Carolina, by Bernice Kelly Harris, *The Carolina Play-Book,* September, 1933.

Last of the Lowries, The, a play of the Croatan outlaws, by Paul Green. Reprinted in pamphlet form from *Carolina Folk Plays,* First Series (New York, Samuel French, 1934).

Leavin's, a legend of the Carolina Mountains, by Janie Malloy Britt, *The Carolina Play-Book,* March, 1937.

Lion and the Second Fiddle, The, a comedy of university life, by Betty Smith and Robert Finch (Chicago, Dramatic Publishing Company, 1938).

Lord's Will, The, a tragedy of a country preacher, by Paul Green. Reprinted in pamphlet form from *The Lord's Will and Other Plays* (New York, Samuel French, 1934).

Loyal Venture, The, a drama of Colonial Carolina, by Wilkeson O'Connell, *The Carolina Play-Book,* March, 1932.

Muley, a comedy of North Carolina, by Chase Webb (Evanston, Illinois, Row, Peterson and Company, 1937).

Murder in the Snow, a drama of old Montana, by Betty Smith and Robert Finch (New York, Samuel French, 1938).

Naked Angel, a folk comedy of Lake Ronkonkoma, New York, by Betty Smith and Robert Finch (New York, Samuel French, 1937).

Near Closing Time, a mystery drama of a small Montana town, by Betty Smith and Robert Finch (Chicago, T. S. Denison and Company, 1938).

New Nigger, a tragedy of the tobacco country, by Fred Howard, *The Carolina Play-Book,* September, 1936.

Night in the Country, A, a folk comedy of Lake Ronkonkoma, New York, by Betty Smith and Robert Finch (Evanston, Illinois, Row, Peterson and Company, 1938).

No 'Count Boy, The, a Negro comedy, by Paul Green. Reprinted in pamphlet form from *The Lord's Will and Other Plays* (New York, Samuel French, 1934).

Pensioner, a play of contemporary social conditions, by Alice Truslow (Published in pamphlet form by Encyclopædia Britannica, Inc., 1935).

AMERICAN FOLK PLAYS

Popecastle Inn, a pirate legend of old Carolina, by Betty Smith and Robert Finch (New York, Samuel French, 1937).

Raleigh, the Shepherd of the Ocean, a pageant-drama by Frederick H. Koch, *The Carolina Play-Book,* June, 1937 (excerpts).

Red Velvet Goat, The, a tragedy of laughter and a comedy of tears, by Josephina Niggli, *One-Act Play Magazine,* July, 1937.

Released, a poetic drama of biblical times, by Betty Smith and Jay G. Sigmund (Franklin, Ohio, Eldridge Entertainment House, 1938).

Saints Get Together, The, a modern morality play of Iowa, by Betty Smith and Jay G. Sigmund (Chicago, Illinois, T. S. Denison and Company, 1937).

Schoolin', a play of the San Francisco "mission district," by Edith Daseking (San Francisco, The Banner Play Bureau, 1933).

Shroud My Body Down, a folk dream, by Paul Green, *The Carolina Play-Book,* December, 1934 (first episode, Scene 1).

Sigrid, farm woman of the prairie, by Margaret Radcliffe, *The Carolina Play-Book,* September, 1934.

Silvered Rope, The, a biblical poetic drama, by Betty Smith and Jay G. Sigmund (Chicago, T. S. Denison and Company, 1937).

Singing Piedmont, a choral drama of the tobacco fields of North Carolina, by Anthony Buttitta, *One-Act Play Magazine,* August, 1937. (Reprinted, New York, Contemporary Play Publications, 1938).

Singing Valley, a Mexican village comedy, by Josephina Niggli, *The Carolina Play-Book,* December, 1936 (excerpts from Act II).

Sleep On, Lemuel, a Carolina Negro comedy, by John W. Parker, *The Carolina Play-Book,* December, 1932.

So Gracious Is the Time, a drama of to-day, by Betty Smith, *One-Act Play Magazine,* June-July, 1938.

Soldadera (Soldier-Woman), a play of the Mexican revolution, by Josephina Niggli, in *The Best One-Act Plays of 1937,* edited by Margaret Mayorga. (New York, Dodd, Mead Company, 1938).

APPENDIX I   561

Still Stands the House, a drama of the Canadian frontier, by
   Gwendolyn Pharis, *The Carolina Play-Book,* June, 1938.
Sunday Costs Five Pesos, a Mexican folk comedy, by Josephina
   Niggli, *One-Act Play Magazine,* January, 1938.
Third Night, The, a play of the Carolina mountains, by Thomas
   Wolfe, *The Carolina Play-Book,* September, 1938.
This Bull Ate Nutmeg, a Mexican folk comedy, by Josephina
   Niggli, in *Contemporary One-Act Plays* (New York, Charles
   Scribner's Sons, 1938).
Thrice-Promised Bride, The, a Chinese folk play, by Cheng-
   Chin Hsiung (London, Thomas Nelson & Sons, Ltd., 1932).
Transient, a play of homeless men, by Walter Spearman (Char-
   lotte, N. C., Mrs. J. M. Woolard, The Herald Press, 1936).
Trees of His Father, The, a tragedy of Iowa farm life, by Betty
   Smith and Jay G. Sigmund (New York, Samuel French,
   1937).
Vine Leaves, a small town comedy of Iowa, by Betty Smith and
   Jay G. Sigmund (New York, Samuel French, 1937).
Washed in de Blood, a Negro ritual drama of rural Georgia, by
   Rietta Winn Bailey, *The Carolina Play-Book,* March, 1938.
Western Night, a poetic drama of Montana cowboys, by Betty
   Smith and Robert Finch (New York, Dramatists Play Serv-
   ice, 1938).
Yours and Mine, a comedy of domestic difficulties, by Ella Mae
   Daniel (Published in pamphlet form by Encyclopædia
   Britannica, Inc., 1935).

2. *The Carolina Play-Book* * (*Articles*)

September, 1931
   "The New Season," by Frederick H. Koch.
   "Paul Green," by Frederick H. Koch.
   "Creative Dramatic Experimentalism," by Archibald
      Henderson.
   "A Native American Theatre," by Paul Green.
December, 1931
   "The Roanoke Island Celebration," by Frederick H.
      Koch.
   "A Junior Theatre," by Harry Davis.

* Published by The Carolina Playmakers, Chapel Hill, N. C.

March, 1932
"The Kenan Professorship," by Robert B. House.
"The State Dramatic Tournament," by Irene Fussler.
June, 1932
"Folk Drama Festival," by Rebecca Cushman.
"American Regional Drama," by Frederick H. Koch.
"Our Fourteenth Season," by Frederick H. Koch.
"The Natural Theatre," by Barrett H. Clark.
"The Making of Strike Song," by Loretto and J. O. Bailey.
September, 1932
"A Log-Cabin Theatre," by Frederick H. Koch.
December, 1932
"Folk Drama Defined," by Paul Green.
"*Alcestis* in the Greek Stadium," by Rebecca Cushman.
March, 1933
"The Shaw-Henderson Festival," by Frederick H. Koch.
June, 1933
"Fishermen All," by Paul Green.
"Greetings from Einstein," by Albert Einstein.
"The World and the Village," by Frank P. Graham.
"For the Theatre and the Drama," by Percy Mackaye.
"The Carolina Dramatic Festival," by Rebecca Cushman.
September, 1933
"The Fifteenth Season," by Frederick H. Koch.
"Playmakers in the West," by Frederick H. Koch.
"*A Midsummer Night's Dream* in the Forest Theatre."
December, 1933
"A Christmas Carol," by Frederick H. Koch.
"The Negro Theatre Advancing," by Frederick H. Koch.
"A Folk Theatre," by Albert Shaw.
March, 1934
"Back to the Stage," by Frederick H. Koch.
"The Festival," by Irene Fussler.
June, 1934
"The First National Folk Festival," by Carl Thompson.
"The Rockefeller Grant," by Alton Williams.
"The Eleventh Dramatic Festival," by Alton Williams.
September, 1934
"Sixteen Years, 1918-1934," by Frederick H. Koch.

APPENDIX I 563

December, 1934
"*Shroud My Body Down.*" (Two photographs of the world première of Paul Green's symphonic drama.)

March, 1935
"The Twelfth Dramatic Festival," by John Parker.

June, 1935
"Thomas Wolfe—Playmaker," by Frederick H. Koch.
"The State Is Our Campus," by John W. Parker.
"*Hamlet* in the Forest," by Samuel Selden.

September, 1935
"Thirty Years of Trail Blazing in American Drama." (This entire issue is devoted to celebrating Frederick H. Koch's thirtieth anniversary as a Playmaker.)

December, 1935
"*The Enchanted Maze.*" (Two photographs of the world première of Paul Green's drama.)
"The Seventeenth Season," by Frederick H. Koch.

March, 1936
"*Soldadera*" *(Soldier-Woman).* (A photograph of a scene from the Mexican folk play by Josephina Niggli.)

June, 1936
"The Setting and a Scene from *Lysistrata.*" (Two photographs.)
"The New Department of Dramatic Art," by Frank Durham.
"The Roland Holt Theatre Collection," by Harry Davis.
"The Thirteenth Festival," by John W. Parker.

September, 1936
"A Negro Sharecropper Play," by Frederick H. Koch.
"Communal Playmaking," by Frederick H. Koch.

December, 1936
"Texas Calls," by Walter Spearman.
"An American National Theatre," by Frederick H. Koch.
"Eighteenth Season," by Frederick H. Koch.

March, 1937
"Nancy Hanks," by Frederick H. Koch.
"The Festival—1937," by Robert Finch.
"Stadia and Night," by Phillips Russell.

June, 1937
"The Drama of Roanoke," by Frederick H. Koch.
"Androcles and the Lion," by Archibald Henderson.
"Shaw in the Forest," by Phillips Russell.

September, 1937
"I Can't Write a Play," by Frederick H. Koch.
"Music in the Theatre," by Paul Green.
"Johnny Q Sees *The Lost Colony*," by Bernice Kelly Harris.
"Playmaking at Banff," by Frederick H. Koch.
"Summer Repertory," by Harry E. Davis.
"Play-Acting," by Frederick H. Koch.

December, 1937
"Cut Is the Branch That Might Have Grown Full Straight," by Maxwell Anderson.
"The Play in the Audience," by Samuel Selden.
"And So It Began," by Bernice Kelly Harris.
"Founding Fathers," by Brooks Atkinson.
"Strolling Players in North Carolina," by Richard G. Walser.
"The Nineteenth Season," by Frederick H. Koch.

March, 1938
"Experimental Production," by Noel Houston.
"On the Presentation of the Bust of Eleanora Duse," by Katherine Pendleton Arrington.
"Negro Ritual Drama," by Frederick H. Koch.

June, 1938
"Western Canada," by Frederick H. Koch.
"American Theatre—A Radio Interview," by Paul Green.
"The Fifteenth Festival," by Frederick H. Koch.

September, 1938
"Thomas Wolfe: Playmaker," by Frederick H. Koch.
"Theatre Fire," by Frederick H. Koch.
"A Folk Theatre," by Albert Shaw.
"*The Merry Wives of Windsor,*" by Betty Smith.
"Forest Theatre Scenery," by Samuel Selden.
"Twentieth Season," by Frederick H. Koch.

APPENDIX I

3. Other Publications

Play Producing for School and Little Theatre Stages, by Frederick H. Koch and Staff Members of The Carolina Playmakers (Chapel Hill, N. C., The University of North Carolina Press, 1935).

Plays for Schools and Little Theatres, by Frederick H. Koch, Betty Smith and Robert Finch (Chapel Hill, N. C., The University of North Carolina Press, 1937).

Play Direction (First Principles), by Samuel Selden (Chapel Hill, N. C., University of North Carolina Extension Div., 1937).

II. REFERENCES IN BOOKS

BAKER, BLANCHE M., *Dramatic Bibliography* (New York, The H. W. Wilson Company, 1933).

CALVERTON, V. F., *The Liberation of American Literature* (New York, Charles Scribner's Sons, 1932).

CHANDLER, FRANK W., and CORDELL, RICHARD A., *Twentieth Century Plays* (New York, Thomas Nelson and Sons, 1934).

CLARK, EMILY, *Innocence Abroad* (New York, Alfred A. Knopf, 1931).

CLARK, BARRETT H., *Maxwell Anderson, the Man and His Plays* (New York, Samuel French, 1933).

CONNOR, R. D. W., *The History of North Carolina* (Chicago and New York, American Historical Society, Inc., 1928).

COUCH, W. T., Ed., *Culture in the South* (Chapel Hill, N. C., University of North Carolina Press, 1934).

ENCYCLOPÆDIA BRITANNICA, *College Theatre and Workshops* (New York, Encyclopædia Britannica, Inc., 1929).

GILDER, ROSAMOND, and FREEDLEY, GEORGE, *Theatre Collections* (New York, Theatre Arts, Inc., 1936).

GREEN, PAUL, "Folk Drama," in *The National Encyclopedia* (New York, P. F. Collier and Son, 1935).

HAINES, HELEN E., *Living with Books* (New York, Columbia University Press, 1935).

HARTMAN, GERTRUDE, and SCHUMACHER, ANN, Eds., *Creative Expression* (New York, John Day Company, 1932).

HEFFNER, HUBERT, SELDEN, SAMUEL, and SELLMAN, HUNTON D., *Modern Theatre Practice* (New York, F. S. Crofts, 1935).

ISAACS, EDITH R., *The American Theatre in Social and Educational Life* (New York, National Theatre Conference, 1932).
LANDIS, BENSON Y., and WILLARD, JOHN D., *Rural Adult Education* (New York, The Macmillan Company, 1933).
Lost Colony, The, souvenir program-book, *The Drama of Roanoke* (Rev. Ed. 1938; Manteo, North Carolina, Roanoke Colony Memorial Association, 1937).
MACGOWAN, KENNETH, "The Little Theatre Movement in America," *National Encyclopedia* (N. Y., P. F. Collier, 1935).
MIMS, EDWIN, *Adventurous America* (New York, Charles Scribner's Sons, 1929).
National Cyclopedia of American Biography, Biography of Frederick H. Koch. Current Volume A, p. 361 (New York, James T. White & Co., 1930).
National Encyclopedia, "Theatre Schools" (New York, P. F. Collier and Sons, 1935).
PATTEN, MARJORIE, *The Arts Workshop of Rural America* (New York, Columbia University Press, 1937).
PERRY, CLARENCE ARTHUR, *The Work of the Little Theatres* (New York, Russell Sage Foundation, 1933).
PLESSOW, GUSTAV L., *Das Amerikanische Kurzschauspiel Zwischen 1910 und 1930* (Halle Salle, Germany, Max Niemeyer Verlag, 1933).
QUINN, ARTHUR HOBSON, *Representative American Plays* (New York, D. Appleton-Century Company, 1930).
ROWE, NELLIE M., *Discovering North Carolina* (Chapel Hill, N. C., University of North Carolina Press, 1933).
ROWE, KENNETH THORPE, *University of Michigan Plays* (Ann Arbor, Michigan, George Wahr, 1932).
SELDEN, SAMUEL, *A Player's Handbook* (N. Y., F. S. Crofts, 1934).
TAYLOR, CARL C., *Rural Sociology* (New York, Harper and Brothers, 1933).
TILLETT, NETTIE S., and YARBOROUGH, MINNIE CLARE, *Image and Incident* (New York, F. S. Crofts, 1933).
TUCKER, S. MARION, *Twenty-Five Modern Plays* (New York, Harper and Brothers, 1931).
WAUGH, FRANK A., *Outdoor Theatres* (Boston, Mass., Richard G. Badger, 1917). Dakota Playmakers.
WHITMAN, CHARLES HUNTINGTON, *Representative Modern Dramas* (New York, The Macmillan Company, 1936).

APPENDIX I

WHITMAN, WILSON, *Bread and Circuses* (New York, Oxford University Press, 1937).

III. PERIODICAL REFERENCES TO THE CAROLINA PLAYMAKERS

Billboard (Cincinnati)
"Native Drama in the Little Theatre," Editorial, November 29, 1930.
Bookman, The (New York)
"Paul Green," by Julian R. Meade, January-February, 1932.
Bridgeport Life (Bridgeport, Conn.)
"College Dramatics," by Carl Glick, February 4, 1933.
Bulletin of the American Library Association, The (Chicago)
Illustrations of the Forest Theatre and the Playmakers Theatre, University of North Carolina, July, 1932.
"Making a Regional Drama," by Frederick H. Koch, August, 1932.
Christian Science Monitor (Boston, Mass.)
"Think the Thought," biography of Shepperd Strudwick, by L. A. Sloper, June 25, 1932.
"The Carolina Playmakers," by Rebecca Cushman, August 20, 1932.
"A Carolina Folk Theatre," by Rebecca Cushman, September 3, 1932.
"Shaw's 'Boswell' Honored at North Carolina Festival," March 2, 1933.
"The Carolina Playmakers," by Rebecca Cushman, July 31, 1933.
"Tiny Tim's Message Once More Rings Out Its Good Will to Men to Firesides All Over the World," by Rebecca Cushman, December 22, 1933.
"Days of Elizabethan Period Revived by Carolina 'Twelfth Night' Revels," by Rebecca Cushman, January 18, 1934.
"American Folk Drama," September 26, 1934.
Current History (New York)
"The American Note in Drama," by Montrose J. Moses, October, 1933.
Delta of Sigma Nu Fraternity, The (Indianapolis)
"Shaw-Henderson Festival," May, 1933.

Emerson (College) Quarterly, The (Boston)
"A Unit Set for *The Taming of the Shrew*," by Elmer Hall, March, 1932.
English Journal, The (Chicago)
"*The Carolina Play-Book*," March, 1933.
Equity Magazine (New York)
"'Dr. Dixie' Is with Us No More," February, 1931.
Holland's, The Magazine of the South (Dallas)
"Southern Personalities—Paul Green—Philosopher and Playwright," by Mary H. Phifer, October, 1931.
"Southern Personalities—Frederick H. Koch," by Winifred Camp, July, 1936.
Landmark, The (London)
"Sixty Weeks of Shakespeare in the United States," by Sir Philip Ben Greet, August, 1932.
"The Folk Theatre of the South-Eastern United States," by Phillip Cummings, January, 1938.
Liberty Magazine (New York)
"To the Ladies!" (Interview with Frederick H. Koch), by Princess Alexandra Kropotkin, September 17, 1932.
Literary Digest, The (New York)
"The Work of The Carolina Playmakers," by David Carb, April 14, 1934.
Momento (Monterrey, Mexico)
"Josefina Niggli," July, 1937.
New Theatre Magazine (New York)
"Drama in Dixie," by Molly Day Thacher, October, 1934.
"Negro Players in Southern Theatres," by J. O. Bailey, July, 1935.
North Carolina Education (Raleigh, North Carolina)
"Centennial Pageant Making," by Frederick H. Koch, November, 1936.
"A Festival of Youth," by Frederick H. Koch, April, 1937.
Ohio Wesleyan Magazine, The (Delaware, Ohio)
A Biographical Sketch of Frederick H. Koch (Ill.), May, 1931.
Players Magazine, The (Peru, Nebraska)
"The Carolina Playmakers Feature *The Taming of the Shrew*" (Ill.), November and December, 1931.

APPENDIX I 569

"Carolina Playmakers Open Fourteenth Season," by Ora Mae Davis, January and February, 1932.
"*Alcestis* in the Greek Stadium" (Ill.), by Rebecca Cushman, January and February, 1933.
"Shakespeare in the Forest Theatre," November and December, 1933.
"Carolina Playmakers Complete Fifteenth Season," by Frederick H. Koch, January-February, 1934.

Saturday Review of Literature, The (New York)
"The Reader's Guide," by May Lamberton Becker, May 27, 1933.
"Thomas Wolfe," by Ann Preston Bridgers, April 6, 1935.

Scholastic (Pittsburgh)
"Folk Chronicler of Carolina (Paul Green)" (Ill.), February 18, 1933.

Southern Folklore Quarterly (Gainesville, Florida)
"Making a Native Folk Drama," by Frederick H. Koch, September, 1937.

State, The (Raleigh, North Carolina)
"The Man Who Made North Carolina Drama Conscious" by Majel Ivey Seay, July 7, 1934.
"The Festival of Youth," by Majel Ivey Seay, April 3, 1937.

Theatre and School (St. Mateo, Cal.)
"Towards an American Folk Drama," by Frederick H. Koch, October, 1933.

Theatre Arts Monthly (New York)
"American Plays" (with illustrations from *Git Up an' Bar the Door* and Paul Green's *The Field God*), July, 1931.
"Adventures in Playmaking," by Carl Carmer, July, 1932.
Strike Song (photograph), July, 1932.
"Paul Green, the Making of an American Dramatist," by Carl Carmer, December, 1932.
"Frederick H. Koch as 'Death' in *Alcestis*" (a photograph), December, 1932.
"Carolina Folk-Comedies," a review, by Carl Carmer, February, 1933.
"Drama and the Weather," by Paul Green, August, 1934.
"Paul Green's *Shroud My Body Down*" (photograph), April, 1935.

Theatre Arts Monthly (continued)
"History Repeats Itself," by Edith J. R. Isaacs (two photographs from *Shroud My Body Down*), July, 1935.
"Paul Green's *The Enchanted Maze*" (photograph), July, 1936.
"Josephina Niggli's *The Red Velvet Goat* (photograph), July, 1937.
"The Carolina Playmakers' Touring Equipment," by Harry E. Davis, July, 1937.
"Paul Green's *Johnny Johnson*" (two photographs), July, 1938.
"Paul Green's *The Lost Colony*" (photograph), July, 1938.
Town Hall Crier, The (New York)
"A Christmas Carol," by Frederick H. Koch (illustrated), December, 1931.

APPENDIX II

THE CAROLINA PLAYMAKERS: PRODUCTIONS AND TOURS

September, 1931, to September, 1938 *

I. ORIGINAL PLAYS PRODUCED

1. *Full-Length Plays*

Strike Song, a new play of Southern mill people, by Loretto Carroll Bailey, December 10-11-12, 1931.
Sad Words to Gay Music, a new comedy in three acts, by Alvin Kerr, February 23-24-25, 1933.
Shroud My Body Down, a folk dream, by Paul Green, December 7-8, 1934.
The Enchanted Maze, by Paul Green, December 6-7 and 9, 1935.
Singing Valley, a comedy of Mexican village life, by Josephina Niggli, July 15, 1936.
The Fair-God (Malinche), a new play of Maximilian of Mexico, by Josephina Niggli, December 3-4-5, 1936.
Sharecropper, a new Negro drama in five scenes, by Fred Howard, February 24-25-26, 1938.

2. *One-Act Plays*

Thirtieth Bill, March 3-4-5, 1932
  Bloomers, a comedy of family life, by Jo Norwood.
  The Common Gift, a tragedy of working women, by Elwyn de Graffenried.

* For the list of Productions and Tours from 1918 to 1931 see Appendix I of the Second Series and Appendix I of the Third Series of *Carolina Folk Plays* (Henry Holt & Company), and Appendix I of *Carolina Folk Comedies* (Samuel French).

AMERICAN FOLK PLAYS

The Loyal Venture, a drama of Colonial Carolina, by Wilkeson O'Connell.

Thirty-First Bill, December 8-9-10, 1932
Creek Swamp Nigger, a Carolina Negro tragedy, by Harry W. Coble.
Davy Crockett, half horse, half alligator, by John Philip Milhous.
Four on a Heath, a grotesque, by Foster Fitz-Simons.
Stumbling in Dreams, a folk comedy of Tin Pan Alley, by George Brown.

Thirty-Second Bill, May 11, 1933
Judgment Comes to Daniel, a folk comedy of eastern North Carolina, by Bernice Kelly Harris.
A Little Boat to India, a springtime farce, by Foster Fitz-Simons.

Thirty-Third Bill, May 12, 1933
Comedy at Five, an American comedy, by Martha Matthews Hatton.
Eternal Spring, a tragedy of prejudice, by Robert Barnett.
Blow Me Down, a comedy of Long Island sailor folk, by William Bonyun.

Thirty-Fourth Bill, May 13, 1933
The Queen Was in the Kitchen, a persistent comedy, by Ellen Stewart.
Etowah Plantation, a legend of the land, 1846-1864, by Eugenia Rawls.
Comedy at Five, an American comedy, by Martha Matthews Hatton.

Thirty-Fifth Bill, December 7-8-9, 1933
Everglades, an episode in the life of Andrew Jackson, by John F. Alexander.
The Head-Ax of Ingfell, a tragedy of the Igorote Hill folk of the Philippines, by Anne B. Walters.
Shadows of Industry, a drama of the financial world, by Vermont C. Royster.
Sing Your Own Song, a comedy—we hope!, by Nat Farnworth.

Thirty-Sixth Bill, May 10, 1934
The Girl with the White Sweater, a fantasy of the Carolina Mountains, by Margaret Siceloff.

Third Verse, a comedy of a small-town newspaper, by Wilbur Dorsett.
Tomorrow, a play of a lodging house, by Douglas Hume.
Thirty-Seventh Bill, May 11, 1934
Third Verse, a comedy of a small-town newspaper, by Wilbur Dorsett.
Where There Is Faith, a sophisticated play of an unsophisticated girl, by Kathleen Krahenbuhl.
Thirty-Eighth Bill, May 12, 1934
Release, a play of courage, by Jean Smith Cantrell.
Where There Is Faith, a sophisticated play of an unsophisticated girl, by Kathleen Krahenbuhl.
Thirty-Ninth Bill, May 14, 1934
Concealed Aim, a drama of a small-town bank, by Carl W. Dennis.
New Rasthenia, a nervous break-down, by Herman Fussler.
Fortieth Bill, February 28 and March 1-2, 1935
Ancient Heritage, a drama of a New England family, by Philip Goddard Parker.
Cottie Mourns, a comedy of Carolina fisherfolk, by Patricia McMullan.
Yours and Mine, a comedy of domestic difficulties, by Ella Mae Daniel.
Forty-First Bill, April 25, 1935
Goldie, a comedy of a Negro Saturday night, by Wilbur Dorsett.
Hunger, a tragedy of Carolina farm folk, by Ella Mae Daniel.
Spare Ribs, a comic drama of the sea, by Donald B. Pope.
Forty-Second Bill, April 26-27, 1935
Ca'line, a Carolina folk comedy, by Bernice Kelly Harris.
Back Page, a newspaper melodrama, by Don Shoemaker.
Metropolitan Feodor, a romantic drama of seventeenth-century Russia, by Philip Goddard Parker.
New Nigger, a tragedy of the tobacco country, by Fred Howard.
Forty-Third Bill, April 30, 1935
Clam Digger, a play of Maine sea-folk, by Jean Ashe.
The Devil's Trampin' Ground, a tragedy of mixed blood, by Sara Seawell.

New Anarchy, a play of the banking crisis, by Philip Goddard Parker.
Pretty, Plump Angel, a play of youth, by Cecilia Allen.
Forty-Fourth Bill, February 27-28-29, 1936
Election, a play of politics in a small Texas town, by Mary Delaney.
Prairie Dust, a play of the Dakota drought, by Gerd Bernhart.
Soldadera (Soldier-Woman), a play of the Mexican revolution, by Josephina Niggli.
Forty-Fifth Bill, April 23, 1936
Awakening, a play of disillusionment, by Eleanor Barker.
An Orchid to You, a comedy of sorority life, by Jean Walker.
Raise a Tune, Sister, a play of Carolina fisherfolk, by Patricia McMullan.
Forty-Sixth Bill, April 24, 1936
The Eternal Comedy, a play of adolescence, by Mary Delaney.
Hangman's Noose, a play of character conflict, by Charles A. Poe.
Hjemlengsel (Home Longing), a Norwegian folk play, by Gerd Bernhart.
Forty-Seventh Bill, April 25, 1936
Azteca, a tragedy of pre-Conquest Mexico, by Josephina Niggli.
The Cry of Dolores, the story of Mexican independence, by Josephina Niggli.
The Red Velvet Goat, a tragedy of laughter and a comedy of tears, by Josephina Niggli.
Sunday Costs Five Pesos, a Mexican folk comedy, by Josephina Niggli.
Forty-Eighth Bill, February 25-26-27, 1937
Sleep On, Lemuel, a Carolina Negro comedy, by John W. Parker.
Leavin's, a legend of the Carolina mountains, by Janie Malloy Britt.
Fire of the Lord, a play of religious fanatics, by Frank Durham.
Funeral Flowers for the Bride, a comedy of the Blue Ridge Mountains, by Beverley DuBose Hamer.

APPENDIX II

Forty-Ninth, Fiftieth and Fifty-First Bills, April 22, 24, and 26, 1937

Drought, a tragedy of rural South Carolina, by Walter Spearman.
The Sun Sets Early, a play of a small college, by William Peery.
Fightin' Time, a comedy of southern Indiana, by Kate May Rutherford.
Toujours Gai, a modern tragedy, by Virginia La Rochelle.
Barge Incident, a play of the New York water-front, by Herb Meadow.
Naughty Boy, a New York suburban comedy, by William T. Chichester.
Cockle Doody Doo, a play of Carolina fisherfolk, by Patricia McMullan.
The Good-bye, by Paul Green.
Lighted Candles, a tragedy of the Carolina highlands, by Margaret Bland.
Abide with Me, a comedy of rural South Carolina, by Walter Spearman.

Fifty-Second and Fifty-Third Bills, April 20-21-22-23, 1938

Pair of Quilts, a folk comedy of eastern North Carolina, by Bernice Kelly Harris.
While Reporters Watched, a Christmas Eve newspaper mystery, by Rose Peagler.
Mary-Marge, a comedy of Carolina fisherfolk, by Ellen Deppe.
One Man's House, a play of a Canadian reformer, by Gwendolyn Pharis.
The Worm Turns, a comedy of adolescent love, by Jean Brabham.
Murder in the Snow, a drama of old Montana, by Betty Smith and Robert Finch.
Three Foolish Virgins, a Carolina folk comedy, by Bernice Kelly Harris.
This Is Villa, a portrait of a Mexican general, by Josephina Niggli.

3. Experimental Productions

FULL-LENGTH PLAYS

Playthings, a comedy of illusion in three acts, by Anthony Buttitta, February 28, 1931.

Rest for My Soul, a play in three acts, by Ann Wishart Braddy, May 28, 1931.

Snow White, a children's play in two acts, by Sallie M. Ewing, May 26, 1932.

A House Divided, a comedy-drama in three acts, by Frederica Frederick, March 8, 1934.

Water, a play of pioneer settlement in California, by Alton Williams, April 13, 1935.

ONE-ACT PLAYS

First Series, December 14, 1931

A Vision of Eugenics, a very modern extravaganza, by Maurice Ferber.

Old Aus Ramsey, a comedy of Carolina mountain folk, by Charles Elledge.

The Mandarin Coat, a very foolish comedy, by Olive Newell.

Those Children, a modern comedy, by Osmond Molarsky.

Whispering Shadows, a tragedy of the blind, by Vernon B. Crook.

Patches, a comedy of family life, by Jo Norwood.

Second Series, February 23, 1932

The Last Two Shots, a mountain tragedy, by Irene Fussler.

Treasures, by Irene Fussler.

King, Queen, and Joker, a drama of royalty, by Irene Fussler.

Third Series, March 7, 1932

Birds of a Feather, a domestic comedy by Jo Norwood.

Granny, a domestic tragedy, by Jack Riley.

The Golden Lioness, a phantasy of Paris in 1750, by Reuben Young Ellison.

Proof, a play about love, by Osmond Molarsky.

APPENDIX II

Fourth Series, May 12, 1932
  Boardin' Out, a mountain folk comedy, by Charles Elledge and Malcolm Seawell.
  Proof, a play about love, by Osmond Molarsky.
  Sleep On, Lemuel, a Carolina Negro comedy, by John W. Parker.
  Granny, a tragedy of North Carolina farm folk, by Jack Riley, *May 23, 1932*

Fifth Series, May 25-26, 1932
  Neighbors of the Dead, a tragedy of heredity (first act of a full-length play), by Vernon Crook.
  Ol' Honeycutt's Boy, a play about a country boy, by Jack Riley.
  The Boss of the House, a Carolina country comedy, by Lubin Leggette.
  Chicken Money, a play of Iowa farm life, by Winifred Tuttle.
  The Battle of Shaw's Mill, a Carolina country comedy, by Charles Elledge and Malcolm Seawell.

Sixth Series, July 15, 1932
  Election Returns, a social tragedy (Act I of a full-length play), by Alonzo Hoyle.
  Freights, a drama of the side-lines, by Marjorie Craig.
  A Revolt in the Nineties, a romance, by Anne Wilson.
  Playing with Fire, a tragedy of country life, by Thea W. Whitefield.
  A Little Cajun, a play of Louisiana folk, by Peg Williamson.
  It's Just Too Bad, a tragedy of college youth, by James Alfred Stanley.
  Blessed Assurance, a Carolina country comedy, by Evelyn McCall.

Seventh Series, November 12, 1932
  Old Ninety-Seven, a tragedy of railroad life, by Wilbur Dorsett.
  Nothing Ever Happens, a modern domestic tragi-comedy, by Elmer R. Oettinger, Jr.
  Gateway, an interlude, by Eugenia Rawls.

578　AMERICAN FOLK PLAYS

    Four on a Heath, a grotesque, by Foster Fitz-Simons.
    Sour Fodder, a play of Iowa small-town folk, by Burdette Kindig.
    Creek Swamp Nigger, a Carolina Negro tragedy, by Harry W. Coble.
    Hell Bent for Honolulu, a college comedy, by William Bonyun.
    And They Lived Happily, a domestic comedy, by Marion Tatum.
    Stumbling in Dreams, a comedy of Tin Pan Alley, by George Brown.
    Davy Crockett, half horse, half alligator, by John Philip Milhous.

Eighth Series, December 14, 1932
    Coal, a play of West Virginia mine folk, by Marguerite McGinnis.
    The State Rests, a play of a small-town court, by Peggy Ann Harris.
    In His Hand, a play of village folk, by Betty Bolton.
    The Elders Play, a problem play of youth, by Sue Roberson.
    Honora Wade, a play of Georgia folk, by Eugenia Rawls.
    Back Door, a Carolina folk comedy, by Wilbur Dorsett.

Ninth Series, March 1, 1933
    Fool's Justice, a Negro tragedy, by Harry W. Coble.
    A Little Boat to India, a springtime farce, by Foster Fitz-Simons.
    Heart Trouble, a comedy of Georgia village folk, by Bradford White.
    Mumsey, a drama of Long Island folk, by Sarah M. W. Huntley.
    One Every Minute, a modern comedy, by Everett Jess.
    Malone, an Irish folk tragedy, by Marion Tatum.

Tenth Series, March 3, 1933.
    The Last Skirmish, a play of West Virginia mountain people, by Marguerite McGinnis.
    Second Edition, a psychological drama, by Robert W. Barnett.
    Lights in the Sky, an American comedy, by William Bonyun.

APPENDIX II

Design for Justice, a social commentary, by Elmer R. Oettinger, Jr.
Comedy at Five, an American comedy, by Martha Matthews Hatton.
Mihalusek's Wager, a drama of Polish military life, by Edward V. Conrad.

Eleventh Series, April 13, 1933

Discontent, a play of industrial strife, by J. M. Ledbetter, Jr.
Blow Me Down, a comedy of sailor folk, by William Bonyun.
And the Poet Laughed, a modern comedy drama, by Burdette Kindig.
Etowah Plantation, a legend of the land, 1846-1864, by Eugenia Rawls.
Tintagil, a dream play, by Martha Matthews Hatton.
Farewell to Glamour, a modern American comedy, by James P. McConnaughey.
My Son, a tragedy of a Southwest trapper, by Frank McIntosh.
The Salted Pup, a comedy of the time of sap and smalle fooles, by John Philip Milhous.

Twelfth and Thirteenth Series, May 25, 1933

The Moon Turns, the conclusion of a youthful romance, by Elmer R. Oettinger, Jr.
Beer on Ice, the burp of a nation, by Harry W. Coble.
Bull Session, an ironic comedy of college life, by George Brown.
For Poland, a tragedy of the Great War, by Ed Conrad.
No Word from the Wise, a little comedy of Small-Town people, by Wilbur Dorsett.
A Mocking Bird Singing, a romance of the South, by Foster Fitz-Simons.
Burgundy for Breakfast, an effervescent farce, by Martha Matthews Hatton.
Three Muggy Rooms in the Bronx, a play of father and son, by George Brown.
Henna Rinse, a play of "Ye Venus Beauty Shoppe," by Marion Tatum.

Fourteenth and Fifteenth Series, November 7, 1933
  Showing at Eight, a play of a small-town moving-picture theater, by Leonard Rapport.
  O Woman, a modern comedy of an ancient tragedy, by Carl G. Thompson.
  November Night, a play of a Pennsylvania mining town, by Margaret Belle McCauley.
  Hell's Dreams, a play of modern life, by Frederica Frederick.
  Diana, a moonlight chase, by Kathleen Krahenbuhl.
  Shadows of Industry, a drama of the financial world, by Vermont C. Royster.
  Sing Your Own Song, a comedy—we hope!, by Nat Farnworth.
  Flight Unending, a tragedy of youth, by Robert W. Barnett.
  Everglades and Hickory, an episode in the life of Andrew Jackson, by John F. Alexander.

Sixteenth Series, December 13, 1933
  Grand Slam, a satiric comedy, by James Thompson.
  Copper Penny, a modern domestic drama, by Douglas Hume.
  Bought with the Vittles, a dude ranch comedy, by Alton Williams.
  Opposite Poles, a play of the divorce problem, by Margaret Siceloff.
  New Rasthenia, a nervous break-down, by Herman Fussler.
  Driftwood, a tragedy of the fisherfolk of eastern Carolina, by Patricia McMullan.
  La Capilla (The Chapel), a legendary romance of Spanish California, by Frederica Frederick.

Seventeenth Series, February 7, 1934
  Over the Doorsill, a play of small-town life, by Harry W. Coble.
  Another Journey, a modern tragedy, by Virgil Lee.
  Borrowed of the Night, a tragedy of youth, by Kathleen Krahenbuhl.
  Moon in the Hawthorne Tree, a Georgia farm tragedy, by Foster Fitz-Simons.
  Prelude, a story of youth, by Vermont C. Royster.

The Stars Are Fire, a comedy of earnest youth, by Nat Farnworth.
John Brown, an episode in his campaign in "Bleeding Kansas," by John F. Alexander.
Oh, Hell, a very modern political satire, by Margaret McCauley.
Shipmates, a play of the water-front, by Donald Pope.

Eighteenth Series, March 8-9, 1934
Cottie Mourns, a comedy of sea island folk, by Patricia McMullan.
Tomorrow, a play of a lodging-house, by Douglas Hume.
The Lo Fan Joss, a subtle thing, by Herman Fussler.
Pretty, Plump Angel, a play of youth, by Cecilia Allen.
Never a Second Time, a romantic interlude, by Leonard Rapport.
Release, a play of courage, by Jean Smith Cantrell.
Third Verse, a comedy of a small-town newspaper, by Wilbur Dorsett.
Unto the Hills, a play of faiths, by Leonard Rapport.
Strange Interlaken, a vignette, by Robert Barnett.
Lifeguards and Fish, a modern comedy of errors, by Margaret Siceloff.

Nineteenth Series, March 22, 1934
Back Page, a newspaper melodrama, by Don Shoemaker.
The Golden Wedding, a romantic comedy, by Alton Williams.
Rich Man! Poor Man! a Marxian romance, by Cecilia Allen.
When Floosies Meet, a comedy of pseudo-artists, by Walter Terry.

Twentieth and Twenty-First Series, May 30, 1934
The Suicide, a modern interpretation of hell, by Sara Seawell.
A Beating of Wings, a poetic tragedy, by Foster Fitz-Simons.
Beginners, a belligerent satire, by Bradford White.
Belle, a small-town tragedy, by Patricia McMullan.
When Doctors Fail, a comedy of faith healing, by W. A. Sigmon.
The Skeleton Rattles His Bones, a modern domestic comedy drama, by Douglas Hume.

Spare-Ribs, a comedy of nautical cookery, by Donald Pope.
Crash, a story of "The Street," by Milton Kalb.

Twenty-Second and Twenty-Third Series, November 1, 1934
Sea Psalm, a tragedy of Carolina sea-folk, by Charles Edward Eaton.
New Anarchy, a play of the banking crisis, by Philip Goddard Parker.
New Nigger, a tragedy of the tobacco country, by Fred Howard.
Clam Digger, a play of Maine sea-folk, by Jean Ashe.
Hunger, a tragedy of North Carolina farm folk, by Ella Mae Daniel.

Twenty-Fourth Series, November 15, 1934
Traficante, a play of Spanish Florida, by Maxeda von Hesse.

Twenty-Fifth Series, December 11, 1934
The Passer-By, a play of Carolina village folk, by Ralph Lyerly.
Ancient Heritage, a drama of a New England family, by Philip Goddard Parker.
Octagon Soap, a Carolina country comedy, by Nancy Lawlor.
Damned Idealist, a college drama, by Charles A. Poe.
Rations, a mountain folk comedy, by Catherine Threlkeld.
Confidentially Speaking, a satire on true-story writing, by Wilbur Dorsett.

Twenty-Sixth and Twenty-Seventh Series, February 5, 1935
Muddy Jordan Waters, a tragedy of the Carolina mountains, by Mildred Moore.
The Villain Gets the Girl, a modern satire in the old style, by Charles A. Poe.
Pensioner, a play of contemporary social conditions, by Alice A. Truslow.
The Devil's Trampin' Ground, a tragedy of mixed blood, by Sara Seawell.
Yours and Mine, a comedy of domestic difficulties, by Ella Mae Daniel.

Twenty-Eighth and Twenty-Ninth Series, March 7, 1935
I Sing Forever, a tragedy of the North Carolina mountains, by Mildred Moore.

APPENDIX II

The Settin' Up, a country wake, by Sara Seawell.
Tsalagi, an historical drama of the Cherokee Indians, by Billy Greet.
And So They Grow, a play of little ladies, by Ellen Deppe.
Wait a While, the first act of a full-length domestic drama, by Kenneth Bartlett.
Goldie, a comedy of a Negro Saturday night, by Wilbur Dorsett.
Crazy-Patch Quilt, a play of the Carolina tobacco country, by Anne Hyman Moore.

Thirtieth Series, *May 13, 1935*
So It Will Last, an eighteenth-century romance, by William Howard Wang.
The Best Butter, a modern tea-room comedy, by Joseph Lee Brown.
Virtue, a satiric interlude, by Leonard Rapport.
Hangman's Noose, a tragedy, by Charles A. Poe.
Bathroom Echoes, or *The Tale of a Tub,* a slightly ribald farce of character, by Walter Terry.

Thirty-First and Thirty-Second Series, *May 29, 1935*
Dark Journey, a drama of a farm family, by Virgil Jackson Lee.
There Ain't No Escape, a comedy of arrested courtship, by Ella Mae Daniel.
Thou Thief!, a play of small-town complacency, by Ralph Lyerly.
Barn Trash, a mountain mystery-comedy, by Mildred Moore.
Penny-Wise, a drama of misunderstanding, by Ellen Deppe.
Queer New World, a Negro comedy-comment, by Wilbur Dorsett.
Debtor's Hell, an historical incident of Colonial Massachusetts, by Jean Ashe.

Thirty-Third and Thirty-Fourth Series, *October 31, 1935*
The School Teacher, a play of character conflict, by Kenneth E. Bartlett.
The Jew, a poetic drama of the Inquisition, by William Howard Wang.
Across the Tracks, a play of Southern slums, by Frank Durham.

Cockle Doody Doo, a play of Carolina fisherfolk, by Patricia McMullan.

Hjemlengsel (Home Longing), a Norwegian folk play, by Gerd Bernhart.

The Red Velvet Goat, a tragedy of laughter and a comedy of tears, by Josephina Niggli.

Thirty-Fifth and Thirty-Sixth Series, *December 12, 1935*

Take Your Choice, a play of college liberalism, by George Starks.

Black Sheep, a tragedy of the color line, by Marjorie Usher.

Election, a play of politics in a small Texas town, by Mary Delaney.

The Other Way, a tragedy of indecision, by Lawrence Wismer.

A Most Lamentable Comedy, a true story, by Barbara A. Hilton.

Horses and Mice, a tragi-comedy of musical playmakers, by Joseph Lee Brown.

Thirty-Seventh and Thirty-Eighth Series, *February 4, 1936*

With Onions, an illogical play of social protest, by Frank Durham.

There Is No Guilt, a play of a pacifist who died, by William Howard Wang.

Transient, a play of homeless men, by Walter Spearman.

The Eternal Comedy, a play of adolescence, by Mary Delaney.

Prairie Dust, a play of the Dakota drought, by Gerd Bernhart.

Raise a Tune, Sister, a play of Carolina fisherfolk, by Patricia McMullan.

Thirty-Ninth and Fortieth Series, *March 5, 1936*

Grandma's Bonnet, a comedy of age, by June Hogan.

Brownstone Front, a modern domestic tragedy, by William Chichester.

Cat Alley, a college comedy, by Kenneth Bartlett.

An Active's Pledge, a play of college fraternity life, by William A. Barwick.

Frame-Up, a play of social protest, by Jane Henle.

An Orchid to You, a comedy of sorority life, by Jean Walker.

APPENDIX II

Forty-First Series, May 12, 1936
  Country Sunday, a play of white justice, by Walter Spearman.
  Mob-Tide, an anti-lynching play, by John Walker.
  Strike-Breaker, a play of protest, by George Starks.
  So Spin the Norns, a play of Norse gods, by Gerd Bernhart.
  Fire of the Lord, a play of religious fanatics, by Frank Durham.

Forty-Second Series, May 27, 1936
  Ocean Harvest, a tragedy of Maine sea-folk, by Jean Ashe.

Forty-Third Series, October 30, 1936
  Ugly Hands, a tragedy of factory women, by Kate May Rutherford.
  And Things Happen, a play of post-war shadows, by Don Watters.
  Waitin', a drama of the Southwest Virginia mountains, by William Peery.
  The Barren Year, a tragedy of a South Carolina farm woman, by David Beaty.

Forty-Fourth and Forty-Fifth Series, December 11, 1936
  Tidal Wave, a tragedy of the South Carolina low country, by Evelyn Snider.
  Cause Unknown, a tragedy of modern youth, by John Walker.
  Who's Boss? a comedy of Negro farm life, by Lubin Leggette.
  Widening the Channel, a play of Piedmont Virginia, by Sally Wills Holland.
  Six Dollars, a tragedy of youth, by Virginia Peyatt.
  Leavin's, a legend of the Carolina mountains, by Janie Malloy Britt.
  In the Jungle, a drama of the "Milk and Honey Route," by William Peery.

Forty-Sixth Series, February 2, 1937
  The Steep Road, by Joseph Feldman.
  Funeral Flowers for the Bride, a comedy of the Blue Ridge Mountains, by Beverley DuBose Hamer.
  Mrs. Juliet, an ironic essay, by David Beaty.
  Rosemary's for Remembrance, a play from the legends of Old Lynnhaven, by Sally Wills Holland.

Abide with Me, a comedy of rural South Carolina, by Walter Spearman.

Forty-Seventh Series, March 4, 1937
The Sun Sets Early, a play of a small college, by William Peery.
Near a Spring, a play of southern Indiana, by Kate May Rutherford.

Forty-Eighth Series, May 7, 1937
Thank Rotary, a play of the Big Brother movement, by William Peery.
Penguin Soup, a Second Avenue nightmare, by Jean Ashe.
Shattered Glass, a play of a woman's frustration, by Marion Hartshorn.
Long Sweetenin', a comedy of the hill folk, by Janie Malloy Britt.

Forty-Ninth Series, May 27, 1937
Courtship at Eight, a play of children's love triangles, by Charlotte Wright.
By Any Other Name, a racial tragedy, by Marion Hartshorn.
From Sullen Earth, a play of rural South Carolina, by Frank Durham.
Earth Treading Stars, a Travelers Aid incident, by Manuel Korn.
The White Doe, a legend of North Carolina Indians, by William Peery.

Fiftieth Series, July 19, 1937
Seventy Times Seven, a Carolina folk play, by William Ivey Long.
"A-Pinin' and A-Dyin'," a mountain comedy, by Emily Polk Crow.
The Ivory Shawl, a folk play of South Alabama, by Kate Porter Lewis.

Fifty-First Series, November 4, 1937
The Cross of Cannair, a social drama of New York in 1887, by Lynette Heldman.
Uncle Smelicue, a Carolina mountain comedy, by Lois Latham.
This Side Jordan, a play of farm life in the Middle West, by Lynn Gault.

It Don't Make No Difference, a folk play of Tin Pan Alley, by Joseph Lee Brown.

Fifty-Second Series, December 9, 1937
Hello, Hanging Dawg, a Carolina mountain comedy, by Lois Latham.
Künstbeflisener (Student of Art), a play of an artist's conflict, by Thad Jones.
Pennies for Their Thoughts, a domestic comedy of an author, by Noel Houston.
Washed in De Blood, a symphonic play of Negro life, by Rietta Winn Bailey.

Fifty-Third Series, February 2, 1938
Hit's Man's Business, a Carolina mountain play, by Lois Latham.
And Darling, Do Be Tactful, a domestic comedy, by Rose Peagler.
The Last Christmas, a drama of death row, by N. Houston.
His Boon Companions, a temperance comedy, by Lynn Gault.

Fifty-Fourth Series, March 3, 1938
Where the Wind Blows Free, a play of the Texas range, by Emily Polk Crow.
Hidden Heart, a comedy of Armenian-American folk, by Howard Richardson.
Still Stands the House, a drama of the Canadian frontier, by Gwendolyn Pharis.
Wings to Fly Away, a Negro ritual drama, by Rietta Winn Bailey.

Fifty-Fifth Series, May 26, 1938
Last Refuge, an outlaw comes home, by Noel Houston.
Chris Axelson, Blacksmith, a folk comedy of western Canada, by Gwendolyn Pharis.
West from the Panhandle, a tragedy of the dust-bowl, by Clemon White and Betty Smith.
Let the Chips Fall, a comedy of domestic intrigue, by Emily Crow.

Fifty-Sixth Series, July 20, 1938
Fresh Widder, a play of Colington Island fisherfolk, by Lacy Anderson.

AMERICAN FOLK PLAYS

Stick 'Em Up, a comedy of frontier New Mexico, by Gordon Clouser.
Me an' De Lawd, a Negro play of eastern North Carolina, by Jameson Bunn Dowdy.
Montana Night, a drama of the Old West, by Robert Finch and Betty Smith.
Triflin' Ways, a comedy of the Missouri Ozarks, by Lealon N. Jones.

II. THE PLAYMAKERS' TOURS

Twenty-Ninth Tour, Eastern North Carolina, February 26-28, 1933
    Davy Crockett, by John Philip Milhous.
    Four on a Heath, by Foster Fitz-Simons.
    Stumbling in Dreams, by George Brown.

Thirtieth Tour, Western and Eastern North Carolina, March 22-25, 1933
    Davy Crockett, by John Philip Milhous.
    Four on a Heath, by Foster Fitz-Simons.
    Stumbling in Dreams, by George Brown.

Thirty-First Tour, North Carolina, Kentucky, Missouri, April 24–May 2, 1934
    On Dixon's Porch, by Wilbur Stout.
    Job's Kinfolks, by Loretto Carroll Bailey.
    Quare Medicine, by Paul Green.

Thirty-Second Tour, Eastern Carolina, Virginia, Maryland, November 19-27, 1934
    The Loyal Venture, by Wilkeson O'Connell.
    Fixin's, by Paul Green.
    Quare Medicine, by Paul Green.

Thirty-Third Tour, Eastern Carolina, Virginia, November 13-26, 1935
    Cottie Mourns, by Patricia McMullan.
    New Nigger, by Fred Howard.
    Tooth or Shave, by Josephina Niggli.

Thirty-Fourth Tour, North Carolina, New Jersey, New York, November 13-20, 1936
    Quare Medicine, by Paul Green.
    New Nigger, by Fred Howard.
    Tooth or Shave, by Josephina Niggli.

Thirty-Fifth Tour, North Carolina, Virginia, Maryland, November 22–December 4, *1937*
  Funeral Flowers for the Bride, by Beverley DuBose Hamer.
  Leavin's, by Janie Malloy Britt.
  Sunday Costs Five Pesos, by Josephina Niggli.

III. OUTDOOR PRODUCTIONS

1. Forest Theatre Productions

A Midsummer Night's Dream, by William Shakespeare, May 19-20, 1933.
The Women Have Their Way, by Joaquin and Serafin Alvarez Quintero, July 7, 1933.
Hamlet, by William Shakespeare, May 25 and 27, 1935.
Lysistrata, by Aristophanes (Gilbert Seldes' Modern Version), May 22-23, 1936.
Androcles and the Lion, by George Bernard Shaw, May 21-22, 1937.
The Merry Wives of Windsor, by William Shakespeare, May 20-21 and 28, 1938.

2. Kenan Stadium Productions

Alcestis, by Euripides, July 11-12, 1932.
Iphigenia in Tauris, by Euripides, July 16 and 19, 1935.

IV. PROFESSIONAL PLAYS PRODUCED

1. Full-Length Plays

Saturday's Children, by Maxwell Anderson, October 22-23-24, 1931.
A Doll's House, by Henrik Ibsen, February 4-5-6, 1932.
Cinderella, by Harry Davis, April 8-9, 1932 (Junior Playmakers).
The Butter and Egg Man, by George S. Kaufman, May 19-20-21, and June 4, 1932.
Uncle Tom's Cabin, dramatized by George L. Aiken, November 3-4-5, 1932.
You Never Can Tell, by George Bernard Shaw, February 2-3-4, 1933.
Ali Baba and the Forty Thieves, by Harry Davis, April 28-29, 1933.

The House of Connelly, by Paul Green, November 2-3-4, 1933.
Princess Ida, by Gilbert and Sullivan, February 2-3, 1934.
The Witching Hour, by Augustus Thomas, March 1-2-3, 1934.
Wappin' Wharf, by Charles S. Brooks, April 21, 1934.
Hay Fever, by Noel Coward, May 25-26, 1934.
The Cradle Song, by G. Martinez Sierra, July 18, 1934.
R. U. R., by Karel Capek, October 25-26-27, 1934.
The Young Idea, by Noel Coward, January 31 and February 1-2, 1935.
Three Cornered Moon, by Gertrude Tonkonogy, October 24-25-26, 1935.
Paths of Glory, by Sidney Howard, January 31 and February 1, 1936.
The Drunkard, by W. H. Smith and a gentleman, October 22-23-24, 1936.
The Pirates of Penzance, by Gilbert and Sullivan, January 29-30-31, 1937.
Personal Appearance, by Lawrence Riley, July 15, 1937.
Johnny Johnson, by Paul Green, October 29-30 and November 2, 1937.
Boy Meets Girl, by Bella and Samuel Spewack, January 27-28-29 and 31, 1938.
Laburnum Grove, by J. B. Priestley, July 14, 1938.
The Blue Bird, by Maurice Maeterlinck, July 18, 1938 (Junior Playmakers).

2. *One-Act Plays*

The Hand of Siva, by Ben Hecht and Kenneth Sawyer Goodman, May 13, 1932.
The Man on the Kerb, by Alfred Sutro, May 13, 1932.
Words and Music, by Kenyon Nicholson, May 13, 1932.
In the Morgue, by Sada Cowan, May 14, 1932.
The Open Door, by Alfred Sutro, May 14, 1932.
Things Is That-A-Way, by E. P. Conkle, May 14, 1932.
Rosalie, by Max Maurey, May 14, 1932.
The Man in the Stalls, by Alfred Sutro, May 23, 1932.
Tomorrow and Tomorrow (Act II, Scene 1), by Philip Barry, May 23, 1932.
The Constant Lover, by St. John Hankin, May 23, 1932.

APPENDIX II 591

The Stronger, by August Strindberg, May 11, 1933.
The Proposal, by Anton Chekhov, May 11, 1934.
Rosalie, by Max Maurey, May 12, 1934.
The House across the Way, by Katherine Kavanaugh, May 14, 1934.
Modesty, by Paul Hervieu, May 14, 1934.
The Twelve Pound Look, by J. M. Barrie, March 2, 1937.
The Flattering Word, by George Kelly, February 12, 1937.
The Boor, by Anton Chekhov, March 2, 1937.

V. OCCASIONAL PERFORMANCES

The Association of American Universities (Annual Meeting), Chapel Hill, November 13, 1931: *Job's Kinfolks,* by Loretto Carroll Bailey; *Magnolia's Man,* by Gertrude Wilson Coffin.
The Goethe Centenary, Chapel Hill, April 19, 1932: *The Masterpieces of Goethe.*
The Shaw-Henderson Festival, Chapel Hill, February 2-3-4, 1933: *You Never Can Tell,* by George Bernard Shaw.
The Dogwood Festival (First Annual), Chapel Hill, April 29, 1933: *Ali Baba and the Forty Thieves,* by Harry Davis.
The United Daughters of the Confederacy (38th Convention), Chapel Hill, October 10, 1934: *Agatha,* by Jane Toy.
A Fifteenth Century Nativity Play (in German), adapted by Meno Spann, December 9, 1934.
The Dogwood Festival (Third Annual), Chapel Hill, April 25-26-27, 1935: See the Forty-First and Forty-Third Bills of New Plays.
The Southeastern Arts Association, Chapel Hill, April 8, 1937: *Leavin's,* by Janie Malloy Britt.
The Ninety-Third Meeting of the American Chemical Society, Chapel Hill, April 12, 1937; *Leavin's,* by Janie Malloy Britt; *Funeral Flowers for the Bride,* by Beverley DuBose Hamer.
Annual Twelfth Night Revels
    The Fourth, January 9, 1932.
    The Fifth, January 7, 1933.
    The Sixth, January 6, 1934.
    The Seventh, January 12, 1935.

The Eighth, January 11, 1936.
The Ninth, January 9, 1937.
The Tenth, January 8, 1938.

Annual Capers
The Eighth, May 28, 1932.
The Ninth, May 27, 1933.
The Tenth, June 2, 1934.
The Eleventh, June 1, 1935.
The Twelfth, May 30, 1936.
The Thirteenth, May 29, 1937.
The Fourteenth, May 28, 1938.

Annual Commencement Performances
The Eighth, June 4, 1932: *The Butter and Egg Man,* by George S. Kaufman.
The Ninth, June 5, 1933: *Henna Rinse,* by Marion Tatum; *Davy Crockett,* by John Philip Milhous; *Good-bye to Alice,* by Foster Fitz-Simons.
The Tenth, June 11, 1934: *Third Verse,* by Wilbur Dorsett; *Where There Is Faith,* by Kathleen Krahenbuhl; *Art for Spite's Sake,* by Walter Terry.
The Eleventh, June 10, 1935: *Yours and Mine,* by Ella Mae Daniel; *Ancient Heritage,* by Philip Goddard Parker; *Goldie,* by Wilbur Dorsett.
The Twelfth, June 8, 1936: *Texas Calls,* by Paul Green; *Sunday Costs Five Pesos,* by Josephina Niggli.
The Thirteenth, June 7, 1937:: *Leavin's,* by Janie Britt; *Funeral Flowers for the Bride,* by Beverley DuBose Hamer.
The Fourteenth, June 6, 1938: *Still Stands the House,* by Gwendolyn Pharis; *Sunday Costs Five Pesos,* by Josephina Niggli.

(1)

Date Due

MAR 18 1946		
JAN 30 '57		
MAY 30 1961		
APR 30 1962		
JUL 22 1964		
MAR 17 '71		